barbri®

California Lecture Handouts

Table of Contents

CAH

Introduction

LECTURE HANDOUTS
INTRODUCTION

Welcome to the BARBRI Substantive Law Lecture Series

California BARBRI provides lecture handouts as part of its review program to help bar candidates in their understanding of the material tested on the bar exam.

These lecture handouts are to be used in conjunction with the BARBRI lecture series for your bar exam preparation. The lecture handouts contained in this volume were created by the individual professors to enable you to follow along in class and to obtain the maximum benefit from the lecture.

BARBRI lecturers perform several critical functions:

- They review and synthesize the material in an organized and digestible manner;

- They emphasize and clarify principles and areas of law that students consistently find perplexing;

- Most importantly, they hone in on areas most often tested so that your studies may be focused.

The lecture handouts in this volume are organized alphabetically by course subject. It is imperative that you bring the respective lecture handout(s) with you to the selected class.

We highly recommend that you bring this book with you to __EACH AND EVERY__ class as no additional copies of the lecture handouts will be available at the lecture sites!

Agency and Partnership

Professor Michael Kaufman

AGENCY AND PARTNERSHIP

OUTLINE AND HYPOTHETICALS

By Professor Michael J. Kaufman
Loyola University Chicago School of Law

AGENCY

THREE AGENCY PROBLEMS:

I.   Liability of Principal to Third Parties for Torts of an Agent

II.   Liability of Principal to Third Parties for Contracts Entered by an Agent

III.   Duties Which Agents Owe to Principals

I.   **LIABILITY OF PRINCIPAL FOR TORTS OF AGENT -- RESPONDEAT SUPERIOR OR VICARIOUS LIABILITY**

    A.   Issue: Whether the principal will be vicariously liable for torts committed by agent.

    B.   Two-Part Test: Principal will be liable for torts committed by agent if: (1)

    _____,

    and (2) the tort was committed by the agent within the _____ of that relationship.

        1.   **The Principal-Agent Relationship**

            a.   Principal-agent relationship requires:

1) Assent

_____

_____

2) Benefit

_____

_____

3) Control

_____

_____

_____

    a) Sub-agents: Will the principal be vicariously liable if the agent gets the help of a "sub-agent" and the sub-agent commits the tort? The principal will be liable for a sub-agent's tort if there is:

_____

_____

_____

_____

_____

    b) Borrowed agents: Will a principal who borrows another principal's agent be vicariously liable for the borrowed agent's tort? The principal will be liable for a borrowed agent's tort if there is:

_____

_____

_____

_____

b.   Contrast **Agents** with **Independent Contractors**

     1)   The key distinction between an agent and an independent contractor is that:

_____

_____

_____

     2)   Vicarious liability rule for independent contractor torts:

_____

_____

_____

     3)   Exceptions:

         a)   _____

_____

_____; and

         b)   _____

_____

_____

Hypo: Tory Victus went to E-Stop-L Gas Station to have her brakes repaired. E-Stop-L Gas Station had an independent contractor arrangement with Brake Repairer. Brake Repairer tortiously repaired Tory's brakes, resulting in an accident. Is E-Stop-L Gas Station liable?

_____

_____

_____

_____

_____

_____

_____

2. **Scope of Principal-Agent Relationship Factors**

    a.   Was conduct "of the kind" agent was hired to perform?

_____

_____

    b.   Did the tort occur "on the job"? <u>Frolic</u> v. <u>Detour</u>:

_____

_____

_____

_____

    c.   Did the agent intend to benefit the principal?

_____

_____

<u>Hypo</u>: Employer instructs Employee to drive across town to deliver files to a branch office. On the way back, Employee stops to pick up shirts at the dry cleaner for work the next day. In the parking lot of the dry cleaner, Employee hits a pedestrian. Is Employer liable?

_____

_____

_____

_____

_____

3. **Intentional Torts**

    a.   Rule

_____

_____

    b.   Exceptions: Intentional torts are within the scope if the conduct was:

        1) _____

        2) _____

        3) _____

II. LIABILITY OF PRINCIPAL FOR CONTRACTS ENTERED BY AGENTS

    A.   Issue: Whether the principal is liable for contracts entered into by its agent.

    B.   One Test: Principal is liable for contracts entered into by its agent if the principal **authorized** the agent to enter the contract.

    C.   There are four types of **authority**: actual express, actual implied, apparent, and ratification.

        1.   **Actual Express Authority:** Principal used words to express authority to agent.

            a.   Rules: Actual express authority can be _____ and _____ , but it is _____ construed.

            b.   Exception:

_____

_____

_____

_____

_____

Hypo: Agent tells Principal that she is an expert in negotiating real estate transactions. Principal whispers into Agent's ear at a party that Principal wants Agent to sell Green Acres Farm. Agent sells Green Acres Farm for Principal. Is Principal bound on the sale?

_____

_____

_____

_____

      c.   Express authority will be revoked by:

          1)   Unilateral act of either the principal or the agent, or

          2)   Death or incapacity of the principal.

Hypo: Paula collects rare books. She hires Alice to find a rare book to complete her collection. Alice searches everywhere for the rare book. As Alice is about to pay for the book, Paula dies. Is Paula's estate bound by the contract?

_____

_____

_____

_____

_____

      d.   Exception:

_____

_____

_____

_____

2. **Actual Implied Authority**

    a.   Authority which the principal gives the agent through conduct or circumstance:

        1)   <u>Necessity</u>. There is implied authority to do all tasks:

_____

_____

_____

        2)   <u>Custom</u>. There is implied authority to do all tasks:

_____

_____

_____

        3)   <u>Prior dealings between the principal and the agent</u>. There is implied authority to do all tasks:

_____

_____

_____

_____

_____

3. **Apparent Authority:** Two-Part Test: (i) Principal "cloaked" agent with the appearance of authority, and (ii) third party reasonably relies on appearance of authority.

<u>Hypo</u>: Charles owns an antique store. A shipment of antique clocks arrives from London. Charles tells his employee Dufus not to sell a special grandfather clock. Charles goes to lunch. Dufus sells the clock. Is Charles bound on the sales contract?

_____

_____

_____

_____

_____

_____

_____

4.   **Ratification:** Authority can be granted after the contract has been entered, if:

  a.   Principal has <u>knowledge</u> of all material facts regarding the contract, <u>and</u>

  b.   Principal accepts its <u>benefits</u>.

  c.   Exception: Ratification <u>cannot alter</u> the terms of the contract.

<u>Hypo</u>: Priscilla gives Agnes a power of attorney to purchase steel drums. Agnes enters a contract to purchase 11,000 wooden barrels. Priscilla tells Agnes, "Great job! I love wooden barrels, but I only need 10,000." Is Priscilla bound?

_____

_____

_____

_____

_____

_____

_____

_____

D.   The Rules of Liability on the Contract

1.   **General Rule**: The principal is liable on its authorized contracts, and therefore as a rule: _____

_____

2.   Exception: The undisclosed principal -- If principal is <u>partially disclosed</u> (only the identity of principal concealed) or <u>undisclosed</u> (fact of principal concealed), <u>authorized agent</u> may nonetheless be liable at the <u>election</u> of the third party.

III. DUTIES AGENT OWES TO PRINCIPAL

A.   In return for reasonable compensation and reimbursement of expenses, agents owe principals:

    1.   Duty of _____.

    2.   Duty to _____

        _____.

    3.   Duty of _____. The agent may never do any of the following:

        a.   Self-dealing: Agent cannot receive a benefit to the detriment of the principal.

        b.   Usurping the principal's opportunity, or

        c.   Secret profits: making a profit at the principal's expense without disclosure.

B.   <u>Hypo</u>: Priscilla authorizes Agnes to buy diamonds. Agnes spots choice diamonds and secretly buys them for herself for $1 million. Agnes then resells the diamonds for $2 million.

    1.   What duties, if any, has Agnes breached?

    2.   What remedies, if any, does Priscilla have against Agnes?

PARTNERSHIP

FIVE ISSUE AREAS:

I.   General Partnership Formation

II.   Liabilities of General Partners to Third Parties

III. Rights and Liabilities Between General Partners

IV.   General Partnership Dissolution

V.   Alternative Unincorporated Business Organizations

I.   GENERAL PARTNERSHIP FORMATION

A.   Formalities

_____

_____

B.   Definition

_____

_____

_____

C.   Sharing of Profits is the Key Factor. Therefore:

_____

_____

_____

_____

_____

10

II.   LIABILITIES OF GENERAL PARTNERS TO THIRD PARTIES

A.   Agency Principles Apply

1.   Partners are agents of the partnership for apparently <u>carrying on usual partnership business</u>.

2.   Therefore, the general partnership is liable for each partner's torts in the scope of partnership business and for each partner's authorized contracts.

B.   **Each General Partner is Personally Liable for All Debts of the Partnership and for:** _____.

1.   Incoming partner's liability for pre-existing debts

_____

_____

_____

2.   Dissociating (withdrawing) partner's liability for subsequent debts

_____

_____

_____

C.   **General Partnership Liability by Estoppel**: One who represents to a third party that a general partnership exists will be liable as if a general partnership exists.

<u>Hypo</u>: Paula convinced her friend Peter to start a sailing school and agreed to lend Peter money to purchase a boat for that purpose. At a party, Paula told a wealthy friend: "My partner Peter and I are starting a sailing school and we need a boat." The wealthy friend offered to sell Paula and Peter a boat and agreed to allow Peter to take it for a test ride the next day. Later that night, however, Peter and Paula fight and decide to drop the sailing school idea. The next day, Peter takes the boat for a ride and tortiously destroys the boat. May the wealthy friend sue Paula for the loss of the boat?

_____

_____

_____

_____

_____

_____

_____

_____

III. RIGHTS AND LIABILITIES BETWEEN GENERAL PARTNERS

A. General Partners Are **Fiduciaries** of Each Other and the Partnership

1. Therefore, general partners owe to each other and the partnership:

_____, which means that general

partners may never engage in _____;

may never _____ partnership opportunities;

and may never make a _____ at the partnership's expense.

2. Action for Accounting

_____

_____

_____

_____

B. Partners' Rights in **Partnership Property** and **Liquidity**

1. Specific Partnership Assets

_____

_____

_____

2.   Share of Profits and Surplus

_____

_____

_____

_____

3.   Share in Management

_____

_____

_____

4.   In order to determine whether the fact pattern involves specific partnership assets or personal property, the test is:

_____

_____

_____

_____

Hypo: John buys a car in John's own name with John's money which John uses in partnership business. John dies. Does John's spouse Yoko get the car or is it a specific asset of the partnership?

_____

_____

_____

_____

C.   **Management**: Absent an agreement, each partner entitled to **EQUAL** control (vote).

Hypo: A, B, and C agree to contribute money and share profits 60-30-10. How do they vote?

_____

_____

D.   **Salary**: Absent an agreement, partners get **NO SALARY**.

Hypo: A and B are partners. A works 96 hours a week. B sleeps all day. Does A get any salary?

_____

Exception:

_____

E.   **Partner's** Share of **Profits** and **Losses**

1.   Absent an agreement, **PROFITS SHARED EQUALLY**

2.   Absent an agreement, **LOSSES SHARED LIKE PROFITS**

Hypos:

a.   If agreement is silent on profits and losses?

_____

_____

b.   If agreement states that "profits are shared 60/40" but is silent on losses. Losses shared?

_____

c.   If agreement states that "losses are shared 60/40" but is silent on profits. Profits shared?

_____

d.   Partner A puts up all of the money. Partner B does all of the work. Partner C gives the partnership its fine name. Partner D does nothing. How are profits shared?

_____

IV. GENERAL PARTNERSHIP DISSOLUTION

A. Key definitions

1. **Dissolution**

_____

_____

_____

_____

_____

2. **The Real End of the Partnership is Called:**

_____

3. **Winding Up**

_____

_____

_____

_____

B. **Partnership's Liability**

1. Old business. The partnership and therefore its individual general partners retain liability on:

_____

_____

2. New business. The partnership and therefore its individual general partners retain liability on brand new business transactions during winding up until:

_____

_____

C.   **Priority of Distribution**

1.   Each level of priority must be fully satisfied before beginning the next level. Order of priority:

a.   First, all creditors must be paid.

_____

_____

_____

b.   Second, all capital contributions by partners must be paid.

_____

_____

c.   Profits and surplus, if any.

_____

_____

2.   Rule: Each partner must be repaid his or her loans and capital contributions, plus that partner's share of the profits or minus that partner's share of the losses.

3.   Distribution Hypos:

a.   A and B dissolve the AyeBee Partnership. In winding up, they liquidate the partnership assets and have a total of $1 million to distribute.   How should that amount be distributed if (1) the partnership owes $600,000 to trade creditors; (2) Partner A loaned the partnership $100,000; and (3) Partner B made capital contributions of $200,000?

_____

_____

_____

_____

b. Suppose, in the prior hypo, that AyeBee Partnership has only $700,000 to distribute?

_____

_____

_____

_____

_____

_____

_____

_____

_____

_____

V. ALTERNATIVE UNINCORPORATED BUSINESS ORGANIZATIONS

A. Limited Partnerships

1. Defined: _____

_____

_____

_____

2. Formation: _____

_____

_____

_____

3. Liability and Control

    a. General Partners: _____

_____

_____

    b. Limited Partners: _____

_____

_____

_____

_____

_____

_____

_____

_____

_____

_____

B. **Registered Limited Liability Partnerships (RLLP)**

1. Formation: _____

_____

_____

2. Liabilities: _____

_____

_____

_____

_____

C.   **Limited Liability Companies (LLC)**

    1.   Defined: _____

        _____

        _____

        _____

    2.   Formation Requirements: _____

        _____

        _____

    3.   Control: _____

        _____

    4.   Limited Liquidity: _____

        _____

        _____

        _____

    5.   Limited Life: _____

        _____

        _____

    6.   Therefore: LLCs = _____

        _____

MINI REVIEW

A.   AGENCY

    1.   **Principal's Liability for Agent's Torts**

       (a) _____

       (b) _____

       (c) _____

    2.   **Principal's Liability for Agent's Contracts**

       (a) _____

          _____

       (b) _____

       (c) _____

       (d) _____

       (e) _____

          _____

    3.   **Duties Agent Owes Principal**

       (a) _____

       (b) _____

       (c) _____

B.   PARTNERSHIP

    1.   **Formation**

       (a) _____

       (b) _____

          _____

2.   **Liabilities to Third Parties**

    (a)   _____

    (b)   _____

3.   **Relations Between Partners**

    (a)   _____

    (b)   _____

    (c)   _____

            _____

4.   **Dissolution**

    (a)   Priority

            _____

            _____

    (b)   Distribution Rule

            _____

            _____

5.   **Alternative Unincorporated Business Organizations**

            _____

            _____

Civil Procedure

Professor Rich Freer

CIVIL PROCEDURE (FEDERAL AND CALIFORNIA)

Big topics:

1. Right court?
Personal jurisdiction
Subject matter
Venue

2. Learning about case
Service of process
Pleadings
Discovery

3. Complex cases
Party joinder

4. Adjudication
Pretrial
Conferences
Trial

5. Appellate Review
Appeal

6. Preclusion
Claim and issue preclusion

FEDERAL CIVIL PROCEDURE

FIRST BIG TOPIC: ARE WE IN THE RIGHT COURT? (to page 11)

I. PERSONAL JURISDICTION (power over the *parties*)

A. Do federal courts need personal jurisdiction over the parties? _____

B. How is it assessed? _____

_____

_____

II. SUBJECT MATTER JURISDICTION (power over the *case*)

A. Basic Idea. Now we know that P will sue D in a particular state. But in what court in that state: the state court or the federal court?

Federal courts can only hear certain types of suits. What are the two main types? _____

_____

_____

_____

B. Diversity of Citizenship Cases. Two requirements: (1) the action must be between "citizens of different states" (or between a citizen of a state and a foreign citizen (alien)) **and** (2) the amount in controversy must exceed $75,000.

1. **Who are "citizens of different states"?** (BTW – "states" includes DC, Puerto Rico)

   Complete diversity rule. No diversity if *any* P is a citizen of the same state as *any* D.

   -- P (CA) sues D-1 (TX) and D-2 (CA). OK? _____

   _____

   _____

   How do we determine a litigant's citizenship?

   a. **Natural person** who is a U.S. citizen, citizenship is the state of her *domicile*. Domicile is established by two factors: (1) Presence in state **AND** (2) intent to make it her permanent home (*e.g.,* paying in-state tuition, registering to vote).

      -- Can a person have more than one domicile at a time? _____

      _____

      -- P (CA) sues D (AZ). After filing, D becomes a citizen of CA. Does that mean diversity is destroyed now that it's California versus California? _____

      _____

      _____

      -- That means: we don't care what happens to citizenships after the case is filed or what the citizenships were before the case was filed.

      -- P (CA) wants to sue D (CA) in federal court. P moves to Utah and sues under diversity jurisdiction. OK? Yes, if P changed her domicile. Here we know she moved to Utah, but we do not know if she has made Utah her domicile. Why?

      _____

      _____

      _____

   b. **Corporation** – citizenship equals: (1) state where incorporated **AND** (2) the *one* state where the corporation has its principal place of business (PPB). So corporations, unlike humans, can have two citizenships.

      -- Dunder-Mifflin Paper Co. is incorporated in PA with its PPB in NY. What is the corporation's citizenship? _____

      _____

-- How do we determine the corporation's PPB? _____

_____

_____

-- We call this the "nerve center." It's usually the headquarters.

c. **Unincorporated association (like partnership, LLC).** Use the citizenship of all members (that includes general and limited partners).

-- Partnership has partners who are citizens of CA, AZ, and NV. What is Partnership's citizenship? _____

_____

_____

d. **Decedents, minors, and incompetents.** Use *their* citizenship, not the citizenship of their representative.

-- Executor (CA) sues on behalf of the estate of Elvis (TN). What citizenship is relevant? _____

_____

2. **Amount in controversy.** In addition to the complete diversity rule, P's good faith claim must *exceed* $75,000 (not counting interest on the claim or costs of litigation).

-- P sues for *exactly* $75,000. OK? _____

_____

--Whatever the plaintiff claims in good faith is OK unless it is *clear to a legal certainty* that she cannot recover more than $75,000. That's rare – *e.g.*, statutory ceiling on recovery.

--Suppose P sues for more than $75,000 but ultimately recovers less than $75,000. Is jurisdiction OK? _____

_____

_____

-- But a P who wins less than $75,000 may have to pay D's litigation costs. (Usually, loser pays winner's costs, which do not include attorney's fees.)

--**Aggregation** means adding two or more claims to meet the amount requirement.

-- P sues D for $40,000 breach of contract and for $50,000 for a totally unrelated claim. The amount is $90,000. Why? _____

_____

_____

_____

-- Plaintiff #1 sues D for $50,000. In the same case, Plaintiff #2 sues D for $40,000. OK? NO! You cannot aggregate these two claims because the case is not by a single P against a single D. _____

_____

_____

-- P sues joint tortfeasors X, Y and Z for $75,000.01. OK? _____

_____

_____

_____

_____

_____

-- **Equitable relief.** P sues D for an **injunction** to tear down part of his house that blocks P's view. Two tests; if *either* is met, most courts say it's OK:

     -- *Plaintiff's viewpoint*: does the blocked view decrease the value of plaintiff's property by more than $75,000?

     -- *Defendant's viewpoint*: would it cost defendant more than $75,000 to comply with the injunction?

3. **Exclusions.** Even if the requirements for diversity of citizenship jurisdiction are met, federal courts will not hear actions involving issuance of divorce, alimony or child custody decree or to probate an estate.

C. **Federal Question Cases.** *Complaint* must show a right or interest founded substantially on a federal law (*e.g.*, federal constitution, legislation). The claim "arises under" federal law.

     1. Is citizenship of the parties relevant? _____

     2. Is the amount in controversy relevant? _____

3. "Well pleaded complaint" rule. It is not enough that some federal issue is raised by the complaint. The P's *claim itself* must "arise under" federal law. So we look at the claim and ignore other material P might have alleged.

-- **Ask:** _____

_____

    --   If the answer is yes, the case can go to federal court under FQ jurisdiction.
    --   If the answer is no, the case cannot go to federal court under FQ.

-- Sharon Stone hires David Epstein to build a house. Epstein then fails to build, but argues that a *federal* environmental statute prohibits building where Sharon wants to build. Sharon sues Epstein for specific performance, and alleges that the federal statute does not apply. So the complaint mentions a federal law and raises a federal issue. But there is no FQ jurisdiction. Why? _____

_____

_____

_____

_____

_____

-- *IMPORTANT*: Diversity and FQ can get a *case* into federal court. Once it is there, though, there may be additional *claims* in that case. *For every single claim, test whether it invokes diversity or FQ.* If so, it can come into the case. What if it does not?

D. Supplemental Jurisdiction.

Can this be used to get a *case* into federal court? _____

_____

Supplemental jurisdiction only works after a case is already in federal court (through diversity or FQ). Now we have an *additional claim in that case* that does not meet diversity or FQ. We might get *that claim* into federal court with supplemental jurisdiction.

1. **The test.** The claim we want to get into federal court must share a "common nucleus of operative fact" with the claim that invoked federal subject matter jurisdiction. This test is *always* met by claims that arise from the same transaction or occurrence (T/O) as the underlying claim. _____

2. **The limitation.** BUT in a diversity case, the plaintiff cannot use supplemental jurisdiction to overcome a lack of diversity.

a. P (Utah) sues D-1 (CA) and D-2 (Utah) on state-law claims in one case. The claims arise from the same transaction. The claims exceed $75,000. The claim by P against D-1 meets diversity of citizenship jurisdiction. The claim by P against D-2 does not. Can the claim by P against D-2 invoke supplemental jurisdiction? After all, the claim meets "the test." Is it OK? _____

_____

_____

_____

b. But P can use supplemental jurisdiction to overcome a lack of diversity for a claim in a FQ case.

-- P (CA) sues D (CA) for (1) violation of federal antitrust laws, and joins a transactionally related claim for (2) violation of state antitrust laws. OK? Claim (1) is OK because it's a FQ. But claim (2) is not FQ (because it's based on state law) and does not meet diversity. Can claim (2) invoke supplemental jurisdiction? YES. It meets "the test" and the limitation does not apply. Why?

_____

_____

_____

c. And P can also use supplemental jurisdiction to overcome a lack of *amount in controversy* for a claim in a diversity case.

-- P-1 (CA) and P-2 (CA) sue D (AZ) on state-law claims. P-1's claim is for $100,000. P-2's claim arises from the same transaction, and is for $50,000. P-1's claim meets diversity. But P-2's claim does not, because even though citizenship is OK, the claim does not exceed $75,000. Can the claim by P-2 invoke supplemental jurisdiction? Yes. This claim meets the test and _____

_____

_____

_____

_____

d. And any party but P can use supplemental jurisdiction to overcome either a lack of complete diversity or amount in controversy in any case (diversity or FQ).

-- SOLID GOLD SUMMARY: So a non-federal, non-diversity claim can be heard in federal court if it meets "the test" *UNLESS* it is:

    a. Asserted by a plaintiff
    b. In a diversity of citizenship (not FQ) case AND
    c. Would violate complete diversity.

3.   **Discretionary factors.** Court has discretion NOT to hear the supplemental claim if: (1) the federal question is dismissed early in the proceedings; or (2) the state law claim is complex, or (3) state law issues would predominate.

E.   **Removal.** A defendant sued in state court might be able to "remove" the case to federal court. Removal is a one-way street -- it transfer a case ONLY from a state trial court to a federal trial court. If improper, federal court can "remand" to state court.

1.   No later than 30 days after *service* of the first document that makes the case removable. Usually, this means 30 days after service of process. But some cases are not removable then and only become removable later (example in hypo 2.e. below).

2.   *General test.* D can remove if the case would invoke diversity or FQ.

    a.   P sues D-1 and D-2. Can D-1 remove? _____

    _____

    b.   P sues D in state court. D files a claim against P in that case. Can P remove? _____

    _____

    _____

    c.   P (AZ) sues D (CA) in AZ state court for tort damages of $500,000. Can D remove? Yes. Why? _____

    _____

    d.   P (Georgia) sues D-1 (CA) and D-2 (Alabama) in an Alabama state court for $500,000. Can D-1 and D-2 remove? No. *Special rule for diversity cases only*: _____

    _____

    _____

    _____

    _____

    -- This exception only applies in diversity cases, never in FQ cases.

e. What if P dismisses the claim against D-2? The case *then becomes removable* because there is no defendant who is a citizen of the forum. So D-1 (the remaining defendant) has 30 days from service of the dismissal of D-2 in which to remove. BUT in a *diversity case*, no removal more than one year after the case was filed in state court.

_____

_____

_____

3. *Where?* The case can only be removed to the federal district embracing the state court in which the case was originally filed.

4. *Procedure for removal:* D files notice of removal in federal court, stating grounds of removal; signed under Rule 11; attach all documents served on D in state action; copy to all adverse parties. Then file copy of notice in state court.

    -- If removal was procedurally improper, P moves to remand to state court; she must do so within 30 days of removal. But if there is no federal subject matter jurisdiction, P can move to remand *anytime* (or the federal court can remand *anytime*). In other words, there is no time limit on raising lack of subject matter jurisdiction. (Similarly, in a case filed originally in federal court, the court must dismiss if there is no federal subject matter jurisdiction.)

    -- A defendant who files a *permissive* counterclaim (or cross-complaint) in state court probably waives the right to remove. Filing a *compulsory* counterclaim in state court, though, probably does not waive the right to remove. (Counterclaims are on p. 16.)

F. **The *Erie* Doctrine.** The question will be whether the court must apply state law on some issue. Black letter: in diversity cases, federal court must apply state ***substantive*** law.

    1. Ask: is there a federal law (like federal constitution or statute or FRCP or Federal Rule of Evidence) on point that directly conflicts with state law? If so, apply the federal law, as long as it is valid. What is this based on? _____

    _____

    _____

      -- BTW, a FRCP is valid if it is "arguably procedural." None has ever been held invalid.

    2. If there is no federal law on point, ask: is this issue one of the easy ones? These are the easy ones: (1) elements of a claim or defense, (2) statute of limitations, (3) rules for tolling statutes of limitations, and (4) conflict (or choice) of law rules. Why are these easy? _____

    _____

3. What if there is no federal law, and it's not an easy one, but federal judge wants to do ignore the state law? If the issue is substantive, she must follow state law. Throw in 3 tests, and come to a reasonable conclusion:

   a. *Outcome determinative:* would applying or ignoring the state rule affect outcome of case? If so, it's probably a substantive rule, so should use state law.
   b. *Balance of interests:* does either federal or state system have strong interest in having its rule applied?
   c. *Avoid forum shopping:* if the federal court ignores state law on this issue, will it cause parties to flock to federal court? If so, should probably apply state law.

III. VENUE

A. Basic idea. Subject matter jurisdiction told us we can take a case to federal court. Venue tells us exactly *which* federal court. The country is divided into federal *districts.* P is suing in federal court and wants to lay venue in a proper district.

B. Local actions. Actions about ownership, possession or injury (including trespass) to **land** must be filed in the district where the land lies.

C. If it's not a local action, it is called _____

_____

In any transitory case (diversity or FQ), plaintiff may lay venue in **"any *district* where . . ."**

   -- **all defendants reside* (special rule in hypo #2 below) or**
   -- **a substantial part of the claim arose.**

1. P (D. Kan.) sues D-1 (E.D. Ca.) and D-2 (D. Colo.) for $200,000 for breach of contract occurring somewhere in the United States. What are proper venues?

   -- One choice: any district where all defendants reside. What's wrong? _____

   _____

   _____

   -- Another choice: any district where a substantial part of claim arose. We need more facts about where (in what district(s)) the breach of contract occurred.

*2. Wayne Newton (D. Nev.) sues D-1 (N.D. Ca.) and D-2 (C.D. Ca.). SPECIAL RULE in cases where all defendants reside in different districts *of the same state,* plaintiff can lay venue in the district in which any of them resides. _____

   _____

   _____

D. Where do defendants "reside" for venue purposes?

1. Where does a human "reside"? _____

   _____

2. Corporations and other business associations "reside" in all districts where they are subject to personal jurisdiction (PJ) when the case is filed!

   -- So a corporation might have two *citizenships,* but it might "reside" in every district in the U.S.

E. Transfer of venue. A federal district court may transfer the case to another federal district court. IMPORTANT: It can only transfer to a district where case *could have been filed.* What does that mean? _____

   _____

   _____

   _____

   _____

1. If venue in original district is *proper*, that court has *discretion* to transfer to another federal district, based on convenience for the parties and witnesses and "the interests of justice." Courts are nervous about this, because transfer overrides P's choice of forum. In deciding whether to transfer, what factors does it look to? _____

   _____

   _____

   -- Public: things like what law applies, what community should be burdened with jury service, keeping local controversy in the local court.
   -- Private: convenience – where are the witnesses and the evidence?

      -- The court to which case is transferred under this statute applies the choice of law rules of original court (even if the plaintiff sought the transfer).

2. If venue in original district is *improper*, court may transfer in the interests of justice or dismiss.

F. Forum Non Conveniens. Like transfer, there is another court that is far more convenient than the one we are in now. But here, the court does not transfer to that court. What does it do? _____

   _____

-- Why does the court dismiss or stay? Because transfer is impossible -- the more convenient court is in a different judicial system (*e.g.,* a foreign country).

-- Decision is based on the same public and private factors as transfer in E.1. above. This requires a *very* strong showing, though, since this results in dismissal or stay.

-- Does it matter that P may recover less in the other court? Not determinative.
-- FNC dismissal almost never granted if P is resident of the present forum.

SECOND BIG TOPIC: LEARNING ABOUT THE CASE (through page 22)

I. SERVICE OF PROCESS

A. **Basic idea.** Must give notice to D. Deliver to D (1) a summons (formal court notice of suit and time for response) and (2) a copy of the complaint.

-- These two documents are called: _____

-- Serve within 120 days of filing case or case dismissed without prejudice (not dismissed if P shows good cause for delay in serving).

B. **Who can serve process?**

-- *Any nonparty* who is at least 18 years old.

     -- Does she have to be appointed by a court? _____

C. **The mechanics -- how is process served?**

     1. **Personal service.** Papers given to D personally. Where? _____

         _____

     2. **Substituted service.** Process is left with D's butler at D's summer home. OK if:

         _____

         _____

         _____

         _____

     3. **Service on D's agent.** Process can be delivered to D's agent. OK if receiving service is within the scope of agency, *e.g.*, agent appointed by contract or by law or corporation's registered agent, managing agent or officer.

4. **State law.** In addition, in federal court we can use methods of service **permitted by state law** of the state where the federal court sits *or* where service is effected.

5. **Waiver by mail.** Mail (regular mail is OK) to D a copy of the complaint and two copies of a waiver form, with a prepaid means of returning the form. If D executes and mails the waiver form to P within 30 days, D waives formal service.

-- What does P do then? _____

_____

_____

-- Suppose D fails to return the waiver form. P then has D served personally or by substituted service. If D did not have good cause for failing to return the waiver form is there a penalty for D? _____

_____

_____

_____

D. **Geographic limitation.** Federal court can serve process outside the state in which it sits ONLY if state law allows (*e.g.,* with a long-arm statute).

E. **Immunity from service.**

-- D is served for a federal civil case while instate to be a witness or party in another civil case. OK? _____

_____

_____

F. **Other documents.** For later papers (*e.g.*, answer, other pleadings, motions, discovery requests and responses), we serve by delivering or mailing the document to the party's attorney (or pro se party). If mailed, add 3 days for any required response.

II. PLEADINGS

A. **Basic idea.** Documents setting forth claims and defenses.

B. **Rule 11.** Requires attorney (or party representing herself, called a *pro se* party) to sign all papers (except discovery documents, which are treated by another rule).

-- With signature, the person is certifying that to the best of her knowledge and belief, *after reasonable inquiry*:

1. The paper is not for an improper **purpose**,
2. Legal contentions are warranted by **law** (or nonfrivolous argument for law change), and
3. **Factual contentions** *and* denials of factual contentions have evidentiary support (or are likely to after further investigation).

-- This certification effective every time position is "presented" to the court (*e.g.*, at signing, at filing, when later advocating a position). _____

_____

_____

-- Sanctions may be levied (they are discretionary) against attorney, firm, or party. Are Rule 11 sanctions supposed to punish or to deter a repeat of bad conduct? _____

_____

_____

-- Can be non-monetary sanctions. Monetary sanctions are often paid to court, not to the other party. Before imposing sanctions, court must give a chance to be heard.

-- If another party violates Rule 11, can a party move for sanctions now? _____

-- You *serve* the motion on other parties but cannot file it. The party in violation has a *safe harbor of 21 days* in which to fix the problem and avoid sanctions. If she does not do so, then the motion can be filed.

-- The court can raise Rule 11 problems on its own ("sua sponte"). If it does – by demanding that a party show cause why there should be no sanctions – does the court have to give the party a safe harbor of 21 days to fix the problem? _____

_____

_____

C. **Complaint.** Filing commences an action.

1. Requirements:

   a. Statement of grounds for *subject matter jurisdiction*;
   b. Short and plain statement of the *claim*, showing entitled to relief;
   c. Demand for *relief* sought.

   -- In stating the claim, federal courts traditionally used "notice pleading," which means you only need enough detail to put the other side on notice. Now, though, the Supreme Court requires more detail.

-- What is the standard? _____

_____

_____

_____

_____

_____

2.   What three matters must be pleaded with even more detail -- with *particularity* or *specificity*? _____

_____

-- Special damages do not normally flow from an event. _____

D. Defendant's response. Rule 12 requires D to respond in one of two ways: (1) by **motion** or (2) by **answer**. To avoid default, when must you do one of these two things? _____

_____

1.   *Motions* (Rule 12). Motions are not pleadings; they are requests for a court order.

   a.   Issues of form: (1) Motion for more definite statement – pleading so vague D can't frame a response (rare); (2) Motion to strike, which is aimed at immaterial things, *e.g.,* demand for jury when no right exists; any party can bring.

   b.   *Rule 12(b) defenses:* (1) lack of subject matter jurisdiction; (2) lack of personal jurisdiction; (3) improper venue; (4) insufficiency of process (problem with the papers); (5) insufficient service of process; (6) failure to state a claim; (7) failure to join indispensable party. These can be raised *either* by motion or answer.

   -- Which of these are called "waivable"? _____

   _____

   -- "WAIVABLE" ONES MUST BE PUT IN THE *FIRST* RULE 12 RESPONSE (MOTION OR ANSWER) OR ELSE THEY'RE WAIVED.

   (1) P sues D. D files a timely motion to dismiss for defective service of process. The court denies the motion, after which D files and serves her answer, asserting as defenses lack of personal jurisdiction and improper venue. OK? NO—she has waived both defenses. Why? _____

   _____

   _____

(2)   At trial, D moves to dismiss for failure to join an "indispensable party" and for failure to state a claim on which relief can be granted. OK? _____

_____

_____

_____

(3)   After trial, D asserts for the first time that the court lacks subject matter jurisdiction. OK? _____

_____

_____

2.   ***The Answer.*** It is a pleading.

   a.   **Timing.** Serve within 21 days after service of process. But if D made a Rule 12 motion, and it is denied, she must serve her answer within 14 days after court rules on motion.

   b.   **What do you do in the answer?**

   (1)   Respond to allegations of complaint: (1) admit; (2) deny; (3) state that you lack sufficient information to admit or deny. Number 3 acts as a denial, but can't be used if the information is public knowledge or is in defendant's control.

   Failure to deny can constitute an admission on any matter except damages. In his complaint, P alleges "D was intoxicated while driving his car." In his answer, D said "P has no proof that I was intoxicated." Did D make a mistake? _____

_____

_____

   (2)   Raise affirmative defenses. These basically say "even if I did all the terrible things plaintiff says, plaintiff still cannot win." Classic affirmative defenses are statute of limitations, statute of frauds, res judicata, self-defense.

   --   P sues D for breach of contract. D answers, denying material allegations. At trial, D introduces evidence that the contract was procured by P's fraud, and is therefore unenforceable. P objects. The evidence is inadmissible because it relates to an affirmative defense that defendant failed to plead. _____

_____

_____

E. **Counterclaim.** This is a *claim* against *an opposing party, e.g.,* D v. P. In federal court, it is part of **D's answer**. The two types of counterclaim.

-- *Compulsory:* arises from the same T/O as P's claim. MUST BE FILED IN THE PENDING CASE, OR IT'S WAIVED. The claim cannot be asserted in another action.

_____

_____

-- *Permissive:* does *not* arise from same T/O as plaintiff's claim. You may file it with your answer in this case or can assert it in a separate case.

-- Lois and Meg, each driving her own car, collide and each is injured. Lois sues Meg to recover for personal injuries. Meg answers and defends the suit and then institutes her own action against Lois to recover for her personal injuries. Case dismissed. Why? __

_____

_____

_____

-- Instead of answering, say Meg moved to dismiss the first case and the court granted the motion. Meg would not have to file a counterclaim in that case, because she was never required to answer. _____

-- If a counterclaim is procedurally OK in federal court, then what do you do? _____

_____

_____

-- So assess whether the counterclaim invokes diversity or FQ jurisdiction. If so, it's OK in federal court. If not, then try supplemental jurisdiction.

F. **Crossclaim.** This is a claim against a *co-party*. It *must* arise from the same T/O as the underlying action.

-- If you have a crossclaim, *must* you file it in the pending case? _____

_____

-- P (CA) sues Draper (NY) and Sterling (NY) for personal injuries of $500,000 arising from a car collision (Draper was driving Sterling's car). Sterling doesn't know who's at fault between the two drivers, but knows his car (worth $200,000) is totaled. Sterling wants to recover $200,000 for the property damage. (No federal question anywhere in this hypo.)

1. Sterling should file a compulsory counterclaim against P. It's against an opposing party and arises from the same T/O as P's claim, so it's a compulsory counterclaim. Now, is there subject matter jurisdiction over the compulsory counterclaim? _____

    _____

    _____

    _____

2. Sterling *may* file a crossclaim against Draper. It's against a co-party and arises from the same T/O as the underlying case, so it's a crossclaim. What about subject matter jurisdiction? _____

    _____

    _____

```
                                    (Draper (NY)
        P (CA) --------------------(
                                    (Sterling (NY)
```

    --So is there supplemental jurisdiction over the crossclaim? Yes. Why? Because it (1) meets "the test" because it arises from the same T/O as the underlying case and (2) this is not a claim by a plaintiff, so "the limitation" on supplemental jurisdiction does not apply. _____

    _____

G. Amending pleadings – think of fact patterns.

1. **Right to amend.**

    -- *Plaintiff* has a **right to amend** *once* _____

    _____

    _____

    -- *Defendant* has a **right to amend** *once* within 21 days of serving his answer.

2. **If there's no right to amend**, seek leave of court; it will be granted if "justice so requires." What factors do courts look to in ruling on this? _____

    _____

    _____

3.   **Variance.** That's where the evidence at trial does not match what was pleaded.

-- P sues for breach of contract; D answers. At trial, P introduces evidence that D assaulted him. D doesn't object. OK? Evidence of assault is admitted into evidence (because D didn't object). At or after trial, P can move to amend the complaint to conform to the evidence. Why? _____

_____

_____

-- This ensures that the pleadings match what was actually tried.

-- Same case, but D does object. Evidence of assault inadmissible because it is at "variance with the pleadings."

4.   **Amendment after the statute of limitations has run ("relation back").**

a. To join a new claim. P files his complaint and has process served on July 1. The statute of limitations runs on July 10. In August, P seeks leave to amend to add a new claim. Is the new claim time-barred because the statute ran on July 10?

-- Rule: Amended pleadings "relate back" if they concern the same conduct, transaction or occurrence as the original pleading.

-- Relation back means you treat the amended pleading as though it was filed when the original was filed, so it can avoid a statute of limitations problem. _____

_____

_____

_____

b. To change a defendant after the statute has run. This will relate back if:

   (1) It concerns the same conduct, transaction, or occurrence as the original;
   (2) The new party knew of the action within 120 days of its filing; and
   (3) She also knew that, but for a mistake, she would have been named originally.

This applies when P sued the wrong D first, but the right D knew about it. Example:
-- P is injured in a Sam's Store. He sues "Sam Store, Inc." before the statute runs and has process served on Sam within 120 days. P should have sued "Samco Ltd." Sam is president of Samco Ltd. and is authorized to receive service. P discovers the problem after the statute runs, and seeks leave to amend to name Samco Ltd. _____

_____

III. DISCOVERY

A. **Required disclosures.** This material must be produced even though no one asks for it.

   1. **Initial disclosures.** Unless court order or stipulation of parties differs, in most cases, within 14 days of the Rule 26(f) conference, must identify persons and give copies (or description) of documents or electronically stored info "likely to have discoverable information that the disclosing party may use to support its claims or defenses," computation of damages and insurance for any judgment.

   2. **Experts.** As directed by court, must identify experts "who may be used at trial," written report containing opinions, data used, qualifications, compensation, etc.

   3. **Pretrial.** No later than 30 days before trial, must give detailed information about trial evidence, including documents and identity of witnesses to testify live or by deposition.

B. **Discovery tools.** These may not be used until after Rule 26(f) conference unless court order or stipulation allows. What is a key issue with discovery tools? _____

   _____

   _____

   _____

   1. **Depositions** (questions can be oral or written (if written, read by court reporter)). Deponent gives sworn oral answers to questions by counsel (or pro se parties). Recorded by sound or video or stenographically and a transcript can then be made.

       -- ***Can depose nonparties or parties. Nonparty should be subpoenaed, however, or she is not compelled to attend.*** Subpoena could be "duces tecum," which requires the deponent to bring material (*e.g.*, documents) with her. Party need not be subpoenaed; notice of the deposition, properly served, is sufficient to compel attendance.

       a. Cannot take more than 10 depositions or depose the same person twice without court approval or stipulation. Deposition cannot exceed one day of seven hours unless court orders or parties stipulate.
       b. Use at trial (all subject to rules of evidence): (1) impeach the deponent; (2) any purpose if the deponent is an adverse party; (3) any purpose if the deponent (regardless of whether a party) is unavailable for trial, unless that absence was procured by the party seeking to introduce the evidence.

       c. Unless she agrees, nonparty cannot be required to travel more than 100 miles from her residence or place where she regularly transacts business for the depo.

       d. Notice of subpoena to a business may require it to designate the right person for deposition (*e.g.,* to depose the person who designed a particular product).

2. **Interrogatories**. Questions propounded in writing *to another party*, to be answered in writing under oath. Must respond with answers or objections within 30 days. Can say you don't know the answer, but only after reasonable investigation; if the answer could be found in business records and it would be burdensome to find it, can allow propounder access to those records.

   -- At trial, cannot use your own answers; others may be used per rules of evidence. Cannot serve more than 25 (including subparts) without court order or stipulation.

3. **Requests to produce**. Requests to *another party (or to non-party if accompanied by subpoena)* requesting that she make available for review and copying various documents or things, including electronically stored info (ESI), or permit entry upon designated property for inspection, measuring, etc. Specify form in which ESI is to be produced (hard copy or electronic). Must respond within 30 days of service, stating that the material will be produced or stating objection.

4. **Physical or mental examination**. *Only available through court order* on showing that party's (or person in party's control, *e.g.*, parent in control of child) health is in actual controversy and "good cause" (i.e., you need it and can't get it elsewhere). Party seeking the order chooses the suitably licensed person to perform the exam. Person examined may obtain copy of report simply by asking for it, but by doing so waives his doctor-patient privilege re reports by his doctors re that condition.

5. **Request for admission**. A request by one party *to another party* to admit the truth of any discoverable matters. Often used to authenticate documents; the propounding party will send copies of the documents to be authenticated with the request. Must respond within 30 days of service. The response is to admit or deny; can indicate lack of information only if indicate you've made a reasonable inquiry. Failure to deny tantamount to admission; can amend if failure not in bad faith.

6. Parties sign substantive answers to discovery under oath. Every discovery request and response is signed by counsel certifying (1) it is warranted, (2) not interposed for improper purpose, and (3) not unduly burdensome. (Remember, Rule 11 does not apply to discovery documents, so this is a separate certification for them.)

7. Duty to supplement. If a party learns that its response to required disclosure, interrogatory, request for production, or request for admission is incomplete or incorrect, what must she do? _____

   _____

C. **Scope of discovery (what information can we get through discovery?).**

   1. **Standard**. What can you discover? _____

      _____

      _____

-- **Relevant** means "reasonably calculated to lead to the discovery of admissible evidence." NOTE—This is broader than "admissible." So you may be able to discover hearsay, even though it would not be admissible at trial. It's OK just so it's reasonably calculated to lead to admissible evidence. _____

2.   **Privileged** matter is not discoverable. _____

_____

_____

3.   **Work product** or "trial preparation materials" (material prepared in anticipation of litigation). Generally protected from discovery.

   --   Howell sues Skipper for losses sustained when a vessel sank. Skipper, fearing the suit, had hired Shore, an attorney, who interviewed Gilligan, a witness to the sinking. Shore (a) had Gilligan write a statement regarding the incident; (b) made a note that based on what Gilligan says, there appears to be no defense; and (c) made a note that Gilligan is stupid and would make a lousy witness at trial.

   -- *All three items are work product, because each was generated in anticipation of litigation.* So start with assumption it is NOT discoverable. BUT

   -- Item (a) (the witness statement by Gilligan) is discoverable if Howell shows: _____

   _____

   _____

   _____

   -- BUT items (b) and (c) are absolutely protected because they are (1) mental impressions, (2) opinions, (3) conclusions, and (4) legal theories.

   -- Does work product have to be generated by a lawyer? _____

   _____

   _____

4.   **Claiming privilege or work product.** If you withhold discovery because it asked for privileged material or work product, you must claim the protection expressly and describe the materials. If you inadvertently produced protected material, notify the other party, who then has to return it pending decision by the court.

5.   **Experts.** Remember, parties are required to produce information about experts who may be used at trial without request from party (p. 19). In addition, a party may take deposition of any expert "whose opinions may be presented at trial."

-- Consulting expert (retained in anticipation of litigation but will not testify at trial): no discovery absent "exceptional need" (probably means not available elsewhere).

D. Enforcement of discovery rules.

1. There are three main ways discovery problems are presented to court.

   a. *Protective order.* Responding party seeks protective order (*e.g.*, request is overburdensome, or involves trade secrets and we want an order limiting disclosure to the litigation or electronically stored information is not reasonably accessible (e.g., deleted files) or request seeks work product);

   b. *Partial violation.* Receiving party answers some and objects to others. If the objections are not upheld, this is a *partial violation*, so we expect a light sanction.

   c. *Total violation.* Receiving party fails completely to attend deposition, respond to interrogatories or to respond to requests for production. This is a *total violation*, so we expect a heavy sanction.

2. Sanctions against a party. (The party seeking sanctions must certify to the court that she tried in good faith to get the info without court involvement.)

   -- If a party fails to produce electronically stored information because it was lost in the good faith, routine operation of an electronic info system, are there sanctions?

   _____

   _____

   a. **Partial violation:** _____

      (1) Can get an *order compelling* the party to answer the unanswered questions, plus costs (including attorney's fees) of bringing motion.

      (2) IF the party violates the order compelling him to answer, RAMBO sanctions plus costs (and attorney's fees re the motion) and could be held in contempt for violating a court order (except no contempt for refusal to submit to medical exam).

   b. **Total violation:** one step. RAMBO plus costs (and attorney's fees re the motion). No need to get an order compelling answers. Go directly to RAMBO.

      -- **RAMBO SANCTIONS** (choices available to judge):
      -- Establishment order (establishes facts as true)
      -- Strike pleadings of the disobedient party (as to issues re the discovery)
      -- Disallow evidence from the disobedient party (as to issues re the discovery)
      -- Dismiss plaintiff's case (if bad faith shown)
      -- Enter default judgment against defendant (if bad faith shown)

THIRD BIG TOPIC: COMPLEX CASES – JOINING PARTIES (to page 28)

A. **Proper parties.** Plaintiff is structuring the case and may want multiple parties on one side or the other – so who *may* be joined as co-parties?

-- Three people are injured when the taxi in which they are riding crashes. May they sue together as co-plaintiffs? Yes, because their claims:

(1) _____

_____ AND

(2) _____

_____

-- May they (or any one of them) sue the taxi driver and the cab company as co-defendants? Yes, because the claims *against the two* (1) arise from the same T/O and (2) raise at least one common question.

-- Then assess subject matter jurisdiction – can the case as structured invoke diversity or federal question jurisdiction?

B. **Necessary and indispensable parties.** Some absentees (non-parties) must be forced to join in the case. Why? Because they're necessary (or "required").

1. **Who's necessary?** An absentee (A) who meets any of these tests:

(1) Without A, the court cannot accord complete relief among existing parties (worried about multiple suits);
(2) A's interest may be harmed if he is not joined (practical harm); or
(3) A claims an interest which subjects a party (usually D) to multiple obligations.

-- Which is most likely on the bar exam? _____

_____

-- Are joint tortfeasors necessary? _____

-- Bob Barker holds 1000 shares of stock in Pricelineisright.com. Shatner claims that he and Bob agreed to buy the stock jointly and that he paid for half the stock. Shatner sues Pricelineisright.com, seeking to have Bob's shares canceled and the stock reissued in their joint names. Is Bob necessary? Yes. He probably meets all three tests for required. Which one seems clearest? _____

_____

_____

2. **Can A be joined?** So Bob is necessary. NOW see if his joinder is "feasible." It is feasible if (1) there is personal jurisdiction over him and (2) joining him will not destroy diversity (the court decides whether Bob is joined as a plaintiff or a defendant). If joinder is feasible, bring Bob into the case.

3. **If A cannot be joined.** What happens if Bob cannot be joined? The court must do one of two things. What are the choices? _____

_____

_____

_____

-- How does the court make that decision? It looks at these factors:

   (a) is there an alternative forum available (maybe a state court)?
   (b) what is the actual likelihood of harm to Bob?
   (c) can the court shape relief to avoid that potential harm?

-- What happens if the court decides to dismiss (rather than proceed without Bob)? _____

HINT: JOINDER RULES THAT START WITH "C" – COUNTERCLAIM, CROSSCLAIM – ARE CLAIMS BETWEEN PRESENT PARTIES. CLAIMS THAT START WITH "I" INVOLVE JOINING SOMEONE NEW TO THE CASE.

C. **Impleader** (third-party practice). A defending party wants to bring in someone new (third-party defendant ("TPD")) for one reason: the TPD may owe indemnity or contribution to the defending party on the underlying claim. There is a right to implead within 14 days after serving answer; after that, need court permission.

-- Pam sues Doris to recover for personal injuries from a car wreck. Doris has a right to indemnity from Insco. (Or perhaps Doris has a right of contribution from a joint tortfeasor.) Steps for impleading the TPD in the pending case:

a. File third-party complaint naming Insco as TPD; and
b. Serve process on the TPD. (So must have personal jurisdiction over TPD.)

TPD

Plaintiff -------------- Defendant

-- After TPD is joined, can plaintiff assert a claim against TPD? Yes, if the claim arises from the same T/O as the underlying case.
-- After TPD is joined, can TPD assert a claim against plaintiff? Yes if the claim arises from the same T/O as the underlying case.

A-24

-- Subject matter jurisdiction. Then, for any of these claims, assess subject matter jurisdiction. Always do it the same way. Does the claim invoke diversity of citizenship or FQ? If so, it's OK.

-- If one of these claims does not invoke diversity or FQ, what do we try? _____

D. **Intervention.** Absentee wants to join a pending suit. She chooses to come in either as plaintiff or as a defendant. The court may realign her if it thinks she came in on the "wrong" side. Application to intervene must be "timely."

   -- Intervention of right. A's interest may be harmed if she is not joined and her interest is not adequately represented now. (Like test #2 for necessary parties.)

   -- Permissive intervention. A's claim or defense and the pending case have at least one common question. Discretionary with court; OK unless delay or prejudice.

   -- Say in a diversity case and the plaintiff intervenor is not diverse from original D (or the defendant-intervenor is not diverse from original P). Is there supplemental jurisdiction over a claim by or against an intervenor? The courts generally say no.

E. **Interpleader.** One holding property forces all potential claimants into a single lawsuit to avoid multiple litigation and inconsistency.

   -- Person with property is called the stakeholder.
   -- Folks who want it are called the claimants.

   -- There are two types of interpleader in federal court: "rule" (FRCP 22) and "statutory." In each, the stakeholder is not sure who really owns the property (maybe she thinks she does) and wants to avoid multiple liability or suits. The types have different standards for diversity of citizenship, amount in controversy, venue, and service of process. In each, the court can enjoin claimants from suing elsewhere. Remember: rule interpleader is a regular diversity case.

      -- To determine diversity of citizenship:

         -- Under rule interpleader: stakeholder must be diverse from *every* claimant.
         -- Under statutory interpleader: one claimant must be diverse from one other claimant (don't care about stakeholder's citizenship).

      -- Amount in controversy: Under the Rule, must exceed $75,000. Under the statute, $500 or more.

      -- Service of process: Under the Rule, treated as a regular lawsuit. Under the statute, nationwide service (so no personal jurisdiction problems over claimants in U.S.).

-- Venue: Rule, like a regular case. Statute, any district where any claimant resides.

-- Hypo: Insco (inc. in Del.; ppb NY) holds a fund of $100,000 under a life insurance policy. After the insured dies, potential claimants to the fund are Bonzo (NJ), Gonzo (MN) and Nonzo (NY). Insco wants to avoid being sued on the policy in three different actions. What can it do? Interplead. But how?

   (1) No rule interpleader because no diversity. Stakeholder is not diverse from every claimant.

   (2) How about statutory interpleader? OK—for diversity, one claimant is diverse from one other. All other requirements met.

F. The Class Action. Representative(s) ("Rep") sues on behalf of class members.

1. Initial requirements. Must demonstrate *all* of these:

   a. *Numerosity*: Too many class members for practicable joinder;
   b. *Commonality*: There are some questions of law or fact in common to class;
   c. *Typicality*: Rep's claims/defenses typical of those of the class; *and*
   d. *Representative is adequate*: Rep will fairly and adequately represent class.

2. Next step. Must fit the case within one of three types:

   a. "Prejudice": class treatment necessary to avoid harm either to class members or to party opposing class. An example is many claimants to a fund. Individual suits might deplete the fund, leaving some without remedy. _____

   _____

   b. Injunction or declaratory judgment (not damages) sought because class was treated alike by other party. Example: _____

   _____

   _____

   c. "Damages": (1) common questions predominate over individual questions; AND (2) class action is the superior method to handle the dispute. Example: _____

   _____

   _____

   _____

   _____

3. The court must determine "at an early practicable time" whether to "certify" the case to proceed as a class action. If the court certifies the class, it must define the class and the class claims, issues, or defenses.

-- What else must the court do if it certifies the class? _____

_____

_____

-- Class counsel must fairly and adequately represent the interests of the class.

4. Does the court notify the class of pendency of the class action? In the Type 3 class, the court must notify class members, including individual notice (usually by mail) to all reasonably identifiable members. The notice tells them various things, including: (a) they can opt out; (b) they'll be bound if they don't; and (c) they can enter a separate appearance through counsel.

-- Who pays to give this notice? _____

-- Is this kind of notice required in Type 1 or Type 2 classes? _____

_____

5. Who's bound by the judgment? All class members, except those who opt out of a Type 3 class action. Is there any right to opt out of a Type 1 or Type 2 class? _____

_____

6. Can the parties dismiss or settle a certified class action? _____

_____

-- And, in all three types of class action, the court gives notice to class members to get their feedback on whether the case should be settled or dismissed. If it's a Type 3 class, the court might give members a second chance to opt out.

7. Subject matter jurisdiction. The class could invoke FQ jurisdiction by asserting a claim arising under federal law.

-- What about a class action brought under diversity of citizenship? For citizenship, consider only the rep (ignore other class members' citizenships). What about amount in controversy? _____

_____

-- So: as long as the rep is diverse from all defendants, and as long as the rep's claim exceeds $75,000, it's OK.

8. *Class Action Fairness Act (CAFA).* This contains a grant of subject matter jurisdiction separate from regular diversity of citizenship jurisdiction. It lets federal courts hear a class action if *any* class member (not just the representative) is of diverse citizenship from *any* defendant and if the aggregated claims of the class exceed $5,000,000. It makes it easier for interstate class actions to go to federal court. There are complicated provisions to ensure that local classes (where most class members and the primary defendants are citizens of the same state) do not stay in federal court; they get dismissed (or, if they were removed from state court, are remanded to state court).

FOURTH BIG TOPIC: ADJUDICATION (to page 33)

I. PRETRIAL ADJUDICATION

A. Voluntary Dismissal. May be allowed on court order (and P may have to pay D's costs). But sometimes P has a right to do so simply by filing a written notice of dismissal.

-- P sues D but, before D answers, files a written notice of dismissal. OK? Yes. P may voluntarily dismiss "without prejudice" before D serves her answer or a motion for summary judgment. What does "without prejudice" mean? _____

_____

_____

-- But if P dismisses the second case by written notice, it is with prejudice, so the claim cannot be reasserted. Is this true even if the first case was filed in state court? _____

_____

_____

B. Default and Default Judgment.

1. Default is a notation by the court clerk on the docket sheet of the case. A claimant gets a default by showing the clerk that D has failed to respond within 21 days after being served with process. D can respond anytime before the default is entered.

2. Getting the default does not entitle the claimant to recover. She needs a *judgment* to enforce and recover money or other remedies. The clerk of court can enter judgment if:

      -- D made no response at all
      -- The claim itself if for a sum certain in money;
      -- Claimant gives an affidavit (sworn statement) of the sum owed; AND
      -- D is not a minor or incompetent.

-- But if any of those four is not true, the claimant must go to the court itself (the judge, not the clerk) for the judgment. The judge will hold a hearing and has discretion to enter judgment. D gets notice of that hearing only if she made some appearance in the case.

3. Default judgment cannot exceed what the claimant demanded in her complaint (or be a different kind of relief. (This is different from a case that goes to trial, in which the claimant can recover more (and a different kind of relief) than she put in her complaint.

   -- D may try to set aside a default by showing good cause and a viable defense. Good cause usually means excusable neglect. D may try to set aside a default judgment on the same basic showing.

C. **Failure to State a Claim.** Under FRCP 12(b)(6), D moves to dismiss for failure to state a claim. It tests only the sufficiency of P's allegations. The court ignores legal conclusions and looks at allegations of fact. It asks this question: _____

_____

_____

-- This tests to see whether the facts alleged state a claim that the law would recognize.

-- In ruling on this motion, does the court look at evidence? _____

_____

_____

(1) Chuck Norris sues Larry King, alleging "while Mr. King and I were bodybuilding, Mr. King asked me how I enjoyed seeing Howard Stern's private parts. No one else heard him, but the statement made me feel cheap." Even assuming it's true, there's no claim here. He would not win a judgment if he showed this. The court will grant King's motion, but will probably let Chuck amend to try to state a claim.

(2) The same motion, if made after D has answered, has a different name, and the California examiners have hit this. What is the name? _____

_____

_____

D. **Summary Judgment.** Moving party must show (1) there's no genuine dispute as to material issue of fact and (2) that she is entitled to judgment as a matter of law.

   -- In summary judgment, can the court look at evidence? _____

_____

-- The court generally views the evidence in the light most favorable to the nonmoving party.

-- The idea of summary judgment is to weed out cases in which we don't need *trial*. Why do we ever have a trial? _____

_____

-- Federline sues the company he founded, Famous For No Reason, Inc. (FFNR), alleging that a representative of the company defamed him by making a derogatory statement to a reporter at a meeting. FFNR files an answer, in which it denies it made the statement. FFNR then moves for summary judgment, attaching affidavits (or declarations) from three wonderful, honest people, who swear that they were at the meeting, and no FFNR representative said anything about Federline.

    -- Affidavits (or declarations) are signed under oath. So they can be used as evidence.

(1)   In response, Federline files no affidavits, but relies on the allegations in his complaint. Summary judgment probably granted. WHY? Federline gave the court no evidence, because pleadings are not evidence (unless verified (under oath)). So the only evidence before the court are FFNR's affidavits from the priest, the rabbi, and the nun. AND __

_____

_____

-- Note: Unverified pleadings are not evidence, but they might be relevant on summary judgment. For example, if D failed to deny an allegation by P, it can be treated as fact.

(2)   Instead, Federline responds with an affidavit from Michael Scott, who swears he heard about the meeting and was told that FFNR made the derogatory statement about Federline. Summary judgment is probably granted here too. WHY? Michael Scott's affidavit is inadmissible (hearsay). So it's the same as the previous hypo. _____

_____

(3)   Instead, Federline responds with deposition testimony from an alcoholic, drug addicted, convicted swindler who swears he was at the meeting and FFNR said derogatory things about Federline. Summary judgment denied. WHY? The evidence for Federline is first-hand knowledge and creates a dispute on a material issue of fact.

_____

_____

_____

_____

II. CONFERENCES AND MEETINGS

A. **Rule 26(f) Conference.** Unless court order says otherwise, at least 21 days before scheduling conference (or scheduling order is due), parties discuss claims, defenses, and settlement. Must form discovery plan, including issues about how electronically stored info will be produced, and present it to court in writing within 14 days.

B. **Scheduling Order.** Unless local rule or court order says otherwise, the court enters an order scheduling cut-offs for joinder, amendment, motions, etc.

C. **Pretrial Conferences.** The court may hold "pretrial conferences" to process the case and foster settlement. Final pretrial conference determines issues to be tried and evidence to be proffered. This is recorded in a pretrial conference order, which *supersedes the pleadings*.

-- The final pretrial conference order is an important document -- it is a roadmap of issues to be tried, evidence to be presented at trial, witnesses, etc. _____

_____

III. TRIAL, JUDGMENT, AND POST-TRIAL MOTIONS

A. **Jury Trial.** (Juries determine FACTS, and are instructed on the law by the judge.)

1. **Right to jury trial in federal court**. Seventh Amendment (which applies ONLY in federal court (not state court)) preserves the right to jury in "civil actions at law," but not in suits at equity. What if a case involves both law and equity?

   -- Suppose a case involves a claim for damages (legal relief) and an injunction (equitable relief). Do we get a jury? _____

   _____

   _____

   _____

   -- In what order will the court usually proceed? _____

   _____

2. Requirement of demand. Must demand *in writing* no later than 14 days after service of the last pleading raising jury triable issue.

3. In the jury selection process ("voir dire"), each side might want to strike (remove) potential jurors. There is no limit on the number of strikes "for cause" (*e.g.*, bias, prejudice, juror is related to a party). But what about "peremptory" strikes? Each side (P and D) gets three.

-- Historically, you didn't need a reason to justify peremptory strikes. Today, however, *peremptory strikes must be used in a race and gender neutral way.* Why?

_____

_____

-- We need at least 6 jurors (a verdict cannot be taken from fewer than 6) and no more than 12. There are no alternate jurors – all participate unless excused for good cause.

4. **Motion for judgment as a matter of law** (JMOL). This is an exceptional order, the effect of which is to take the case away from the jury.

   -- When brought? After the other side has been heard at trial. So usually defendant can move twice: at close of plaintiff's evidence and at close of all evidence at trial. Plaintiff: only at close of all evidence.

   -- Standard for granting motion. _____

   _____

   _____

   _____

   -- Court views evidence in the light most favorable to the nonmoving party.

B. **Renewed motion for judgment as a matter of law (RJMOL).** SAME AS JMOL BUT COMES UP AFTER TRIAL.

1. Situation: judge did not grant motion for JMOL, and the case went to the jury. Jury returns a verdict for one party, and the court enters judgment on the basis of the verdict. Now the losing party files a renewed motion for judgment as a matter of law.

   – If RJMOL is granted, the court enters judgment for the party that lost the jury verdict! Move within 28 days after entry of judgment.

2. Standard: same as with motion for judgment as a matter of law. (So, if granted, the jury reached a conclusion reasonable people could not have reached.)

3. IF YOU DID NOT MOVE FOR JMOL AT TRIAL, YOU CANNOT BRING THE RJMOL MOTION.

C. **Motion for a new trial.**

1. Situation: judgment entered, but errors at trial require a new trial. Something happened that makes the judge think the parties should start over and re-try the case. Move within 28 days after judgment.

2. Grounds: (1) prejudicial (not harmless) error at trial makes judgment unfair (*e.g.*, wrong jury instruction; evidentiary ruling); (2) new evidence that could not have been obtained with due diligence for the original trial; (3) prejudicial misconduct of party or attorney or third party or juror (*e.g.*, juror conducted independent investigation of accident); (4) judgment is against the weight of the evidence (serious error of judgment by jury); (5) excessive or inadequate damages.

3. Compare: grant of new trial is less drastic than grant of renewed motion for judgment as a matter of law. Why? _____

_____

_____

-- RJMOL results in taking judgment away from one party and giving it to the other.

D. Motion to set aside judgment.

Grounds	Timing
1. Clerical error	Anytime
2. Mistake, excusable neglect	Reasonable time (never more than 1 year)
3. New evidence that could not have been discovered with due diligence for a new trial motion	Reasonable time (never more than 1 year)
4. Judgment is void	Reasonable time (no maximum)

FIFTH BIG TOPIC: APPELLATE REVIEW

A. Basic idea. United States Court of Appeals to review what federal district court did.

B. Final judgment rule. Generally, there is a right to appeal only from final judgments. That means the ultimate decision by the trial court of the merits of the entire case. File notice of appeal *in trial court* within 30 days after entry of final judgment.

-- To determine if it's a final judgment, ask: after making this order, does the trial judge have anything left to do on the merits of the case? _____

_____

_____

Would these be final judgments?

-- Grant of a motion for new trial?_____

_____

--   Denial of a motion for new trial? _____

_____

_____

--   Grant of motion to remand to state court? _____

--   Grant or denial of renewed motion for judgment as a matter of law? _____

_____

C.   Interlocutory (non-final) review. May be appealable even though not final judgments.

1.   Interlocutory orders reviewable as of right: orders granting, modifying, refusing, etc. injunctions; appointing, refusing to appoint receivers; findings of patent infringement where only an accounting is left to be accomplished by trial court; orders affecting possession of property, *e.g.,* attachments.

2.   Interlocutory Appeals Act. Allows appeal of nonfinal order if trial judge certifies that it involves a controlling issue of law as to which there is substantial ground for difference of opinion *and* the court of appeals agrees to hear it.

3.   "Collateral order" exception. Appellate court has discretion to hear ruling on an issue if it (a) is distinct from the merits of the case, (b) involves an important legal question, and (c) is essentially unreviewable if parties must await a final judgment (*e.g.*, claim of immunity from suit, such as a state's claim of Eleventh Amendment immunity from suit for damages).

4.   When more than one claim is presented in a case (*e.g.*, claim and counterclaim), or when there are multiple parties, the trial court may expressly direct entry of a final judgment as to one or more of them if it makes an express finding that there is no just reason for delay.

5.   Extraordinary writ. Not technically an appeal, but an original proceeding in appellate court to compel the trial judge to make or vacate a particular order. Not a substitute for appeal; available only to enforce a clear legal duty.

6.   Class action. Court of appeals has discretion to review order granting or denying certification of class action. Must seek review at the court of appeals (not in the trial court) within 14 days of order. Appeal does not stay proceedings at trial court unless trial judge or court of appeals so orders. _____

_____

CALIFORNIA CIVIL PROCEDURE

FIRST BIG TOPIC: ARE WE IN THE RIGHT COURT? (to page 45)

I. PERSONAL JURISDICTION

A. **Basic idea.** This involves one question: can P sue D *in this state*? That's all. It is *not* concerned with what COURT we go to in that state -- that is subject matter jurisdiction.

-- Whether there's personal jurisdiction is a **two-step analysis**:

   1. Satisfy a statute (*e.g.*, a state long-arm statute), AND
   2. Satisfy the Constitution (Due Process).

   -- Is the analysis different depending on whether the case will be filed in federal court or state court? _____

   _____

   _____

   -- Though both steps in the two-step analysis should be mentioned, one has been far more important on the California bar exam. Which one? _____

   _____

   _____

   _____

B. **In personam jurisdiction.** P wants to impose a personal obligation on D. Jurisdiction is over the person, not her property, because of some contact between D and the forum state.

   1. **Statutory analysis.** Most states have a series of statutes that allow personal jurisdiction in different situations, such as personal jurisdiction over defendants who (1) are served with process in the state, or (2) are domiciled in the state, or (3) do certain things (*e.g.*, commit a tortious act, conduct business) in the state.

   In California, though, the statutory analysis is easier. Why? _____

   _____

   _____

   _____

   _____

2. **Constitutional analysis.** (*International Shoe*).

    Test: does defendant have "such minimum contacts with the forum so that exercise of jurisdiction does not offend traditional notions of fair play and substantial justice"?

    -- Though this is amorphous, there are some easy cases. If D is **domiciled** in the forum or **consents**, or is **present in the forum when served with process** (at least if not forced or tricked into forum), those are "traditional bases" and almost always meet the constitutional test. Tougher cases involve lesser contact.

    -- Factors in the constitutional analysis:

    a. **Contact**. There must be a relevant tie between D and the forum state. There are two factors to be addressed here.

        (1) The contact *must* result from **purposeful availment**: D's voluntary act.

        _____

        _____

        _____

        _____

        _____

        -- What are examples of purposeful availment? _____

        _____

        _____

        _____

        _____

        _____

        _____

        (2) **Foreseeability**. What does this mean? _____

        _____

        _____

        _____

b. **Fairness (fair play and substantial justice).** If there is a relevant contact, now we assess whether the exercise of jurisdiction would be fair or reasonable under the circumstances. Factors:

(1) **Relatedness** between the contact and plaintiff's claim. We are assessing the quality of D's contact with the forum. What question do we ask? _____

_____

_____

_____

_____

-- If the answer is yes, the court might uphold jurisdiction even if the defendant does not have a great deal of contact with California. Where the claim is related to D's contact with the forum, it is called: _____

_____

_____

-- What if the claim does not arise from D's contact with the forum? Then, jurisdiction is OK ONLY if the court has *general personal jurisdiction.* To have this, what must be true? _____

_____

_____

_____

-- So a D with continuous and systematic ties with the forum may be sued there for a claim that arose anywhere in the world; that is general personal jurisdiction. But a D with limited ties with the forum can only be sued there for a claim arising from those activities; that is specific jurisdiction.

-- Examples of continuous and systematic ties: _____

_____

_____

(2) **Convenience**: D may complain that the forum makes it tough to litigate because it's far from D's home and maybe it's tough to get D's witnesses and evidence to the forum. Standard: the forum is OK unless it puts D at a *severe disadvantage in the litigation.* _____

_____

_____

_____

(3) **State's interest**, *e.g.*, provide forum for its citizens. _____

_____

SUMMARY OF CONSTITUTIONAL TEST:
My Parents Frequently Forgot to Read Children's Stories.

Minimum contacts	Fair play & substantial justice
— purposeful availment	— relatedness of contact and claim
— foreseeability	— convenience
	— state's interest

-- **HYPO**: Doofus makes valves in PA and sells them to a company in NY. The NY company then puts the Doofus valves into its widgets and sells the widgets nationwide. A Doofus valve in one of these widgets explodes in California. So the Doofus valve got into California, but Doofus did not send it there. Would in personam jurisdiction over Doofus in California be constitutional?

   1. Minimum Contacts. Is there a contact between Doofus and California? YES, the Doofus valve blew up here. _____

   -- But was this contact the result of **purposeful availment** by Doofus of California? Very tough question. Argue both ways and come to a reasonable conclusion.

   -- Maybe no: because a third party (the NY manufacturer) sent the valves to California. _____

   _____

   -- Maybe yes: because Doofus makes money from the sales by the NY company into California. _____

   _____

   _____

-- Is it **foreseeable** that Doofus could get sued in California? Maybe—if Doofus knows its valves get to California and that valves can explode and hurt people. _____

_____

2. *Fairness*. Is there **relatedness**? Yes! The claim arises directly from the contact between Doofus and California. So if Doofus had very little contact with California, jurisdiction might be OK because there is relatedness.

-- On the other hand, if Doofus had continuous and systematic ties with California, the case for jurisdiction here would be especially strong. _____

_____

_____

-- **Convenience.** Doofus may complain that litigation in California is difficult and expensive, and it's tough to get its witnesses there from PA. But it has to show that it is so gravely inconvenient as to put it at a severe disadvantage in the litigation. _____

_____

_____

_____

-- **State's interest.** The forum state (California) might have an interest in providing a courtroom for its people who are harmed by allegedly careless out-of-state manufacturers. _____

_____

Assess each factor and come to a reasonable conclusion.

-- <u>*Special note about the Internet*</u>. A Nevada hotel maintains an *interactive* website, on which Californians can get rate information, make reservations, and get driving directions from California to the hotel. This supported specific jurisdiction in California over the Nevada hotel. Maintaining a passive website, providing only information, in another state, is probably not a relevant contact with California. _____

_____

_____

_____

C. **In rem and quasi in rem jurisdiction.** Here, jurisdiction is not over D herself, but over her property in the forum. The statutory basis is an attachment statute (e.g., allowing court to attach property claimed by non-resident). Constitutionally, the Supreme Court held that in all cases, even in rem and quasi in rem, D must satisfy the *International Shoe* test. So the constitutional analysis is the same as in personam.

II. SUBJECT MATTER JURISDICTION

A. **Basic idea.** Here, we've decided we have personal jurisdiction over D in California and that we'll sue in state (not federal) court. There is one basic trial court in California – the Superior Court. Each of the 58 counties has one Superior Court.

B. **Superior Court.** The Superior Court has *general subject matter* jurisdiction. What does that mean? _____

_____

    -- Are there any kinds of cases the Superior Court cannot hear? Yes, but very few. There are some federal question cases that must go to federal court, but very few. They include bankruptcy, federal securities and antitrust, and patent infringement. Outside of those, the Superior Court can hear any case, including cases that would invoke federal question or diversity of citizenship jurisdiction.

    -- Within the Superior Court, there are different classifications of cases.

        1. **Limited Civil Cases.** These are civil cases in which the amount in controversy

_____

_____

_____

        -- If P demands exactly $25,000, is that a limited civil case? _____

_____

_____

        -- In a limited civil case, generally the court cannot grant a permanent injunction or declaratory judgment or determine title to land. Also, there is limited discovery (we'll see that on p. 57) and you cannot file a "special demurrer."

        -- Key limitation: in a limited case, _____

_____

_____

2. Unlimited Civil Cases. These include civil cases in which the plaintiff seeks general equitable relief (like a permanent injunction or declaratory judgment). What about a case seeking damages? It is unlimited if the amount in controversy:

_____

_____

_____

3. Small Claims Cases. These are heard in a small claims division of the superior court. Procedures are simple. What is the amount in controversy for these?

-- If plaintiff is an individual: $7,500 or less.
-- If plaintiff is an entity: $5,000 or less.

C. Classification and Reclassification.

1. Plaintiff initially determines what kind of case it is.

-- In doing so, what do we consider? The "amount of the demand, or the recovery sought, or the value of the property, or the amount of the lien" in controversy.

-- Does this include attorney's fees, interest on the claim, or costs? _____

_____

-- If plaintiff files a limited civil case, she must note the classification in the caption of the complaint. _____

_____

2. Reclassification.

-- If a case is misclassified or if subsequent events make it clear that the original classification should be changed, does the court lose subject matter jurisdiction?

_____

_____

-- **Automatic.** If P amends her complaint in a way that changes the classification (raises or decreases the amount in controversy from limited to unlimited or unlimited to limited), what happens? _____

_____

_____

-- **On motion.** A party can move to reclassify. Or the court can reclassify on its own motion. What is required here? _____

_____

_____

_____

_____

-- In determining whether to reclassify, can the court consider the merits of the underlying claim? _____

_____

_____

_____

-- Can the court consider materials beyond the pleadings, such as a judicial arbitration award (p. 64) and settlement conference statement? _____

_____

_____

_____

-- If there is a motion to reclassify, the court may reclassify **from unlimited to limited** when the judge is convinced that the matter _____

_____

_____

_____

_____

-- If there is a motion to reclassify, the court may reclassify **from limited to unlimited** when the judge is convinced that _____

_____

_____

_____

3.   **Effect of multiple claims.** Rule: the entire case is either limited or unlimited. So no case is mixed, with some limited and some unlimited.

-- P asserts three unrelated claims against D – one for $12,000, one for $8,000, and one for $6,000. Can this be filed as an unlimited civil case? _____

_____

_____

_____

_____

-- P-1 asserts a claim of $26,000 against D and P-2 asserts a claim of $14,000 against D in the same case. Can this be filed as an unlimited civil case? _____

_____

_____

-- P sues D for $20,000 in a limited civil case. D files a *cross-complaint* against P for $26,000. What happens? _____

_____

_____

_____

-- P sues D for $26,000 in an unlimited case. D files a cross-complaint against P for $12,000. What happens? _____

_____

_____

III. VENUE

A.   **Basic idea.** Now we know the case will be filed in state court in California. But where?

-- In federal court, we lay venue in an appropriate federal district. What is the relevant place for laying venue in state court? _____

_____

B.   **Local actions.** Cases for the recovery of land, or determination of an interest in land, or for injury to land are local actions.

-- In a local action, where do we lay venue? _____

_____

C. **If it's not a local action, it's a "transitory" action.** What are the venue choices for transitory cases?

   -- **General rule:** venue is OK in a county: _____

   _____

   _____

   _____

   -- *Additional* **venue in contract cases:** venue is *also* OK in the county where: _____

   _____

   _____

   _____

   -- *Additional* **venue in personal injury or wrongful death:** venue is *also* OK in the county where: _____

   _____

   -- If D is a corporation, venue is OK in the county where (1) it has its principal place of business, or (2) where it entered or is to perform a contract, or (3) where the breach occurred or liability arises.

   -- If D is an unincorporated business, venue is OK in county of PPB if that is on file with secretary of state. Otherwise, where any member or partner resides.

   -- What if all the defendants are non-residents of California? Venue is OK: _____

   _____

D. **Transfer of venue.** We're moving the case from the Superior Court in one county in California to the Superior Court in another county in California.

   -- If the original venue is *improper*, D can move to transfer to a proper county. When should this motion be made? _____

   _____

   _____

-- If the original venue is proper, a court may, on motion, transfer if:

    1. There is reason to believe impartial trial cannot be had in the original venue; or
    2. Convenience of witnesses and ends of justice would be promoted; or
    3. No judge is qualified to act.

-- If the court grants the motion, it transfers to a county on which the parties agree. What if they do not agree? _____

_____

E.   **Inconvenient forum** (forum non conveniens). As in federal court, this is where a court dismisses (or stays) because the far more convenient and appropriate court is in a different judicial system (*e.g.,* state court in Missouri or a court in a foreign country).

    -- By statute in California, state courts may dismiss or stay on motion (by a party or by the court itself). It must find that "in the interest of substantial justice an action should be heard in a forum outside [California]." The court looks at the same sorts of public and private factors as in federal court. _____

    -- If the court grants the motion, it may do so on condition, *e.g.,* that D waive a personal jurisdiction or statute of limitations objection in the other forum.

SECOND BIG TOPIC: LEARNING ABOUT THE CASE (to page 59)

I. SERVICE OF PROCESS

A.   **Basic idea.** D must be served with process (summons and a copy of the complaint)

B.   **Who may serve process?** _____

_____

C.   **Methods of service.**

    1. **Personal service.** Good anywhere in the state (same in federal court).

    2. **Substituted service.** Different from federal court (p. 11) in some ways.

      -- Can only use substituted service to serve an individual if personal service "cannot with reasonable diligence" be had. So you must try personal service first and only if not possible can you use substituted. Then the requirements are:

      -- Must be made at D's usual abode or mailing address (not counting a post office box);
      -- Must be left with a competent member of the household who is at least age 18;
      -- That person must be informed of the contents; and
      -- Process must also be mailed by first-class mail, postage prepaid to D.

When is such substituted service deemed effective? _____

_____

3. **Corporations and other businesses.** Deliver process to agent for service of process or to an officer, or general manager. These people may be served personally or process left with someone apparently in charge at her office during usual office hours. _____

_____

_____

4. **Service by mail.** Copy of summons and complaint and two copies of acknowledgment (waiver form) are mailed to D, with self-addressed stamped envelope addressed to P. Works like waiver in federal court (p. 12), except this is considered "service" and not "waiver or service." Two other points:

      1. D has 20 days (instead of 30 days in federal court) to return the form, and

      2. _____

         _____

         _____

         _____

5. **Service by publication.** Only on affidavit from plaintiff's attorney that D cannot be served, after demonstrating reasonable diligence to serve D in another way.

D. **Service outside California.**

-- Can be made out of state in any manner allowed by California law OR by mail, postage prepaid, return receipt requested. If by mail, deemed complete tenth day after the mailing.

E. **Immunity?** D, a nonresident, is served with process in Bakersfield while in California to be a witness or party in a civil case. Is D immune from being served with process for a California state court case? _____

_____

F. **Subsequent documents.** As in federal court, can be delivered or mailed. If mailed, add 5 days to time required for response (10 days if out of state). (Federal court we add 3 days.)

II. PLEADINGS

A. **Basic idea.** Timing and some of the terminology are different from federal court. In state practice, we have: complaint, answer, *demurrer*, various motions, and *cross-complaint*.

B. **Fact pleading.** California uses "fact pleading" instead of "notice pleading." That means state courts require more detail in pleadings than federal court.

C. **Frivolous litigation.** There are two general statutes in state practice.

1. California has a statute that mirrors Federal Rule 11. It works just like Federal Rule 11, which we saw on page 12 of this handout, with one exception.

   -- Different from federal court: the 21-day safe harbor applies not only in motions brought by a party, but also when the court raises the issue on its own.

2. Another California statute allows the court to order a party or his attorney or both to pay expenses and attorney's fees incurred by another party because of bad faith or frivolous tactics in litigation.

   -- "Frivolous" means something completely without merit or for the sole purpose of harassing an opposing party. _____

   _____

   _____

   -- There must be a motion (by party or the court) and opportunity to be heard.

D. **Complaint.** Pleading by the plaintiff. As in federal court, filing commences the action.

1. **Contents:**

   a. **Statement of facts constituting the cause of action**, stated in ordinary and concise language. _____

   _____

   b. **Demand for judgment** for the relief to which the pleader claims to be entitled.

   -- Must P allege subject matter jurisdiction? _____

   -- Remember the complaint in a limited civil case must state it is limited. _____

   -- If P seeks damages, must she state the amount? _____

   -- *Exception #1:* in what kinds of cases is P forbidden from stating a damages amount in the complaint? _____

   _____

   _____

-- *Exception #2:* also, whenever P claims *punitive damages*, she is forbidden from stating the amount in the complaint. _____

-- So in a personal injury or wrongful death case, how can D find out about the amount of actual damages? And anytime there's a claim for punitive damages, how does D find out about the amount? _____

_____

_____

_____

_____

     -- If P fails to provide the SOD, D can move for a court order requiring P to do so.

-- Also, in personal injury or wrongful death cases, and anytime P seeks punitive damages, what must P do before taking D's default? _____

_____

_____

_____

_____

2.   Remember the requirement of "fact pleading." What does this mean for the plaintiff?

_____

_____

_____

_____

3.   Heightened pleading requirements. The big one: circumstances constituting fraud must be pleaded with particularity. So must these: civil conspiracy, tortious breach of contract, unfair business practices, and product liability claims among multiple defendants resulting from exposure to toxins.

4.   **Fictitious defendants.** If P is genuinely unaware of the identity of a D, she may name the D as a "Doe" defendant. She must also allege that she is unaware of the D's true identity and *must state the cause of action against the "Doe" defendant* (that's a "charging allegation").

-- P, while walking in the crosswalk, is hit by a car driven by D-1. D-1 had been rear-ended by a car driven by D-2, which knocked D-1's car into P. After the wreck, D-2 flees; he had been driving a stolen car. P sues D-1 by name and sues D-2 as a "Doe" defendant. P also alleges that she is unaware of D-2's true identity and states a charging allegation against D-2. Is this OK? _____ _____

_____

-- Fictitious defendants may come up with statute of limitations issues – page 55.

5. Verified pleadings. These are signed under oath by the party. They are rare, but are required, for example, in shareholder derivative suits and for suits against government entities. Remember, verified pleadings can be treated as affidavits.

E. **Defendant's response.** Defendant must respond in an appropriate way within *30 days* after service of process is deemed complete. _____

_____

1. **General demurrer.** This can used to assert some defenses. Which is the most important? _____

_____

_____

_____

_____

-- This is like the federal motion to dismiss for failure to state a claim (p. 29). So the court takes factual allegations as true and limits its assessment to the complaint (and matters of which it takes judicial notice). If sustained, usually the court will let P try again. Can be aimed at the entire complaint or individual causes of action.

-- Watch for this to test substantive elements of a cause of action. _____

_____

-- What else can be raised by general demurrer? _____

_____

-- Can these defenses be raised in the answer instead? _____

-- Or could be in a motion "for judgment on the pleadings" if it raised after D has pleaded and time for demurrer has expired.

-- Is a general demurrer considered a pleading? _____

_____

2. **Special demurrer.** This can be used to assert many (pretty minor) defenses.

-- The complaint is **uncertain, ambiguous or unintelligible.** This is like the federal motion for more definite statement. _____

_____

-- The complaint is **unclear about which theories of liability** are asserted against each of the defendants.

-- **Lack of legal capacity.**

-- **Existence of another case between the same parties on the same cause of action.**

-- **Defect or misjoinder of parties.**

-- **Failure to plead whether a contract is oral or written.**

-- **Failure to file a "certificate of merit."** This is required to sue architects, engineers, or land surveyors for professional negligence. In such cases, P's attorney must file a certificate certifying that she consulted with a professional and there is reasonable cause to file the case. _____

_____

-- Lack of certificate can be raised by motion to strike (p. 52).

-- Can these various defenses be raised in the answer instead? _____

_____

-- What if they are not raised by demurrer or answer? _____

_____

-- As with the general demurrer, the court treats allegations of fact as true and limits assessment to what's in the complaint and matters of judicial notice.

-- Is a special demurrer considered a pleading? _____

-- When are special demurrers not available? _____

_____

3. **Terminology.** Motions are either "granted" or "denied." What about demurrers? ____

_____

_____

4. **Motion to quash service of summons.**

-- This is used to assert what defenses? _____

_____

_____

_____

_____

*THIS MOTION MUST BE MADE **BEFORE** OR **WITH** A DEMURRER, ANSWER, OR A MOTION TO STRIKE, OR ELSE D WAIVES THESE DEFENSES.*

-- P sues D. D files an answer in which he asserts the affirmative defense of lack of personal jurisdiction. D has waived the defense of lack of personal jurisdiction. _____

_____

_____

_____

_____

-- P sues D. D files a motion to quash service of summons at the same time as a demurrer, answer, or motion to strike. Is that OK? _____

_____

_____

-- If the court denies the motion to quash, D must "plead" within 15 days.

-- If the court denies the motion, the only way to get appellate review is to seek a writ of mandate from the Court of Appeal within 10 days of service of the written notice of entry of the order denying her motion. So you cannot wait until final judgment to raise the issue in the Court of Appeal.

5. **Motion to dismiss or stay for inconvenient forum (forum non conveniens).** What is the timing for bringing this motion? _____

_____

_____

_____

6. **Motion to strike.** A party can file this to strike all or part of any pleading. The court may strike "irrelevant, false, or improper matter." _____

-- P files a malpractice case against an architect, engineer, or land surveyor without a "certificate of merit" from P's lawyer. D can attack the complaint with a special demurrer or could move to strike the entire complaint.

-- **Anti-SLAPP motion to strike.** The legislature has been concerned about strategic lawsuits against public participation (SLAPP). These are suits brought to chill the valid exercise of free speech and petition. When P sues D for an act D took in furtherance of her free speech right or right to petition the government, D can make an anti-SLAPP motion to strike.

   -- D must make a showing that P's cause of action arises from protected activity. If D makes that showing, what happens? _____

_____

_____

_____

-- Because so many anti-SLAPP motions were made, the legislature limited availability of the motion. So D is not supposed to make the motion if P's case is truly in the public interest or on behalf of the general public. _____

_____

_____

-- A defendant who wins an anti-SLAPP motion can sue the person who sued her for malicious prosecution. This is called a SLAPPback suit.

7. **Answer.** This is like the answer in federal court.

-- General denial: this is a short document, in which D simply denies each and every allegation of P's complaint. This is permitted if D can do so consistent with rules about frivolous litigation.

-- In stating affirmative defenses, be careful to _____

_____

_____

-- If P filed a verified (under oath) complaint, D must file a verified answer.

-- Can an answer include a demand for recovery against P, e.g., damages? _____

_____

8. **Timing.** No later than *30 days* after service of process is deemed complete, D must (to avoid default) file an answer or demurrer or one of the motions noted. But a motion to strike does not extend the time in which to demur.

F. **Claims by Defendant.** As in federal court, D can assert a claim (1) against the plaintiff (an opposing party), (2) against a co-defendant, or (3) against an impleaded third-party defendant. In federal court these claims had different names – (1) counterclaim, (2) cross-claim, and (3) impleader.

-- In California state courts, all three of these claims have the same name. They are all called _____

_____

-- The cross-complaint must be a separate document from the answer.

1. *Cross-Complaint against P.* Like the federal counterclaim, except it is not part of the answer (it is a separate document). This is to be filed before or at the same time as the answer.

    a.   It is against an opposing party (e.g., D v. P).

    b.   What if the cross-complaint by D against P arises from the same transaction or occurrence as P's cause of action against D? _____

_____

_____

_____

    c.   What if the cross-complaint by D against P does not arise from the same T/O as P's cause of action? _____

_____

2. *Cross-Complaint against co-party.* Like the federal crossclaim. May be filed anytime before the court has set a trial date.

    a. It is a claim against a co-party, by a defending party.

    b. It *must* arise from the same T/O as the underlying dispute.

    c. It is *never* compulsory. The party may assert it here as a cross-complaint or may sue in a separate case.

3. *Cross-Complaint against third-party defendant (TPD).* Like federal impleader (third-party complaint). May be filed anytime before the court has set a trial date. It is never compulsory – so you don't have to file it. _____

_____

_____

4. The person against whom any cross-complaint is asserted must do what? _____

_____

_____

5. If the cross-complaint is asserted against one who has not yet appeared in the case, it must be served with summons. _____

G. Amending pleadings.

1. Plaintiff has a right to amend (amendment as a matter of course) before defendant files an answer or demurrer. After demurrer but before hearing on the issue raised by demurrer, any party may also amend once as a matter of course.

2. Any party can seek leave to amend anytime. Same standard as I federal court. _____

_____

3. Amendment to conform to the evidence is available. _____

_____

4. After sustaining a demurrer or granting a motion to strike, the court will usually do so "with leave to amend." This allows P to try again. If the court sustains a demurrer or grants a motion to strike "without leave to amend," P cannot try again.

5. Relation back is available to add new claims after the statute of limitations has run, if the new claim relates to the same general facts as originally alleged.

6.   Relation back to change a defendant after the statute of limitations has run is OK if there was a "misnomer" – P sued the wrong D but the right D knew about it. _____

_____

7.   Relation back and fictitious defendants. Relation back is OK if:

a. Original complaint was filed before the statute of limitations ran and *contained charging allegations against the fictitious defendant(s).* _____

_____

b. P was genuinely ignorant of the identity of the Doe defendant(s) and

c. P pleaded that ignorance in the original complaint. _____

_____

_____

_____

_____

_____

_____

III. DISCOVERY

A.   Are there required disclosures? _____

_____

B.   Discovery tools. P must get a court order to take discovery from D within 10 days after D was served with process (within 20 days to take D's deposition).

1.   **Depositions** (oral and on written question). Same as in federal court as to the basics, so can depose a party or a non-party. But you should subpoena a non-party to ensure attendance. Can only depose a person once unless court orders otherwise.

-- Different from federal: No presumptive time limit on deposition (federal court it's one day of 7 hours unless court orders or parties agree otherwise). Also, in state court there is no presumptive limit on the number of depositions to be taken in the case (federal court it's no more than 10 unless court orders or parties agree).

2.   **Interrogatories**. Same as in federal court as to basics, so can only be sent to parties.

-- There are form interrogatories approved by the Judicial Council. There is no limit to the number of form interrogatories that can be served on other parties.

-- If a party wishes to draft specific interrogatories to serve on another party, the interrogatories may not contain subparts. What is the maximum number of drafted interrogatories allowed in an unlimited civil case? _____

_____

_____

_____

_____

_____

3. **Requests to produce (inspection demand).** Like requests to produce in federal court. Re electronically stored info (ESI), specify form desired (hard copy or electronic).

-- Is there a statutory limit on how many of these can be served without court permission in an unlimited civil case? _____

-- In federal court, these can be used to get information from a non-party if accompanied by a subpoena. The California basic statute does address using these to get information from a non-party. But it is possible to get discovery of things from a non-party. How? _____

_____

_____

_____

_____

-- For business records, you can just subpoena them without taking a deposition.

4. **Medical examination.** Same as in federal court, so you have to get a court order. Except in state court, in one kind of case, D has a right to demand one physical examination of P. What kind of case? _____

_____

-- In California, if it is a physical exam, the lawyer for that person has the right to attend the examination. If it is a mental exam, the lawyer can attend only if there is a court order allowing it.

5. **Request for admission.** Same as in federal practice.

-- What is the maximum number of requests for admission that can be served on a party in an unlimited civil case? _____

_____

-- But there is no limit on the number of requests to admit the genuineness of documents.

6. **Discovery in limited civil cases.** There are strict limits on use of discovery devices.

-- How many depositions can a party take? _____

-- How many interrogatories, inspection demands, and requests for admission can each party propound to another party? _____

_____

_____

-- In a limited civil case, can the parties ever get additional discovery? _____

_____

7. **Supplemental discovery – in unlimited cases only.** Unlike in federal court, there is no standing duty to supplement discovery responses, as long as the information given was accurate and complete when given. Instead, the requesting party can propound a "supplemental interrogatory" to elicit later-acquired information bearing on answers previously made. Also, she can propound a "supplemental demand for inspection," which demands inspection of later-acquired or later-discovered documents or things.

-- How many times can a party propound a supplemental interrogatory or request for production? _____

_____

_____

_____

C. **Scope of discovery.**

1. **Standard**: can discover anything "relevant to the subject matter involved in the pending action." This is slightly broader than the federal standard (relevant to a "claim or defense"). _____

_____

2. **Relevant** includes material that is "reasonably calculated to lead to the discovery of admissible evidence." _____

3. As in federal court, **privileged** matter is not discoverable. When a discovery request would intrude on privileged matter (e.g., confidential communication between attorney and client), the responding party must object with **particularity**.

4. **Privacy**. The California Constitution recognizes a right of privacy, which can be claimed to limit discovery. It is not absolute, however.

    -- How does a court determine whether to allow discovery? _____

    _____

    _____

    _____

5. **Work product**. In federal court, it can be generated by the party or any representative of a party, not just by attorneys.

    -- Is the rule the same in California courts? _____

    _____

    _____

    _____

    -- A pro se party (not represented by a lawyer) can generate work product if it would be WP if done by an attorney.

    -- A party can only get discovery of work product if the court determines that denial of discovery will unfairly prejudice the party seeking discovery or will result in injustice.

    -- BUT a writing that reflects an attorney's impressions, conclusions, opinions, or legal research is *never* discoverable.

6. **Experts**. Any party may request the simultaneous exchange of expert *witness* information. Then each party must exchange a list of experts to be called at trial, declare the nature and substance of testimony, and the expert's qualifications. You can also demand reports by the expert. A party may then take a deposition of the expert.

    -- If a party does not exchange this information, the court may exclude its expert from testifying.

    -- Generally, can you discover info of *consulting* experts (who will not testify at trial)? _____

D.   Enforcement of discovery rules.

1.   Parties generally must meet and confer to work out problems before seeking court orders. A party failing to do so is subject to monetary sanction of expenses, including attorney's fees, incurred by the other party as a result of the failure to meet and confer.

2.   California law prohibits "misuse" of discovery, such as not playing by the rules, making unjustified objections, abusive motions, failing to confer, refusal to respond, etc. By statute, a court may sanction any person – including parties and attorneys – guilty of misusing the discovery process. The person to be sanctioned must be given notice and a chance to be heard.

-- Sanctions include: (1) monetary sanction (expenses and attorney's fees incurred by other party because of misuse), (2) establishment order, (3) refusal to allow party to support its position with evidence at trial, (4) striking pleadings, (5) entering default judgment against D or dismissing P's cause of action.

-- The court will usually start with monetary sanctions and move through the hierarchy as warranted. It has broad discretion in selecting the appropriate sanction. The court will look, among other things, to whether the abuse is willful.

-- When a party seeks sanctions for discovery abuse, what must it indicate in the motion? _____

_____

_____

3.   A party may seek a protective order to protect against unwarranted annoyance, embarrassment, oppression, burden or expense. _____

_____

_____

4.   A party can object that ESI is not reasonably accessible because of undue burden or expense, but must identify the categories of sources that are not accessible. _____

_____

THIRD BIG TOPIC: COMPLEX CASES – JOINING PARTIES (to page 61)

A.   Proper plaintiffs and defendants. Who *may* be joined? Basically the same as in federal court. _____

_____

B.   Necessary and indispensable parties. Who *must* be joined. Like federal practice.

C. **Impleader.** Remember, this is a cross-complaint in state practice. _____

_____

D. **Intervention.** Identical to federal practice for intervention of right. Similar to federal practice for permissive intervention, but statute requires the applicant have "an interest in the matter in litigation, or in the success of either of the parties."

E. **Interpleader.** Procedurally the same as in federal practice. In federal practice, it is clear that the person instituting interpleader may claim that she owns the property interpleaded. It is not clear in California whether that is OK – maybe the stakeholder can interplead only if she does not claim to own the property.

F. **The Class Action.** The state statute uses vastly different language than the Federal Rule.

1. **Requirements.** The California statute speaks of "when the question is one of a common or general interest, of many persons, . . . and it is impracticable to bring them all before the court, one or more may sue or defend for the benefit of all." What does the state requirement mean? _____

_____

_____

_____

_____

-- In considering whether there is a "well-defined community of interest," what will the court consider? _____

_____

_____

_____

_____

2. **Types of class actions.** In federal court, there are three types of classes. What about in state court? _____

_____

3. Notice may be given to the class by publication. Individual notice is not required.

-- In federal court the cost of notice is borne by the representative. How about in state court? _____

_____

_____

_____

4. All class members who do not opt out are bound by the class judgment. Opt out may be allowed by the court.

5. California does not require the court to appoint class counsel.

6. Settlement or dismissal must be approved by the court. _____

_____

7. Determining amount in controversy. Suppose a class has 26,000 members, each of whom has been harmed $1. What is the amount in controversy for determining whether this is a limited or unlimited civil case? _____

_____

_____

FOURTH BIG TOPIC: ADJUDICATION (to page 67)

I. PRETRIAL ADJUDICATION

A.   Voluntary dismissal.

-- P can move to dismiss anytime before trial starts. The decision is for the court to make. Is such a dismissal without prejudice? _____

_____

-- If P moves for voluntary dismissal after trial starts, it may be granted only with prejudice, unless the parties stipulate otherwise or the court finds good cause to dismiss without prejudice.

B.   Involuntary dismissal. All courts (federal and state) have authority to dismiss for failure to prosecute, failure to abide by court orders or rule and, of course, for the various reasons that can be raised by demurrer, motions to quash, etc.

-- California state courts have discretion to dismiss if the case has not been brought to trial (or defendant has not been served with process) within two years of filing.

-- Mandatory dismissal: in California state courts, case must be dismissed if _____

_____

_____

_____

_____

_____

C. **Default and default judgment.** D fails to respond to the complaint within 30 days of the effective date of service of process on her. The procedure is very similar to that in federal court, with these differences.

1. D must be given notice of the application for entry of default.

2. Default judgment can be entered by the clerk without a judge's involvement if

> -- D made no response at all
> -- the claim is on a contract or judgment
> -- the claim is for a sum certain in money
> -- D was not served by publication AND
> -- P provides an affidavit stating relevant facts

  -- But if any of those is not true, the claimant must go to the court itself (the judge, not the clerk) for the judgment. The judge will hold a hearing and may enter judgment.

3. Default judgment cannot exceed what the claimant demanded in her complaint or be a different kind of relief. This is different from a case that goes to trial, in which the claimant can recover more (and a different kind of relief) than she put in her complaint.

4. D may move to set aside default or default judgment and for leave to defend the action if service of process did not result in actual notice of the suit to D within the time to respond. Notice of motion must be accompanied by an *affidavit* attesting the lack of notice was not the result of trying to avoid notice or of inexcusable neglect.

  -- Motion must be filed within reasonable time, not to exceed the earlier of these: 6 months after service of written notice of default or default judgment or two years after entry of default judgment.

D. **Failure to plead facts constituting a cause of action.** Instead of the Federal Rule 12(b)(6), in state court how does D usually raise this? _____

_____

_____

E.   Motion for summary judgment. The standard is the same as in federal court (p. 29).

> -- The elements for P's cause of action are W, X, Y, and Z. After discovery, D moves for summary judgment and shows that P has no evidence to support element X. What if P does not proffer evidence of element X? _____
>
> _____
>
> _____

1. The moving party must file and serve a separate statement of material facts she claims to be undisputed, with supporting evidence for each fact. If she does not, the motion can be denied.

    -- If the moving party files and serves such a statement and evidence, the opposing party must respond by indicating the facts she believes to be in dispute and supporting evidence for each fact. If she does not, the court may grant summary judgment.

2. The moving party must serve all papers at least 75 days before the hearing on the motion. Opposition papers must be filed at least 14 days before the hearing. Reply papers by the moving party must be filed no more than 5 days before the hearing.

II. CASE MANAGEMENT AND ALTERNATIVE DISPUTE RESOLUTION

A.   Case management conference. Rules of Court require the court to hold initial case management conference within 180 days after filing of complaint. At the conference, the court reviews service, pleadings, discovery issues, potential problems with discovery of electronically stored info (ESI), appropriateness of alternative dispute resolution (ADR), settlement, trial date, etc. Before the conference, parties must meet and confer and file a "Case Management Statement" addressing such issues. Court issues case management order. This is like the Federal Rule 26(f) conference (p. 31), but there is no requirement that the parties form a discovery plan to submit to the court.

B.   "Fast track." Court reviews each case to determine suitability for case management program. Such cases are actively managed to meet goals of disposition.

Unlimited cases: 75% to be disposed of within 12 months of filing, 85% within 18 months of filing, and 100% within 24 months of filing.

Limited cases: 90% within 12 months, 98% within 18 months, 100% within 24 months.

C.   Additional conferences. The court may order mandatory settlement conference (or the parties may request one). Parties submit settlement conference statement in advance, detailing the demand or offer. Additional conferences may be held as needed.

D.   Sanctions. Court may sanction party or attorney for failing to comply with rules or orders. E.g., may dismiss defendants not served within 60 days of filing. Sanction terminating the case are OK only if the failure to comply was the fault of the party and not the attorney.

E. **Alternative dispute resolution (ADR).** Each county's Superior Court has an ADR program, aimed at reducing case congestion. In larger counties, unlimited civil cases, unless exempted, are submitted to "judicial arbitration" if the judge is of the opinion that P will ultimately obtain $50,000 or less. Consumer class action and probate cases are among those that cannot be subject to judicial arbitration.

-- In judicial arbitration the court refers the case to an arbitrator, who holds a hearing; rules of evidence do not apply. She renders a decision that becomes a judgment unless a party demands trial de novo. But if that party does not fare better in trial than in the arbitration, she may be liable for the other side's costs from the date of the rejection, the other side's expert witness fees, and interest on the claim from the date of rejection (not from date of the judgment). With judicial arbitration, the parties have discovery rights.

-- In "contractual arbitration," parties agree in writing to arbitrate a dispute. Such contracts are valid if not the product of unconscionability or illegality. Usually no right to discovery unless parties agree. Arbitrator's decision is final. It can be vacated by a court only on very narrow grounds and not for legal error (unless parties stipulated to judicial review for legal errors).

III. TRIAL, JUDGMENT, AND POST-TRIAL MOTIONS

A. **Recovery.**

-- In her complaint, P claims damages of $100,000. Does that limit the amount she can recover if the case goes to trial? _____

_____

-- Remember, though, in limited civil cases, _____

_____

_____

B. **Jury trial.**

1. **Right to jury.** The California Constitution grants right to jury trial, largely along the same law/equity split as the Seventh Amendment (p. 31). Some matters are handled differently from federal court, though.

   -- You get a jury to determine issues of fact relating to causes of action at law, not equity. If case involves both law and equity, jury determines the facts on the law cause of action and judge determines the facts on the equity cause of action. BUT, unlike federal court, generally here _____

   _____

   _____

-- P's complaint states an equity cause of action, for an injunction against future trespass, and also seeks incidental damages for past trespass. In federal court there is a right to have a jury determine the facts relating to damages. What about in California state courts? _____

_____

_____

_____

_____

_____

2. **Requirement of demand.** A party must "announce" her demand for jury at the time the case is set for trial or within five days after notice of the setting of trial. Usually, this is made in the case management statement. Failure to demand constitutes waiver.

3. **Number of jurors.** In state court, there are _____ jurors in civil cases unless the parties agree in open court to a lesser number.

-- If a juror is excused for illness or other reason, an alternate juror takes her place. If there is no alternate, trial continues unless a party objects.

4. **Selection.** In the voir dire process, each party is entitled to six peremptory challenges and unlimited challenges for cause.

-- Peremptory challenges may not be used on the basis of "race, color, religion, sex, national origin, sexual orientation, or similar grounds." _____

_____

_____

5. **Verdict.** In federal court, the jury verdict must be unanimous unless the parties agree otherwise. In state court, what is required? _____

_____

_____

_____

6. **Motion for directed verdict.** This is what the federal courts call motions for judgment as a matter of law. Standard: reasonable people could not disagree as to the result. Parties can move for this only at the close of all evidence.

-- If D moves for this at the close of P's opening statement or at the close of P's evidence at trial, it is often called _____

_____

7. **Motion for judgment notwithstanding the verdict (JNOV).** What the federal courts call renewed motion for judgment as a matter of law. _____

-- Standard: same as directed verdict. So the court is saying the jury reached a conclusion reasonable people could not have reached. Same as in federal court.

-- Timing: must file notice of intention to move either before entry of judgment or the earlier of these:
       -- 15 days of mailing or service of notice of entry of judgment or
       -- 180 days after entry of judgment.

-- Difference from federal: Party making the motion is NOT required to make motion for directed verdict at trial. _____

C. Motion for a new trial.

1. Timing. Same as JNOV (immediately above).

2. Bases. Same as in federal court: something convinces the court that the parties should retry the case. Proper only if the court concludes "that the error complained of has resulted in a miscarriage of justice." _____

_____

3. One ground for new trial is excessive or inadequate damages. What is the standard for ordering new trial on this ground? _____

_____

_____

-- To avoid a new trial, the court might offer (or suggest) *remittitur* or *additur*.

-- **Remittitur** – playing hardball with the P. P suffered minor damage, but the jury awarded $200,000. The court finds the damages figure shocks the conscience. It can order new trial or offer remittitur. This gives P a choice: take a lesser amount (which the court sets) or go through new trial. Is remittitur OK in state and federal court? _____

_____

-- Can the court simply lower the figure as determined by the jury? _____

_____

-- **Additur** -- playing hardball with the D. P suffered very serious harm, but the jury awarded only $30,000. The court finds the damages figure shocks the conscience. It can order new trial or offer additur. This gives D a choice: pay a greater amount in damages (which the court sets) or go through new trial. Is additur OK in state and federal court? _____

_____

_____

_____

_____

D. **Motion to set aside judgment.** A party may move to set aside judgment because of "mistake, inadvertence, surprise, or excusable neglect." This might be possible in a default judgment case, where the party or lawyer simply goofed up and didn't respond.

-- The motion *must* include an "affidavit of fault" by the party or lawyer demonstrating the mistake, etc. If the ground is shown, the court must set aside the judgment. Court may order the party/lawyer to pay expenses and attorney's fees incurred by the other side.

-- Timing for such a motion: reasonable time, not to exceed six months after entry of the judgment.

FIFTH BIG TOPIC: APPELLATE REVIEW (to page 68)

A. **Basic idea.** In an unlimited case, we appeal from the Superior Court to the California Court of Appeal. Appeal is to the district of the Court of Appeal to which the county is assigned.

-- Timing: generally, the notice of appeal must be filed in the trial court within:
   -- 60 days after mailing or service of the "notice of entry" of judgment or
   -- 180 days after entry of judgment if no notice is served.

-- Judgments in limited civil cases and small claims matters are appealed to the appellate department of the Superior Court.

B. **Final judgment rule.** Like federal courts, California follows the final judgment rule. So generally one cannot appeal until the merits of the entire action are resolved. _____

-- P sues D-1 and D-2. The trial court enters summary judgment in favor of P against D-2. That would not be a final judgment in federal court because the cause of action by P against D-1 is still pending. In state court, however, a judgment as to one of several parties is considered a final judgment and can be appealed. _____

_____

_____

C. **Interlocutory (non-final) review.**

   1. By statute, these are appealable:

      -- Order granting a motion to quash service of summons;
      -- Order granting a dismissal or stay of a case for forum non conveniens;
      -- Order granting new trial;
      -- Order denying a motion for JNOV;
      -- Order denying (not granting) certification of an entire class action;
      -- Order granting, dissolving, or refusing to grant or dissolve an injunction;
      -- Order directing party or attorney to pay monetary sanctions of over $5,000.

   2. Collateral order rule: Court of Appeal may hear appeal on (1) an issue collateral to the merits of the case (2) that the trial court has decided finally, if (3) it directs payment of money or performance of an act.

   3. **Extraordinary writ.** If an order is not otherwise appealable, the aggrieved party may seek a writ of mandate (to compel a lower court to do something the law requires) or prohibition (to stop a lower court from doing something the law does not allow). _____

      _____

      _____

      _____

      -- The writ is issued to an inferior court (e.g., Court of Appeal to Superior Court).

      -- Such a writ is *extraordinary,* not routine.

      -- Party seeking writ must demonstrate (1) that she will suffer *irreparable harm* if the writ is not issued (i.e., lower court result is unusually harsh or unfair), (2) the normal route of appeal from final judgment is inadequate, (3) she has a beneficial interest in the outcome of the writ proceeding.

         -- When is extraordinary writ the *only* way to seek review by an appellate court?

         _____

         _____

         _____

   ## SIXTH BIG TOPIC: PRECLUSION (through page 72)

A. **Basic idea.** Whenever there has been an earlier case, watch for these issues, which concern the preclusive effect of a prior judgment on the merits. The question is whether a *judgment* already entered (Case 1) precludes litigation of any matters in another case (Case 2).

--   If Case 2 is in a different court system (*e.g.*, federal or state) from Case 1, which system's law applies regarding claim and issue preclusion? _____

_____

_____

     -- So Case 1 is in federal court, where judgment is entered. Case 2 is in California state court. What law of claim and issue preclusion does the state court judge use? __

_____

_____

--   Suppose the judgment in Case 1 has been appealed (or the time for appealing has not yet expired). Is that judgment entitled to claim or issue preclusion effect?

     -- Federal law: _____

     -- California law: _____

--   Claim and issue preclusion are affirmative defenses, so defendant should raise them in her answer. How is the issue often presented on the bar exam? _____

_____

_____

B.   **Claim preclusion (or res judicata).** This stands for the proposition that you only get to sue on a cause of action (or claim) once. So if you have a cause of action (or claim) you only get one case in which to vindicate all rights to relief for it. **Requirements**:

   1.   Case 1 and Case 2 were brought by the **same claimant against the same defendant**. Note: not just same parties, but same guy suing the same guy in both cases. _____

_____

   2.   **Case 1 ended in a valid final judgment *on the merits*.** General rule: Unless the court said otherwise when it entered the judgment, any judgment is "on the merits" UNLESS it was based on: _____

_____

_____

_____

     -- So is a default judgment "on the merits"? _____

-- Is a judgment based upon discovery abuse "on the merits"? _____

3. Case 1 and Case 2 asserted the **same cause of action (or claim).**

   -- Federal law: "claim" means _____

   _____

   -- California law: you get one "cause of action" for each right invaded. So if a single accident caused both personal injuries and property damage, there would be two causes of action – one for the body and one for the property. What is this theory called? _____

   _____

HYPO: Case 1: P sues D for personal injuries sustained in an auto collision. A valid final judgment on the merits is entered. Case 2: P sues D for property damage from the same crash. Should the court enter summary judgment for Epstein in Case 2 under the doctrine of claim preclusion?

   (1) Were both cases brought by the same claimant against the same defendant? _____

   _____

   (2) Did Case 1 end in valid final judgment on merits? _____

   (3) Did both cases involve the same claim (federal) or cause of action (state)?

       -- Federal law: Yes, because both cases involve the same T/O. So dismiss the second case under claim preclusion. _____

       _____

       -- California law: _____

       _____

       _____

       _____

HYPO: P and D are parties to a contract under which D is required to make monthly payments. When P files Case 1, D has failed to make six such payments. Under federal and California law, are there six separate claims here or only one claim or cause of action? _____

   _____

   _____

C. Issue preclusion (collateral estoppel). This is narrower. It precludes relitigation of a particular *issue* litigated and determined before. That issue is deemed established in Case 2, so it cannot be relitigated. Requirements:

1. Case 1 ended in a valid, final judgment on the merits.

2. The same issue was actually litigated and determined in Case 1. _____

    _____

    _____

    _____

3. The issue was essential to the judgment in Case 1. Without this issue, the judgment in Case 1 would have been different.

4. *Against whom* can issue preclusion be asserted? Only against one who was a party to Case 1 (or who was represented by a party). THIS IS REQUIRED BY DUE PROCESS. _____

    _____

    _____

5. *By whom* can issue preclusion be asserted?

    -- Traditional view (mutuality): only by one who was a party to Case 1. THIS IS *NOT* REQUIRED BY DUE PROCESS, AND SOME COURTS HAVE REJECTED IT TO ALLOW "NONMUTUAL" ASSERTION OF ISSUE PRECLUSION. So "nonmutual" means it's being used *by* one who was not a party in Case 1. That person may be the defendant or the plaintiff in Case 2.

    a. *Nonmutual defensive issue preclusion* (used by one who was not a party in Case 1, but who is D in Case 2).

        -- DJ, driving Becky's car, is involved in a collision with Joey. Assume Becky is vicariously liable for DJ's acts. Case 1: Joey sues DJ. DJ wins, based on a finding that Joey was negligent, which caused the wreck. The court enters final judgment for DJ. Case 2: Joey sues Becky. Can Becky assert issue preclusion as to the finding of Joey's negligence?

        (1) Did Case 1 end in a valid, final judgment on the merits? _____

        (2) Was the same issue litigated and determined in Case 1? _____

        _____

A-71

(3) Was that issue essential to the judgment in Case 1?_____

_____

_____

(4) Is issue preclusion being asserted *against* one who was party to Case 1? ___

_____

(5) BUT, is it being asserted BY someone who was NOT party to Case 1. Under mutuality rule, could not be done. How do we handle this under federal and California law? _____

_____

_____

_____

b. *Nonmutual offensive issue preclusion* (used by one who was not a party in Case 1 and is P in Case 2).

-- Same facts, except Case 2 is brought by Becky against Joey. She sues to impose upon Joey liability for damage to her car from the wreck Joey had with DJ. Becky wants to assert collateral estoppel as to the finding in the first case that Joey was negligent. Can she?

(1)-(4) As above, the first four requirements are all met.

(5) The only tough part is the fifth, because issue preclusion is asserted nonmutually. And here, the person asserting it is a plaintiff. Under the mutuality rule, could not be done.

-- Federal and California law allow this only if it is "fair." Factors:

(a) Joey had a full and fair opportunity to litigate in Case 1;
(b) Joey could foresee multiple suits;
(c) Becky could not have joined easily in Case 1; and
(d) There are no inconsistent judgments on record. If there had been multiple litigation, and sometimes Joey was found negligent and sometimes not, it would be unfair to let Becky get issue preclusion on a negligence finding.

LET'S CUT TO THE CHASE. WITH LIMITED TIME, WHAT IS THE STUFF I SHOULD PROBABLY FOCUS ON?

1.

2.

3.

4.

5.

6.

7.

8.

LAST POINT (I promise): If you have any questions, call me. E-mail is not a good option for me, so call. If I'm not there, leave your question and phone number and I'll call back. My phone number is: _____

Comparison of Major Documents and Names

Document	**Federal Court**	**State Court**
P's initial pleading	Complaint	Complaint
D's standard responsive pleading	Answer	Answer
D's claim v. P	Counterclaim	Cross-Complaint
Party's claim v. co-party	Cross-Claim	Cross-Complaint
D's claim v. TPD	Impleader	Cross-Complaint
Time to respond (after effective date of service of process)	21 days	30 days

To raise:

-- Failure to state claim	Motion to dismiss 12(b)(6)	General demurrer
-- Lack of personal jurisdiction	Motion to dismiss	Motion to quash service of summons
-- Lack of subject matter jurisdiction	Motion to dismiss	General demurrer
Major waiver problems	Waive personal jurisdiction, venue, process, and service of process if not put in first Rule 12 response (motion or answer)	Waive special demurrer issues if not put in answer or demurrer

Waive personal jurisdiction if not raised by special appearance (e.g., motion to quash service of summons) before or with demurrer or answer or motion to strike |

Community Property

Professor Michael Waterstone

California Community Property

By

Professor Michael Waterstone, Loyola Law School, Los Angeles

INTRODUCTION

It is easy to identify CP essay question on bar exam:

- Parties in fact pattern are identified as Herb and Wendy, Hank and Wilma (H &W).

- Question ALWAYS ends "answer according to California law."

- In all of my hypos (and on exam), story starts with H & W married and domiciled in CA except where otherwise noted.

   o Bar exam question will involve characterizing assets in the context of divorce or separation, death of one of spouses, or assertion of creditor's claim.

I.   BASIC PRINCIPLES

These statutory definitions apply **unless** the character of an asset has been altered by (i) the parties' agreement (premaritial or during marriage); (ii) parties' conduct; or (iii) how title was taken.

Separate Property (SP):

- Property owned by either spouse before marriage; or

- Property acquired during marriage by gift, will, or inheritance; or

- Property acquired during marriage with the expenditure of separate funds.

   - *Example – W inherits $10,000 from mother's estate, which she uses to buy IBM stock.* The IBM stock would be SP, because she used the inheritance which was SP.

- We call this **"source"** rule or **"tracing."**

- The rents, issue, and profits derived from separate property.

Community Property (CP): Property, other than separate property, acquired by either spouse during marriage. The most common examples are (i) salary or wages earned by either spouse, and (ii) the income from community assets.

- *Examples* – Prize money won by W on quiz show is CP (acquired from wife's labor); Bonus paid by H's employer which was wrapped in gift box is CP (compensation, not gift).

There is a **community presumption**: all assets acquired during the marriage are presumptively community property. Absent a showing of the parties' agreement or that title was taken in a form that overcomes the community presumption, the burden of proof that a particular asset is separate property is on the party so contending.

California has **extended its community property system** – as of 2004, the community property system applies to *registered domestic partners* upon filing a Declaration of Domestic Partnership with the Secretary of State, retroactive to January 1, 2000. It is available only to (i) same sex couples, and (ii) elderly opposite-sex couples receiving Social Security benefits.

- Everything same, except not H & W. (Harry and Hal, or Wilma and Wendy).

- In *In re Marriage Cases* (2008), the California Supreme Court held that the California Family Code section providing that only a marriage between a man and a woman is valid or recognized in California was unconstitutional under the California state constitution. Subsequently, the voters approved Proposition 8, amending the California Constitution to provide that "only marriage between a man and a woman is valid or recognized in California." In *Strauss v. Horton* (2008), the California Supreme Court held that Prop. 8 was a permissible constitutional amendment, but that it could not be applied retroactively to invalidate lawful marriages of same-sex couples contracted prior to the effective date of Proposition 8, November 5, 2008. Prop 8 now being challenged in federal court.

  - Therefore, same-sex couples lawfully married after *In re Marriage Cases* but before the effective date of Proposition 8 may claim community property rights as **spouses**, not as domestic partners.

A.   When does the economic community end?

Hypo 1 - Hal and Wynn, having difficulties in their marriage, agree to a trial separation for six months. Hal moves into his own apartment on May 10, 2005. When the trial period ends November 10, 2005, Hal and Wynn discuss their future. Hal, who still is in love with Wynn, begs her to "give me another chance," but Wynn tells him that "the situation is hopeless." Wynn files for divorce in March 2006. Between May 10 and Nov. 10, 2005, Wynn invests $15,000 of her earnings to buy 300 shares of Able stock. Between November 10 and the time of filing for divorce, Hal invests $10,000 of his earnings to buy Baker stock.

- *When did the economic community end?*

    1. _____ AND

    2. _____ .

When was this met in the hypo? _____ .

- *Classify Able and Baker stock.*

    - Able stock (acquired between May 10 and Nov. 10) – _____

    - Baker stock (acquired after Nov. 10th and before divorce filing) – _____

Hypo 2 - Doctor Harry leaves Wanda and moves in with his nurse. Harry and the nurse set up housekeeping on a houseboat in Marina Del Rey. Thereafter, Harry never had sex with Wanda. But Harry occasionally went home to eat with Wanda and the kids, took Wanda to dinner on several occasions, took Wanda along to medical association meetings, and (classy guy) regularly took his laundry home.

- *Does this show the intent of either party not to resume marital relation?*

    _____

- *Until divorce filed, earnings are _____ .*

3

Hypo 3 - During marriage to Hal, Wendy (a law professor) wrote a casebook published by West Publishing Co. The book was not mentioned in the divorce proceeding. Six months after the divorce Wendy receives an $8,000 royalty payment from West. Wendy contends that the $8,000 is her SP because she owned the copyright and she now owns the book. *Is she correct?*

o _____. The copyright and all royalty payments were _____.

For community property not divided on divorce, the court retains *continuing jurisdiction* to award CP that was not previously adjudicated, and on motion the omitted or unadjudicated CP will be divided 50-50 *unless* the court finds that *"the interests of justice require an unequal division."*

o But if Wendy wrote the book before marriage, royalty payments would be _____ even if received during the marriage.

B. How is community property handled on divorce?

Hypo 4 - At the time of their divorce, H & W own the following assets as community property: a house ($300,000); furnishings, cars, and other tangible personal property ($20,000); and stocks and bonds ($500,000), for a total of $820,000. H is an engineer; W (who has only a high school education) has not worked since their first child was born. Citing the disparities in earning power and career potential of the parties, and the fact that W was awarded custody of the couple's minor children, in making a division of CP the trial court (a) divides the tangible personal property equally; (b) awards the house to W; and (c) awards $200,000 of the securities to W and $300,000 to H. As a result, W takes property worth $510,000 and H takes property worth $310,000.

• *Is this proper?*

o _____. Absent a property settlement agreement, all community property must

be _____.

o Disparity in earning power can be considered only as to

_____.

- Suppose, instead, that the court divided the tangible property equally ($10,000 each), awarded the house ($300,000) to W, and awarded securities worth $100,000 to W and $400,000 to H, with the result being that each ends up with assets worth $410,000. *Was this non-pro rata division proper?*

  - General rule: _____. Each and every community asset (and liability) must be

    _____.

  - **Economic Circumstances exception** – can have non-pro rata division, giving particular asset wholly to one spouse and "cash out" other spouse with other assets (with each spouse getting 50% of total value).

    - **Examples** of this exception:

      - *Family residence* – (very common) Family residence *and* loss of family home would uproot couple's minor children.

      - *Closely held corporation* - All 100 shares of closely held corporation are CP; W is CEO of corporation.

      - *Pension* - Awarding all of H's pension to H, other assets to W, so they can go their separate ways.

- *Statutory exceptions* to "equal 50/50 division on divorce" rule, with one spouse ending up with *more* than 50% of total value:

  - One spouse **misappropriates** CP, whether before or during pendency of divorce.

  - One spouse has incurred **educational debts**; treated separately as separately incurred debt (take law school loans with you!)

- One spouse incurred **tort liability** *not* based on activity for benefit of the community.

- **Personal injury** award is CP but on divorce is awarded to injured spouse (unless interests of justice require otherwise).

- "Negative community" – **community liabilities exceed assets**; relative ability of spouses to pay debt is considered (concern is protect creditors).

C. What rules govern lifetime and testamentary gifts of community property?

Hypo 5 - Unbeknownst to Winkie, Hobie gives Apple stock (CP) worth $40,000 to his deadbeat brother Buddy. When Winkie finds out about the gift (the stock is then worth $100,000), *what are her options?*

- Winkie can _____ because neither spouse can make

  a gift of CP without the other spouse's _____.

  - The power to manage CP is *not* equal to the power to give it away.

- *Alternatively*, on divorce, WInkie can take equal offsetting CP assets to recover her ½ CP.

- What if Winkie only learns about the gift *after* Hobie's death?

  - Winkie can _____.

  - Winkie's recovery will be from either _____ or_____; whichever is easiest.

- The *same* result would apply if Hobie, the insured under a $100,000 CP life insurance policy, names a third party as a beneficiary (e.g., girlfriend). Winkie can recover her ½ CP, from either the beneficiary OR Hobie's estate.

- Only *exception* to party not being able to give CP away is when US government savings bonds are involved.

  - In this case, federal law trumps, and there is **federal preemption**.

  - So even if Hobie uses $20,000 CP to buy United States Series EE Savings Bonds in the name of "Hobie, payable on death to Buddy," Winkie cannot recover her ½ community interest in bonds.

Hypo 6 - Harry buys Blackacre with community funds. Not being totally familiar with California's community property system, and because the deed conveying Blackacre names Harry as grantee, Harry thinks Blackacre is his SP. He dies leaving a will that says:

1. I, Harry, own Blackacre as my separate property. I devise fee simple title therein to my sister Sally.

2. I give and bequeath all the rest, residue, and remainder of my property to my wife Wanda if she survives me, otherwise to my brother Bob.

At the time of Harry's death, Blackacre is worth $100,000. Harry and Wanda own other community property worth $400,000.

- *Did Harry have testamentary power to devise the entire interest in Blackacre to Sally?*

  - _____. Each spouse has the power of testamentary disposition over *all* of his SP, but only over ½ of the CP.

- *Does this mean that Wanda gets to keep her one-half interest in Blackacre and take Harry's ½ CP under the second paragraph of will?*

  - _____. They key term is_____.

- Harry's will purports to bequeath the entire interest in a community asset. Wanda has therefore been put to a choice (an "election"). She *cannot* read the will selectively ("I'll take the residuary estate under ¶2, but I protest the gift in ¶1"). Rather, she has to read *all* of the will. If Wanda elects to **take under the will** and receive her residuary estate, she will take ½ of Harry's CP ($200,000), but she has to allow the will to operate to devise Blackacre to Sally.

- Alternatively, Wanda can elect to **take against the will**, by claiming her ½ CP in Blackacre. But she then must relinquish all testamentary gifts in her favor. In this case, Harry's will is read as though Wanda died before him, meaning that Wanda does not take Harry's ½ CP in residuary estate under ¶2 of the will.

- *What will Wanda do?* _____.

  - If she takes under the will, she will wind up with $400,000 (her ½ CP ($200,000) + Harry's ½ CP ($200,000)). If she elects against the will, she will wind up with $250,000 (her ½ CP ($200,000) + ½ Blackacre ($50,000).

D. What rules govern acquisitions on credit during the marriage?

Hypo 7 - Hal buys a lot near Big Bear Lake for $50,000, paying $10,000 in community funds and $40,000 with a loan from Bank. At the Bank's insistence, Willow signs the note for the loan along with Hal. The deed to the lot names "Hal" as the grantee.

- At the time of the purchase, the lot is at least 20% _____because of the $10,000 down payment from community funds. *What about the other 80% acquisition on credit?*

  - Funds borrowed during marriage, and goods purchased during marriage, are

    _____. This is the _____.

  - *However,* borrowed funds (and credit purchases) are classified according to the

    _____. We look at where the lender is looking for satisfaction of the debt.

- *What would be the result if the lender was primarily relying on Hal or Willow's general standing in the community, or was relying primarily on Hal's personal creditworthiness or reputation?*

  o The note would be a _____ obligation, and the lot would be_____.

- *What would be the result if the loan was secured by a mortgage on land in Los Angeles worth $50,000 which Hal owns as his SP?*

  o The note would likely be a _____obligation; the lot would be _____CP and _____SP.

  o But remember, the controlling test is **primary intent of the lender.** Thus, it still could be shown that (e.g.,) Bank was primarily looking to Hal's credit standing, in which case the note and lot would be _____.

E.   Confidential relationship raises fiduciary duty; presumption of undue influence

Spouses are subject to fiduciary duties that arise from their confidential relationship, imposing a duty of the highest good faith and fair dealing with each other. If one spouse gains an advantage from a transaction, a **presumption of undue influence** arises. That spouse has the burden of proof to show she did not breach her fiduciary duty.

- Under a 2002 statute, a grossly negligent and reckless investment of community funds is a breach of a spouse's fiduciary duty.

- Example – if H invests community funds in Alchemy, Inc., a start-up company with a "sure-fire formula to turn lead into gold," it would be a presumptive breach of the H's fiduciary duty.

II.   ALTERING THE CHARACTER OF ASSETS BY AGREEMENT

Absent any contrary agreement, the statutory definitions of SP and CP control. But California has always allowed the parties to opt out of the CP and SP characterizations by agreement, either as to **particular assets** or as to **all acquisitions.**

These agreements can be made *before* marriage (and thus governed by the Uniform Premarital Agreement Act) or be made *during* the marriage. When, by agreement during the marriage the character of an asset is changed (from SP to CP, from CP to SP, or from one spouse's SP to the other spouses SP), this results in a **transmutation.** Transmutation can be by **gift** (e.g., H gives jewelry inherited from his mother to W on her birthday; jewelry is W's SP), or by **agreement.**

Unlike most contracts, no consideration is required for either a premarital agreement or for a transmutation during marriage.

A.   Premarital agreements

General rule – Premarital agreements must be in **writing, signed** by both parties. Oral agreements are invalid. There are *two exceptions* to this general rule.

- *Exception #1 –* Where oral agreement is _____.

Hypo 8– To induce Winkie to marry him, Hobie orally agrees to name her as beneficiary of his $100,000 life insurance policy. The parties marry, and Hobie changes the beneficiary designation to make Winkie the beneficiary. Later, after a heated argument, Hobie changes his policy to make his sister Sue the beneficiary. Hobie dies shortly thereafter. Winkie now sues Sue, offering proof of the oral agreement; Sue contends that evidence of the agreement is barred by the writing requirement for premarital agreements.

- ○ *Winkie argues that her marrying Hobie in reliance on the agreement is sufficient performance of the oral contract to make it an exception to the writing requirement. Is she correct?*

  - ▪ _____. Marriage alone is not sufficient performance to make it an exception to the writing requirement because

  _____.

- ○ *Winkie argues that evidence of Hobie's actions is still admissible to prove the existence of a premarital agreement as to the insurance. Is she correct?*

  - ▪ _____. By naming her as beneficiary, Hobie did what he promised and acted consistent with the existence of a contract. This conduct substitutes for requirement of writing.

- *Exception #2 –* _____ based on _____.

Hypo 9 – Wanda (who is single) executes a will leaving all of her property to her nephew Norman. Wanda later meets Howie. Howie agrees that if Wanda marries him, he will make no claim against Wanda's estate at the time of Wanda's death. They marry. Wanda dies, and Howie brings a claim for his share of the will against Wanda's estate (which he would otherwise get under California's omitted spouse statute).

   o *In probate court, evidence of Howie's oral promise is offered by independent witnesses. Howie argues that the evidence is inadmissible because of the premarital agreement writing requirement. Is the evidence admissible?*

      ▪ _____. Wanda relied on Howie's promise, and he is now estopped from asserting the writing requirement.

In a premarital agreement, what can parties agree to? _____.

- Parties can agree that after marriage, each party's salary and wages will be that parties SP; that neither will claim a family allowance in other's estate; that an agreement will govern disposition of property on separation, divorce, or death.

   o *Exception* – Parties cannot agree to limit either party's contribution to

      _____. This is prohibited by statute.

There are two defenses to enforcement of a premarital agreement:

- **Defense 1** - Not signed voluntarily

   o Background – *Marriage of Bonds* (Cal. S. Ct. 2000): in 1987, on trip to Montreal, BB meets Swedish masseuse. Whirlwind courtship; BB's lawyer drafts premarital agreement saying each keep earnings as SP. She was told she get attorney; declines, saying "that is the way we do it Sweden." Flew to Vegas and married next day. Marriage doesn't last, she tries to render agreement unenforceable, saying not signed voluntarily. Court held agreement enforceable, reasoning it was an informal wedding and she could have postponed it if she wanted attorney to review the agreement. Court suggested that it would have been different if she was presented with take-it-or-leave it agreement 30 minutes before formal wedding. California legislature not happy.

- o 2001 statute (response to Bonds) - A premarital agreement shall be deemed **not voluntary** (and thus **unenforceable**) unless court finds that party challenging agreement:

    i. Was represented by **independent legal counsel** at time agreement signed (or waived in separate writing); AND

    ii. Was given at least **7 days** to sign; AND

    iii. If not represented by independent counsel, was **fully informed in writing** (in language in which party proficient) of terms and basic effect of agreement. Party must execute document declaring that they got information and identifying who provided it.

- **Defense 2** – Unconscionability

    - o Unconscionability claims divide into two areas, those involving **spousal support** and those involving **anything else.**

        - *Spousal support* – in *Pendleton v. Fierman* (Cal. S.Ct. 2000), the California Supreme Court held that right to spousal support can be waived or modified in premarital agreement.

            - CA Legislature Response (2001): Provision in premarital agreement regarding spousal support is **unenforceable** on one of two grounds:

                a. Party challenging was

                _____at time signed; OR

                b. Provision is _____
                (even if party represented by independent legal counsel).

- *Anything else* – Agreement unenforceable if **unconscionable when made** AND (i) no full and fair **disclosure** of other party's property or financial obligations; (ii) right to disclosure not **waived** in writing; and (iii) party challenging had no adequate **knowledge** of other party's property or financial circumstances.

  o By statute, unconscionability is a _____ to be decided by the _____, not a question for the jury.

B.   Marital agreements (transmutations)

Before 1985, oral transmutations were permitted, whether by express agreement or agreement -in-fact.

After 1985, must be (1) in *writing*; (2) *signed* by spouse whose interested is adversely affected; and (3) must *explicitly state* that a change in ownership is being made.

- Applies to **all transmutations**: SP into CP; CP into SP; one spouse's SP into other spouse's SP.

- Usual exceptions to the writing requirement (statute of frauds) (e.g., estoppel, partial performance) do <u>not</u> apply.

- *Only exception*- gifts of tangible property of personal nature (e.g., inherited jewelry) which "are not substantial in value taking into account the circumstances of the marriage."

  (2/10 - $15K painting paid for with SP funds, given as gift to other spouse; still SP – no transmutation)

Hypo 10 – Hal owns AT&T stock worth $80,000; Wendy owns Exxon stock worth $20,000. Over breakfast one day in late 1984 or early 1985, Hal says, "I think it would be a good idea for all of our stock to be owned as CP." Wendy says, "Great!"

- *If conversation took place in 1984, what result?*

  _____and _____.

  - Rationale – spouses cannot be expected to act formally.

  - Problem – in divorce proceedings, it becomes messy – no written record.

- *If conversation took place in 1985, what result?*

  _____.

Hypo 11 – H executes will that says "I own no SP. All of my property, real and personal, is CP of my wife and me." H & W get divorced. In proceedings, H claims that some of his assets are SP. W procures Xerox copy of H's will, saying it shows a transmutation. *Is H's will admissible in divorce proceeding as evidence of a written transmutation agreement?*

- _____. By statute, in any proceeding commenced before the death of the person who made the will or created a revocable trust, a statement in a will or

  revocable trust as to the character of the property _____ as evidence of transmutation.

III.   EFFECT OF HOW TITLE IS TAKEN

A.   Property acquired before 1975: Married woman's special presumption

Married Woman's Special Presumption- Where CP was used to take written title in a married woman's name before 1975, and the title did not indicate CP or joint tenancy was intended, the property is presumptively wife's SP. Still need to know even though more than 30 years old.

- This is an exception to the general principle that an asset titled in one spouse's name does not overcome the community presumption.

  - Rationale – paternalism - before 1975, except for W's earnings H had sole management of CP. So if title taken in W's name, H must have intended gift.

- Is the presumption rebuttable as against a third-party bona fide purchaser who buys asset from W in reliance on fact that is titled in W's name, and therefore must be W's SP? _____.

- Is the presumption rebuttable as between H & W? _____.

    - E.g. – H could rebut presumption by showing he did not intend to make a gift to W; but had some other reason for taking title in her name (H concerned about creditors' claims, or W took title in her name w/out H's knowledge or consent).

Hypo 12 – Hobie and Winkie Gates are married. Before 1975, and with Hobie's participation, community funds are used to purchase Greenacre. *Does the special presumption arise...*

- If title is taken in the name of "Winkie Gates (or Winkie Gates, "a married woman?")"

    - _____. Greenacre is W's _____.

- If title is taken in the name of "Winkie Gates and Sam Slade" (Winkie's brother)?

    - _____. Winkie Gates and Sam Slade hold Greenacre as _____.

- If title is taken in the name of "Hobie Gates and Winkie Gates, husband and wife" (or "Mr. and Mrs. Hobie Gates")?

    - _____. Greenacre is _____.

- If title is taken in the name of "Hobie Gates and Winkie Gates, as joint tenants with right of survivorship?"

    - _____. Greenacre is held by HG and WG as _____.

- If title is taken in the name of "Hobie Gates and Winkie Gates" (with no reference to their marital status)?

    - _____, although H & W hold Greenacre as _____.

        - Hobie's ½ is held as CP.

        - Winkie's ½ is held as her SP.

        - At divorce, W winds up with 75% (her ½ and ½ of H CP) and H winds up with 25% (1/2 of CP).

To summarize, what you need to know is that the married woman's special presumption applies in one of three situations:

1. Title is taken in W's name alone before 1975 (property is W's SP).

2. Title in name of W & H before 1975, but title is <u>not</u> taken in joint tenancy form, and <u>not</u> as "husband and wife" or "Mr. & Mrs." (property is ½ W SP, ½ CP).

3. Title in name of W and some third party before before 1975 (W would be tenant in common with third party).

B.   Presumptions that arise from taking title in "joint and equal form"

"Joint and equal form" means the title lists both spouses names – "Harry and Wanda Smith," "Harry and Wanda Smith, husband and wife," "Mr. and Mrs. Harry Smith," or "Harry and Wanda Smith as joint tenants."

Hypo 13 – In 1978, H & W purchase a home for $60,000, using $15,000 of W's SP and $45,000 of CP. Title is taken as "Harry and Wanda Smith." W later contributes $10,000 of her SP for improvements.

- *When **H dies**, W seeks to "trace" and show that the house is ¼ SP because of her down payment. W also seeks reimbursement for improvements made with her SP.*

- o **Marriage of Lucas (Cal. S. Ct. 1980)** On similar facts, held that by taking title as joint tenants (which by statute made house CP), property was presumptively CP. Taking title in a form that raised a CP presumption was inconsistent with idea that W intended to reserve a SP interest. W's subjective intent was irrelevant. Absent proof of an agreement that W was to have a SP interest, by taking title in CP form W must have intended gift to community. Unless such an agreement is established, W has *no* separate ownership interest and has *no* claim for reimbursement.

- o In case involving death of one party, **Lucas** is still law. So W has

  _____, unless she can establish that there was agreement that W was to have SP interest or W was to be reimbursed.

- *In **divorce action**, W seeks to "trace," and show that the house is ¼ W's SP because of down payment, and W seeks reimbursement for improvements made with her SP.*

  - o The California legislature has passed two **anti-Lucas statutes** on the *ownership* and *reimbursement* issue when the issue arises on **divorce or separation.**

  - o *Ownership* (Family Code § 2581) – For purposes of division of property on divorce or separation, property acquired during marriage in joint and equal form is presumptively CP, and is subject to equal division on divorce. CP presumption can be rebutted by:

    - Express statement in the deed or other instrument of title that the property (or portion thereof) is SP; or

    - Written agreement by the parties that the property (or portion thereof) is SP.

  - o *Reimbursement* (Family Code §2640) – For purposes of division on divorce or legal separation, spouse who made contributions of SP to the acquisition or improvement of CP is entitled to reimbursement without interest for contributions to **D**own payment, **I**mprovements, or **P**rincipal payments on mortgage (acronym is "DIP."). But no reimbursement for SP used to pay interest on mortgage, taxes, insurance, or maintenance.

17

- So if no express statement in the deed or other writing indicating any SP interest,

  W _____ be able to claim ¼ of the house as SP because of the down

  payment, but _____ receive reimbursement (without interest) for her contributions to DIP.

Hypo 14 – Using $25,000 of CP funds and $25,000 of his SP funds, Harry purchases a vacation property for $50,000 cash. On divorce several years later, property is worth $90,000.

- *If the deed names "Harry and Wanda Smith, husband and wife," as grantees*, the anti-Lucas statutes apply. On divorce, the property is _____ (unless H's SP ownership interest is specified in deed or is recognized in separate written agreement between H & W). H is entitled to reimbursement without interest for DIP.

- *But if deed names "Harry Smith,"* as grantee, the anti-Lucas statutes do <u>not</u> apply because property was not taken in joint and equal form. Under the source rule and tracing, the property is _____.

Hypo 15 – Using $5,000 in CP funds and $5,000 of Wanda's SP, Harry and Wanda purchase a Picasso painting for $10,000. Although the receipt names "Mr. and Mrs. Harry Smith" as the buyers, there is no title document. The parties later divorce.

- The Picasso is _____ under the source rule.

- The anti-Lucas statutes do not apply because no title document or deed is involved. A receipt is not enough.

IV. EFFECT OF PARTIES' ACTIONS ON CHARACTERIZATION OF ASSETS

A. Installment purchase pre-marriage; debt paid down with CP post-marriage

Hypo 16 – Wanda, who is single, buys house for $100,000, paying $20,000 down and signing a note (secured by a mortgage) for the $80,000 balance. Thereafter, until her marriage to Harold, Wanda makes mortgage payments that reduce the loan balance by $10,000 (to $70,000). After the marriage, Wanda continues to make the mortgage payments out of her salary (CP) until the note is paid in full. Wanda dies leaving a will that devises "all my property" to her nephew Norman. The house is now worth $500,000. *Who takes what?*

- _____ – installment purchase before marriage, payment with CP funds after marriage (or during marriage W inherits land subject to mortgage and pays off note with CP funds), the community estate takes a pro rata portion of the property, measured by the amount (percentage) of **principal debt reduction** attributable to the expenditure of community funds.

- numerator: principal debt reduction attributable to CP $70,000
  denominator: purchase price $100,000

- The house is: _____.   House ($500,000) is $350,000 CP; $150,000 Wanda SP. Norman winds up with $325,000 (1/2 of W's CP ($175,000) + W's SP ($150,000).

  - Note – CP component measured by amount of principal debt reduction attributable to community funds, *not mortgage interest, property taxes*, or *insurance*.

Hypo 17 – same facts, except that note not paid off in full when Wanda divorces Harold (or one of them dies). Wanda buys house for $100,000, paying $20,000 down and signing a note (secured by a mortgage) for the $80,000 balance. Thereafter, until her marriage to Harold, Wanda makes mortgage payments that reduce the loan balance by $10,000 (to $70,000). At the time Wanda and Harold get divorced, the house is valued at $500,000, and the principal balance of the note has been reduced to $50,000. Thus the principal balance has been reduced by $20,000 with community funds (Wanda's salary). *Between Wanda and Harold, who takes what?*

  - Same proration rule – the community estate takes a pro rata portion of the property, measured by the amount (percentage) of principal debt reduction attributable to the expenditure of community funds.

  - numerator   principal debt reduction attributable to CP $20,000
    denominator   purchase price $100,000

  - The house was: _____. House ($500,000) is $100,000 CP, $400,000 Wanda SP. Wanda ends up with $450,000 (her SP ($400,000) + her ½ CP ($50,000); Harold winds up with $50,000 (his ½ CP).

Hypo 18 – In 1994, Hugh, while single, takes out a $100,000 **whole life insurance policy** (cash value; investment feature) that names his mother as beneficiary. Hugh pays the first annual premium of $2,000 and all subsequent premiums out of his salary. Hugh marries Wilma in 2000 (having made six premium payments before the marriage), and dies in 2004 (having made four additional premium payments during the marriage) without changing the beneficiary designation. *Who takes the policy proceeds?*

- In classifying ownership of **whole life insurance policies**, _____.

- Therefore, the life insurance policy was _____ and

  _____. Wilma will get _____.

Hypo 19 – Same facts, except that the $100,000 life insurance policy was a **term life insurance policy** (pure insurance with no cash surrender value (car insurance)); the annual premiums were paid by H's employer (or could be H paid first premium with SP). H marries W, and dies in 2004 (having made final payments with community funds).

- The term insurance policy was _____ SP and _____ CP.

- Rule for term insurance is that the last premium determines the character.

B.   Community funds used to improve SP

Hypo 20 – Hobie owns a house at the time of his marriage to Winkie. Thereafter, Hobie spent $50,000 out of his salary (CP) to add a family room to the back of the house, to put in a swimming pool, and to build a redwood deck around the pool. These improvements increase the value of the house from $200,000 to $280,000. Winkie has filed for divorce. *Do these expenditures for improvements give the community a proportionate share of the ownership of the house?*

- _____. This situation is governed by the real property doctrine of _____. The improvements become part of the property. Expenditure of CP does not change ownership character of house.

- *What are Winkie's rights?*

- o Winkie can bring a claim for _____ for the community. The

    community gets _____.

- The Anti-Lucas statutes do not apply because _____trigger anti-Lucas.

Hypo 21 – Suppose, instead that Winkie owned the house as her SP. Thereafter, Hobie spent $50,000 out of his salary (CP) to add the family room, swimming pool, and redwood deck. Those improvements increased the value of the house and land from $200,000 to $280,000. *In a divorce proceeding, is Hobie entitled to assert a community reimbursement claim for the expenditure of community funds on Winkie's separate property?*

- There is a **split of authority!** You need to argue **both ways!**

    - o **No reimbursement** –These facts (CP expended other spouse's SP) give rise to presumption of gift to W's separate estate; presumption of gift can be overcome only by evidence of an agreement to reimburse community estate.

    - o **Reimbursement** – Other cases rejected presumption of gift and granted reimbursement.

Hypo 22 – Henry and Wanda own a house as CP. The deed names "Henry and Wanda Harris" as grantees. Thereafter, Henry spends $50,000 of his SP to add a family room, swimming pool, and redwood deck. The improvements increase the value of the house from $200,000 to $280,000. *In a divorce proceeding, can Henry assert a reimbursement claim?*

- _____. This situation is governed by _____. When asset is held in joint and equal form, and SP is expended to improve CP, upon *divorce*, the party who expended SP would get reimbursement (without interest) for DIP (down payment, improvements, principal payments).

    - o If issue arises on *death* of one of the spouses, the situation would be governed

        by_____, and there would be _____unless there was proof of an agreement to reimburse.

To recap the reimbursement rules triggered by improvements:

- If H expends CP to improve own SP (feathering his nest), community has reimbursement claim for the greater of the cost of improvements or the enhanced value.

- If H expends CP to improve other spouse's SP, there is a split of authority on whether there is reimbursement or not.

- If H expends SP to improve community property, we are governed by anti-Lucas statutes (divorce) or *Lucas* (death).

C.   Comingled bank accounts

Hypo 23 – Herb owned substantial SP at the time of his marriage to Wilma, including $200,000 in a savings account on which Herb was the only authorized signatory. During the marriage (which ended in divorce after 15 years), Herb deposited his salary checks and additional separate funds into the account. From time to time, Herb made withdrawals and wrote checks to pay family living expenses, and also to buy various assets, title to which was taken in Herb's name. At the time of the divorce action, the amount on deposit is $60,000. Herb seeks to prove that *all* assets purchased from the account are his SP by *recapitulation accounting:* he totals all family living expenses over 15 years of marriage, and shows that family living expenses exceeded 15 years of community income by a substantial margin. Therefore, Herb argues that all CP must have been exhausted, and he "must have" used SP to purchase assets.

- *Is Herb correct?* _____. The mere fact that SP funds are commingled with CP funds does not transform or transmute the SP into CP. But the **burden of proof** is on H to show that **each asset** was purchased with SP funds.

    o Problem with *recapitulation* theory is that it does not show that CP funds were unavailable when each asset was purchased.

    o There is a **family expense presumption** – It is presumed that expenditures for family expenses (food, housing, clothing, recreation, etc.) were made with community funds (to the extent they were available), even though separate funds were available.

- But because of commingling and inadequate records, some family expenses may have been paid with SP funds, in which case the

  presumption is _____.

  To defeat this presumption, H would need an_____.

- To satisfy his burden of proof, Herb can use one of two accounting methods:

  - _____:

    - E.g., Herb's records show that on 9/20/95 the account balance dropped to $3,000; that H deposited $20,000 of his separate funds on that date; on 9/22 Herb wrote a $5,000 check to pay his daughter's tuition bill at private school (exhausting CP), and that on 9/24 Herb withdrew $10,000 to buy 200 shares of stock.

  - _____:

    - E.g., At a time when $15,000 was in account, Herb deposited $12,000 of SP funds; two days later he wrote a $12,000 check to buy 200 shares of stock. Direct tracing requires that (a) sufficient separate funds were available, and (b) that H intended to use SP funds to buy the asset.

V. CHARACTERIZATION PROBLEMS RAISED BY CERTAIN ASSETS

A. Business owned before marriage greatly increases in value during the marriage

Hypo 24 – Wendy owned a computer software company in San Jose worth $100,000 at the time of her marriage to Hal in 1986. When the couple divorce in 1996, the business is worth $4 million.

Hal contends that a substantial portion of the business is CP. He points out that because of the increased volume of business in the 1990's, Wendy worked long hours and on weekends; they rarely took vacations; that Hal stayed home to watch their daughter; that Wendy drew a modest salary; and thus the great increase in the business was from W's labor (a community asset).

23

Wendy contends that the increase in value stemmed from her incredibly good fortune and timing; that only an idiot couldn't have made a fortune when the computer and microchip business exploded in San Jose in the 1990's; that she had hired two Cal Tech graduates whose ideas contributed to the business's growth; and that the salary and bonuses she drew out of the business were substantial – far above the going rate for similar positions. Therefore, since the business was her SP at the time of the marriage the business is entirely her SP.

Who wins?

- There are two relevant tests: **Pereira** and **Van Camp.** You need to discuss **both**.

- For **Pereira**, think **P_____**.

  o Use where spouse's time, skill, and effort are major factors in growth of business. Look for instances where spouse contributed creative ideas or develops new techniques, and/or worked long hours and only drew modest salary.

    ▪ E.g. - H owned modest real estate business at time of marriage; worth $3 million at time of divorce. H claimed he was passive investor who got caught up in the real estate boom, but the court found that H was unusually skillful in developing raw land, supervising financing and construction, and negotiating lucrative leases of commercial properties.

  o Pereira formula – **P_____**; the rest is _____.

    ▪ Pay interest (legal rate of 10% annum) on value of business at time of the marriage.

      - In hypo 24, if H & W had been married for ten years, W is entitled to the initial $100,000 (value of business at time of marriage) plus $100,000 in interest (10 x 10,000 (interest at 10%)). Therefore, the business is 5% her SP ($200,000/$4,000,0000) and the balance is CP.

- For **Van Camp**, think **V**_____ **C**_____.

  o Use where capital investment was the major factor in the business's growth, and spouse's skills and efforts were less of a factor. Look for instances where spouse was paid substantial salary and large bonuses (meaning the community was compensated).

    ▪ Ex. – H owns Ford dealership at time of marriage in 1947, business grows dramatically due to increased demand for cars after WWII.

  o Van Camp formula – **V**_____ **C**_____; the rest is _____.

    ▪ Start with value of spouse's services at market rates (how much would executives in similar positions be compensated on the market?) MINUS family expenses paid from community funds EQUALS community component. The balance is SP.

      • In hypo 24, if H&W married for 10 years, and the market rate for executives in comparable positions was $100,000 and living expenses were $80,000/year, the value of the community component would be $200,000. The business would be 5% CP ($200,000/$4,000,000) and the balance W's SP.

      • $100,0000 x 10 years = $1,000,000   value of community labor
        - $80,000 x 10 years = - $800,000 family expenses paid from CP
        community component: $200,000

- California Supreme Court has said that court is not bound either to adopt **Pereira** or **Van Camp.** May select whichever formula will achieve substantial justice between the parties.

B.   Pension benefits

Hypo 25 – H had worked for Shell Oil Co. for 10 years at the time he married W in 1982; the marriage ended by divorce in 1992, and H will be eligible to retire in 2002. In all of these years, H was a participant in Shell's qualified pension plan, where the pension benefit is measured by years of service. H was not eligible for retirement at the time of the divorce action. W contends that a portion of the pension benefit is CP. *Is she right?*

- _____. Employee retirement benefits accumulated during marriage, whether or not vested at the time of divorce, are

  _____.

- Use a *proration rule*:

  Numerator: _____   <u>10</u>

  _____

  Denominator: _____   30

  Pension would be _____.

- Given that H is not yet eligible for retirement, in awarding W a share of the benefit, what form should the decree take? *Two options*:

  o 1 – "_____" – if and when received, she gets her share (1/6, which is half of 1/3 CP share).

  o 2 – "_____" – by awarding other assets of equal value.

Hypo 26 – same facts as Hypo 25 (H had worked for 10 years before marriage, 10 years during marriage), except that H was eligible for retirement at the time of the divorce action. W seeks payment of her community share of H's pension benefit even though H has not retired. *Is she entitled?*

- _____ Since H could have retired at the time of the divorce, his retirement benefit had

  _____.

  o H's election not to retire _____.

- If a nonparticipant spouse ("NPS") in a qualified pension plan **divorces** a participant spouse, her community property interest is recognized; under federal law she can get a qualified domestic relations order ("QDRO") and receive payments from the plan.

- What if the marriage ended by death rather than divorce. *Does the NPS have a devisable interest in a qualified plan if she predeceases the participant?*

    - _____. There is federal preemption under the Employment Retirement Income Security Act ("ERISA"), which trumps CP laws. Her interest is terminated when she predeceased the participant.

Hypo 27 – same facts as hypo 25 (H had worked for 10 years before marriage, 10 years during marriage), but H was also covered by Shell's disability insurance program. Shortly before the divorce, H suffers an on-the-job injury and is given disability retirement; under the Shell plan H received **disability pension** of $900/month. Also, H is awarded a **workers' compensation benefit** of $150/week. W claims a community interest in the disability and workers' compensation benefits, arguing that these benefits were derived from H's labor, and should be treated the same as pension benefits. *Is W right?*

- _____. Disability retirement benefits and workers' compensation benefits are

    treated as _____.

- Thus, disability retirement and workers' compensation benefits are classified according

    to _____.

    - What if H could elect to take, at his option, either a regular retirement benefit at $1,200/month or disability retirement at $900/month; H chooses disability retirement. *Does W have CP interest in H's retirement benefit?*

        - _____. H cannot elect to defeat her community interest.

- What about **severance pay**?

    - No clear rule (Courts of Appeal are split) – *argue both ways!*:

        - H's severance pay is SP because it replaced lost earnings which after a divorce or permanent separation would be H's SP; OR

        - H's severance pay is CP because it arose from a collective bargaining agreement and was thus earned by employment during marriage.

C.   Stock options

A stock option gives an employee (typically an executive) an option to purchase shares of the company's stock at a set price on a certain date in the future. Stock options typically provide that they are not "vested," and that the option-holder must be employed by the company as of the date the option becomes exercisable for the option to vest. If the option is awarded during marriage but does not vest until after the economic community has ended, the **proration formula** that is used in determining what portion of the option is CP and what portion is SP depends on the **primary intent of the employer in granting the option.**

Hypo 28 – Hank, married to Wynn, was employed by the Ajax Company on June 10, 1998. On June 10, 2004, Ajax Company granted Hank a stock option entitling him to purchase 5,000 shares of Ajax common stock if he is still employed by the company on June 10, 2008. Hank and Wynn are divorced in 2006; the economic community ended when Hank and Wynn permanently separated (with an intent not to resume the marital relation) on June 10, 2006.

- The divorce court determines that the stock options were awarded primarily to reward Hank for his past services, as a form of deferred compensation. The court should employ the **Marriage of Hug** proration formula, under which the starting point for both the numerator and denominator of the fraction is the date of employment. The fraction is then multiplied by the number of shares of stock that can be purchased under the options:

  Numerator: <u>years from the date of employment to date economic community ends</u>
  Denominator: years from date of employment to date options become exercisable

  $$\frac{\_\_\_\_ \text{ years employment to date economic community ended}}{\_\_\_\_\_ \text{ years employment to date option becomes exercisable}} = \_\_\_\_\_ \text{ CP}$$

  Subject to equal division on divorce.

- Suppose, instead that the divorce court determines that the stock options were awarded primarily to encourage Hank to remain with the company. The court should employ the **Marriage of Nelson** proration formula, under which the starting point for both the numerator and denominator of the fraction is the date the options are granted. The fraction is multiplied by the number of shares of stock that can be purchased under the options:

Numerator: <u>years from date options are granted to date economic community ends</u>
Denominator: years from date options granted to date options become exercisable

___ years from date option granted to date economic community ends
_____ = ___ CP

___ years from date option granted to date option becomes exercisable

Subject to equal division on divorce.

D.   Goodwill of a professional practice

Hypo 29 – Winkie is a CPA with a solo practice. At the time of her divorce from Hobie, she is netting $100,000/year after expenses. If she went on the job market, she could earn $60,000/year as an associate. Winkie's firm has $100,000 in capital assets; at a 10% return, these assets would earn $10,000/year. Hobie contends that the "goodwill" of Winkie's professional practice, which Winkie opened a year after marriage to Hobie, is community property. *Is Hobie right?*

- _____. Goodwill of a professional practice (to the extent acquired during the marriage)

    _____.

    - Goodwill are those qualities that generate income *beyond that* derived from (1) the professional's labor; and (2) reasonable return on capital and physical assets.

    - Goodwill is primarily established by expert witness testimony as to its value.

Hypo 30 – Winkie is a partner in a small firm. The partners have a buy-sell agreement which provides that any partner who dies or leaves the firm will receive $5,000 for his or her interest in the partnership. Winkie contends that the buy-sell agreement puts a $5,000 cap on the value of her goodwill in the partnership for purposes of division on divorce. *Is she right?*

- _____. It is a factor but not conclusive.

E.   Educational expenses

Hypo 31 – Hobie and Winkie are married shortly after Hobie graduates from USC with a degree in history and Winkie graduates from nursing school. They both want to go to medical school, but realize they cannot both do so at the same time. Because Winkie's prospects for employment as a nurse are better than Hobie's, they decide that Winkie will work the night shift in an emergency room while Hobie gets his MD. Four years (and $120,000 in GSL) later, it is graduation day. Hobie tells Winkie he has good news and bad news. The good news is that he will finally be a doctor. The bad news is he is filing for divorce. *Is Hobie's professional degree "property" that is subject to division on divorce?*

- _____. To what then is Winkie (actually the community) entitled?

  - _____ if the education

    _____.

  - *Is reimbursement available if the educational expenses were incurred before marriage and the loans were paid with community funds after the marriage?*

    _____.

- Defenses to reimbursement of community estate for educational expenses:

  - Community has already substantially benefited from the earnings of the educated spouse. If more than 10 years have elapsed since the degree was awarded, the presumption is that the community has substantially benefited, meaning that unless presumption is rebutted, no reimbursement.

  - OR if other spouse also received a CP-funded education.

- What about $120,000 in GSL loans used to finance H's education?

  - They are _____.

VI. TORT AND CONTRACT LIABILITY; MANAGEMENT PROBLEMS

Hypo 32 – During marriage, Winkie is injured in an automobile accident in which her husband Hobie was the negligent driver. Winkie collects $75,000 in a settlement with Hobie's insurance company.

- Where the other spouse was a tortfeasor, the tort recovery is _____.

    o Why? Otherwise, he would benefit from his wrongful act.

Hypo 33 – Suppose, instead that Winkie was injured in an automobile accident in which a *third party* was the negligent driver. Two years later, Winkie collects $100,000 in a settlement with the driver's insurance company.

- Where damages are recovered from a third party, the tort recovery is _____.

    o However, in a property division on *divorce* or *legal separation*, the $100,000 will

       be awarded _____, so long as the $100,000

       _____.

    o This will be the result *unless* the interests of justice, including economic need, require otherwise.

        ▪ But on either spouse's *death*, the $100,000 will be treated as _____.

Hypo 34 – Same facts as hypo 33, except that Winkie was the *negligent driver.* She suffered a judgment of $200,000, of which $100,000 was covered by liability insurance. In recovering the remaining $100,000, *what assets can the judgment creditor reach, and in what order?*

- The rule is that _____.

- But we also need to look at what money creditors are able to recover first.

    o If W was performing an act for the benefit of the community (e.g., driving to work, or driving the kids in a car pool),

        ▪ The liability is first satisfied from _____, and then from _____.

31

- o If W was not performing an act on behalf of the community (e.g., driving to SP vineyard to talk to foreman, or driving to liaison with her boyfriend)

    - ▪ The liability is first satisfied from _____, and then from _____.

        - • Can a judgment creditor reach H's SP?

        _____.

Management Rules:

- • General Rule – *equal management powers* – Each spouse has equal management and control over all community property, and thus has full power to buy or sell CP and contract debts without the other spouse's joinder or consent.

    - o *Personal Belongings Exception* – One spouse cannot sell or encumber personal property used in family dwelling (furniture, clothing, etc.) without written consent of other spouse. Transaction voidable by other spouse at any time.

    - o *Business exception* – Applies when a spouse operates a business interest that is all or substantially all community *personal* property and has primary management and control of all the business. While this spouse can act alone in all transactions, if the spouse sells, leases, or otherwise encumbers substantially all of the *personal* property used in the business, must give written notice to other spouse.

Hypo 35 – Hank and Winona own a ranch as CP, but title to the ranch is in Hank's name. Hank sells the ranch to Bob (or leases it for more than one year), telling Bob that he is single. Winona learns about the sale 10 months after the sale. She demands that Bob reconvey the ranch to Hank and Winona, and offers to refund the purchase price. *Can Winona void the transfer?*

- • _____. For conveyances of CP real property, _____.

    There is a _____.

    - o What about Bob's rights as a bonafide purchaser? _____.

    - o What if Bob knew or should have known that Hank was married?

        _____.

- **General rule** – Neither spouse can transfer or encumber their ½ interest in real CP (house). Only entire interest can be transferred or encumbered.

  - *Exception* – A spouse can unilaterally encumber her ½ interest in real CP to pay the family attorney representing her in a divorce action –

    _____.

Hypo 36 – During marriage, H incurs debts of $40,000 owed to various suppliers in connection with his business, and incurs $30,000 in medical expenses (not covered by insurance) by reason of illness.

- *Can CP be reached in satisfaction of $40,000 business debt?* _____. Spouses have

  _____, and either spouse can _____.

  - *Can CP be reached if debt was incurred by H before marriage to W?*

    - _____, with one exception: The earnings of a nondebtor spouse cannot be reached for premarital debts if held in a separate account (in which the other spouse has no right of withdrawal) and not commingled with other CP funds.

  - *Can W's SP be reached in satisfaction of $40,000 business debt?*

    - _____. W is _____.

- *Can W's SP be reached in satisfaction of H's $30,000 medical bills?*

  - _____. The Family Code provides that each spouse has the duty to support the other spouse and minor children. This means that each spouse is personally liable for the other spouse's

    _____.

  - If CP funds are available to pay medical bills,

    _____.

     ○   *Can W's SP be reached in satisfaction of $30,000 in H's medical bills if (when debt incurred), W & H had separated and economic community had ended?*

          ■ _____. For purposes of family code, _____.

Hypo 37 – In a property settlement agreement entered into by Hobie and Winkie as part of their divorce, stocks and bonds (which were CP) are awarded to Winkie. At the time of the divorce, H owed $40,000 to a supplier. After the divorce, the supplier obtains a judgment against Hobie, but only collects $10,000 from him. The supplier then seeks to reach the securities awarded to Winkie. *What result?*

- After divorce, a creditor *cannot* reach CP awarded to a spouse unless that spouse:

     ○ _____ or _____.

VII.   MULTISTATE PROBLEMS/CONFLICT OF LAWS

Hypo 38 – Henry and Wynn, married in Kansas (a non-community property state) in 1990, moved to California in 1998, bringing with them 2,000 shares of IBM stock which Henry had acquired from his salary. They also own a farm in Kansas (the deed names Henry as grantee) acquired from Henry's salary. Wynn has never been employed. After their move to California, they get divorced. At the time of the divorce, there are 2,400 shares of IBM stock in Henry's name (resulting from stock dividends) and the Kansas farm is worth $40,000. *What division of these items should be made in the divorce proceeding?*

- The 2,400 shares of IBM stock are

    _____.

     ○ **Rule** – Property acquired while the couple was domiciled in a non-community property state, which would have been classified as community property had it been acquired under the same circumstances in California, is *quasi community property*.

- On these facts, with respect to the IBM stock, Henry is the *acquiring spouse*, and Wynn is the *non-acquiring spouse*. On divorce, *quasi community property* is treated the same as *true community property*, and divided 50-50.

- But if Harry inherited property in Kansas, it is not quasi-CP because it would be SP if acquired in California.

- The farm in Kansas:

  o For purposes of division on *divorce*, "foreign" real property is

  _____.

  o What about the fact that California has no jurisdiction over Kansas land?

    - No problem. In making 50-50 division, a California court could award the Kansas land to Henry and other assets of equal value to Wynn, OR require Henry to execute any conveyances that are necessary (court does have personal jurisdiction over Henry).

Hypo 39– same facts as Hypo 38, except that the marriage ends not by divorce but by Henry's death. Henry leaves a will that bequeaths "all my property" to the couple's daughter Dorkie. Henry is survived by Wynn and Dorkie. *What distribution?*

- As to the 2,400 shares of IBM stock, as Henry was the "acquiring spouse,"

  _____.

- As to the farm in Kansas ("foreign real property"), for purposes of division on death,

  foreign real property, _____.

Hypo 40 – same facts as Hypo 39, except that it is Wynn (the "non-acquiring spouse") who dies, leaving a will that bequeaths "all my property" to daughter Dorkie. *Does the non-acquiring spouse have any power of disposition over quasi-CP if she dies before the acquiring spouse?*

COMMUNITY PROPERTY

- _____. The quasi-CP system gives protection only if

  _____.

  - Rationale - if Henry and Wynn had continued to live in Kansas, on Henry's death Wynn would be protected from disinheritance by Kansas's elective share statute. The quasi-CP statute is designed to replace that protection.

Hypo 41 – same facts as Hypo 40, except that the couple moved to California not from Kansas but from Texas (another CP state). *Are the IBM stock and Texas ranch quasi CP, meaning that Wynn, as the non-acquiring spouse, has no ownership interest to pass by will?*

- _____. Both are _____.

VIII. PROPERTY ACQUIRED OUTSIDE THE MARITAL RELATION

Hypo 42 – Hobie Gates and Winkie Waters are living together in California, but they are not married. Pooling their resources 50-50, they buy a house, taking title in the name of "Hobie Gates and Winkie Waters, husband and wife." *How is title held?*

- California does _____(where people live together and hold themselves out as married).

  - *Exception* – Where common law marriage _____.

- *Do Hobie and Winkie hold title to the house as CP?* _____. Only spouses and registered domestic partners can have CP. They own it as

  _____.

Hypo 43 – Marvin and Michelle have gone out for five years. When Michelle asks about marriage, Marvin replies, "Out of the question. I'll tell you what, though. If you will move in with me, cook and clean for me and … provide other services, we can have all of the benefits of marriage anyway." Michelle does so, even though it means forsaking a promising acting career. Ten years later, they split. In the meantime, Marvin has accumulated assets worth $400,000 from selling tax shelters. *What are Michelle's rights?*

- The property relationships between Marvin and Michelle are governed by

_____.

Would need to do contract analysis as to whether contract existed on these facts.

  - As long as the contract is not based solely on sexual services.

Hypo 44 – After Daphne moved from Texas to California, she met and fell in love with Luther, an attorney. When Daphne asked about marriage, Luther (knowing it to be false) told Daphne that they did not need to go through a ceremonial marriage because California recognizes common law marriages. On that basis, Daphne moved in with Luther, and they lived together as husband and wife for ten years – when Daphne learns the truth and moves out. During their ten years together, Daphne and Luther acquired property worth $200,000 from Luther's earnings.

- In a relationship with Luther, Daphne is called a _____.

  - The test is whether she _____
    that they were lawfully married.

  - If so, the assets acquired by Luther and Daphne are called_____,

    and when they split, the assets are split _____.

    - One California Court of Appeal case has held that if Luther was "bad faith partner," he is not entitled to ½ property earned by her labor (which would otherwise be CP, subject to 50/50 split).

- If Daphne was aware that they were not lawfully married, their relationship is characterized as unmarried cohabitants. Absent a contract (express or implied), Luther

  _____and Daphne _____.

Constitutional Law

Professor Erwin Chemerinsky

CONSTITUTIONAL LAW

by Erwin Chemerinsky

OVERVIEW OF ORGANIZATION

I.   The Federal Judicial Power

      A.   The requirement for cases and controversies

            1.   Standing. Standing is the issue of whether the plaintiff is the proper party to bring a matter to the court for adjudication.

                  a.   Injury. The plaintiff must allege and prove that he or she has been injured or imminently will be injured

                        i.   Plaintiffs only may assert injuries that they personally have suffered

                        ii.   Plaintiffs seeking injunctive or declaratory relief must show a likelihood of future harm

1

b. Causation and redressability. The plaintiff must allege and prove that the defendant caused the injury so that a favorable court decision is likely to remedy the injury.

c. No third party standing. A plaintiff cannot assert claims of others, of third parties, who are not before the court.

   i. Exception: third party standing is allowed if there is a close relationship between the plaintiff and the injured third party

   ii. Exception: third party standing is allowed if the injured third party is unlikely to be able to assert his or her own rights

   iii. Exception: an organization may sue for its members, if
      — the members would have standing to sue;
      — the interests are germane to the organization's purpose;
      — neither the claim nor relief requires participation of individual members

d. No generalized grievances. The plaintiff must not be suing solely as a citizen or as a taxpayer interested in having the government follow the law.

   Exception: taxpayers have standing to challenge government expenditures pursuant to federal statutes as violating the Establishment Clause

2. Ripeness. Ripeness is the question of whether a federal court may grant pre-enforcement review of a statute or regulation.

   a. The hardship that will be suffered without preenforcement review

   b. The fitness of the issues and the record for judicial review

3.   Mootness. If events after the filing of a lawsuit end the plaintiff's injury, the case must be dismissed as moot.

    a.   Exception: wrong capable of repetition but evading review

    b.   Exception: voluntary cessation

    c.   Exception: class action suits

4.   The political question doctrine. The political question doctrine refers to constitutional violations that the federal courts will not adjudicate.

    a.   The "republican form of government clause"

    b.   Challenges to the President's conduct of foreign policy

    c.   Challenges to the impeachment and removal process

    d.   Challenges to partisan gerrymandering.

B.   Supreme Court review

1.   Virtually all cases come to the Supreme Court by writ of certiorari

    a.   All cases from state courts come to the Supreme Court by writ of certiorari

      b.   All cases from United States courts of appeals come to the Supreme Court by writ of certiorari

      c.   Appeals exist for decisions of three-judge federal district courts

      d.   The Supreme Court has original and exclusive jurisdiction for suits between state governments

2.   Generally, the Supreme Court may hear cases only after there has been a final judgment of the highest state court, of a United States Court of Appeals, or of a three-judge federal district court

3.   For the Supreme Court to review a state court decision, there must not be an independent and adequate state law ground of decision. If a state court decision rests on two grounds, one state law and one federal law, if the Supreme Court's reversal of the federal law ground will not change the result in the case, the Supreme Court cannot hear it.

C.   Lower federal court review

1.   Federal courts (and state courts) may not hear suits against state governments

      a.   The principle of sovereign immunity

            i)   The Eleventh Amendment bars suits against states in federal court

    ii) Sovereign immunity bars suits against states in state courts or federal agencies

   b. Exceptions. States may be sued under the following circumstances

    i) Waiver is permitted

    ii) States may be sued pursuant to federal laws adopted under section 5 of the Fourteenth Amendment. Congress cannot authorize suits against states under other constitutional provisions.

    iii) The federal government may sue state governments.

    iv) Bankruptcy proceedings.

   c. Suits against state officers are allowed
     — state officers may be sued for injunctive relief;
     — state officers may be sued for money damages to be paid out of their own pockets
     — state officers may not be sued if it is the state treasury that will be paying retroactive damages

  2. Abstention. Federal courts may not enjoin pending state court proceedings

II. The Federal Legislative Power

 A. Congress's authority to act

  1. There must be express or implied Congressional power

  2. The necessary and proper clause

3. The taxing/spending power and the commerce power

    a. Congress may tax and spend for the general welfare

    b. The Commerce Power
        i) Congress may regulate the channels of interstate commerce

        ii) Congress may regulate the instrumentalities of interstate commerce and persons or things in interstate commerce

        iii) Congress may regulate economic activities that have a substantial effect on interstate commerce. (In the area of non-economic activity, a substantial effect cannot be based on cumulative impact.)

4. The Tenth Amendment as a limit on Congressional powers. The Tenth Amendment states that all powers not granted to the United States, nor prohibited to the states, are reserved to the states or the people.

    a. Congress cannot compel state regulatory or legislative action. Note: Congress can induce state government action by putting strings on grants, so long as the conditions are expressly stated and relate to the purpose of the spending program.

    b. Congress may prohibit harmful commercial activity by state governments.

5. Congress' power under section 5 of the Fourteenth Amendment. Congress

may not create new rights or expand the scope of rights. Congress may act only to prevent or remedy violations of rights recognized by the courts and such laws must be "proportionate" and "congruent" to remedying constitutional violations.

B.   Delegation of powers

    1.   No limit exists on Congress' ability to delegate legislative power.

    2.   Legislative vetos and line-item vetos are unconstitutional. For Congress to act, there always must be bicameralism (passage by both the House and the Senate) and presentment (giving the bill to the President and sign or veto). The President must sign or veto the bill in its entirety.

    3.   Congress may not delegate executive power to itself or its officers

III.   **The Federal Executive Power**

A.   Foreign policy

    1.   Treaties. Treaties are agreements between the United States and a foreign country that are negotiated by the President and are effective when ratified by the Senate.

a.   Treaties prevail over conflicting state laws

b.   If a treaty conflicts with a federal statute, the one adopted last in time controls

c.   If a treaty conflicts with the United States Constitution, it is invalid

2.   Executive agreements

a.   Definition. An executive agreement is an agreement between the United States and a foreign country that is effective when signed by the President and the head of the foreign nation.

b.   Executive agreements can be used for any purpose

c.   Executive agreements prevail over conflicting state laws, but never over conflicting federal laws or the Constitution

[See chart on the following page]

CONSTITUTIONAL LAW – CHART 1

TREATIES AND EXECUTIVE AGREEMENTS

	IS SENATE APPROVAL REQUIRED?	CONFLICTS WITH STATE LAW	CONFLICTS WITH FEDERAL STATUTE	CONFLICTS WITH CONST.
TREATIES	YES	TREATY CONTROLS	WHICHEVER WAS ADOPTED LAST IN TIME CONTROLS	CONST. CONTROLS
EXECUTIVE AGREEMENTS	NO	EXECUTIVE AGREEMENT CONTROLS	FEDERAL STATUTE CONTROLS	CONST. CONTROLS

3. The President has broad powers as Commander-in-Chief to use American troops in foreign countries

B. Domestic affairs

1. The appointment and removal power

    a. The appointment power

        i. The President appoints ambassadors, federal judges and officers of the United States

        ii. Congress may vest the appointment of inferior officers in the President, the heads of departments or the lower federal courts

        iii. Congress may not give itself or its officers the appointment power

    b. The removal power. Unless removal is limited by statute, the President may fire any executive branch office.

        i. For Congress to limit removal, it must be an office where independence from the President is desirable and

        ii. Congress cannot prohibit removal, it can limit removal to where there is good cause

2. Impeachment and removal. The President, the Vice President, federal judges and officers of the United States can be impeached and removed from the office for treason, bribery, or for high crimes and misdemeanors

    a. Impeachment does not remove a person from office

b.   Impeachment by the House of Representatives requires a majority vote; conviction in the Senate requires a 2/3 vote

3.   The President has absolute immunity to civil suits for money damages for any actions while in office. However, the President does not have immunity for actions that occurred prior to taking office.

4.   The President has executive privilege for presidential papers and conversations, but such privilege must yield to other important government interests

5.   The President has the power to pardon those accused or convicted of federal crimes

IV.   Federalism

A.   Preemption. The Supremacy Clause of Article VI provides that the Constitution, and laws and treaties made pursuant to it, are the supreme law of the land.

1.   Express preemption

2. Implied preemption

    a. If federal and state laws are mutually exclusive, federal law preempts state law

    b. If state law impedes the achievement of a federal objective, federal law preempts state law

    c. If Congress evidences a clear intent to preempt state law, federal law preempts state law

3. States may not tax or regulate federal government activity (Inter-governmental immunity)

B. The dormant commerce clause and the privileges and immunities clause of Article IV

    1. Definitions

        a. The dormant commerce clause (Negative implications of the commerce clause)

        b. The privileges and immunities clause of Article IV

        c. The privileges or immunities clause of the Fourteenth Amendment

    2. Does the state law discriminate against out-of-staters?

3. Analysis if the law does <u>not</u> discriminate

    a. The privileges and immunities clause of Article IV does not apply

    b. If the law burdens interstate commerce, it violates the dormant commerce clause if its burdens exceed its benefits

4. Analysis if the law discriminates against out-of-staters

    a. If the law burdens interstate commerce, it violates the dormant commerce clause unless it is necessary to achieve an important government purpose

        i.   Exception: Congressional approval

        ii. Exception: The market participant exception. A state or local government may prefer its own citizens in receiving benefits from government programs or in dealing with government-owned businesses.

    b. If the law discriminates against out-of-staters with regard to their ability to earn their livelihood, it violates the privileges and immunities clause of Article IV unless it is necessary to achieve an important government purpose

        i)   The law must discriminate against out-of-staters.

        ii)   The discrimination must be with regard to civil liberties or important economic activities.

        iii) Corporations and aliens cannot use the privileges and immunities clause.

        iv)   The discrimination must be necessary to achieve an important government purpose.

[See chart on the following page]

CONSTITUTIONAL LAW – CHART 2

DORMANT COMMERCE CLAUSE/PRIVILEGES AND IMMUNITIES CLAUSE OF ARTICLE IV

DOES THIS STATE OR LOCAL GOVERNMENT'S ACTION DISCRIMINATE AGAINST OUT-OF-STATERS?

YES

NO

Violates the Dormant Commerce Clause if it places a burden on interstate commerce unless it is necessary to achieve an important government purpose. Two exceptions:
a) Congressional approval of discrimination.
b) Market participant exception.

Violates the Privileges and Immunities Clause of Article IV if it discriminates against individuals with regard to important economic activities or civil liberties unless it is necessary to achieve an important government purpose.

If the government is burdening interstate commerce, balance the benefit to the state against the burden on interstate commerce (if the benefit exceeds the burden, the law is upheld; if the burden exceeds the benefit, the law is struck down).

Privileges and Immunities Clause of Article IV is inapplicable.

CONSTITUTIONAL LAW – CHART 3

Comparison of the Dormant Commerce Clause and the Privileges and Immunities Clause of Article IV

<u>Dormant Commerce Clause</u>	<u>Privileges and Immunities Clause</u>
• Does not require discrimination against out-of-staters in order to apply	• Requires discrimination against out-of-staters in order to apply
• Requires a burden on interstate commerce	• Requires discrimination with regard to civil liberties or important economic activities
• Corporations and aliens can sue under it	• Corporations and aliens cannot sue under it
• Exceptions: Congressional approval and the market participant exception	• No exceptions

      C.   State taxation of interstate commerce

             1.   States may not use their tax systems to help in-state businesses

             2.   A state may only tax activities if there is a substantial nexus to the state

             3.   State taxation of interstate businesses must be fairly apportioned

      D.   Full faith and credit. Courts in one state must give full faith and credit to judgments of courts in another state, so long as:

             1.   The court that rendered the judgment had jurisdiction over the parties and the subject matter.

             2.   The judgment was on the merits.

             3.   The judgment is final.

V.   The Structure of the Constitution's Protection of Individual Liberties

      A.   Is there government action?

             1.   The Constitution applies only to government action. Private conduct need not comply with the Constitution

2.   Congress, by statute, may apply constitutional norms to private conduct

    a.   The Thirteenth Amendment can be used to prohibit private race discrimination

    b.   The commerce power can be used to apply constitutional norms to private conduct

    c.   Congress cannot use section 5 of the Fourteenth Amendment to regulate private behavior

3.   Exceptions: situations where private conduct must comply with the Constitution

    a.   The public function exception. The Constitution applies if a private entity is performing a task traditionally, exclusively done by the government.

    b.   The entanglement exception. The Constitution applies if the government affirmatively authorizes, encourages, or facilitates unconstitutional activity. Key examples:

        i)   Courts cannot enforce racially restrictive covenants.

ii)   There is state action when the government leases premises to a restaurant that racially discriminates.

iii)   There is state action when a state provides books to schools that racially discriminate.

iv)   There is no state action when a private school that is over 99% funded by the government fires a teacher because of her speech.

v)   There is no state action when the NCAA orders the suspension of a basketball coach at a state university.

vi)   There is state action when a private entity regulates interscholastic sports within a state.

vii)   There is not state action when a private club with a liquor license from the state racially discriminates.

B.   The application of the Bill of Rights

1.   The Bill of Rights applies directly only to the federal government

2.   The Bill of Rights is applied to state and local governments through its incorporation into the due process clause of the Fourteenth Amendment. Except:

a.   The Third Amendment right to not have a soldier quartered in a person's home.

b.   The Fifth Amendment right to grand jury indictment in criminal cases.

c.   The Seventh Amendment right to jury trial in civil cases.

d.   The Eighth Amendment right against excessive fines

C.   Levels of scrutiny

    1.   Rational basis test

    2.   Intermediate scrutiny

    3.   Strict scrutiny

[See chart on the following page]

CONSTITUTIONAL LAW – CHART 4
THE LEVELS OF SCRUTINY

	MEANS?	ENDS?	LEAST RESTRICTIVE ALTERNATIVE ANALYSIS?	BURDEN OF PROOF
RATIONAL BASIS TEST	RATIONALLY RELATED	LEGITIMATE CONCEIVABLE PURPOSE	NO	CHALLENGER
INTERMEDIATE SCRUTINY	SUBSTANTIALLY RELATED	IMPORTANT ACTUAL PURPOSE	NO	GOVERNMENT
STRICT SCRUTINY	NECESSARY	COMPELLING ACTUAL PURPOSE	YES	GOVERNMENT

VI.   Individual Rights

A.   Definitions

    1.   Procedural due process

    2.   Substantive due process

    3.   Equal protection

B.   Procedural due process

    1.   Has there been a deprivation of life, liberty, or property?

        a.   Definitions

            i.   A deprivation of liberty occurs if there is the loss of a significant freedom provided by the Constitution or a statute

            ii.   A deprivation of property occurs if there is an entitlement and that entitlement is not fulfilled

        b.   Government negligence is not sufficient for a deprivation of due process. Generally, there must be intentional government action or at least reckless action for liability to exist. However, in emergency situations, the government is liable under due process only if its conduct "shocks the conscience."

c.   Generally, the government's failure to protect people from privately inflicted harms does not deny due process

2.   What procedures are required?

      a.   The test: Balance

            i)   The importance of the interest to the individual

            ii)   The ability of additional procedures to increase the accuracy of the fact-finding

            iii)   The government's interests

      b.   Examples

[See chart on the following page]

CONSTITUTIONAL LAW – CHART 5
PROCEDURAL DUE PROCESS

Has the government deprived a person of life, liberty (a significant freedom secured by the Constitution or Statute), or property (an entitlement to a continued receipt of a benefit)?

YES / \ **NO**

What procedures must government supply?

Government need not provide procedural due process.

BALANCE:
a) Importance of interest to the individual;
b) Ability of additional procedures to increase the accuracy of the fact finding; and
c) The government's interests

C.   Economic liberties

1.   Only a rational basis test is used for laws affecting economic rights. The Constitution provides only minimal protection for economic liberties.

2.   The takings clause. The government may take private property for public use if it provides just compensation.

    a.   Is there a taking?

        i)   possessory taking—Government confiscation or physical occupation of property is a taking.

        ii)   regulatory taking—Government regulation is a taking if it leaves no reasonable economically viable use of the property.

NOTE: Government conditions on development of property must be justified by a benefit that is roughly proportionate to the burden imposed; otherwise it is a taking

NOTE: A property owner may bring a takings challenge to regulations that existed at the time the property was acquired

NOTE: Temporarily denying an owner use of property is not a taking so long as the government's action is reasonable.

b.   Is it for public use?

c.   Is just compensation paid?

[See chart on the following page]

CONSTITUTIONAL LAW –
THE TAKINGS CLAUSE – CHART 6

Government may take private property for public use if it pays just compensation

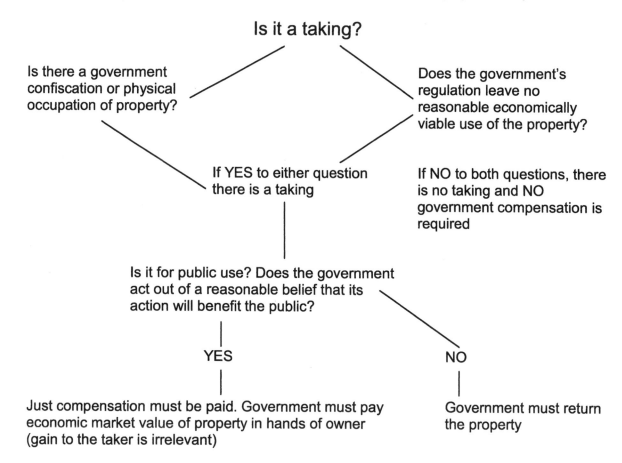

Is it a taking?

Is there a government confiscation or physical occupation of property?

Does the government's regulation leave no reasonable economically viable use of the property?

If YES to either question there is a taking

If NO to both questions, there is no taking and NO government compensation is required

Is it for public use? Does the government act out of a reasonable belief that its action will benefit the public?

YES

NO

Just compensation must be paid. Government must pay economic market value of property in hands of owner (gain to the taker is irrelevant)

Government must return the property

3. The contracts clause. No state shall impair the obligations of contracts.

    a. Applies only to state or local interference with existing contracts

    b. State or local interference with private contracts must meet intermediate scrutiny
    — Does the legislation substantially impair a party's rights under an existing contract?
    — If so, is the law a reasonably and narrowly tailored means of promoting an important and legitimate public interest?

    c. State or local interference with government contracts must meet strict scrutiny

    d. The ex post facto clause does not apply in civil cases. (An ex post facto law is a law that criminally punishes conduct that was lawful when it was done or that increases punishment for a crime after it was committed). Retroactive civil liability only need meet a rational basis test. (A bill of attainder is a law that directs the punishment of a specific person or persons without a trial.)

D. Privacy is a fundamental right protected under substantive due process

    1. The right to marry

    2. The right to procreate

    3. The right to custody of one's children

4.   The right to keep the family together

5.   The right to control the upbringing of one's children

6.   The right to purchase and use contraceptives

7.   The right to abortion

     a.   Prior to viability, states may not prohibit abortions, but may regulate abortions so long as they do not create an undue burden on the ability to obtain abortions.

        — Example: a requirement for a 24 hour waiting period for abortions is not an undue burden.
        — Example: a requirement that abortions be performed by licensed physicians is not an undue burden
        — Example: the prohibition of "partial birth abortions" is not an undue burden.

        After viability, states may prohibit abortions unless necessary to protect the woman's life or health.

     b.   The government has no duty to subsidize abortions or provide abortions in public hospitals

     c.   Spousal consent and notification laws are unconstitutional

     d.   Parental notice and consent laws for unmarried minors. A state may require parental notice and/or consent for an unmarried minor's abortion so long as it creates an alternative procedure where a minor can obtain an abortion by going before a judge who can approve the abortion by finding it would be in the minor's best interests or that she is mature enough to decide for herself

8. The right to privacy protects a right to engage in private consensual homosexual activity

9. The right to refuse medical treatment

    i. Competent adults have the right to refuse medical treatment, even life-saving medical treatment.

    ii. A state may require clear and convincing evidence that a person wanted treatment terminated before it is ended.

    iii. A state may prevent family members from terminating treatment for another.

10. There is not a constitutional right to physician-assisted death.

E. The second amendment right to bear arms

F. The right to travel

1. Laws that prevent people from moving into a state must meet strict scrutiny

2. Durational residency requirements must meet strict scrutiny

3. Restrictions on foreign travel need meet only the rational basis test

G.   The right to vote

1.   Laws that deny some citizens the right to vote must meet strict scrutiny, but regulations of the electoral process to prevent fraud only need be on balance desirable

2.   One-person - one-vote must be met for all state and local elections

3.   At-large elections are constitutional unless there is proof of a discriminatory purpose

4.   The use of race in drawing election district lines must meet strict scrutiny

5.   Counting uncounted votes without standards in a presidential election violates equal protection

H.   There is no fundamental right to education

[See chart on the following page]

CONSTITUTIONAL LAW – CHART 7

Fundamental Rights
Key Examples

Rights triggering strict scrutiny	Rights triggering "Undue burden test"	Not a fundamental right (Only rational basis review)	Level of scrutiny unknown
• Right to marry • Right to procreate • Right to custody of children • Right to keep family together • Right to control raising of children • Right to purchase and use contraceptives • Right to travel (covered under Equal Protection, §VII-H) • Right to vote (covered under Equal Protection, §VII-H) • Freedom of speech (covered under First Amendment, §VIII) • Freedom of association (covered under First Amendment, §VIII) • Free exercise of religion (if the law burdening religion is not a neutral law of general applicability) (covered under First Amendment, §VIII)	• Right to abortion	• Right to practice a trade or profession • Right to physician-assisted death • Right to education	• Right to engage in private consensual homosexual activity • Right to refuse medical treatments • Right to possess firearms

VII.   Equal Protection

A.   An approach to equal protection questions

1.   What is the classification?

2.   What level of scrutiny should be applied?

3.   Does this law meet the level of scrutiny?

B.   Constitutional provisions concerning equal protection

1.   The equal protection clause of the Fourteenth Amendment applies only to state and local governments

2.   Equal protection is applied to the federal government through the due process clause of the Fifth Amendment

C.   Classifications based on race and national origin

    1.   Strict scrutiny is used

    2.   How is the existence of a racial classification proven?

        a.   The classification exists on the face of the law

        b.   If the law is facially neutral, proving a racial classification requires demonstrating both discriminatory impact and discriminatory intent

        Example: discriminatory use of peremptory challenges based on race denies equal protection

    3.   How should racial classifications benefiting minorities be treated?

        a.   Strict scrutiny is applied

        b.   Numerical set-asides require clear proof of past discrimination

        c.   Educational institutions may use race as one factor in admissions decisions to help minorities

        d.   Public school systems may not use race as a factor in assigning students to schools unless strict scrutiny is met.

D.   Gender classifications

      1.   Intermediate scrutiny is used

      2.   How is the existence of a gender classification proven?

           a.   The classification exists on the face of the law

           b.   If the law is facially neutral, proving a gender classification requires demonstrating both discriminatory impact and discriminatory intent

                Example: discriminatory use of peremptory challenges based on gender denies equal protection

      3.   How should gender classifications benefiting women be treated?

           a.   Gender classifications benefiting women that are based on role stereotypes will not be allowed

           b.   Gender classifications that are designed to remedy past discrimination and differences in opportunity will be allowed

E. Alienage classifications

   1. Generally, strict scrutiny is used

   2. Only a rational basis test is used for alienage classifications that concern self-government and the democratic process

   3. Only a rational basis test is used for Congressional discrimination against aliens

   4. It appears that intermediate scrutiny is used for discrimination against undocumented alien children

F. Discrimination against non-marital children

   1. Intermediate scrutiny is used

   2. Laws that deny a benefit to all non-marital children, but grant it to all marital children are unconstitutional

G.   Rational basis review is used for all other types of discrimination under the Constitution

1.   Age discrimination

2.   Disability discrimination

3.   Wealth discrimination

4.   Economic regulations

5.   Sexual orientation discrimination

[See chart on the following page]

CONSTITUTIONAL LAW – CHART 8

EQUAL PROTECTION

EQUAL PROTECTION ISSUES CAN BE DIVIDED INTO 3 QUESTIONS:		

1 - WHAT IS THE CLASSIFICATION?

Two ways to determine the existence of classifications:

a)   The classification is on the face of the law; or

b)   If the law is facially neutral, there is both a discriminatory intent for the law and a discriminatory impact to the law.

2 - WHAT IS THE LEVEL OF SCRUTINY?

Strict Scrutiny	Intermediate Scrutiny	Rational Basis Test
Law must be necessary to achieve a compelling government purpose.	*Law must be substantially related to an important government purpose.*	*Law must be rationally related to a legitimate government interest.*
• Race • National origin • Alienage - generally • Travel (but not foreign travel) • Voting	• Gender • Illegitimacy • Undocumented alien children	• Alienage classifications related to self government and the democratic process • Congressional regulation of aliens • Age • Disability • Wealth • All other classifications

3 - DOES THIS LAW MEET THE LEVEL OF SCRUTINY?

VIII. The First Amendment

A. Free speech methodology

1. Content-based v. content-neutral restrictions

    a. Content-based restrictions on speech generally must meet strict scrutiny. Two type of content based laws:
       — subject matter restrictions (application of the law depends on the topic of the message)

       — viewpoint restrictions (application of the law depends on the ideology of the message)

    b. Content-neutral laws burdening speech generally need only meet intermediate scrutiny

2. Prior restraints

    a. Court orders suppressing speech must meet strict scrutiny. Procedurally proper court orders must be complied with until they are vacated or overturned. A person who violates a court order is barred from later challenging it.

    b. The government can require a license for speech only if there is an important reason for licensing and clear criteria leaving almost no discretion to the licensing authority. Licensing schemes must contain procedural safeguards such as prompt determination of requests for licenses and judicial review

3. Vagueness and overbreadth

    a. Vagueness. A law is unconstitutionally vague if a reasonable person cannot tell what speech is prohibited and what is allowed

b. Overbreadth. A law is unconstitutionally overbroad if it regulates substantially more speech than the constitution allows to be regulated.

c. Fighting words laws are unconstitutionally vague and overbroad

4. Symbolic speech. The government can regulate conduct that communicates if it has an important interest unrelated to suppression of the message and if the impact on communication is no greater than necessary to achieve the government's purpose

5. Anonymous speech is protected

6. Speech by the government cannot be challenged as violating the First Amendment.

B. What speech is unprotected or less protected by the First Amendment?

1. Incitement of illegal activity. The government may punish speech if there is a substantial likelihood of imminent illegal activity and if the speech is directed to causing imminent illegality.

2. Obscenity and sexually-oriented speech

a. The test

i. The material must appeal to the prurient interest

ii. The material must be patently offensive under the law prohibiting obscenity

iii. Taken as a whole, the material must lack serious redeeming artistic, literary, political or scientific value

b. The government may use zoning ordinances to regulate the location of adult bookstores and movie theaters

    c.   Child pornography may be completely banned, even if not obscene (To be child pornography, children must be used in production of the material).

    d.   The government may not punish private possession of obscene materials; but the government may punish private possession of child pornography

    e.   The government may seize the assets of businesses convicted of violating obscenity laws

    f.   Profane and indecent speech is generally protected by the First Amendment

        i)   Exception: over the broadcast media

        ii)   Exception: in schools

3.   Commercial speech

    a.   Advertising for illegal activity, and false and deceptive ads are not protected by the First Amendment

    b.   True commercial speech that inherently risks deception can be prohibited

        i.   The government may prevent professionals from advertising or practicing under a trade name

ii. The government may prohibit attorney, in-person solicitation of clients for profit

iii. The government may not prohibit accountants from in-person solicitation of clients for profit

c. Other commercial speech can be regulated if intermediate scrutiny is met

d. Government regulation of commercial speech must be narrowly tailored, but it does not need to be the least restrictive alternative.

4. Defamation

a. If the plaintiff is a public official or running for public office, the plaintiff can recover for defamation by proving falsity of the statement and actual malice

b. If the plaintiff is a "public figure'" the plaintiff can recover for defamation by proving falsity of the statement and actual malice

c. If the plaintiff is a "private figure" and the matter is of "public concern," that state may allow the plaintiff to recover for defamation by proving falsity and negligence by the defendant. However, the plaintiff may recover presumed or punitive damages only by showing actual malice

d. If the plaintiff is a "private figure" and the matter is not of "public concern," the plaintiff can recover presumed or punitive damages without showing actual malice

[See chart on the following page]

CONSTITUTIONAL LAW – CHART 9

DEFAMATION

PLAINTIFF	LIABILITY STANDARD	DAMAGES	BURDEN OF PROOF
Public Official	Actual Malice	Compensatory Presumed/Punitive	Plaintiff Must Prove Falsity
Public Figure	Actual Malice	Compensatory Presumed/Punitive	Plaintiff Must Prove Falsity
Private Figure, Matter of Public Concern	Negligence and Actual Injury	Compensatory for Actual Injury; Presumed or Punitive Damages Require Actual Malice	Plaintiff Must Prove Falsity
Private Figure, Matter of Private Concern	Unclear - Negligence	Compensatory for Actual Injury; Presumed or Punitive Damages Do Not Require Actual Malice	Unclear - Burden on Defendant to Prove Truth

5. Privacy

    a. The government may not create liability for the truthful reporting of information that was lawfully obtained from the government

    b. Liability is not allowed if the media broadcasts a tape of an illegally intercepted call, if the media did not participate in the illegality and it involves a matter of public importance

    c. The government may limit its dissemination of information to protect privacy

6. Speech by government employees on the job in the performance of their duties is not protected by the First Amendment.

7. Other government restrictions based on the content of speech must meet strict scrutiny

C. What places are available for speech?

1. Public forums—government properties that the government is constitutionally required to make available for speech.

    a. Regulations must be subject matter and viewpoint neutral, or if not, strict scrutiny must be met.

b.   Regulations must be a time, place, or manner regulation that serves an important government purpose and leaves open adequate alternative places for communication

c.   Government regulation of public forums need not use the least restrictive alternative

d.   City officials cannot have discretion to set permit fees for public demonstrations

2.   Designated public forums—government properties that the government could close to speech, but chooses to open to speech. The same rules apply as for public forums.

3.   Limited public forums – government properties that are limited to certain groups or dedicated to the discussion of only some subjects. The government can regulate speech in limited public forums so long as the regulation is reasonable and viewpoint neutral.

4.   Non-public forums—government properties that the government constitutionally can and does close to speech. The government can regulate speech in non-public forums so long as the regulation is reasonable and viewpoint neutral.

5.   There is no First Amendment right of access to private property for speech purposes

[See chart on the following page]

CONSTITUTIONAL LAW – CHART 10

PLACES AVAILABLE FOR SPEECH

	SUBJECT MATTER NEUTRAL?	VIEWPOINT NEUTRAL?	METHOD OF REGULATION ALLOWED?	INTEREST REQUIRED?
PUBLIC FORUMS (e.g., sidewalks, parks)	YES	YES	TIME, PLACE, OR MANNER	IMPORTANT
DESIGNATED PUBLIC FORUMS (i.e., non-public forums that the government opens to speech)	YES	YES	TIME, PLACE, OR MANNER	IMPORTANT
LIMITED PUBLIC FORUMS (i.e., government property that the government opens to certain groups or discussion of some subjects)	NO	YES	REASONABLE	LEGITIMATE
NON-PUBLIC FORUMS (e.g., military bases, airports)	NO	YES	REASONABLE	LEGITIMATE
PRIVATE PROPERTY	NO FIRST AMENDMENT RIGHT TO USE PRIVATE PROPERTY FOR SPEECH PURPOSES			

D.   Freedom of association

      1.   Laws that prohibit or punish group membership must meet strict scrutiny. To punish membership in a group it must be proven that the person:

            a.   actively affiliated with the group;

            b.   knowing of its illegal activities; and

            c.   with the specific intent of furthering those illegal activities.

      2.   Laws that require disclosure of group membership, where such disclosure would chill association, must meet strict scrutiny

      3.   Laws that prohibit a group from discriminating are constitutional unless they interfere with intimate association or expressive activity

E.   Freedom of religion

      1.   The free exercise clause

            a.   The free exercise clause cannot be used to challenge a neutral law of general applicability.

b. The government may not deny benefits to individuals who quit their jobs for religious reasons

2. The establishment clause

 a. The test

  i. there must be a secular purpose for the law

  ii. the effect must be neither to advance nor inhibit religion

  iii. there must not be excessive entanglement with religion

 b. The government cannot discriminate against religious speech or among religions unless strict scrutiny is met.

 c. Government sponsored religious activity in public schools is unconstitutional. But religious student and community groups must have the same access to school facilities as non-religious groups

 d. The government may give assistance to parochial schools, so long as it is not used for religious instruction. The government may provide parents vouchers which they use in parochial schools.

CONSTITUTIONAL LAW – CHART 11

An approach to constitutional law questions

Ask: Who is the actor in the question?

Congress	President or Federal executive branch	Federal Courts	State/local government	Private (non-government actor)
The issue is either or both	The issue is either or both	The issue is:	The issue is:	The issues are:
1) Does Congress have the authority to act? (outline, esp. § II) and/or 2) Has Congress violated a limit on its power? (outline, esp.§§ VI, VII, VIII)	1) Has the President/ Executive branch exceeded the scope of executive powers? (outline, esp. § III) and/or 2) Has the President/ Executive branch violated a limit on government power? (outline, esp. §§ VI, VII, VIII)	Does the federal court have the authority to hear the case? (outline, esp. § I)	Has the state/local government violated a limit on its power? (outline, esp. §§ IV, VI, VII, VIII)	1) Is there state action? (outline § V) and, if so, 2) Does it violate the Constitution? (outline, esp. §§ VI, VII, VIII)

Contracts

Professor David Epstein

CALIFORNIA CONTRACTS
(INCLUDING ARTICLE 2 SALES)

By

Professor David G. Epstein
University of Richmond Law School
depstein@richmond.edu

Overview of lecture:

1. Applicable law
2. Formation of contracts
3. Terms of contract
4. Performance
5. Remedies for unexcused nonperformance
6. Excuse of nonperformance
7. Third-party problems

"Armadillos from Texas play rap, eating tacos."

VOCABULARY

A. Unilateral contract - results from **an offer** that expressly requires performance **as the only possible method of acceptance**

B. Bilateral contract – all other offers, usually offer that is silent as to acceptance

Bilateral contract unless (1) reward, prize, contest (2) offer expressly requires **performance for acceptance**

(1) NBC offers Ashlee Simpson $25,000 to sing "Autobiography" on "Saturday Night Live." Ms. Simpson agrees to sing, is there a contract? _____ What if Ms. Simpson does not do what she agreed to do, what if she "lipsyncs" instead of sings_____

C.   Quasi contract   -   Equitable remedy
Elements
        P has conferred a benefit on D, *and*
        P reasonably expected to be paid, *and*
        D realized unjust enrichment if P not compensated

Measure of Recovery
        Contract price is not the measure of recovery. Focus on value of benefit conferred. The contract price is a ceiling if P is in default.

FIRST ISSUE: APPLICABLE LAW

OVERVIEW OF APPLICABLE LAW

You are responsible for parts of (i) the "common law" of contracts (largely case law) and (ii) UCC law of sales (largely statutory).

I. **"COMMON LAW"**

II. **ARTICLE 2 OF THE UCC**
Article 2 applies to contracts that are primarily *sales of goods*. Most, but not all, UCC rules are the same as the common law rules. The factors that determine whether Article 2 applies are thus:

(i) type of transaction--sale

(ii) subject matter of transaction--goods, *i.e.*, tangible, personal property

Real estate - common law

(2) Conviser, the guy who invented BRI, contracts to buy **a house**. Does Article 2 apply? _____

Services contract - common law

(3)   Conviser contracts with Epstein to **wash** his 2011 Rolls. Does Article 2 apply? _____

Sale of goods - UCC 2

(4)   Conviser contracts to **buy** Epstein's 1973 **Cadillac for $400**. Does Article 2 apply?

_____

Mixed deal: general rule -- all or nothing/more important part

(5)   Under Conviser's agreement with Epstein to buy Epstein's **car**, Epstein is also obligated to provide Conviser with two **lessons** in parallel parking a 1973 Cadillac. Does Article 2 apply if there is a disagreement about the parking lessons? _____

(6)   Conviser contracts to buy a new Duncan Glo-Yo **yo-yo** and receive ten **lessons** from Yo-Yo Ma for $40,000. Does Article 2 apply if there is a dispute about the Duncan yo-yo?

_____

Mixed deal - exception -- if **contract divides payment**, then apply UCC to sale of goods part and common law to the rest

(7)   Same facts as (6) above except that contract provides that Conviser will pay **$10 for the yo-yo and $39,990 for the lessons**. Does Article 2 apply if there is a dispute about the Duncan yo-yo? _____

III.   NO REVISED ARTICLE 2

IV.   ARTICLE 2A OF THE UCC
Article 2A applies to leases of goods. Not leases of land or buildings. NOT ON MULTISTATE BAR. NOT ON CALIFORNIA BAR.

SECOND ISSUE: FORMATION OF A CONTRACT

OVERVIEW OF FORMATION
A contract is an agreement that is legally enforceable. Accordingly, look first for an agreement. Then, second, determine whether the agreement is legally enforceable.

In looking for an agreement, watch for information in the question about (i) the initial communication ("offer") and (ii) what happens after the initial communication ("termination of the offer") and (iii) who responds and how she responds ("acceptance").

I.   **INITIAL COMMUNICATION: OFFERS**

        A.   General Test: Manifestation of Commitment
        An offer is a **manifestation** of an intention to contract – words or conduct showing **commitment**. The basic test is whether a reasonable person in the position of the offeree would believe that his or her assent creates a contract.

        B.   Specific Problems to Watch For
        1.   Content
            a.   Missing <u>price</u> term in <u>sales</u> contract
                (i)   Sale of real estate - common law - price and description required, not an offer

(8)   Can a communication from S to B relating to S's sale of Blackacre to B be an offer even though nothing is said about price? Offer? _____

                (ii)   Sale of goods - Article 2 - no price requirement

(9)   Can a communication from S to B relating to S's sale of her car to B be an offer even though nothing is said as to price? _____

            b.   Another specific content problem to watch for: Vague or ambiguous *material* terms not an offer under either common law or UCC
            [Appropriate, fair, reasonable]

(10)   Can a communication from S to B relating to S's sale of her car to B be an offer if it provides for the sale for a fair price? [Compare with 9] _____

            c.   Yet another content problem: Requirements contracts/output contracts

A contract for the sale of goods can state the quantity of goods to be delivered under the contract in terms of the buyer's requirements or seller's output.
[All, only, exclusively, solely]

    (i)   Whether requirements or output contract

(11)   B "offers" to buy grits from S for five years. There is not a specific quantity term in the "offer"; instead, it provides that B shall purchase **all** its grits from S. Offer?_____

    (ii)   Increase in requirements. Buyer can increase requirements so long as the increase is in line with prior demands. Not unreasonably disproportionate limitation on increases.

(12)   Same facts as (11). B buys **1,000** pounds of grits in each of the first three years of the agreement. B then orders **1,020** pounds the fourth year. What result? _____

    2.   Context
    a.   General rules: An advertisement is <u>not</u> an offer

    b.   Exceptions
    (i)   An advertisement can be an offer if it is in the nature of a reward. For example, Carbolic Smoke Ball Company promises 100 pound reward to anyone who catches the flu after using its smoke ball as directed.

    (ii)   An advertisement can be an offer if it specifies quantity and expressly indicates who can accept. For example, Lefkowitz Department Store advertises "1 fur coat $10 – first come, first served."

II.   **WHAT HAPPENS AFTER INITIAL COMMUNICATION:**
TERMINATION OF OFFERS [four methods]
An offer *cannot* be accepted if it has terminated. An offer that has been terminated is "dead."

A.   <u>First Method of Termination:</u> **Lapse** of Time - time stated or reasonable time

(13)   During the break, I write in your notes that I will sell you my 1973 Cadillac for $400. The writing fails to indicate how long the offer will be kept open. Can you accept the offer **five years** from now? _____

B.   <u>Second Method of Termination of an Offer:</u> **Death** of a Party Prior to Acceptance

1.   General rule: Death or incapacity of either party after the offer but before acceptance terminates offer.

2.   Exception: Irrevocable Offers (see below)

C.   <u>Third Method of Termination of Offer</u>: <u>Words or Conduct of Offeror</u>; *i.e.*, **Revocation** of an Offer

1.   How an offer is revoked

     a.   **Unambiguous** statement by offeror to *offeree* of unwillingness or inability to contract, or

     b.   **Unambiguous** conduct by offeror *indicating an unwillingness or inability to contract that* **offeree** *is aware of*

(14)   On January 15, I offer to sell Sharon Stone my 1973 Cadillac for $400. The next day, while standing in the shower, I exclaim, "I have changed my mind. I do not want to sell my Cadillac to Sharon Stone." Is the offer to Ms. Stone revoked? _____

(15)   On January 15, I offer to sell Sharon Stone my Cadillac for $400. The next day I sell my Cadillac to Conviser. Is the offer to Ms. Stone revoked? _____

(16)   On January 15, I offer to sell Sharon Stone my Cadillac for $400. The next day I sell my Cadillac to Conviser. Ms. Stone sees Conviser driving my Cadillac on January 16 and **learns** from him that he has bought it. Is the offer to Ms. Stone revoked? _____ Can she still accept? _____

(17)   [multiple offers not revocation] On January 15, I offer to sell Sharon Stone my Cadillac for $400. The next day I make the same offer to Conviser. Ms. Stone learns that I have made the offer to Conviser. Is the offer to Ms. Stone revoked? _____

2.   *Which offers are irrevocable, i.e., cannot be revoked.*
Be sure you know vocabulary – know the difference among ***"irrevocable," "revocable," and revoked****. [Generally offers can be freely revoked by the offeror. There are four different situations in which an offer cannot be revoked i.e., is irrevocable.*

     #1   Option: An offer cannot be revoked if the offeror has not only made an offer but also (i) promised to not revoke (or promised to keep the offer "open") AND (ii) this promise is supported by payment or other consideration ("option")

(18)   **[Option]** S offers to sell B her car for $400. B pays S $10 for S's promise "to keep the offer open for a week." Can S still revoke the offer? _____ Can B accept the offer ten days later? _____

(19)   **[Not an option]** S offers to sell her car to B for $400. S promises "to keep the offer open for a week." Can S revoke? _____

> #2   *UCC "Firm Offer Rule": An offer cannot be revoked for up to three months if (i) offer to buy or sell goods, (ii) signed, written promise to keep the offer open, and (iii) party is a merchant. (Merchant is GENERALLY a person in business.)*

(20)   S, a used car dealer, offers to sell B a 1973 Cadillac for $400. The offer is in writing, signed by S, and expressly promises it will be kept open for a week. Can S revoke? [COMPARE WITH 18] _____

(21)   S, a used car dealer, offers to sell B a 1973 Cadillac for $400. The offer is oral and includes a promise that it will be kept open for a week. Can S revoke? _____

(22)   S, a used car dealer, offers to sell B a 1973 Cadillac for $400. The written offer is signed by S and states it will not be revoked for six months. Can S revoke? _____

(23)   S, a used car dealer, offers to sell B a 1973 Cadillac for $400. The written offer is signed by S and states it will not be revoked but does not state a time period. Can S revoke?

_____

(24)   S, a used car dealer, offers to sell B a 1973 Cadillac for $400. The written offer is signed by S. Can S revoke? _____

(25)   S offers to sell B her house for $100,000, and the written offer states that it cannot be revoked for the next 4 months. Can S revoke? _____

> (#3)   *An offer cannot be revoked if there has been (1) reliance that is (2) reasonably foreseeable and (3) detrimental.*

(26)   G is a general contractor who is bidding on a contract to build a new hotel, using various subcontractors. S, a subcontractor, submits a bid to G to do the painting work for $100,000. G uses S's bid in making its bid and is awarded the hotel construction contract. Can S still revoke its bid? _____

> (#4)   *The start of performance pursuant to an offer to enter into a unilateral contract makes that offer irrevocable for a reasonable time to complete performance.*
> (i)   Unilateral/performance

(27)   O offers P $1,000 to paint O's house. O's offer states that it can be accepted only by performance. P starts painting. Can O still revoke? _____

> (ii)   Unilateral/mere preparation

(28)   O offers P $1,000 to paint O's house. O's offer states that it can be accepted only by performance. P buys paint. Does this trigger rule #4 so that O cannot revoke? _____ Does this trigger rule #3 so that O cannot revoke? _____

> D.   **Fourth Method of Termination of an Offer**: Words or Conduct of the Offeree -**Rejection**
> Watch for one of the following three methods of indirect rejection - (1) counteroffer, (2) conditional acceptance of (3) additional terms. First two apply to all contracts; additional terms rule (3) does not apply to contracts for sale of goods, i.e. common law only
>
> > 1.   First Method of Indirect Rejection - **Counteroffer**
> > Counteroffer generally terminates the offer and becomes a new offer. Thus generally, where a counteroffer has been made there is no express contract unless that counteroffer has itself been accepted. Counteroffers need to be distinguished from bargaining. Bargaining does not terminate the offer. And, counteroffers do not terminate options.

(29)   **[Counteroffer general rule]** S offers Blackacre to B for $10,000. B responds, "I will only pay $9,000."   Can B later accept S's offer to sell for $10,000?_____

(30)   **[Bargaining]** S offers Blackacre to B for $10,000. B's response is "Will you take 9,000?"   Can B later accept S's offer?_____

(31)   **[Counteroffer: option exception]** On January 15, S offers Blackacre to B for $10,000. B pays S $2 for S's promise not to revoke the offer until April 5. On March 3, B makes a counteroffer to S of $9,000.   Can B still accept S's offer? _____

> > 2.   Second Method of Indirect Rejection - **Conditional Acceptance**
> > A conditional acceptance terminates the offer. Look for a response to an offer with the word "accept" followed by one of these words or phrases: **"if," "only if," "provided," "so long as," "but"** or **"on condition that."**

(32)   L offers to lease an apartment to T by sending T a signed lease that is silent about arbitration of disputes. T adds a paragraph that states that T "accepts **provided that** all disputes shall be resolved by arbitration of disputes" and signs. Has T accepted L's offer creating an express contract?_____ If after receiving T's conditional acceptance, L sends T the keys to the apartment, is there a contract? _____ Is the arbitration term a part of the contract?_____

(33)   B sends S a purchase order for polyester pant suits. The purchase order makes no mention of arbitration of disputes. S sends an acknowledgment form that provides for

arbitration of disputes and states "accept **only if** you agree that all disputes shall be submitted to arbitration." No further communications or actions. Has S accepted B's offer creating an express contract? _____ If S sends B the polyester pant suits and B pays for them, is there a contract? _____ Is the arbitration term a part of the contract? _____

> 3. Third Method of Indirect Rejection - Additional Terms to a Common Law Contract: **Mirror Image Rule**
> Under common law, a response to an offer that adds new terms is treated like a counteroffer rather than an acceptance.

(34)   L offers to lease a building to T by sending T a signed lease that is silent about arbitration of disputes. T adds a sentence that states that "All disputes shall be resolved by arbitration of disputes" and signs. Has T accepted L's offer creating an express contract? _____ Can T later accept L's offer? _____

> 4. *Additional Terms Still Acceptance Under UCC Article 2 (2-207): seasonable expression of acceptance*
> *A fact pattern in which there is (i) offer to buy or sell goods and (ii) a response with additional terms raises two separate questions:*
> *a. First question: Is there a contract?*
> *Under the UCC, a response to an offer that adds new terms, [but does not make the new terms a condition of acceptance] is generally treated as an acceptance -- is generally a "seasonable expression of acceptance." Whether the parties are merchants is irrelevant in answering this first question.*

(35)   B sends S a signed purchase order for grits that is silent about arbitration of disputes. S responds by sending back a signed acknowledgment form that states that "All disputes shall be resolved by arbitration." Is there a contract? [compare with (33)] _____

> *b. Second question: Is the additional term a part of the contract?*
> *The additional term is a part of the contract only if (i) both parties are merchants AND (ii) additional term is not "material" {fact question} AND (iii) the additional term is not objected to by offeror.*

(36)   Epstein offers to sell his 1973 Cadillac to Conviser for $400. Conviser responds: "I accept. Deliver it on Saturday." No further communications or actions. Is there a contract? _____ With Saturday delivery as a contract term? _____

(37)   Same facts as (36) but Conviser's response is, "I accept if the car is delivered on Saturday." Is there a contract? _____

III. ACCEPTANCE OF AN OFFER

Look at the offer for information about how the offer was accepted and who accepted.

A.   METHOD OF ACCEPTANCE

1. The offer can control the method of acceptance (e.g., offer states that it can only be accepted by performance), the time that a distance acceptance is effective (e.g., offer states that its acceptance is effective only when it has been received at offeror's Richmond office), or whether the offeree must give notice that it has accepted by performance (e.g., acceptance by performance will not be effective until offeror has been so notified).

2. On most bar exam questions, the offer is silent as to the method of acceptance, time of acceptance or notice of acceptance. Instead, bar exam questions on acceptance usually involve one of the following fact patterns:

(#1)   Possible acceptance fact pattern: the offeree starts to perform
Watch for fact patterns with three characteristics. First, verbal offer, second, no words in response, and third, **start** of performance.
    a.   General rule: start of performance is acceptance. Starting to perform is treated as an implied promise to perform and so there is a bilateral contract.

(38)   O offers P $1,000 to paint his house. The offer is silent as to method of acceptance. P starts painting the house. Has P accepted O's offer? _____

    b.   Exception: Start of performance is not acceptance of unilateral contract offers. Completion of performance is required. Again, start of performance is an implied promise to perform. Offers to enter into unilateral contracts cannot be accepted by a promise. If offer requires "performance" for acceptance, then "performance" for purposes of acceptance of that offer means completion of performance.

(39)   O offers P $1,000 to paint his house. O's offer states that it can be accepted only by performance, not by promising to perform. P starts painting O's house. Has P accepted O's offer so that he is contractually obligated to continue painting O's house? _____[Compare with (38) and with (27)]

(#2)   *possible acceptance fact pattern: distance and delay in communications*

The offeror and the offeree are at different places and there are delays in receipt of communications. Four rules. First, all communications OTHER THAN ACCEPTANCE are effective only **when received**. Second, acceptance is GENERALLY effective **when mailed**. Third, if a rejection is mailed before an acceptance is mailed, then neither is effective until received. Fourth, you cannot use the mailbox rule to meet an option deadline.

(40)   Conviser receives a letter from Epstein offering to sell Conviser his 1973 Cadillac for $400. On January 10, Conviser mails his letter of acceptance. On January 11, Conviser receives a letter from Epstein revoking the offer. Is there a contract?_____

(41)   Conviser receives a letter from Phish inviting him to replace Trey in a new version of the group. On August 8, Conviser mails a letter to the group rejecting their offer. On August 9, he changes his mind and mails a letter of acceptance. What result if the rejection letter arrives first?_____

(42)   B and S execute an option contract that gives B the option to buy Blackacre from S for $100,000. The option contract provides that it expires on July 13 at 5 p.m., EST. B sends S a letter on July 13 at 4:50 p.m. EST, exercising the option and agreeing to buy Blackacre for $100,000. Can S revoke her offer at 6:00 p.m. EST July 13? _____

(#3)   possible acceptance fact pattern: the seller of goods sends the "wrong" goods
a.   General Rule: Acceptance and Breach

(43)   B orders 100 red widgets. S sends 100 blue widgets. Is there a contract?_____
A breach of contract?_____

b.   Accommodation (i.e., explanation) Exception: Counteroffer and No Breach

(44)   B orders 100 red widgets. S sends 100 blue widgets with the explanation "out of red, hope that you can use blue instead." Is there a contract? _____ Breach of contract?____

B.   Who Can Accept?
Generally, an offer can be accepted only by (1) a person who knows about the offer at the time she accepts (2) who is the person to whom it was made. Offers can not be assigned; options can be assigned unless the option otherwise provides. [We will see later that contract rights can be assigned]

(45) **[Rewards and knowing of the offer]** I offer a $500 reward to the person who finds my lost dog. You find and return my dog, not knowing of the reward. Is that acceptance of my offer?_____

(46) **[Non-assignability of offers]** I offer to sell you my 1973 Cadillac for $400. Can you sell the offer to Conviser so that he can accept the offer? _____

(47) **[Assignability of options]** You pay me $10 for a ten-day option to buy my Cadillac for $400. Can you sell the option to Conviser so that he can now exercise the option and accept the offer? _____

IV.   FORMATION: SECOND VIEW/OVERVIEW

Again, remember that a contract is more than an agreement. Some agreements are not legally enforceable. Legal reasons for not enforcing an agreement include (1) lack of consideration or a consideration substitute for the promise at issue; (2) lack of capacity of the person who made that promise; (3) Statute of Frauds; (4) existing laws that prohibit the performance of the agreement; (5) public policy; (6) misrepresentations; (7) nondisclosure; (8) duress; (9) unconscionability; (10) ambiguity in words of agreement; and (11) mistakes at the time of the agreement as to the material facts affecting the agreement.

V.   REASON FOR NOT ENFORCING AGREEMENT: LACK OF CONSIDERATION <u>OR</u> CONSIDERATION SUBSTITUTE

A.   What Is Consideration?
The doctrine of consideration is of limited practical significance. In most transactions, particularly most commercial agreements, there will be no issue as to consideration. Article 2 of the UCC has further reduced the practical significance of consideration in modification.

In dealing with consideration questions on the bar exam, go through the following three steps. First, identify the promise breaker, i.e., the person who is not doing what she promised to do. Second, ask whether that person asked for something in return for her promise, i.e., bargained for something. Third, look at the person who is trying to enforce the promise and ask what requested legal detriment that person sustained. In sum, look for bargained-for legal detriment.

B.   Possible consideration Issues
1.   "Bargained for"
Asked for by the promisor IN EXCHANGE for her promises. Consideration fact patterns have people doing stuff that they were asked to do.

(48) L rents an apartment to T. One month before the lease expires, L sends T a letter promising to renew the lease at the same rental rate. T paints the apartment.

Notwithstanding her promise to T, L increases the rent. T sues L for breach of contract. L asserts no contract because no consideration. Is T's painting the apartment consideration for L's promise to renew the lease at the same rental rate?_____

2.   "Legal detriment"

(49)   I make the following promise to you: "Stop listening to records by Kinky Friedman, (www.kinkajourecords.com) for two months and I'll pay you $100." You don't listen to Kinky Friedman records, not "Asshole From El Paso", not "Why Did You Bob Your Nose, Girl?", not "They Ain't Making Jews Like Jesus Anymore", not any of his other "classics". Notwithstanding your "forbearance," I don't pay. You sue for breach of contract. Is there consideration, *i.e.,* bargained-for legal detriment, supporting my promise to pay you $100?_____

3.   Promise as consideration

(50)   On April 15, B and S enter into a written agreement in which B promises to buy S's house and S promises to sell his house to B, with B's payment and S's transfer of title to occur on June 6.   Is there consideration for B's promise to buy?_____ Is there consideration for S's promise to sell?

(51)   Illusory promise exception: Same facts as (50) except S promises to sell unless she changes her mind. Is there consideration for B's promise to buy? _____

4.   Adequacy of consideration
Not relevant in contract law.

5.   "Past consideration"
a.   General rule: *not* consideration

(52)   Apu saves Lisa's life. Homer is so grateful that he promises to pay Apu $3,000. Homer later changes his mind. Is there consideration for Homer's promise so it is legally enforceable? _____

b.   Exception: <u>expressly</u> requested by promisor *and* expectation of payment by promisee

(53)   Homer sees Lisa in danger and **asks Apu to save her**, knowing that Apu would expect to be paid. After Apu saves Lisa, Homer promises to pay Apu $3,000.   Is this promise legally enforceable?_____

6.   "preexisting contractual or statutory duty rule" [Common law different from Article 2]
a.   Common law

    (i)   General Rule: doing what you are already legally obligated to do is not new consideration for a new promise to pay you more to do merely that. Under common law new consideration is required for contract modification.

(54)   Kinky Friedman contracts with Lil Jon to perform as the opening act at a crunk show at Town Hall for $15,000. Notwithstanding the contract, the Kinkster refuses to sing unless he is paid $20,000, not $15,000. Lil Jon promises to pay Kinky $20,000. Kinky performs. Lil Jon only pays Kinky $15,000. Is there consideration for Lil Jon's promise to pay the additional $5,000? _____ Is that promise legally enforceable? _____

    (ii)   Exception: addition to or change in performance

(55)   What if Lil Jon promised to pay Kinky the additional $5,000 if he will sing Tom Lehrer's "I Am Spending Hanukkah in Santa Monica" instead of Kinky's usual opening song, "Get Your Biscuits in the Oven and Your Buns in the Bed"?

_____

    (iii)   Exception: Unforeseen Difficulty So Severe as to Excuse Performance

(56)   The sound system at Town Hall is inoperative. Lil Jon agrees to pay Kinky an additional $5,000 if he will still perform. Kinky performs. Is the promise to pay the additional $5,000 legally enforceable?_____

    (iv)   Exception: third party promise to pay

(57)   Same facts as (61) except Conviser, not Lil Jon, promises to pay Kinky the additional $ 5,000. Is Conviser's promise to pay the additional $5,000 enforceable? _____

    b.   *Article 2*
        Article 2 does not have a pre-existing legal duty rule. New consideration is not required to modify a sale of goods contract. Good faith is the test for changes to an existing sale of goods contract.

(58)   S contracts to sell grits to B for $1,000. S subsequently tells B that it cannot deliver the grits for less than $1,300. B promises by telefax to pay the additional $300. S delivers the grits. Is there new consideration for B's new promise to pay $300 more?___ Is that new promise nonetheless legally enforceable?_____

7.   Part payment as consideration for release, i.e., promise to forgive balance of debt
        Key is whether debt is due and undisputed. If debt is due and undisputed, then part payment is <u>not</u> consideration for release.

a.   Due and undisputed

(59)   D owes C $3,000. The debt is due and undisputed. C and D agree that D will pay $2,000 in exchange for a release, i.e., C's promise that she will not take any action to collect the remainder of the debt. D pays $2,000. Did C receive new consideration for her new promise to release the balance of the debt?_____Is the debt settlement legally enforceable?_____

b. Not yet due (or disputed)

(60)   Same facts as (59) except the $3,000 debt was due on January 15. C agrees to take $2,000 on or before January 11 in full satisfaction of the debt. D pays the $2,000 on January 11. Did C receive new consideration for his new promise to release?_____

D. CONSIDERATION SUBSTITUTES
A promise is legally enforceable even though there is no consideration if there is one of the following consideration substitutes.

1. Seals
Majority Rule Is Now That Seal Is <u>Not</u> a Consideration Substitute

2. A **written** promise to satisfy an obligation for which there is a legal defense is enforceable **without consideration**.

(61)   D owes C $1,000. Legal action to collect this debt is barred by the statute of limitations. D **writes** C, "I know that I owe you $1,000. I will pay you $600." Is there new consideration for D's new promise? _____ Can C enforce the new $600 promise?_____

3.   Promissory Estoppel (Detrimental Reliance)
    a.   Elements
        (1)   Promise

        (2)   Reliance that is reasonable, detrimental and foreseeable

        (3)   Enforcement necessary to avoid injustice

    b.   Comparison of consideration and promissory estoppel

(62)   L leases a building to T. L sends T a letter promising to renew the lease without a rent increase. T paints the building. Notwithstanding her promise and T's painting the building, L increases the rent. T sues L for breach of contract. Is T's painting the building "consideration"?_____ Promissory estoppel? [compare with (48)]_____

VI.   REASON FOR NOT ENFORCING AGREEMENT: DEFENDANT PROMISSOR'S LACK OF CAPACITY
    A.   Who lacks capacity to contract?

1.   infant - under 18

2.   mental incompetents - lacks ability to understand agreement

3.   intoxicated persons *if other party has reason to know*

B.   Consequences of incapacity
1.   Right to disaffirm by person without capacity

(63)   Conviser hires Eric Cartman to lecture on Contracts for $100 a lecture.   If Cartman does not do the lectures, can Conviser enforce the agreement? _____

(64)   If Cartman does the lectures and Conviser does not pay him, **can Cartman enforce** the agreement?_____

2.   Implied affirmation by retaining benefits after gaining capacity (ratification)

(65)   S sells B a car on credit. B is only 17. B does not pay S but refuses to return the car. B later turns 18. B keeps the car without complaint or objection. Can S now enforce the agreement that B made when she was 17?_____

3.   Quasi-contract liability for necessaries
A person who does not have capacity is legally obligated to pay for things that are necessary such as food, clothing, medical care or shelter but that liability is based on quasi-contract law, not contract law.

(66)   X, a person who is mentally incompetent, leases an apartment from L. The lease agreement provides for $400 a month rent; L's other tenants are only paying $300 a month for a comparable apartment. Can L enforce the agreement to pay $400 a month? ____ Is there any other basis for requiring X to pay for this requested necessary?_____

VII.   REASON FOR NOT ENFORCING AGREEMENT: STATUTE OF FRAUDS DEFENSE

A Statute of Frauds is a statute designed to prevent fraudulent claims of the existence of a contract. Statute of Frauds makes it harder to make such a false or fraudulent claim by requiring the claimant have proof that a contract exists before the claimant gets its day in court. The proof required to satisfy the Statute of Frauds is generally proof of either (1) performance (2) or a writing signed by the person who is asserting that there was no such agreement.

Statute of Frauds is in essence a barrier between a litigant's asserting a contract claim and a trial on that claim. If a contract claim is "within the Statute of Frauds" then the Statute of Frauds's requirement of "special proof" (performance or a writing) must be satisfied to get through that Statute of Frauds barrier to have a trial.

      A.   Contracts *Within* The Statute Of Frauds
      (1)   Promises to **Answer for** the Debts of Another
             [suretyship]

      Not merely a promise to pay but rather a promise to pay if someone else does not. LOOK FOR A GUARANTEE.

(67)   S Store sells P paint on credit for $400. S Store sues Conviser for the $400, alleging Conviser promised to pay for the paint. Conviser files a motion to dismiss based on the Statute of Frauds. Is Conviser's alleged promise within the Statute of Frauds? _____

(68)   S Store sells P paint on credit to be used in painting **Epstein's** house. S Store sues Conviser alleging that Conviser promised to pay for the paint if P did not pay. Conviser files a motion to dismiss based on the Statute of Frauds. Is Conviser's alleged promise within the Statute of Frauds? _____

      LOOK ALSO FOR THE MAIN PURPOSE EXCEPTION. If the "main purpose" of the obligation allegedly guaranteed was to benefit the guarantor, then not even that guarantee is within the Statute of Frauds

(69)   Same facts as (68) except that S Store sells P paint to use in painting **Conviser's** house Is Conviser's alleged promise within the Statute of Frauds? _____

      (2)   Service contract not "**capabl**e" of being performed within a year **from the time of the contract**. (i.e., more than one year)
      (a)   specific time period, more than a year - S/F applies

(70)   P sues D for breach of an alleged 3 year employment contract. D files a motion to dismiss based on the Statute of Frauds. Is this within the Statute of Frauds? _____

(71)   Same facts as (70) except that P also claims that the 2 year employment contract could be terminated on thirty days' notice. Is this within the Statute of Frauds? _____

      (b)   specific time, more than a year from date of contract - S/F applies

(72)   Kenny G sues Club Putz for breach of an alleged January 15, 2010 contract to perform on December 24, 2011. Club Putz files a motion to dismiss based on the Statute of Frauds. Is this within the Statute of Frauds? _____

(73)   P claims that O agreed to employ her for a year, starting next month. Is this within the Statute of Frauds? _____

       (c)   task (nothing said about time) - Statute of Frauds does not apply. Recall the language of the Statute: "not capable of being performed" within a year. "Capable" in essence means theoretically possible with unlimited resources; ignore what actually happens; key is what might have happened with unlimited resources.

(74)   P claims that D hired him on January 15, 2011, to cut all of the trees on D's land. Is this within the Statute of Frauds? _____

       (d)   life - Statute of Frauds does not apply

(75)   P claims that D hired her to work for her for the rest of P's life. P is only 21 years old and in great health. Is this within the Statute of Frauds?_____

       (3)   Transfers of Interest in Real Estate (with exception for leases of year or less)

(76)   P claims that D agreed to build a house on Blackacre. Is this within the Statute of Frauds? _____

(77)   P claims that D agreed to sell Redacre for $400. Is this within the Statute of Frauds?_____

(78)   P claims that D agreed to sell an easement on Greenacre. Is this within the Statute of Frauds?_____

(79)   P claims that D agreed to lease Blackacre for one year. Is this within the Statute of Frauds? _____

       (4)   *Sale of goods for $500 or more*

(80)   Conviser sues Epstein, claiming that Epstein agreed to sell him his 1973 Cadillac for $500. Epstein files a motion to dismiss based on the Statute of Frauds. Is this within the Statute of Frauds?_____

(81)   Same facts as (80) except that Conviser claims that the agreed upon price was $400.____

    C.   How Is Statute Of Frauds Satisfied?
        If Statute of Frauds is applicable, then requirements of the Statute of Frauds must be met ("satisfied") in order for the agreement to be

enforceable.   If the requirements of the Statute of Frauds are not satisfied, there is a Statute of Frauds defense. And, if there is a Statute of Frauds defense **asserted and established,** there is no legally enforceable agreement – no contract liability.

READ QUESTION CAREFULLY TO SEE WHAT IS ASKED. Question might ask, "Is the Statute of Frauds satisfied?" or question might ask, "Is there a Statute of Frauds defense?" or question might ask "Is there contract liability?"

1.   Performance
       The Statute of Frauds can be satisfied by performance. The six rules for satisfaction of the Statute of Frauds by performance vary depending on whether the contract is a real estate transfer contract, services contract, or a sale of goods contract.

a. Performance and Transfer of Real Estate (#1)
       Part performance satisfies the Statute of Frauds in transfers of real estate. Part performance requires any two of the three: (i) improvements to the land, (ii) payment and (iii) possession.

(82)   B claims that S orally agreed to sell Blackacre to B for $10,000. When S refused to deed Blackacre to B, B sues for breach of contract. S asserts a Statute of Frauds defense. B is in possession of Blackacre and made improvements. Does S have a Statute of Frauds defense?_____

(83)   Same facts as (82) except that all that B has done is pay S $10,000. Does S have a Statute of Frauds defense?_____

b. Performance and Services Contracts
       (i)   Full performance by either party satisfies the Statute of Frauds. (#2)

(84)   Conviser and Ludacris agree that (i) Ludacris will write new mini review materials and (ii) Conviser will advertise the course as the Ludacris Mini Review for the next five years. Is this within the Statute of Frauds? _____ Ludacris completes the materials. Conviser continues to call the course the Conviser Mini Review. Ludacris sues Conviser for breach of contract. Conviser asserts a Statute of Frauds defense (in essence contending that there is no contract – that Ludacris is fraudulently claiming that there is a contract). Is the Statute of Frauds satisfied? _____ Does Conviser have a Statute of Frauds defense?_____

       (ii)   Part performance of a services contract does not satisfy the Statute of Frauds. (#3)

(85)   P agrees to work for D for three years. P works for 13 months and then D fires her without cause. P sues D for breach of contract. D asserts a Statute of Frauds defense. Is the Statue of Frauds satisfied by P's working for 13 months?_____   Does D have a Statute of Frauds defense?_____   Can P recover under contract law for the 13 months of work she had done?_____ Under quasi-contract?_____

> b.   *Part Performance and Sale of Goods Contracts*
>   (i)   *Seller's Part Performance Ordinary goods*
> *General rule is that part performance of a contract for the sale of goods satisfies the Statute of Frauds but*
>
> *only to the extent of the part performance. More specifically, look to see if question is about*

(86)   **Delivered goods. (#4)**   S orally agrees to sell 2,000 sacks of grits to B for $10,000. S delivers 600 sacks of grits. S sues B for payment for the 600 sacks that have been delivered. B asserts a Statute of Frauds defense. Does B have a Statute of Frauds defense?_____

(87)   **Undelivered goods. (#5)**   Same facts as (86) except that B sues S for failure to deliver the remaining 1400 sacks. S asserts a Statute of Frauds defense. Does S have a Statute of Frauds defense? _____

> (ii)   *Seller's Part Performance Specially Manufactured Goods*
> *If the contract is for the sale of goods that are to be specially manufactured, then the Statute of Frauds is satisfied as soon as the seller makes a "substantial beginning". This means that the seller has done enough work that it is clear that what she is working on is specially manufactured, i.e., custom made or made to order.   (#6)*

(88)   S sues B alleging B breached a contract for a $500 pair of cowboy boots by telling S after S had made a "substantial beginning" that she did not want the boots. B asserts a Statute of Frauds defense.   Does B have a Statute of Frauds defense?_____

> 2.   Writing
> The requirements of the Statute of Frauds can also be satisfied by a writing. Remember (1) not every writing satisfies the requirements of the Statute of Frauds and (2) the requirements of the Statute of Frauds can be satisfied without a writing [as we just learned in the performance materials].
> a.   Statutes of Fraud other than the UCC's
> Look at the contents of the writing OR WRITINGS--all material terms test [who and what].

(89) "Your offer of January 15th is hereby accepted" s/ Dana Scully. Does this writing satisfy the Statute of Frauds?_____

(90) "The law firm of Hewes & Associates ("HA") hereby agrees to employ Harriet Miers as an attorney for three years at $200,000 a year." s/Patty Hewes for the firm. HA wrongfully dismisses Ms. Miers. She sues for breach of contract. HA asserts a Statute of Frauds defense. Did the writing satisfy the Statute of Frauds so that HA does not have a Statute of Frauds defense? _____

> Look also at who signed the writing. The writing satisfies the Statute of Frauds so that there is no Statute of Frauds defense only if the writing has been signed by the person who is asserting the
>
> Statute of Frauds defense – by the person who is saying that there is no such agreement.

(91) Same writing as (90). Ms. Miers breaches. HA sues Ms. Miers for breach of contract; she asserts a Statute of Frauds defense. Does the writing satisfy the Statute of Frauds?

_____

> b. *Article 2 Statute of Frauds*
> *Again, look to the contents of the writing and who signed the writing. The writing must indicate that there is a contract for the sale of goods and contain the quantity term [how many].*

(92) S sues B for breach of an alleged contract to buy hominy grits for $500. The only writing is the following: "I agree to buy 100 pounds of grits" S/B Does the writing satisfy the Statute of Frauds?_____

> *Generally, the writing must be signed by the person asserting the Statute of Frauds defense (i.e., the defendant). The UCC, however, has an exception to this general rule: based on that person's failure to respond to a signed writing. Both parties must be merchants and the person who receives a signed writing with a quantity term that claims there is a contract fails to respond within ten days of receipt.*

(93) S, a grits distributor, receives the following fax from B, a grits store: "As we agreed during our telephone conversation today, you will be sending me 200 sacks of grits." s/B. S does not respond. S never sends the grits. B sues S for breach of contract. S asserts a Statute of Frauds defense. Has the Statute of Frauds been satisfied even though S did not sign anything?_____

> 3. *Judicial Admission*

This is based on the common-sense recognition that if the defendant asserting a Statute of Frauds defense admits in a pleading or testimony that he had entered into an agreement with the plaintiff, the purpose of the Statute of Frauds--protection against fraudulent or otherwise false claims of an agreement -is fulfilled and so the Statute of Frauds is satisfied – no Statute of Frauds defense.

D.   Use of Statute of Frauds on the Bar Exam for Questions Other Than Whether There is a Statute of Frauds Defense to Enforcement of Agreement
1.   Authorization to enter into contract for someone else.
Issue is when do RULES OF LAW REQUIRE that a person have written authorization in order to execute a contract for someone else. RULES OF LAW REQUIRE that the authorization must be in writing that contract only if the contract to be signed is within the Statute of Frauds, *i.e.,* the authorization must be of "equal dignity" with the contract.

(94)   Landlord (L) sues Sharon Stone for breach of a one year apartment lease that Epstein entered into on her behalf. Does contract law require that L have written evidence of Epstein's authority to act on behalf of Sharon Stone?_____

2.   Contract modification
a.   When do RULES OF LAW REQUIRE written evidence of modification of a written contract?

Sometimes, there is no LEGAL requirement of written evidence of an alleged modification of a written contract. Resolve any LEGAL issue of whether such written evidence of the modification is needed by (1) looking at the deal with the alleged change and (2) determining whether the deal with the alleged change would be within the Statute of Frauds. If the deal with the alleged change would be within the Statute of Frauds, then the alleged modification agreement must be in writing.

(95)   T leases a building from L for one year. L claims they later agreed to increase the term to 3 years. Does contract law require written evidence of the alleged modification?_____

(96)   T leases a building from L for three years. T later claims that they agreed to reduce the duration of the lease from three years to one year. Does contract law require written evidence of the alleged modification? _____

(97)   Conviser contracts to buy 600 bottles of Thunderbird wine from Epstein for $600. Conviser later claims that they agreed to modify the contract to reduce the price to $3. Does contract law require written evidence of the alleged modification agreement?_____

b. What if the agreement is in writing and requires that all modifications be in writing?

> *Under common law*, contract provisions requiring that all modifications be in writing are not effective – ignore contract language.

(98) R employs E for eleven months. They sign a contract. It provides that all modifications have to be in writing. E claims that they later agreed to reduce the employment term to seven months. R alleges that there was no such later agreement. Is a writing required AS A MATTER OF LAW? _____

(99) Same facts as (98) except that E claims that they later agreed to extend the employment term to seven years. Is a writing required?_____

Under UCC contract provisions requiring written modifications are effective unless waived

(100) Epstein contracts to sells his Cadillac to Conviser for $400. They sign a contract providing that all modifications must be in writing. Epstein claims that they later agreed to raise the price to $499. Conviser refuses to pay $499. Is a writing required as A MATTER OF LAW [even though $499 is less than 500]_____

VIII. OTHER REASONS FOR NOT ENFORCING AN AGREEMENT: ILLEGALITY, PUBLIC POLICY, MISREPRESENTATION, NON DISCLOSURE, DURESS

A.   Illegal Subject Matter/Illegal Purpose
If the subject matter is illegal, the agreement is not enforceable. If the subject matter is legal but the purpose is illegal, the agreement is enforceable only by the person who did not know of the illegal purpose.

(101) **[Illegal subject matter]** Epstein agrees to pay $7,000 to Sarah Silverman to injure Conviser. If Silverman does not injure Conviser, can Epstein recover from Silverman for breach of contract?_____

(102)   **[Illegal purpose]** Silverman contracts with Delta for a non-refundable ticket to fly
from Los Angeles to Chicago where Conviser is. If Silverman does not pay for the ticket, can Delta recover from Silverman for breach of contract?_____

B.   Public Policy
Courts can refuse to enforce an agreement because of public policy. Look for an exculpatory agreement that exempts intentional or reckless conduct from liability or a covenant not to compete without a reasonable need or reasonable time and place limits.

C.   Misrepresentation
Look for a (i) statement of "fact" before the contract, (2) by one of the contracting parties or her agent , (3) that induces the contract, (4) that is false. No wrongdoing required for material misrepresentations.

(103)   S tells B that the house had no termites. B agrees to buy the house in reliance on S's representation.   S honestly believes that the house has no termites, but the house has termites. Can B rescind the agreement to buy the house?_____

     D.   Nondisclosure
          Generally, a person making a contract has no duty to disclose what she knows. E.g., B is contracting to buy land for a new Walmart but does not have to disclose that fact to sellers. Wrongdoing requirement for nondisclosure. Look for fiduciary-like relationship or concealment.

(104)   In selling her house to B S puts carpets and heavy furniture over the termite damage and does not tell B about the termites. Can B rescind?_____

     E.   Duress: Physical or economic
          1.   Elements of economic duress
               (a)   "bad guy" - improper threat which is usually threat to breach existing contract

               AND

               (b)   "vulnerable guy" - no reasonable alternative

          2.   Most common example of economic duress

(105)   D has a contract to supply 1,000 pounds of kosher grits to P for Chanukah sales in 2011. D refuses to perform this contract until P agrees to buy 4,000 pounds of cheese grits in 2012. P has no other source of kosher grits and so agrees. D delivers the kosher grits. Can P get out of the agreement to buy 4,000 pounds of cheese grits in 2012?_____

IX.   REASONS FOR NOT ENFORCING AGREEMENT: UNCONSCIONABILITY
This doctrine, originally applicable only to sales of goods but (1) now a part of contracts law generally, (2) empowers a court to refuse to enforce all or part of an agreement. The two basic tests, (3) unfair surprise (procedural) and oppressive terms (substantive) , are (4) tested as of the time the agreement was made (5) by the court. *Under 2A, a court may grant relief from a consumer lease even though no provision of the lease is unconscionable, if there is unconscionable conduct in inducing or enforcing the lease.*

X.   REASON FOR NOT ENFORCING AGREEMENT, I.E., AMBIGUITY IN WORDS OF AGREEMENT *[Raffles v. Wichelhaus]*
There will be no contract if
(1)   parties use a <u>material</u> term that is open to at least two reasonable interpretations, and

     (2)   each party attaches different meaning to the term, and

(3)   neither party knows or has reason to know the term is open to at least two reasonable interpretations.

(106)   B and S contract for cotton to be delivered on the Peerless. B intends the October Peerless; S intends the December Peerless. Neither B nor S knows that there are two ships named Peerless. Can S enforce an agreement to buy the cotton on the December Peerless?_____

(107)   What result in (106) if B (but not S) knows that there are two ships named Peerless?

_____

XII.   FINAL REASON FOR NOT ENFORCING AGREEMENT: MISTAKE OF FACT EXISTING AT TIME OF CONTRACT

Distinguish mistake of fact from (1) mistake in judgment or (2) uncertainty or (3) risk allocated to party asserting mistake. Also, don't mistake "mistake" which is an incorrect belief as to facts not based on either what the other party has said or what the contract says with "misunderstanding" which focuses on words in contract or with "misrepresentation" which focuses on words before contract.

A.   **Mutual** Mistake of **Material** Fact and **Not Assumed Risk**

(108)   S and B contract for the sale of a cow named Rose for $80. Both were certain that Rose was barren. Rose turned out to be fertile and worth $750. S refused to deliver Rose. B sued for breach of contract. What result?_____

B.   **Unilateral** Mistake of Material Fact
Generally, courts have been reluctant to allow a party to avoid a contract for a mistake made by only one party. Look for situations in which the other party had reason to know of the mistake, i.e., **palpable mistake.**

(109)   BRI gets bids from 10 vendors for new hoodies. Nine of the bids were more than $100,000. The other bid by X which BRI accepted was for $30,000 because X made a mistake as to the number of BARBRI hoodies. Can X rescind the contract because of its unilateral mistake?_____

THIRD ISSUE: TERMS OF THE CONTRACT

OVERVIEW OF TERMS
Look first for information about words used by people making the contract. Then, look also for information about past or similar deals. And, third, think about UCC warranty, delivery and risk of loss terms if it is a sale of goods.

I.   PARTIES' WORDS AND THE PAROL EVIDENCE RULE
A.   Overview

FOR PURPOSES OF THE BAR EXAM, the parol evidence rule is like an evidence rule in the sense that the (1) issue is whether evidence is admissible and (2) purpose for which the evidence is to be introduced is often determinative. The underlying premise is that the final written version of a deal is more reliable than anything said or written earlier. The essence of the parol evidence rule is the exclusionary effect of written contract on earlier (or contemporaneous) agreements as a possible source of terms of the contract.

And, remember, no "e" in "parol."

B.   Vocabulary of parol evidence

1.   Integration
Written agreement that court finds is the final agreement, triggers the parol evidence rule

2.   Partial integration
Written and final, but not complete

3.   Complete integration
Written and final and complete

4.   Merger clause
Contract clause such as "This is the complete and final agreement."

5.   Parol evidence
- Words of party (or parties)
- Before integration, i.e., before agreement was put in written form.
- Oral or written

6.   Reformation
- Equitable action to modify written contract to reflect actual agreement

C.   Triggering facts
1.   Written contract that court finds is the final agreement; AND

2.   Oral statement made at the time the contract was signed OR earlier oral or written statements by the parties to the contract

D.   Parol evidence fact patterns
1.   Changing/**contradicting** terms in the written deal

Regardless of whether the writing is a complete or partial integration, the parol evidence rule prevents a court from admitting evidence of earlier agreements for the purpose of contradicting the terms in the written contract.

(110) **General rule – cannot use parol evidence to change/contradict**: S contracts in writing to sell B 1,000 chickens a month for 12 months. B sues for reformation of the written contract, claiming that S told him just as they were signing the contract that S would deliver as many chickens as B needs during the 12 month contract term and offers evidence of pre-contract telefaxes from S supporting this claim. Can the court admit this evidence that change/contradicts the terms of the contract? _____ What about evidence of post-contract statements and telefaxes?_____

>   ## 2. Mistake in integration
>   A court may, however, consider evidence of such terms for the limited purpose of determining whether there was a mistake in integration, i.e., a mistake in reducing the agreement to writing.

(111) **Mistake in integration:** Same written contract as (110). Various earlier letters state that the deal is that S will deliver 1,200 chickens a month for 10 months. If B sues for reformation, can this evidence be admitted for the limited purpose of determining whether there was a mistake in putting the agreement in writing? _____

>   ## 3.   Getting out of a written deal.
>   And, regardless of whether the writing is a complete or partial integration, the parol evidence rule does not prevent a court from admitting evidence of earlier words of the parties for the limited purpose of determining whether there is a defense to the enforcement of the agreement such as misrepresentation, fraud, duress.

(112) **Defense exception:** Same basic facts as (110): S contracts in writing to sell B 1,000 chickens a month for 12 months. B claims that S told him just as they were signing the contract that S would deliver as many chickens as B needs during the 12 month contract term, and offers evidence of pre-contract telefaxes supporting this claim. If B sues for rescission, can the court admit this evidence for the limited purpose of determining whether there is a misrepresentation defense to the enforcement of the agreement?_____

>   ## 4.   Explaining term in the written deal
>   And regardless of whether the writing is a complete or partial integration the parol evidence rule does not prevent a court from admitting evidence of earlier agreements to resolve ambiguities in the written contract.

(113) S contracts in writing to sell B chickens. B contends that the word "chickens" in the contract means only fryers while S contends that the term includes boiling hens. Can the

court consider evidence of pre-contract statements by B and S as to what they mean by the word "chicken"?_____

> 5. **Adding to the written deal**
> The parol evidence rule prevents a court from admitting evidence of earlier agreements as a source of consistent, additional terms unless the court finds (i) that the written agreement was only a partial integration or (ii) that the additional terms would ordinarily be in a separate agreement.

(114) S contracts in writing to sell B chickens. The written contract does not specify how the chickens are to be packaged and wrapped. Can the court admit evidence of earlier agreements between S and B as to how the chickens are to be packaged and wrapped for the purpose of determining whether such packaging terms should be added to the terms of the written contract? _____

> E. Comparison of Parol Evidence Rule and Statute of Frauds
> What fact will most often trigger Statute of Frauds question? _____
>
> What fact is required to trigger parol evidence rule question?_____

II. CONDUCT AND COURSE OF PERFORMANCE AND . . .

The words of the parties are not the only source of contract terms. Conduct can also be a source of contract terms. On the bar, such conduct takes one of three forms. Courts look **first** to course of performance, **second** to course of dealing, **third** to custom and usage to explain words in contracts or to fill gaps in contracts: Consider again the example of a written contract for the sale of "chickens."

> 1. Course of performance - same people, same contract
> S contracts to sell 1,000 chickens a month to B for 12 months. The first three shipments are boiling hens, and B does not complain.
>
> 2. Course of dealing - same people, different but similar contract
> S contracts to sell 1,000 chickens a month to B for 12 months. Under prior chicken contracts, S sent B boiling hens, and B complained.
>
> 3. Custom and usage - different but similar people, different but similar contract
> S contracts to sell 1,000 chickens a month to B for 12 months. It is customary in the chicken industry to use the word "chicken" when the deal covers chickens up to six pounds including boiling hens.

III. *UCC FOR TERMS IN SALES OF GOODS CONTRACTS ("default" terms)*

> A. *Delivery Obligations Of Seller Of Goods If Delivery By Common Carrier*

If there is an agreement as to place of delivery by a common carrier, then the question is what does the seller have to do to complete its delivery obligation. There are two possible UCC answers to that question.

1. Shipment contracts

One possibility is that the contract is a shipment contract which means that the seller completes its delivery obligation when it (i) gets the goods to a common carrier, and (ii) makes reasonable arrangements for delivery and (iii) notifies the buyer.

(115) S, a Snook, Texas pet store, contracts to deliver armadillos to B, a Buffalo, New York pet store. What are S's delivery obligations if this is a shipment contract?

_____

2. Destination contracts

The other possibility is that the contract is a destination contract which means that the seller does not complete its delivery obligation until the goods arrive where the buyer is.

3. *Determining whether contract is a shipment or destination. Most contracts with delivery obligations are shipment contracts. Watch for the use of FOB--free on board (city) - as source for determining whether the contract is a shipment contract or a destination contract. FOB followed by city where the seller is or where goods are means shipment contract; FOB followed by any other city means destination contract.*

(116) Same facts as (115), i.e., Snook seller and Buffalo buyer. What if the contract provides for the shipment of the armadillos to Chicago, F.O.B., Chicago?_____

B. Risk Of Loss
1. *What is a risk of loss problem?*

Risk of loss issues arise where (i) after the contract has been formed but before the buyer receives the goods (ii) the goods are damaged or destroyed and (iii) neither the buyer nor the seller is to blame.

For example, a grocer in New Ulm, Minnesota ordered coffee from a New York seller. Even though the coffee was shipped in the best available containers, rats "infiltrated" the coffee while it was in transit. The coffee was delivered; the grocer paid for the coffee. The grocer then opened the packages of coffee and wrote the following letter of complaint:

Schentlemens in New York:

*Der last two pecketches ve got from you off koffe was
mit rattschidt gemitz. Der Koffee may be gute enuff,
but der rattsdurds schbeels the trade. Ve did not see
der rattschidt in der sambles vich you sent us for
examination. It takes so much time to peck der
rattsturds from the koffee. Ve order der kelen koffee
and you shipt schidt mit der koffee; it vas a
muschtake, YA? Ve like you to schipp us der koffee
in van sak und der rattschidt in a udder sak. Den ve
mix it to suit our kostorner.*

*Write please if ve shudt shipp der schidt bak and keep
der koffee or if ve shudt keep der schidt and schipp
der koffee back or ship der whole schidten verks bak.
Ve vant to do rite in der madder, but ve don't like dis
rattschidt bizziness.*

Mit mutch respeckts,
Karl Brummenschidt

2. *What are the possible consequences in a risk of loss problem?
When, AFTER THE CONTRACT HAS BEEN ENTERED INTO,
goods are lost or damaged WITHOUT THE FAULT of the buyer or
seller, which party has the risk of loss: the buyer or the seller? If
the risk of loss is on the buyer, he has to pay the full contract price
for the lost or damaged goods. If the seller has the risk of loss, no
obligation on the buyer; possible liability on seller for nondelivery.*

3. *What are the risk of loss rules?
There are four risk of loss rules. None involve "title." Title is
irrelevant. Do rule #1 first, if it does not apply, then #2 and if does
not apply, then*

   #1 *Agreement: Agreement of the parties controls*

   #2 *Breach: Breaching party is liable for any uninsured loss
   even though breach is unrelated to problem.*

(117)   What if the seller in the coffee hypo, S, was two weeks late in delivering
the coffee?

   #3 *Delivery by common carrier other than seller: Risk of loss
   shifts from seller to buyer at the time that the seller
   completes its delivery obligations.*

(118) What if the coffee was shipped from New York by the New York seller by common
carrier, F.O.B. New York? _____

> **#4**   *No agreement, no breach, no delivery by a carrier ("catch-all"): The determining factor is whether the seller is a merchant. WHETHER THE BUYER IS A MERCHANT IS IRRELEVANT. Risk of loss shifts from a merchant-seller to the buyer on the buyer's "receipt" of the goods; risk of loss shifts from a non-merchant seller when he or she "tenders" the goods.*

(119)   B buys a stove from S, a used appliance dealer. S tells B that he can pick up the stove at the loading dock. Before B can drive his truck to the loading dock, lightning strikes the stove. Does B have to pay for the damaged stove? _____

(120)   B, a used appliance dealer, buys a used stove from S. S tells B to pick up the stove at his convenience that the stove is on S's back porch. Later, vandals damage the stove before B gets it. Does B have to pay for the damaged stove? _____

> **C.**   *Warranties Of Quality*
>   **1.**   *Express*
>   *Look for words that promise, describe or state facts or for use of sample or model. Distinguish from sales talk which is more general, an opinion.*

(121)   Which of the following is/are an express warranty:
    (a)   "all steel"
    (b)   "top quality"
    (c)   guaranteed to operate for two years
    (d)   seller's showing buyer a sample

    _____

>   **2.**   *Implied warranty of merchantability.*
>   *When any person buys any goods from any merchant, a term is automatically added to the contract by operation of law--that the goods are fit for the ordinary purpose for which such goods are used.*
>   *a.*   *Triggering fact: seller is a merchant WHICH HERE MEANS IT DEALS IN GOODS OF THAT KIND.*
>   *b.*   *Warranty: goods are fit for ordinary purposes*

(122)   Conviser buys a "gold" chain from Golden Fleece Fine Jewelry Store. Nothing was written or said about the quality of the chain. When Conviser puts the new chain on, his seven chest hairs fall out. Can Conviser recover from the seller on a breach of warranty theory?_____

(123)   Conviser buys a car from the Golden Fleece Fine Jewelry Store. One day later. Conviser cannot get the car to start. Can Conviser recover from the seller on a breach of warranty theory?_____

3.   *Implied warranty of fitness for a particular purpose*
   a.   *Triggering facts: buyer has particular purpose; buyer is relying on seller to select suitable goods; seller has reason to know of purpose and reliance.*
   b.   *Warranty: goods fit for particular purpose*

(124)   Bubba Conviser, Richard's country cousin, tells a clerk at a shoe store that he needs some shoes to wear to interviews with Wall Street firms. The clerk shows and sells Bubba a pair of white, patent leather loafers. The Wall Street lawyers take one look at Bubba's shoes and terminate the interview. Is there an implied warranty of merchantability?___ Has it been breached? _____

(125)   Same facts as (124). Is there an implied warranty of fitness for a particular purpose? ___

D.   *Contractual Limitations On Warranty Liability*
   1.   *Disclaimer [E.g.,]: Eliminates IMPLIED warranties "there are no warranties"*
      a.   *Express warranties generally cannot be disclaimed*

      b.   *Implied warranties of merchantability and fitness can be disclaimed in EITHER of the following ways*
         (1)   CONSPICUOUS language of disclaimer, mentioning merchantability OR
         (2)   "as is" or "with all faults"

(126)   B buys a big screen television "as is" from S TV Store. Shortly after B turns the television on in her home, it explodes. Can B sue S for breach of the implied warranty of merchantability?_____

   2.   *Limitation of remedies: Does not eliminate warranties, simply limits or sets recovery for any breach of warranty.*

      ▪   *possible to limit remedies even for express warranties*

      ▪   *general test is unconscionability*

      ▪   *prima facie unconscionable if breach of warranty on consumer goods causes personal injury*

(127)   B buys an oven from S. The contract provides that "All operating parts are guaranteed for two years" and "Warranty liability shall be limited to replacement parts." A defective heating element causes a fire which causes $100 of property damages. If B sues S for breach of contract, what can B recover?_____

FOURTH ISSUE: PERFORMANCE

I. *SALE OF GOODS PERFORMANCE CONCEPTS*

    A.   *Goods concepts (six concepts)*

First: Perfect Tender

You need to know three things about "perfect tender" for the bar exam. First, "perfect tender" only applies to sales of goods. Second, "perfect tender" means that the seller's performance must be perfect: perfect goods, perfect delivery. Third, a less than perfect tender by the seller generally gives the buyer the option of rejection of the delivered goods.

(128)   B and S enter into a contract for 200 green widgets. S delivers 199 green widgets and one yellow widget.   Is that a perfect tender?_____

Second: Rejection Of The Goods: General Rules

There are only two things you need to know about rejection of goods for the bar exam. First, you need to be able to distinguish rejection of an offer from rejection of the goods. Second, if the seller does not meet the perfect tender standard, the buyer has the option to retain and sue for damages or reject "all or any commercial unit" and sue for damages. This rejection alternative is limited by CURE "INSTALLMENT CONTRACT and ACCEPTANCE."

(129)   Rejection of an offer. S offers to sell B 200 green widgets for $1,000. B rejects the offer. Is there a contract? _____

(130)   Rejection of the goods. S offers to sell B 200 green widgets for $1,000. B accepts S's offer. S sends 199 green widgets and one yellow widget. If B rejects the goods, is there a contract?_____

Third: Cure

In some instances, a seller who fails to make a perfect tender will be given a "second chance," an option of curing. Note that a seller does not always have the opportunity to "cure," and that the buyer cannot compel the seller to cure.

    (a)   Seller's reasonable ground to believe would be "ok"
           In very limited situations, a seller has the option of curing even after the contract delivery date. The statutory test is whether the seller has reasonable grounds for believing that the improper tender would be acceptable, perhaps with a money allowance. Look for information in the question about prior deals between that buyer and seller with such an allowance.

(131) B and S enter into a contract for 2000 green widgets. S delivers yellow widgets. Previously, B had accepted widgets in colors different from what he had ordered. After delivery, B notifies S he rejects the widgets because they are yellow. Can S cure?____

> *(b)   Time for performance has not yet expired.*

(132) B ordered green widgets from S to be delivered **no later than 6/6.** S delivers **yellow widgets on 5/5.** B notifies S that she is rejecting the yellow widgets. Can S cure?_____

> ### *Fourth: Installment Contracts*
> *An installment contract REQUIRES or AUTHORIIZES (i) delivery of the goods in separate lots (ii) to be separately accepted. The buyer has the right to reject an installment only where there is a substantial impairment in that installment that can't be cured.*
> *Be sure that you see the differences between (1) entering into an installment sales contract that provided for multiple deliveries and acceptances and (2) buying something on credit and paying for it in monthly installments.*

(133) S and B enter into a contract for the delivery of 10 kegs of beer at 6 p.m. for **each night of the bar review course, payment on delivery.** One night S delivers 9 kegs at 6:30 p.m. Can B reject that installment? _____

> ### *Fifth: Acceptance Of The Goods*
> *(1)   Effect of acceptance of the goods: Again, if the buyer accepts the goods, it cannot later reject them.*
> *(2)   Effect of payment: Payment without opportunity for inspection not acceptance*

(134) Epstein buys a "hair replacement system" from Hair Direct by calling Hair Direct's 800 number and using his credit card. Obviously, Epstein's new hair has not yet arrived. Has Epstein accepted the goods?_____

> *(3)   Effect of buyer's keeping goods' implied acceptance-- LOOK FOR THE BUYER'S KEEPING THE GOODS WITHOUT OBJECTION: more specifically look for a fact pattern that states when buyer first received goods and when buyer first complained to seller.*

> ### *Sixth: Revocation Of Acceptance Of The Goods*
> *Remember that if a buyer accepts the goods, it can NOT later reject the goods. In limited circumstances, a buyer can effect a cancellation of the contract by revoking its acceptance of the goods. The requirements for revocation are as follows:*

> i.   *nonconformity substantially impairs the value of the goods, and*
>
> ii.   *excusable ignorance of grounds for revocation or reasonable reliance on seller's assurance of satisfaction, and*
>
> iii.   *revocation within a reasonable time after discovery of nonconformity*

(135)   In July, B buys a sleeping bag from S. The contract provides that the sleeping bag is insulated for temperatures as low as 10 degrees. B uses the sleeping bag for various warm weather camping adventures throughout the summer. When B goes camping in October, she learns that the sleeping bag is not insulated for temperatures as low as 10 degrees. Can B reject the goods?_____ Can B revoke her acceptance of the goods?_____

> 7.   *Comparison Of Rejection Of The Goods And Revocation Of Acceptance Of The Goods*

TWO DIFFERENT WAYS OF BUYER'S RETURNING GOODS AND RECOVERING ANY PAYMENT

		Rejection	Revocation
1.	Timing	Early, before acceptance	Later, after acceptance
2.	Standard	Generally, perfect tender	Substantial impairment
3.	Other Requirements	1. seasonably notify seller 2. hold the goods for seller 3. follow reasonable seller instructions	
4.	Consequences	1. Goods back to seller 2. No buyer payment obligation	

> B.   *Payment*
> *Other performance of sale of goods contract is payment. Two payment problems to watch for: (1) open price term means reasonable price at time of delivery, (2) price to be fixed by buyer or seller means that price must be so fixed in good faith*

II.   COMMON LAW PERFORMANCE CONCEPTS
Again "perfect tender" is not a common law concept. The common law counterpart to perfect tender is substantial performance. In a sale of goods contract, if the seller makes a perfect tender then the buyer must perform by paying the contract price. In a common law contract, if one party substantially

Epstein California Contracts

performs then the other party must pay or otherwise perform. More on the substance of substantial performance later.

Epstein California Contracts   Epstein California Contracts

FIFTH ISSUE: REMEDIES FOR AN UNEXCUSED NONPERFORMANCE

I. **NONMONETARY REMEDIES (IN REM)**
   A.   Specific Performance/Injunction
          Equitable remedy. Look for <u>adequacy of remedy at law</u> or unclean hands, or other parties' equities.
                    1.   Contracts for sale of real estate

(136)   S contracts to sell Blackacre to B. S breaches. Can B get specific performance?_____

(137)   S contracts to sell Blackacre to B. S breaches and sells Blackacre to X, a bona fide purchaser. Can B still get specific performance? _____

                    2.   *Contract for sale of goods: Unique goods: antiques, art, custom-made or other appropriate circumstances*

(138)   S contracts to sell an antique desk to B. S breaches. Can B get specific performance?_____

                    3.   Contract for services: No specific performance, possible injunctive relief

(139)   Epstein contracts with BRI to lecture for BRI.   Epstein breaches. Can BRI obtain a court order requiring Epstein to lecture for BRI?_____

(140)   Same facts as (139). Can BRI obtain a court order barring Epstein from lecturing for a competing bar review course? _____

   B.   *Reclamation*
          Right of an unpaid seller to get its goods back. Key facts are that (i) the buyer must have been insolvent at the time that it received the goods, and (ii) the seller demands return of goods within 10 days of receipt (this "10-day rule" becomes a "reasonable time rule" if before delivery there had been an express representation of solvency by the buyer), and (iii) the buyer still has goods at time of demand.

(141)   On January 15, S sells B grits on credit. The grits are delivered to B on January 22. B is insolvent on January 22d. S learns of B's financial difficulties and demands return of the grits on January 27th. B still has the grits on January 27th. Can S get the grits back by reclamation? _____

(142)   Same facts as (141) except that B sold the grits to C for $1,000 on January 25_____

II. MONEY DAMAGES FOR BREACH OF CONTRACT: GENERAL CONCEPTS

A. Overview
1. Policy: Compensate plaintiff, not punish defendant

2. Vocabulary
EXPECTATION
Incidental
CONSEQUENTIAL
Avoidable
Certainty
Reliance
Liquidated

B. Measure of damages
1. General approach – protection of expectation
Expectation simply means that people who contract expect the other person will not breach. Expectation damages protect that expectation. Accordingly, (1) determine dollar value of performance without breach, (2) then determine dollar value of performance with breach, and (3) compare the two to determine the amount of damages.

(143) P contracts to paints O's house for $1,000, payable when P completes the work. P breaches -- does not paint the house. O hires another painter who charges $1,400. O sues P for breach of contract. What is the measure (amount) of O's damages that O can recover from P for P's breach of contract?_____

(144) P contracts to paint O's house for $1,000, payable when P completes work. P anticipates making $200 profit from this contract. O breaches after P has started work and used $100 of paint and labor. P sues O for breach of contract. What is the measure of P's damages?_____

Damages Rules for Sales of Goods
Part 7 of Article 2 reflects the general contract damages policy of putting the innocent party where it would have been had the contract been performed., i.e., expectation. There are two relevant facts: (1) who breached and (2) who has the goods. Thus, there are four basic Article 2 damages fact patterns and four sets of rules.
1. Seller breaches, buyer keeps the goods **[Fair market value if perfect-fair market value as delivered].**

(145) S sells B an antique car for $30,000. B pays the $30,000, and S deliers the car. Although the contract provided that all parts of the car were authentic and original, some were not. B keeps the car and sues for breach of contract. The jury finds that at the time and place of B's acceptance of the car, the car as delivered was only worth $20,000; the jury also

finds that if the car had been delivered as contracted, it would have been worth $34,000. How much can B recover?_____

> **2.   *Seller breaches, seller has the goods* ([market price at time of discovery of the breach-contract price] or [replacement price-contract price]).**

(146)   S contracts to sell B carpeting for $5,000. S never delivers the carpeting (or S delivers the carpeting and B rejects it because it is not a perfect tender). At the time B learned of the breach, the market price of comparable carpeting is $6,600. How much can B recover? _____

(147)   What if B pays $7,000 for replacement carpeting?_____

> **3.   *Buyer breaches, buyer keeps the goods* [contract price].**

(148)   B contracts to buy carpet from S. Contract price is $800. B receives the carpeting and does not pay for it. The market price for that carpet is now $900. How much does B owe?_____

> **4.   *Buyer breaches, seller has the goods* contract price--resale price and, in some situations, provable lost profits.**

(149)   Epstein contracts to sell his 1973 Cadillac to Conviser $1,000. Conviser breaches. Epstein then sells the Cadillac to Sharon Stone for $800._____

(150)   Same facts as (149) except that Sharon Stone pays Epstein $1,000._____

(151)   **[Lost profits for lost volume seller]** S&M Leather contracts to sell leather clothing to Conviser for $1,000. (Assume that Conviser is buying goods that are part of S&M's regular inventory--"off the rack" so to speak.) Conviser breaches. S&M sells the very same items to Karl Rove for $1,000. Can S&M recover any damages from Conviser? _____ If so, how much?_____

What if S&M's profit margin is 20% of the sales price? _____

> *D. Additions and Limitations*

> > 1.   *Plus INCIDENTAL damages*
> >   *Costs incurred in dealing with the breach such as costs of storing rejected goods in a sale of goods or finding a replacement in a services contract – always recoverable*

(152)   P contracts to paint O's house for $1,000. P breaches. O spends $20 finding another painter, X, who agrees to paint the house for $1,000. What is the measure of O's damages?_____

2.   *Plus foreseeable CONSEQUENTIAL (special) damages*

The term "consequential damages" is very important. And very confusing. Consequential damages does not mean all damages caused as a consequence of the breach. Rather think of damages as being either (1) general damages, i.e., kind of loss that any person would sustain or (2) consequential damages, i.e., kind of loss that is special to this plaintiff. Consequential damages are limited to damages arising from P's special circumstances and recovery of consequential damages is limited to situations in which D had reason to know of these special circumstances at the time of the contract.

(153)   **[No consequential damages]** M contracts with C carrier to transport goods to another village for repair for $100. C breaches by nonperformance. M is unable to find anyone else who will transport the goods for less than $150 and pays T $150 to transport the goods. M sues C for breach of contract. What is the measure of M's damages?

_____

(154)   **[Consequential damages—not recoverable]** Same facts as (153). C's breach resulted in a 5 day delay and M lost $1,000 in profits from the closure of M's mill. M sues C for breach of contract. What is the measure of M's damages?_____

(155)   **[Consequential damages – recoverable]** Same facts as (154) except that M told C before the contract that the mill was closed because of the broken shaft and would remain closed until the shaft was repaired and returned. What is the measure of M's damages?

_____

3.   *Less AVOIDABLE damages*
         No recovery for damages that could have been avoided without undue burden on plaintiff. Burdens of pleading and proof on defendant.

(156)   **Continuing to perform.** P contracts to paint O's house for $1,000. P anticipates that she will make $200 profit from painting O's house. O breaches after P has incurred $100 of costs for paint and labor. Notwithstanding O's breach, P finishes painting O's house. How much can P recover? _____

(157)   **Turning down other opportunities.** P contracts to paint O's house for $1,000. P anticipates that she will make $200 profit from painting O's house. O breaches. X offers P $500 to paint her fence. P anticipates she would make $100 from painting X's fence. P declines X's offer. How much can P recover from O? _____

2.   *CERTAINTY limitation and RELIANCE alternative*
         Reasonable certainty test. Look for fact pattern involving a services contract and plaintiff engaged in new business or a new business activity. Consider reliance recovery as an alternative to expectation.

(158) Epstein, who has never promoted anything (other than himself), contracts with Kinky Friedman for a Texas Jewboys reunion concert (first time in 20 years) in Jasper, Alabama. Kinky breaches two months before the concert.   Epstein sues for breach of contract, alleging that he expected to sell 3,000 tickets at $30 a ticket (even though no one in Jasper, Alabama knows Kinky Friedman, Epstein, or anybody Jewish). Should Epstein be able to recover the $90,000 as damages protecting his expectation interest?

_____

(159) Same facts as (158) with the additional fact that, prior to Kinky's breach, Epstein has spent $2,000 arranging for and promoting the Kinky Friedman Texas Jewboys Reunion concert. Should Epstein be able to recover the $2,000?_____

E.   *Contract provisions regarding damages, i.e., LIQUIDATED damages Look for contract provision fixing amount of damages. Issue will be validity: concern is whether provision is too high – a penalty. Tests are (1) damages were difficult to forecast at time contract was made and (2) provision is a reasonable forecast.*

(160) B contracts to build store for O. Contract fixes damages for delay at $10,000. Is this liquidated damages? _____ Valid liquidated damages? _____

SIXTH ISSUE: EXCUSE OF NONPERFORMANCE OF CONTRACT BECAUSE OF SOMETHING THAT HAPPENED AFTER CONTRACT WAS MADE

Overview: Look for information in fact pattern about (1) nonperformance of contract and (2) something happening after contract.

I. EXCUSE BECAUSE OTHER GUY'S NONPERFORMANCE

II. IMPROPER PERFORMANCE

A. Common law and material breach rule
   1. Four general rules.
   First, damages can be recovered for any breach. Second, only a material breach by one guy excuses the other guy from performing. Third, whether a breach is material is a fact question (and so whether a breach is material is not likely to be a bar exam question). Fourth, if there is substantial performance then the breach is not material. If the breach is material, then the performance was not substantial.

   a.   Problems with the Quantity (Amount) of Performance

(161)   P contracts to paint 10 identical apartments for O for $10,000. P breaches after painting 2 apartments. Was P's breach a material breach?_____Under contract law, is O obligated to pay P $10,000? _____Under contract law, is O obligated to pay P for painting the two apartments? _____ Under quasi-contract?_____

Divisible contract exception. In a "divisible contract" there can be a contract law recovery for substantial performance of a divisible part even though there has been a material breach of entire contract. On the bar, look at whether price is stated as a lump sum or on a per performance basis.

(162)   Same facts as (161) except that the contract states that P will be paid $1,000 an apartment, _____

_____

   b.   Problems with the Quality of Performance

(163)   O hires P to paint his house white for $1,000. P, a big fan of the group Gogol Bordello, http://www.youtube.com/watch?v=p_8114DXlwM paints the house purple.   Did P substantially perform? _____Is O excused from performing, i.e., excused from paying anything? _____ Can O recover money damages?_____

(164)   O hires P to paint his house white for $1,000. P paints the house white but fails to paint one of the closets. O has to pay another painter $25 to paint the closet with paint left by Did P substantially perform?_____ Is O excused from performing, i.e., excused from paying anything?_____ Can O recover money damages? _____

(165)   O hires B to build a house for $100,000. Contract states that B will use only copper Reading brand pipe. B instead uses copper Cohoe brand. Court finds that copper Cohoe pipe is roughly comparable to copper Reading pipe and that use of Cohoe pipe only reduces the value of the house by $1,000. O refuses to pay B anything. B sues. Is O excused by B's breach? _____ Can O recover money damages? _____

> ### A.   Article 2 and perfect tender rule again
> Never do material breach or divisible contracts in sale of goods problems. Do perfect tender and installment contract. If B gets 199 green widgets instead of the 200 she ordered, she can reject the goods and will be excused from performing (paying) unless installment contract.

II.   EXCUSE BECAUSE OF NON-OCCURRENCE OF AN EXPRESS CONDITION
Overview of what you need to know: (i) what is an express condition, (ii) how can you identify an express condition, (iii) how can an express condition be satisfied, and (iv) how can an express condition be excused.

> ### A.   What An Express Condition Is
> An express condition is a mutually agreed upon promise modifier. It is language in a contract – not merely language in a response to an offer – that does not create a new obligation, but merely limits obligations created by other language in the contract.
>
> Express conditions in contracts are created by language in the contract. **Watch for words such as "if", "only if", "provided that", "so long as", "subject to", "in the event that", "unless", "when", "until", and "on condition that, "in the contract".** Most contracts and most bar exam fact patterns do NOT have express conditions.

(166)   Conditional acceptance. S offers to sell B his house for $100,000. **B responds** that she will buy the house "**if** a mortgage at no more than 6% can be obtained." Is there a contract? _____

(167)   Express Condition. S and B enter into an **agreement that states** that B will buy S's house for $100,000 "**if** a mortgage at no more than 6% can be obtained." Is there a contract?_____ Notwithstanding B's best efforts, B cannot obtain a mortgage at 6% or less. Does B have to buy the house?_____

> ### B.   What is the standard for determining whether an express condition has occurred, i.e. been "satisfied"?
> General rule – strict compliance is required for "satisfaction" of a condition

(168)   B contracts to buy S's house. The contract states "This sale is **subject to** the house's being appraised at $200,000". If the house is appraised at $195,000 is B obligated to perform?_____

(169)   B contracts to build O's house. The contract states "O's payment for B's work is **conditioned on** B's using only copper Reading pipe." B instead uses comparable copper Cohoe pipe. Has the condition been satisfied so that O has to perform, i.e., pay for the house? [compare with (165)] _____

> D.   **How Can an Express Condition Be Eliminated?**
> Non-occurrence of an express condition is an excuse, i.e., GENERALLY, if the express condition does not occur, all remaining contract obligations are excused. Sometimes, however, the occurrence of the express condition is eliminated (excused) which means that even though the express condition did not occur, there is no excuse for the performance of remaining contract obligations.
>
> > 1. Waiver/estoppel.
> > Identify the person who benefits from or is protected by the express condition. Then look for a statement by that person giving up the benefits and protection of the express condition. Estoppel is based on a statement by the person protected by the express condition BEFORE the conditioning event was to occur and requires reliance. Waiver is based on a statement by the person protected by the express condition AFTER the conditioning event was to occur and does not require reliance.

(170)   B contracts to buy S's house. The contract provided that the sale was conditioned on B's obtaining a mortgage interest rate of 6% or less. B is unable to get a loan of less than 6.5%. B still wants to buy the house.   Can S now refuse to sell the house because the condition was not satisfied?_____

> > 2. Prevention
> > If the party protected by the express condition hinders or prevents the occurrence of the express condition, then the express condition is excused and the contract must be performed.

(171)   House sale contract between B and S is conditioned on the house being appraised at $200,000. The house is appraised at $195,000, and B refuses to buy the house. What result if S sues B for breach of contract and is able to establish that (i) the house should have been appraised at $205,000 and that (ii) B bribed the appraiser? _____

_____

[The concepts illustrated above apply to both express "conditions precedent" and express "conditions subsequent." Almost all express conditions are "conditions precedent" – conditions that must occur before there is any obligation to perform. The **non-occurrence** of an express condition precedent excuses performance. Express conditions subsequent are express conditions that occur subsequent to the start of performance. The **occurrence** of an express condition subsequent excuses any further performance. For example, you and Spike Lee agree that he will sell you his Knicks courtside seats for $10 a game until the Knicks are in first place.]

III.   EXCUSE OF PERFORMANCE BY REASON OF THE OTHER PARTY'S ANTICIPATORY REPUDIATION

Anticipatory repudiation is an **unambiguous** statement or conduct indicating (i) that the repudiating party will not perform (ii) made prior to the time that performance was due. Anticipatory repudiation by one party excuses the other party's duty to perform. It also <u>generally</u> gives rise to an immediate claim for damages for breach unless the claimant has already finished her performance.

(172)   P contracts to paint O's house with payment to be made on July 13. On March 10, **before** P has finished painting, O tells P that she is doing a great job but that O is not going to pay. Is P excused from continuing to perform?_____

(173)   Same facts as (172). If P stops painting and sues O on March 11, can P recover damages for breach of contract on March 11 even though the contract date for payment was July 13?_____

(174)   P contracts to paint O's house for $1,000 with payment to be made on July 13. On March 25, **after** P has finished painting the house, O tells P that he has done a great job but that O is not going to pay. If P sues O on March 26, can P recover damages for breach of contract on March 26 even though the contract date for payment was July 13?

_____

Anticipatory repudiation can be reversed or retracted so long as there has not been a material change in position by the other party. If the repudiation is timely retracted, the duty to perform is reimposed but performance can be delayed until adequate assurance is provided.

(175)   Same facts as (172) except that, before P finds another painting job or moves her painting equipment, O tells P that he has changed his mind again, that he will pay P for painting the house, and that the money has been placed in an escrow account. Can O recover damages for breach of contract if P does not paint the house?_____

IV. INSECURITY

Recall that anticipatory repudiation requires an unambiguous statement or conduct indicating that a party will not perform. What if the words or conduct of a party merely makes performance uncertain? Look for this in sale of goods problems. If the words or conduct of one party give "reasonable grounds for insecurity", then the other party can in writing demand adequate assurance and if it is "commercially reasonable" can suspend performance until it gets adequate assurance. The three concepts again are (1) reasonable grounds for insecurity and (2) written demand for adequate assurance and (3) commercially reasonable to stop performance

(176) In January, B contracts to buy custom-made widgets from S. Contract requires B to pay 25% of price in March and requires S to deliver widgets no later than April 5. In February, B learns that S was late on all January widget deliveries to other customers and that a substantial number of the widgets delivered were defective. B, in writing, demands adequate assurance. Is B excused from making the March payment until S provides adequate assurance? _____

V.   EXCUSE BY REASON OF A LATER CONTRACT

A.   Rescission (cancellation)
       The key is whether performance is still remaining from each of the contract parties. (executory)

(177) P contracts to paint O's house for $1,000 with payment to made when the work is completed. P begins work. Before P completes the work, P and O agree to rescind the contract. Is the rescission valid?_____

(178) P contracts to paint O's house for $1,000 with payment to be made when the work is completed. After P completes the work, P and O agree to rescind the contract. Is the rescission valid?_____

B.   Accord and Satisfaction (substituted *performance*)
       You need to know (i) what an accord is and what a satisfaction is and (ii) the effect of the making of the accord, and (iii) the effect of getting no satisfaction.
       1.   Meaning of "accord", "satisfaction"
              On bar exam, accord questions will have an agreement by the parties to an already existing obligation to accept a different **performance** in satisfaction of the existing obligation.

(179) D borrows $1,000 from C and agrees to pay the loan with interest. Later D and C agree that IF D delivers 20 widgets by the end of the month, THEN the debt will be excused. Is this an accord?_____

              2.   Effect of accord AND SATISFACTION
       a.   If the new agreement ('the accord') is performed (satisfaction), then performance of the original obligation is excused.

(180)   D borrows $1,000 from C and agrees to pay the loan with interest. Later D and
C agree that IF D delivers 20 widgets by the end of the month, THEN the debt will be
excused.   D delivers the 20 widgets before the end of the month. C sues D on the debt.
What result?_____

b.   If the accord is not performed, then the other party can sue
on either the original obligation or the accord

(181)   D borrows $1,000 from C and agrees to pay the loan with interest. Later D and
C agree that IF D delivers 20 widgets by the end of the month, THEN the debt will be
excused. D does not deliver the widgets. Can C recover on the original loan agreement?
_____ Can C recover from D on the accord_____

C.   Modification (substituted *agreement*)
Modification is an agreement by parties to an existing obligation to accept
a different **agreement** in satisfaction of the existing obligation.

(182)   D borrows $1,000 from C and agrees to repay the loan with interest. Later D and C agree
that D will deliver 20 widgets by the end of the month instead of paying $1,000 with
interest. D does not deliver the widgets. Can C recover on the original loan agreement?

_____

D.   Novation (substituted *person*)
You need to know (i) what novation is, (ii) who is liable after a novation
and (iii) what the factual and legal differences between a novation and a
delegation are.
1.   What is a novation?
A novation is an agreement between BOTH parties to an existing
contract to the substitution of a new party, *i.e.*, same performance,
different party.

(183)   P contracts to paint O's house. Subsequently, P, O, and X agree that
X will do the work instead of P, i.e., will replace P. Is this a novation?

_____

2.   Who is liable after a novation?
Novation excuses the contracted for performance of the party who
is substituted for or replaced.

(184)   Same facts as (183). X does not paint the house. Can O recover damages from P for
breach of contract?_____

3.   How is delegation different from novation?
Novation requires the agreement of BOTH parties to the original
contract and excuses the person replaced from any liability for
nonperformance. Delegation does not require the agreement of
both parties and does not excuse.

(185) P contracts to paint O's house. Subsequently, P, without consulting O, asks X to do the work and X agrees. X doesn't paint the house. Can O recover damages from P for breach of contract?_____

VI. EXCUSE OF PERFORMANCE BY REASON OF A LATER, UNFORESEEN EVENT

Performance of contractual duties (other than a contractual duty to pay money) can be excused under impossibility or impracticability or frustration of purpose if

(i)   something happens after contract formation but before the completion of contract performance; and

(ii)   that something that happens was unforeseen; and

(iii)   that something that happens makes performance impossible or commercially impracticable or frustrates the purpose of the performance.

Possible differences between impossibility and impracticability include (i) former is objective/latter subjective; (ii) former means can't be done while latter means can only be done with EXTREME and UNREASONABLE difficulty and expense. Bar questions are more likely to focus on whether there is any basis for excusing performance than on whether that basis should be called impossibility or impracticability.   Bar exam questions often turn on your understanding. (1) which party is arguing that his performance is excused, (2) what her performance is (3) whether post-contract occurrence affected her **ability** to perform not just the **cost** of her performance.

A.   Damage or destruction of subject matter of contract AFTER contract

(186) P contracts to paint O's house for $1,000. After P begins painting, the house burns down. Is P excused from performing on this contract so that P is now free to take another painting job?_____

(187) B contracts to build a house for O for $100,000. After B begins work, the house burns down. Is B excused from performing on this contract so that B is now free to take another construction job?_____

If sale of goods [like Karl and his coffee] do risk of loss first. If risk of loss is on the seller <u>and</u> the buyer sues for damages for seller's nonperformance, then:

(188) **[Seller's risk of loss and destruction].** Epstein contracts to sell Conviser his 1973 Cadillac for $700. After the contract but before the risk of loss has passed to Conviser, Epstein's Cadillac is destroyed by an unseasonable flood. When Epstein fails to perform the contract (i.e., fails to deliver the Cadillac) Conviser sues Epstein for breach of contract. Is Epstein's nonperformance excused?_____

(189) **[Seller's risk of loss and destruction—different answer].** Epstein contracts to sell Conviser 100 sacks of grits for $300. After the contract but before the risk of loss has

passed to Conviser, Epstein's grits are destroyed by an unseasonable flood. When Epstein fails to deliver grits, Conviser sues Epstein for breach. Is Epstein's nonperformance excused? _____

> B.   Death AFTER contract
> 1. General effect of debt on contract obligations
> Death does <u>not</u> make a person's contract obligations disappear.

(190) D borrows $10,000 from C and signs a contract promising to repay the $10,000. D dies, leaving an estate of $30,000. Under contract law, can C recover the $10,000 from D's estate? _____ Is contract performance excused by D's death? _____

(191) Conviser contracts with P to paint his house for $25,000. After contracting but before Conviser's paying or P's painting, P dies. Conviser hires another painter AP, who charges $30,000 for painting Conviser's house. Conviser sues P's estate for breach of k, seeking expectation damages of $5,000. Is P's contract nonperformance excused by P's death? _____ Under contract law, can Conviser recover the $5,000 from P's estate? _____

> 2.   Party to contract who is "Special" person

(192) Owen Wilson contracts with HBO to star in the made for television movie: "Law School Legend --- The David Epstein Story". Before filming starts, Wilson dies. HBO sues Wilson's estate for breach of contract. Is Wilson's nonperformance of the contract excused by impossibility? _____

> C.   Subsequent law or regulation
> 1.   Later law makes performance of contract illegal –
> excuse by impossibility

(193) Conviser contracts with the Gold Club to be the featured dancer in the club's legendary "Bottoms Up Review." After the contract but before Conviser dances, the town passes a new law outlawing nude dancing. Nonetheless, Conviser comes to the club nude, ready to dance. Is the Gold Club excused from performing? _____

> 2.   Later law makes mutually understood purpose of contract
> illegal - excuse by frustration of purpose

(194) Conviser tells his plastic surgeon (P) that he needs plastic surgery so that he will be a "lean, mean, nude dancing machine" when he dances at the Gold Club. Conviser and P agree that Conviser will pay P $7,000 and P will do liposuction and other "more intimate" plastic surgery. After the agreement but before the surgery, the town passes a law outlawing nude dancing. Is Conviser excused from performing the surgery contract? (Krell v. Henry) _____

SEVENTH ISSUE: THIRD PARTY PROBLEMS

You will be tested on three different kinds of third-party problems: third party beneficiaries, assignments of contract rights and delegation of contract duties.

I.   A PERSON TRYING TO ENFORCE A CONTRACT SHE DID NOT MAKE: THIRD PARTY BENEFICIARY

You will need to be able to (1) identify a problem as a third-party beneficiary problem, (2) use the vocabulary of third-party beneficiary law, (3) deal with efforts to cancel or modify a third-party beneficiary contract, (4) figure out who can sue whom and (5) assert any available defenses.

A.   Identifying Third-Party Beneficiary Problems
Look for two parties contracting with the intent of benefit to a third party. For example,

(195) Epstein takes out an insurance policy with Allstate Insurance. The insurance contract provides that (i) Epstein will make annual premium payments of $3,000 and (ii) Allstate will pay Sharon Stone $250,000 on Epstein's death. When Epstein dies, does Ms. Stone have a contract law right to recover $250,000 from Allstate?_____

(196) B and S enter into a contract in which S agrees to provide 100 sacks of grits to T and B agrees to pay S $200 for S's providing the grits to T. When S fails to deliver the grits, can T recover from S under contract law? _____

B.   Knowing the Vocabulary
(1)   Third-party beneficiary
Not a party to the contract. Able to enforce contract others made for her benefit. [T (196)]

(2)   Promisor
Look for person who is making the promise that benefits the third party. [S in (196)]

(3)   Promisee
Look for person who obtains the promise that benefits the third party. [B in (196)]

(4)   Intended/incidental
Only intended beneficiaries have contract law rights. Intent of parties to contract determines whether intended or incidental.

(5)   Creditor/donee
Intended beneficiaries are either donees or creditors. Usually donees. Look at whether beneficiary was a creditor of the promisee.

C.   Dealing With Efforts to Cancel or Modify
The test is whether the third party knows of and has relied on or assented as requested. If so, her rights have vested and the contract cannot be canceled or modified without her consent unless the contract otherwise provides.

(197)   Same facts as (196). Can B and S cancel the grits contract before T learns of the contract? _____

(198)   Same facts as (196). Can B and S cancel the contract after T learns of the contract and relies on it?_____

D.   Who Can Sue Whom?
Four "bar exam important" rules
(1)   Beneficiary Can Recover from Promisor

(199)   Can T recover from S for breach of contract if T does not get the grits?_____

(2)   Promisee Can Recover from Promisor

(200)   If B pays $100 for the grits and S never delivers the grits to T, can B recover from S for breach of contract?_____

(3)   General rule. Beneficiary can not recover from Promisee .

(201)   Can T recover from B for breach of the grits contract if T does not get the grits?_____

(4)   Limited exception: Creditor Beneficiary can recover from Promisee BUT ONLY on pre-existing debt

(202)   Can T recover from B if B owed T $100 before B ordered the grits to satisfy that debt and the grits were never delivered? _____

E.   Defenses
If the Third Party Beneficiary sues the Promisor, the Promisor can assert any defense that he would have had if sued by the Promisee.

(203)   The check S receives from B bounces. S does not deliver grits to T. T sues S for breach of contract. Does S have any defense?_____

II.   A PERSON TRYING TO ENFORCE A CONTRACT SHE DID NOT MAKE: ASSIGNMENT OF RIGHTS

You need to know (1) what an assignment of a contract is, (2) the vocabulary of assignment, (3) the limitations on assignment, (4) the requirements for assignments, (5) the rights of assignee and (6) how to deal with multiple assignments.

A. What An Assignment Is: Transfer of rights under a contract, involves two separate steps: first step - contract between only two parties; and second step - one of the parties later transfers rights under that contract to a third party. Need to see the difference between assignment of an offer and assignment of a contract. Need to see the difference between assignment of a contract and third party beneficiary.

(204) Epstein offers to sell you his 1973 Cadillac for $400 to be paid on Tuesday with the car to be made available to you at the University of Richmond Law School's student parking garage on Thursday. Can you assign the offer to Conviser?_____

(205) Epstein offers to sell you his 1973 Cadillac for $400 to be paid on Tuesday with the car to be made available to you at the University of Richmond Law School's student parking garage on Thursday. You accept the offer. Can you assign the contract to Conviser?_____

(206) On January 15, Batman contracts with Gotham to provide security services for a year; the contract provides that Batman is to be paid $300,000 for the services. Batman later transfers his rights under the contract to Robin. Is this an assignment of a third party beneficiary contract?_____

(207) On January 15, Batman contracts with Gotham to provide security services for a year; this January 15 contract provides that Gotham will pay Robin $300,000 for Batman's services. Is this an assignment of a third party beneficiary contract?_____

B. Vocabulary
    1. Assignor: Party to the contract who later transfers rights under the contract to another. [Batman in (206)]

    2. Assignee: Not a party to the contract. Able to enforce the contract because of the assignment. [Robin in (206)]

    3. Obligor: Other party to the contract. [Gotham in (206)]

C. Limitations On Assignment
    1. If There Is a Contract Provision Regarding Assignment
       If fact pattern includes language of contract regarding assignability, determine whether contract (a) prohibits assignments or (b) invalidates assignments.
                    (a)   prohibition: Language of prohibition takes away the right to assign but not the power to assign which means that the assignor is

liable for breach of contract but an assignee who does not know of the prohibition can still enforce the assignment.

(208)   Batman-Gotham contract provides "<u>rights hereunder are not assignable</u>." Notwithstanding this contract provision, Batman assigns the right to the $300,000 payment to Robin who does not know about the contract provision. Can Robin collect from Gotham?____ Can Gotham recover from Batman for breach of contract?____

        (b)   invalidation: Language of invalidation takes away both the right to assign and the power to assign so that there is a breach by the assignor and no rights in the assignee.

(209)   Batman-Gotham contract provides "<u>all assignments of rights under this contract are void</u>." Notwithstanding this contract provision, Batman assigns the right to the $300,000 payment to Robin who does not know about the contract provision. Can Robin collect from Gotham?_____

IF ANY DOUBT IN YOUR MIND AS TO WHETHER PROHIBITION OR INVALIDATION, THEN PROHIBITION

        2.   If There Is Nothing in Fact Pattern About Contract Law Regarding Assignability . . . .
Even if a contract does not in any way limit the right to assign, common law bars an assignment that substantially changes the duties of the obligor.
        a.   assignment of right to payment (never substantial change)

(210)   Batman assigns his rights to payment under the contract with Gotham to Robin, *i.e.*, Gotham is to pay Robin, not Batman. Does this substantially change the duty of the obligor so that the assignment is not enforceable?_____

        b.   assignments of right to contract performance other than right to payment (usually substantial change on bar)

(211)   Gotham assigns its rights to security services under the contract with Batman to Metropolis, *i.e.* Batman is to defend Metropolis, not Gotham. Does this substantially change the duty of the obligor so that the assignment is not enforceable?_____

        D.   Requirements for Assignment

General rule is that consideration is <u>not</u> required but gratuitous assignments (and only gratuitous assignments) can be revoked.

(212) Batman assigns the right to payment under the contract with Gotham to the University of Richmond Law School for no consideration. Is this a valid assignment? _____

(213) Same facts as (212). Before Gotham pays Richmond, Batman changes his mind. Can Batman revoke the assignment to Richmond and obtain the $300,000 payment from Gotham himself? _____

E.   Right Of Assignee
      1.   Assignee can recover from the obligor.

(214) Batman contracts to perform security services for Gotham for $300,000. Batman then assigns his rights under the contract to Robin, and Batman performs the contract. When Gotham refuses to pay Robin, Robin sues Gotham. Can Robin collect from Gotham for breach of contract? _____

      2.   Assignor for consideration <u>cannot</u> recover from obligor

(215) After assigning the contract with Gothom to Robin for $10 and doing all of the work himself, can Batman collect from Gotham? _____

      3.   Obligor has same defenses against assignee as it would have against assignor.

(216) If Batman fails to perform the services, can Robin still collect from Gotham? _____

      4.   Payment by obligor to assignor is effective until obligor knows of assignment. Similarly, modification agreements between obligor and assignor are effective if the obligor did not know of the assignment.

(217) You rent furniture from Acme Furniture Rentals. In March, Acme assigns your rental contract to Baker Rents. You do not know of the assignment and so make your next two rental payments to Acme. Baker then sues you for the two payments it has not received. Can assignee Baker recover from you the obligor? _____

      5.   Implied warranties of assignor IN AN ASSIGNMENT FOR VALUE

            Recall that it is possible to make an assignment without consideration, a gratuitous assignment. In some respects, assignments for consideration are treated differently than

such gift assignments. One such difference is that in an assignment for
consideration only, the assignor warrants (1) the right assigned actually exists and (2) the right assigned is not subject to any then existing defenses by the obligor and (3) the assignor will do nothing after the assignment to impair the value of the assignment. Assignor, however, does not warrant what the obligor will do after the assignment.

(218) X signs a note promising to pay Y $1,000. Y assigns the note to Z for $800. X was an infant when he signed the note and refuses to pay Z. Can assignee Z recover from assignor Y?_____

(219) Epstein assigns the right to royalties from his splendid West bankruptcy casebook to Sharon Stone for $1,000. Epstein then writes West and releases it from any obligation to pay royalties. Can Ms. Stone collect from Epstein for breach of implied warranty of assignment? _____

(220) Epstein assigns the right to royalties from his splendid West contracts casebook to Sharon Stone for $1,000. Two days later, West files for bankruptcy and refuses to pay any royalties. Can Ms. Stone collect from Epstein for breach of implied warranty of assignment? _____

       F.   Multiple Assignments
            1.   All gratuitous assignments
                  General rule: last assignee generally wins

(221) Batman gives the right to the $300,000 payment from Gotham to the University of Richmond Law School on January 15. On April 5, Batman makes a gift of the same payment right to the UJA. Which assignee has greater rights? _____

            2.   Assignments for Consideration

                 a.   General rule: First assignee for consideration wins.

(222) On February 2, Batman assigns his rights under the contract with Gotham to Robin for $1. On March 3, Batman assigns his rights under the same contract with Gotham to Conviser for $250,000. Whom should Gotham pay?_____

                 b.   Very Limited Exception
                      A subsequent assignee takes priority over an earlier assignee for value only if he both (i) does not know of the earlier assignment and (ii) is the first to obtain (1)

payment, (2) a judgment, (3) a novation, OR (4) indicia of ownership ["four horsemen" rule].

(223) **[Exception Not Applicable]** As before, Batman assigns to Robin for consideration and then assigns to Conviser for consideration. Conviser does not know of the assignment to Robin and Conviser is the first to notify Gotham that he is an assignee. Gotham learns of the earlier assignment to Robin before it pays Conviser. To whom should Gotham make the payment?

III. **DISPUTES ARISING FROM A PERSON'S PERFORMING A CONTRACT SHE DID NOT MAKE: DELEGATION OF DUTIES**
You need to know (1) what a delegation is, (2) relationship of assignment and delegation, (3) which duties are delegable, and (4) what are the consequences of delegation.

A. What delegation Is
Party to a contract transferring work under that contract to third party. For example, P contracts to paint O's house for $1,000. P (delegating party) and X (delegatee) agree that X will paint O's (obligee) house.

B. Relationship of assignment and delegation
A contract creates both rights and duties. For example, if P contracts to paint O's house for $1,000, then P has a duty to paint and a right to payment and O has a duty to pay and a right to the painting of her house. Assignment is the transfer by a party to a contract of his rights or benefits under the contract to a third party who was not a party to the contract. Delegation is the transfer by a party to a contract of his duties or burdens under the contract to a third party who was not a party to the contract.

Often a contracting party makes both an assignment and a delegation of his rights and duties under the contract to a third party. Often the multistate examiners use the term "assignment" in a problem involving an assignment and a delegation and even in a problem involving only a delegation.

(224) P contracts with O to paint O's house for $1,000. P and X agree that X will do the painting and collect the $1,000 from O. Is this an assignment, a delegation or both an assignment and a delegation?_____

(225) Same facts as (224) except that P and X agree that X will do the painting and P will pay X $1,000. Is this both an assignment and a delegation?

---

(226) Same facts as (225). X does the painting, and X does a great job. Can X recover the $1,000 from O? **NO**

>   C.   Which duties are delegable
>   Generally contractual duties are delegable. The limitations on delegation are very limited. Delegations are permitted unless either (1) contract prohibits delegations or *prohibits assignments* or (2) "personal services contract" calls for VERY SPECIAL skills

(227) Same facts as (226). Can P recover the $1,000 from O? _____

(228) Same facts as (226) except contract provides "No delegations." Can P recover the $1,000 from O? _____

(229) Again, same facts as (226) except contract provides "No assignments." Can P recover the $1,000 from O? _____

(230) Chipper Jones has a contract with the Atlanta Braves. No contract provision regarding assignments or delegation. Can he delegate performance to Epstein?

_____

>   D.   Nonperformance by delegate. What if, after delegation, the third party delegatee does not perform?
>   1.   Delegating party always remains liable.
>
>   2.   Delegatee liable only if she receives consideration from delegating party.

(231) **Delegation without consideration:** P contracts to paint O's house for $1,000. X then agrees with P that she (X) will do the painting for P because P is a good friend. X does not do the work. Can O recover from P? _____

(232) Same facts as (231). Can P recover from X? _____

(233) Same facts as (231). Can O recover from X? _____

(234) **Delegation for consideration:** P contracts to paint O's house for $1,000. P and X then agree that X will do the work and P will pay X $900. X does not do the work. Can O recover from P? _____

(235) Same facts as (234). Can P recover from X? _____

(236) Same facts as (234). Can O recover from X? _____

CONTRACTS IN AN EVEN SMALLER "CONCENTRIC CIRCLE" (LESS THAN 5 FULLPAGES (BIG PRINT)

I.   **APPLICABLE** LAW
     If sale of goods, look for some special Article 2 rule.

II. CONTRACT **FORMATION**
     #1 Offer
     - Actual intent largely irrelevant
     - Missing terms [other than price in sale of land] ok – no "all material terms" requirement for offers
     - Watch for "appropriate","fair" or "reasonable" which are disqualifying vague terms
     - Watch for "all", "exclusively", "only", "solely" which manifest commitment and give rise to requirements contract or output contract

     #2 Termination of offer
     - Revocation of offers and where is Sharon Stone
     - "Firm offer" rule – writing signed by merchant expressly promising to keep offer open (bar exam certainty)
     - Counteroffers kills offers
     - Watch for acceptance followed by "if", "provided", "so long as", "on condition that" which means rejection
     - Mirror image requirement for common law but not sale of goods.
     - In sale of goods, distinguish additional term which means contract generally without additional term from conditional acceptance which means no express contract

     #3 Acceptance
     - Offer can control method and time of acceptance but on bar rarely does
     - Bilateral world so most offers can be accepted by promise or the implied promise resulting from start of performance.
     - Start of performance pursuant to offer to enter into unilateral contract make offer irrevocable but is not acceptance
     - Acceptance (and only acceptance) effective when sent unless (1) meeting an option deadline or (2) following a rejection

     #4 Lack of consideration as reason not to enforce agreement
     - Promise breaker must have asked for something in return for her promise (bargained for)
     - Promise can be consideration
     - Peppercorn can be consideration.
     - Stuff done before promise (past consideration) not consideration
     - Doing only what you are already obligated to do (pre-existing duty) not consideration
     - No consideration required to modify Article 2 contract

- No new consideration in settlement of due and undisputed debt
- Foreseeable, detrimental reliance (promissory estoppel) is substitute for consideration.

#5 Statute of Frauds as a reason not to enforce agreement

- "Promise to answer for the debts of another" so limited (guarantee only/main purpose exception) that is generally wrong answer
- Watch for Kenny G and performance more than a year away
- "Task" never a Statute of Frauds problem
- Not one year real estate lease
- Full performance (BUT NOT PART PERFORMANCE) of service contracts
- Sale of goods whether dispute as to goods delivered
- Real estate part performance by 2 of 3
- Writing look for contents and who signed
    o Who and what and defendant signed if common law
    o How many and defendant signed if Article 2 unless "answer the damned letter" rule

#6 Misrepresentation as a reason not to enforce agreement
- Even if honest and innocent so long as material and relied on
- Distinguish nondisclosure (must be wrongful) and mistake

#7 Mistake of fact unlikely

III.   CONTRACT **TERMS**

#1 Precontract words of parties and parol evidence rule
- Vocabulary
    o Integration
    o Parol evidence
    o Merger clause
- Admissibility and purpose of proffer
    o Admissible to explain ambiguity
    o Admissible to establish defense
    o Admissible to establish mistake in integration (clerical error)
    o Admissible to add term, unless complete integration
    o Inadmissible to contradict or otherwise change

#2   Conduct
- 1st Course of performance: same people, same contract
- 2d Course of dealing: same people, earlier contract
- 3d Custom and usage: other people, similar contracts

#3   UCC
- Delivery obligations of seller if shipment contract
    o Get goods to common carrier

- o Make delivery arrangements
- o Notify buyer
  - Risk of loss if common carrier turns on whether shipment contract
  - Risk of loss if not common carrier turns on if seller is merchant
    - o Receipt rule for merchant sellers
    - o Tender rule for others
  - Disputes over quality of delivered goods
    - o Fit for ordinary purpose is seller regularly sells
    - o Fit for buyer's special purpose if seller knows

    - o Look for "as is" / "with all faults" to disclaim implied warranties
    - o Look for limitation of remedies of express warranties

IV.   SELLER'S **PERFORMANCE** OF SALE OF GOODS CONTRACT

#1   Perfect tender (read literally)

#2   Rejection of goods option for buyer if not perfect tender unless installment contract

#3   Rejection limited by seller's option to cure if
- Early delivery
- Reasonable in light of past deals

#4   Rejection not possible after acceptance
- Buyer's payment without opportunity to inspect not acceptance
- Buyer's keeping goods without objection is acceptance

#5   Revocation of acceptance
- Substantial impairment (i.e., something really bad wrong)
- Not discoverable earlier

V.   BREACH OF CONTRACT **REMEDIES**

#1   Specific performance
- Only if money damages inadequate
- Generally wrong answer

#2   Reclamation
- Delivery of goods on credit to buyer insolvent at time of receipt
- Timely (generally 10 days from buyer's receipt of goods)

#3   Money damages
- Generally expectation damages – compensate by putting P in same position as if contract had been performed without breach
  - o #1 Determine dollar result of performance without breach
  - o #2 Determine dollar result of performance with breach
  - o #3 Compare #1 and #2
- More than one question on consequential damages
  - o Look for special facts about buyer that caused it to sustain special loss

o Recoverable only if other party knew special facts at time of contract

o Remember Conviser and Rove in their sets of leathers

VI. **THINGS HAPPENING AFTER CONTRACT THAT EXCUSE PERFORMANCE**

#1 Other party's material breach

#2 Other party's anticipatory repudiation
- Unequivocal words or conduct.
- Watch for whether nonrepudiating party had already performed to determine when there can be recovery of money damages

#3 Nonoccurrence of express condition
- Determining whether there is an express condition
   o Modifies other contract duties, not create new duties
   o **If, only if, provided that, so long as, in the event that, unless, when, until, and on condition that**
   o IF IN DOUBT, not a condition
- Strict compliance test for satisfying condition.
- Excuse of condition: focus on word or conduct of person protected by condition
   o Waiver
   o Prevention

#4 Later agreement
- Accord AND satisfaction
   o If no satisfaction, liability under accord OR original deal
   o Distinguish substituted agreement from accord and satisfaction
- Novation
   o Mutually agreed upon replacement party that excuses
   o Distinguish novation from delegation

#5 Later occurrences that affect the ABILITY to perform or MUTUALLY
     UNDERSTOOD PURPOSE of performance
- Death of party generally not an excuse
- Later illegality of performance of purpose generally an excuse
- Destruction of subject matter of contract is two part reading comprehension test
   o First, reading facts, what is the contract performance obligation
   o Second, comprehending facts, how does later occurrence affect ability to perform
- Later performance becoming more expensive is no excuse.

VII. **THIRD PARTY PROBLEMS**

#1 Third party beneficiary

- Like life insurance: two people contracting with "intent" to benefit third party
- On bar, intended third party beneficiary will be named in contract
- Promisor is contract party whose promise more directly benefits third party.
- Third party can recover from promisor
- Alternatively, promise can recover from promisor.
- Third party cannot recover from promise on the contract

#2   Assignment
- Two people contracting and then later, one of the two (the assignor) transfers to a third party (the assignee) his rights under the contract against the other party to that contract (the obligor).
- No consideration required for assignments but assignments without consideration can be revoked and have no implied warranties
- Assignment cannot "substantially change duties of obligor"
  - o Not an issue in assignment of right to payment
  - o Issue in assignment of right to services
- Contract provisions usually treated as prohibition which means that assignee who did not know of contract prohibition still has rights of assignee
- Assignee can recover from obligor.
- Assignor cannot recover from obligor unless assignment was without consideration.
- Obligor has same defenses against assignee as it would have against assignor
- Multiple assignments
  - o Last in time if none for consideration
  - o Otherwise, first assignee for consideration

#3   Delegation
- Two or more people contracting and then later one of the two transfers duty to perform
- Need to be able to distinguish (1) a delegation and assignment from (2) a delegation for consideration.
- Delegatee is legally obligated only if delegation and assignment or delegation for consideration.
- Delegating party is always liable after delegation.

Concluding Advice

1.   Read the Conviser Mini Review.

2.   Epstein's top 11 for 2011

     #1 Statute of Frauds

#2 Parol evidence rule
#3 Money damages
#4 Revocation of offer
#5 Rejection of goods/Revocation of acceptance of goods
#6 Delegation/Novation
#7 Third party beneficiary
#8 Rejection of offer
#9 Assignment
#10 Warranty
#11 Risk of Loss

3.   Whenever you are in Charlottesville, Virginia, eat at my sons' restaurant, EPPIES on the Downtown Mall, eppiesrestaurant.com.

Corporations

Professor Michael Kaufman

CALIFORNIA CORPORATIONS

TEACHING HYPOTHETICALS

By Professor Michael Kaufman
Loyola University Chicago School of Law

Six test issues:
1. corporate formation
2. issuance of stock
3. action by and liability of directors and officers
4. rights of shareholders
5. fundamental corporate changes
6. federal securities laws

I. CORPORATE FORMATION

A. PRE-INCORPORATION CONTRACTS -- PROMOTERS AND SUBSCRIBERS

1. **Promoters** -- Promoters are persons acting on behalf of a corporation not yet formed.

   a. The <u>corporation</u> becomes liable on a promoter's preincorporation contract when the corporation <u>adopts</u> the contract by:

   1) _____; or

   2) _____

   _____

   b. The <u>promoter</u> remains liable on pre-incorporation contracts until there has been a <u>novation</u>; *i.e.,* an agreement between the promoter, the corporation, and the other contracting party that the corporation will replace the promoter under the contract.

1) Who is liable if the promoter enters a contract, and the corporation is never formed?

_____

_____

2) Who is liable if the promoter enters a pre-incorporation contract, and the corporation is formed, but merely adopts the contract?

_____

_____

c.   Promoters are <u>fiduciaries</u> of each other and the corporation. Therefore, promoters cannot make a <u>secret</u> <u>profit</u> on their dealings with the corporation.

1) Sale to corporation of property acquired by promoter <u>before</u> becoming a promoter: profit recoverable by corporation only if sold for more than fair market value.

2) Sale to corporation of property acquired by promoter <u>after</u> becoming a promoter: any profit recoverable by the corporation.

On January 10, Paula begins working as a promoter for the Vegan Corned-Beef Deli, Inc. On March 10, Paula buys a ton of vegan corned-beef for $10,000. On April 3, Paula sells the vegan corned-beef to the corporation for $20,000. May the corporation sue Paula? _____

_____

_____

2.   <u>Subscribers</u> -- Persons or entities who make written offers to buy stock from a corporation not yet formed.

1/10, S signs a preincorporation subscription agreement, offering to buy 100 shares of C Corp., a corporation not yet formed. One week later, S changes her mind. Can S revoke?

_____

_____

B.   FORMATION REQUIREMENTS – DE JURE CORPORATE STATUS

1.   **Incorporators**

_____

_____

2.   The Articles <u>must</u> include:

a.   *Authorized shares* – _____

_____

b.   *Purpose*

1)   <u>general</u> purpose and <u>perpetual</u> duration - presumed

Can the articles of Bubba's Bountiful Biscuits, Inc. indicate that the corporation's purpose is to "engage in all lawful activity in perpetuity"?

_____

_____

_____

2)   Specific statement of purpose and ultra vires rules

What if the articles of Bubba's Bountiful Biscuits, Inc. indicate that the corporation's purpose is to "sell Southern-style sausage biscuits" and the corporation later sells T-Shirts as well as the biscuits? Selling T-shirts is an ultra vires activity. What are the consequences?

_____

_____

_____

_____

_____

c.   *Agent* -- and address of registered office (registered agent is the corporation's official legal representative)

     d.   ***Incorporators***

     e.   ***Name of corporation***

         Can I form a corporation with the name Bubba's Bountiful Biscuits?

         _____

3.   By-Laws – The corporation need not adopt By-laws. The board has the power to adopt and amend the by-laws, unless the Articles give the power to the Shareholders.

C.   DE FACTO CORPORATION DOCTRINE

A business failing to achieve <u>de jure</u> corporate status nonetheless is treated as a corporation, if the organizers have made a good faith, colorable attempt to comply with corporate formalities and have no <u>knowledge</u> of the lack of corporate status.

D.   LEGAL SIGNIFICANCE OF FORMATION OF CORPORATION

1.   A corporation is a separate legal person.

2.   **Generally, shareholders are not personally liable for debts of corporation.** This is the principle of limited liability, which means that the shareholder is liable only for the price of her stock.

E.   PIERCING THE CORPORATE VEIL

General rule: a shareholder is not liable for the debts of a corporation.

Except: *"Piercing the corporate veil"* to avoid fraud or unfairness.

1.   *Alter Ego--Failure to Observe Sufficient Corporate Formalities, or*

2.   *Undercapitalization -- Failure to Maintain Sufficient Funds to Cover Foreseeable Liabilities*

        X is the shareholder and Chief Executive Officer of Glowco, Inc., a corporation that hauls and disposes of nuclear waste. Glowco does not carry insurance. Glowco has an initial capitalization of $1,000. X commingles personal and corporate funds. V is injured when one of Glowco's trucks melts down. Can V sue X?

        _____

_____

_____

_____

_____

_____

_____

_____

_____

_____

_____

Remember: courts are generally more willing to PCV for a tort victim than for a contract claimant.

F.   FOREIGN CORPORATIONS

A corporation incorporated outside the state that wishes to engage in regular intrastate

business must qualify by filing a Certificate of Authority with the Secretary of State that

includes: _____.

II.   ISSUANCE OF STOCK –
WHEN A CORPORATION SELLS ITS OWN STOCK

A.   CONSIDERATION -- what must the corporation receive when it issues stock?

1.   *par value* means "_____"

C Corp. is selling 10,000 shares of $3 par stock. It must receive at least

_____

2.   *acquiring property with par value stock*

Can C Corp. issue 5,000 shares of $3 par stock to acquire Green Acres?

_____

_____

3. *no par* means "no minimum issuance price." Therefore: _____

    _____

    _____

4. *treasury stock*

    Treasury stock is stock that was previously issued and had been reacquired by the corporation. It can then be re-sold. Treasury stock is deemed to be:

    _____

    C Corp. is selling $3 par treasury stock. It must receive at least:

    _____

    _____

5. *consequences of issuing par stock for less than par value*

    C Corp. issues 10,000 shares of $3 par to X for $22,000.

    Can C Corp. recover $8,000 from its directors?

    _____

    _____

    Can C Corp. recover $8,000 from X?

    _____

    _____

B. PREEMPTIVE RIGHTS

1. What are preemptive rights?

    Preemptive right is the right of **an existing shareholder** to maintain her percentage of ownership by buying stock whenever there is a **new issuance** of stock for **cash**.

S owns 1,000 shares of C Corp. There are 5,000 shares outstanding. C Corp. is planning to issue an additional 3,000 shares for cash. If S has preemptive rights, then S has the right to

_____

_____

_____

2. What if the articles of incorporation are silent or the bar exam question does not indicate whether the articles of C Corp. provide for preemptive rights?

_____

_____

III. DIRECTORS AND OFFICERS

A. STATUTORY REQUIREMENTS-DIRECTORS

1. Corporations must have a Board with at least _____ member.

2. Shareholders elect directors.

3. Shareholders can <u>remove</u> a director before her term expires. On what basis?

_____

4. *Valid Meeting*

   a. Unless all directors consent in writing to act without a meeting, a meeting is required.

   b. *Notice* of directors' meeting can be set in bylaws.

   c. *Proxies* are not allowed. Also, no voting agreements. But conference calls now generally valid

   d. *Quorum* -- must have a majority of *all* directors to take action (unless a different percentage is required in bylaws).

   e. *Vote* -- To pass a resolution, however, all that is required is a majority vote of those *present*.

      So, if there are 9 directors, at least _____ directors must attend the meeting to constitute a quorum. If 5 directors attend, at least _____ must vote for a resolution in order for it to pass.

      f.   Each director is presumed to have concurred in Board action unless her dissent or abstention is recorded <u>in writing</u> (i.e. minutes or letter to corporate secretary).

B.   LIABILITY OF DIRECTORS TO THEIR OWN CORPORATION AND SHAREHOLDERS

1.   Directors have a ***duty to manage*** the corporation. Directors may delegate management functions to a committee of one or more directors that recommends action to the Board.

2.   In managing the corporation, the directors are protected from liability by the ***Business Judgment Rule.*** The ***Business Judgment Rule*** is a presumption that the directors manage the corporation in good faith and in the best interests of the corporation and its shareholders. As such, directors will not be liable for innocent mistakes of business judgment.

3.   Directors, however, are <u>fiduciaries</u> who owe the corporation duties of care and loyalty.

4.   **Duty of Care** -- A director owes the corporation a duty of care. She must act with the care that a **prudent** person would use with regard to her own business, unless the Articles have limited director liability for a breach of the duty of care.

      Heffner, a director of Hedonists' Hot Tubs, Inc., after studying the issue thoroughly, votes to hire a religious singing ensemble to promote the company's line of hot tubs with built-in wine coolers and video cameras. The idea is a disaster. Has Heffner breached his duty of care?

_____

_____

_____

_____

_____

_____

_____

_____

5. **Duty of Loyalty** -- a director owes the corporation a duty of loyalty. A director may not receive an <u>unfair</u> benefit to the detriment of the corporation or its shareholders, unless there has been material <u>disclosure</u> and <u>independent ratification</u>.

    a.   <u>Self-dealing</u> -- director who receives an unfair benefit to herself (or her relative, or another one of her businesses) in a transaction with her own corporation.

    b.   <u>Usurping corporate opportunities</u> -- director receives an unfair benefit by usurping for herself an opportunity which the corporation would have pursued.

    c.   <u>Ratification</u> -- Directors may defend a claim by obtaining <u>independent</u> ratification through: (a) a majority vote of <u>independent</u> directors, (b) majority vote of a committee of at least 2 <u>independent</u> directors, or (c) majority vote of shares held by <u>independent</u> shareholders.

Alice, one of ten directors of Diamond Merchants Inc., spots choice diamonds and buys them for herself for $1 million. Alice then resells those diamonds to her corporation for $2 million. Alice, however, disclosed her conduct to the Board, and at a Board meeting attended by the other 9 board members, 5 of the members voted to ratify her transaction. What liabilities, if any, does Alice have?

_____

_____

C.   OFFICERS

1.   Owe same duties of care and loyalty as directors

2.   Are <u>agents</u> of the corporation and bind the corporation by their authorized activities

3.   Corporations must have a President, Secretary and Treasurer

4.   Directors have virtually unlimited power to select officers, and may remove them from office at any time – but the corporation will be liable for breach of contract damages.

D.   INDEMNIFICATION OF DIRECTORS AND OFFICERS

Director or Officer has incurred costs, attorneys' fees, fines, a judgment or settlement in the course of corporate business; she seeks reimbursement from the corporation.

1.   The corporation may **NEVER** indemnify a director who:

_____

2.   The corporation **MUST ALWAYS** indemnify if:

_____

3.   The corporation **MAY** indemnify if:

a.   Liability to third-parties or <u>settlement</u> with the corporation.

b.   Director or officer shows that she acted in good faith and that she believed her conduct was in the corporation's best interest.

c.   Who may determine whether to grant permissive indemnity?

1)   _____

2)   _____

3)   _____ ; or

4)   _____

IV. RIGHTS OF SHAREHOLDERS

A. SHAREHOLDER DERIVATIVE SUITS

1. In a derivative suit, a shareholder is suing to enforce the *corporation's* cause of action.

    Always ask: could the corporation have brought this suit? If so, it's a derivative suit.

2. What are the requirements for bringing a shareholder derivative suit?

    a. *contemporaneous stock ownership*

    _____

    _____

    _____

    b. *must generally make demand on directors* that they cause their own corporation to bring suit

    _____

    _____

    _____

B. VOTING

1. *Who has the right to vote at an upcoming meeting where voting occurs?*

    _____

    _____

    _____

2. *Shareholder Voting by Proxies*

    a proxy is a (i) writing (fax or e-mail generally valid), (ii) signed by record shareholder, (iii) directed to secretary of corporation, (iv) authorizing another to vote the shares; (v) valid for only 11 months.

On June 2, S, who is the record owner on the record date, sends a signed letter to secretary of C Corp. authorizing Alice to vote her shares. Can Alice vote S's shares at the annual meeting in July?

_____

_____

_____

What if, prior to the meeting, S writes to the secretary of C Corp. that she now wants Betty to vote her shares at that meeting?

_____

_____

_____

Can S revoke her proxy even though it states that it is irrevocable?

_____

_____

S (the record owner) sells B her shares after the record date but before the annual meeting. S gives B an irrevocable proxy to vote the shares at the annual meeting. Can S revoke this proxy?

_____

_____

_____

3. *Where do shareholders vote?*

   a. properly noticed annual meeting

   _____

   _____

   _____

b. specially noticed special meeting (called by the board, the president or the holders of 10% of voting shares)

_____

_____

_____

_____

4. **QUORUM:** There must be a quorum represented at the meeting. Determination of a quorum focuses on the number of *shares* represented, not the number of shareholders. A quorum requires a majority of outstanding shares when the meeting begins, unless otherwise provided in Articles.

X Corp. has 120,000 shares outstanding. X Corp. has 700 shareholders. What or who constitutes a quorum?

_____

_____

_____

_____

5. **VOTE**: If quorum is present, action is approved if the votes cast in favor of the proposal exceed the votes cast against the proposal.

X Corp. has 120,000 shares outstanding. 80,000 shares are represented at the meeting, but only 50,000 shares vote on a particular proposal. How many shares must vote *for* the proposal in order for it to be accepted by the shareholders?

_____

_____

_____

_____

6. *Pooled or Block Voting Methods*

Shareholders who own relatively few voting shares decide that they can increase their influence by agreeing to vote alike. How can they do so?

a. Voting Trusts _____

_____

_____

b. Shareholder Voting Agreements _____

_____

_____

_____

7. **CUMULATIVE VOTING FOR DIRECTORS**

a. You own 1,000 shares of stock in C Corp. C Corp has nine directorships open for election. You believe that Martha Stewart should be director of C Corp.

1) Under traditional, straight voting, how many votes can you cast for Martha?

_____

2) Under cumulative voting, you may multiply the number of shares times the number of directors to be elected:

_____

_____

_____

b. The articles of C. Corp. are silent as to whether shareholders can vote cumulatively. Can C's shareholders still vote cumulatively?

_____

_____

C. **RIGHT OF SHAREHOLDER TO EXAMINE THE BOOKS AND RECORDS OF THE CORPORATION - ANY SHAREHOLDER SHALL HAVE ACCESS UPON NOTICE AND AT PROPER TIMES.**

D. **DIVIDENDS** (to be declared in Board's <u>discretion</u> unless the corporation is <u>insolvent</u> or would be rendered insolvent by the dividend) (Board members are liable personally for unlawful distributions, but have a defense of good faith reliance on financial officer's representations regarding solvency).

1. *Priority of Distribution*

The board of directors of C Corp. decides to declare dividends totaling $400,000.

Who receives dividends if the outstanding stock is:

a. 100,000 shares of common stock

_____

b. 100,000 shares of common and 20,000 shares of preferred with $2 dividend preference

_____

_____

_____

c. 100,000 shares of common and 20,000 shares of $2 preferred that are participating

_____

_____

_____

_____

d. 100,000 shares of common and 20,000 shares of $2 preferred that are cumulative (and no dividends in the three prior years)

_____

_____

_____

E. SHAREHOLDER AGREEMENTS TO ELIMINATE CORPORATE FORMALITIES (CLOSELY-HELD CORPORATIONS)

1.   Requirements: _____

_____

_____

_____

2.   Consequences: _____

_____

_____

_____

F. PROFESSIONAL CORPORATIONS

1.   Licensed Professionals (i.e., lawyers, accountants, medical professionals) may incorporate as Professional Corporation ("PC").

2.   Requirements:

    a.   Organizers file Articles with name designated "Professional Corporation" or "PC."

    b.   The shareholders must be licensed professionals.

    c.   The corporation may practice only one designated profession.

3.   Consequences:

    a.   The professionals are liable personally for their own malpractice.

    b.   But, the professionals are not liable personally for each other's malpractice or the obligations of the corporation itself.

G. SHAREHOLDER LIABILITIES

1.   As a rule: shareholders are not liable for corporate obligations

2.   Except:

    a.   Piercing the corporate veil to render shareholder liable;

    b.   <u>Controlling</u> shareholders owe a fiduciary duty to minority shareholders; and

    c.   Controlling shareholders are liable for selling corporation to a party who <u>loots</u> the corporation, unless reasonable measures were taken to investigate the buyer's reputation and plans for the corporation.

V.   FUNDAMENTAL CORPORATE CHANGES

A.   RECOGNIZED FUNDAMENTAL CORPORATE CHANGES

1.   Merger (A becomes B); Consolidation (A and B become C); Dissolution (A dissolves)

2.   <u>Fundamental</u> (not ministerial) Amendment of the Articles; <u>Sale</u> (not purchase) of Substantially All of the Corporation's Assets

B.   PROCEDURAL STEPS

1.   Resolution by Board at a Valid Meeting.

2.   Notice of Special Meeting

3.   Approval by _____ of all _____ to vote, and by

    _____

    _____

    _____

    <u>Except:</u>   No shareholder approval required for "short-form" merger where a parent corporation that owns 90% or more of the stock in its subsidiary merges with the subsidiary.

4.   Possibility of dissenting shareholder right of appraisal.

    a.   A shareholder who does not vote in favor of a fundamental change has the right to force the corporation to buy her shares at fair value.

    b.   actions by shareholder to perfect the right

<ol>
<li>Before shareholder vote, file written notice of objection and intent to demand payment;</li>
<li>Do not vote in favor of the proposed change;</li>
<li>Make prompt written demand to be bought out.</li>
</ol>

    c.   What happens if the shareholder and the corporation cannot agree on fair value?

---

5.   File Notice with the State (i.e., Articles of Merger)

VI.   FEDERAL SECURITIES LAW CONSIDERATIONS

A.   ANTI-FRAUD--SECTION 10(b) OF THE SECURITIES EXCHANGE ACT OF 1934

1.   The essential elements of a §10(b) action are:

    a.   <u>Scienter</u> -- _____

    b.   <u>Deception</u> --

        1)   <u>Liar</u> – misrepresentation of a material fact, or failure to disclose a material fact in breach of a fiduciary duty to disclose.

        2)   <u>Insider Trading</u> –

            a)   <u>Misappropriator</u> – one who misappropriates (_i.e._ steals, converts) material nonpublic information and uses it to purchase or sell securities;

            b)   <u>Tipper</u> -- one who tips inside information for <u>personal benefit</u> to another who trades on it; or

            c)   <u>Tippee</u> -- one who receives inside information and trades on it with <u>knowledge</u> that the information was disclosed in breach of the tipper's fiduciary duty..

    c.   In connection with the <u>actual</u> purchase or sale of securities.

2.   In addition, in a private action for damages, investors must also prove:

    a.   <u>Reliance</u> – investors actually relied on fraud, or invested at a market price infected by fraud (_i.e._ fraud on the market).

    b.   <u>Loss Causation</u> – the fraud not only induced investors to purchase or sell, but also caused their economic losses.

Ronco Corp. intentionally issues a misleading press release that Pickens has expressed an interest in acquiring a major block of its stock. The release fails to indicate that it is Slim Pickens and not Boone Pickens who is interested. In reliance on this press release, Conviser does not sell his Ronco stock. Does Conviser have a Section 10(b) cause of action?

_____

_____

_____

_____

_____

B.   **SECTION 16(b)—SHORT-SWING TRADING PROFITS**

    1.   When does 16(b) apply?

        a.   Big corporations: Reporting corporation – (1) listed on a national exchange or (2) at least 500 shareholders and $10 million in assets

        b.   Big shot defendant--officer, director, or more than ten percent shareholder

        c.   Type of transaction

            buying and selling stock within a single six-month period (short-swing trading) [Fraud is not required. No requirement of inside information.]

    2.   What happens when 16(b) applies?

All "profits" from such "short-swing trading" are recoverable by the corporation. If, <u>within six months</u> before or after <u>any sale</u>, there was a <u>purchase at a lower price than the sale price</u>, there is a <u>profit</u>.

C. SARBANES-OXLEY ACT OF 2002

1. Reporting Corporations

2. CEO and CFO must **certify** that based on the Officer's **knowledge**, reports filed with the Securities and Exchange Commission (SEC) do not contain falsehoods.

3. Willfully certifying a false report could bring $5 million fine and 20 years.

4. If false reports have to be corrected and restated, the corporation (directly or derivatively) may recover Officer's benefits made from trading the company's securities within 12 months after the false reports were filed, and may recover incentive-based compensation received during that period.

5. Corporations (directly or derivatively) may also recover any benefits made by officers from trading corporation's stock during "black out" periods when employees are prohibited from trading in their retirement plan's securities.

6. Therefore: _____

_____

MINI REVIEW

I.   Formation: _____

_____

_____

_____

II.   Issuance: _____

_____

III.   Dir./Off/Liability: _____

_____

_____

_____

IV.   Shareholder Rights:

      1.   Derivative Suits: _____

      2.   Voting: _____

      3.   Proxies: _____

      4.   Quorum: _____

      5.   Vote: _____

      6.   Cumulative Voting: _____

      7.   Dividends: _____

_____

_____

      8.   Eliminating Formalities (Closely-held): _____

_____

_____

      9.   PC: _____

V.   Fundamental Changes: _____

_____

_____

VI.   Federal Securities Laws:

   1.   §10(b): _____

   2.   §16(b): _____

   3.   SOA: _____

   _____

Criminal Law

Professor Robert Hull

CRIMINAL LAW

By Professor Bob Hull

OVERVIEW

PART ONE: CRIMES AGAINST THE PERSON

Criminal Homicide Crimes: Murder and Manslaughter

Other Person Crimes: Assault, Battery, Kidnapping

PART TWO: CRIMES AGAINST PROPERTY

Theft Crimes: Larceny, Embezzlement, False Pretenses, Robbery

Structure Crimes: Arson and Burglary

PART THREE: PRELIMINARY CRIMES

Attempt, Solicitation, Conspiracy

PART FOUR: ACCOMPLICE LIABILITY

PART FIVE: DEFENSES AND STATE OF MIND

PART ONE: CRIMES AGAINST THE PERSON

Criminal Homicide Crimes: Murder and Manslaughter

I.   **Murder: A** _____**committed with** _____.

     A.   **Homicide:** Killing of another human caused by the defendant.

          1.   "Caused by the defendant"

              a.   Defendant acted _____ to cause death.

              b.   Defendant's _____ caused death and defendant by statute, contract, relationship or voluntary undertaking had a duty to act.

              c.   Act of a _____ contributed to cause death.

                 1)   Vicarious liability: A defendant may be liable for the crime of another if the defendant (1) _____ the crime; or (2) an _____ with the one who commits the crime; (3) is an _____ to the one who commits the crime; or (4) under the _____.

                 2)   Was the third party act _____?

EXAMPLE: Defendant shoots victim and victim rushed to hospital. Surgeon negligently attempts to remove bullet and victim dies as a result. Non-negligent surgery would have saved victim's life. Defendant is still an actual and proximate cause of death (as is Surgeon too) because intervening _____ is _____ and Defendant is criminally liable for the homicide.

              d.   Death was a _____ of defendant's act or omission.

B. **Malice:** The mental state required for murder.

1. Intent to kill

   a. Defendant's words

   b. Deadly weapon doctrine: Use of a deadly weapon in a _____.

2. Intent to inflict _____.

3. Depraved heart: Reckless indifference to _____ high risk of death

EXAMPLE (Depraved heart): A shoots a gun at a target in a vacant lot, knowing that houses are in range. Bullet misses target and kills person in the house.

COMPARE (No depraved heart): A shoots a gun at an abandoned commercial building at midnight. Unknown to A, a homeless man was asleep in the building and is killed by A's bullet.

4. Felony Murder Rule: Homicide committed during the perpetration of an _____ felony.

   a. During the perpetration: From _____ until felon reaches a place of _____.

   b. Inherently dangerous felonies: Burglary, Arson, Rape, Robbery and Kidnapping (BARRK)

      1. Minority rule: Some states also include _____ felonies committed in a _____ manner.

EXAMPLE: Swindler induces terminal cancer patient to pay for worthless herbal cure Swindler misrepresents as a miracle cure. Patient forgoes proper medical treatment in reliance. Patient dies.

Swindler's crime (false pretenses) is not "inherently dangerous" but was committed in a dangerous manner sufficient under minority rule to uphold a felony murder conviction.

c.   Felony must be _____ from the act that caused death:

EXAMPLE (No independent felony):   A shoves B into a glass window (Battery). The battery felony is the act that caused B's death cannot be used to support a felony murder charge against A.
Note: This would be _____ .

EXAMPLE (Independent felony): A broke and entered B's home intending to steal from B (Burglary). While inside, B startled A and A stabbed and killed B. The burglary is an independent felony and can be used to support a felony murder charge against A.

d.   A defense to the felony is a defense to a felony murder charge.

EXAMPLE: A holds a gun to B's head and says "burn down C's house or I will kill you." While A aims the gun at him, B sets fire to C's house. Unknown to B, C was asleep in the house and died in the fire. B cannot be convicted of felony murder for the death of C based on arson as the underlying felony because duress is a defense to arson.

e.   Vicarious Liability: All felons are liable for death caused by a co-felon.

   No felony murder under majority rule if _____ (police officer, store owner, etc.) kills a _____ .

   Some states will excuse felons from felony murder liability if a non-felon kills another non-felon while resisting the felony.

EXAMPLE: Felon holds up storeowner at gunpoint, storeowner attempts to shoot felon but shot misses and kills shopper. Some states will find felons liable for felony murder, others will not.

f.   Proximate cause: The felony must be the proximate cause of the homicide (i.e., the homicide must be a foreseeable result of the felony).

EXAMPLE (Foreseeable): A and B commit a bank robbery and speed away from the bank with the police in hot pursuit. While speeding, the felons' car strikes a kills a pedestrian in a crosswalk. The death of the pedestrian is a foreseeable result of the felony. A and B will both be liable for felony murder.

COMPARE: (Not foreseeable): A and B commit a bank robbery. While driving slowly and carefully away from the bank, their car strikes and kills a child who suddenly ran directly into their path. The death of the child is an unforeseeable result of the felony. The felons will not be liable for felony murder.

C.   **Involuntary Manslaughter:** A homicide committed _____ _____ under one of the three following circumstances.

  1.   Intent to inflict _____ bodily injury: Defendant kills victim with no intent to kill or seriously injure, but did have intent to inflict some slight bodily injury. This is typically a non-aggravated (no weapon) battery or assault that causes death of victim.

  2.   Criminal _____: Defendant kills victim while acting in a more than ordinary negligent manner but the Defendant's conduct does not present a high enough risk of death for depraved heart recklessness. Defendant's conduct is a "gross deviation" from the standard of care that a reasonable person would observe.

EXAMPLES: (1) Defendant shoots a bullet at a distant passing freight train and kills a transient who was hiding in a freight car. (2) While driving 85 MPH (20 MPH over speed limit), Defendant unable to avoid striking another vehicle and kills the other driver.

3.   "Misdemeanor-Manslaughter" Rule: Defendant kills while committing a _____ (i.e., felony not sufficient for felony murder rule) or a _____ (inherently wrongful) _____ as opposed to a malum prohibitum (wrongful only because prohibited by statute) crime.

EXAMPLE (Non-inherently dangerous felony): Defendant sells an unregistered stolen rifle (a statutory felony). While arguing with the buyer the Defendant accidentally pulls the trigger, killing the buyer. Defendant can be charged with involuntary manslaughter.

EXAMPLES OF MALUM IN SE: Killings that occur while the defendant was committing misdemeanor battery, larceny, public intoxication, or in possession of drugs have been found to be malum prohibitum and <u>sufficient</u> for involuntary manslaughter.

EXAMPLES OF MALUM PROHIBITUM: A killing that occurs while the defendant was driving on a suspended license, passing through a toll gate without paying the toll, unlawfully possessing a firearm, or unlawfully defacing the flag is not sufficient for involuntary manslaughter.

D. **Justification:** If a homicide (or any other crime) is justified, the defendant is _____ or the crime.

1. Self-Defense: The defendant may use _____ to protect against an imminent deadly attack. Deadly force must be _____ and _____ to repel the attacker.

   a. No duty to retreat: The defendant need not retreat before using deadly force, unless defendant is the _____(started the fight), and safe retreat is available.

      1) Minority rule: Defendant must retreat before using deadly force if safe retreat available, unless Defendant in his/her home, a police officer, or victim of a violent felony.

   b. Defendant is the initial aggressor: Defendant cannot assert self-defense as a justification unless:

      1) The defendant initial aggressor _____ clearly communicates to victim intent to stop fighting).

      2) The defendant initially used _____ force and is now faced with attacker suddenly using deadly force.

      3) If _____ is available, the initial aggressor must retreat before using deadly force.

2. Defense of others: Defendant can use deadly force if _____ to defend another.

    a. "Victim" not entitled to self-defense: Can a defendant use deadly force to protect a criminal or initial aggressor who had no right to use self-defense against their "attacker"?

    Under the majority rule, a defendant may claim defense of others if the victim _____ to have the right to use deadly force, even if the "other" does not actually have that right.

    Under the minority rule, a defendant can use no more force than the person they are defending ("_____ of person defended")

EXAMPLE: D encounters Victim who appears to be under unjustified violent attack by C. Under the majority rule, D may use deadly force if necessary and reasonable to defend Victim, regardless of whether Victim was the initial deadly aggressor or if C was an undercover police officer making a lawful arrest of Victim. Under the minority rule, D stands in the shoes of Victim and cannot use deadly force to defend Victim unless Victim was privileged to use deadly force in self-defense.

3. Crime Prevention: A police officer or private person may use deadly force if reasonably necessary to prevent the commission of a _____.

4. Apprehension/Arrest of Criminal: A police officer or private person may use deadly force if reasonably necessary to prevent apprehend/arrest a _____ _____.

NOTE: A private citizen can only use deadly force if the person apprehended with deadly force is actually guilty of the dangerous felony. A private citizen is not entitled to make a reasonable mistake (we don't encourage vigilantism).

5. Reasonable Mistake: A defendant may use deadly force based on a reasonable mistake as to self-defense, defense of others (majority only), and crime prevention. Only a _____can use deadly force to apprehend or arrest based on a reasonable mistake.

6. Defense of Habitation/Property: As a general rule, a defendant cannot use deadly force to protect home or other property.

    a. Exception: Deadly force can be used to protect occupants of home from violent intruder or if intruder intends to commit a felony inside.

E. Excuse: If a homicide (or any other crime) is excused, the defendant is _____for the crime.

1. Youth/Infancy: Common law rules apply.

    a. Under age of 7: No criminal liability.

    b. Between 7 and 14: Rebuttable presumption of no criminal liability.

    c. Over 14: Treated as an adult.

    NOTE: All states have juvenile or family courts to adjudicate criminal cases against minors.

2. Insanity: There are four tests that can apply (and on the essay points are awarded for discussing all four).

    a. M'Naghten or "Right/Wrong" test:

        1) Defendant, as a result of mental defect, did not know the _____OR could not _____ the _____ and _____of his acts.
            NOTE: Focus is on _____ impairment, not _____ability.

9

b.   Irresistible Impulse test:

    1)   Defendant, as a result of mental defect, was unable to
_____ his conduct or _____ his
conduct to the law.
NOTE: Focus is on volitional ability, not cognitive. Need not
be sudden event.

c.   ALI/Model Penal Code Test:

    1)   Defendant lacked the _____
either to appreciate the _____of his conduct or to
_____to the requirements of
the law.
NOTE: Focus is on both volitional (conform conduct) and
cognitive (appreciate wrongfulness).

d.   Durham Test: (No longer followed anywhere, but still worth 5 points
on an essay to discuss it.)

    1)   Defendant is not guilty if his crime was the _____
of a mental disease or defect.

3.   Intoxication: If the defendant is intoxicated (alcohol, illegal or legal
drugs, etc.) at the time of the crime, the intoxication may excuse
criminal liability.

    a.   Voluntary intoxication: Exists when the defendant
_____and _____ consumes an
intoxicating substance. Voluntary intoxication is _____
to crimes requiring no intent (strict liability), _____
criminal intent or _____.

However, voluntary intoxication can negate _____
intent but only if the defendant is so intoxicated he cannot form
the specific intent required for the crime. It can also preclude a
finding of _____ if the Defendant is charged
with First Degree Murder.

b.   Involuntary intoxication: Exists when the defendant
_____ (forced to consume) or
_____ (voluntarily consume without
knowledge substance consumed was an intoxicant).
Involuntary intoxication is a defense to all crimes if the
intoxication renders the defendant "insane" under the
applicable test.

NOTE: A minority of states recognize a _____
defense where evidence of defendant's mental defect while
insufficient for insanity, is admissible to prove the defendant
did not have or could not form the intent required for the crime.

F.   Mitigation: An intentional killing that would otherwise be
murder will be mitigated to _____
under both of the following situations:

1.   Provocation: An intentional killing will be mitigated to
voluntary manslaughter if the defendant experiences
_____. The provocative act must
be one that would cause both subjective and objective
passion and no "cooling off" occurred.

a. Subjective passion: The defendant must have been
_____ losing self-control and
did not _____ before killing the victim.

b. Objective passion: The provocation must be one that
would have caused a _____ to lose
self-control and a reasonable person would not have
cooled off in the time lapse between the provocation and
the time of the killing.

EXAMPLES OF "REASONABLE" PROVOCATION:
Defendant's who are struck by the victim who inflicts a "staggering
blow" to the defendant or if the defendant "catches spouse in act of
adultery" with the victim.

11

2. Good Faith Mistake: A defendant who intentionally kills victim under good faith, but _____, mistaken belief as to _____ (so-called "imperfect self defense"), _____ or _____ can successfully argue their homicide crime should be mitigated to voluntary manslaughter.

G. **Degrees of Murder:** At common law there were no degrees of murder. However, by statute today all states have at least two degrees of murder.

1. First Degree Murder: There are two common types of first degree murder:

   a. Premeditated and Deliberate Intent to Kill:

      1) Premeditated: The intent to kill is premeditated if the defendant had _____ (even for a brief few seconds) to think about killing the victim before doing so.

      2) Deliberate: The intent to kill is deliberate if the defendant acted in a _____ frame of mind ("cold blooded").

NOTE: Usually, deliberation is the bigger issue. If the defendant was at all angry, excited or suffering any type of mental disturbance, that will likely lead to a finding the killing was not deliberate.

   b. Felony Murder Rule: A murder that satisfies the felony murder rule AND is based on one of the _____ if the state's first degree murder _____ (usually BARRK felonies) will be sufficient for first degree murder.

NOTE: First Degree Murder can only be based on malice established under intent to kill or the felony murder rule. Intent to inflict great bodily harm murder or depraved heart murder are (at most) <u>second degree</u> murder

2. Second Degree Murder: All other murders that do not qualify as first degree murder are second degree murder.

SUMMARY OF HOMICIDE CRIMES

MURDER: Homicide with malice and no justification, excuse or mitigation. Finish with degrees of murder.

INVOLUNTARY MANSLAUGHTER: Homicide without malice and no justification or excuse.

VOLUNTARY MANSLAUGHTER: Homicide with malice but with mitigation.

Other "Person" Crimes: Assault, Battery, Kidnapping

A. **Assault:** There are two kinds of criminal assault.

1. Attempted battery: Defendant attempts (but is unsuccessful) to cause imminent harmful contact with victim.

NOTE: The "attempted battery" assault is a _____ crime.

2. Intentional creation of reasonable apprehension of contact: Defendant attempts to cause victim to reasonably apprehend imminent harmful contact.

B. **Battery:** The unlawful application of force to another person causing bodily injury or offensive contact.

C. **Kidnapping:** The confinement of another person involving either _____ or _____ of the victim. (No ransom required.)

PART TWO: CRIMES AGAINST PROPERTY

Theft Crimes: Larceny, Embezzlement, False Pretenses

NOTE: All the theft crimes are specific intent crimes.

I. **LARCENY:** The trespassory taking and carrying away of the personal property of another with the intent to permanently deprive.

    A. **Tresspassory:** Defendant must take possession of victim's property without the _____ of the victim. For consent to exist, the victim must consent before the taking.

EXAMPLE (Consent of victim after taking): Defendant takes victim's watch from victim's desk when victim was in another room. When victim returns and sees Defendant wearing victim's watch, victim says, "Oh, go ahead and keep it...I was going to give it to you anyway." This consent is too late. Defendant's taking of the watch was by trespass.

    B. **Taking and Carrying Away:** Defendant must move the property as part of attempt to take possession. _____ _____ is enough!

EXAMPLE (Slight movement): Defendant knows he has no money, goes into grocery store, picks up rib-eye steak with intent to steal it, but immediately changes mind and puts steak back. This is larceny, not attempted larceny, because Defendant moved the property by trespass with intent to steal it.

    C. **Personal Property of Another:** Larceny is a crime against _____, not _____. An owner can commit larceny over property he owns if the owner gives possession of it to the victim.

EXAMPLE: Defendant owns a car and takes it to repair shop and agrees to pay for needed repairs. If Defendant later uses spare key and takes car back from repair shop without paying bill or obtaining consent from repair shop, Defendant can be charged with larceny because repair shop had rightful possession of car until repair bill paid.

D. **With intent to permanently deprive:** Defendant must have the specific intent to keep the property (no intent to return) and the intent must exist at the _____ _____.

    1. Defendant takes then abandons victim's property: The intent to permanently deprive exists if the defendant abandons the victim's property creating a _____ _____ (e.g., leaving victim's car in high crime area vs. parked in front of victim's house).

    2. Defendant takes with intent to return: The intent to permanently deprive does not exist if the defendant intends only to borrow the item and return it later. This may lead to tort liability (trespass to chattels) but is not a crime.

II. **LARCENY BY TRICK:** Same definition as larceny, but the taking occurs with the victim's apparent consent. But the consent is negated because acquired by the defendant's misrepresentation ("trick").

EXAMPLE: Defendant asks to "borrow" Victim's camera without disclosing Defendant's secret intent to steal the camera. Victim gives Defendant possession of the camera because Victim believes Defendant intends to return it. Defendant is guilty of larceny by trick.

III. **EMBEZZLEMENT:** The fraudulent conversion of the property of another by one in rightful possession.

    A. **Fraudulent conversion:** The defendant must deal with victim's property in some manner inconsistent with victim's grant of possession of the property to the defendant.

EXAMPLE: Victim (store owner) gives Defendant (store manager) the possession of the company car to drive it to and from work and to call on store customers. If Defendant takes the car on a cross-country vacation trip or loans the car to a friend to use, a fraudulent conversion has occurred.

    B. **By one in rightful possession:** The victim must first voluntarily give the defendant rightful possession of the property that the defendant _____ fraudulently converts.

IV. **FALSE PRETENSES:** The acquisition of _____ to defendant's property by a _____ with the intent to defraud.

   A. **Acquisition of Title:** The victim must intend to pass title (ownership) not just possession. This is usually when the victim intends to _____ the property to the defendant.

   B. **False representation:** Like larceny by trick, the victim is falsely induced into the transaction. But this transaction is for the passing of _____, not just possession.

V. **ROBBERY:** A larceny (same elements as above) committed from the victim's person or presence by force or threat of force of immediate bodily harm.

   A. **From victim's person or presence:** The defendant must take the property from the victim's _____ (wallet, purse) or from the victim's _____ _____ (property in same room or house is sufficient).

   B. **By force or threat of force of immediate bodily harm:** The defendant must use force or threaten immediate bodily harm to accomplish the taking (or immediately reacquire it if victim momentarily resists and retakes possession briefly).

      1. Immediate bodily harm: Threats of _____ bodily harm, or immediate or later _____ harm are not sufficient for robbery (but would be sufficient for _____).

Structure Crimes: Arson and Burglary

I. **ARSON:** The burning of a protected structure of another with malice.

   A. **Burning:** There must be some <u>charring</u> of some part of the structure (wall, ceiling, beams, etc.) caused by fire. A charring of non-fixtures (furniture, paintings, etc.) is not sufficient.

B. **Protected Structure:** At common law, the structure had to be the dwelling house of another. Today, most states protect _____ _____(residential, industrial, commercial, etc.).

C. **Of another:** The protected structure must be in the rightful _____ of another when burned. Thus, a landlord who burns a house rented to a tenant can commit arson.

D. **Malice:** A defendant is guilty of arson if committed with (1) the _____ the structure or (2) with knowledge of the _____ of the structure burning.

II. **BURGLARY:** The trespassory _____ of the protected structure of another at nighttime with the intent to commit a felony therein. (Specific intent crime)

A. **Tresspassory:** Defendant's entry into the structure must be without the consent of the rightful possessor.

B. **Breaking:** Defendant's entry into the structure must involve some _____ of a door or window or by majority rule today some use of _____ (constructive breaking) to gain entry.

EXAMPLE (No breaking): One night, Defendant intends to enter Victim's home and steal Victim's property inside. When Defendant arrives at Victim's home, the door is wide open. Defendant's entry is not a breaking.

EXAMPLE (Constructive breaking): One night, Defendant intends to enter Victim's home and steal Victim's property inside. Defendant dresses up as cable repair tech to gain entry. Even though Victim opens door and invites Defendant to enter, Defendant's entry is a breaking.

C. **Entering:** Some portion of Defendant's _____ (or some object defendant uses to commit the felony inside—a hook to steal a purse, etc.) must enter the structure.

D. Protected Structure: At common law, it had to be a dwelling of another. Today, like for arson, most states extend burglary to include _____ (residential, commercial, industrial).

E. Of another: Like arson, burglary is a crime against possession so the structure must be in the _____ of another. Again, a landlord can burglarize his own unit if the unit is rented to a tenant.

F. At night: At common law, the entry had to occur at night. Today, most states have eliminated the nighttime requirement.

G. With the intent to commit a felony therein: The intent to commit a felony must exist _____ occurs. A later formed intent to steal (after entry) does not qualify.

PART THREE: PRELIMINARY CRIMES

Attempt, Solicitation, Conspiracy (All three are Specific Intent Crimes)

I. ATTEMPT: Defendant is guilty of attempt if Defendant commits an act of perpetration with the intent to commit the intended (target) crime.

A. Act of perpetration: Defendant must do more than merely prepare to commit the crime; the defendant must take a _____ _____ toward its commission or come _____ to completing the intended crime.

B. With the intent to commit the crime: Defendant must have the specific intent to commit the target crime.

EXAMPLE (No specific intent): Defendant drives his auto at very high speed through a school zone and strikes a school child. If the child dies, Defendant is very likely guilty of murder under depraved heart malice. If the child lives, Defendant is _____ of attempted murder because _____ is the only intent sufficient for attempted murder.

C. Defenses: Merger and Impossibility

1. Merger: Attempt merges into the target crime so a defendant who actually commits the intended crime cannot be convicted and punished for both attempt and the intended crime.

2. Impossibility—Legal and Factual: If the defendant does not succeed in committing the target crime, it may be because the target crime was either legally or factually impossible. Legal impossibility is a good defense; factual impossibility is not.

   a. Legal Impossibility: Exists when the _____ defendant intends to commit are _____ in the jurisdiction.

EXAMPLE: Defendant, believing it is arson to burn down your own house, douses his home with gasoline (overt act) and is about to strike a match when arrested by the police and charged with attempted arson.
Result: Defendant is not liable for attempted arson because the acts he intended to commit had he succeeded are not the crime of arson. Since an arson conviction would be legally impossible, so is an attempted arson conviction.

   b. Factual Impossibility: Exists when the acts defendant intended to commit would be a crime, if the facts were as defendant _____ them to be.

EXAMPLE: Defendant, believing that Victim has a wallet in his back pocket, reaches into to steal the wallet but finds instead the pocket is empty. Defendant can be convicted for attempted larceny because his target crime (larceny) was only factually impossible. Had the facts been as Defendant believed (the wallet was in Victim's pocket), he would have succeeded. Thus, it is just and fair to convict him of attempted larceny.

II. **SOLICITATION:** Defendant is guilty of solicitation if Defendant _____ or _____ another to commit a crime.

    A. **Vicarious liability:** If the party solicited actually commits the requested crime, the solicitor will also be liable for the crime.

III. **CONSPIRACY:** Defendant is guilty of conspiracy if Defendant enters into an agreement with another party to for an unlawful objective and some overt act is performed in furtherance of the unlawful objective.

    A. **Agreement:** An agreement can exist by _____ or it can be _____. Co-conspirators need not meet or even know each other exist; so long as they are working toward a common unlawful goal an agreement exists.

    B. **With another party:** Majority rule requires _____ conspirators to _____ to commit the unlawful objective. An agreement with an undercover police officer who only feigns agreement is not a conspiracy.

        Minority rule (MPC) follows the _____ conspiracy rule and provides that "one guilty mind" is enough for conspiracy if the guilty mind believed the other party was actually agreeing to commit the unlawful purpose.

        Wharton's Rule: If the target crime requires two parties (e.g., dueling), then there is no conspiracy to duel unless there are three or more parties. (For conspiracy, you always need one more party than is required to commit the unlawful objective).

    C. **For an unlawful objective:** The goal of the conspiracy must be a _____.

D. **Overt Act:** At common law, only the agreement was required. Today, most states also require that one of the conspirators perform an "overt act" in furtherance of the unlawful purpose. Just about anything (buying supplies, planning escape route, etc.) will qualify as an overt act so not really testable on the exam.

E. **Vicarious Liability:** All conspirators are liable for any crime committed by any other conspirator so long as that crime was (1) _____ and (2) in _____of the conspiracy.

EXAMPLE: A and B agree to commit an armed robbery of a bank and both drive to the bank to commit the robbery. A encounters resistance from a teller and shoots and kills the teller. B (and A, of course) will be liable for the murder of the teller because it was reasonably foreseeable that someone might get killed in an armed robbery and A killed the teller in order to accomplish (reasonable furtherance of the goal of the conspiracy) the robbery.

F. **Defenses to Conspiracy: Withdrawal and Impossibility**

1. Withdrawal: Defendant must timely _____ to all other co-conspirators that Defendant is no longer a participant in the conspiracy.

   a. Timely communicate: Defendant must communicate intent to withdraw _____ the target crime occurs.

   b. Effect: Liable for _____, not for _____.

      If a co-conspirator provides a timely withdrawal, he will have no liability for any subsequent crimes committed by the other members of the conspiracy. But, the withdrawing conspirator remains liable for conspiracy.

      1) Withdrawal that thwarts crime: Under the minority rule (MPC), if the withdrawing conspirator goes to the police in time to permit the police to stop the target crime, the conspirator will not be liable for conspiracy or the target crime.

21

2. Impossibility: (Same as attempt)

3. Merger? No, conspiracy _____
into the target crime. A conspirator can be
convicted and separately punished for both
conspiracy and the target crime.

PART FOUR: ACCOMPLICE LIABILITY

More than one party may participate in a crime. Two issues: What do we call
them and what is their liability?

I. **Parties to a Crime:** Under the majority rule today, a party to a crime
may be a principal, accomplice or an accessory after the fact.

A. **Principal:** One who, with the intent to commit the crime,
causes the crime to occur.

B. **Accomplice:** One who, with the intent the crime be committed,
_____ the principal.
NOTE: Silent approval is not sufficient.

C. **Accessory after the Fact:** One who, with the intent to help a
felon escape or avoid arrest or trial, receives, relieves, or assists
a known felon after the felony has been completed.

II. **Liability of a Party:**

A. **Principal and Accomplices:** All accomplices (and the
principal) are liable for the crimes the principal committed that
the accomplice assisted, counseled or encouraged.

1. Other Crimes: Accomplices are also liable for other
crimes committed by the principal so long as the other
crimes were _____.

COMPARE: A co-conspirator is only liable for other crimes committed by other conspirators if the crime was both foreseeable and in reasonable furtherance of the conspiracy.

EXAMPLE: A and B agree to kidnap a woman and hold her for ransom. A has prior sexual offenses and B makes A promise A will not harm the woman. When B leaves A alone with the woman, A rapes the woman.

Can B be convicted of rape?

First: B has no direct liability because A, not B, committed the rape.

Second: As an accomplice to the kidnapping, B will be liable for the rape A committed only if the rape was _____.

No, not foreseeable because A promised he would not harm the woman? Yes, foreseeable because B knew of A's sexual offenses and left A alone with her?

Third: As an co-conspirator with A for kidnapping, B will be liable for the rape only if the rape was both (1) _____ and (2) in _____ of the conspiracy.

Foreseeable? (Same as above)
In reasonable furtherance of conspiracy? No, because purpose of conspiracy was kidnapping for ransom, sexual offense of victim does not further that goal.

B.   **Accessory after the fact:** Under the majority rule, an accessory after the fact is not liable for the crimes committed by the principal, but instead for a separate crime of "obstructing justice" which usually carries a lesser punishment (up to a five year sentence).

PART FIVE: DEFENSES and STATE OF MIND

I.   DEFENSES

A.   Insanity, Intoxication, Infancy, Self-Defense, Defense of Others (see Murder—Excuses)

B.   Duress: A defendant's criminal liability (except an intentional homicide) is excused if the crime is committed under the threat of imminent death or great bodily harm.

EXAMPLE: A holds a gun to B's head and says "burn down C's house or I will kill you." While A aims the gun at him, B sets fire to C's house. Unknown to B, C was asleep in the house and died in the fire. B cannot be convicted of arson because the crime is excused by duress.
Also, B cannot be convicted of felony murder for the death of C based on arson as the underlying felony because duress is a defense to arson (and felony murder is not an intentional homicide).

C.   Entrapment: A defendant's will have not liability for a crime if committed because defendant was entrapped by government officials.

1.   Not _____ to commit crime: To succeed on an entrapment defense (an affirmative defense so defendant has the burden of proof) the defendant must show the criminal plan _____ and defendant was _____ to commit the crime prior to the contact with the government.

D.   Mistake of Fact: Reasonable and Unreasonable

1.   Reasonable mistake of fact: If the defendant makes a reasonable mistake of fact or is ignorant of a fact that negates the required mental state for the crime, defendant is _____ of that crime.

EXAMPLE: Homeowner wakes up in the middle of the night and hears an intruder coming in through a window. Homeowner grabs a loaded pistol and sees what appears to be a gun in the intruder's hand pointed at him. Homeowner shoots and kills the intruder who turns out to be the unarmed teenage son attempting to sneak into his room while texting on a mobile phone. If Homeowner's mistake as to the threat posed by the intruder was reasonable, Homeowner will not be liable for murder or any lesser offense.

    2.   Unreasonable mistake of Fact (Specific Intent): If the defendant is mistaken or ignorant of a fact, but the mistake is unreasonable under the circumstances, then the mistake is a defense only if the crime is a specific intent crime.

COMPARE: Factual impossibility applies only to Attempt and Conspiracy crimes. Mistake of fact applies to all other crimes, except those with no mental state (Strict Liability crimes).

E.   **Mistake of Law (No defense):** A mistake or ignorance of the law is no defense if charged with violation of that law.

II.   **STATE OF MIND (MENTAL STATES)**

    A.   **General criminal intent:** Battery and Rape and Assault
        1.   Key defense: Reasonable mistake of fact

    B.   **Specific criminal intent:** Assault when based on an Attempted Battery, all the theft crimes, Burglary, all the Preliminary Crimes, First Degree Murder based on intent to kill (or Felony Murder where underlying felony requires specific intent), and all statutory crimes with words like "_____" or "_____" as part of their elements.

        1.   Key defenses: Reasonable or unreasonable mistake of fact, voluntary intoxication

    C.   **Strict Liability crimes:** Rare on the exam. Must be a crime with no mental state required.

        1.   Only defense: Defendant performed no voluntary act.

Criminal Procedure

Professor Chad Noreuil

Chad Noreuil
Clinical Professor of Law
Arizona State University
Sandra Day O'Connor College of Law
Tempe, Arizona

INTRODUCTION

_____

_____

_____

_____

_____

_____

_____

_____

_____

_____

_____

_____

_____

_____

I.   Overview of Key Amendments in Criminal Procedure

    A. Fourth Amendment: prohibition against unreasonable search and seizure.

    B. Fifth Amendment:

        1. Privilege against compulsory self-incrimination;

        2. Prohibition against double jeopardy.

    C. Sixth Amendment:

        1. Right to a speedy trial;

        2. Right to a trial by jury;

        3. Right to confront witnesses;

        4. Right to assistance of counsel.

    D. Eighth Amendment: prohibition against cruel and unusual punishment.

        1. The death penalty;

        2. Prisoner rights.

II.   Exclusionary rule: a remedy of American constitutional procedure whereby someone who has been the victim of _____ or a _____ can (among their other remedies) have the product of that illegal search or that coerced statement **excluded** from any subsequent criminal prosecution.

    A. The limitations on exclusion

        1. Exclusion does not apply to _____ proceedings.

            a. A grand jury witness may be compelled to testify based on _____ evidence.

        2. Exclusion is not an available remedy in _____.

3. In order to qualify for exclusion the search in question must either violate the federal constitution or a _____.

4. Exclusion is not an available remedy in _____ proceedings.

5. The use of excluded evidence for _____.

    a. Since 1980, **ALL** illegally seized real or physical evidence may be admitted to _____ of the defendant's trial testimony.

    b. Note: only the defendant's trial testimony may be impeached – not the testimony of _____.

6. Exclusion is not an available remedy for violations of the _____ in the execution of search warrants.

B. "The Fruit of the Poisonous Tree" doctrine

1. The doctrine will not only exclude illegally seized evidence, but will also exclude **all** evidence obtained or derived from _____.

2. There are three ways that the government can break the chain between an original, unlawful police action and some supposedly derived piece of evidence:

    a. The government could show that it had _____ _____ for that evidence, independent of that original police illegality.

    b. Inevitable discovery: the police would have inevitably discovered this evidence anyway.

3

        c. Intervening _____ on the part of the
           defendant.

Hypo #1: Defendant is illegally arrested on Friday night. On Saturday he gets out on bail. On Monday he hires and consults an attorney. On Tuesday he voluntarily returns to the police station and confesses. Will that Tuesday confession be fruit of the illegal Friday night arrest?

    C. The Exclusionary Rule and convictions

        1. A conviction will _____ be overturned
           because improperly obtained evidence was admitted at trial.

        2. On appeal, a court will apply the _____
           test.

        3. Under the test, a conviction _____ if the
           conviction would have resulted despite the improper evidence.

III.   Fourth Amendment

    A. The Fourth Amendment protects citizens from _____
       searches and seizures.

    B. Arrests and detentions

        1. An arrest must be based on _____.

        2. Arrest warrants are generally not required before arresting
           someone in a _____.

3. However, a non-emergency arrest of an individual
    _____ **does require** an arrest warrant.

4. Station house detention: The police need probable cause to arrest
    you and compel you to come to the police station either for
    _____ or _____.

5. **Note**: An unlawful arrest, by itself, _____
    on a subsequent criminal prosecution.

C. Investigatory detentions (*Terry* Stops)

1. The police have the authority to briefly detain a person even if they
    lack probable cause to arrest. In order to make such a stop, the
    police must have a _____
    supported by _____ of criminal
    activity.

2. Whether the police have reasonable suspicion depends on the
    _____.

3. Automobile stops: The police may stop a car if they have at least
    _____ that the law has
    been violated.

    a. Exception: _____.

4. Traffic Stops and Police dogs: During routine traffic stops, a
    _____ is not a _____ so long as the police do
    not extend the stop beyond the time needed to issue a ticket or
    conduct normal inquiries.

D. Search & Seizure and your model for answering any search and seizure question:

    1. STEP ONE: Governmental conduct?

        a. The _____ – on or off duty.

        b. Any _____ acting at the direction of the public police.

            (1) Privately paid police actions do NOT constitute governmental conduct UNLESS they are

            _____.

            (2) Examples of privately paid police:

                (a) Store _____;

                (b) Subdivision police;

                (c) Campus police.

    2. STEP TWO: Reasonable expectation of privacy?

        a. Automatic categories of standing:

            (1) If you _____ you always have standing to object to the search of the place you own.

            (2) You _____ the premises searched, whether you have ownership interest or not. **Example**: Grandchild living at grandparents' home.

(3) _____ have standing to object
     to the legality of the search of the place they are
     staying.

b. An important "sometimes" category of standing: You own
    the property seized.

    (1) If you own the property seized you have standing
        only if you have a reasonable expectation of privacy
        in the _____.

Hypo #2: Homer and his girlfriend Marge are walking down the street when Homer sees
police officers walking toward them. In a somewhat nonchalant manner, Homer takes
drugs out of his pocket and stuffs them into Marge's purse. Homer is arrested, and he
later admits that the drugs were his. Does Homer have standing to object to the search
of Marge's purse?

c. The "No Standing" Categories. You have NO expectation
    of privacy, and therefore no standing for anything that you
    _____ everyday.
    The following is a list of things held out to the public, the
    seizure of which implicates **no right of privacy**:

    (1) The sound of _____.

    (2) The style of _____.

    (3) The paint on the outside of your car.

    (4) Account records _____.

    (5) Monitoring the _____on
        a public street or in your driveway.

(6) Anything that can be seen across the _____ _____.

(7) Anything that can be seen from flying over in the public air space.

(8) The _____ emanating from your luggage or car.

(9) Your _____ set out on the curb for collection.

3.   STEP THREE: Did the police have a valid search warrant?

    a. There are two core requirements for a facially valid search warrant: _____ and _____.

        (1) The standard for **probable cause**: A _____ _____ that contraband or evidence of a crime will be found in the area searched.

        (2) **Particularity**: The warrant must state with particularity the _____ and the _____.

        (3) Warrants and the use of informants

           (a) If an officer's affidavit or probable cause is based on informant information, its sufficiency is determined by the _____ _____

           (b) An informant's _____, and _____ are all relevant factors in making this determination.

(c) A valid warrant can be based **in part** on an informant's tip even though that informant is

_____.

b. "No Knock" entry permitted in the execution of search warrants if exigent circumstances exist:

(1) An officer need not "knock and announce" if knocking and announcing would be

_____, _____, or inhibit the investigation.

(2) Biggest fear of inhibiting the investigation:

_____.

4. STEP FOUR: If the warrant is not valid, does an officer's _____ save the defective search warrant?

a. The general rule is that an officer's _____ _____ on a search warrant overcomes defects with the probable cause or particularity requirements.

b. Four exceptions to a good faith reliance on a defective search warrant:

i. The affidavit underlying that warrant is so _____ _____that no reasonable police officer would have relied on it.

Hypo #3: An affidavit states that the officers "have it on good information and do believe that there are drugs at Scooter's house," but states nothing else. Is this affidavit legally sufficient?

ii. The affidavit underlying the warrant is so
     _____
     _____ that no reasonable
     officer would have relied on it.

iii. The police officer or prosecutor
      _____ or _____ the
      magistrate when seeking the warrant.

iv. If the magistrate is _____, and
     therefore has wholly abandoned his or
     her neutrality.

5. STEP FIVE: If warrant is invalid and cannot be saved by the good faith defense or if the police never had any warrant at all, then you move to last step: **Exceptions to the warrant requirement**:

    a. Search incident to a _____.

        (1) The arrest must be _____. If the arrest is unlawful then the search is unlawful.

        (2) The arrest and search must be contemporaneous in _____ and _____.

Hypo #4: Defendant is lawfully arrested in Philadelphia at noon and the police later search him in Pittsburgh at 5pm. Is this a valid search incident to arrest?

(3) Geographic scope limitation: What can be searched? The person and the areas in to which he can reach either to _____ or to _____.

(4) Search incident to arrest & automobiles: The police may search the interior of the auto incident to arrest ONLY IF:

(a) The arrestee is _____ and still may gain access to the interior of the vehicle; or

(b) The police reasonably believe that evidence of the offense _____ _____may be found in the vehicle.

Hypo #5: The police arrested defendant for driving on a suspended license shortly after he stepped out of his car. Defendant was then handcuffed and placed in a squad car. The police then searched the passenger compartment of defendant's car and found cocaine in a jacket in the car. Is this a valid search incident to arrest?

Hypo #6: While on patrol in her squad car, Officer LaGuerta sees a car swerving across the center lane and driving erratically. The Officer stops the car, and approaches the driver side window. The man in the car and the car itself reek of alcohol, and the man's speech in slurred. After administering a sobriety test (which the driver failed), the driver is arrested, handcuffed and placed in the back of the locked squad car. Officer LaGuerta then searches the man's car and finds drugs and an illegal handgun. Will these items be admissible at the man's trial?

Hypo #7: While on patrol in their squad car, Officers Ponch and John observe a car speed past them going well over the posted speed limit. Ponch approaches the driver side window and asks for the driver's license and registration. While pulling out his license, a bag of crack cocaine and a pipe falls out of the man's pocket, which Ponch observes. Ponch asks the driver to step out the car and then informs the driver that he is under arrest. While reading the driver his *Miranda* rights and attempting to handcuff him, the man breaks free and runs off. Officer Ponch chases after him. Officer John, now with bad knees, does not join the chase, but instead searches the driver's car. Officer John finds recently stolen jewelry under the passenger seat. Is this a valid search incident to arrest?

(c) **Note**: Many states recognize the _____ exception to this rule, which justifies a warrantless search if an officer faces an emergency that threatens the _____ or _____ of an individual or the public.

b. The automobile exception:

(1) In order for the police to search anything or anybody and fall under the automobile exception they must have _____.

(2) **Note**: If -- but only if -- before searching anything or anybody the police have probable cause then they can search _____. This includes the entire interior compartment, and the trunk. Moreover, if there is probable cause, the police may open (without a warrant) any package, luggage or other container which could _____ they had probable cause to look for whether that package, luggage or other container is owned by the passenger or the driver.

Hypo #8: The DC police have over 30 reports that drugs are being sold out of the back of a car. The police know everything about the car, the make, the model, the license number but they know nothing about the drug seller. A DC police officer, aware of the 30 reports, sees the car go by driving at a lawful speed. The officer stops the car, but he does not arrest the driver. He orders the driver out of the car and searches the car. The officer finds a box under the passenger seat, opens the box and finds drugs. Will the drugs be admissible?

Hypo #9: The DC police have over 30 reports that stolen TVs are being sold out of the back of a van. The police know everything about the car, the make, the model, the license number but they know nothing about the TV seller. A DC police officer, aware of the 30 reports, sees the car go by driving at a lawful speed.   The officer stops the van, but he does not arrest the driver. He orders the driver out of the van and searches the car. The officer finds a small six inch by six inch box under the passenger seat, opens the box and finds drugs. Will the drugs be admissible?

(3) The probable cause necessary to justify the warrantless search of an auto under the automobile exception **can** arise _____.
BUT the probable cause must arise before

_____.

Hypo #10: A Denver police officer pulls over a car to give a speeding ticket. The car was stopped but nobody was searching anybody when the police officer noticed that the car, driver, and passenger fit a description just broadcast of people involved in the theft of auto parts. And then the police officer looks in the back seat and sees lug nuts, wrenches, and other things that suggest the theft of auto parts. The officers seize the auto parts and arrest the occupants. Is this a valid search?

c. Plain view

(1) To constitute a valid plain view seizure the police officer must be _____ at the location where he or she does the viewing of the item seized.

(2) It must be _____ _____ that the item is contraband or a fruit of a crime.

Hypo #11: A police officer for no reason runs through the front door of your apartment and then sees the big pile of marijuana in plain view. Is this a valid exception to the warrant requirement?

    d. Consent

       (1) For consent to be valid, the consent must be
       _____ and _____.

Hypo #12: The police come to your house and say, "we have a warrant. Do you mind if we look around?" You respond by saying, "Okay, go ahead." Drugs are found in your house and you are arrested, but the warrant subsequently turns out to be invalid. Is the evidence still admissible because you consented to the search?

       (2) Third Party consent

          (a) **Rule**: where two or more people have an equal right to use a piece of property, either can consent to its warrantless search. However, if both people are present and one person consents to the search and the other does **not** consent, then the one who _____ controls.

    e. Stop and frisk

       (1) A *Terry* stop is a brief detention for the purpose of _____.

       (2) The legal standard for stopping:
       _____.

       (3) The reasonable suspicion standard is
       _____ the probable cause standard.

(4) A *Terry* "frisk" is a pat down of the outer clothing and body to _____.

(5) A *Terry* frisk is justified by _____
_____.

Hypo #13: While on patrol in a high crime area, police officers notice a man standing on the corner wearing a red bandana and red shoes (typical colors of the Bloods street gang). The officers pull over and observe the man for fifteen minutes and the man never moves from the street corner. Suspecting him of being a drug dealer, the police approach him and say they would like to ask him a few questions. The man says he needs to leave the area and refuses. If the police persist, is this a valid *Terry* stop?

Hypo #14: NY police officers observe two teenage boys pushing a baby carriage down the street at midnight, and they notice that where the baby was supposed to be, there was a computer terminal. When the boys see the officers, they quickly turn in the opposite direction and speed up their pace. Can the police stop and frisk the boys?

Hypo #15: Officers stop a man on reasonable suspicion, pat him down and feel something in his pocket, which turns out to be a weapon. Is the weapon admissible?

Hypo #16: Officers stop a man on reasonable suspicion, pat him down and feel something in his pocket. The officers reach inside and pull out evidence of a previous crime reported in the neighborhood - but **not** a weapon. Is the evidence admissible?

(6) **Note**: If probable cause arises during an investigatory stop, the detention can become _____ and the officer could then conduct a full search incident to that arrest.

(7) **Auto stops**: If a vehicle is properly stopped for a traffic violation and the officer reasonably believes that a driver or passenger may be armed and dangerous, the officer may (1) _____ _____ of the suspected person, and (2) may _____, so long as it is limited to the areas in which a weapon may be placed.

f. Evanescent Evidence, Hot Pursuit, and Special Needs searches

(1) Evanescent evidence is evidence that _____ if the police took the time to get a warrant. **Example**: A police officer can scrape under a suspect's fingernails without getting a warrant because if you took the time to get a warrant the defendant might go wash his hands.

(2) Hot pursuit of a fleeing felon. **Rule of thumb**: If the police are not within _____ behind the fleeing felon, it is **not** a valid hot pursuit exception.

Hypo #17: A cab driver with a CB Radio hears the broadcast of a fleeing felon on the police radio. The cab driver sees the person run into a house. The cab driver calls the police, and they arrive about 8 minutes later. The police enter the house without a warrant, search and find a gun and a whole bunch of bloody clothes – all linking the guy to the crime. Is the evidence admissible?

         (a) **Note**: If the police are truly in hot pursuit they can enter anyone's home without a warrant, and any evidence they see in plain view will be

             _____.

    (3) Inventory searches: Before incarceration of an arrestee, the police may search (1) the arrestee's _____ and/or (2) the arrestee's entire _____.

    (4) Public school searches

         (a) Public school children engaged in

         _____
can be randomly drug tested.

         (b) Warrantless searches of public school children's _____, such as _____ and/or _____ is permissible to investigate violations of school rules.

(c) A school search will be held to be reasonable only if:

    i. It offers a _____ _____ of finding evidence of wrongdoing;

    ii. The measures adopted to carry out the search are _____ _____to the objectives of the search; and

    iii. The search is *not* _____ _____.

E. Wiretapping and eavesdropping:

    1. All wiretapping and eavesdropping requires a _____.

    2. Exceptions: "Unreliable ear" and "uninvited ear" (no warrant necessary).

        a. Everybody in this society assumes the risk that the person to whom he is speaking will either consent to the government monitoring the conversation or _____ and therefore has no basis for a Fourth Amendment objection as a warrantless search.

        b. A speaker has no Fourth Amendment if she makes no attempt to _____.

IV.   Confessions

      A. *Miranda* warnings

          1. When *Miranda* warnings are required, the suspect must be given the following information:

             a. You have a right to remain silent;

             b. Anything you say can be used against you in court;

             c. You have the right to an attorney; and

             d. If you can't afford an attorney, one will be appointed for you if you so desire.

          2. The trigger for required *Miranda* warnings:

                  _____.

             a. Custody

                (1) Legal standard for custody: You are in custody if, at the time of the interrogation, you are

                      _____.

                    (a) The "not free to leave" standard covers being in a police car or being in jail, but you could also be _____ or in a hospital bed.

                    (2) In 1984 the Supreme Court said that_____ _____and routine _____ are **not** "custodial."

b. Interrogation

(1) Under the Fifth Amendment *Miranda* doctrine, interrogation is defined as any conduct where the police knew or should have known that they might

_____

from the suspect.

(2) *Miranda* warnings are not required prior to the admissibility of what's known as a

_____.

Hypo #18: Donna was arrested and taken to police headquarters where she was given her *Miranda* warnings. Donna indicated that she wished to phone her lawyer and was told she could do so after her fingerprints had been taken. While being fingerprinted, however, Donna blurted out "paying a lawyer is a waste of money because I know you have me." At trial, Donna's motion to prevent the introduction of the statement she made while being fingerprinted will most probably be:

A) Granted, because Donna's request to contact her attorney by telephone was reasonable and should have been granted immediately.

B) Granted, because of the "fruit of the poisonous tree doctrine."

C) Denied, because the statements were volunteered and were not the result of interrogation.

D) Denied, because fingerprinting is not a critical stage in the proceeding requiring the assistance of counsel.

Correct Answer _____

3. *Miranda* Waiver

   a. A *Miranda* waiver must be _____,
_____, and _____.

   b. Courts will employ a _____
test in making this determination.

Hypo #19: Defendant is detained and read *Miranda* warnings. At the end of the warnings, the defendant remains silent. The cops then ask if the defendant would like to waive his rights and talk to them. The defendant shrugs his shoulders in response. Is this a valid waiver?

4. Invoking your *Miranda* rights

   a. Invoking the right to remain silent

      (1) Invoking the right to silence must be

         _____.

      (2) The police may reinitiate questioning after the defendant has invoked the right to silence if they wait a significant amount of time, _____ _____, and the questions are limited to a crime that was _____ _____.

   b. Invoking the right to counsel

      (1) The request for counsel can be invoked only by an _____.

(2) If the accused invokes his right to counsel, all
   questions must cease until (1) the accused is
   _____ or (2) the
   accused _____.

(3) **Note**: The police may not even question about a
   _____ (as
   they might be able to where the accused merely
   invokes the right to remain silent).

Hypo #20: The police arrest Bilbo Baggins and bring him to the station for questioning. After rigorously questioning him about a murder, Bilbo says, "I don't like the way you're treating me. I want to talk to my lawyer right now." The police continue to interrogate Bilbo, and Bilbo finally makes incriminating statements about the crime. Will Bilbo's incriminating statements be admissible at his criminal trial?

B. Fifth Amendment right to counsel vs. Sixth Amendment right to counsel

   1. Once the defendant asserts his right to terminate the interrogation
      and requests an attorney, _____ of the
      interrogation by the police without his attorney present violates his
      _____ right to counsel.

   2. The United States Supreme Court has created the Fifth
      Amendment Right to Counsel and it only arises in one
      circumstance:

      a. When a suspect on hearing the *Miranda* Warnings says, "I
         want a lawyer," the Supreme Court has interpreted this to
         mean that the suspect needs the help of an attorney with
         the process of _____,
         and therefore the police may not reinitiate interrogation on
         any topic without his attorney present.

    3.   The Fifth Amendment Right to counsel is NOT offense specific.

    4.   All other times (other than hearing the *Miranda* Warnings) you getting a lawyer invokes your Sixth Amendment Right and your Sixth Amendment Right _____ offense specific. And the attorney would only have to be present at the interrogation if the defendant were being asked questions about that attorney's case.

Hypo #21: Defendant McNeil is arrested and charged with burglary. He is given a court appointed attorney. McNeil cannot make bail so he remains in jail for two weeks. After two weeks, the police came to McNeil's cell, gave him the *Miranda* Warnings, he waives them, and the police ask him questions about an unrelated murder. He makes incriminating statements about the murder. McNeil is then charged with murder. In an effort to avoid those damaging statements and their admission in the murder case, McNeil argues that "my attorney from the burglary case should have been present when I was being interrogated." Are the statements relating to the murder charges admissible?

V.   Pretrial identification

   A. There are two substantive bases on which you can attack a pretrial identification technique:

      1. Denial of the right to counsel

         a. Post-charge _____ (standing in a line); and _____ (one-on-one) give rise to the right to counsel.

         b. **But note**: There is no right to counsel when they go out to show the victim or witness _____.

    c. Other stages where there is **NO** right to counsel:

        (1) Taking of _____ samples.

        (2) Taking of _____ samples.

        (3) Pre-charge lineups.

        (4) Preliminary hearings to determine _____
            _____.

        (5) Brief recess during _____ at trial.

        (6) Parole and _____ revocation
            proceedings.

2. Denial of due process

    a. Certain pretrial identification techniques are so
        _____and
        so substantially likely to produce a misidentification that
        they_____.

3. The remedy for a denial of pretrial due process is to _____
the in-court identification. The victim or witness will **not** be allowed
to identify the person in court.

4. **Note**: the denial to the right to counsel or the denial of due process
will _____ get the remedy of excluding
the in-court identification. The state can defeat the suspect's claim
for that remedy by showing an adequate _____
_____ for that in-court identification (independent
of that bad line-up).

VI. Pre-trial procedures

    A. Bail

        1. Bail issues are _____.

        2. Preventive detention **is** Constitutional.

    B. Grand juries

        1. Exclusion does **not** apply to the conduct of grand juries. Accordingly, a grand jury witness may be compelled to testify based on _____ evidence.

        2. The proceedings of grand juries are _____. Defendant has no _____ and no _____.

VII. Prosecutorial duty to disclose exculpatory information

    A. A prosecutor's failure to disclose evidence, whether willful or _____, violates the Due Process Clause and may be grounds for reversal of a conviction.

    B. A failure to disclose exculpatory information will constitute grounds for reversing a conviction if:

        1. The evidence is _____, and

        2. Prejudice has resulted, meaning there is a _____ _____ that the result would have been different had the information been disclosed.

VIII. Trial

    A. Right to an unbiased judge

        1. Bias means having a _____ in the outcome of the case or some _____ against the defendant.

Hypo #22: Judge Judy told defendant Smith when she sentenced him last time, "Smith if you come back through my court again this year I'm going to give you the maximum." Smith was arrested again and sent back before Judge Judy again. Is she now biased?

    B. Right to jury trial

        1. The constitutional right to jury trial attaches anytime the defendant is tried for an offense for which the maximum authorized sentence _____. If the maximum authorized sentence is up to or including 6 months, there is no constitutional right to jury trial.

        2. Number and unanimity of jurors

            a. The minimum number of jurors permissible is _____. If a court uses this minimum number of jurors, the verdict must be _____.

            b. **Note**: There is no federally protected constitutional right to a unanimous twelve juror verdict. The Supreme Court has approved the non-unanimous verdicts of _____ and _____.

3. The cross sectional requirement

    a. You have the right to have the jury pool reflect a _____ _____ of the community; but – you have no right to have the _____ reflect a fair cross section of the community.

4. The use of peremptory challenges for racial and gender based discrimination.

    a. A peremptory challenge is a challenge to exclude a prospective juror _____. EXCEPT: It is unconstitutional for the prosecutor or the defense to exercise preemptory challenges to exclude from the jury prospective jurors on account of their _____ or _____.

C. Right to counsel

1. A criminal defendant's right to counsel applies to all _____ of a prosecution, including trial.

2. Ineffective assistance of counsel

    a. **Rule**: there must be deficient performance by counsel and, but for such deficiency, the result of the proceeding _____.

    b. Typically, such a claim can only be made out by specifying _____ of trial counsel.

3. Right to self-representation

    a. A defendant has the right to defend himself so long as his waiver of trial counsel is _____ and

_____ , and he is _____
to proceed *pro se*.

      b. **Note**: a defendant can be found mentally competent to stand trial, yet incompetent to represent himself, as determined by _____.

D. Right to confront witnesses

    1. The absence of face-to-face confrontation between the defendant and accused does **not** violate the Sixth Amendment when preventing such confrontation _____ and
_____.

    2. A defendant who is _____ may be removed from the courtroom, thereby relinquishing his right of confrontation.

IX.   Guilty pleas and plea bargaining

A. The Supreme Court will not disturb guilty pleas _____.

B. If a defendant pleads guilty, the judge must specifically address the defendant on the record about the following:

    1. The nature of the charge; and

    2. The judge must tell the defendant the _____
_____and any _____
_____; and

3. The judge must tell him that he has a right to plead not guilty and to _____; and

4. All of this must be _____.

C. Four good bases for withdrawing a guilty plea after sentence:

1. The plea was _____ (some mistake in plea taking ceremony);

   a. Note: A plea is not involuntary merely because it was entered in response to the prosecution's _____

   _____.

2. Lack of jurisdiction;

3. Ineffective assistance of counsel;

4. Failure of the prosecutor to keep _____

   _____.

Hypo #23: Defendant Smith agrees to plead guilty in exchange for the prosecutor's promise to consolidate all the charges and make no sentence recommendation. Prosecutor consolidates all charges. Smith pleads guilty, and the judge accepts the plea. The judge then asks the prosecutor for a sentence recommendation and the prosecutor replies, "The State recommends the maximum sentence allowed." May the defendant withdraw his plea?

X. Death penalty

A. Any death penalty statute that does not give the defendant a chance to present _____ is unconstitutional.

B. There can be no _____ for imposition of
    the death penalty.

C. The state may not by statute limit the _____;
    all relevant _____ must be admissible or the
    statute is unconstitutional.

D. Only a _____ – not a judge – may determine the aggravating factors
    justifying imposition of the death penalty.

XI. Double jeopardy

A. Jeopardy attaches in a jury trial when _____.
    In a bench trial, jeopardy attaches when the _____.

B. Jeopardy does not generally attach when the proceedings are _____.
    Example: It is okay to have a criminal prosecution for tax fraud, and then
    a civil proceeding to collect the back taxes.

C. Exceptions permitting retrial:

    1.   Jury is unable to_____.

    2.   Mistrials for_____.

    3.   A retrial after a _____ is **not**
             double jeopardy.

4.   Breach of an agreed upon plea bargain by the defendant.
        Rule: When the defendant breaches a plea bargain
        agreement, his plea and sentence can be withdrawn and the

        _____.

Hypo #24: Heidi and Spencer (dating but not married) commit murder. Heidi cooperates with the investigation and is allowed to plead to second-degree murder in exchange for her testimony against Spencer at his trial. Spencer is convicted of first-degree murder, based largely on Heidi's testimony. Months later, Spencer successfully appeals his conviction on other grounds, and he is granted a new trial. Heidi refuses to testify at Spencer's retrial. Does double jeopardy prevent the prosecutor from recharging Heidi with first-degree murder?

D. Two crimes do not constitute the same offense if each crime requires
    proof of _____ that the other does not.

Hypo #25: Homer sits through a three-hour property lecture, and becomes very tired. He gets into his car, falls asleep, and hits and kills two people. Homer realizes what has happened, but he's really hungry, so he drives home. Homer is tried in separate trials for manslaughter **and** hit and run from that single transaction. Does double jeopardy preclude the prosecution of both crimes?

1. Lesser included offenses: Being put in jeopardy for a greater
    offense _____ for any lesser included offense.
    Example: The crime of robbery includes the two lesser crimes of
    larceny and assault. If you are tried for robbery, you _____
    be retried for the lesser included offense of larceny. Similarly, if
    you are first put in jeopardy for the lesser included offense
    (larceny), you _____ later be retried for the greater
    offense (robbery).

        a. **Exception**: If a person is tried and convicted on a charge of battery, and the victim of the battery later dies due to the injuries, the person can also then be prosecuted for
_____.

E. Separate Sovereigns

    1. Double Jeopardy bars retrial for the same offense by _____
_____.

Hypo #26: Paris is in possession of an illegal drug, which violates both federal drug laws and the state's drug laws. Can Paris be prosecuted under both the state drug laws and the federal drug laws or would this be double jeopardy?

XII. Fifth Amendment privilege against compelled testimony

A. The Fifth Amendment Privilege against self-incrimination can be asserted by anyone in _____ case. Anyone asked a question under oath in any kind of case, wherein the response might tend to
_____ is entitled to a Fifth Amendment privilege.

    1. You must assert that privilege the _____ the question is asked or you will have _____ your Fifth Amendment privilege for all subsequent criminal prosecutions.

    2. The privilege must be claimed in _____ to prevent the privilege from being waived for a later criminal prosecution.

    3. If the individual responds to the questions instead of claiming the privilege during a civil proceeding, he _____ later bar that evidence on Fifth Amendment grounds.

B. The scope of the protection

   1. The Fifth Amendment protects citizens from

       _____.

   2. The Fifth Amendment does **not** protect citizens from having the government use _____ in ways to incriminate them.

   3. Examples of non-testimonial evidence that the prosecution can compel a person to produce:

       a.   A person's _____ sample;

       b.   A person's _____ sample;

       c.   A person's _____ sample;

       d.   A person's _____ sample.

C. The Fifth Amendment and prosecutorial conduct

   1. It is unconstitutional for the prosecutor to make a negative comment on the defendant's _____ or on a defendant _____ after being given the *Miranda* warnings.

   2. **Exception**: The prosecutor **can** comment on the defendant's failure to take the stand when the comment is in response to defense counsel's assertion that defendant _____ _____.

   3. When a prosecutor impermissibly comments on a defendant's silence, the _____ test applies, and thus, the prosecutor's conduct may not be fatal to an otherwise sound conviction.

Hypo #27: During closing argument, the prosecutor makes the following statements: "Defendant is a cold-blooded murderer. Several witnesses testified to this, and it was clear that their words and mannerisms were truthful. The defendant is as guilty as the day is long, and he deserves to be convicted. Moreover, he didn't even take the stand in his own defense, so he must be guilty." Are the prosecutor's statements permissible?

       D. The Fifth Amendment privilege can be eliminated in three ways:

           1. Under grant of _____.

           2. No possibility of incrimination

              a. **Example**: If the _____
                 has run on the underlying crime, you are not entitled to a
                 Fifth Amendment Privilege.

           3. Waiver

              a. The criminal defendant who _____
                 waives the Fifth Amendment privilege as to all legitimate
                 subjects of cross examination.

XIII. GENERAL NOTES AND TIPS

Essay Writing Workshops

Professor Richard Sakai

barbri®

ESSAY

WORKSHOPS

Professor Richard T. Sakai

i

TABLE OF CONTENTS

Essay Workshops

By

Professor Richard T. Sakai

SCOPE OF COVERAGE FOR THE CALIFORNIA BAR EXAM

ESSAYS

The essay examination instructions of the Committee of Bar Examiners ask you to answer the essays according to "legal theories and principles of general application" unless you are asked to use California Law. The scope is as follows:

BUSINESS ASSOCIATIONS – Corporations, Sole Proprietorships, Partnerships, Joint Ventures, Limited Liability Companies and Agency.

CIVIL PROCEDURE – Federal Rules of Civil Procedure and California Code of Civil Procedure, and the differences.

COMMUNITY PROPERTY – California law

CONSTITUTIONAL LAW – U.S. Constitution

CONTRACTS – Majority rule with significant minorities and UCC Articles 1 & 2 (Part 1, §101-107, Part 2, §201-210, Part 3, § 301-311) (when applicable)

CRIMINAL LAW – Majority rule, Common Law and modern statutes

CRIMINAL PROCEDURE – U.S. Constitution

EVIDENCE – Federal Rules of Evidence and California Evidence Code, and the Differences.

PROF RESPONSIBILITY   – California Rules of Professional Conduct, relevant sections of the California Business and Professions Code, ABA Model Rules and Code, and leading case law.

REAL PROPERTY   – Majority rule with significant minorities and common law.

REMEDIES   – Majority rule with significant minorities.

TORTS   – Majority rule with significant minorities.

TRUSTS   – Majority rule with significant minorities.

WILLS   – California Probate Code and California Law.

TUESDAY MORNING   THURSDAY MORNING

California Bar Examination

Answer all three questions.
Time allotted: Three hours

Your answer should demonstrate your ability to analyze the facts in the question, to tell the difference between material facts and immaterial facts, and to discern the points of law and fact upon which the case turns. Your answer should show that you know and understand the pertinent principles and theories of law, their qualifications and limitations, and their relationships to each other.

Your answer should evidence your ability to apply the law to the given facts and to reason in a logical, lawyer-like manner from the premises you adopt to a sound conclusion. Do not merely show that you remember legal principles. Instead, try to demonstrate your proficiency in using and applying them.

If your answer contains only a statement of your conclusions, you will receive little credit. State fully the reasons that support your conclusions, and discuss all points thoroughly.

Your answer should be complete, but you should not volunteer information or discuss legal doctrines which are not pertinent to the solution of the problem.

Unless a question expressly asks you to use California law, you should answer according to legal theories and principles of general application.

CALIFORNIA BAR EXAM SUBJECTS

Constitutional Law

Contracts

Crimes

Evidence

Real Property

Torts

Business Associations

Civil Procedure

Community Property

Professional Responsibility

Remedies

Wills and Trusts

BUSINESS ASSOCIATIONS
(Agency, Partnership & Corporations)

AGENCY

I. AGENCY

    A.   Formation
        1.   Capacity
        2.   Consent
        3.   Method of formation
            a.   By action
            b.   By operation of law

    B.   Duties owed by agent
        1.   Duty of loyalty
        2.   Duty of obedience
        3.   Duty of care

    C.   Duties owed by principal
        1.   Duty to compensate or reimburse
        2.   Duty to cooperate
        3.   Duty under contract

    D. Remedies
        1.   To agent
        2.   To principal

II. CONTRACT LIABILITY

    A.   Does the agent have authority?
        1.   Actual or Apparent Authority
        2.   Ratification
        3.   Termination

    B.   Contract Liability to Third Parties
        1.   Third party v. Principal
        2.   Third party v. Agent
        3.   Principal v. Third party

IV. TORT LIABILITY – RESPONDEAT SUPERIOR

    A.   Employer/Employee Relationship
    B.   Conduct within scope of employment

PARTNERSHIP

I. **Formation**
    A. Contract rules apply
    B. Intent
    C. Factors to imply a partnership
    D. Partnership by Estoppel

II. **Partnership property**
    A. Partner's intent
    B. Factors to determine property within partnership
    C. Partner's rights

III. **Liabilities owed to third parties**
    A. Agency theories
    B. Imputing knowledge to the partnership
    C. Civil liabilities
    D. Criminal liabilities

IV. **Dissociation and Dissolution**
    A. Methods
    B. Terminating apparent authority
    C. Continued authority to wind up
    D. Distributing assets

V. **Limited Partnership**
    A. Created by statute
    B. Liability limited to capital contribution
    C. Liability and right of limited partner
    D. Dissolution and distribution of assets

VI. **Limited Liability Partnership**

VII. **Limited Liability Limited Partnership**

CORPORATIONS

I. FORMATION OF CORPORATION

   A.   Formation of corporation - de jure, de facto, and corporation by estoppel

   B.   Pierce "corporate veil" - Fraud, undercapitalization and alter ego theories

   C.   Unpaid stock

   D.   Watered stock

II. CAPITAL STOCK STRUCTURE

   A.   **Subscription Agreements** (revocability)

   B.   **Consideration for stock.**
      1.   Money paid, labor done, property received
      2.   Tangible or intangible property or benefit
         a.   Promissory notes
         b.   Contracts for future services

   C.   **Redemptions and Repurchases of Stock**

III. STOCK TRANSACTIONS (SALES AND PURCHASES)

   A.   **Common Law Duty** (owed existing shareholders and generally required "privity" as compared to transactions carried out on stock exchanges).
      1.   Tort of fraud or misrepresentation

   B.   **Rule 10b-5** (Federal securities action)
      1.   Three major requirements
         a.   Interstate commerce
         b.   Fraudulent conduct
            (1)   May be overt act or omission to act
            (2)   Materiality
            (3)   Scienter
         c.   May be in connection with either purchase or sale
      2. Insider trading - abstain from trading or disclose inside information.
         a.   Fiduciary relationship required
         b.   Tippers must have an improper purpose
         c.   Tippees liable if tipper breached and tippee knew that tipper breached
         d.   Misappropriation theory brought by government against any trader who misappropriated information from any source

    C.   **Section 16(b)**
        1.   This requires:
            a.   Large corporation
                (1) Traded on national exchange, _or_
                (2) 500+ shareholders _and_ $10 million in assets
            b.   Defendant is
                (1) officer,
                (2) director, or
                (3) 10% shareholder
            c.   Purchase and sale of stock within six month period.
                (_Highest_ sales are matched with _lowest_ purchases to maximize recovery)
        2.   There are _no_ defenses, e.g., good faith of defendant.

IV. OPERATION AND MANAGEMENT OF CORPORATION

    A.   **Promoters**
        1.   Promoter _always_ liable until there is novation.
        2.   Corporation _never_ liable until there is adoption.

    B.   **Shareholders**
        1.   Voting Rights
            a.   Meeting
                (1) _Unanimous_ written consent (no meeting required)
                (2) Annual meeting
                (3) Special meeting
            b.   Proxies
                (1) Requirements
                    (a) written
                    (b) signed
                (2) Expiration - 11 months unless it says otherwise
                (3) Revocable unless coupled with an interest
            c.   Effective Shareholder Action
                (1) Quorum necessary
                (2) Majority of quorum wins
                (3) Cumulative voting (for directors only)
            d.   Shareholder Agreements to Control Voting
                (1) Pooling Agreements
                (2) Voting Trusts
                    (a) on file
                    (b) expires in 10 years
                (3) Stock Transfer Restriction Agreements (must be _reasonable_ restriction)
        2.   Preemptive Rights - Only applicable to
            a.   newly authorized stock
            b.   sold for cash

10

3. Dividends
   a. No right to them
   b. Irrevocable once declared
      (1) Insolvency exception
   c. Payable out of:
      (1) Earned surplus - always
      (2) Stated Capital - never
      (3) Other surplus accounts - depending on state
4. Inspection Rights
   a. May only inspect records, books, shareholder lists, etc., i.e., what's on paper (as compared to inspecting factory)
   b. Need proper purpose
5. Derivative Suits
   a. Requirements
      (1) Shareholder at time of and when suit brought
      (2) Prior demand on board of directors unless futile. (If demand turned down in good faith - that's it!)
      (3) Bond
   b. If suit is successful the recovery goes to corporation and individual is reimbursed for litigation costs
6. Controlling Shareholders
   a. Controlling shareholder must refrain from obtaining a special advantage or to cause corporation to take action prejudicing minority shareholders.
   b. Controlling shareholders are treated as "insiders" under Securities Exchange Act.

C. **Directors**
   1. Effective Board Action
      a. Need quorum
      b. Majority of quorum wins
      c. Voting agreement not allowed; no proxies
   2. Board Vacancy may be filled by other directors or shareholders
   3. Director Duties
      a. Duty of Care
         (1) good faith
         (2) due care of ordinarily prudent person
         (3) best interest of corporation
      b. Duty of Loyalty
         (1) Insider trading
         (2) Self-dealing (Interested director transaction) O.K. if either:
            (a) Fair
            (b) Or, in many states if approval, after full disclosure of material facts, by a vote of the disinterested

11

        i) Directors or
        ii) Shares
     (c) Remedy is rescission.
    (3) Corporate Opportunity Doctrine
     (a) Note: Remedies are:
        i) damages
        ii) constructive trust or
        iii) corp gets opportunity at cost
    (4) Compete with corporation – unrelated business is not conflict of interest.
     (a) Note: Remedies are
        i) damages
        ii) injunctive relief

D. **Officers**
 1. Agents of Corporation
 2. Bar exam issues essentially same as for directors, e.g., duties of care and loyalty.

V. FUNDAMENTAL CORPORATE CHANGES

A. **Mergers**
 1. Directors and shareholders of <u>both</u> corporations must approve, the latter by majority of shares entitled to vote
 2. Short form merger does not require shareholder approval.
 3. Appraisal Rights of Dissenting Shareholder
  a. Requirements:
   (1) Written objection before meeting
   (2) Vote against merger or abstain from voting
   (3) File written claim

B. **Sale of Assets**
 1. If sale, lease or exchange of substantially all of the corporate assets is outside the ordinary course of business, then majority of directors and majority of shares entitled to vote must approve.
 2. De Facto Merger
  a. Sale of assets may be a de facto merger, may trigger possible recission or appraisal rights.
  b. Purchasing corporation may be liable for debts and liabilities.

C. **Amendment of Articles**
 1. Corporation can amend articles. No appraisal rights.
 2. Board of directors may amend or repeal bylaws unless articles exclusively reserve power to shareholders.

D. **Dissolution and Liquidation**
 1. Majority of directors and majority of shares entitled to vote must approve (no quorum concept).
 2. If liquidation, pay outside creditors first.

BUSINESS ASSOCIATIONS QUESTION 1

Abby, chief executive officer of Oilco, was eating lunch with several fellow Oilco executives when she saw her business school classmate, Barb, sit down at the next table. Abby was aware that Barb was a prominent local stockbroker. In an unusually loud voice, Abby stated to her fellow executives, "I bet my former classmate would give her left arm to know that tomorrow we are going to announce a tender offer for ALT Corporation."

Barb overhead this remark and when she returned to her office, bought 10,000 shares of ALT Corporation for her own account.

Barb also telephoned the Mutual Fund Complex (Mutual) and told its chief executive officer, "If you are smart, you will buy ALT Corporation this afternoon." Within one hour Mutual placed an order to buy 50,000 shares of ALT, using Barb as a broker.

That afternoon, Barb visited Cora, a neighbor whom she intensely disliked and who, at Barb's recommendation, had recently purchased ALT stocks. Barb told Cora that she had heard that ALT shares were about to decrease in value and because she felt badly that it was upon her advice that Cora had purchased ALT shares, she was willing to buy the ALT shares from Cora at the current stock exchange price without charging any commission. Cora immediately sold her one hundred shares of ALT stock.

The following morning, Oilco announced it was making a tender offer for ALT Corporation shares at a price 50% above its current market price. Approximately one month later, the tender offer was completed, with Barb and Mutual receiving profits of approximately 50% on their shares. Abby has not purchased any ALT shares for more than three years.

1. Has Abby, Barb, or Mutual violated Rule 10b-5 under Section 10(b) of the Federal Securities Exchange Act? Discuss.

2. Has Barb incurred any potential non-statutory civil liability? Discuss.

I. **10b-5 violations under Federal Securities Exchange Act**
Sec. 10b prohibits "any manipulative or deceptive device" in connection with the purchase or sale of a security

   A. **Requirements for 10b-5 violations**

       1. The transaction must involve interstate commerce or be traded on national stock exchange
       2. Fradulent conduct
       3. With regard to purchase or sale of securities

   B. **Abby** - did not buy or sell, however, Abby may be subject to liability.

       1. Abby's liability as a <u>tipper</u>
         a. Abby is a fiduciary of Oilco and thus owes a duty not to disclose material, nonpublic information.
         b. The information was material.
         c. Abby did act knowingly because she spoke loudly and specifically referred to her former classmate, Barb.
         d. Abby must personally benefit, directly or indirectly - here reputational interest.
         e. As a result of above, Abby is a proper defendant. There are proper plaintiffs since Cora did sell at the time that Barb or Mutual purchased.

   C. **Barb**

       1. Tippee liability for buying stock for own account
         a. All the elements for a 10b-5 violation are present.
         b. The issue is whether Barb was a tippee so that she had a duty to disclose inside information.
           1) Barb's liability derives from tipper's (Abby's) obligation
           2) Abby had breached, and Barb, being a prominent stockbroker, knew Abby was Oilco's CEO.
         c. Thus, Barb must disgorge her profits.

2. Tipper liability - tipping Mutual to buy
   a. Barb's liability as a <u>tipper</u> is dependent on the same elements as Abby. However, the problem here is that Barb can argue she had no fiduciary duty to ALT or Oilco.

   b. In some jurisdictions, Barb would be liable under a misappropriation theory

3. Buying Cora's ALT stock
   a. Here, Barb would also be subject to 10b-5 liability. Barb intentionally misrepresented ALT's future upon which Cora relied and sold her shares to Barb.
   b. The only fact to be determined is whether Barb used any instrumentality of interstate commerce.

D. **Mutual** - purchased ALT stock on Barb's suggestion

1. Mutual's liability would be under a tippee theory. However, Mutual's liability hinges on whether it knew or should have known that Barb's recommendation was based on inside information.

2. Mutual would also argue that they did not receive any information anyway.

II. Barb's non-statutory civil liability

A. **Misrepresentation or Deceit as to Cora**
   1. Barb intentionally misrepresented the facts about ALT to Cora, which induced Cora
   2. Barb would be liable for her profits, or Cora can seek to impose a constructive trust
   3. In addition, punitive damages may be appropriate given Barb's malicious intent.

B. **At common law, Barb was not an insider.**

BUSINESS ASSOCIATIONS QUESTION 2

Artis, a respected computer engineer, invented a unique computer device, but she lacked sufficient financial resources to manufacture and market it. Artis presented to Ben, a wealthy acquaintance, a business plan for producing and selling the device. Ben and Artis agreed that: 1) Artis would form a corporation named "Compco" to manufacture and market the device; 2) Ben would provide the financing by contracting with the corporation to loan it $1 million; and 3) Ben would receive periodic loan payments, a number of shares of the corporation equal to the number that would be issued to Artis and 20% of the net profits of the corporation for ten years.

Artis caused the articles of incorporation to be prepared for the corporation as a close corporation. She also caused to be prepared a loan agreement in which Ben and Compco were the parties. The agreement contained the provisions to which Artis and Ben had agreed. Artis signed the agreement as president of Compco, and Ben promptly funded the $1 million loan. Under state law, legal existence of the corporation would begin only when the articles were filed with the secretary of state. However, through inadvertence the articles were not filed with the secretary of state until ten days after the loan agreement was executed and the loan funded. Artis was duly elected as sole officer and director of Compco. Thereafter, the computer device was manufactured, Compco enjoyed some initial business success, made payments on the loan and paid 20% of its net profits to Ben.

Compco authorized only 1,000 no par common shares for an issue price of $1,000 per share. Compco issued 200 shares to Artis in return for her assignment of all rights in her invention to Compco and 200 shares to Ben pursuant to the loan agreement. Compco issued 500 shares to others in return for their payment of $1,000 per share. Artis caused the remaining 100 shares to be issued as a gift to her friend, Carla, a busy and successful computer marketing expert, in an attempt to induce Carla to provide free marketing advice to Compco, which was facing increasing competition. However, after receiving the stock, Carla refused to provide any advice.

Recently, Compco has operated at a loss, and Ben has not received any further payments under the loan agreement.

Questions on next page

1. Are Compco and/or Artis liable to Ben for the payments due under the loan agreement? Discuss.

2. Is Artis liable to Compco for having issued stock to herself and to Carla, and if so, what is the basis of any such liability? Discuss.

3. Is Ben liable to Compco because he was issued stock in Compco and, if so, what is the basis of any such liability? Discuss.

4. Is Carla liable to Compco because she was issued stock in Compco and, if so, what is the basis of any such liability?

Business Associations Question 2

1. Compco and/or Artis liability for loan payments

   a. Compco's liability
      1) Breach of Contract
      2) Compco argue not liable for promoter contract, however a corporation is liable if:
         a) novation or
         b) adoption - received loan and made payments

   b. Artis liability
      1) Promoter liability
         a) Personally liable unless novation
         b) Here no evidence of novation.

2. Artis liability to Compco

   a. 200 shares issued to herself
      1) Stock must be supported by consideration, exchange for property
      2) Her invention was property
      3) Good faith assessment of adequacy of consideration
         a) duty of care
         b) duty of loyalty
   b. 100 shares issued to Carla
      1) Future services not consideration
      2) Fiduciary duty of care - seeking marketing advice
      3) Fiduciary duty of loyalty - friend

3. Ben's liability to Compco

   a. Loan adequate consideration? - promissory notes - modernly, sufficient consideration.
   b. A gift? Watered stock?

4. Carla's liability to Compco

   a. No consideration - contracts for future services - watered stock?
   b. Carla argues she made no enforceable promise

BUSINESS ASSOCIATIONS QUESTION 3

Alfred, Beth, and Charles orally agreed to start ABC Computers ("ABC"), a business to manufacture and sell computers. Alfred contributed $100,000 to ABC, stating to Beth and Charles that he wanted to limit his liability to that amount. Beth, who had technical expertise, contributed $50,000 to ABC. Charles contributed no money to ABC but agreed to act as salesperson. Alfred, Beth, and Charles agreed that Beth would be responsible for designing the computers, and that Charles alone would handle all computer sales.

ABC opened and quickly became successful, primarily due to Charles' effective sales techniques.

Subsequently, without the knowledge or consent of Alfred or Charles, Beth entered into a written sales contract in ABC's name with Deco, Inc. ("Deco") to sell computers manufactured by ABC at a price that was extremely favorable to Deco. Beth's sister owned Deco. When Alfred and Charles became aware of the contract, they contacted Deco and informed it that Beth had no authority to enter into sales contracts, and that ABC could not profitably sell computers at the price agreed to by Beth. ABC refused to deliver the computers, and Deco sued ABC for breach of contract.

Thereafter, Alfred became concerned about how Beth and Charles were managing ABC. He contacted Zeta, Inc. ("Zeta"), ABC's components supplier. He told Zeta's president, "Don't allow Charles to order components; he's not our technical person. That's Beth's job."

Charles later placed an order for several expensive components with Zeta. ABC refused to pay for the components, and Zeta sued ABC for breach of contract. Not long afterwards, ABC went out of business, owing its creditors over $500,000.

1. How should ABC's debt be allocated? Discuss.

2. Is Deco likely to succeed in its lawsuit against ABC? Discuss.

3. Is Zeta likely to succeed in its lawsuit against ABC? Discuss.

[July 2010 #4]

CIVIL PROCEDURE
[See lecture for California Civil Procedure for California rules]

I. **DOES THE COURT HAVE THE AUTHORITY TO DECIDE THE DISPUTE?**

    A. **Does the court have authority over the parties?**
        1. Personal Jurisdiction
            a. Traditional ways of asserting jurisdiction
                1) domicile
                2) presence in state when served
                3) consent
                    a) appearing in the action
                    b) by contract
                    c) appointment of agent for service
                    d) implied consent, e.g., non-resident motorist statutes
            b. Assertion of jurisdiction over non-residents
                1) state long-arm statute, and
                2) minimum contacts
                    a) purposeful availment
                    b) foreseeability
                3) traditional notions of fair play and substantial justice
                    a) relatedness between claim and contact (less important if contact is great)
                    b) convenience
                    c) state's interest
        2. In rem jurisdiction
        3. Quasi in rem jurisdiction
        4. Notice--service of process

    B. **Does the court have authority over the subject matter?**
        1. Subject matter jurisdiction
            a. State courts are generally courts of unlimited jurisdiction. The only limits are statutory
            b. Federal courts only have jurisdiction over two types of claims:
                1) federal questions
                2) diversity actions
                    a) complete diversity
                    b) good faith allegation over $75,000
            c. Removal
            d. Supplemental jurisdiction

    C. **Is the court the proper place to resolve the dispute?**
        1. Venue in federal courts
            a. district where any defendant resides, if all defendants in same state;
            b. where a substantial part of the claim arose, or
            c. if no district meets a. or b.:
                1) in diversity cases, district where any defendant is subject to personal jurisdiction or
                2) in other cases, where any defendant may be found.
            d. Improper or inappropriate venue

        1)   transfer

        2)   forum non conveniens

II. WHAT LAW GOVERNS THIS DISPUTE?

A. Erie Doctrine

    1. Federal courts are required to apply state substantive law to nonfederal causes of action

    2. The Necessary and Proper Clause allows federal courts to apply federal procedural rules. In addition, federal courts will apply some state "procedural" rules when those rules have no bearing on the mechanics of the federal court system

III. ARE THE PLEADINGS PROPER?

A. Federal courts use notice pleading - the pleading must put the opposing party on notice of the claim. By contrast, some states use code pleading

B. Complaint
    1. statement of subject matter jurisdiction
    2. statement of the claim
    3. demand for relief

C. Defendant's response
    1. Answer
    2. Rule 12 motion (watch waivable defenses)

D. Counterclaim
    1. Compulsory
    2. Permissive
    3. Supplemental jurisdiction, if needed, for compulsory

E. Cross-claims - Supplemental jurisdiction (if needed)

F. Amendments and Supplemental pleadings

G. Rule 11
    1. Certification
    2. Sanctions

IV. ARE THE PROPER PARTIES AND CLAIMS BEFORE THE COURT?

A. Joinder of Parties
    1. Compulsory Joinder - necessary parties should be joined if possible
    2. Permissive Joinder - If joinder of necessary party not feasible (e.g., would destroy diversity jurisdiction), court must either proceed without absentee or dismiss the case.

B.   Joinder of Claims
    1.   Class Actions
        a.   Initial requirements
            1)   Class is so numerous that joinder of all members is impracticable
            2)   Questions of law or fact common to the class
            3)   The claims of the representative parties are typical of the class
            4)   The representative parties will fairly and adequately protect the interest of the class

        b.   Types
            1)   "prejudice"
            2)   injunction/declaratory judgment
            3)   common question predominate

    2.   Intervention
        a.   Intervention as of right
        b.   Permissive intervention
        c.   Supplemental jurisdiction (if needed) for intervention of right or defendant

    3.   Impleader
        a.   Indemnity or contribution
        b.   Other claims: TPD v. plaintiff and plaintiff v. TPD
        c.   Supplemental jurisdiction (if needed) for impleader and TPD v. plaintiff

    4.   Interpleader
        a.   Rule 22 Interpleader
        b.   Statutory Interpleader

V.   HAVE THE PARTIES PROPERLY PROPOUNDED AND REPLIED TO DISCOVERY?

A.   Types of discovery
    1.   Depositions
    2.   Interrogatories
    3.   Requests to Produce
    4.   Physical or Mental Examinations
    5.   Requests for Admission
    6.   Required disclosures

B.   Scope of discovery
    1.   Anything reasonably calculated to lead to admissible evidence
    2.   Privileged matter not discoverable
    3.   Work product

C.   Enforcement of discovery rules (sanctions)
    1.   Total or partial failure to provide discovery: motion to compel plus costs and certify good faith attempt to obtain discovery
    2.   Sanctions include:
        a.   Treat matters as admitted

           b.   Disallow evidence on an issue
           c.   Establish the issue adverse to the violating party
           d.   Strike the pleadings
           e.   Dismiss the cause of action or the entire action (bad faith)
           f.   Enter a default judgment (bad faith)
           g.   Hold in contempt, except for refusal to submit to physical or mental exam.
       3.   Immediate or Automatic sanction

VI.   CAN THE DISPUTE BE RESOLVED WITHOUT A TRIAL?

   A.   12(b)(6) - failure to state claim

   B.   Dismissal
         1.   Voluntary
         2.   Involuntary

   C.   Summary Judgment
         1.   The moving party must show that there is no triable issue of fact and entitled to judgment as matter of law
         2.   Partial summary judgment can be granted

VII.   IF THERE IS A TRIAL, WHO WILL DECIDE THE MATTER?

   A.   Seventh Amendment guarantees a right to jury trial for actions at common law, but not for equitable actions. State constitutional provisions and statutes also guarantee jury trials

   B.   Written demand

   C.   When an action contains legal and equitable claims, legal claim tried first to a jury

   D.   The verdict can be a general verdict, a special verdict or a general verdict with interrogatories

   E.   If there is a jury, can the jury be disregarded?
         1.   Nonsuit
         2.   Judgment as a Matter of Law
         3.   Renewed Motion for Judgment as a Matter of Law
         4.   Motion for New Trial

VIII.   CAN THE DECISION BE APPEALED?

   A.   The Final Judgment Rule requires a final judgment of the entire case before an appeal may be taken

   B.   Exceptions to the Final Judgment Rule
         1.   Pretrial orders involving temporary remedies
         2.   Final judgment on collateral matters
         3.   Interlocutory orders of great importance that may be determinative of the ultimate decision

IX. IS THE DECISION BINDING IN FUTURE CASES?

A. Res Judicata (Claim Preclusion)
  1. When there is a final judgment on the merits, res judicata prevents re-assertion of the claimant's cause of action
  2. "On the merits" is any judgment except one based on jurisdiction, venue or indispensable parties (or if first court said it was not on merits)

B. Collateral Estoppel (Issue Preclusion)
  1. Issues of fact actually litigated and essential to a judgment in a first action are conclusive in a subsequent, although different, action between the plaintiff and defendant or their privies
  2. Default and consent judgments do not involve litigation of the merits and therefore do not give rise to collateral estoppel

C. Who is bound by the judgment?
  1. Parties are bound
  2. Privies to parties are also bound including those who control the litigation and will be affected by the outcome
  3. Strangers are not bound, but may take advantage of collateral estoppel if jurisdiction rejects mutuality doctrine
  4. Other jurisdictions
    a. The Constitution requires that full faith and credit be given to public acts, records and judicial proceedings of sister states. Federal statutes compel recognition of federal court judgments
    b. Full faith and credit is only required when the court had personal jurisdiction over the parties and the court issued a final judgment on the merits
    c. Full faith and credit is not required for foreign country judgments.

CIVIL PROCEDURE - QUESTION 1

Paul was injured two years ago by a defectively constructed machine while working in an industrial plant in State A. The machine had been manufactured by Manco, a State B Corporation. Doctor (Doc) treated Paul for his injuries in a State A hospital (Hospital). During the course of the treatment, Doc prescribed medication to which Paul was allergic. Paul's condition worsened gradually after that, but it is unclear whether this decline was due to the drug or to the progression of his injuries.

Paul sued Hospital in a State A state court for negligence. Hospital's defense was (1) that it was not responsible for the acts of Doc because he was an independent contractor, (2) that Doc had not been negligent, and (3) that the worsening of Paul's condition had resulted from the injury, rather than from the medication. After a trial before a judge sitting without a jury, the court ruled that Doc had not acted negligently and that he was not an agent of Hospital. The court further ruled that it need not reach the causation issue. No appeal was taken.

Paul later died from his condition, and Wanda, his widow, who had lived in State A for five years, returned to her original home in State C, located about 1,500 miles from State A. As executor of Paul's estate, she sued Manco and Doc for the injuries to and death of Paul. The suit was filed in a State C state court.

Manco sells its products in forty states and has a small sales office in State C. For fifteen years, Manco has sold its industrial machinery in State C, its sales there having ranged from $400,000 to $500,000 a year. The machine that injured Paul was originally sold to Dealer, located in State A, who in turn sold it to Paul's employer. Manco was served by mail at its corporate headquarters as provided for under the State C long arm statute.

Doc lives and practices medicine only in State A but he was personally served with process at an airport hotel in State C. Doc, who was on a highly-publicized speaking tour, arrived in State C on the morning of his speech, and left four hours later to speak in another state.

It is undisputed that (1) State C asserts personal jurisdiction to the full extent permitted by the United States Constitution, and (2) Wanda's suit was not barred by the statute of limitations.

Manco timely moved to dismiss the complaint as to it on the ground that the court lacked personal jurisdiction over Manco. The motion was denied.

Doc timely moved to dismiss the complaint as to him on the grounds that the court lacked personal jurisdiction over him. The motion was denied. Subsequently, Doc timely moved to dismiss the complaint on the grounds that the suit against him was barred by the principles of res judicata and collateral estoppel. A certified copy of the judgment in Paul's suit against Hospital was attached to the motion. The motion was denied.

Did the court rule correctly on:

  a.   Manco's motion to dismiss? Discuss.

  b.   Doc's motion to dismiss on grounds of lack of personal jurisdiction? Discuss.

  c.   Doc's motion to dismiss on grounds of res judicata and collateral estoppel? Discuss.

29

Civil Procedure Question 1

a.   Manco's motion to dismiss

1.   Personal jurisdiction
   a.   State C long arm statute
   b.   No traditional bases because Manco not a resident of C and corporate headquarters in B.
   c.   Minimum contacts
      1)   Purposeful availment? has maintained small office for 15 years in C, sells $400,000 to $500,000 – benefited and protected by C's laws
      2)   Foreseeability – selling products in state C makes it foreseeable Manco will be sued in C.
   Reasonable?
      1)   Relationship to cause of action – Manco sold machine to Dealer in A, who sold it to employer in A. Injury in A. Wanda moved to C.
      2)   State C's interest – protecting citizens sufficient?
      3)   Convenience – State C is 1,500 miles from State A Office

b.   Doc's motion to dismiss

1.   Personal jurisdiction when D is present in forum
   a.   Doc personally served in C
      1)   Doc came to lecture
      2)   presence not gained by trick or fraud

c.   Doc's motion on res judicata and collateral estoppel

1.   Res Judicata – claim preclusion
   a.   Identity of parties – Doc not a party
   b.   Claim resolved favorably for moving party

2.   Collateral Estoppel – issue preclusion
   a.   Wanda as executor was a party
   b.   Negligence issue actually determined in State A decision
   c.   Negligence issue not essential because issue of agency was sufficient to justify judgment in Paul v. Hospital
   d.   Mutuality – relaxed or eliminated when defendant asserts

CIVIL PROCEDURE QUESTION 2

Pat, involuntarily hospitalized in a State A hospital, filed a *pro se* complaint in federal district court in State A naming in the caption the following defendants: the United States, State A, Smith and Jones. The complaint alleged that State A violated State A law by hospitalizing him and that Smith, a hospital orderly, viciously beat him. The only allegation concerning Jones appeared immediately after the allegation concerning Smith and stated, "Regarding Jones: see Smith above." There was no mention of the United States other than in the caption.

Pat further alleged that the defendants' actions violated his federal civil rights under 42 U.S.C. §1983, that he was a citizen of State B, and all defendants were State A citizens. He requested damages of $6,000,000 on his claim against State A, $37,500 from Smith and $37,500 from Jones.

Each defendant moved, on the basis of the pleadings alone, to dismiss the complaint on the ground that the court lacked jurisdiction. State A also moved for its dismissal on the basis that it was not a proper defendant. The United States, Smith and Jones also moved for their dismissals on the basis that the claims against them were not sufficiently pleaded. Pat responded that his complaint was "just fine."

The trial judge, relying only on the pleadings, ruled as follows:

1. The court has jurisdiction;

2. State A is not a proper defendant; and

3. The claims against the United States, Smith and Jones are sufficiently pleaded.

Was the court correct as to each of these rulings? Discuss.

31

Civil Procedure Question 2

a.   **Subject Matter Jurisdiction**

1.   Federal Question
     a.   The federal question must appear as part of the
          plaintiff's cause of action set out in a well-pleaded
          complaint. Here, Pat has based his claim under a
          federal civil rights statute.
     b.   In addition, the court could exercise supplemental
          jurisdiction.
2.   Diversity of citizenship
     a.   Diversity of citizenship requires no plaintiff and no
          defendant is from the same state.
          1)   Here, Pat is from State B and all defendants are
               from State A.
     b.   Amount in controversy must be a good faith allegation
          exceeding $75,000, exclusive of interest and costs.
          1)   As to State A = $6 mil
          2)   As to Smith and Jones, $37.5 each
               a)   Pat can aggregate claims against several
                    Ds only if Ds are jointly liable to P.
               b)   However, the total does not exceed 75K.
3.   Supplemental Jurisdiction
     a.   The federal court has discretion to exercise pendent
          jurisdiction over a state law claim if the two
          claims derive form a common nucleus of operative
          fact and if a plaintiff would ordinarily
          be expected to try all issues in one proceeding.
     b.   Here, Pat has asserted a claim under the federal
          statute and State A law.

b.   **State A is not a proper D**

1.   The 11th Amendment prohibits a federal court from hearing
     a private party's claims against a state government.
2.   State A may waive immunity, which it has not done here.

c.   **Claims not sufficiently pleaded**

1.   Pat's complaint should contain a short statement of the
     grounds for the court's jurisdiction, of the claim that
     the pleader is entitled to relief and a demand for relief.
2.   As to the US, Pat did not provide any of the above and
     only inserted the US in the caption.
3.   As to Smith and Jones, it appears that the allegations in
     the complaint are sufficient as to Smith but not Jones.
4.   A party can move for a more definite statement.

CIVIL PROCEDURE QUESTION 3

Pat was living in State X when he was arrested and charged with violating a State X criminal statute. Because of overcrowding in State X Penitentiary, however, Pat was forced to await trial while incarcerated in the security wing of Delta Hospital (D), a private hospital for persons with psychiatric disorders, located and incorporated in the neighboring state of Y.

Pat filed a class action complaint against D in a federal district court in State X on behalf of himself, on behalf of 25 similarly situated inmates who were incarcerated at D awaiting trial in State X and on behalf of all such future inmates. The complaint alleged violations of the State Y Prisoners' Rights Act, which guarantees prisoners, inter alia, the right to safe food. The complaint alleged that the food served at D was often spoiled and contaminated with vermin droppings and that, as a result, he suffered continual gastrointestinal disorders. Pat requested $70,000 in damages and an injunction prohibiting D from serving tainted food. D was properly served with a copy of the complaint.

Before D responded to the civil complaint, Pat's brother paid Pat's bail. As a result, Pat is no longer detained at D and has returned to State X.

The federal district court:

1. Denied a motion by D to dismiss for lack of jurisdiction;

2. Declined to certify the class on the ground that the class was not large enough;

3. Declined a motion by D to change venue to a federal district court in State Y; and

4. Granted a motion by D to dismiss the action as moot.

Was each of the rulings correct? Discuss.

33

Civil Procedure Question 3

1. Denial of D's motion to dismiss for lack of jurisdiction

    a. Federal Subject Matter Jurisdiction
      1)   Federal Question – not met here since P's claim based on State Y law
      2)   Diversity of Citizenship
         a)   Parties
            (1) P is named representative whose domicile is in State X since he does not intend to stay in State Y.
            (2) D, hospital, as a corporation can be a citizen of its principal place of business and where incorporated. Here, D is located and incorporated in State Y.
         b)   Amount in controversy – over $75,000
            (1) P claimed $70,000 in damages
            (2) P also requested an injunction – consider value of right to be protected or extent of injury to be prevented – tainted food
            (3) Complaint dismissed only if there is no legal possibility that recovery will exceed jurisdictional amount.

    b.   Personal Jurisdiction
      1)   Assume State X has a long arm statute
      2)   Minimum contacts
         a)   D purposefully availed itself of State X's laws by accepting prisoners from State X
         b)   Foreseeable to D that it could be sued over care of State X prisoners.
      3)   Reasonable to assert jurisdiction
         a)   Cause of action connected to contacts
         b)   Convenience because State X is neighbor of State Y
         c)   State X has an interest over its prisoners

2. Declined class certification because the class was not large enough

    a.   Certification of class actions require numerosity, common questions, typicality and fair and adequate representation.
    b.   Here, issue is numerosity – joinder of all members is impracticable.
      1)   26 inmates (including P) plus future inmates
      2)   Inconsistent results

3.   Denied D's motion to change venue

    a.   Venue is proper where any D resides, events occurred or in diversity cases, where any D is subject to personal jurisdiction. To transfer to another venue the transferee court must have subject matter jurisdiction, personal jurisdiction and venue.

        1)   Original venue did not exist in State X but D is subject to personal jurisdiction in State X (see above).

        2)   Even if proper in State X, court may transfer for convenience factors to State Y.

4.   Granted D's motion to dismiss as moot

    a.   There must a genuine case or controversy.
    b.   If a matter has been resolved, it is dismissed as being moot. Here, P was no longer detained at D.
    c.   Exception if matter is capable of repetition or in class actions if other members' claims are still viable. Here, the food may still be contaminated and injunctive relief is still viable for remaining and future inmates.

CIVIL PROCEDURE QUESTION 4

Diane owns a large country estate to which she plans to invite economically disadvantaged children for free summer day camp. In order to provide the children with the opportunity to engage in water sports, Diane started construction to dam a stream on the property to create a pond. Neighbors downstream, who rely on the stream to irrigate their crops and to fill their wells, immediately demanded that Diane stop construction. Diane refused. Six months into the construction, when the dam was almost complete, the neighbors filed an application in state court for a permanent injunction ordering Diane to stop construction and to remove the dam. They asserted causes of action for nuisance and for a taking under the United States Constitution. After a hearing, the state court denied the application on the merits. The neighbors did not appeal the ruling.

Thereafter, Paul, one of the neighbors and a plaintiff in the state court case, separately retained Lawyer and filed an application for a permanent injunction against Diane in federal court asserting the same causes of action and requesting the same relief as in the state court case. Personal jurisdiction, subject matter jurisdiction, and venue were proper. The federal court granted Diane's motion to dismiss Paul's federal court application on the basis of preclusion.

Infuriated with the ruling, Paul told Lawyer, "If the court can't give me the relief I am looking for, I will take care of Diane in my own way and that dam, too." Unable to dissuade Paul and after telling him she would report his threatening comments to criminal authorities, Lawyer called 911 and, without identifying herself, told a dispatcher that "someone is on his way to hurt Diane."

1. Was the state court's denial of Diane's neighbors' application for a permanent injunction correct? Discuss. Do not address substantive property or riparian rights.

2. Was the federal court's denial of Paul's application for a permanent injunction correct? Discuss. Do not address substantive property or riparian rights.

3. Did Lawyer commit any ethical violation when she called 911? Discuss.

Answer according to both California and ABA authorities.
[July 2009 #5]

COMMUNITY PROPERTY

I. ANALYSIS APPROACH

Step 1: **State basic presumptions of California community property law.**

Step 2: **Are there any issues which affect all or most items of property?**

Step 3: **Divide the question by item of property (usually organized by the call of the question).**

Step 4: **Analyze the character of each item of property.**

    a.   When was the asset acquired? What presumptions apply?

    b.   Where was the asset acquired?

    c.   What was the source of funds used to acquire the asset? What presumptions apply?

    d.   Have any actions been taken by the parties which change the character of the property?

    e.   Are there any special rules which apply to this property?

    f.   What is the resulting character of the property?

Step 5: **Discuss preemption issues, if any.**

Step 6: **For each item of property, analyze what will be done with it for purposes of the question**

II. WRITING AN ESSAY
A. **Start your essay by explaining the basic presumptions which govern the law of community property:**

"California is a community property state. All property acquired during the course of a marriage is presumed to be community property. All property acquired before marriage or after permanent separation is presumed to be separate property. In addition, any property acquired by gift, devise or bequest is presumed to be separate property.

"In order to determine the character of any asset, courts will trace back to the source of funds used to acquire the asset. A mere change in form of an asset does not change its characterization. With these basic principles in mind, we can now turn to the specific items of property involved in this instance."

B. **Analyze any issues, which affect all (or most) of the assets**

    1. For example, in some questions there is a transmutation which affects all of the assets. You may want to discuss an issue like this at the outset.

    2. Likewise, you might want to discuss the basic rules regarding what happens to the property at divorce or at death depending on the type of question:

> "At divorce, the community assets will be equally divided in kind unless some special rule requires deviation from the equal division requirement."

> **OR** "At death, the decedent can leave all of his separate property and one half of the community property. If the decedent dies intestate, the surviving spouse is automatically entitled to the decedent's share of the community property and 1/3 to all of the decedent's separate property depending on whether the decedent left issue or parents surviving."

C. **Separate each item of property.**

    1. Isolate each asset acquired by the spouses and use a heading to break up your discussion by asset.

    2. Isolate any liabilities incurred by the spouses and use a heading to break up your discussion by liability.

D. **For each asset or liability, discuss the basic presumptions, which govern the asset or liability.**

    1. For each asset or liability, determine whether any special classification exists and set forth the special classification rule.

        a. **Personal injury awards** are CP if the cause of action arose during marriage. If the cause of action arose before marriage or after permanent separation, the award is SP. At divorce, CP personal injury awards will be awarded entirely to the injured spouse unless the interests of justice require otherwise. Personal injury awards against the other spouse are always the SP of the injured spouse.

        b. **Retirement benefits** are CP if earned during the course of the marriage. For retirement pensions and other retirement benefits earned before and during marriage, courts use the time rule to determine how much of the pension is attributable to CP labor and how much is attributable to SP labor.

        c. **Disability pay and worker's compensation benefits** are either CP or SP depending on the wages they are designed to replace. To the extent disability benefits are taken in lieu of retirement benefits, disability benefits are treated as retirement benefits.

d.   Courts are split on **severance pay**. If it arises on the bar exam, raise arguments on both sides. Courts which treat severance as SP do so because they believe the severance pay replaces future wages which would have been received.

e.   **Stock options** are a form of employee compensation and they are treated as CP or SP depending on when they were earned. Courts use the time rule to determine the respective CP and SP shares.

f.   **Business and professional goodwill** is CP if earned during marriage.

g.   **Education and training** are not CP. The community may be entitled to reimbursement however when CP funds are used to pay for education or training and the education enhances the earning capacity of the spouses. The CP is not entitled to reimbursement where the community has already benefitted from the education or training; where the other spouse has also received community-funded education; or, where the need for spousal support is reduced by the education or training.

2.   **Property acquired with community and separate funds**.

a.   When property is acquired with community and separate funds and no title presumption applies, the community and separate property interests are determined by apportioning their respective contributions. (*Marriage of Moore*).

1)   The most common situation is when a spouse acquires property prior to marriage, but uses CP funds to pay off the mortgage.

2)   Example: Hal acquires a home for $100,000, paying $20,000 down and obtaining a mortgage for $80,000. One month later he marries Wanda. During the marriage, community funds have been used to pay off $30,000 on the mortgage. Hal and Wanda are now getting divorced. How should the property be divided?

"When community and separate funds are used to purchase an asset, the CP and SP acquire a pro rata ownership interest in the asset. To determine the respective shares of ownership, you start by figuring out the percentage that each contributed to the purchase price. The SP initially contributed $20,000 plus a mortgage of $80,000. The mortgage is SP because it was acquired prior to marriage and the intent of the lender must have been to rely on H's SP. From this amount, we must subtract the amount the CP contributed to pay off the mortgage ($30,000). Thus, the SP contributed $20,000 + $80,000 - $30,000 = $70,000. The CP contributed $30,000 of the initial purchase price. The SP share is $70,000/$100,000 or 7/10; the CP share is $30,000/$100,000 or 3/10. At divorce, the SP is entitled to its actual contribution to the purchase price ($20,000) plus 7/10 of the appreciation; the CP is entitled to $30,000 plus 3/10 of the appreciation."

    b.   By contrast, when CP is used to improve the SP of a spouse, the CP does not obtain a pro rata ownership interest in the asset but may be entitled to reimbursement.

        1)   When a spouse uses CP to benefit the SP of the other spouse, a gift is presumed.

        2)   When a spouse uses CP to benefit the spouse's own SP, the CP is entitled to reimbursement. The CP is entitled to the cost of the improvement or the increase in value of the SP whichever is greater.

3.   **Actions by the spouses altering the character of property.**

    a.   Antenuptial agreements (agreements before marriage) are enforceable, but must be in writing to satisfy the statute of frauds.

    b.   Transmutations (agreements during marriage)

        1)   Define what it is: "A transmutation is an agreement between spouses to change the character of an asset or series of assets."

        2)   Explain the requirements: "Prior to 1985, a transmutation could be oral, written or inferred from the conduct of the parties. After 1985, however, a transmutation must be in writing to be enforceable."

        3)   Apply to the facts: "Here, there (was/was not) a valid transmutation because..."

    c.   Married Woman's Special Presumption

        1)   Define what it is: "The Married Woman's Special Presumption (MWSP) is a special presumption which applies to property taken in the married woman's name alone prior to 1975. According to the MWSP, property taken in the name of a married woman prior to 1975 is presumed to be her separate property. The MWSP is based on the fact that prior to 1975 the husband was given sole management and control of the community assets and thus,

any property in the woman's name was
presumed to have been a gift to her."

    2) Explain the limits on MWSP: "The MWSP does
not apply to assets where some intent other
than a gift is shown or where the woman
controlled how title to the asset was
taken."

    3) Apply the MWSP to the asset in question:
"Here, the MWSP (does/does not) apply
because...."

d. Taking assets in joint title. What happens to
jointly titled property differs depending on whether
the property is being divided at divorce or at death.

    1) First, identify whether the characterization is
taking place at divorce or at death.

    2) Set forth the applicable rule completely:

"At death, Lucas applies. Under Lucas,
when a married couple takes title in joint and
equal form, it is inconsistent with the
preservation of a separate property interest in
the asset. Any SP used to acquire the asset is
presumed to be a gift of the SP unless there is
an oral or written agreement to the contrary."
or

"At divorce, the rules vary depending on
when the asset was acquired. Under California
Family Law, when a married couple takes title
to an asset in joint tenancy after 1984,
the asset is presumed to be community property
for purposes of divorce. The legislation was
later revised so that property taken by a
married couple in any joint form after 1987
is now presumed to be community property for
purposes of divorce. Thus, any SP used to
acquire the jointly title asset does not give
the SP a pro rata ownership interest in the
asset. However, the SP is entitled to
reimbursement for its contributions to the
purchase price of a jointly titled asset.
Jointly titled assets acquired before 1984
are governed by Lucas."

    3) Apply the applicable rule to the facts of the
case and state your conclusion.

e. Community labor enhancing the value of SP.

    1) When community labor is used to enhance the
value of a separate property business, the
community is entitled to share in the
increased value of the SP.

a)   Explain why CP has any interest:
"Here, although H's business is SP,
the CP is entitled to a share of the
appreciation of that business because
H's labor during the course of the
marriage was used to increase the value
of the business."

b)   Explain the different formulas for
calculating the CP's interest and
explain how they apply to the facts.

"Pereira accounting is used when the
increase in value of a separate property
business is primarily the result of
community labor. Using Pereira you determine
the value of the SP at the beginning of the
business and give it a fair rate of return
over the course of the marriage. Normally
this is the legal interest rate (10% simple
interest) calculated annually. The SP is
given the initial value plus the fair rate
of return. The remainder is CP. Here, if
Pereira accounting were used, ...(apply to
facts)."

"Van Camp accounting is used when the
increase in value of a business is primarily
the result of the unique nature of the SP
asset. Using Van Camp, you determine what a
fair salary would be for the community
labor. You multiply that by the years of the
marriage. You subtract any salary already
received and any amounts paid for community
expenses. The result is your CP share. The
rest is SP. Here, if Van Camp accounting
were used, ... (apply to facts)."

c)   Explain which method should be applied:
Example: "Here, Van Camp accounting should
be used. The principal reason for the
increase in value of the business was not
H's labor, but rather the increase in the
value of the product sold by the business
due to war time rationing by the
government."

42

E. **After characterizing the property, explain what happens to it for purposes of the question.**

1. **Distribution at Divorce.**
   a. State the basic rule: "The basic rule at divorce is to divide each community asset equally in kind. Thus, each spouse is given one-half of each community asset."
   b. Explain whether there are any reasons to deviate from the equal division rule.
      1) misappropriation by one spouse
      2) liabilities exceed assets
      3) educational debts will be assigned to the spouse who received the education.
      4) tort liabilities will be assigned to the tortfeasor spouse if the liability was not for the benefit of the community.
      5) family home may be awarded to the person Who is given custody of the minor children.

2. **Distribution at Death.**
   a. If the spouse dies with a will, the spouse is entitled to dispose of all of his or her separate property and one-half of the community property.
   b. If the spouse dies without a will, the community property is awarded entirely to the surviving spouse. Between one-third and all of the decedent's separate property will be awarded to the surviving spouse depending on whether there are issue or parents surviving.

3. **Quasi-Community Property**
   a. Explain what it is: "Quasi-Community property is property acquired by the couple while living in another jurisdiction which would have been classified as community property had the parties been domiciled in California."
   b. Explain what happens at divorce: "At divorce, quasi-community property is treated exactly like community property."
   c. Explain what happens at death: "At death, the surviving spouse has a one-half interest in the quasi-CP titled in the decedent's name. The decedent does not have an interest in the quasi-CP titled in the survivor's name."

4. **Management and Control During Marriage**
   a. Explain the basic rule: "The general rule is that during the marriage the spouses have equal management and control of all the community assets."

43

b. Explain whether there is an applicable exception to the equal management rule:
1) Real property transfers: both spouses must join.
2) Personal belongings including clothing and furniture.
3) Spouse managing a business is given primary management and control.
4) Bank accounts in the name of one spouse alone.

F. Discuss any preemption issues if they exist.

1. **Preemption**
   a. Explain the basic concept: "Under the Supremacy Clause, federal law preempts inconsistent state laws. In some instances, federal law preempts California from applying community property concepts to certain assets."

   b. Explain whether preemption applies or not:
   1) Preempted
      a) federal homestead claims
      b) military life insurance benefits
      c) U.S. Savings Bonds
      d) Social Security benefits

   2) Not preempted
      a) railroad retirement benefits
      b) military retirement benefits
      c) copyrights

COMMUNITY PROPERTY QUESTION 1

All the following events occurred in California.

Shortly after he graduated from college in 1978, Harry purchased a home for $40,000, taking title in his name. Harry's father gave him the $10,000 down payment and Harry borrowed the balance of the purchase price on a note secured by a 30 year mortgage for the remainder. A month later, Harry married Wilma and began work for ABDO Corporation. Harry made all mortgage payments from his ABDO earnings. The house is now worth $500,000.

A homemaker until their children were grown, Wilma enrolled in a local public university and in 1997 earned a professional credential in landscape architecture. Her tuition and other educational costs were paid by Harry from his ABDO earnings.

In 2002, using a $50,000 inheritance from her father, Wilma established a remarkably successful landscape business, Flora, Inc. In 2006, Wilma was offered $600,000 for Flora even though the physical assets were worth only $50,000. Wilma rejected the offer.

In 2008, Harry was permanently and totally disabled in a hunting accident. In satisfaction of his claim for personal injuries, he received a $400,000 settlement, which he used to purchase a portfolio of corporate stocks now worth $600,000.

Harry can no longer work at ABDO because of his disability. He now receives ABDO disability benefits, which provide two-thirds of his monthly pre-injury salary. The disability payments will continue until 2015 when Harry turns 60. He will then receive ABDO early retirement benefits, which will be three-fourths of his pre-injury monthly salary.

Harry and Wilma have decided to obtain a dissolution of their marriage.

1. How should the following assets be classified and distributed on dissolution:
    A. The house? Discuss.
    B. Flora, Inc? Discuss.
    C. The corporate stocks? Discuss.
    D. The ABDO disability payments? Discuss.
    E. The future ABDO retirement benefit payments? Discuss.

2. Should any adjustment in the distribution be made in order to reflect the cost and value of Wilma's education? Discuss.

45

Community Property Question 1

Harry and Wilma

1. **Classification and Distribution of assets**

A. **The house**

    1.   Characterization
        a.   SP - Harry acquired before marriage in his name
    2.   CP gets pro rata interest - <u>Moore</u>
        a.   Harry used $10,000 SP as down payment, i.e. 1/4 of price of $40,000
        b.   Harry used CP earnings of $30,000 to pay off mortgage, i.e. 3/4 of price
        c.   CP gets 3/4 and Harry's SP gets 1/4
            1)   Harry's SP interest = his original $10,000 + 1/4 of the appreciation
            2)   CP interest = $30,000 + 3/4 of appreciation. Thus, Wilma and Harry would split
    3.   Equal division rule

B. **Flora, Inc.**

    1.   Characterization
        a.   Trace acquisition to SP inheritance of $50,000
    2.   Appreciation of SP during marriage - Wilma offered $600,000 although assets worth $50,000
        a.   Goodwill of business - thus CP to be equally divided
        b.   If used, <u>Pereira</u> - SP gets return on original investment, CP gets balance
        c.   <u>Van Camp</u> - CP awarded reasonable salary, SP gets balance
        d.   Preferable method here is <u>Pereira</u> because of Wilma's efforts.

C. **The corporate stocks**

    1.   Characterization - trace
        a.   Personal injury award during marriage is CP
    2.   Distribution upon divorce
        a.   Personal injury damages traceable to stocks
        b.   Awarded entirely to Harry unless commingled with other CP
    3.   The $200,000 appreciation would follow its source and thus would be CP

D.   The ABDO disability payments

    1.   Characterization
        a.   Disability pay is CP if intended to replace marital earnings, here 2/3 of monthly salary
    2.   Distribution
        a.   CP until parties separate; thereafter, Harry's SP.

E.   The future ABDO retirement benefit payments

    1.   Characterization
        a.   CP to the extent the right to benefits earned during marriage
    2.   Distribution
        a.   Time Rule - apportion SP and CP interests according to the total years worked and years during marriage

2.   Wilma's education

A.   Characterization
    1.   Education is not a community asset

B.   Distribution
    1.   CP entitled to reimbursement when community funds used to pay for education and the education substantially enhances the spouse's earning capacity.
    2.   Reimbursement reduced if community has already substantially benefited
        a.   Rebuttable presumption of 10 years has passed.
        b.   CP should not be reimbursed.

COMMUNITY PROPERTY QUESTION 2

Two years ago, Mike and Flo, who were not married but were living together in California, signed an agreement stating they would "share" subsequent acquisitions and disbursements "just as if we were married." Shortly thereafter Flo was seriously injured and she had to quit her job.

The pair lived on Mike's wages as a bartender, from which he paid $500 a month in support of his children from a prior marriage. In January of last year, Mike inherited $20,000, which he put into a savings account in his name alone.

Flo received $400,000 in settlement of her personal injury claims. Flo invested half of her settlement in diamonds and half in bonds in her name alone.

Recently Mike took the diamonds and sold them to Bud for $100,000. Mike soon lost this money while gambling in Las Vegas. Flo was unaware of the removal and sale of the diamonds or of the gambling losses.

Mike has left Flo and has sued her to enforce their agreement. Flo has denied the validity of the agreement and has also asserted appropriate counterclaims. Flo has cross-complained against Bud seeking recovery of the diamonds.

The bonds Flo bought are still worth $200,000, and Mike's savings account contains $20,000. During the time Mike and Flo lived together, Mike paid $18,000 from his wages in child support.

On what theory or theories may:

1. Flo assert rights against Mike because of his child support payments? Discuss.
2. Flo assert rights in or to the $20,000 savings account? Discuss.
3. Mike assert rights in or to the bonds? Discuss.
4. Flo assert rights against Mike as a result of the taking and sale of the diamonds? Discuss.
5. Flo assert rights against Bud arising out of his acquisition of the diamonds? Discuss.

Answer according to California law.

COMMUNITY PROPERTY QUESTION 2

<u>Mike and Flo</u>

<u>The agreement</u>

1. Valid, enforceable contract
2. Valid, enforceable antenuptial agreement
   a. Writing
   b. Not against public policy and likely there was disclosure
3. Treat under California community property rules

1. <u>Child support</u>
   a. Generally, debts during marriage are CP
      1) Exception: child support payments from prior marriage.
   b. CP entitled to reimbursement if SP available
      1) Here, Mike inherited $20,000, his SP
      2) Flo entitled to ½ of CP share

2. <u>Savings account</u>
   a. Mike's inheritance is his SP
   b. Savings account in his name alone
   c. Savings account is Mike's SP unless subject to child support (above) or he commingled

3. <u>Bonds</u>
   a. Trace bonds to ½ of personal injury settlement
   b. Flo injured after agreement
      1) Settlement would be CP
      2) Placing bonds in her name does not change character
   c. CP personal injury awards are given to injured spouse upon dissolution, unless justice requires otherwise
      1) Flo can argue Mike has sufficient SP and the bonds were not commingled
      2) Flo may be entitled to all but at least ½

4. <u>Diamonds</u>
   a. Trace diamonds to personal injury settlement -- CP
   b. Equal management and control over CP
      1) Mike took and sold diamonds below value and lost the money
      2) Flo may have no right to reimbursement unless she successfully argues a gift without her consent or Mike deliberately misappropriated

5. <u>Rights against Bud</u>
   a. Flo may seek to void Mike's transaction with Bud as raised above.
   b. Bud would defend, arguing he was a bona fide purchaser

COMMUNITY PROPERTY QUESTION 3

In 1998, Henry and Wilma, residents of California, married. Henry had purchased shares of stock before marriage and kept these shares in his brokerage account. The shares in the account paid him an annual cash dividend of $3,000. Henry deposited this income in a savings account held in his name alone.

In 1999, Wilma was hired by Tech Co. Wilma was induced to work for Tech Co. by the representation that successful employees would receive bonuses of company stock options. Later that year, Wilma was given options on 1,000 shares of Tech Co. stock. These stock options are exercisable in 2006, as long as Wilma is still working for Tech Co.

In 2003, because of marital difficulties, Wilma moved out of the home she had shared with Henry. Nevertheless, the couple continued to attend marriage counseling sessions that they had been attending for several months. Later that year, Henry was injured in an automobile accident. Afterwards, Henry and Wilma discontinued marriage counseling and filed for dissolution of marriage.

In 2004, Henry settled his personal injury claim from the automobile accident for $20,000. The settlement included reimbursement for $5,000 of medical expenses that had been paid with community funds.

Henry had a child by a prior marriage and, over the course of his marriage to Wilma, had paid out of community funds a total of $18,000 as child support.

    1. When making the final property division in Henry and Wilma's dissolution proceeding, how should the court characterize the following items:
      a. Henry's savings account? Discuss.
      b. Henry's personal injury settlement? Discuss.
      c. Wilma's stock options? Discuss.

    2. Should the court require Henry to reimburse the community for his child support payments and, if so, in what amount? Discuss.

Answer according to California law.

[July 2005 #1]

51

COMMUNITY PROPERTY QUESTION 4

In 2000, Harry and Wanda, California residents, married. Harry was from a wealthy family and was the beneficiary of a large trust. After their marriage, Harry received income from the trust on a monthly basis, and deposited it into a checking account in his name alone. Harry remained unemployed throughout the marriage. Wanda began working as a travel agent. She deposited her earnings into a savings account in her name alone.

In 2003, Harry and Wanda purchased a vacation condo in Hawaii. They took title in both their names, specifying that they were "joint tenants with the right of survivorship." Harry paid the entire purchase price from his checking account, which contained only funds from the trust. Harry and Wanda orally agreed that the condo belonged to Harry.

In 2004, Harry purchased a cabin in the California mountains to use when he went skiing. He paid the entire purchase price of the cabin from his checking account, and took title to the cabin in his name alone.

In 2005, Wanda commenced a secret romance with Oscar. During a rendezvous with Oscar, Wanda negligently operated Oscar's car, causing serious personal injuries to Paul, another driver.

In 2006, Wanda received an e-mail advertisement inviting her to invest in stock in a bioengineering company. She discussed the investment with Harry, who thought it was too risky. Wanda nevertheless bought 200 shares of stock, using $20,000 from her savings account to make the purchase. She put the stock in her name alone.

In 2007, Harry and Wanda separated. Shortly thereafter, as a result of the car accident, Paul obtained a money judgment against Wanda.

Harry and Wanda are now considering dissolving their marriage. The condo and cabin have increased in value. The stock has lost almost all of its value.

{Interrogatories on next page}

1. In the event of a dissolution, how should the court rule on Harry's and Wanda's respective rights and liabilities with regard to:

   a. The condo in Hawaii? Discuss.
   b. The cabin in the California mountains? Discuss.
   c. The stock in the bioengineering company? Discuss.

2. What property can Paul reach to satisfy his judgment against Wanda? Discuss.

Answer according to California law.

[July 2010 #6]

CONSTITUTIONAL LAW

I. **JUSTICIABLE CASE OR CONTROVERSY (RAMPSE)**

    A. **Ripeness**

    B. **Abstention**

    C. **Mootness**

    D. **Political Question**

    E. **Standing**

    F. **Eleventh Amendment**

II. **WHAT KIND OF CONSTITUTIONAL ISSUE?**

    A. **Separation of Powers – Branches of Government**
        1. Judicial (see above under Justiciability)
        2. Executive (foreign and domestic powers and limitations, especially executive privilege)
        3. Legislative (source of power and limitations)

    B. **Federal Legislative Powers**
        1. Source of power
            a. Commerce Clause
            b. Spending
            c. Taxing
            d. Taking Property
            e. Citizenship
            f. Civil Rights
            g. Foreign Affairs
            h. War
            i. Elections
        2. Necessary and Proper Clause
        3. Limitations on power of 10th Amendment

    C. **State Interference with Federal System**
        1. Preemption
        2. Dormant Commerce Clause
            a. Discrimination against out-of-state interests
            b. Undue burden on interstate commerce
        3. Privileges & Immunities Clauses, art. IV and 14th Amendment.

III. **Individual Rights - (SSTRREPS)**
   A.   **S**tate Action - analyze first

   B.   **S**peech
        1.   Prior Restraint
        2.   Vagueness or Overbreadth
        3.   Content Regulation or Content Neutral
            a.   Content Regulations - Advocacy of Unlawful Conduct, Defamation, Obscenity, Fighting Words, Commercial Speech. Know the tests for each.
            b.   Content Neutral - Time, Place & Manner, Public Forums, Symbolic Expression, Freedom of Association. Know tests for each; generally compelling state interest standard.

   C.   **T**aking (5th Amendment)
        1.   Taking must be for public use
        2.   Taking requiring just compensation v. a regulation under police power not requiring just compensation.
        3.   Just compensation? Usually fair market value

   D.   **R**eligion
        1.   Establishment Clause
            a.   Secular Purpose
            b.   Secular Effect
            c.   No undue entanglement
        2.   Free Exercise Clause

   E.   **R**etroactive Legislation
        1.   Impairment of Contract
        2.   Ex Post Facto Laws
        3.   Bills of Attainder

   F.   **E**qual Protection
        1.   Classification or Fundamental Interest
            a.   Fundamental Interest, e.g. 1st Amendment, Travel, Voting - requires Strict Scrutiny
            b.   Classification
                1)   Suspect - race and alienage, requiring strict scrutiny
                2)   Quasi suspect - gender and illegitimacy, requiring middle tier analysis
                3)   Other classes - wealth, age, and others requiring rational basis

2. Scrutiny
   a. Strict Scrutiny - compelling state interest and means necessary to achieve state interest
   b. Middle Tier - important state interest and means substantially related
   c. Rational Basis - legitimate state interest and means rationally related

G. **P**rocedural Due Process
   1. Life, Liberty or Property Interest
   2. What process is due?

H. **S**ubstantive Due Process
   1. Privacy - Marriage, Procreation, Child rearing
   2. Strict Scrutiny

CONSTITUTIONAL LAW

I.   **JUSTICIABLE CASE OR CONTROVERSY (RAMPSE)**
   A.   Ripeness
   B.   Abstention
   C.   Mootness
   D.   Political Question
   E.   Standing
   F.   11th Amendment

II. **GOVERNMENTAL POWER**
   A.   Separation of Powers
   B.   Federal Power
      1.   Enumerated Powers
      2.   10th Amendment
   C.   State Police Power
   D.   State interference with Federal system
      1.   Preemption
      2.   Dormant Commerce Clause
      3.   Privileges & Immunities

III. **INDIVIDUAL RIGHTS (SSTRREPS)**
   A.   **S**tate Action
   B.   **S**peech
      1.   Prior restraint
      2.   Vagueness or Overbreadth
      3.   Content Regulation
      4.   Indirect Regulation
   C.   **T**aking (5th Amendment)
      1.   Taking for public use
      2.   Just compensation
   D.   **R**eligion
      1.   Establishment Clause
      2.   Free Exercise Clause
   E.   **R**etroactive Legislation
      1.   Impairment of contract
      2.   Ex post facto
      3.   Bills of attainder
   F.   **E**qual Protection
      1.   Classification or Fundamental right
      2.   Scrutiny
         a.   Strict scrutiny
         b.   Middle tier
         c.   Rational basis
   G.   **P**rocedural Due Process
      1.   Life, Liberty or Property interest
      2.   What process is due?
   H.   **S**ubstantive Due Process
      1.   Marriage, Procreation, Privacy
      2.   Strict Scrutiny

CONSTITUTIONAL LAW QUESTION 1

To prepare herself for a spiritual calling to serve as a pastor at City's jail, Ada enrolled in a nondenominational bible school. After graduating, Ada advised the pastor of her own church that she was ready to commence a ministry and asked that her church ordain her. While sympathetic to her ambition, Ada's pastor accurately advised her that their church did not ordain women.

Ada began going to City's jail during visiting hours and developed an effective ministry with prisoners, particularly women inmates who increasingly sought her counsel. Ada noticed that ordained ministers who visited the jail received special privileges denied to her.

Dan, the jail supervisor, told Ada that ministers who were ordained and endorsed by a recognized religious group were designated "jail chaplains" and, as such, were permitted access to the jail during nonvisiting hours. He told Ada that she too could be designated a jail chaplain if she obtained a letter from a recognized religious group stating that it had ordained her as a minister and had endorsed her for such work.

Ada replied that her church was not part of any recognized religious group and would not ordain her anyway because she was a woman. She asked Dan nonetheless to designate her a jail chaplain because of the effectiveness of her work.

Dan refused to designate Ada a jail chaplain or to allow her the access enjoyed by jail chaplains. He acted pursuant to jail regulations adopted to avoid security risks and staff involvement in making determinations as to who was really a "minister."

Ada has brought suit in federal court to obtain an injunction requiring that she be designated a jail chaplain or be granted access to City's jail equivalent to those who have been designated jail chaplains. Ada's complaint is based on the grounds that the refusal to designate her a jail chaplain violates rights guaranteed to her and the prisoners by the First Amendment to the U.S. Constitution and also violates rights guaranteed to her by the equal protection clause of the Fourteenth Amendment to the U.S. Constitution.

How should Ada's suit be decided? Discuss.

Constitutional Law Question 1

I. Ada's suit – Justiciable case or controversy? Ada alleges City's jail violates rights guaranteed "to her and the prisoners" by the First Amendment
   A. Ada's standing
      1. Injury in fact – denied being a jail chaplain or allowed access; asserts violations of 1st & 14th Amendments
      2. Causation – Dan/City's refusal
      3. Redressability – Injunction will require Dan/City to give Ada rights denied to her
   B. Prisoners
      1. Generally, no third party standing
      2. However, plaintiff may assert if she has suffered injury and:
         a. third parties find it difficult to assert own rights – may not be difficult here because prisoners could sue to see Ada, or
         b. plaintiff's injury adversely affects her relationship with third parties – Ada increasingly sought by women prisoners.

II. Individual Rights
   A. State Action – City is subdivision of state
   B. 1st Amendment applicable through 14th Amendment
   C. 1st Amendment Free Exercise of Religion Clause
      1. Ada was told jail chaplains must be ordained and endorsed by a recognized religious group to enjoy special privileges
         a. Court cannot declare Ada's religious beliefs to be false, but can inquire into the sincerity of her belief
         b. Strict scrutiny
            1) compelling state interest?
               a) security risks
               b) avoiding staff involvement
            2) means necessary/narrowly tailored?
               a) only ministers from certain religious groups not security risks?
               b) less restrictive alternatives available
         c. Prison Regulations usually upheld if reasonably related to legitimate penological interests.

D. 1st Amendment Establishment Clause
    1. Sect preference?
        a. If so, then strict scrutiny
        b. If none, then below
            1) Prison rule upheld if
                a) Secular purpose – security, avoid staff involvement
                b) Secular effect – "recognized religion" advances and inhibits but only affects visiting hours
                c) Excessive governmental entanglement with religion – jail officials must decide which religions are recognized

E. 14th Amendment – Equal Protection Clause
    1. Fundamental right – see 1st Amendment above
    2. Classification – Gender
        a. Intent to discriminate?
            1) not facial
            2) discriminatory impact – Ada's religion does not ordain women, though no facts to show City knew this until Dan was told
            3) difficult to show discriminatory motive or purpose unless City knew
        b. Quasi-suspect classification – gender – intermediate scrutiny
            1) important governmental interest – must be genuine - security
            2) discrimination substantially related
        c. If no intent to discriminate, then rational basis standard applies

CONSTITUTIONAL LAW QUESTION 2

A City ordinance enacted several years ago requires payment of an annual tax of $500 by each household in City with two or more children. The tax applies only to people who have become residents of City since the effective date of the ordinance. Its stated purpose is to reimburse City in part for the additional public school expenses and costs of recreational facilities attributable to the new residents.

Paul and Pat, husband and wife, became residents of City since the effective date of the tax ordinance and live alone with no children. They have filed suit against City in federal court for a judgment declaring that the ordinance violates their rights under the U.S. Constitution to familial privacy, to due process, and to equal protection.

During discovery, Paul and Pat revealed that they are medically unable to conceive a child and have applied to adopt twins. Although the court had ordered that this information remain confidential and all references to it were ordered sealed, City's attorney has disclosed the information in a press release. Paul and Pat have amended their complaint to allege another claim against City: i.e., that the disclosure by City's attorney violated their privacy rights under the U.S. Constitution, entitling plaintiffs to an injunction prohibiting further disclosures and allowing the court to impose sanctions for violation of its confidentiality order.

City has moved to dismiss the entire complaint on the following grounds: (1) the plaintiffs lack standing to challenge the tax ordinance, and (2) that, in any event, none of the alleged constitutional rights claimed by Paul and Pat were violated by City.

How should the court decide City's motion to dismiss? Discuss.

City's motion to dismiss – Standing

    A.   Standing requires:

        1.   Injury in fact

            a.   City ordinance applies only to people w/ 2 or more children who became residents after the ordinance's enactment.

            b.   Because Paul & Pat has applied to adopt twins, there is an imminent threat of injury

        2.   <u>Causation</u> – injury must be traceable to gov't action.

        3.   <u>Redressability</u> – a ruling in favor of the litigant must eliminate the threatened harm.

    B.   Ripeness

        1.   Where there is an immediate threat of harm, as in this case, the case is ripe.

II.   Constitutional challenges: Familial privacy, due process, equal protection.

    A.   State Action – City's ordinance

    B.   Familial privacy: Substantive due process

        1.   14th Amendment due process clause applies to local governments

        2.   Various privacy rights including marriage, procreation and childrearing are fundamental rights.

        3.   Regulations affecting privacy rights are subject to strict scrutiny.

            a.   Compelling state interest? Partially reimbursing city for expenses and recreational facilities.

            b.   Necessary to achieve purpose? May have less restrictive alternatives.

    C.   Due Process

        1.   Under 14th Amendment due process clause, government shall not take a person's life, liberty or property interest without due process of law.

        2.   A legitimate liberty or property interest must be denied. Here there is none.

    D.   Equal Protection

        1.   Under the 14th Amendment, P&P are entitled to equal treatment under the law

        2.   Classifications – facial discrimination

        3.   Rational basis standard

            a.   Legitimate state interest - fiscal

        b.   Means rationally related - increase in expenses due to use by new, larger families

4.   Fundamental right?
    a.   Right to travel
    b.   P&P argue durational requirement affects right to travel, however only affects travel between cities, not states.

E.   Violation of privacy rights
    1.   First Amendment
        a.   Prior restraint, to be valid must be narrowly tailored to achieve a compelling, or at least, significant governmental interest.
        b.   Here, court was probably trying to protect P&P's privacy, a significant interest, although the nondisclosure order may not have been necessary.
        c.   Collateral bar rule: If prior restraint proper, then City Attorney must have appealed immediately.

    2.   Invasion of Privacy
        a.   Publication of private facts and offensive to a reasonable person.
        b.   First Amendment requires a showing of constitutional malice.

CONSTITUTIONAL LAW QUESTION 3

The National Highway Transportation and Safety Administration (NHTSA), a federal agency, after appropriate hearings and investigation, made the following finding of fact: "The NHTSA finds that, while motor vehicle radar detectors have some beneficial purpose in keeping drivers alert to the speed of their vehicles, most are used to avoid highway speed-control traps and lawful apprehension by law enforcement officials for violations of speed-control laws." On the basis of this finding, the NHTSA promulgated regulations banning the use of radar detectors in trucks with a gross weight of five tons or more on all roads and highways within the United States.

State X subsequently enacted a statute prohibiting the use of radar detectors in any motor vehicle on any road or highway within State X. The State X Highway Department (Department) enforces the statute.

The American Car Association (ACA) is an association comprised of automobile motorists residing throughout the United States. One of ACA's purposes is to promote free and unimpeded automobile travel. ACA has received numerous complaints about the State X statute from its members who drive vehicles there.

In response to such complaints, ACA has filed suit against the Department in federal district court in State X, seeking a declaration that the State X statute is invalid under the Commerce Clause and the Supremacy Clause of the United States Constitution. The Department has moved to dismiss ACA's complaint on the ground that ACA lacks standing.

1. How should the court rule on the Department's motion to dismiss on the ground of ACA's lack of standing? Discuss.

2. On the assumption that ACA has standing, how should the court decide ACA's claim that the State X statute is invalid under the Commerce Clause and the Supremacy Clause of the United States Constitution? Discuss.

[February 2004 #5]

Constitutional Law Question #3

I. Organizational Standing

    A. Injury in fact to members – no one cited

    B. Injury related to organization's purpose – "free and unimpeded" auto travel

    C. Individual participation not required

II. Commerce Clause

    A. Federal power to regulate interstate commerce

    B. State power under police power

    C. State X law discriminate against interstate commerce?
      1. State X law broader than federal regulation
      2. State X law does not favor local interests

    D. Does State interest outweigh burden on interstate commerce?
      1. Burden of inconsistent regulations
      2. Strong State interest to provide safe roads

III. Supremacy Clause

    A. Federal law is supreme

    B. State law invalid when conflicts with federal statutes and regulations or frustrates federal regulations or prevents a federal objective

    C. Here, State X law does not conflict because it is broader than Federal regulations and does not frustrate or prevent federal regulations and objective.

CONSTITUTIONAL LAW QUESTION 4

In an effort to "clean up Columbia County," the County Board of Supervisors recently passed an ordinance, providing as follows:

"(1) A Review Panel is hereby established to review all sexually graphic material prior to sale by any person or entity in Columbia County.

(2) Subject to subsection (3), no person or entity in Columbia County may sell any sexually graphic material.

(3) A person or entity in Columbia County may sell an item of sexually graphic material if (a) the person or entity first submits the item to the Review Panel and (b) the Review Panel, in the exercise of its sole discretion, determines that the item is not pornographic.

(4) Any person or entity in Columbia County that fails to comply with subsection (2) or (3) is guilty of a misdemeanor, and is punishable by incarceration in jail for one year or by imposition of a $5,000 fine, or by both."

Videorama, Inc., a local video store, has brought an action claiming that the ordinance violates the First Amendment to the United States Constitution.

What arguments may Videorama, Inc. reasonably make in support of its claim, and is it likely to succeed? Discuss.

[July 2006#2]

CONSTITUTIONAL LAW QUESTION 5

In a recent statute, Congress authorized the United States Secretary of Transportation "to do everything necessary and appropriate to ensure safe streets and highways." Subsequently, the Secretary issued the following regulations:

Regulation A, which requires all instructors of persons seeking commercial driving licenses to be certified by federal examiners. The regulation details the criteria for certification, which require a minimum number of years of experience as a commercial driver and a minimum score on a test of basic communication skills.

Regulation B, which requires that every bus in commercial service be equipped with seatbelts for every seat.

Regulation C, which provides that states failing to implement adequate measures to ensure that bus seatbelts are actually used will forfeit 10 percent of previously appropriated federal funds that assist states with highway construction.

The State Driving Academy, which is a state agency that offers driving instruction to persons seeking commercial driving licenses, is considering challenging the validity of Regulation A under the United States Constitution. The Capitol City Transit Company, which is a private corporation that operates buses within the city limits of Capitol City, is considering challenging the validity of Regulation B under the United States Constitution. The State Highway Department, another state agency, is considering challenging the validity of Regulation C under the United States Constitution.

1. What constitutional challenge may the State Driving Academy bring against Regulation A, and is it likely to succeed? Discuss.

{Interrogatories continued on next page}

2. What constitutional challenge may the Capitol City Transport Company bring against Regulation B, and is it likely to succeed? Discuss.

3. What constitutional challenge may the State Highway Department bring against Regulation C, and is it likely to succeed? Discuss.

[July 2009 #4]

CONTRACTS

I. DOES THE UCC APPLY?

A. The UCC governs all contracts for the sale of goods
B. The UCC also has special rules governing transactions between merchants
C. If UCC does not apply, e.g. service contracts - then apply Common Law

II. IS THERE A VALID CONTRACT? – Mutual Assent and Consideration

A. **Offer**
   1. Manifestation of a present intent to contract demonstrated by a promise, undertaking or commitment
   2. Definite and certain terms
   3. Communicated to an identified offeree

B. **Has the offer been terminated?**
   1. Lapse of time
   2. Revocation: words or conduct of the offeror terminating the offer
      a. effective when received by offeree
      b. unless the offer is irrevocable
         1) option contract
         2) Merchant's Firm Offer under UCC
         3) detrimental reliance
   3. Rejection: words or conduct of the offeree rejecting the offer
      a. effective when received
      b. counteroffer acts as rejection
   4. Termination by operation of law
      a. death or insanity of either party
      b. destruction of subject matter of the contract
      c. supervening illegality

C. **Acceptance**
   1. Under common law, acceptance must mirror the offer
   2. Under the UCC, an acceptance which adds terms to the offer is valid.

      Between merchants, the additional terms become part of the contract unless they materially alter the contract, unless the offeror objects or unless the offer is limited to its terms. UCC § 2-207 ("battle of the forms").

    3.   Method of acceptance
        a.   promise to perform
        b.   starting to perform
        c.   complete performance
    4.   Mode of acceptance
        a.   manner authorized by offer
        b.   any reasonable manner
    5.   Effective upon dispatch
        a.   mailbox rule
        b.   limits on mailbox rule

D.   Consideration
    1.   Bargained for exchange
    2.   Legal detriment or legal benefit
        a.   adequacy generally irrelevant
        b.   past consideration
        c.   "pre-existing" duty rule
        d.   part payment to settle existing debt
        e.   payment to settle legal claim
        f.   payment of debt barred by statute of limitations
    3.   Promissory estoppel or detrimental reliance as a substitute for consideration

E.   Defenses to formation
    1.   Statute of frauds
    2.   Mistake
    3.   Illegality
    4.   Incapacity
    5.   Unconscionability
    6.   Duress
    7.   Fraud

III. TERMS OF THE CONTRACT

A.   Interpretation of terms
    1.   Custom and usage in the industry
    2.   Course of dealing between the parties

B.   Mistake and ambiguous terms

C.   Parol Evidence Rule

D.   Modification
    1.   Additional consideration needed under common law

2. Under UCC, no consideration needed so long as in good faith
3. Modification may need to satisfy Statute of Frauds

IV. THIRD PARTIES RIGHTS OR OBLIGATIONS

A. Third party beneficiaries
1. Intended or Incidental TPB?
2. Creditor or Donee TPB?
3. Have rights vested?
4. Who can sue whom?
   a. TBP v. promisor
   b. promisee v. promisor
   c. TBP v. promisee

B. Assignment of rights
1. Assignments are generally valid unless they materially alter the obligor's duty or risk, or unless they are prohibited by law
2. Does obligor have defenses against assignee?
3. What happens when there is more than one assignment of the same right?

C. Delegation of duties
1. Delegation of duties is permitted except where prohibited by the contract, where the duties involved personal judgment and skill or where the delegation would change the obligee's obligations.
2. Obligee may sue delegator and delegatee.

V. PERFORMANCE

A. Conditions
1. Types of conditions
   a. Express, implied, or constructive
   b. Precedent, concurrent, subsequent
2. Satisfaction of conditions
3. Excuse of conditions
   a. Wrongful prevention
   b. Voluntary disablement
   c. Anticipatory repudiation
   d. Waiver
   e. Estoppel

B. Discharge of duties
1. Impossibility – objective test

        a.   death or physical incapacity
        b.   illegality
        c.   destruction of subject matter
   2.   Impracticability
        a.   extreme and unreasonable difficulty that was unanticipated
        b.   subjective test

   3.   Frustration of purpose
   4.   Rescission
   5.   Novation
   6.   Accord and satisfaction

C.   **Breach**

VI.   REMEDIES

A.   **Damages**
   1.   Compensatory
        a.   expectation damages (benefit of the bargain) or reliance damages
        b.   consequential damages must be foreseeable
   2.   Liquidated damages
        a.   actual damages difficult to calculate at the time the contract was formed
        b.   amount is a reasonable forecast of damages
   3.   Punitive damages

B.   **Duty to mitigate**

C.   **Restitution - Quasi-contractual relief**

D.   **Specific Performance**

E.   **Recission**

F.   **Reformation**

CONTRACTS

I. **Which law governs?**

II. **Formation of Contract**
    A.   Mutual Assent
        1.   Offer
        2.   Acceptance
    B.   Consideration
        1.   Bargained for exchange
        2.   Promissory Estoppel

III. **Defenses to Formation**
    A.   Statute of Frauds
    B.   Mistake/Ambiguity
    C.   Illegality
    D.   Incapacity
    E.   Unconscionable
    F.   Fraud, Duress

IV. **Contract Terms**
    A.   Interpretation of terms
    B.   Modification
    C.   Parol Evidence Rule

V. **Third Parties**
    A.   Third Party Beneficiaries
    B.   Assignment/Delegation

VI. **Performance**
    A.   Conditions
        1.   Types
        2.   Excuse
        3.   Satisfaction
    B.   Discharge of Duty
        1.   Impossibility, Impracticability
        2.   Frustration of Purpose
        3.   Modification
        4.   Mutual Recission
        5.   Novation
        6.   Accord & Satisfaction
    C.   Breach - Major vs. Minor Breach

VII. **Remedies**
    A.   Compensatory Damages
    B.   Consequential Damages
    C.   Restitution
    D.   Recission or Reformation
    E.   Specific Performance

CONTRACTS QUESTION 1

Clark is a wholesale distributor of office supplies. Jones operates a novelty supply company. On May 1, Clark received a written order from Jones for 30,000 pens at 50 cents each, the price listed in Clark's catalogue. The order from Jones stated that the pens were to be specially imprinted by Jones with a political slogan and were being purchased for resale by Jones to Davis, a candidate for the United States Senate. The order specified for delivery of half of the pens by August 1 and the remainder by October 1.

On May 5, Clark sent to Jones a written confirmation, which acknowledged the quantity, price, delivery dates, and purpose of the purchase. Both the order and the confirmation were on forms containing a number of printed clauses. The printed clauses were substantially the same on both forms, except that Clark's confirmation included an additional clause stating that all disputes about the transaction were to be resolved by arbitration.

On June 30, Jones telephoned Clark and told him that another distributor had offered Jones the same pens at 45 cents each and that Jones intended to switch his order to the other distributor unless Clark agreed to lower his price. Rather than lose the sale, Clark grudgingly agreed to lower the price to 45 cents for Jones' order.

On July 30, Clark shipped the first 15,000 pens and, on August 2, Clark accepted Jones' payment for them at 45 cents each. On August 10, Jones wrote to Clark canceling the second half of the order because Davis had withdrawn from the senatorial race due to poor health. When he received the letter of cancellation, Clark had not yet ordered the second shipment of pens from the manufacturer.

Clark sued Jones for breach of contract in state court, seeking damages based on the original 50 cents price for the remaining 15,000 pens.

What arguments should each party make, and how should the case be decided? Discuss.

Contracts Question 1

I. UCC governs
   A. The UCC governs the sale of goods.
   B. Contract is for the sale of pens. UCC applies.
   C. Special rules when the contract is between merchants

II. Contract Formation
   A. Offer
      1. Jones's May 1 written order was a promise by Jones to buy 30,000 pens at 50 cents each
   B. Acceptance
      1. Clark sent a written confirmation, which acknowledged all the elements of the order
      2. Jones argues arbitration clause a part of contract
      3. "Battle of the Forms" – UCC 2-207
   C. Consideration
      1. Clark's promise to ship the pens and Jones' promise to pay

III. Defenses/Statute of Frauds
   A. Sale of goods over $500
   B. Merchant's confirmatory memo – Clark's confirmation

IV. Modification
   A. UCC contract modifications sought in good faith are binding
   B. Jones argues Clark agreed; Clark argues "grudgingly agreed"

V. Anticipatory Repudiation
   A. Party unequivocally and explicitly indicates that he will not perform – Clark argues Jones canceled
      1. Sue immediately
      2. Suspend performance and wait until the performance date to sue
      3. Treat the repudiation as an offer to rescind and treat the contract as discharged

VI. Discharge/Frustration of Purpose
   A. Supervening, not reasonably foreseeable event destroys the purpose of the contract – Davis' serious illness but contract's purpose not destroyed

VII. Remedies
   A. The non-breaching party to a contract is entitled to expectation damages
   B. The non-breaching party has a duty to mitigate damages

CONTRACTS QUESTION 2

In February, Carrier, a trucking company, and Maker, a manufacturer, negotiated an agreement under which Carrier promised to provide for two years all the transportation services required by Maker in exchange for monthly payments based on the number of packages transported. In response to Carrier's concerns over proposed legislation that would restrict its ability to use more efficient "triple-trailer" trucks, the parties agreed that Carrier could terminate the contract if such legislation were enacted. No such law was ever passed.

Carrier drafted a document embodying the agreed terms and, on March 1, sent two signed copies to Maker with a request that Maker sign and return one copy. Although Maker did not sign the document, the parties immediately began doing business according to its terms. During the next six months, Maker paid all of Carrier's monthly invoices on time. During the same period, Carrier declined two potentially lucrative offers from other manufacturers because performance of the agreement with Maker required most of Carrier's capacity.

In September, Maker began to have concerns about the cost of Carrier's service. Maker sent a letter to Transport, one of Carrier's competitors, describing Maker's needs, Maker's agreement with Carrier, and the amount charged by Carrier. Transport offered to provide comparable transportation services at a lower cost. On September 20, Maker sent a fax to Carrier stating that Maker would no longer use Carrier's services as of November 1. Carrier responded with a fax to Maker, which stated that Maker had no right to terminate the contract. On September 21, Maker suspended all business with Carrier and began doing business with Transport. Maker also refused to pay an invoice submitted by Carrier for transportation services rendered in September.

What, if any, rights and remedies does Carrier have against:

1. Maker?   Discuss.

2. Transport?   Discuss.

Contracts Question 2

I. <u>Carrier v. Maker</u>
   A.   Common law governs this service contract
   B.   Formation of Contract
      1.   Mutual assent
         a.   The parties "negotiated an agreement"
         b.   Maker may argue price and quantity terms were indefinite. Court will imply a reasonable price and good faith applies.
      2.   Consideration
         a.   Exchange of promise to provide services in exchange for promise to pay monthly
         b.   Maker will argue it made an illusory promise because parties were not mutually bound
         c.   However, this is a requirements contract, i.e. Carrier promised to provide all transportation services "required by Maker"

   C.   Defense to Formation
      1.   Statute of Frauds
         a.   Two year contract requires a writing
         b.   Carrier memorialized terms in writing but Maker did not sign. Maker sent a letter to Transport.
         c.   Exceptions
            1)   Performance - 6 months and Maker paid but for service contract, there must be full performance
            2)   Promissory estoppel - Carrier declined 2 other lucrative offers

   D.   Performance
      1.   Anticipatory repudiation
         a.   Maker's fax on 9/20 and suspended performance on 9/21
         b.   Carrier can sue immediately, wait and sue or suspend performance
      2.   Maker breached

   E.   Remedies
      1.   Damages
         a.   Compensatory - benefit of bargain - ascertainable?
         b.   Duty to mitigate

      c.   Consequential - reasonably foreseeable that Carrier would give up other jobs

   2.   Restitution - unjust enrichment - September

  3.   Specific performance but damages at law adequate and specific performance generally not granted in service contract cases.

II.   <u>Carrier v. Transport</u>
    A.   Tortious interference with contract
        1.   Valid contract between Carrier and Maker
        2.   Transport knew of contract through Maker's letter
        3.   Transport intentionally interfered when it offered to provide comparable services at a lower cost
        4.   Transport's interference induced Maker to breach
        5.   Carrier suffered damages
    B.   Remedies
        1.   Damages - specific and foreseeable?
        2.   Restitution - to prevent unjust enrichment
        3.   Injunction but damages are adequate remedy

CONTRACTS QUESTION 3

In January, in response to an inquiry, Seller sent Buyer a letter offering to sell 10,000 tires, assorted sizes to be selected by Seller and delivered at the rate of 1,000 each month for ten months. This letter stated the price for each size and specified that payment was due on delivery of each shipment. Buyer sent a letter agreeing to purchase 10,000 tires, assortment to be specified by Buyer. Buyer's letter contained its standard provision that any disputes arising under the agreement were to be resolved by commercial arbitration. The letter also contained Buyer's specification of the size assortment for the first month's shipment of tires.

On February 1, Seller's driver arrived with the first installment, which consisted of the assortment specified in Buyer's letter. The driver left the tires without asking for payment. Four days later Buyer sent Seller a check for the first installment and a letter specifying the assortment for the second installment. On March 1, Seller's driver arrived with the second installment, again containing the assortment specified in Buyer's letter. Again the driver left the tires without getting payment.

Three days later Buyer sent a check for the second installment and specifications for the third installment. On April 1, Seller's driver arrived, but the assortment was not exactly what Buyer had specified. Buyer accepted the tires anyway and seven days later sent a check for the third installment, along with specifications for the fourth installment.

On May 1, Seller's driver arrived, again with an assortment that was not exactly what Buyer had specified. Buyer agreed to take delivery, but Seller's driver insisted on payment. When Buyer was unable to pay, Seller's driver refused to leave the tires and took them back to Seller's warehouse.

Buyer called Seller to complain about the driver's refusal to leave the tires and insisted upon immediate redelivery. Buyer said he would pay "as usual, a few days after delivery." Seller refused and told Buyer, "If you don't like it, why don't you take me to arbitration?"

{Continued on next page}

Buyer replied, "Look, I have no intention of arbitrating this dispute. But I'm not accepting that last shipment unless it meets my specifications precisely and unless you allow me the same leeway for payment as with past shipments."

Seller sued Buyer for breach of contract. Buyer simultaneously filed a counterclaim against Seller and moved the court for an order staying suit and compelling arbitration. Seller opposed the motion.

1. How should the court rule on the motion for an order staying the suit and compelling arbitration? Discuss.

2. What are the rights and obligations of Seller and Buyer, and who should prevail on the merits of the litigation? Discuss.

Contracts Question 3

<u>Seller v. Buyer</u>
1. Staying the suit and compelling arbitration - court should stay suit and compel arbitration if the arbitration clause was a term in a valid contract

    A. UCC governs
        1. Tires = goods
        2. Seller and buyer = merchants
    B. Contract Formation
        1. Offer
            a. Buyer sent an inquiry
            b. Seller's January letter - communicated and intended on certain and definite terms:
                1) subject matter - tires
                2) quantity - 10,000
                3) price - stated for each size
                4) performance - sizes to be determined by Seller and payment due on delivery, 1,000 tires per month
        2. Acceptance - in a reasonable manner.
            a. Buyer's letter - UCC 2-207
                1) Buyer agreed to purchase 10,000 tires
                2) Buyer also included size to be specified by Buyer and arbitration clause
                3) Additional terms between merchants part of contract unless:
                    a) offer limited acceptance - it did not
                    b) there was no objection - Seller did not object; in fact, Seller later suggested Buyer arbitrate
                    c) material alteration - change the risks or the remedies available? Seller seemed to assent.
                        (1) arbitration may not have materially altered the contract
                        (2) if treated as different term, may be knocked out.
        3. Consideration - tires for promise to pay
        4. Valid contract including arbitration clause.

2. Rights and Obligations
   A.   Performance
        1.   Conditions – Payment due on delivery of each shipment
        2.   Installment contract – delivery of 1,000/month – there is a breach only if defects materially impair value of entire contract

              a.   February 1 and March 1 – Seller delivered installments according to Buyer's specs. without requiring payment. Buyer paid later.
              b.   April 1 – Seller delivered nonconforming installment, but Buyer accepted and paid later.
              c.   May 1 – Seller refused delivery when Buyer could not pay. Buyer was willing to accept delivery though not conforming to specs.
              d.   Seller waived right to payment on delivery
              e.   Buyer's specs. may control and if so, Buyer can reject nonconforming goods even though Buyer waived as to prior nonconforming deliveries.

   B.   Obligations
        1.   Buyer can require installments meet Buyer's specs. and was not obligated to pay on delivery.
        2.   Buyer did not breach by failing to pay on May 1
        3.   Seller not excused from delivery conforming goods on May 1.

CONTRACTS QUESTION 4

Susan is the Chief Operating Officer of WestTel, a telecommunications company. Felix is the Chief Executive Officer of CodeCo, a software company. About a year ago, Susan and Felix negotiated and signed a valid written contract under which WestTel purchased from CodeCo a license to use and sell software that prevents interception of telephone communications during transmission. Susan was assisted in the negotiations by Larry, an in-house attorney then employed by WestTel.

Throughout the negotiations, WestTel insisted that the license from CodeCo be an exclusive license for WestTel to use and sell the software in the national cellular telephone market. The only language bearing on the subject in the contract stated that, "WestTel shall have the use" of the software. The contract contained a clause stating that the written contract represents the entire agreement of the parties.

Susan was given oral assurances by Felix that the language quoted above would be interpreted by CodeCo to mean that WestTel was granted the exclusive license and that CodeCo would not license the software to others in the national cellular telephone market. Larry advised Susan that he was satisfied with Felix's oral assurances.

Last week, Susan saw an ad in a trade journal announcing that NewCom, a competitor of WestTel, was marketing a new national cellular phone service using the same anti-interception software produced by CodeCo. She immediately called Felix to inquire about the NewCom ad and remind him of WestTel's exclusive license. Felix confirmed that CodeCo had licensed the same software to NewCom and denied that WestTel had an exclusive license.

Susan then called NewCom and informed its chief executive officer that WestTel had the exclusive license for the use of the software and that, if NewCom went forward with its plan to use the software in the national market, WestTel would sue New Com. She was told that if she wanted to discuss it further she should talk to Larry, NewCom's in-house attorney who had negotiated the NewCom/CodeCo contract.

Continued on next page

It turns out that at the time Larry was assisting Susan with the WestTel/CodeCo negotiations, NewCom had contacted Larry and offered him a job. NewCom knew when it offered him the job that Larry was participating in the WestTel/CodeCo negotiations. Larry quit WestTel about six months ago and joined NewCom's legal staff.

When Susan confronted Larry and reminded him of his advice about the exclusivity of the WestTel/CodeCo deal, Larry responded only with, "Well, you signed it."

1. What theories, if any, might WestTel reasonably assert against CodeCo to establish and enforce a right to an exclusive license and what is the likely outcome on each theory?

2. Should WestTel prevail in actions for tortious interference with the WestTel/CodeCo contract against:
   a. CodeCo? Discuss.
   b. NewCom? Discuss.
   c. Larry? Discuss.

3. What, if any, ethical duties has Larry breached? Discuss.

Contracts Question 4

1. WestTel's theories to establish and enforce exclusive license
    A. To establish exclusive license
        1) Parol Evidence Rule: Evidence of prior or contemporaneous agreements that modify, contradict or vary contract terms are inadmissible if the contract is intended as a complete and final expression of the parties.
            a) Here, WestTel will argue extrinsic evidence should be admitted to interpret the words, "WestTel shall have the use," to mean an exclusive license.
            b) However, CodeCo will argue merger clause as barring evidence.
        2) Fraud in the inducement makes contract voidable
            a) WestTel will argue Felix's assurances went to a material factor
            b) Susan reasonably relied.
    B. To enforce an exclusive license
        1) Reformation - based on fraud, WestTel can seek to reform the contract to reflect the original agreement of the parties.
        2) Recission would cancel the contract
        3) Specific Performance
            a) Inadequate remedy at law - damages will not compensate WestTel though software may not be unique
            b) Definite and certain terms - questionable given above
            c) Feasible - court could issue negative injunction
            d) Mutuality - both parties can seek specific performance
            e) Defenses - none
2. Tortious interference with contract
    This tort requires a valid contract, D's knowledge of the contract, intentional interference that induces a breach and causes damages.
    A. Against CodeCo
        1) This tort requires third party interference
        2) CodeCo is not liable because it is an original party to the contract
    B. Against NewCom
        1) WestTel would argue NewCom knew of the contract with CodeCo through Larry.
        2) NewCom will argue it did not know and there was no interference, only competition.

93

        C.   Against Larry
            1)   Larry knew of the negotiations with and assurances to WestTel
            2)   Larry negotiated the NewCom/CodeCo contract

3.   Larry's ethical duties

        A.   Duty of Loyalty
            1)   Conflict of interest between WestTel and NewCom Larry should not have taken the job. Larry should have disclosed

        B.   Duty of Confidentiality
            1)   Duty of silence as WestTel's counsel Larry likely revealed or used confidential information while working for NewCom while negotiating contract with CodeCo.

        C.   Duty of Competence
            1)   Duty to act with the legal knowledge and skill reasonably necessary for representation.
            2)   Larry may have breached given his advice to WestTel

CONTRACTS QUESTION 5

Developer had an option to purchase a five-acre parcel named The Highlands in City from Owner, and was planning to build a residential development there. Developer could not proceed with the project until City approved the extension of utilities to The Highlands parcel. In order to encourage development, City had a well-known and long-standing policy of reimbursing developers for the cost of installing utilities in new areas.

Developer signed a contract with Builder for the construction of ten single-family homes on The Highlands parcel. The contract provided in section 14(d), "All obligations under this agreement are conditioned on approval by City of all necessary utility extensions." During precontract negotiations, Developer specifically informed Builder that he could not proceed with the project unless City followed its usual policy of reimbursing the developer for the installation of utilities, and Builder acknowledged that he understood such a condition to be implicit in section 14(d). The contract also provided, "This written contract is a complete and final statement of the agreement between the parties hereto."

In a change of policy, City approved "necessary utility extensions to The Highlands parcel," but only on the condition that Developer bear the entire cost, which was substantial, without reimbursement by City. Because this additional cost made the project unprofitable, Developer abandoned plans for the development and did not exercise his option to purchase The Highlands parcel from Owner.

Builder, claiming breach of contract, sued Developer for the $700,000 profit he would have made on the project. In the meantime, Architect purchased The Highlands parcel from Owner and contracted with Builder to construct a business park there. Builder's expected profit under this new contract with Architect is $500,000.

What arguments can Developer make, and what is the likely outcome, on each of the following points?

1. Developer did not breach the contract with Builder.
2. Developer's performance was excused.
3. In any event, Builder did not suffer $700,000 in damages.
   Discuss.

[Feb. 2009#5]

CRIMINAL PROCEDURE

I. **4th AMENDMENT**
   A. Arrest
      1. Standards - felony, misdemeanor
      2. Detentions
   B. Search & Seizure
      1. Governmental conduct
      2. Reasonable expectation of privacy
      3. Search with or without a warrant?
         a. With a warrant
            1) probable cause
            2) scope of warrant
            3) neutral and detached magistrate
            4) proper execution
            5) good faith
         b. Without a warrant
            1) incident to lawful arrest
            2) automobile
            3) plain view
            4) consent
            5) stop and frisk
            6) exigent circumstances
      4. Persons or places searched
         a. public schools
         b. probationer
         c. border searches
         d. wiretapping
         e. body searches
      5. Exclusionary rule
         a. harmless or reversible error
         b. fruit of poisonous tree
         c. inevitable discovery or independent source
         d. admissible to impeach

II. **5th AMENDMENT**

   A. Incriminating statements
      1. Privilege against self incrimination protects compelled testimonial evidence
      2. Miranda
         a. custodial interrogation
         b. warning
         c. waiver
         d. voluntary
   B. Double Jeopardy
      1. Attaches in jury or bench trial
      2. Exceptions - hung jury, mistrial

97

3. Same offense or lesser included, unless new evidence
4. Does not apply to separate sovereigns

III. 6th AMENDMENT

    A. Right to Counsel
       1. Right at post charge lineup or show up
       2. Critical stages of a prosecution
       3. No right at photo ID or taking of physical evidence
       4. Waiver & right to defend oneself
       5. Effective assistance of counsel
    B. Right to a Speedy Trial
       1. Totality of circumstances
       2. Attaches once D is arrested or charged
    C. Right to a Jury Trial
       1. Serious offenses – 6 months
       2. Number and selection of jurors
       3. Death penalty – juror's view must not prevent or substantially impair ability to perform duties
       4. Guilty pleas must be voluntary and intelligent
    D. Right to Confront Witnesses (also consider Hearsay)
       1. Observe witness demeanor and opportunity to cross examine
       2. Right not absolute
          a. Disruptive defendant
          b. Co-defendant's confession

IV. 8th AMENDMENT

    A. Cruel and Unusual Punishment
       1. Punishment proportionate to offense
       2. Death penalty
          a. Not inherently violative of 8th Amendment
          b. Jury should be allowed to consider mitigating circumstances
          c. Can be imposed for felony murder if D participated in a major way and acted with reckless indifference
          d. Jury can consider impact on victim's family
          e. Cannot be imposed on mentally retarded and minors
       3. Status crimes but no violation for imposition for acts

V. 14th AMENDMENT
    A. Due Process
       1. Burden of proof on prosecution
       2. Unnecessarily suggestive identifications

CRIMINAL LAW

I.   **PRINCIPLES OF CRIMINAL LAW**
A.   Actus Reus
B.   Mens Rea
C.   Concurrence
D.   Causation

II. **ACCOMPLICE LIABILITY**
A.   **Elements of accomplice liability**
    1.   Must be aiding, abetting and counseling the crime - active aiding required. Mere presence not enough even if by his presence he seems to be consenting to the crime or even if he fails to notify the police.
    2.   Liability: the crime itself and all other foreseeable crimes
B.   **Defenses**
    1.   Withdrawal
        a.   if the person merely encouraged the commission of the crime he must repudiate his encouragement
        b.   if person provided some material (e.g., gun) must do all possible to retrieve it
        c.   alternative: notify authorities or take some action to prevent the commission of the crime
        d.   must be before the chain of events leading to the commission of the crime becomes unstoppable
    2.   **Accessory After the Fact**
        a.   Helping someone escape
            (1) not liable for the crime itself
            (2) a separate lesser charge

III. **INCHOATE OFFENSES - Solicitation, Conspiracy and Attempt**

A.   **Solicitation**
    1.   Element: Asking someone to commit a crime
    2.   Defense: The refusal of the solicitee is no defense

B.   **Conspiracy**
    1.   Elements:
        a.   an agreement
        b.   an intent to agree
        c.   an intent to achieve the unlawful purpose or objective of the agreement
    2.   Liability: each conspirator is liable for all crimes of other conspirators if foreseeable and in furtherance of the conspiracy

3. Defense
    a. no impossibility defense
    b. can only withdraw from liability for future crimes - no withdrawal from liability for the conspiracy itself
    c. no merger: can be convicted of conspiracy to rob and robbery for example

C. Attempt
  1. Elements:
    a. specific intent
    b. a substantial step in the direction of the commission of the crime (mere preparation not enough)
  2. Defenses:
    a. factual impossibility no defense
    b. majority rule - legal impossibility is a defense
    c. abandonment no defense after the substantial steps have been begun

IV. COMMON LAW CRIMES

A. Crimes against the Person
  1. Homicide
    a. Murder
      1) Malice aforethought
        a) Intent to kill
        b) Intent to commit serious bodily injury
        c) wanton and reckless - abandoned and malignant heart
        d) felony murder rule
      2) Degrees
    b. Voluntary Manslaughter
      1) Adequate Provocation
      2) Heat of Passion - no cooling time
    c. Involuntary Manslaughter
      1) Unintentional killing
      2) Misdemeanor Manslaughter
  2. Assault and Battery
  3. Rape
  4. Kidnapping
  5. Mayhem

B. Crimes against Personal Property - Theft
  1. Larceny
  2. Embezzlement
  3. False Pretenses
  4. Receiving Stolen Property

C. Crimes against Person and Personal Property
1. Robbery
2. Extortion

D. Crimes against Real Property
1. Arson
2. Burglary

E. Crimes against the Public
1. Forgery
2. Misprison, Compounding a Felony
3. Bigamy

V. DEFENSES

A. Self-Defense
B. Defense of Others
C. Defense of Property
D. Insanity
1. M'Naughten
2. Irresistible Impulse
3. ALI Substantial Capacity
4. Durham Product
E. Intoxication
1. Voluntary
2. Involuntary
F. Entrapment
G. Mistake
H. Age, Infancy
I. Necessity
J. Duress
K. Crime Prevention

CRIMINAL PROCEDURE & LAW QUESTION 1

Al and Bill offered Clara, whom they had just met in a bar, a ride to her home when the bar closed. She accepted, but the two men instead drove her to a remote area where first Bill, and then Al, forcibly raped her. When Clara attempted to push Al away, he subdued her by choking her. Bill watched, but took no part in Al's activities. Clara died as a result of the choking.

Al and Bill were arrested. After receiving proper notice of their <u>Miranda</u> rights, which they waived, each admitted raping Clara. Al denied having intent to kill when he choked Clara, and Bill denied having either an intent that she be killed or knowledge that Al would use deadly force in raping her.

At their joint trial on charges of felony murder and rape, evidence of these events and the defendants' statements was admitted. The court, over defendants' objections: (1) excused for cause, on the prosecutor's motion, three jurors who expressed unqualified opposition to the death penalty; (2) excluded, at both the guilt and penalty phases of the trial, evidence proffered by Bill that he was mentally retarded; and (3) admitted at the penalty phase of the trial evidence offered by the prosecutor regarding the emotional impact of Clara's death on her family. The jury convicted both defendants of first degree felony murder in the commission of the rape and returned penalty verdicts of death for each defendant.

In a post-trial hearing, the defendants moved to vacate the verdicts on the basis of juror misconduct. The court refused to admit the affidavit of juror X that juror Y was intoxicated during one afternoon of the guilt phase trial. The motion to vacate the verdicts was denied and the court sentenced Al and Bill to death.

In defendants' appeals from the judgments of death, how should the court rule on arguments that:
1. The evidence was insufficient to support the conviction of Bill for first degree felony murder? Discuss.
2. The court erred in excusing the three jurors? Discuss.
3. The court erred in excluding the evidence of Bill's retardation? Discuss.
4. The court erred in excluding the evidence of juror intoxication and denying the motion to vacate? Discuss.
5. The court erred in admitting the evidence of the impact of Clara's death on her family? Discuss.
6. Imposition of the death penalty on Al, assuming he had no intent to kill, and on Bill, assuming he neither intended to kill nor participated in the killing, violates the Eight Amendment prohibition of cruel and unusual punishment? Discuss.

CRIMINAL PROCEDURE & LAW QUESTION 1

People v. Al & Bill

I.   Bill's conviction
    A.   First degree felony murder
        1.   B's liability depends on A's guilt
            a.   B did no act but watched
        2.   Malice - felony murder rule
            a.   Underlying felony - rape
            b.   First degree because inherently violent
        3.   Accomplice liability - Aided and abetted A?
            a.   Mere presence insufficient
            b.   But B participated and watched

II. Excluding three jurors
    A.   6th Amend. right to impartial jury trial - only absolute opposition to imposition of death penalty may excuse juror
        1.   Juror's view should not prevent or substantially impair performance of duty
        2.   Here, appears unqualified opposition

III. Excluding evidence of B's retardation
    A.   Guilt phase
        1.   Would be error if relevant - did not allege insanity [note: could raise insanity tests]
            a.   Negate intent - but rape is general intent crime and not relevant to accomplice liability.
            b.   Could be relevant to confession
    B.   Penalty phase
        1.   Must be allowed to present mitigating circumstances
        2.   8th Amend. does prohibit execution of murderer who is mentally retarded

IV. Excluding evidence of juror intoxication
    A.   Jury verdict may be set aside for juror misconduct
        1.   Most states require independent evidence
            a.   Here affidavit of X re: juror Y
            b.   Denial of motion to vacate valid
        2.   Some states allow impeachment of verdict by jurors. Motion to vacate here depends on whether Y's conduct was harmless

V.   Admitting evidence of impact on Clara's family
    A.   Introduced at penalty phase - Victim impact statements admissible to assess defendant's moral culpability.

Continued on next page

VI.   8th Amendment - Cruel & unusual punishment
    A.   Supreme Court has held death penalty can be imposed on a defendant under felony murder if defendant participated in a major way and acted with reckless indifference
    1.   A - acted with intent by raping and choking
    2.   B - participated in rape and acted with reckless disregard by watching and not stopping A.

CRIMINAL PROCEDURE & LAW QUESTION 2

Duce and Cody were arrested for an armed robbery. Duce was taken to the police station, where she was interrogated without Miranda warnings. After three hours of questioning, a police officer asked Duce if she would consent to a search of her automobile. Duce consented and a search of her car revealed a handgun and items stolen in the robbery, which were seized by the officers. When told what the officers found, Duce confessed to driving the getaway car in the robbery.

Cody, who did not know that Duce had confessed, then confessed and named Duce as the driver of the getaway car.

At their joint trial on a charge of robbery, Duce moved to exclude her confession from evidence based solely on the failure of the police to give her Miranda warnings. Based only on that violation, the court granted the motion to exclude her confession. Duce also moved to exclude from evidence the handgun and the stolen items seized from her automobile, claiming that she was not aware that she had a right to refuse consent to search. The prosecutor conceded that the police had no authority to search the car absent consent, but asserted that Duce's consent was obtained without coercion. The court denied the motion, finding that the consent was voluntary.

The handgun and the stolen items seized from Duce's car were admitted into evidence at the joint trial of Duce and Cody over objections by each defendant. Cody's confession, redacted to eliminate any reference to Duce, was admitted into evidence against Cody.

At trial Duce testified, denying that she drove the getaway car and that she knew the handgun or the stolen items were in her car. She testified that she had loaned her car to Cody on the day of the robbery. In rebuttal the prosecutor called a police officer who testified, over objection by Duce, to the contents of Duce's confession and to the contents of Cody's complete unredacted confession implicating Duce as the driver of the getaway car.

Assume that in each instance all appropriate constitutional and evidentiary objections were made.

1. Did the court err in admitting the handgun and the stolen items seized from Duce's car against Duce and Cody? Discuss.
2. Did the court err in admitting the police officer's testimony about Duce's confession? Discuss.
3. Did the court err in admitting the police officer's testimony about Cody's complete unredacted confession? Discuss.

107

1. **Handgun and Stolen Items**
   A. Duce
      1. 4th Amendment – prohibits unreasonable search & seizure and applies to states by 14th Amendment
         a. Government conduct – police
         b. Reasonable expectation of privacy – Duce's car
         c. Search without warrant – prosecutor conceded consent was only basis for warrantless search
            1) Consent must be voluntary and intelligent
               a) Knowledge of consent not required, but is a factor to determine voluntariness
               b) Duce consented and didn't appear to be coerced, though preceded by 3 hours of questioning
            2) Duce had apparent authority to consent
   B. Cody
      1. No reasonable expectation of privacy
2. **Duce's Confession**
   A. 5th Amendment – prohibits compelled self-incrimination and applies to the states by the 14th Amendment
      1. Custodial interrogation
         a. Custodial – Duce was arrested
         b. Interrogation – Duce questioned for 3 hours and police told Duce what the search found
      2. Miranda warnings not given – never waived
      3. Duce confessed to driving getaway car
         a. Was the confession voluntary or coerced?
            1) Never given Miranda
            2) Duce made confession after being told what police found – spontaneous?
         b. Could be used to impeach Duce's testimony so long as her confession was voluntary
3. **Cody's Unredacted Confession**
   A. 6th Amendment – right to confront witnesses and applicable to the states by the 14th Amendment
      1. Generally, statement of a co-defendant implicating the other co-defendant is inadmissible.
      2. However, Cody's confession admissible if:
         a. all portions referring to other defendant eliminated – but here unredacted, or
         b. if confessing defendant takes stand and is subject to cross examination– Cody did not, or
         c. if the confession is used to rebut the other defendant's argument that his confession was obtained involuntarily – here offered to rebut Duce's testimony.

CRIMINAL PROCEDURE AND LAW QUESTION 3

Al, Bob, and Charlie planned to bring 50 cases of whiskey ashore from a ship anchored in the harbor near their town and sell it to a local bar owner. They believed the whiskey had been produced abroad and was subject to a federal import duty. They also knew that smuggling items into this country without paying duty required by the Tariff Act is a crime. In fact, however, the whiskey in this shipment had been produced in the United States.

The three met at Al's house on Monday and agreed to bring the whiskey ashore by rowboat on Friday night. On Wednesday, however, Bob called Al to say that he and his wife were going to visit relatives that weekend and Bob would not be able to help bring the whiskey ashore. Al said that was all right, that he and Charlie could handle the boat and the whiskey, but that Bob would naturally be cut out of the profits on this job.

When Charlie learned from Al that there would be just the two of them he became apprehensive, but he was afraid of what Al might do to him if he tried to back out. Therefore, on Thursday, Charlie informed the police of Al's plan and did not show up on Friday night. Al was arrested on Friday night as he came ashore, alone, with the whiskey and was loading it into a truck he had stolen from a nearby Coast Guard parking lot.

Al, Bob, and Charlie have been charged with theft of the truck and conspiracy to import dutiable goods without payment of duty.

Al has also been charged with attempt to import dutiable goods without payment of duty. He has told Len, his attorney that he plans to testify that he knew all along that the whiskey was produced in the United States.

Based on the above facts:

1. Should Al, Bob, or Charlie be convicted of:
   (a) Conspiracy to violate the Tariff Act? Discuss.
   (b) Theft of the truck? Discuss.

2. Should Al be convicted of attempt to import dutiable goods without payment of duty in violation of the Tariff Act? Discuss.

3. If Al insists on testifying he knew the whiskey was produced in the United States, what, if anything, should Len do? Discuss.

1. Al, Bob or Charlie

    A. <u>Conspiracy to violate the Tariff Act</u>

        1.   Conspiracy requires:
   - a. agreement between 2 or more - here, all three met on Monday and agreed
   - b. intent to enter into the agreement - all agreed to bring the whiskey ashore by rowboat.
   - c. intent by at least 2 to achieve the objective of the agreement - met here but, see below.
   - d. Most states require an overt act - no overt act by Wednesday, so Bob may be absolved.

        2.   Defenses
   - a. Mistake of fact, i.e. the whiskey was actually produced in U.S., is no defense because Tariff Act appears to be a strict liability offense. Further, if the facts were as they believed, smuggling the whiskey without paying duty would have been a crime.
   - b. Withdrawal is no defense to conspiracy, but may be as to crimes committed in furtherance. Withdrawal requires an affirmative act notifying all conspiracy members, and if defendant has provided assistance, must neutralize the assistance.
     (1) Bob - merely visiting relatives and would not be able to help bring the whiskey ashore - rather weak.
     (2) Charlie - informed the police but not Al.
   - c. Duress - Charlie - but requires threat of imminent infliction of death or great bodily harm.

    B.   <u>Theft of truck</u>
   1. Al - guilty because he had stolen truck
   2. Bob and Charlie - see withdrawal above. If withdrawal a good defense for crimes in furtherance, must discover when Al stole the truck.
   3. Accomplice liability may be argued.

2. Should Al be convicted of attempt?

    A.   Attempt requires an act beyond preparation with intent to commit a crime- here Al believed the whiskey was produced abroad, intended to smuggle it without paying duty and was loading it on the truck.

B. Defenses
    1. Factual impossibility is no defense - fact that whiskey was not produced abroad is no defense.
    2. Legal impossibility - here Al would be claiming that no matter what he did, he could not have violated the Tariff Act because the whiskey was domestic. However, this is factual impossibility.

3. **If Al insists on lying, what should Len do?**
    A. Len owes Al duties of loyalty and confidentiality
    B. Len owes duty to court - must try to persuade Al not to commit perjury or to recant, or try to withdraw, or not participate, or must reveal the perjury.

CRIMINAL PROCEDURE AND LAW QUESTION 4

Dan stood on the steps of the state capitol and yelled to a half-dozen people entering the front doors: "Listen citizens. Prayer in the schools means government-endorsed religion. A state church! They can take your constitutional rights away just as fast as I can destroy this copy of the U.S. Constitution."

With that, Dan took a cigarette lighter from his pocket and ignited a parchment document that he held in his left hand. The parchment burst into flame and, when the heat of the fire burned his hand, he involuntarily let it go. A wind blew the burning document into a construction site where it settled in an open drum of flammable material. The drum exploded, killing a nearby pedestrian.

A state statute makes it a misdemeanor to burn or mutilate a copy of the U.S. Constitution.

It turned out that the document that Dan had burned was actually a copy of the Declaration of Independence, not of the U.S. Constitution, as he believed.

Dan was arrested and charged with the crimes of murder and attempting to burn a copy of the U.S. Constitution. He has moved to dismiss the charge of attempting to burn a copy of the U.S. Constitution, claiming that (i) what he burned was actually a copy of the Declaration of Independence and (ii) the state statute on which the charge is based violates his rights under the First Amendment to the U.S. Constitution.

1. May Dan properly be found guilty of the crime of murder or any lesser-included offense? Discuss.

2. How should the court rule on each ground of Dan's motion to dismiss the charge of attempting to burn a copy of the U.S. Constitution? Discuss.

[July 2007 #5]

CRIMINAL PROCEDURE & LAW QUESTION 5

Don arrived home at night and found Vic assaulting Don's wife. Vic escaped before Don could apprehend him. Convinced that the legal system would never bring Vic to justice, Don spent three months searching for Vic so that he could take care of the matter himself.

Alex, whom Don did not know, had his own reasons for wanting Vic dead. Alex heard of Don's desire to locate and retaliate against Vic. Hoping that Don would kill Vic, Alex sent Don an anonymous note giving Vic's location. Don, taking a pistol with him, found Vic where the note said he would be. After a heated argument in which Don accused Vic of attempting to rape his wife and Vic denied the accusation, Don shot Vic in the head.

Vic was rushed to a hospital where he was preliminarily diagnosed as "brain dead" and placed on life support systems for three days during which follow-up studies confirmed the permanent cessation of all brain function. A hospital physician then disconnected the life support systems, which had kept Vic's heart and respiratory systems functioning, and Vic was pronounced dead.

Don and Alex were both charged with murder. Evidence of the above facts was admitted at trial. The prosecutor argued that the murder was willful, deliberate, and premeditated and that it was committed during the commission of felonies of assault with a deadly weapon and burglary. Alex was alleged to have aided and abetted Don. The court instructed the jury on aiding and abetting and on premeditated murder, felony murder, burglary, and assault with a deadly weapon, but ruled that there was no evidence to warrant instructions on manslaughter. The jury convicted both Don and Alex of first degree murder. Both have appealed.

1. How should the appellate court rule on Don's arguments that:
    a. The uncontradicted evidence established that the hospital physician, not Don, killed Vic? Discuss.
    b. The court erred in instructing on murder in the commission of a felony? Discuss.
    c. The court should have instructed on manslaughter? Discuss.

Question 2 on next page

2.   How should the appellate court rule on Alex's arguments that:

   a.   The evidence is insufficient to support his conviction as an aider and abettor? Discuss.

   b.   The evidence is insufficient to support his conviction of first degree murder even if it does support a finding that he aided and abetted Don? Discuss.

NOTE: The following answer is a typed reproduction of an applicant's actual handwritten answer, except for minor corrections in spelling and punctuation. It is reprinted here for the sole purpose of giving students an example of an actual answer. This answer earned a "75."

1.   Don's arguments
     Hospital physician's actions:
The issue is whether the hospital physician killed Vic, rather than Don.

To find out who killed Vic, the court will look for the cause of Vic's injuries. The court will then trace the result of the injuries to the victim's death and look for any superceding, intervening cause that reduces or relieves Don of any liability.

Vic was injured by Don when Don shot Vic in the head. Vic's injury was the gunshot in the head. Therefore, the cause of Vic's injury was Don's act of shooting Vic in the head.

A person is declared dead when they are "brain dead" and all brain function has ceased. Vic was brain dead when admitted to the hospital and was considered "dead" when the doctor found the follow up studies showed Vic's brain was not functioning. Therefore, since Don shot Vic in the head and the injury Vic received from that shot was being "brain dead," Don, not the physician killed Vic.

According to the facts, Vic was already dead when the physician removed Vic's life support systems. Since Vic's brain stopped functioning before he was removed from life support, he was "dead" before he was removed from life support.

     3 days passage of time
The passage of three days between Vic's injury and Vic's death does not relieve Don of liability either because Vic died within a year of receiving the gunshot from Don. Thus, since Don shot Vic and Vic received an injury "brain dead" and that injury led to his clinical death, Don, not the physician, killed Vic.

     Commission of a felony
Burglary is the breaking and entering into the dwelling of another with the intent to commit a felony. There are no facts to suggest that Don broke and entered into Vic's dwelling. The facts only state that Don found Vic where the note said he (Vic) would be. There is no evidence that Don found Vic at Vic's or anyone else's house. Therefore, unless there was a breaking and entering with intent to commit a felony, there is no burglary. Obviously, Don committed a felony by shooting Vic, however it is unclear what Don's intent was when he was looking for Vic. Don did take a gun with him, however it is uncertain whether he intended to use the

116

gun to assault, injure or frighten Vic. Assault is the fear or anticipation of imminent touching. Here there are no facts to show that Don assaulted Vic.

If Don put into Vic a fear of imminent, unlawful touching, Don assaulted Vic. The facts are that Don and Vic had a heated argument only. There are no facts to say the Don "assaulted" Vic during the argument. A heated argument alone is not assault.

Therefore the appellate court should rule for Don for the trial court erred in instructing the jury for murder in the commission of a felony because there was no evidence of any felonies committed other than Don shooting Vic.

Manslaughter

Manslaughter is the killing of another that was either justifiable, reasonable or done without the requisite intent for common law murder.

Here Don will argue there should have been an instruction to the jury on voluntary manslaughter. This requires Don to have had adequate provocation and to have committed the killing in the heat of passion. The provocation Don must have had is that which would provoke a reasonable man in the same situation.

Don will argue he was both adequately provoked and in the heat of passion. Provocation because he found Vic assaulting Don's wife. The reasonable man would be provoked because the victim's action towards the wife was egregious. The heat of passion argument arises because Vic denied assaulting Don's wife even though Don caught Vic doing just that.

The prosecution will argue the manslaughter instruction was unnecessary because Don spent 3 months searching for Vic to get even. This they will argue is more than enough time for the reasonable man to cool off and there was no longer provocation.

The court should not have instructed on manslaughter.

2. ### Alex
Aider and Abettor

An aider and abettor purposely assists, aids, helps, encourages or otherwise causes the perpetrator of the given crime to commit the crime through the assistance of the aider and abettor.

There is ample evidence of Alex's assistance, purpose assistance to help Don kill Vic.

117

First, Alex knew that Don wanted to locate and retaliate against Vic. Vic also had "his own reasons" for wanting to kill Vic. Therefore, Alex was reasonably certain that when he provided Don with Vic's location, Don would retaliate and likely kill Vic.

Alex purposefully provided the information because he wanted Vic dead. Therefore, Alex purposefully aided Don in finding Vic. As such, since Alex knew of the likely consequences, Alex is guilty because Alex knowingly, purposefully helped Don find Vic so Don could kill Vic.

Alex does not escape liability because he did not agree with Don that they were both going to kill Vic. No conspiracy is required.

Court should rule against Alex.

First Degree Murder

First degree murder requires the willful homicide of another with premeditation and deliberation or murder done in the commission of a felony. First degree murder is also present where the defendant's act is so outrageous as to be done with certainty a death will result.

Here Alex's willful indifference towards Vic's life is present because (1) he knew Don wanted to kill Vic for assaulting Don's wife, therefore he knew by providing the address, Vic was certain to die. (2) Alex hoped that Don would kill Vic and was certain he would do so. Alex assisted in Don's act of killing because he premeditated and deliberated to give Don's location so Don could kill Vic.

Rule for prosecution, evidence sufficient for 1st degree murder.

EVIDENCE

I. **FORM**
   In what way is the evidence being introduced?
   A.   Sequence of witness examination - direct, cross, etc.
   B.   Objections to questions and answers

II. **PURPOSE**
   What is the purpose for introducing the evidence?
   A.   Logical relevance
      1.   Tendency in reason to prove...
      2.   Special relevancy problems: Similar happenings, experiments, prior suits or K's, negative evidence

   B.   Legal relevance
      1.   Extrinsic policy exclusions
         a.   Liability insurance
         b.   Subsequent remedial conduct
         c.   Settlement Offers
         d.   Payment or offer to pay medical expenses
         e.   Guilty pleas
      2.   Prejudicial Impact vs. Probative Value

   C.   Character
      1.   Civil cases
         a.   Character in issue by virtue of case
         b.   Habit
      2.   Criminal cases
         a.   Open Door Rule
         b.   "MIMIC"

III. **PRESENTATION**
   How is the evidence being presented?
   A.   Witness
      1.   Competency - age and mental
      2.   Personal knowledge
      3.   Impeachment
         a.   Character
            1)   Truth or veracity
            2)   Look to form of character evidence
               a)   Opinion and reputation
               b)   Specific Acts
         b.   Bias, Motive
         c.   Defects in memory, perception, knowledge
         d.   Inconsistent statements

B. Document reliability
   1. Authentication
   2. Best Evidence Rule
C. Opinion Testimony
   1. Lay opinion
   2. Expert opinion
D. Judicial Notice
E. Burdens of proof
F. Presumptions

IV. **HEARSAY**

Any out of court statements introduced?

A. Definition
   1. Out of court
   2. Statement
   3. To prove truth of matter asserted
B. Exceptions
   1. Admissions
      a. Party
      b. Vicarious
      c. Adoptive (Tacit)
      d. Co-conspirator statements
   2. Unavailability exceptions
      a. Declarations against interest
      b. Dying declarations
      c. Former testimony
   3. Reliability exceptions
      a. Excited utterances
      b. Present sense impressions
      c. Bodily condition
      d. Present state of mind
   4. Documentary exceptions
      a. Past recollection recorded
      b. Business records
      c. Official records
   5. Others
      a. Ancient documents
      b. Learned treatises
      c. Federal catch all

V. **PRIVILEGES**

Any privileged relationship involved?

A. **Approach**
   1. Privileged Relationship?
      a. Professional
      b. Marital
         1) Spousal testimonial privilege
         2) Confidential marital communications
   2. Confidential communication?
   3. Holder of Privilege? Waived?
   4. Exceptions

Evidence Writing Exercises

I.   Applicable Rules

A.   Logical Relevance – Evidence is logically relevant if it tends to prove or disprove a material fact, i.e. it makes a fact of consequence to the outcome of the action more probable than it would be without the evidence.

B.   Hearsay

1.   Hearsay is defined as an out of court statement offered to prove the truth of the matter asserted.

2.   If a statement is hearsay, and no exception to the rule applies, the evidence must be excluded upon appropriate objection. The reason for excluding hearsay is that the adverse party was denied the opportunity to cross-examine the declarant.

3.   Exceptions to the Hearsay Rule based on reliability

   a.   Excited Utterance – a statement relating to a startling event, made while under the stress of the event and before the declarant had time to reflect, is admissible.

   b.   Present Sense Impression – comments made concurrently with the sense impression of an event that is not necessarily exciting may be admissible. There is little time for a calculated misstatement, and the contemporaneous nature of the statement makes it reliable.

II. Hypotheticals

The following hypotheticals are excerpts from past California Bar Essay questions on Evidence.

Question 1

While traveling through an intersection governed by a traffic light, Ann's car was struck by a dark blue sports car, which sped from the scene. An eyewitness took the license plate number of the blue car, which was registered to Dave. Ann brought a negligence action against Dave for injuries to herself and her passenger, her four year old daughter, Jane. Dave counterclaimed, alleging Ann was negligent.

Ann's first witness, Bob, testified that he arrived at the scene within minutes of the accident, heard Jane crying, and heard Jane state that "the blue car went through the red light and hit us."

Was the testimony properly admitted?

Question 2

In a rape prosecution against Roe, the following events occurred at the trial by jury:

Adam, a neighbor of the victim, Tess, testified that within five minutes after the rape was alleged to have occurred, Tess ran to his house sobbing and said that she had just been raped by a man with a large brown blemish on his left arm.

Assume proper objections were timely made. Did the court err in admitting the testimony? Discuss.

III. Writing Tips and Examples
Hypothetical Question #1

Bob's Testimony
       1.   Relevance
          a.   Define:
              e.g. "To be relevant, Bob's testimony must have a tendency in reason to prove that someone was negligent, i.e. that it is more probable that someone was negligent than without Bob's testimony."
          b.   Apply:
              e.g. "Here, Bob's testimony is logically relevant because he repeats a percipient witness's (Jane's) statement that a blue car ran a red light and struck Ann's car. Thus, Bob's testimony makes it more probable than not that the blue car was negligent." OR
       "Here, Bob's testimony makes it more probable than not that the blue car was negligent because it tends to show it ran a red light and struck Ann's car."
          c.   Conclude:
              e.g. "Thus, Bob's testimony is relevant."

       2.   Hearsay
          a.   Define:
              e.g. "Hearsay is an out of court statement offered to prove the truth of the matter asserted."
          b.   Apply
              1)   If hearsay is a major threshold issue and you have time, consider analyzing each element, albeit quickly, e.g.:
              "Here, Bob repeats Jane's statement at the scene of the accident, i.e. her out of court statement. It is a statement because Jane was communicating a fact that the blue car ran the red light and struck Ann's car. Lastly, Bob's testimony is being offered to prove the truth that the blue car ran the red light and hit Ann's car."
              2)   In the alternative, you can simplify by writing in an integrated style, joining law and fact in a single sentence, e.g.: "Bob's testimony is hearsay because he repeats Jane's out of court statement made at the accident scene to prove the truth that the blue car ran the red light and struck Ann's car. Thus, it is hearsay."

          c.   Exceptions
              1)   Define: - e.g. "Unless an otherwise hearsay statement is subject to an exclusion or an exception, it is inadmissible." (Of course, you could make this statement after showing a statement is indeed hearsay)

2)   State an applicable exception as a heading, e.g.:
<u>Excited Utterance</u>
3)   Define: An excited utterance is reliable because it is a statement relating to a startling event made under the stress of that event.
4)   <u>Apply:</u>
e.g. Again, you may break into its components or you can summarily write about the elements, integrating law and fact:
<u>Example of breaking into elements:</u>
"Here, the startling event was the automobile accident. The statement relates to the startling event because Jane reported how the accident occurred, i.e. that the blue car ran the red light and hit Ann's car. Lastly, the statement must be made under the stress of the event. Here, Ann would argue that Bob heard Jane still "crying," thus proving she was still under the stress of the accident. However, Dave would argue Jane's statement was not reliable because Bob heard Jane's statement "within minutes" of the accident, thus suggesting Jane may not have been under stress and had sufficient time to reflect. However, Dave will successfully argue that at four years old, Jane would not fabricate a statement within minutes of an accident. Jane personally witnessed what had happened because she identified the color of the traffic light and the car. Thus, Jane's statement was reliable. Bob's testimony is admissible."

<u>Example of an integrated answer</u>
"Here, Bob's testimony qualifies as an admissible excited utterance because he repeated what he heard Jane describe about the car accident, a startling event. Most importantly, Jane was under the stress of the event because she was crying when she made the statement. Moreover, Jane, a four year old, made the statement within minutes of the accident, thus guaranteeing its reliability."

d.   State another applicable exception:
<u>Present Sense Impression</u>
1)   Define: A present sense impression is a statement made concurrently with the sense impression of an event that is not necessarily exciting.
2)   Apply: "Jane's statement must be made contemporaneous with her observation. Again, similar to the Excited Utterance above, the reliability of her statement turns on whether "within minutes" is too remote. Lastly, given Jane's tender age, it is unlikely she calculated her statement. Therefore, it will likely be admitted."

EVIDENCE QUESTION 1

A car driven by Dunn collided with Empire Trucking Co.'s truck driven by Kemper. Kemper died at the scene. Dunn and Dunn's passenger, Paul, were seriously injured. Paul sued Empire for personal injuries. Paul attempted to serve Sigel, an Empire mechanic who was on duty the day of the collision, with a subpoena to appear at the trial, but the process server could not locate Sigel. The following occurred at the jury trial.

1. Paul called the investigating police officer, Oliver, who testified that he talked to Wit at the scene a half hour after the collision. Oliver wrote down Wit's statement and attached it to his report. Oliver testified that Wit told him that he ran over to the scene from the curb and spoke to the driver of the car, Dunn, who told Wit: "I'm not going to make it and I want you to know the truth-the truck ran the red light."

2. Paul called a court reporter who properly authenticated the trial transcript of Sigel's testimony in *People v. Dunn*, a reckless homicide case relating to the same incident, in which Sigel testified that on the morning of the incident he warned Kemper that the brakes on the truck were defective, but Kemper drove the truck anyway. The transcript was admitted into evidence.

3. Paul called Dunn who testified that she had a green light and was driving below the speed limit when defendant's truck struck her car.

4. Empire offered into evidence a properly authenticated copy of the conviction of Dunn for reckless homicide based on this incident. Paul's objections to this offer were sustained.

5. Empire asked Dunn on cross examination: "Q. Isn't it true your insurance carrier reached a settlement with Paul and as part of that written agreement, you agreed to testify on Paul's behalf today?" Paul's objections to this question were sustained.

Assume that all appropriate objections were made. Was the evidence in items (1), (2), and (3), properly admitted, and were the objections in (4) and (5) properly sustained? Discuss.

Evidence Question 1

1. <u>Police Officer Oliver's testimony</u>

    a. Relevance - to prove Kemper's negligence and to show Empire may be vicariously liable.
    b. Probative value outweighs any prejudicial impact
    c. Personal knowledge
    d. Hearsay
        1) Out of court statements of Dunn and Wit offered to prove the truth that the truck ran the red light
        2) Multiple hearsay
            1) <u>Dunn to Wit</u>
                (1) Dying Declaration but Dunn available
                (2) Excited Utterance - "ran over to scene"
                (3) Present Sense Impression
            2) <u>Wit to Oliver</u>
                (1) No exceptions apply. Not reliable because ½ hour after collision and Wit has no duty to report the truth
                (2) FRE catch all?
            3) Oliver's report - not offered and even if offered, Wit had no duty to report the truth

2. <u>Trial transcript of Sigel's testimony</u>

    a. Relevance - impute knowledge to Empire
    b. Probative value outweighs prejudice
    c. Authentication - "properly authenticated"
    d. Hearsay
        1) Sigel's statement made out of this court's proceeding offered for truth? Or nonhearsay because offered to prove notice?
        2) If hearsay, multiple
            a) <u>Sigel to Kemper</u>
                (1) Nonhearsay - effect on hearer
                (2) Vicarious admission
            b) Transcript
                (1) Former testimony
                    (a) Sigel unavailable
                    (b) Similar motive and opportunity to cross exam? Empire was not a party

3. <u>Dunn's testimony</u>

    a. Relevance - to disprove any fault by Dunn
    b. Personal knowledge
    c. Lay Opinion - "below the speed limit"

128

4. Dunn's conviction

    a. Relevance - to prove Dunn was at fault and to impeach
    b. Prejudicial impact
    c. Impeachment - Character - prior felony conviction, less than 10 years old
    d. Hearsay but prior felony convictions are admissible

5. Cross examination of Dunn

    a. Leading Question - permissible on cross
    b. Compound Question
    c. Relevance - to show bias
    d. Legal Relevance - Offers to settle excluded to promote settlement negotiations; evidence of liability insurance excluded to promote coverage; however, admissible to impeach.

EVIDENCE QUESTION 2

Mary Smith sued Dr. Jones, alleging that Jones negligently performed surgery on her back, leaving her partly paralyzed. In her case-in-chief, Mary called the defendant, Dr. Jones, as her witness. The following questions were asked and answers given:

[1]   Q.   Now, you did not test the drill before you used it on Mary Smith's vertebrae, did you?

[2]   A.   No. That's not part of our procedure. We don't ordinarily do that.

[3]   Q.   Well, since Mary's operation, you now test these drills immediately before using them, don't you?

      A.   Yes.

[4]   Q.   Just before you inserted the drill into my client's spine, you heard Nurse Clark say "The drill bit looks wobbly," didn't you?

      A.   No. I did not.

      Q.   Let me show what has been marked as plaintiff's exhibit number 10. [Tendering document] This is the surgical report written by Nurse Clark, isn't it?

      A.   Yes.

[5]   Q.   In her report she wrote: "At time of insertion I said the drill bit looked wobbly," didn't she?

      A.   Yes. That's her opinion.

      Q.   Okay, speaking of opinions, you are familiar with the book, *General Surgical Techniques* by Tompkins, aren't you?

      A.   Yes.

      Q.   And it is authoritative, isn't it?

      A.   Some people think so.

[6]   Q.   And this book says, at page 255, "Always test drill bits before using them in spinal surgery," doesn't it?

      A.   I guess, so, but again that's his opinion.

      Q.   Now, you've had some trouble yourself in the past?

      A.   What do you mean?

[7]   Q.   Well, you were accused by two patients of having sexually abused them, aren't you?

      A.   That was all a lot of nonsense.

[8]   Q.   But you do admit that in two other operations which you performed in 1993 the drill bit which you were using slipped during back surgery, causing injury to your patients?

      A.   Accidents do happen.

What objection or objections could Dr. Jones' attorney reasonably have made to the question or answer at each of the places indicated above by the numbers in the left-hand margin, and how should the court have ruled in each instance? Discuss.

1. "You did not test the drill, did you"
   1. Relevant to prove negligence
   2. Leading question not allowed on direct unless witness is the adverse party or a hostile witness
   3. Argumentative question because of double negative

2. "No, That's not part of our procedure ..."
   1. Nonresponsive answer
   2. Move to strike or have jury disregard nonresponsive parts

3. "since Mary's operation, you now test ..."
   1. Relevant to prove negligence
   2. Legally irrelevant because it is a subsequent remedial measure to prove fault

4. "You heard Nurse Clark say ..."
   1. Hearsay
   2. Exceptions
      a) Admissions - Party, Vicarious, Adoptive (Silent)
      b) Present sense impression
      c) State of mind

5. "In her report ..."
   1. Double Hearsay
      a) "I said ..."
         1) see above
      b) Her report
         1) Business record
         2) Best evidence rule; authentication

6. Reference to book
   1. Hearsay
   2. Learned treatise
   3. Impeachment evidence

7. "Accused by two patients of having sexually abused them ..."
   1. Character evidence
      a) Not admissible to prove conduct in conformity
      b) Impeachment - does not go to honesty and prejudicial

8. "in two other operations ..."
   1. Improper character evidence - conduct in conformity and impeachment

[An actual answer follows on next page]

Evidence Question 2
NOTE: The following answer is a reproduction of an applicant's actual typewritten answer, except for minor corrections in spelling and punctuation. It is reprinted here for the sole purpose of giving students an example of an actual answer. This answer earned a "75."

ITEM 1

Form
Leading questions are not allowed on direct exam. Here, D had been called as a witness for plaintiff (P), so the testimony was on direct.

However, since the witness was also the opposing party, he was a <u>hostile witness</u>. Such witnesses are subject to leading questions.

Therefore, the objection should have been overruled.

Relevance
The evidence was logically relevant for its tendency to prove D had knowledge and control of the surgical drill.

It was legally relevant to show that he knew how to operate it. This was not more prejudicial than probative.

The objection should have been overruled.

Assumes facts not in evidence
The fact that a drill was used on Mary's vertebra by this doctor has not been admitted to evidence.

The objection should have been sustained.

ITEM 2

Relevance
The answer, "NO" was logically relevant to show the drill was tested. It was legally relevant because it was probative to D's fulfillment of his duty of care, relevant to the action for negligence.

However, the rest of the response was irrelevant for reasons stated below.

Nonresponsive to the question asked
Although the first part of the answer was acceptable, the words following were nonresponsive considering that they exceed the first part.

However, the court could have allowed additional questions to be asked or it could have considered an explanatory addition to the first part.

Assumes facts not in evidence

The question refers to surgical procedures, which had not yet to been introduced into evidence.

ITEM 3

Relevance
It was logically relevant to show D's control over the operating procedures.

However, it is presumed logically irrelevant because it was more prejudicial than probative.

Subsequent remedial measures are inadmissible to prove negligence. Remedial measures should be encouraged. Therefore, this statement should not be admitted to prove guilt.

They can be admitted if the court found that the evidence was offered for a purpose other than to prove negligence. But, the rule specifically precludes subsequent remedial measures which was the case here, since the measures addressed occurred "since Mary's operation."

Objection should have been sustained.

ITEM 4

(a) Just before ... spine

Relevance
It was logically relevant for its tendency to prove the operation procedures. It was legally relevant because it was more probative than prejudicial.

Assumes facts not in evidence
The procedures used in the operation had not yet been admitted into evidence.

(b) You heard Nurse Clark say ...

Hearsay
Hearsay is an out of court statement offered for the truth of the matter asserted. It is inherently unreliable and is not admissible unless an exception applies. Nurse Clark's statment was made in the operating room, out of this court, and was offered for its truth.

Present sense impression
A present sense impression is a statement made by a declarant while observing an event and the observation is about the event.

Here, Nurse Clark made the statement while observing the drill. She said that it "looks wobbly." Therefore, it qualifies as a present sense impression.

Objection should have been overruled.

ITEM 5

Relevance
It was logically relevant to show that Clark recorded the statement.

Best Evidence Rule (BER)
The BER requires the admittance into evidence of an original writing if the contents of that writing is in issue.

Here, the contents are in issue because D has denied that Clark made the statement and her surgical report says she did.

Therefore, the record should have been admitted into evidence.

Hearsay
The report is hearsay because writings made out of court offered for their truth are hearsay and are not admissible unless an exception applies.

Business Records Exception
Business records are admissible if they are made in the normal course of business and are prepared by the person in control of them and are authenticated.

Here, although the report is a surgical report, the hospital is not in the business of writing reports, it is in the business of healing. Clark has not authenticated the report.

Therefore, the objection should have been retained.

ITEM 6

BER
The BER requires presentation of the book at trial for exam by the other party. Here, it was referred to but was not at trial.

Hearsay
The book, as confirmed by D, an expert surgeon, has been shown to be authoritative since some doctors rely on it.

As such, the proper way for its admission required it be read into evidence. That is what P's attorney attempted to do.

Objection should have been overruled.

ITEM 7

Relevance
It was logically relevant to show his relationship with his other patients. However, it was more prejudicial than probative.

This case was about negligence, not sexual abuse. The introduction of this would confuse the issues, mislead the jury and waste court time.

The court should have ruled the evidence irrelevant.

Improper character evidence

Although Dr. Jones was accused by two patients, specific instances of prior bad acts are inadmissible to show conduct in conformity in the instant case.

Here, the accusations are not offered to show he acted in conformity but they are also not offered on his truthfulness.

Therefore, the use was improper.

ITEM 8

Relevance

It is logically relevant to prove that he has injured surgery patients in the past. It is not prejudicial than probative because it specifically relates to the negligence allegation.

Improper character evidence

Character evidence of specific prior bad acts cannot be admitted to prove conformity therewith in this case. However, if the court decides the facts are more probative than prejudicial, they can be admitted to show any other relevant fact.

MIMIC Rule

Under this rule, specific bad acts can be admitted to show motive, intent, mistake (absence of) and common plan or scheme.

The court would have to decide if two prior events which happened 6 years ago establish a common plan or scheme, or any of the other factors.

If they do, the objection should have been overruled. If not, it should have been sustained.

EVIDENCE QUESTION 3

Dave brought his sports car into the local service station for an oil change. While servicing the car, Mechanic checked the brakes and noticed that they needed repair. The following events occurred:

(1) Mechanic commented to Helper, "Dave had better get these brakes fixed. They look bad to me."

(2) Mechanic instructed Helper (who did not himself observe the brakes) to write on the work order: "Inspected brakes - repair?", which Helper then wrote on the work order. However, Helper currently does not remember what words he wrote on the work order.

(3) Many hours later when Dave picked up his car, Helper overheard Mechanic say to Dave, "I think your brakes are bad. You'd better get them fixed."

(4) Dave responded, "I am not surprised. They've felt a little funny lately."

(5) Later that day, when Helper was walking down Main Street, he heard the sound of a collision behind him, followed by a bystander shouting: "The sports car ran the red light and ran into the truck."

The sports car involved in the accident was the one that Dave had just picked up from Mechanic. Polly owned the truck. Polly sued Dave for negligence for damages sustained in the accident. Polly's complaint alleged that the accident was caused by the sports car running the red light because the sports car's brakes failed. Polly's theory of liability is that Dave knew or should have known that his brakes were bad and that driving the car under those circumstances was negligent.

Polly called Helper as a witness to testify as to the facts recited in items (1) through (5) above, and she also offered into evidence the work order referred to in item number (2).

Assume that in each instance, appropriate objections were made.

Should the court admit the evidence offered in items numbers (1) through (5), including the work order referred to in item number (2)? Discuss.

[July 2007 #3]

EVIDENCE QUESTION 4

While driving their cars, Paula and Dan collided and each suffered personal injuries and property damage. Paula sued Dan for negligence in a California state court and Dan filed a cross-complaint for negligence against Paula. At the ensuing jury trial, Paula testified that she was driving to meet her husband, Hank, and that Dan drove his car into hers. Paula also testified that, as she and Dan were waiting for an ambulance immediately following the accident, Dan said, "I have plenty of insurance to cover your injuries." Paula further testified that, three hours after the accident, when a physician at the hospital to which she was taken asked her how she was feeling, she said, "My right leg hurts the most, all because that idiot Dan failed to yield the right-of-way."

Officer, who was the investigating police officer who responded to the accident, was unavailable at the trial. The court granted a motion by Paula to admit Officer's accident report into evidence. Officer's accident report states: "When I arrived at the scene three minutes after the accident occurred, an unnamed bystander immediately came up to me and stated that Dan pulled right out into the path of Paula's car. Based on this information, my interviews with Paula and Dan, and the skidmarks, I conclude that Dan caused the accident." Officer prepared his accident report shortly after the accident.

In his case-in-chief, Dan called a paramedic who had treated Paula at the scene of the accident. Dan showed the paramedic a greeting card, and the paramedic testified that he had found the card in Paula's pocket as he was treating her. The court granted a motion by Dan to admit the card into evidence. The card states: "Dearest Paula, Hurry home from work as fast as you can today. We need to get an early start on our weekend trip to the mountains! Love, Hank."

Dan testified that, as he and Paula were waiting for the ambulance immediately following the accident, Wilma handed him a note. Wilma had been identified as a witness during discovery, but had died before she could be deposed. The court granted a motion by Dan to admit the note into evidence. The note says: "I saw the whole thing. Paula was speeding. She was definitely negligent."

Assuming all appropriate objections were timely made, should the court have admitted:

(Questions on opposite page)

1. Dan's statement to Paula about insurance? Discuss.
2. Paula's statement to the physician? Discuss.
3. Officer's accident report relating to:
    a. The unnamed bystander's statement? Discuss.
    b. Officer's conclusion and its basis? Discuss.
4. Hank's greeting card? Discuss.
5. Wilma's note? Discuss.

Answer according to California law.

[July 2009 #3]

PROFESSIONAL RESPONSIBILITY

I. **THE ATTORNEY'S DUTY TO THE CLIENT**

    A. **The duty of loyalty**

    B. **The duty of silence**

    C. **The duty of competence**

    D. **The duty of financial integrity**

II. **THE ATTORNEY'S DUTY TO THIRD PARTIES**

    A. **The duty to opposing parties in litigation**

    B. **The duty to accept representation**

    C. **The special duty of prosecutors**

III. **THE ATTORNEY'S DUTY TO THE COURT**

    A. **The duty of candor**

    B. **The duty of honesty**

    C. **The duty to witnesses and jurors**

IV. **THE ATTORNEY'S DUTY TO THE PROFESSION**

    A. **The duty to avoid unauthorized practice of law**

    B. **The duty to avoid false or misleading advertisements**

    C. **The duty to not improperly solicit clients**

PROFESSIONAL RESPONSIBILITY QUESTION 1

Attorney Ann is a member of the State Bar of California and represents primarily low-income tenants. Frank, a friend of Ann, told her about an apartment complex that appeared to be very run down and to have many elderly tenants. Ann visited the building and was shocked at its dilapidated and unsafe conditions.

Ann sent a letter to each of the tenants in the building, which stated:

> It has come to my attention that there may be ILLEGAL and UNSAFE conditions at your apartment building!
>
> I am an attorney experienced in this type of case, and I am willing to represent you in a lawsuit against your landlord regarding these conditions. CALL TODAY!

Tom, a tenant, called Ann in response to the letter and told her he wanted to hire her to sue Landlord. He said that another tenant named Barbara, who is 82 years old and speaks only Spanish, also wanted to hire Ann.

Ann met with Tom and Barbara. Since Ann speaks very little Spanish, and Tom is bilingual, he acted as a translator. It became clear that Tom's interest was in obtaining a money judgment and that Barbara's interest was in obtaining an injunction requiring the landlord to make repairs. Ann, Tom and Barbara signed a contingency fee agreement for Ann to represent Tom and Barbara in a lawsuit against Landlord. Under the agreement, Ann would receive 40% of any recovery in the case. Ann also separately agreed with Frank that she would pay him 10% of any fees she recovers in return for his having told her about the apartment complex.

Ann filed a lawsuit against Landlord. The suit had a sound legal basis, and she handled it in a professionally competent manner.

Ann and Tom worked together closely on the case, and before the case was resolved, he asked Ann to date him. He also gave her a free airline ticket to accompany him on a trip to Hawaii, which she accepted. Eventually, Landlord made a written settlement offer to pay money damages only, which Ann conveyed to Tom. Tom, without consulting Barbara, told Ann that he and Barbara accepted the offer. Ann concluded the settlement.

What professional responsibility issues are raised by Ann's conduct? Discuss.

Professional Responsibility Question 1

<u>Attorney Ann</u>

<u>Advertisement</u>
1.   Attorney advertising enjoys limited 1st Amendment protection. State may regulate misleading, deceptive or untruthful advertising.
2.   Here, targeted mailing to persons in need of representation. Ann must clearly indicate this is advertising material.
3.   The advertisement is potentially misleading, e.g. ILLEGAL and UNSAFE conditions.

<u>Duty of Loyalty: Joint representation</u>
1.   Conflict of interest between two clients, Tom and Barbara
2.   Ann could represent both if secured their waivers after disclosure and consent.

<u>Duty of Confidence</u>
1.   Disclosure of information when Ann met with Tom and Barbara and Tom translated.

<u>Fee Agreement</u>
1.   In California, must disclose in writing the method of calculating the fee and deduction of costs.
2.   The fee must be reasonable

<u>Fee splitting agreement</u>
1.   Is Frank a lawyer?
     a.   If yes, fee splitting permitted but requires client awareness and consent
     b.   If not, not permitted - runner

<u>Ann & Tom's relationship</u>
1.   Did Ann use her position to coerce relationship or did Tom pursue Ann?
2.   Continuing relationship may adversely affect Barbara

<u>Duty to Communicate - Settlement offer</u>
1.   Ann did not communicate with Barbara
2.   Offer was adverse to what Barbara wanted

PROFESSIONAL RESPONSIBILITY QUESTION 2

Attorney Ann is a member of the Board of Directors of Californians Against Poverty (CAP), a non-profit corporation. Two years ago, CAP received a grant from the Department of Labor to provide computer training to unemployed individuals. The Department of Labor now wants to audit CAP's books to verify the grant expenditures. CAP's executive director, Dave, has taken the position that CAP's books are confidential and has refused to allow the audit.

Since Ann is the only attorney on the Board of Directors, Dave asked her to assist him in presenting the issue to the CAP Board of Directors. Ann concluded that an argument could be made that the audit request is too broad and is not specifically authorized by the grant documents. However, in the course of discussing the proposed audit, Dave informed Ann that the real reason he opposed the audit was that he used grant funds to purchase two personal computers for his children to use at home. This is a violation of the terms of the federal grant and, arguably, a violation of federal criminal statutes.

At the next meeting of the CAP Board of Directors, Dave presented the matter without making any mention of any misuse of funds. Ann said nothing, and the Board adopted a resolution opposing the audit. Dave then asked Ann to represent CAP on a *pro bono* basis to file an action against the Department of Labor to enjoin the audit.

1. What, if any, ethical issues are raised by Ann's role as an attorney and a member of CAP's Board? Discuss.

2. Is Ann ethically required to disclose to the Board Dave's misuse of funds? Discuss.

3. Can Ann ethically represent CAP on a *pro bono* basis in a suit to enjoin the audit? Discuss.

145

Professional Responsibility Question 2

1. Ethical issues – Ann's role as attorney and CAP Board Member
   A. Fiduciary duties as board member
      1) Duty of care
      2) Duty of loyalty
      3) These duties may conflict with her ethical duties
   B. Duties as attorney
      1) Duties owed to client
         a) Who is client? CAP? Board of Directors? Dave? If Dave, in his personal or professional capacity?
         b) Duty of Loyalty – Conflict of interest created in fiduciary duties owed to CAP and to potential client – Ann must disclose
         c) Duty of confidentiality – Dave might expect as to matters disclosed to Ann. However, duty of silence conflicts with fiduciary duties
         d) Duty of Candor and Honesty – Ann owes duties to the court and to third parties. These duties may be compromised if she represents Dave or CAP

2. Must Ann disclose to CAP Board?
   A. Ann owes fiduciary duties to CAP re: opposing the audit and disclosing the real reason.
      1) Duty of care
      2) Duty of loyalty
   B. Disclosure may constitute ethical breach to Dave, if an attorney client relationship exists
      1) Ann should have informed Dave her duty was owed to CAP and that Dave should seek counsel.
      2) Ann may not report Dave's crime
   C. If Ann represented CAP (questionable), then Ann must report to CAP Board.
      1) Ann should advise CAP to obtain outside counsel
      2) Ann should disclose and resign

3. Can Ann represent CAP?
   A. If Ann did represent CAP, she would be covering up Dave's crime and would breach her duty of honesty and candor to both the court and Dep't of Labor
   B. If Ann argued for CAP, she would be advancing a frivolous claim.

PROFESSIONAL RESPONSIBILITY QUESTION 3

There was recently a major release of hazardous substances from a waste disposal site in County. Owen is the current owner of the site. Fred is a former owner of the site.

Hap is the producer of the hazardous substances disposed of at the site. As a result of the hazardous substance release, County has identified the site as a priority cleanup target, and has notified Owen, Fred, and Hap that they are the responsible parties who must either clean up or pay to clean up the site. County advised each responsible party of his degree of culpability. In the event each responsible party does not pay his share of the cleanup costs, County is entitled to impose joint and several liability on each of them.

In an effort to facilitate the resolution of County's demand, Owen, the wealthiest responsible party, arranged for Fred, Hap, and himself to meet with Anne, his tax lawyer. At the meeting, Owen offered to pay the attorney fees of all three of them in exchange for their agreement to be represented by Anne. Fred and Hap accepted Owen's offer and Anne distributed identical retainer agreements to each of them, which they signed.

What ethical violations, if any, has Anne committed? Discuss.

[July 2010#2]

PROFESSIONAL RESPONSIBILITY QUESTION 4

Alex, an attorney, represents Dusty, a well-known movie actor. Dusty had recently been arrested for battery after Vic reported that Dusty knocked him down when he went to Dusty's home trying to take photos of Dusty and his family. Dusty claims Vic simply tripped.

Paul, the prosecutor, filed a criminal complaint against Dusty. Suspecting that Paul was anxious to publicize the arrest of a high-profile defendant as part of his election bid for District Attorney, Alex held a press conference on the steps of the courthouse. He told the press: "Any intelligent jury will find that Dusty did not strike Vic. Dusty is the innocent victim of a witch-hunt by a prosecutor who wants to become District Attorney."

Meanwhile, Paul received a copy of the police report describing Dusty's alleged criminal behavior. Concerned that the description of Dusty's behavior sounded vague, Paul asked the reporting police officer to destroy the existing police report and to draft one that included more details of Dusty's alleged criminal behavior.

Paul interviewed Dusty's housekeeper, Henry, who witnessed the incident involving Dusty and Vic. Henry told Paul that Dusty did not knock Vic down. Paul told Henry to avoid contact with Alex.

Paul has not been able to obtain Vic's version of the events because Vic is on an extended trip abroad and will not be back in time for Dusty's preliminary hearing.
Confident that Dusty is nevertheless guilty, Paul has decided to proceed with the preliminary hearing.

1. What ethical violation(s), if any, has Alex committed? Discuss.
2. What ethical violation(s), if any, has Paul committed? Discuss.

Answer according to both California and ABA authorities.

[July 2009 #2]

REAL PROPERTY

I. **POSSESSORY INTERESTS: ESTATES IN LAND**

    A.   Present possessory interests
        1.   Fee simple absolute
        2.   Defeasible fees
            a.   Fee simple determinable
            b.   Fee simple subject to condition subsequent
            c.   Fee simple subject to executory limitation
        3.   Life estates
    B.   Future interests
        1.   In grantor
            a.   Possibility of reverter
            b.   Right of entry
            c.   Reversion
        2.   In grantee or third person
            a.   Executory interests
            b.   Remainders
        3.   Attributes
            a.   Waste
            b.   Fixtures
        4.   Validity
            a.   Destructibility
            b.   Shelley's Case
            c.   Worthier Title
            d.   Restraints on alienation
            e.   Restraints on marriage
            f.   Rule against Perpetuities
        5.   Class gifts

II. **LANDLORD-TENANT**

    A.   **Nature of leasehold**
        1.   Tenancy for years
        2.   Periodic tenancy
        3.   Tenancy at will
        4.   Tenancy at sufferance - hold-over doctrine

    B.   **Tenant's Duties**
        1.   Duty to repair
            a.   General doctrine
            b.   Affirmative waste
            c.   Permissive waste
            d.   Defenses
            e.   lease shifted burden of repair to tenant
            f.   tenant must promptly report deficiencies to landlord

      2. Duty to not use premises for illegal purpose
        a. General doctrine
        b. Occasional unlawful conduct exception
        c. Landlord remedies
      3. Duty to pay rent
      4. Abandonment of premises by tenant
        a. General doctrine
        b. Landlord remedies
        c. Constructive eviction and tenant remedies

   C. **Landlord's duties**
      1. Duty to deliver possession
      2. Quiet enjoyment
      3. Warranty of habitability

   D. **Assignments and subleases**

III. **CONCURRENT ESTATES**

   A. **Joint Tenacy**

   B. **Tenancy in Common**

IV. **EASEMENTS**

   A. **General doctrine**

   B. **Affirmative easement**

   C. **Negative easement**

   D. **Creation by implication**

   E. **Enforcement**

   F. **Termination**
      1. release
      2. merger
      3. condemnation of the servient estate
      4. destruction of the servient estate
      5. end of necessity
      6. prescription
      7. abandonment
      8. estoppel

   G. **Easements by prescription**
      1. General doctrine
      2. Continuity requirement
      3. Use must be exclusive

V.   LICENSES, PROFITS, COVENANTS & SERVITUDES

    A.   License - general doctrine
       1.   license estoppel theory
       2.   license coupled with an interest
       3.   invalid easement as license

    B.   Profits - general doctrine
       1.   exclusive v. non-exclusive
       2.   profits v. ownership

    C.   Covenants - general doctrine
       1.   affirmative covenant
       2.   negative covenant

    D.   Equitable servitudes - general doctrine
       1.   remedy
       2.   enforcement

VI.   SUPPORT
    A.   Lateral Support
       1.   Support of land in natural state
       2.   Support of land with buildings

    B.   Subjacent Support
       1.   Support of land with buildings
       2.   Interference with underground waters

VII. CONVEYANCING

    A.   Land sale contracts

    B.   Deeds

    C.   Covenants of title

    D.   Recording

    E.   Mortgages
       1.   Effect of foreclosure
       2.   Land records - unrecorded transactions

VIII. ADVERSE POSSESSION
    A.   General doctrine
    B.   Requirements
       1.   open and notorious possession
       2.   actual and exclusive possession
       3.   continuous possession
       4.   hostile while under claim of right

REAL PROPERTY

I. **Classify the interest and was it validly created?**
    A. Ownership interests
        1. Present possessory estates
            a. Fee simple absolute
            b. Defeasible fees
            c. Life estate
        2. Future interests
            a. Of the grantor
            b. Of the grantee
        3. Concurrent estates
            a. Joint tenancy
            b. Tenancy in common
        4. Landlord Tenant (Non-freehold estates)
        5. Adverse possession
    B. Nonpossessory interests
        1. Easement
        2. License
        3. Profit
        4. Covenant running with the land
        5. Equitable servitude
        6. Lateral and Subjacent Support

II. **State the characteristics of the interest**
    A. Attributes
    B. Rights and Duties

III. **State any limitations to the interest**
    A. Exceptions or termination
    B. Public land use

IV. **Conveyancing**
    A. Contracts for the sale of land
    B. Deeds
    C. Delivery
    D. Title
    E. Recording
    F. Mortgages

V. **Remedies**

REAL PROPERTY QUESTION 1

In 2005, Grant subdivided a tract of land into two parcels, A and B. He then sold Parcel B to Nell, and thereafter, Parcel A to Owen. Owen constructed a house on Parcel A, close to the boundary with Parcel B. In March 2006, Owen leased Parcel A to Tim under a ten-year lease. The lease provided for an annual rent payable in monthly installments. Since 2005, first Grant and then Owen allowed Nell access to Parcel B by use of a road through Parcel A.

In January 2010, Nell notified Owen of her intent to construct a building on Parcel B near the common boundary. Nell's contractor excavated for a deep basement for the new building. In March 2010, that portion of Parcel A land under Owen's house subsided, causing material damage to the house. Owen refused to repair the damage, insisting that Nell or her contractor should do so. Tim moved out and refused to make further payments of rent during the balance of the lease. Owen then refused to allow Nell further access over Parcel A.

1.   What are Owen's rights against Tim for the remaining monthly rent payments? Discuss.

2.   What are Owen's rights against Nell for damage to the house? Discuss.

3.   Does Nell have a right to continue use of the road through Parcel A? Discuss.

Real Property Question 1

I.   **Owen v. Tim**
    A.   Classification - Leasehold
        1.   "10 yr. lease" = tenancy for years
            a.   Monthly rent does not alter characterization
            b.   Statute of Frauds satisfied
    B.   Attributes of tenancy for years
        1.   Tenant has possessory interest; Owner has reversionary interest
        2.   Tenant has a duty to pay rent.
            a.   At common law, tenant's duty to pay rent was independent of owner's obligations.
            b.   Modernly, tenant's duty dependent on owner's covenants under the lease.
        3.   Tim will argue Owen breached his implied covenant of Quiet Enjoyment
            a.   Actual eviction or partial eviction?
            b.   Constructive eviction
                1.   Premises uninhabitable?
                2.   Did Owen cause injury?
        4.   Tim will also assert Implied warranty of habitability.

II. **Owen v. Nell**
    A.   Classification - Right to lateral support.
    B.   Attributes - Owen has the right to have his land supported in its natural state by the adjoining land.
        1.   Nell would be strictly liable for not supporting the land in its natural state if land would have subsided without the improvements.
        2.   If land improved would not have collapsed in its natural state, Owen must prove Nell was negligent.
            a.   Did Nell owe a duty of care, which was breached?
            b.   Nell will argue the contractor was an independent contractor
            c.   Nell will argue that Owen did not mitigate his damages

III. **Nell v. Owen**
    A.   Classification - Easement
    B.   Attributes - Nell has an affirmative right to use, but has no right to possess and enjoy the land.
        - Owen has right to possess but he cannot interfere with Nell's use.
    C.   Creation of the easement
        1.   Easement by implication
            a.   common ownership
            b.   reasonable necessity
    D.   If Nell can't prove an easement, then Nell has a license, but probably irrevocable.

REAL PROPERTY QUESTION 2

Donna asked her neighbor, Stan, to give her a roadway easement across his property so Donna could have better access to her own property. Stan agreed and asked Len, his lawyer, to prepare a deed granting an "easement for a road thirty feet wide" along a designated path. Len prepared the deed, which Stan signed and instructed Len to give to Donna. Unbeknownst to Stan, Len was also Donna's attorney and had advised her to obtain an easement from Stan.

Stan died that night. Although he was aware of Stan's death, Len gave the deed to Donna the next day. Donna never recorded the deed.

One year later, Donna constructed a gravel road 15 feet wide along the designated path. Donna continued to farm her land and use the road. She has repaired the road, but not improved it. Stan's son Paul inherited Stan's farm and has never objected to Donna's activities.

After another 21 years elapsed, Donna announced plans to convert her farm to a commercial complex. She now intends to use the road as the complex's main entrance, widening it to 30 feet, paving it, and putting utilities under the pavement.

Paul objects to Donna's plans for the road. A paved road will interfere with his farming. The area is changing and some farms have converted to commercial use, but Paul wants to continue farming.

1. What rights and interests do Donna and Paul each have in the road?   Discuss.

2. May Donna, over Paul's objection, carry out her plans for the road?   Discuss.

3. Has Len violated any rules of professional conduct? Discuss.

1. Donna's rights
    a. Express Easement Appurtenant
        1) define
        2) Statute of Frauds – deed sufficiently described conveyance?
        3) Delivery of deed – escrow situation
    b. Prescriptive Easement
        1) define elements
        2) open & notorious – used and repaired
        3) actual & exclusive – used and repaired
        4) continuous - over 20 years
        5) hostile - P never objected
    c. Easement by Necessity - here only "better access"
    d. Irrevocable license - graveled and repaired

    Paul's rights
    a. Transfer of servient estate – new owner takes subject to the burden of the easement unless new owner is a BFP
        1) Valuable consideration - Paul inherited the land
        2) Notice
            a) No actual notice – Paul did not know
            b) No record notice – Donna did not record
            c) Inquiry notice - gravel road visible

2. Donna's plans
    a. If express easement - foreseeable use within scope?
        1) Road width
        2) Commercial complex
        3) Underground utilities
    b. If prescriptive easement - limited to actual use

3. Len - professional responsibilities
    a. Duty of loyalty - conflict of interest
        1) Disclose
        2) Written Consent
    b. Duty of confidentiality

REAL PROPERTY QUESTION 3

Sam and Paul entered into a written contract on September 1, 1999, for the sale by Sam to Paul of a mountain lakefront lot improved with a residence (the "parcel") for $100,000. The contract was silent as to the quality of title Sam would convey, but provided that a quitclaim deed would be used. Paul failed to tender the agreed-on price on the performance date. Sam sued Paul for specific performance on July 5, 2000. Paul defended the suit on the ground that Sam's title is not marketable.

Sam's claim of title goes back to Owen, who owned an unencumbered fee simple absolute in the parcel. The parcel, which was accessible only during the summer months, had been occupied by Owen and Owen's family as a summer vacation home since 1980. In 1984, Owen conveyed the parcel by recorded deed to "my daughter, Doris, and my son, George, so long as they both shall live, and then to the survivor of them."

Owen died testate in 1987. Owen's will made no specific reference to the parcel, but the residuary clause left to Doris "all my other property not specifically disposed of by this will." Doris and George and their families continued to use the vacation home each summer. Doris died testate in April 1988, her will "devising and bequeathing all my estate to my son, Ed."

George executed a deed in May 1988, purporting to convey a fee simple absolute in the parcel to Cain. Cain and his family occupied the parcel during the summers of 1988 through 1996. In May 1997, Cain conveyed the parcel to Sam. Sam's family occupied it during the summers of 1997 through 1999.

The statute of limitations on actions to recover land in this jurisdiction is 10 years. There is no statute or decision by an appellate court either repudiating or affirming the common law doctrine of destructibility of contingent remainders.

Who should prevail in Sam's suit against Paul? Discuss

[For a sample outline and answer, see the California Essay Exam Book, Real Property]

REAL PROPERTY QUESTION 4

Larry leased in writing to Tanya a four-room office suite at a rent of $500 payable monthly in advance. The lease commenced on July 1, 2006. The lease required Larry to provide essential services to Tanya's suite. The suite was located on the 12th floor of a new 20-story office building.

In November Larry failed to provide essential services to Tanya's suite on several occasions. Elevator service and running water were interrupted once; heating was interrupted twice; and electrical service was interrupted on three occasions. These services were interrupted for periods of time lasting from one day to one week. On December 5, the heat, electrical and running water services were interrupted and not restored until December 12. In each instance Tanya immediately complained to Larry, who told Tanya that he was aware of the problems and was doing all he could to repair them.

On December 12, Tanya orally told Larry that she was terminating her lease on February 28, 2007 because the constant interruptions of services made it impossible for her to conduct her business. She picked the February 28 termination date to give her ample opportunity to locate alternative office space.

Tanya vacated the suite on February 28 even though between December 12 and February 28 there were no longer any problems with the leased premises.

Larry did not attempt to relet Tanya's vacant suite until April 15. He found a tenant to lease the suite commencing on May 1 at a rent of $500 payable monthly in advance. On May 1, Larry brought suit against Tanya to recover rent for the months of March and April.

On what theory could Larry reasonably assert a claim to recover rent from Tanya for March and April and what defenses could Tanya reasonably assert against Larry's claim for rent? Discuss.

[July 2007 #1]

REAL PROPERTY QUESTION 5

Since the early 1960s, Artist has had a year-to-year lease of the third floor of a small loft building which, like most buildings in the area, has mixed commercial and light manufacturing uses. Artist has used her space, as other local craftspeople have used theirs, for both residential and studio purposes. She has enjoyed the serenity of her unit and the panoramic views of the distant hills and of the nearby park to which she has had easy access.

In July 1998, Landlord rented a lower floor of the building to Machinist, whose operations are extremely noisy. Artist's complaints about the noise to both Machinist and Landlord have been to no avail.

At about the same time, Developer began building a large office tower nearby which will block Artist's view when completed. The office building will provide needed employment for the community.

The State Power Department, a State governmental agency, has also begun construction of electric and communications lines for Developer's office building. For the next several years the State Power Department construction will block a path across an undeveloped lot which separates Artist's neighborhood from the park. The path has been regularly used for many years by Artist and other neighborhood residents because the only other access to the park is by a much longer circuitous street route.

1. What are Artist's rights and remedies, if any, against Landlord, Machinist and Developer? Discuss.

2. What are Artist's rights and remedies, if any, against State Power Department for blocking the path? Discuss.

An actual answer follows

Real Property Question 5

NOTE: The following answer is a typed reproduction of an applicant's actual handwritten answer, except for minor corrections in spelling and punctuation. It is reprinted here for the sole purpose of giving students an example of an actual answer. This answer earned a "70."

1. A) A has a periodic tenancy. The building is used for residential and commercial purposes, <u>not</u> residential only purposes. Therefore, certain warranties are not applicable to <u>commercial leases</u>. While people have used the building for both purposes - commercial and residential - we must analyze the <u>implied warranties</u> and if any are breached by landlord (LL), Artist (A) may sue.

   B) We must also determine if Machinist's (M) actions interfere with A's use and enjoyment of her third floor space. If M is substantially interfering with A's floor, A could consider claiming a <u>private nuisance</u> cause of action against M.

   C) The next issue to consider would be if A has a claim of an <u>easement for light, space and air</u> against Developer(D). If she can successfully claim this, she may have to raise an <u>injunction</u> claim to prevent the completion of the large office tower.

   Our facts are silent concerning any zoning restrictions on the building of LL. Most leases contain several implied warranties. One warranty is the <u>implied warranty of habitability</u>; another <u>warranty is the implied warranty of quiet enjoyment.</u> These warranties are not applicable to commercial leases.

   A will argue that LL has violated both implied warranties listed above. These warranties allow a person in a landlord/tenant relationship to enjoy her rental unit and be able to live in this unit comfortably. These have been breached due to Machinist's leasing below her.

   LL will argue both warranties do not apply because the units have mixed commercial and light manufacturing uses. So, M may do his job.

   However, A will claim that her <u>notice</u> of the other flats indicated that many were living and working in their rental units. A relied on the quiet nature of the apartment units when she leased the unit.

If A's claims are held viable, A has options against LL. She can consider a <u>constructive eviction</u>: due to LL's breach allowing her to move out within a reasonable time and not pay rent. Since LL will argue that there would be no <u>actual eviction</u> because commercial units use the building, if A moves out she will be held responsible for rent due until the LL finds a new tenant to mitigate his losses.

<u>A v M</u>

A will claim that M's work is a <u>private nuisance</u>. A private nuisance is any act that substantially interferes with someone's use of their property.

Here, M's operations are extremely noisy and both A and her development as an artist. A will try to establish that M's noise substantially interferes with her use.

If A establishes a private nuisance cause of action, she could attempt to enjoin M from further noise. She could initially try to get a temporary restraining order (TRO) to restrain M from making noise. A could also try to get a preliminary injunction from the court. These two methods require the court to balance issues for both sides and also require hearings.

<u>A's remedy against M</u>
<u>Injunction</u>
    <u>Inadequate remedy at law</u>
        Money damages would be speculative for A's issues.
    <u>Property right</u>
        As shown above, A has a property right as a tenant.
    <u>Feasibility</u>
        It would be feasible for the court to levy a fair and sound judgment.
    <u>Balancing</u>
        Court will balance the interests. The court could get both sides to adhere to the judgment without too much time or supervision.
    <u>Defenses</u>
        There do not appear to be any issues of laches or unclean hands.

<u>Damages</u>
The limitation on damages: They must be certain and foreseeable (<u>Hadley v. Baxendale</u>), causal and unavoidable. A would have a duty to mitigate.

She could try to recover loss of rental use and diminution in value or lost profits if a business, although profits are usually too speculative.

A v. State Power Department (SPD)

A will claim that she and her neighbors have an easement by necessity or prescription. If she raises the easement against SPD, she will try to enjoin SPD from building the building.

The injunction here would involve a property right and set up as follows:

Inadequate Remedy at Law - property is the issue here and there could be multiple lawsuits by the neighborhood.

Property right - property right via the easement.

Feasibility - feasible for the court to remedy the situation.

Balance - the court will balance the hardship of walking the circuitous route vs. keeping the easement of access vs. SPD's hardship, needs and desires for construction of the electric lines.

Defenses - There seem to be no issues of laches or unclean hands or anything else present in our facts.

Regarding A's easement claim, she and her neighbors may claim an easement by necessity. This is rather weak since they are not prevented from going to the park; it just takes longer.

Prescriptive easements are easements like "adverse possession." There must be continual and actual and open use of the easement. The facts state that the easement has been used for many years. It appears to be continual and open. So A should successfully claim an easement by prescription; then get an injunction to prevent the construction as discussed.

REMEDIES

I. **ALWAYS LOOK FIRST TO LEGAL REMEDIES THEN LOOK TO EQUITABLE REMEDIES.**

   A. **First, evaluate the adequacy of legal remedies.**
      1. Legal remedies are:
        a. Damages: Money
        b. Restitution:
          (1) Money
          (2) Replevin: recovery of specific personal property
          (3) Ejectment: recovery of specific real property

   B. **After you have determined what legal remedies are,** or may be inadequate, you can move on.
      1. Equitable remedies are:
        a. Restitution:
          (1) Constructive trust: court-imposed obligation on the defendant to convey specific property to the plaintiff
          (2) Equitable lien: court-imposed security interest in specific property owned by the defendant
        b. Injunction:
        negative or mandatory order (in contract, a specific performance decree)

II. **ORDER OF PROGRESSION IN ANALYZING TORT PROBLEMS**

   A. **Damages**: Injury to the plaintiff arising out of the tort.
      1. Actual damages: Compensatory damages that seek to put plaintiff back where he was before the tort. Actual damages in tort look to the past.
      2. Nominal damages: A small, or nominal, amount of money available when no actual damages can be proved.
      3. Punitive damages: Punitive damages punish and deter. They do not compensate for actual injury suffered by the plaintiff. Remember that there must be some proportionality between actual or nominal damages and punitive damages. Further, wealthy defendants pay more than poor defendants.

B. **Restitution**: Benefit unjustly retained by the defendant. There does not need to be any injury to plaintiff.
   1. Legal remedies:
      a. Money: Look for benefit to the defendant. Sometimes called "waive the tort and sue in assumpsit"
      b. Replevin: Recovery of specific personal property
      c. Ejectment: Recovery of specific real property

   2. Equitable remedies:
      a. Constructive trust: Obligation to convey specific property to the plaintiff.
      b. Equitable lien: Security interest in specific property.

C. **Injunction**: Order to the defendant to refrain from doing something (negative injunction), or to do something (mandatory or affirmative injunction).

III. ORDER OF PROGRESSION IN ANALYZING CONTRACT PROBLEMS

A. **Damages**: Injury to the plaintiff arising out of a breach of contract by the defendant.
   1. Expectation damages: This is the benefit plaintiff expected to get out of the contract. Expectation damages look to the future.
   2. Consequential damages: These are damages to plaintiff in addition to the lost expectation. They must be foreseeable at the time the contract was entered into.
   3. Liquidated damages: These are damages specified in the contract. For a liquidated damages clause to be valid, actual damages must be difficult to calculate, and the amount specified in the clause must be a reasonable approximation. If the clause is invalid, it is called a penalty. If the parties' intent is clearly expressed, liquidated damages may serve as a true alternative to performance.

B. **Restitution**:
   1. Money restitution: Benefits unjustly retained by the defendant when there is a void or unenforceable contract, or where the plaintiff chooses not to sue on the contract, permitting recovery in quasi-contract or quantum meruit. Remember that a breaching party may sometimes recover in restitution even though he or she has breached.

C. **Specific Performance**: Order to the defendant to specifically perform the contract.

D. **Special Remedies sometimes available:**
    1. Rescission: In rescission, the contract is void or voidable, and the deal is called off.
        Grounds for rescission:
        a. Mistake
            1) Mutual
            2) Unilateral
        b. Misrepresentation
            1) Innocent
            2) Fraudulent
        c. Defenses
            1) Unclean hands
            2) Laches
            3) Election of Remedies
            4) Estoppel
    2. Reformation: In reformation, the contract is valid and enforceable, but the written form of the contract is wrong. The contract is rewritten correctly and is then enforced.
        Grounds for reformation:
        a. Mistake
            1) Mutual
            2) Unilateral
        b. Misrepresentation
        c. Defenses
            1) Laches
            2) Sale to BFP
            3) Parol Evidence Rule, Statute of Frauds and Negligence are not good defenses.

IV. **CHECKLIST FOR GRANTING INJUNCTIVE RELIEF IN TORT**

IPFBD – "I Put Five Bucks Down"

Look first for a breach of legal obligation. Has the defendant committed a tort, or is he or she about to?

A. Are the legal remedies **INADEQUATE**?
    1. Damages and money restitution: Damages may be inadequate because they are too speculative or too small to compensate fully for the actual injury. There may be a multiplicity of suits. The injury may be irreparable. There may be injury to land.

2.   Replevin: Replevin may be inadequate if the defendant can keep the property by posting a bond. Or the sheriff may be unable to find the property.

3.   Ejectment: Ejectment (plus mesne damages) is an adequate remedy if the plaintiff only wants a trespassing defendant off his or her land. Ejectment is an inadequate remedy if the plaintiff wants removal of an encroaching structure.

B.   Is a **PROPERTY RIGHT** involved?
Point out that most courts today protect both property and personal rights by injunction.

C.   Is an injunctive decree **FEASIBLE**?
1.   Must the court exercise too much supervision?
2.   Is a negative or a mandatory injunction appropriate?

D.   Should the hardships be **BALANCED**?
1.   Balancing may be required in two situations:
   a.   Encroachment: If the encroachment is intentional, there will be no balancing. Plaintiff will always win on this issue. If the encroachment is innocent (including negligent), the court will balance, but will lean strongly in favor of the plaintiff seeking removal of the encroachment.
   b.   Nuisance: Always balance the hardships in a private nuisance case.

E.   **DEFENSES?**
1.   Laches: The effect of the passing of time. Has the plaintiff's inaction encouraged or allowed the defendant to act to his detriment?
2.   Unclean hands: Plaintiff must come into equity with "clean hands." Must be related to the transaction in the suit.
3.   Freedom of speech: First Amendment rule against prior restraint. See exceptions for national security, and for trade libel, particularly in conjunction with another business tort.
4.   Criminal act: Equity maxim, "Equity will not enjoin a crime." See exceptions for nuisance and public nuisance, and partial exception for crime that also constitutes a tort.

V.   **CHECKLIST FOR GRANTING SPECIFIC PERFORMANCE RELIEF IN CONTRACT**

IDFMD – "I'm Doing Fine Mom & Dad"

Look for a breach of a legal obligation. Is there a valid contract? Has the defendant breached the contract or is he or she about to?

A. Are the legal remedies **INADEQUATE**?
1. Damages and money restitution: Damages may be too speculative or too small to compensate fully for the injury. There may be a multiplicity of suits. There may be an irreparable injury. Plaintiff may seek to recover a unique chattel. A contract for purchase or sale of land may be involved.
2. Replevin: Defendant can post a bond. The sheriff may be unable to find the property.
3. Ejectment: (Typically not involved in an action on a contract.)

B. Are the terms of the contract sufficiently **DEFINITE AND CERTAIN?**
1. Remember that the terms of a contract may be sufficiently certain to constitute a valid contract, but an equity court may still be unwilling to grant specific performance of that contract if it cannot tell exactly what the parties intended.

C. Is a specific performance decree **FEASIBLE**?
1. Is there jurisdiction over the parties or the property? Watch for land outside the state.
2. Is there too much supervision by the court?
3. Is a negative injunction appropriate? Watch for personal service contracts where the employee tries to breach and to work for a competitor.

D. Is there **MUTUALITY** of obligation?
1. Remember that the old test was whether the remedy of specific performance was mutually available (i.e., to both parties) at the time of contracting. The new test is the security of performance test. Under the new test, ask whether the performance of the plaintiff's obligations can be secured to the satisfaction of the court.

E. **DEFENSES**?
1. Laches: The effect of the passing of time. Has the plaintiff's inaction encouraged or allowed the defendant to act to her detriment?
2. Unclean hands: Plaintiff must come into equity with "clean hands." Must be related to the transaction in the suit.

3. Freedom of Speech: First Amendment rule against prior restraint.

4. Hardship: In a suit to specifically enforce a contract, a court of equity may refuse to enforce a contract in which there is inadequate consideration (low price) and there are onerous terms.

REMEDIES QUESTION 1

Henry was an agent for Insco. Over a period of several months, he embezzled a total of $50,000. The shortage in his accounts was not discovered until after Henry died, one month after his final embezzlement.

Henry gave $5,000 of the embezzled money to the Red Cross.

Henry deposited $25,000 of the embezzled money in his savings account at Bank. At the time of the deposit, the account contained $20,000 of Henry's own money. He later withdrew $30,000 from the account, all of which he lost in a week of betting at a race track. Using his own money from his then current earnings, Henry bought a lottery ticket on which he won $15,000, all of which he deposited in the savings account. That was the last transaction involving the account before Henry died.

Henry spent $10,000 of the embezzled money for the premium on a life insurance policy on which his wife, Susan, is the beneficiary. The policy had a face value of $100,000, and the insurance company paid that amount to Susan upon Henry's death. Susan was not aware of the policy nor the embezzlement until after Henry's death. Susan has invested the $100,000 in a certificate of deposit.

Insco is able to determine the foregoing but is unable to determine what Henry did with the remaining $10,000 of the embezzled money. The inventory in Henry's probate estate lists the savings account at Bank and personal property worth $10,000. Insco cannot establish that any of the embezzled funds were used to acquire any of the personal property in the estate.

What are Insco's rights and remedies against:

1.   The Red Cross? Discuss.

2.   The funds in Henry's savings account with Bank? Discuss.

3.   Susan's certificate of deposit? Discuss.

4.   The personal property in Henry's estate? Discuss.

What are Insco's <u>rights and remedies</u> against:

1. **The Red Cross**
    A. Damages - Insco can recover for conversion

    B. Restitution
        1. Replevin
        2. Quasi-Contract - Insco must waive the tort and sue
            a. Red Cross received the money and was unjustly enriched

    C. Constructive Trust
        1. Equitable restitutionary remedy
        2. Insco must prove a res, here the $5,000
        3. Red Cross not a BFP

    D. Equitable Lien - no acquisition of other property

Insco can recover its $5,000.

2. **The Funds in Henry's savings account with Bank**
    A. Equitable lien - commingling and tracing
        1. $25,000 is traceable to the savings account.
        2. The Lowest Intermediate Balance Rule
            a. Recovery can never be greater than the least amount in the account.
            b. The lowest intermediate balance was $15,000 which Insco can recover.
        3. An alternative theory is that Henry deposited money to replenish Insco's misappropriated money.

3. **Susan Certificate of Deposit**
    A. Constructive Trust
        1. Insco must trace the purchase of the life insurance policy and show the policy's proceeds was used to purchase the CD.
        2. Constructive trust will apply to the increase

    B. Susan was not a BFP.

4. **The personal property in Henry's estate**
    A. Constructive trust and equitable lien unavailable.
    B. Compensatory Damages
            a. Insco should be restored to its original position before the tort.

REMEDIES QUESTION 2

Al planned to build a large shopping center in a suburban area. Betty agreed in writing to sell Al her 100 acre farm located in the center of the proposed development. Al deposited with Betty, a portion of the purchase price, the balance to be paid upon delivery of the deed by Betty. At the time their written contract was entered into, Al told Betty only that he was buying her land and 200 acres from other local farmers for a "big project."

Relying upon Betty's agreement, Al purchased the surrounding 200 acres from other farmers. He paid them the same price he had contracted to pay Betty, $1,000 an acre. This price was $200 an acre over market value.

Claude, hoping to build his own shopping center on other nearby land, paid Betty $100,000 to refuse to convey her property to Al. Betty falsely notified Al that she could not complete the sale because she had discovered a defect in her title. Al reluctantly accepted return of his deposit. Without Betty's land, Al could not develop the shopping center as planned, and he has offered his 200 acres for sale.

Claude purchased the land for his shopping center from local farmers for $500 an acre, $300 below the former market value, because land values in the entire area plummeted once Al offered his 200 acres for sale. Claude's shopping center is nearing completion.

Al has recently learned of Claude's arrangements with Betty.

What legal and equitable remedies does Al have:

1. Against Betty? Discuss.

2. Against Claude? Discuss.

REMEDIES QUESTION 2

A.   Al v. Betty

Al has two theories: Breach of contract and Tort of Misrepresentation.

A.   Breach of Contract
1.   Valid and enforceable land sale contract
2.   Betty breached when she fraudulently told Al she could not complete the sale
3.   There was no mutual recission or release
4.   Remedies
   a.   Compensatory damages -- benefit of bargain measured by difference between market and contract price. Here, yields Al nothing.
   b.   Consequential damages -- must be foreseeable at formation. Al told Betty the purchase was for a "big project."
   c.   Restitution -- unjust enrichment. Betty received $100,000 from Claude
   d.   Punitive damages not available
   e.   Specific Perfomance
      1)   Inadequate remedy at law -- land and damages inadequate
      2)   Definite and certain terms -- contract
      3)   Feasibility -- court force Betty to convey to Al, but Claude's shopping center nearly completed
      4)   Mutuality -- Al can perform
      5)   Defenses -- none

B.   Misrepresentation
1.   Betty intentionally misrepresented a material fact upon which Al reasonably relied to his detriment
2.   Remedies
   a.   Damages - forseeable actual loss; $200/acre
   b.   Punitive damages -- Betty's act willful and malicious
   c.   Restitution -- money received from Claude or constructive trust over $100,000
   d.   Injunction -- feasible?

176

2. **Al v. Claude**

    A.   Tortious interference with contract
        1.   Claude knew of the Al/Betty contract and intentionally interfered by inducing Betty to breach
        2.   Remedies
            a.   Damages -- actual loss
            b.   Punitive damages -- Claude acted willfully and maliciously
            c.   Restitution -- constructive trust
            d.   Injunction
                1)   Inadequate remedy at law -- land
                2)   Property interest -- land
                3)   Feasibility -- nearly completed
                4)   Balancing -- not permanent injunction
                5)   Defenses -- laches?

REMEDIES QUESTION 3

Barry is the publisher of *Auto Designer's Digest,* a magazine that appeals to classic car enthusiasts. For years, Barry has been trying to win a first place award in the annual Columbia Concours d'Elegance ("Concours"), one of the most prestigious auto shows in the country. He was sure that winning such an award would vastly increase the circulation of his magazine and attract lucrative advertising revenues. This year's Concours was scheduled to begin on June 1, with applications for entry to be submitted by May 1.

Sally owned a 1932 Phaeton, one of only two surviving cars of that make and model. The car was in such pristine condition that it stood a very good chance of winning the first place prize.

On April 1, Barry and Sally entered into a valid written contract by which Barry agreed to buy, and Sally agreed to sell, the Phaeton for $200,000 for delivery on May 25. In anticipation of acquiring the Phaeton, Barry completed the application and paid the nonrefundable $5,000 entry fee for the Concours.

On May 10, Sally told Barry that she had just accepted $300,000 in cash for the Phaeton from a wealthy Italian car collector, stating "That's what it's really worth," and added that she would deliver the car to a shipping company for transport to Italy within a week.

1. Can Barry sue Sally before May 25? Discuss.

2. What provisional remedies might Barry seek to prevent Sally from delivering the Phaeton to the shipping company pending resolution of his dispute with Sally, and would the court be likely to grant them? Discuss.

3. Can Barry obtain the Phaeton by specific performance or replevin? Discuss.

4. If Barry decides instead to seek damages for breach of contract, can he recover damages for: (a) the nondelivery of the Phaeton; (b) the loss of the expected increase in circulation and advertising revenues; and (c) the loss of the $5,000 nonrefundable entry fee? Discuss.

[July 2008 #4]

TORTS

Example of a structure for an answer:

[**State the issue**] "Plaintiff is suing Defendant for a battery."

[**State the prima facie case**] "To establish a prima facie case for battery, Plaintiff must prove …"

[**Apply law to facts**] "Here, Plaintiff will show …" (make sure your discussion analyzes each element of the cause of action)

[**State your conclusion**]

[**Raise applicable defenses**] "Defendant may assert the privilege of self-defense. Defendant must show …"

[**If applicable, raise General Considerations**] "Defendants may be vicariously liable under respondeat superior. To establish this, Plaintiff must show …"

I. INTENTIONAL TORTS

A. Prima Facie Cases

1. BATTERY: a <u>harmful or offensive contact</u> with <u>plaintiff's person</u>
2. ASSAULT: a <u>reasonable apprehension</u> by plaintiff of an <u>immediate</u> harmful or offensive contact with his/her person
3. FALSE IMPRISONMENT: an act <u>confining</u> the plaintiff to a <u>bounded</u> area
4. INTENTIONAL INFLICTION OF EMOTIONAL DISTRESS: <u>outrageous</u> conduct causing <u>severe emotional distress</u>
5. TRESPASS TO CHATTELS/CONVERSION: <u>some</u> (tc)/<u>great</u> (c) <u>damage</u> to plaintiff's personal property interest
6. TRESPASS TO LAND: a <u>physical invasion</u> of plaintiff's <u>land</u>
7. NUISANCE: Unreasonable interference with use and enjoyment of property. Public or private nuisance.

B. Defenses

1. CONSENT:
   a. Was the privilege available on these facts?
      (1) Did plaintiff have capacity?
      (2) Was consent expressly given?
      (3) Implied by custom and usage <u>or</u> plaintiff's conduct?
   b. If yes, did defendant stay within scope?
2. DEFENSE PRIVILEGES (self-defense, defense of others, defense of property):
   a. Was privilege available on these facts?

             (1)   self-defense: <u>reasonable belief</u> that tort is being or about to be committed on defendant

             (2)   defense of others: tort is <u>in fact</u> being committed or about to be committed on third person

             (3)   defense of property: <u>reasonable belief</u> that tort is being or about to be committed on property

        b.   If yes, did defendant use <u>reasonable force</u>?

    3.   NECESSITY (Applicable <u>only</u> to property torts): If private necessity, defendant pays for actual damages.

F. Miscellaneous intentional torts

    1.   Wrongful Institution of legal proceedings and Abuse of process

    2.   Business torts

        a.   Interference with contractual relationships

        b.   Interference with prospective advantage

            (1)   Problem - damages are speculative

        c.   Trade libel

            (1)   Special damages required

            (2)   Modernly, courts will grant injunction

II. DEFAMATION/PRIVACY

A. Defamation

    1.   Common Law Prima Facie Case

        a.   Defamatory statement

        b.   Of and concerning Plaintiff

        c.   Publication

        d.   Damages - injury to reputation -- presumed if libel or slander within four slander per se categories; otherwise, special damages required.

    2.   Constitutional Issues

        a.   Plaintiff must prove falsity

        b.   Fault

            1)   Status of Plaintiff

            2)   Status of Subject Matter

            3)   Standards of Fault

                a)   New York Times Malice

                b)   Gertz v. Welch Negligence

    3.   Defenses

        a.   truth (if the matter is not one of public concern)

        b.   absolute or qualified privilege

B. **Invasion of Privacy**
1. Appropriation by defendant of plaintiff's name or picture for defendant's commercial advantage
2. Intrusion into plaintiff's privacy or seclusion
3. Publication of facts placing plaintiff in a false light
4. Publication of private facts about plaintiff

III. NEGLIGENCE

A. **Prima Facie Case**
1. Duty of Care
   a. foreseeable plaintiff
   b. standard of care
2. Breach
   a. fact discussion as to whether defendant met adopted standard of care
   b. violation of statute
   c. res ipsa loquitur
3. Causation
   a. actual (causation in fact)
   b. proximate (based on lack of foreseeability)
      (1) direct cause case
      (2) indirect cause case
4. Damages

B. **Defenses**
1. contributory negligence
2. assumption of the risk
3. comparative negligence

IV. STRICT LIABILITY

A. **Strict Liability for dangerous and trespassing animals**

B. **Strict Liability for Abnormally Dangerous Activities**
1. Activity involves serious risk of harm
2. activity cannot be performed without risk of serious harm regardless of due care, and
3. activity is not common in particular community.

V. PRODUCTS LIABILITY

A. **Theories**
1. Strict products liability
2. Negligence
3. Implied warranties
4. Express warranty/misrepresentation

B. **Strict products liability**
1. Defective Products: three types
   a. product is defectively manufactured
   b. product is defectively designed
      (1) product was not safe for its intended use, or
      (2) product could have been made safe without serious impact on its price or utility
   c. failure to adequately warn
2. Two formulas: Consumer expectation and Balancing
3. Causation
   a. actual
   b. proximate
4. Damages
   a. same as negligence - many courts will deny recovery if only economic loss is involved

C. **Negligence (same as any negligence action)**
1. Duty
   a. standard of care
   b. foreseeable plaintiff
2. Breach (note: here, unlike strict products liability, defendant's fault must be established)
3. Causation
   a. actual
   b. proximate
4. Damages

D. **Implied Warranty**
1. Implied warranty of merchantability or fitness for ordinary purpose
2. Implied warranty of fitness for a particular purpose

E. **Express Warranty/Misrepresentation**

VI. **GENERAL CONSIDERATIONS**

A. **Are there two or more defendants?** If so, think about:
1. vicarious liability (liability for someone else's tortious conduct)
   a. respondeat superior
      1) employer/employee relationship
      2) tort committed within the scope of employment
   b. Independent contractor - generally, principal not liable except:
      1) inherently dangerous activity or
      2) nondelegable duty

      c.   Also, Partner or Joint Venturer, Driver of
             of automobile, bailees, children and
             patron of tavern

   2.   joint and several liability
       a.   releases
       b.   contribution
       c.   indemnification

B.   **Did someone die?** If so, think about survival acts/wrongful death acts

C.   **Is Defendant an immediate family member, government or charity?** If so, think about tort immunities

TORTS – PROBLEM SOLVING APPROACH

I. **INTENTIONAL TORTS**
    A. Assault
    B. Battery
    C. False Imprisonment
    D. Intentional Infliction of Emotional Distress
    E. Trespass to chattels/Conversion
    F. Trespass to land/Nuisance
    G. Defenses – Consent, Defensive force, Necessity

II. **DEFAMATION/INVASION OF PRIVACY**
    A. Defamation
        1. Defamatory Statement
        2. Of and concerning plaintiff
        3. Publication
        4. Damages
        5. Defenses
        6. Constitutional issues
            a. Falsity
            b. Fault
    B. Invasion of Privacy
        1. Misappropriation
        2. Intrusion
        3. False Light
        4. Publication of Private Facts

III. **NEGLIGENCE**
    A. Duty – foreseeable Plaintiff, standard of care
    B. Breach of duty
    C. Factual cause
    D. Proximate cause
    E. Damages
    F. Defenses – contributory neg., comparative neg., assumption of risk

IV. **STRICT LIABILITY**
    A. Animals
    B. Inherently dangerous activities

V. **PRODUCTS LIABILITY**
    A. Strict Products Liability – defective product
    B. Negligence – standard of care
    C. Express Warranties/Implied Warranties
    D. Defenses

VI. **GENERAL CONSIDERATIONS**
    A. Vicarious Liability
    B. Joint liability
    C. Wrongful death
    D. Immunities

TORTS QUESTION 1

Transco, a common carrier, hauls toxic chemicals by train through an area where Paul operates a commercial greenhouse. Concerned about the risks if there were spillage from one of the boxcars containing the chemicals, Transco hired Diana, a consultant, to assess the risk. Diana concluded there was little or no risk to nearby property owners if any such spillage occurred, and she so advised Transco.

Thereafter, one of Transco's trains containing a known toxic chemical derailed because the train engineer suffered a heart attack while operating the engine. The engineer was obese and, five years earlier, had taken a leave of absence because of a mild heart attack he had suffered. The derailment caused chemical spillage near Paul's property, and Paul closed his greenhouse business out of fear that the spillage would damage his greenhouse plants and cause him to get cancer. In fact, no lasting damage resulted from the spill.

Six months after the accident, Paul moved back into his previously vacated premises and began operating the greenhouse again. Paul's fear for his health from possible exposure to the chemical continued, however, and subsequently he suffered severe anxiety and depression because of this fear.

On what theory or theories, if any, can Paul recover damages from, and what defenses may reasonably be raised by:

1. Transco?   Discuss.

2. Diana?   Discuss.

Torts Question 1

1. <u>Paul v. Transco</u>

    A. <u>Strict Liability - Abnormally Dangerous Activity</u>
        1. Abnormally dangerous activity if involves a substantial risk of harm no matter how much care is exercised.
        2. 3 requirements:
            a. Risk of serious harm - toxic chemicals; but Diana's conclusion
            b. Activity cannot be performed without risk of serious harm no matter how much care is taken - toxic chemicals; Diana's conclusion
            c. Activity is not commonly engaged in by community - Paul's greenhouse; more facts
        3. Causation - same as negligence below
        4. Damages - same as negligence below
        5. Defense - Assumption of risk
    B. <u>Negligence</u>
        1. Vicarious liability
            a. Acts of engineer imputed to Transco
            b. Diana likely independent contractor
        2. Duty
            a. Standard of care - reasonable carrier; not as common carrier
            b. Foreseeable P? Cardozo and Andrews views
        3. Breach of Duty
            a. Paul -> engineer known to be obese and to have suffered heart attack while operating train.
            b. Transco -> engineer's attack was mild and 5 years ago.
            c. Paul -> res ipsa loquitur
                1) trains normally do not derail without negligence
                2) Transco in exclusive control
                3) Paul not at fault
        4. Factual cause - But for Transco's negligence, Paul would not have closed his greenhouse and suffered health problems.
        5. Proximate cause
            a. Heart attack foreseeable?
            b. Business interruption foreseeable?
            c. Anxiety and depression foreseeable?
        6. Damages
            a. No lasting damage
            b. Business loss
            c. 6 months passage of time

        7. Defenses

   a. Contributory negligence
   b. Assumption of risk
   c. Comparative fault
C. <u>Trespass to Land</u> - but no entry on to Paul's land
D. <u>Nuisance</u>
  1. Unreasonable interference with use and enjoyment of property.
  2. Public or private nuisance
E. <u>Infliction of Emotional Distress</u>
  1. Intentional infliction - requires extreme and outrageous conduct
  2. Negligent infliction - Paul must be in zone of danger and suffer physical injuries
  3. Defense - Paul's unreasonableness

2. <u>Paul v. Diana</u>

 A. <u>Negligence</u>
  1. Duty
   a. Standard of care as like consultant
   b. Foreseeable plaintiff
  2. Breach of Duty - no breach on facts
  3. Factual and Proximate Cause - Diana argues she was neither.
  4. Damages
 B. <u>Indemnity and Contribution</u> - Diana would seek from Transco if she is found liable.

TORTS QUESTION 2

After paying for his gasoline at Delta Gas, Paul decided to buy two 75-cent candy bars. The Delta Gas store clerk, Clerk, was talking on the telephone, so Paul tossed $1.50 on the counter, pocketed the candy, and headed out. Clerk saw Paul pocket the candy, but had not seen Paul toss down the money. Clerk yelled, "Come back here, thief!" Paul said, "I paid. Look on the counter." Clerk replied, "I've got your license number, and I'm going to call the cops." Paul stopped. He did not want trouble with the police. Clerk told Paul to follow him into the back room to wait for Mark, the store manager, and Paul complied. Clerk closed, but did not lock, the only door to the windowless back room.

Clerk paged Mark, who arrived approximately 25 minutes later and found Paul unconscious in the back room as a result of carbon monoxide poisoning. Mark had been running the engine of his personal truck in the garage adjacent to the back room. When he left to run an errand, he closed the garage, forgot to shut off the engine, and highly toxic carbon monoxide from the exhaust of the running truck had leaked into the seldom used back room. Mark attributed his forgetfulness to his medication, which is known to impair short-term memory.

Paul survived but continues to suffer headaches as a result of the carbon monoxide poisoning. He recalls that, while in the back room, he heard a running engine and felt ill before passing out.

A state statute provides: "No person driving or in charge of a motor vehicle shall permit it to stand unattended without first stopping the engine, locking the ignition, removing the key from the ignition, setting the brake thereon and, when standing upon any perceptible grade, turning the front wheels to the curb or side of the highway."

1. Can Paul maintain tort claims against (a) Clerk for false imprisonment and (b) Mark for negligence? Discuss.

2. Is Delta Gas liable for the acts of (a) Clerk and (b) Mark? Discuss.

[July 2006 #1]

1. a. <u>Paul v. Clerk</u> – for false imprisonment, Paul must prove that Clerk intentionally confined Paul to a bounded area and causation.

    1. Intent – follow him and wait in back room until Mark arrived
    2. Confinement to a bounded area – back room; up to 25 minutes
        a. There can be no reasonable means of escape – only door unlocked. No windows; no apparent way for Paul to get out
    3. Causation – Clerk threatened Paul he would call cops and had Paul wait in room. Paul stayed for 25 min. until Mark arrived

    4. Defenses
        a. Shopkeeper's Privilege
            1. reasonable belief that Paul stole – didn't see Paul pay, saw him pocket the candy, leaving, and called him a thief
            2. must confine reasonably – physical and time
                a) Put in room to wait for mgr.
                b) 25 min.
        b. Consent
            1) Paul complied but didn't want trouble with police.
            2) Paul didn't consent to be confined for 25 min.

    b. <u>Paul v. Mark</u> – for negligence, Paul must prove Mark owed him a duty, that Mark breached the standard of care, which factually and proximately caused his injury.

    1. Duty
        a. Paul was a patron on the premises in zone of danger; Mark argue he didn't know P was in room and room was infrequently used
        b. Standard of care – reasonable person; possibly as possessor of land to an invitee

    2. Breach
        a. reasonable person – would not leave engine on while running an errand; Mark argue he is forgetful because of medication
        b. If Mark held to possessor of land, did not make premises safe

  c. Statute – negligence per se?
    1) Paul in protected class? Paul argue
      statute to protect against carbon
      monoxide poisoning; Mark argue statute
      to protect pedestrians and others on
      road, not in a small room.
    2) Paul's injury the type to be prevented?
      Mark argue to prevent cars from running
      or rolling away while unattended. The injury
      to be prevented is hitting someone

3. Factual cause – but for Mark leaving the truck running,
  Paul would not have been injured. In the alternative,
  Mark's negligence was a substantial factor in causing
  Paul's injury

4. Proximate cause – limit to holding Mark liable?
  a. intervening act of Clerk
    1) intentional acts usually not foreseeable
    2) however, foreseeable that employee would
      detain a suspected shoplifter
  b. consequences foreseeable?
    1) unforeseeable a person would suffer injury
      in an seldom used room
    2) foreseeable Paul would suffer headaches from
      carbon monoxide poisoning, especially when he
      was in a windowless room adjacent to the
      garage

5. Damages – Paul was unconscious when found, suffers
  headaches from carbon monoxide poisoning

6. Defenses
  a. Contributory Negligence - Mark would argue Paul did
    not conform to a standard of care for his own
    safety by staying in the small room. However, there
    is no evidence Paul could smell the carbon
    monoxide. Further, he didn't know he could escape.
  b. Assumption of risk would require Paul knew of the
    risk, which he did not and he did not voluntarily
    assume it

2. Delta Gas – vicarious liability

 a. Respondeat Superior holds the employer liable for acts
  of its employees done in the scope of employment.

 b. Clerk

    1)   Clerk was working for Delta at the time he put Paul in the back room.

        2)   Presumably Paul was acting within the scope because as a clerk, he should detain those who steal. Further, he had Paul wait for the manager.

        3)   However, Clerk was on the phone and Delta would claim this was not within the scope

c.   Mark
    1)   Mark had left to run an errand. If the errand was personal, Delta would argue he was not in the scope
    2)   However, if the errand was a minor deviation, Delta would be vicariously liable.
    3)   Mark had left the engine of his personal truck running, which might indicate he was not working
    4)   However, Clerk had Paul wait for Mark, so likely Mark was at work. As the manager, he would handle thefts.

TORTS QUESTION 3

Dan, a student in a state university law school, posted on the law school bulletin board the following typed notice:

> Professor James gave an "A" grade last semester to a woman in return for sexual favors. The facts are widely known and talked about.

The statement about sexual favors was true of a different teacher also named James (Teacher James) who had been fired from his job at a nearby college as a result. Dan knew that Teacher James had been fired but did not know why. Dan honestly believed that Professor James was the one who had given the "A" grade in return for the sexual favors. On the day after Dan posted the typed notice, Ned, editor of Daily Record, the local newspaper, published in the Daily Record a clear picture of the posted notice, commenting only that the notice was posted on the local school bulletin board.

Professor James had given only one "A" grade the previous semester. This was to a woman named Pam, who had never been intimate with Professor James. Her grade had appeared alongside her secret examination number on Professor James's list of grades, which had been posted on the bulletin board. Pam was never identified publicly by Professor James or the school as the recipient of the "A" grade.

1. What legal claims and defenses should be asserted in a suit by Professor James against Dan, Ned, and Daily Record, and how should the claims and defenses be resolved? Discuss.

2. What legal claims and defense should be asserted in a suit by Pam against Dan, Ned, and Daily Record, and how should the claims and defenses be resolved? Discuss.

Torts Question 3

Prof. James v. Dan

    1.   <u>Defamation</u>

        a.   Defamatory?
           1)   lower esteem and reputation - sex for grades
           2)   Statement of "fact" – "The facts are widely known and talked about."

        b.   Of and concerning plaintiff?
           1)   The statement stated "Prof. James."

        c.   Publication to a third person?
           1)   Communicated - placed on bulletin board

        d.   Damage
           1)   At common law, this publication would be libel and actual damage presumed.
           2)   Modernly, it would be libel per se, i.e. on its face, and damage presumed.

        e.   Constitutional issues
           1)   Falsity ... here the statement was false.
           2)   Fault
               a)   Prof. James a public official or figure?
                  (1)   Public official - Professor at a state university?
                  (2)   Public figure - no facts to show that he injected himself voluntarily into a controversy nor that he achieved pervasive fame and notoriety.
              b)   Matter of public concern?
                  (1)   The content of the speech goes to the integrity of grading, the form was written and posted and the context was the law school bulletin board
              c)   Here, a negligence standard applies and Dan had a duty to investigate.
              d)   Thus, Prof. James can recover if he can prove actual damage.
              e)   Constitutional malice? - Dan "honestly believed"

        f.   Privileges
           1)   Qualified privilege of common interest?

2. Invasion of Privacy - False Light

    a. The publication was a major misrepresentation that would be highly offensive to a reasonable person.

    b. However, the matter is in the public interest, thus Prof. James must prove Dan acted with constitutional malice.

3. Intentional Infliction of Emotional Distress

    a. Did Dan act with intent and extreme and outrageous conduct?

Prof. James v. Ned and Daily Record

1. The same discussion applies here.
2. As republishers, Ned and Daily Record can be held liable.

Pam v. Dan, Ned and Daily Record

1. Defamation

    a. While defamatory, the statement must be "of and concerning P." Here, Pam must prove colloquium, i.e. the statement was made about her.

    b. In corporate the prior lawsuit.

2. Incorporate other theories from above.

TORTS QUESTION 4

Peters, a suburban homeowner, decided to resurface with bricks the concrete area surrounding his pool. He purchased from Homeco, a local home improvement store, a concrete cutter manufactured by Conco, which had a blade manufactured by Bladeco. He then took the concrete cutter home and assembled it following the instructions provided by Conco.

The blade that Peters purchased was clearly labeled "Wet." Although no instructions or warnings came with the blade, Conco included several warnings throughout the instructions to the concrete cutter stating, "If using a wet blade, frequently water the blade and surface being cut to avoid risk of blade degradation." No other warnings relating to the blade were included with the concrete cutter.

Peters began cutting the concrete with the concrete cutter without using water. Less than five minutes into the job he noticed that the cutter was vibrating excessively. He turned the machine off by hitting the "kill switch" located near the blade at the bottom of the cutter, with his right foot. The cutter's handle did not have a "kill switch." After carefully examining the concrete cutter and blade, Peters became convinced that nothing was wrong and continued to operate it. Nevertheless, within seconds, the concrete cutter again began vibrating violently.

As Peters reached with his right foot to hit the "kill switch" again, the blade broke into pieces, forced off the cutter's safety guard, spiraled into Peters' right foot and caused permanent injuries.

On what theory or theories might Peters recover damages from and what defenses may reasonably be raised by:

1. Conco? Discuss.

2. Baldeco? Discuss.

3. Homeco? Discuss.

Torts Question 4

1. Conco
   1. Products Liability
      a. Strict product liability
         1) Proper parties
         2) Defective product?
            a) Manufacturing defect?
            b) Design defect
               (a) Consumer expectation test
               (b) Feasibility of alternative design
            c) Failure to warn
               (1) inadequate warning – "Wet" and blade degradation
               (2) specific risk warning needed
            d) Causation and damages
         3) Defenses
            a) Assumption of risk
            b) Misuse
            c) Comparative fault

      b. Negligence
         1) Manufacturer's standard of care
         2) Breach
         3) Causation
         4) Damages
         5) Defenses – Assumption of risk, contributory or comparative fault

      c. Implied Warranties
         1) Merchantability
         2) Fitness for a particular purpose

2. Bladeco – component manufacturer
   1. Strict products liability – see above
   2. Negligence – breach – reasonable to rely on Conco?
   3. Implied Warranties
   4. Indemnification or contribution

3. Homeco – retailer
   1. See above theories – duty to inspect?
   2. Indemnification or contribution

TORTS QUESTION 5

Manufacturer designed and manufactured a "Cold Drink Blender," which it sold through retail stores throughout the country. The Cold Drink Blender consists of three components: a base that houses the motor, a glass container for liquids with mixing blades inside on the bottom, and a removable cover for the container to prevent liquids from overflowing during mixing. A manufacturer's brochure that came with the Cold Drink Blender states that it is "perfect for making all of your favorite cold drinks, like mixed fruit drinks and milk shakes, and it even crushes ice to make frozen drinks like daiquiris and piña coladas," and cautioned, "Do not fill beyond 2 inches of the top."

Retailer sold one of the Cold Drink Blenders to Consumer. One day, Consumer was following a recipe for vegetable soup that called for thickening the soup by liquefying the vegetables. After deciding to use her Cold Drink Blender for this purpose, Consumer filled the glass container to the top with hot soup, placed it on the base, put the cover on top, and turned the blender on the highest speed. The high speed rotation of the mixing blades forced the contents to the top of the container, pushed off the cover, and splashed hot soup all over Consumer, who was severely burned by the hot soup.

Consumer filed a lawsuit against Manufacturer and Retailer, pleading claims for strict products liability and negligence. In her complaint, Consumer stated that the Cold Drink Blender was not equipped with a cover that locked onto the top of the container in such a way as to prevent it from coming off during operation and that the failure to equip the blender with this safety feature was a cause of her injuries.

Manufacturer moved to dismiss the complaint against it on the following grounds:
(1) Consumer's injury was caused by her own misuse of the Cold Drink Blender which, as implied by its name, was intended for mixing only cold substances.
(2) Consumer's injury was caused by her own lack of care, as she overfilled the Cold Drink Blender and operated it at high speed.
(3) The design of the Cold Drink Blender was not defective since it complied with design standards set forth in federal regulations promulgated by the federal Consumer Products Safety Commission, which do not require any locking mechanism.

Continued on next page

Retailer moved to dismiss the complaint against it on the following ground:
(4) Retailer played no part in the manufacture of the Cold Drink Blender and therefore should not be held responsible for a defect in its design.

How should the court rule on each ground of both motions to dismiss? Discuss.

[July 2007 #2]

WILLS & TRUSTS
Road Map For Wills Questions

1. Execution of Wills

   a. <u>Attested Wills</u> - Signature plus 2 witnesses present at the same time.
                       - Interested witness presumption

   b. <u>Holographic Wills</u> - Signature and material provisions in T's handwriting

   c. <u>Testamentary Capacity</u> - Undue influence, Insane delusion, fraud

   d. <u>Conflict of Laws</u>

2. Revocation of Wills

   a. <u>Revocation</u> - by subsequent will, physical act or operation of law

   b. <u>Dependent Relative Revocation</u> - cancels a revocation based on mistaken assumption of law or fact

3. Components of Wills

   a. <u>Integration</u> - papers present at execution with intent

   b. <u>Republication by Codicil</u> - Will speaks at date of codicil

   c. <u>Incorporation by Reference</u> - 1) writing in existence at execution, 2) will shows intent to incorporate, 3) writing sufficiently described in will

   d. <u>Acts of Independent Significance</u> - identify beneficiaries or property by lifetime acts with independent motive

4. Interpretation of Wills

   a. <u>Admission of Extrinsic Evidence</u> - distinguish patent and latent ambiguity
   b. <u>Lapse</u> (Death of Beneficiary Before T) - Anti-lapse statute applies to kindred of T or kindred of T's surviving, deceased or former spouse.
   c. <u>Ademption</u> - by extinction (specific gift not owned by T at death)
                - by satisfaction (substitute lifetime why?

gift to beneficiary, in writing)

5. Intestate Succession

a. <u>Share of surviving spouse</u> - community and separate property share

b. <u>Share of not passing to surviving spouse</u> - issue, parents, parents= issue, etc.

c. <u>Special Problems</u> - adoption, stepchildren, advancements (requires writing that lifetime gift is advance payment of intestate share.

d. <u>Simultaneous Death</u> - I/S: Must prove by C&C evidence heir survived D by 120 hours; Will: Must prove by C&C evidence beneficiary survived T.

6. Rights of Surviving Spouse and Children

a. <u>Pretermitted Spouse</u> - spouse omitted from premarital will receives intestate share (C/P plus up to 1/2 of S/P unless: 1) omission was intentional as shown in will, 2) spouse provided transfers outside will, or 3) spouse made valid agreement waiving right to share in decedent's estate.

b. <u>Pretermitted Children</u> - child omitted from prebirth will (child born after will executed) receives intestate share unless: 1) omission was intentional as shown in will, 2) T had other children and left estate to parent of omitted child, or 3) T provided for child by transfers outside will.

7. Bars to Succession

a. <u>Homicide</u> - A person who feloniously and intentionally kills decedent is not entitled to any benefit from D's estate by will, trust, intestacy, life insurance, joint tenancy or otherwise.

b. <u>Elder Abuse</u> - A person found liable by clear and convincing evidence of elder abuse will be treated as if s/he predeceased decedent. Includes physical abuse, neglect or fiduciary abuse.

c. <u>No Contest Clause</u> - Will be enforced unless beneficiary, with reasonable cause, brings contest on grounds of forgery, revocation, or invalid transfer to person who drafted instrument.

Road Map For Trusts Questions

1. Creation of a Valid Trust - 7 elements of a valid trust:

a. **Settlor/Trustor** - Creator who often provides assets to create trust

b. **Delivery** - Handing over property from settlor to trustee

c. **Trustee** - Person holding legal title to trust property and managing assets

d. **Intent** - Settlor must intend to create trust in the present

e. **Trust Property (Res)** - Must be presently existing property interest

f. **Beneficiaries** - Person(s) holding equitable title and receiving benefit of assets

g. **Valid Trust Purpose** - Purpose cannot violate law or public policy

2. Types of Trusts

a. **Discretionary Trusts** - Trustee has discretion to pay income or principal

b. **Mandatory Trust** - trustee lacks discretion; must pay per the terms of the trust

c. **Spendthrift Trusts** - Limits voluntary and involuntary alienation

d. **Honorary Trusts** - Not a valid trust as lack human beneficiaries, but trustee can carry out settlor's wishes to care for animal, maintain grave.

e. **Secret Trusts** - Fact of the trust is secret; promise enforceable by C/T.

f. **Semi-Secret Trusts** - Trustee named but beneficiaries are secret; unenforceable

g. **Revocable Trusts** - Settlor retains right to amend or revoke during lifetime

h. **Totten Trusts** - Bank account for benefit of third party

i. **Charitable Trusts** - Trust for charitable purposes that benefits large number of unidentifiable beneficiaries (ex. Medicine, education, science, research)

3. Modification and Termination of Trusts

a. **General Rule** - If the settlor and all beneficiaries consent, trust may be modified or terminated (only possible when settlor is alive)

b. **The Claflin Doctrine** - Trust cannot be modified or terminated, even if all beneficiaries agree, if to do so would be contrary to a material purpose of the settlor. Material purpose includes spendthrift, support, discretionary trusts.

c. **Changed Circumstances** - In Cal. court may modify or terminate trust (upon petition by trustee or beneficiary) if changed circumstances mean continuation in the same manner would defeat purpose of the trust.

4. Trust Administration and Trustees Duties

a. **Fiduciary Duty** - Trustee owes fiduciary duty to administer the trust solely in the interest of the beneficiaries. A breach can mean personal liability for trustee.

b. **Duty of Care** - Trustee must exercise degree of care, skill and caution of a reasonable person in managing her own property.

1) **Duties Relating to Care of Trust Property**
   (a) Duty to collect and protect trust property

   (b) Duty to earmark trust property

   (c) Duty not to commingle trust funds with the trustee's own

   (d) Duty not to delegate investment decisions

   (e) Duty to maintain marketability of trust property

   (f) Duty to keep trust property productive

   (g) Duty to diversify investment

206

(h) Duty not to speculate

(i) Duty to account to trust beneficiaries

2) The Prudent Investor Rule - Trustee has duty to invest and manage trust assets as a prudent investor would, in light of purposes, terms, distribution requirements and other circumstances of the trust.

c. **Duty of Loyalty**

1) Self-Dealing - Trustee cannot buy or sell trust assets for trustee or spouse; trustee cannot borrow trust funds.

(a) If trustee engages in self-dealing, courts apply the <u>no further inquiry rule</u>. Trustee=s good faith and reasonableness of transaction are irrelevant.

(b) Remedies for beneficiaries:

(1) <u>Ratify the Transaction</u> - Waive the breach if outcome is positive
(2) <u>Surcharge the Trustee</u> - Sue for any resulting loss
(3) <u>Trace and Recover the Property</u> - except if purchaser is a BFP

2) Conflict of Interest - Trustee breaches duty of loyalty by not acting in best interest of beneficiaries. E.g. Selling trust property to buyer just to increase value of trustee's own property. Remedies include <u>ratification and surcharge</u>.

WILLS & TRUSTS QUESTION 1

Tess, a widow and resident of State X, a state with the same probate code as California, died in 2010. She was survived by a son, Bill, and a daughter, Jan. After Tess's death, a document was found that appeared to be her will. It is printed will form, such as one would purchase at a stationery store. Several lines are written in what appears to be Tess's handwriting, including her signature and a date at the bottom of the document. The date indicates that the document was signed just after Bill was born and one year before Tess adopted Jan, who was ten years old at the time of the adoption. The documents provides (the handwritten portions are underlined):

> *I, Tess, being of sound mind, hereby revoke all previous will and codicils. I make the following testamentary disposition of my property: Everything to Bank in trust, to pay the income to those persons named on the accompanying list until they are 21 years of age, as needed for their support and education, each to receive an equal share of principal upon reaching that age.*
>
> *Dated this ninth day of May 1977.*
> *Tess*
> *Witnessed: 1. [left blank]*
> *2. [left blank]*

Paper-clipped to the will form are six newspaper clippings. Each is a story about a needy child.

In 1979, Tess had established an inter vivos trust of $100,000 for Jan. In 1986, Tess told Jan that a trust had been created for Jan in lieu of leaving Jan anything in Tess's will. Jan later reported Tess's statement to her husband, Harry, but to no one else.

Bill and Jan each want that part of their mother's estate to which each claims he or she is legally entitled. Harry thinks Jan is being greedy, and would testify, if necessary, to what Jan told him about Tess's statement of intention regarding the trust. Jan denies that Tess told her any such thing, and does not want Harry to testify to the contrary.

Tess's net assets at her death consists of $1,000,000 cash.

1. Is Tess's will valid? Discuss.
2. Is the testamentary trust valid, and if not, what result? Discuss.
3. If the testamentary trust is valid, to what share of the estate, if any, are each Bill and Jan entitled? Discuss.
4. In a judicial proceeding regarding the rights of Bill and Jan in Tess's estate: **a)** would Harry's testimony be admissible, **b)** assuming it is admissible, could he testify against Jan's wishes; and **c)** could Harry's testimony affect the outcome? Discuss.

1.   Is Tess's will valid?
  A.   Formalities
    1)   Formal attested will fails for want of witnesses
    2)   Holographic will valid because material provisions and signed by Tess

2.   Is testamentary trust valid, and if not, what result?
  A.   Trust validity
    1)   Requires settlor, trustee, beneficiary, corpus, intent and valid purpose
    2)   Issue = definite and ascertainable beneficiaries – newspaper clippings
      a)   Integration
      b)   Incorporation by reference
      c)   Independent legal significance
    3)   Probably valid
  B.   If not valid, then resulting trust for Tess's heirs

3.   To what share is Bill and Jan entitled?
  A.   Pretermitted or Omitted children
    1)   Bill – Not omitted child because he was born before document signed
    2)   Jan
      a)   Adopted child has same status as biological child and time of adoption controls
      b)   However, Jan provided outside the will through 1963 inter vivos trust
  B.   Neither Bill or Jan are entitled

4.   Harry's testimony
  A.   Admissible?
    1)   Logically relevant to prove Tess's intent
    2)   Double Hearsay
      a)   Tess -> Jan
        (1)   State of mind – here past belief
        (2)   FRE catch all exception?
      b)   Jan -> Harry
        (1)   Admission
        (2)   Possible state of mind
  B.   Can Harry testify against Jan's wishes?
    1)   Spousal testimonial privilege – not criminal proceeding
    2)   Confidential marital communications privilege – Jan can assert
  C.   Could Harry's testimony affect outcome?
    1)   Yes because of omitted child issue above

210

TRUST QUESTION 2

Tom is trustee of a trust created by Abe in 1998. The corpus consists of stocks and bonds worth $150,000, an apartment house appraised at $650,000 in a neighborhood, which is becoming increasingly industrial, and a vacant lot. Yearly net income from the stocks and bonds is $12,000, and from the apartment house is $36,000. Tom has held the lot for five years, not wanting to sell it at a sacrifice because of the uncertainty of zoning and the location of a proposed highway. The trust instrument directs Tom to pay the income from the trust to Abe for life and, at Abe's death, to divide the corpus between Abe's children, Ben and Cathy.

At the end of 2003, Tom sold the vacant lot for $50,000, the fair market value. He also sold some stocks for $35,000, realizing a $10,000 gain. Tom used this money along with $25,000 of accumulated rental income to build an addition to the apartment house.

In another 2003 transaction Tom sold for $25,000 stocks that had been purchased for $25,000, and lent the proceeds to PQ Corp. at 1% below the prevailing interest rate. The loan is secured by a first mortgage on unimproved realty worth $30,000. For several years, Tom has performed substantial services for PQ Corp. as a consulting engineer. He owns 100 shares of its common stock. There are 1,000,000 PQ shares outstanding.

1. Has Tom breached his duties as trustee and, if so, what are his liabilities to the beneficiaries? Discuss.

2. Has Abe received all the income to which he is entitled? Discuss.

[For sample outline and answer see California Essay Exam Book, Wills & Trusts]

1.	Breach of Duties and Liabilities to the beneficiaries

    a.	Trustee duties
        1)	Duty of loyalty - self-dealing
        2)	Duty of care
            a)	Duty to preserve property
            b)	Prudent investor rule

    b.	Vacant lot
        1)	Duty to produce income - duty to sell
            a)	Prudent investor rule - held on to property for five years without income

    c.	Apartment building
        1)	Duty to sell - "changing neighborhood"
            a)	Prudent investor rule
        2)	Violation of express trust instructions - use of accumulated rental income to pay for apartment addition
        3)	Duty to diversify - concentrating funds into single asset

    d.	Sale of Stock and Loan to PQ Corp.
        1)	Stock - Prudent investor rule
        2)	Loan
            a)	Prudent investor rule - insufficient security
            b)	Duty of loyalty
                (1)	Conflict of interest?
                (2)	Self-dealing

2.	Abe's income

    a.	Express trust provision
        1)	Tom applied rental income, which was Abe's
        2)	Tom denied income on vacant lot
        3)	Abe denied income on loan because below market

WILLS & TRUSTS QUESTION 3

In 2001 Tom, a resident of California, executed a valid typewritten and witnessed will. At that time, Tom was married to Wynn. Tom also had two nephews, Norm, and Matt, who were the children of his deceased sister, Sue.

Tom's will made the following dispositions:
Article 1: I leave $10,000 to my friend Frank.
Article 2: I leave my shares in Beta Corp stock to my friend Frank.
Article 3: I leave $80,000 to my sister Sue's issue.
Article 4: I leave the residue of my estate to my wife.

The $10,000 figure in Article 1 was crossed out and $12,000 was handwritten in Tom's hand above the $10,000 figure. Next to the $12,000 Tom had handwritten, "Okay. 2/15/02."

In 2003 Tom and Wynn had a child, Cole.

In 2004, Matt died in a car accident. Matt was survived by his children, Lynn and Kim.

Tom died in 2005. Tom was survived by Wynn, Cole, Norm, Frank, and his grandnieces, Lynn and Kim. At the time of his death, Tom owned, as separate property, $500,000 in cash. He also had 100 shares of Beta Corp stock, titled in Tom's name, which he had purchased with his earnings while married to Wynn. The Beta stock was valued at $1.00 per share at the time of Tom's death.

What rights, if any, do Wynn, Cole, Norm, Frank, and his grandnieces Lynn and Kim have in Tom's estate? Discuss.

Answer according to California law.

[February 2007 #4]

213

NOTE: The following answer is a reproduction of an applicant's actual typed answer with no corrections. It is reprinted here for the sole purpose of giving students an example of an actual answer. This answer earned a "65". (Figure out why!)

This question deals with the distribution of Tom's estate. At death Tom owned $500k worth of separate property and 100 shares of Beta Stock and so the question is how will this property be distributed.

Because Tom died in California, California community property laws apply and he has the right to devise all of this separate property and half of his community property in this will.

Article 1: 10k to my friend, Frank

The gift of 10K to Frank is a general gift because the money is not unique property nor does the will say that it must come from a specific account. The question is whether Frank will be able to receive this money because on the face of the will, the amount was crossed out.

Revocation by physical act: Wynn will argue that Tom revoked the general gift to Frank in his will by the physical act of crossing out the figure of 10k.

Valid Codicil: A valid codicil must meet the same requirements as a valid will. In this case Tom made the changes to his valid typewritten will by hand and thus to be valid the codicil must meet the requirements of a valid holographic will. Here the first requirement that the material information is not met because while Tom wrote in the amount of 12k on the will, the Frank's name, material information concerning who gets the property, is typed from the original valid will.

Dependent Relative Revocation: Frank would then argue he should receive the gift anyway because had Tom known that he was not giving Frank a valid gift of 12k, he would not have crossed out the 10k. He would argue that Tom would want him to have the gift of 10k rather than nothing. Frank would argue that this is evident in the fact that he increased the value of the gift plus the fact that Tom liked him so much he gave in the addition stock as a gift.

If the court believes this then Frank will get the 10k instead of nothing. If the court does not believe this then the 10k will go into the residuary and ultimately go to Wynn.

214

Article 2: Beta Stock

In his will Tom then gave Frank his Beta stock. This is a specific gift in that it is unique because it was "my share," or Tom's shares of stock.

While it was in Tom's name alone, the stock itself was paid for with community property money. All money made during marriage is considered community property because it is made using each spouse's time, labor and skill which is a community property asset.

Gift: To argue that this was a gift to the community, the court would have to find that there was some donative intent by Wynn that Tom hold this property on his own. But there are no facts in the question indicating this intent by Wynn. Thus this argument would fail.

He has indicated that he wants to give it to Frank, then at most Wynn can invalidate 50 shares of the stock and return it as her community property share. Wynn also has the option to offset the amount of the value of the gift of the stock, the $50.00 and just take it from Tom's other assets.

Article 3: 80k to my sister Sue's issue

This is a general gift because the gift of money is not unique. The issue is whether this labeling of the gift to Sue's issues is valid.

Facts of Independent Significance: In this case although from the face of the will it is unclear who Sue's issues are this is fact of independent significance is that the identities of Sue's issues is a fact that exist regardless if the will existed or not.

Sue did in fact have 2 children, Norm and Matt. Thus technically, the will should be able to give the 80k for them to share.

Lapse and Anti-lapse: The problem here is that Matt died in 2004 after Tom had created his will. Thus under the tradition rules, Matt's gift of 40k would fail because he is not longer alive. But under the newer anti-lapse doctrine, the gift would not fail and would in fact go to any of Matt's issue. Here Matt has left two children, Lynn and Kim. Thus they would be able to share in Matt's gift.

Thus for the distribution of the 80k, Norm would get 40k and Lynn and Kim would each get 20k.

Article 4: Residue to my wife

Tom's wife is Wynn thus she stands to inherit whatever is left of Tom's separate property and half of his community property.

Thus if the court finds that Frank is to get the 10k and the gift of 80k to Sue's kids are valid then Wynn could stand to get 410k of Tom's separate property. In addition, she could possibly receive either $50 or 50 shares of the Beta stock.

Pretermitted heirs: In this case Tom has a pretermitted heir in that Tom and Wynn had a child, Chloe, in 2003 after Tom had created his will in 2001. The argument is that had Tom updated his will, he would have no likely provided for Cole. Thus Cole could stand to inherit a share in the same amount had Tom died in intestacy. Based on the facts, given Tom only has Wynn and Cole. Thus Cole is entitled to inherit at least 1/3 of Tom's assets and Wynn would receive at least 1/3 as well. Thus each person's gift would be decreased accordingly to provide Cole his 1/3 share equal to $170k.

There is also the argument that while Tom did not provide for Cole in his will, he did provide for him by giving enough money to Wynn to take care of Cole in the amount stated above and especially since Cole was only 2 when Tom died and this is just a baby. Thus if the courts agree with this argument then none of the gifts would have to be touched.

Evidence

Professor Victor Gold

EVIDENCE
By Victor Gold, victor.gold@lls.edu

I. Introduction.

A. What Law Controls on the Bar Exam? Federal Rules of Evidence (FRE) apply on the multistate bar exam (MBE). Essays can test on the FRE and/or California law. If the essay question tells you what law applies, *just follow the directions*. This means that, if the question tells you to apply California law, then apply California law. Similarly, if the question tells you to apply the FRE, then apply the FRE. If the essay question does not tell you what law applies, *apply the FRE.* Federal and California law are consistent on most issues. We will discuss the distinctions on day 3.

B. Tips on how to answer MBE questions.

1. "Inadmissible because it is not the best evidence."

2. "Inadmissible because of the Dead Man's Statute."

3. "Inadmissible because the evidence is self serving and prejudicial."

4. "The statement is part of the res gestae."

5. T.V. Objections. "The witness is not on trial!" "The evidence calls for an inference upon an inference!"

C. Tips on Essay questions. Coverage of issues must be broad but shallow.

FEDERAL RULES OF EVIDENCE

I.   Relevance. Irrelevant evidence is inadmissible. Relevant evidence *might* be admissible.

    A. Relevance defined. Evidence is relevant if it has *any tendency* to make the existence of any fact that is of consequence to the determination of the action *more or less probable* than it would be without the evidence.

        1. "Of consequence." Action for breach of contract. Defendant testifies that, when he said "I accept your offer" he secretly was joking and had no subjective intent to enter into a contract. Relevant?

        2. "More or less probable." Murder prosecution. Witness testifies he saw Defendant holding a gun shortly before the fatal shooting. Relevant?

        3. Distinguish relevance from probative value.

    B. Discretion to exclude relevant evidence. Even if evidence is relevant, court has discretion to exclude if probative value is substantially outweighed by *unfair prejudice, confusion, or waste of time*. Look for emotionally disturbing evidence or evidence admissible for one purpose but inadmissible for another purpose.

C. Exclusion of relevant evidence for policy reasons. Remember, even if evidence is relevant, it might not be admissible.

    1. *Liability Insurance.* Evidence of liability insurance is inadmissible to prove culpable conduct like negligence or defendant's ability to pay a judgment.

        a. Action for personal injuries suffered in automobile collision. To prove negligence and ability to pay judgment, plaintiff offers defendant's liability insurance policy, which shows defendant has $500,000 of coverage. Admissible?

        b. *Evidence of insurance is admissible to prove anything else.* Same case. Defense witness testifies plaintiff was speeding. Plaintiff offers evidence that witness is president of defendant's insurance company. Admissible?

        c. Same case. Plaintiff claims defendant's employer is vicariously liable for defendant's negligent driving. Employer claims driving was not within scope of defendant's employment. In rebuttal, plaintiff offers evidence that employer paid for defendant's auto liability insurance. Admissible?

    2. *Subsequent remedial measures or repairs.* Evidence of safety measures or repairs after an accident is inadmissible to prove culpable conduct and, in a products liability action, is inadmissible to prove defective product design.

        a. Personal injury action. Plaintiff fell allegedly due to slippery stairs in defendant's building. To prove negligence, plaintiff offers evidence that, shortly after the accident, defendant installed a surfacing that makes stairs slip-proof. Admissible?

b. *Remedial measures evidence is admissible to prove anything else.* Same case. Defendant claims that maintenance of the stairs was tenants' responsibility, not his. Is the repair evidence admissible to prove who was responsible for the stairs?

c. *Admissible to rebut defense of no feasible precaution.* Personal injury action. Plaintiff walked into a glass door that was practically invisible. Defendant alleges there was nothing he could have done to avoid the accident. Plaintiff offers evidence that, after accident, defendant installed warning stickers on the doors. Admissible? What if defendant merely alleged the door was "safe"?

d. Action for products liability. Is the evidence of subsequent remedial measures admissible to prove defective product design?

3. *Settlements, offers to settle and pleas.* In a *civil case*, evidence of settlements, offers to settle, and related statements are inadmissible to prove liability or fault. In a *criminal case*, pleas later withdrawn, offers to plea and related statements are inadmissible to prove guilt. This includes not just pleas of guilty but also nolo.

a. *Exception to settlement rule where no claim filed or threatened:* Two cars collide. First driver leaps out of his car and, before second driver can speak, first driver says "It was all my fault. I should never have let my dog drive. Let's settle." Admissible?

b. *Exception to settlement rule where no dispute as to liability or damages:* Suit on promissory note. Defendant said "I admit I owe you the full $10,000 you are claiming, but I'll only pay you $5,000. Take it or leave it!" Admissible?

4. *Payment or offers to pay medical expenses.* Evidence of payments or offers to pay medical expenses is inadmissible when offered to prove liability for the injuries in question. But related statements are still admissible.

    a. Plaintiff falls down stairs in defendant's building. Defendant visits plaintiff in the hospital and says "I'll pay your hospital bill. I shouldn't have dropped that banana peel on the stairs." Admissible?

    b. *Distinguish between rule regarding settlement offers and rule regarding payment of medical expenses.* Same case. Defendant says "If you will sign a release, I will pay your hospital bill. I shouldn't have dropped that banana peel on the stairs." Admissible?

D. Similar occurrences. Usually evidence is irrelevant if it is not about the specific people & events in issue. When is evidence about *other* people or events relevant? Answer: When there are certain *similarities* between that evidence and the people & events at issue.

1. *Similar occurrences sometimes admissible to prove causation.* Plaintiff had Roadkill McNuggets at McDonalds. He got sick and was rushed to the hospital. He sues McDonalds. To prove that the food caused his illness, plaintiff testifies that the food-poisoning patient in the next bed at the hospital was Ronald McDonald, who plaintiff saw eating McNuggets in the *same restaurant* at the *same time*. Relevant?

2. *Prior accidents or claims of plaintiff usually irrelevant.* Plaintiff falls down stairs in defendant's building. To show that plaintiff is clumsy and was responsible for his fall, defendant offers evidence that two other times in his life plaintiff fell and was hurt. Relevant?

a *Exception for pattern of fraudulent claims.* Same case. Plaintiff sued after each prior fall. Each of plaintiff's prior suits were dismissed because accident was faked. Relevant?

b. *Exception for preexisting condition.* Same case. In a prior fall, plaintiff broke his keester, the same injury plaintiff claims to have suffered here. Relevant?

3. *Previous similar acts relevant to prove intent.* Action for employment discrimination on the basis of gender. Plaintiff, who was denied a job by defendant, offers evidence that in 100 other instances, when a qualified female applicant applied for a job, defendant always hired a male. Relevant?

4. *Evidence relevant to rebut a defense of impossibility.* Plaintiff alleges he was drinking a bottle of Whoopsi Cola and noticed an eyeball in the bottle just a second too late to avoid swallowing it. Whoopsi claims this is impossible because there are electronic eyeball detectors throughout its bottling plant. During a recess, plaintiff is thirsty and buys another bottle of Whoopsi Cola. Before twisting the cap off, plaintiff notices another eye staring back at him from inside. Is this second bottle relevant?

5. *Comparable sales relevant to establish value.* Where value of property is an issue, such as in a condemnation case or to prove amount of damages where property destroyed, evidence of sales price of similar property in same area and sold at same time is relevant.

6. *Habit evidence admissible.* Habit of a person to act in a certain way is relevant and admissible to show the person acted in accordance with the habit on the occasion in question.

    a. *Distinguish habit from character (which is often inadmissible). Character evidence says something general about a person and conveys a moral judgment.* Personal injury action arising out of auto collision. Plaintiff alleges defendant ran a stop sign. Defendant calls a witness who has been a passenger in defendant's car many times. The witness testifies the defendant is a *careful* driver. Admissible?

    b. *Compare: Habit describes specific conduct and makes no moral judgment.* Same case. Defendant's witness has been passenger in defendant's car many times. Witness testifies that each time defendant arrives at a stop sign, he completely stops behind the stop line. Admissible as habit evidence?

    c. *Habit = frequently repeated conduct.* Same case. Witness offers to testify that she rode with defendant twice and that, on each occasion, he acted as described above. Admissible as habit evidence?

7. *Routine practice evidence.* Routine business practice is relevant to show that conduct of the entity was in conformity with that practice on the occasion in question.

8. *Industrial custom evidence relevant to prove standard of care in negligence case.* Plaintiff is a bus passenger. While getting off a bus, plaintiff gets his foot caught in the door and is dragged to the end of the line. He sues, alleging the bus company was negligent for not installing a safety device that prevents the bus from moving when the door is not fully closed. Defendant offers evidence that no bus company employs such device. Relevant?

II. Character Evidence.

    A. Introduction. Four question approach.

       1. What is the purpose for which the character evidence is offered? Three possibilities:

          a. Offered to prove character because *character is an issue in the case*.
          b. Offered to prove character as *circumstantial evidence of a person's conduct* on the occasion in question.
          c. Offered to *impeach or support* the credibility of a witness.

       2. What *method or technique* is used to prove character?

          a. Specific acts of conduct
          b. Opinion
          c. Reputation

       3. Is it a *civil or criminal* case?

       4. Does the evidence prove a *pertinent* character trait?

    B. Character evidence in *civil* cases. Character evidence is *inadmissible* to prove conduct except where civil claim is based on sexual assault or child molestation. In such a case, defendant's prior acts of sexual assault or child molestation are *admissible* to prove conduct in this case.

       1. Action for injuries in auto collision. To prove defendant drove negligently, plaintiff calls witness who testifies defendant has reputation as a reckless driver. Admissible?

       2. Same case. Defendant calls witness who offers to testify that, in his opinion, defendant is a careful driver. Admissible?

       3. Civil action for assault arising out of defendant's alleged molestation of plaintiff, a child. Defendant denies the molestation. Plaintiff offers evidence that defendant molested other children. Admissible?

4. *Character evidence admissible where character in issue.* Suit for *defamation of character*. Plaintiff alleges that defendant was going around town saying plaintiff is a dishonest businessman, thus damaging his reputation. Defendant calls plaintiff's former business partner who offers to testify that he is familiar with plaintiff's conduct and that, in fact, plaintiff is a dishonest businessman. Admissible?

   a. Other civil cases where character is in issue are negligent entrustment (suit against parents claiming they were negligent to give the car to their teenage son, who they knew to be reckless), child custody disputes, and loss of consortium cases. What methods to prove character are OK when character is in issue? Answer: All methods (i.e., specific instances of conduct, opinion, and reputation).

C. Character evidence in *criminal* cases: Is character evidence admissible to prove conduct of defendant? Of the victim? There are two doors to the admissibility of such evidence. Both are closed when the prosecution begins its case. *Usually* only the defendant can open these doors. *Usually* they are opened separately.

   1. Admissibility of evidence of *defendant's* character to prove conduct. *Prosecution cannot be first to offer such evidence. The door is closed at the start of trial when the prosecution begins its case in chief.*

      Exceptions: (1) In cases of sexual assault or child molestation, prosecution can be first to offer evidence that defendant committed other acts of sexual assault or child molestation, (2) Where court has admitted evidence of victim's character offered by defendant, prosecution can be first to offer evidence that defendant has same character trait. (See hypo (d) page 12 for example.)

      a. *Trial begins with the door closed.* Defendant is charged with *non-sexual* assault of an elderly woman. He claims self-defense because, he says, she attacked him first. Defendant looks like an angel, but has a record of violent assaults. During its case in chief, the state offers evidence of this criminal record. Admissible?

b. *Exception for sexual assault/child molestation.* What if this is a prosecution for *sexual* assault and defendant's priors were rape convictions?

c. *Defense can open the door.* Same case as "a" above. On cross, prosecution witness testifies defendant has reputation for being non-violent. Admissible?

d. *Prosecution then can offer pertinent character evidence to rebut because defendant opened the door.* Same case as "a" and "c". Prosecution in rebuttal calls witness to testify that defendant has reputation for violence. Admissible?

e. *Evidence must always concern a pertinent character trait.* What if prosecution offered rebuttal evidence that defendant has a reputation for dishonesty?

f. *Assuming the door is open, reputation and opinion evidence are admissible on direct examination by any party, but not specific instances evidence.* Same case. Defendant calls witness to testify that he once saw defendant attacked but defendant did not retaliate or even defend himself. Admissible?

g. *On cross examination by any party, reputation, opinion, and specific instances are all admissible.* Same case. Defendant calls witness who testifies that, in his opinion, the defendant is gentle. On cross-exam, can prosecutor ask, "Did you know that the defendant kicked his evidence professor?"

h. Same case. Witness in "g" answers "No, I never heard of the professor incident." Can Prosecutor call the professor and, on direct, ask about the attack?

2. Admissibility of evidence of *victim's* character. Most of the same rules apply. Prosecution cannot be first to offer character evidence to prove conduct: the trial begins with the door to the victim's character *closed*. There are two ways defendant can open the door: (i) if defendant offers evidence of victim's character, prosecution may rebut, (ii) in a homicide case, if defendant offers evidence victim attacked first, prosecution may offer evidence of victim's character for peacefulness.

On direct exam, reputation and opinion permitted but no specific instances. On cross, reputation, opinion and specific instances permitted.

a. *Trial begins with the door closed.* Same case (Defendant is charged with *non-sexual* assault of an elderly woman. He claims self-defense because she attacked him first.) During its case in chief, prosecution offers evidence that the little old lady who is alleged victim has a reputation for being peaceful and gentle. Admissible?

b. *Victim attacked first exception.* Same case except defendant on cross-exam of prosecution witness elicits testimony that victim attacked first. Is prosecution evidence that victim had reputation for being peaceful now admissible? What if this was a homicide prosecution?

c. *Defendant can open the door.* Same case (the assault). Defense calls witness to testify that the little old lady is called "Psycho" back at the old-age home because she has a reputation for being violent. Admissible?

d. *The doors usually open separately, but there is one exception.* Same case. After court admits defense evidence of *victim's* violent character, prosecution offers evidence of *defendant's* violent character. Admissible?

e. *Character rules apply only if evidence offered to prove character.* Same case. To support claim of self-defense, accused testifies on direct that he struck the lady only after she removed knitting needle from her purse and that, on the only other occasion accused saw her with knitting needles, she stabbed a boy scout trying to help her cross the street. Admissible?

3. Rape *shield statute.* There are special rules, in criminal and civil cases involving rape or other sexual assault, limiting defense evidence of alleged victim's character when offered to prove consent. Criminal rules: *Reputation and opinion* evidence *inadmissible.* Specific instances of alleged victim's conduct *admissible* only to prove (i) third party is source of semen or injury, or (ii) prior acts of consensual intercourse between defendant and alleged victim. Civil rules: *Reputation, opinion, and specific instances* evidence is *admissible* if probative value substantially outweighs unfair prejudice and, in the case of reputation evidence, plaintiff put her reputation in issue.

4. Specific instances of defendant's bad conduct may be admitted to prove *anything other than character* that is relevant. MIMIC = Motive, Intent, Mistake [absence of mistake], Identity, Common Plan or Scheme.

   a. *Motive.* Vice president of bank loses $ gambling. To cover his losses, he embezzles $ from the bank. Fearing that the bank will discover that cash is missing, he sets the bank on fire. VP is now on trial for *arson* and prosecutor offers evidence of defendant's gambling and embezzlement. Admissible?

   b. *Intent (absence of mistake).* Murder prosecution. Victim, the Roadrunner, was shot. Defendant Coyote claims it was accidental. Prosecution offers evidence that, in the week before shooting, defendant tried to drop an anvil on the victim and gave victim a birthday cake with sticks of dynamite for candles. Admissible?

   c. *Identity.* Prosecution for bank robbery. Defendant claims he was not the robber. Witnesses testify that robber wore a ski mask, pink ballet tutu, and swim flippers. Prosecution offers evidence that defendant has two prior robbery convictions and in each case defendant wore an identical costume. Admissible?

      1) *Similarity and Uniqueness required to prove identity.* Murder prosecution. Victim was stabbed in the heart. Prosecution offers evidence of defendant's previous conviction in which he stabbed another person in the heart. Admissible to prove identity?

13

d. *Common plan or scheme.* Defendant charged with bank robbery in which robbers escaped in an ice cream truck. Prosecutor offers evidence that day before the robbery defendant stole that ice cream truck. Admissible?

e. *Discretion to exclude MIMIC evidence for unfair prejudice.* Prosecution for bank robbery. To prove motive, prosecution offers evidence defendant needed money to support heroin habit and was unemployed because he was just released from prison after convictions for child molestation and puppy cruelty. Admissible?

III. Testimonial Evidence.

A. Competency = Who can testify. Four requirements.

1. *Personal knowledge.* Murder prosecution. Witness testifies she dreamed defendant committed the crime. Admissible?

a. *Distinguish between personal knowledge & hearsay objections. Does the fact testified to = the fact perceived? If not, PK is the objection.* Murder prosecution. Prosecution witness testifies "Defendant shot the victim." Witness is blind and bases testimony on what she heard someone else say. Proper objection? (Hint: Did witness perceive Defendant shooting or did witness perceive a statement being made?)

b. *Does the witness quote someone or explicitly refer to someone's out of court statement? If so, hearsay is the objection.* Same case. Witness testifies, "The sheriff told me that the defendant shot the victim." Proper objection?

c. *Perceptions may be limited.* Murder prosecution. Witness testifies he saw the defendant shoot the victim, but admits lighting was poor. Admissible?

2. *Present recollection.* Witness must testify from present recollection, not from some record regarding matters the witness once knew but has now forgotten.

3. *Communication.* Witness must be able to relate perception either directly or through interpreter.

4. *Sincerity.* Witness must take oath or make affirmation to tell truth.

5. Almost all other grounds for disqualification have been abolished. Only the judge and the jurors are absolutely disqualified from testifying.

   a. Witness admits to being an atheist and states he does not believe he will be punished by God if he lies. Is the witness competent?

   b. Three year old says she saw the accident and promises to tell "what really happened and not make-up something." Witness competent?

   c. Witness was convicted of perjury and psychiatrist says witness is insane, a pathological liar, and a member of Congress. Witness competent?

   d. During investigation of the case, police hypnotized witness to help him recall what he saw. Witness competent?

B. Objections to form of testimony and questions. Need for *timely* and *specific* objection or else the objection is waived.

1. *Calls for narrative.* Antitrust litigation. Plaintiff's witness was at meetings where defendants fixed prices. Counsel asks "Tell us what happened at each of those meetings." Witness rambles for an hour, describing how defendants used drugs and tortured puppies while fixing the price of widgets. What's the proper objection?

2. *Unresponsive.* Same case. Plaintiff's attorney asks witness, "Was price discussed at the meetings?" Witness answers, "They spent most of the time torturing puppies." Objection?

3. *Usually no leading on direct.* Same case. Plaintiff's attorney calls plaintiff and, on direct exam, asks, "Isn't it true that defendants have been fixing prices?" Objection?

4. *Leading OK on cross.* Same case. On cross-exam, defense counsel asks plaintiff, "Isn't it true that you had your fingers crossed when you swore to tell the truth?" Is this leading? Is it improper?

   a. *Cross must stay within scope of direct.*

5. *Leading OK on direct if adverse witness, hostile witness, witness needing help.* Same case. Plaintiff calls defendant and, on direct exam, asks "Isn't it true that you wrote the book "Price Fixing for Fun and Profit?" Improper leading question?

6. *Assumes facts not in evidence.* Suit for divorce. Assume no evidence has yet been offered on physical abuse. Wife's counsel asks, on cross of husband, "When did you stop beating your wife?" Proper objection?

7. *Argumentative.* Same case. Husband testifies that since his wedding he has never even looked at another woman. On cross, wife's counsel asks "Do you expect the jury to believe that baloney?" Proper objection?

8. *Compound.* Same case. On cross-exam, wife's counsel asks "Isn't it true that you cheated on your wife and beat her?" Proper objection?

C. Witness use of documents during testimony. *Watch for hearsay issues!*

1. Personal injury action. Plaintiff calls emergency room physician to testify as to injuries. Doctor states she has seen so many patients she can't recall plaintiff. Counsel shows doctor the emergency room records and doctor states "It says here plaintiff suffered a broken keester." Objection?

2. *Refreshing recollection.* Same case. Doctor says she can't recall plaintiff. This time counsel asks doctor if seeing hospital records might refresh her memory. The doctor answers yes and counsel hands her the records. The doctor silently reads records and then says, "Now I remember. He had a broken keester." Is this permissible?

3. *Anything can be used to refresh recollection.* Same case. To refresh doctor's recollection, counsel hands her Exhibit A, plaintiff's broken keester. Permissible?

4. *The opponent may inspect and offer into evidence anything used to refresh.* Same case. To refresh the doctor's recollection, counsel hands her a note stating, "The correct answer is 'a broken keester.'" Does the direct examiner now have a problem?

5. *Recorded recollection exception to hearsay rule.* Same case. Doctor reads the emergency room report but still can't remember plaintiff's case. What should plaintiff's counsel do?

    Elements of the exception:

    a. The witness once had *personal knowledge* of the facts.

    b. The document was *made* by the witness or under the witness' direction or was *adopted* by the witness. Adoption = another person made the record and witness did or said something to indicate she agreed with contents.

    c. The document was written or adopted at a time when the facts were *fresh in the witness' memory.*

    d. The document was *accurate* when made.

    e. The witness now has *insufficient recollection* to testify as to the matters contained in the document.

D. Opinion testimony. Normally *inadmissible*. Lay and expert opinion may be admitted only under the following rules.

1. Lay opinion. Admissible if rationally based on the witness' perceptions and helpful to the trier of fact. Cannot be based on scientific or other specialized knowledge. "Helpful" = the lay opinion gives jury MORE information than would testimony limited to describing witness' perceptions.

   a. Action for injuries in auto collision. Witness testifies, "In my opinion the car was going about 80 miles per hour. I got a good look at it." Is this (i) based on witness' perception, (ii) rationally based, (iii) helpful to the jury?

   b. Under above test, lay opinion permitted as to: speed of auto, sanity, intoxication, emotions, value of witness' property.

   c. *Legal conclusions are not "helpful" because they give jury LESS information than testimony describing witness' perceptions.* Same case. Witness testifies, "In my opinion, defendant was driving negligently." Admissible?

2. Expert opinion. 5 requirements for admissibility. Opinion must be (i) helpful to jury, (ii) witness must be qualified, (iii) witness must believe in opinion to reasonable degree of certainty, (iv) opinion must be supported by a proper factual basis, and (v) opinion must be based on reliable principles that were reliably applied;

   a. *Helpful = expert uses specialized knowledge to reach conclusion the average juror could not figure out for herself.* Murder prosecution. PhD in criminology offers opinion that, based on fact defendant's fingerprints were on murder weapon, defendant must be guilty. Helpful? Compare: Fingerprint expert offers opinion that the prints on the weapon match defendant's fingerprints. Helpful?

b. *Qualifications.* Murder prosecution. Victim died when a toilet exploded. Defense claims it was an accident. Prosecution calls a plumber, who quit school after the sixth grade, to testify that, based on twenty years of professional experience with toilets, it is impossible for one to explode accidentally. Admissible, even though witness lacks a PhT? What if the plumber offers an opinion as to cause of death?

c. *Degree of Certainty.* Same case. Physician testifies for defense that victim may have died of a drug overdose before toilet went ballistic. But Dr. admits this is speculation and that he is uncertain. Is the opinion admissible?

d. *Opinion must be based on one of the following: (i) admitted evidence, (ii) personal knowledge, or (iii) inadmissible evidence reasonably relied upon.*

1) Same case. Prosecution calls police forensic scientist who investigated crime scene. May she base an opinion on what she saw at the scene?

2) Same case. Prosecution calls Dr. Bidet, the famous French expert on exploding toilets. Dr. Bidet has no personal knowledge of the facts. May he base opinion on already admitted testimony of police forensic scientist?

3) Same case. Prosecution calls pathologist whose knowledge is based on a lab report that has been ruled inadmissible hearsay. After testifying she customarily relies on such reports when rendering professional opinions at the hospital where she works, pathologist then offers opinion as to victim's cause of death. Admissible?

e. *Opinion must be based on reliable principles that were reliably applied: Daubert/Kumho standard.* Murder prosecution. Defendant is Professor Gold. Prosecution expert testifies that a new DNA testing technique reveals perpetrator must be a bald law professor. While the validity of the technique is not generally accepted among scientists in the field of genetics, it has been *peer reviewed and published* in scientific journals, has been *tested and is subject to retesting,* has a *low error rate,* and has *a reasonable level of acceptance.* Admissible?

f. Same case. Pathologist admits her opinion has logical inconsistencies, she did not consider other pertinent evidence or alternative explanations. Admissible?

g. *Learned treatise hearsay exception. LT is admissible to prove anything stated therein if it is an accepted authority in field.* Same case. Prosecution's toilet expert testifies that it's impossible for a toilet to explode accidentally. On cross-examination, defense reads from page 747 of volume 6 of Professor Plunge's seminal work, On The Toilet, which states "Toilets have been known to explode accidentally in seismically active areas." Admissible?

E. Evidence of Witness Credibility. *Watch out for hidden hearsay issues when a prior statement of a witness is offered to attack or support credibility!*

1. *Evidence to support credibility. Inadmissible unless credibility is attacked first.* Murder prosecution. Defense alibi witness testifies defendant was with him at the movies when murder occurred. Prosecution does not cross-examine. To support credibility, defense offers evidence that the alibi witness gave a consistent statement to the police shortly after defendant was arrested. Admissible?

   a. *Prior consistent statement is not hearsay and admissible for all purposes if made before bribe or inconsistent statement. Otherwise, it is inadmissible for any purpose.* Same case. The witness gives the alibi testimony. On cross-examination, prosecutor asks witness, "Didn't defendant give you a bribe of $1000 *last week*?" On redirect, is evidence of witness' consistent statement (supporting the alibi) made *yesterday* admissible? A consistent statement made *two weeks ago*?

Consistent Statement   Bribe   Consistent Statement   Trial

2. *Impeachment.* Three step approach to admissibility of impeachment evidence: (i) Is source of impeachment extrinsic evidence or testimony at this proceeding of witness being impeached? (ii) If extrinsic, is it admissible given impeachment technique? (iii) Any other foundation requirements?

   Definition of Extrinsic Evidence: Any evidence other than testimony given at this proceeding by the witness being impeached. E.G., extrinsic evidence = testimony of other witnesses, writings, prior statements of the witness who is now testifying .

a. *Impeachment by Contradiction.* Extrinsic evidence inadmissible to contradict on collateral matter. Collateral matter = a fact not material to the issues in the case that says nothing about witness' credibility other than to contradict the witness.

   1) Murder prosecution. Prosecution witness testifies he saw the crime at 3 a.m. while coming home after a visit with his grandma. Can defense call witnesses to testify that the prosecution witness really was visiting his mistress?

   2) Same case. Prosecution witness claims he saw the murder while on his way home from his grandma's. Defendant offers testimony of another witness that prosecution witness really was on his way home from a bar, where he had spent the preceding six hours drinking heavily. Admissible?

b. *Impeachment by Prior Inconsistent Statement (PIS).* Action for personal injuries in auto accident. Plaintiff's witness testifies that defendant ran red light. On cross-exam, defendant asks, "Didn't you tell the police that defendant had the green light?" Witness answers, "Yes." What is this relevant to prove? What is this admissible to prove?

   1) *PIS of witness who testifies at trial = not hearsay if given under oath at trial or deposition. Otherwise = hearsay and inadmissible if offered to prove truth.* Same case. Plaintiff's witness testifies defendant ran the red light. On cross, defendant asks "Didn't you testify at your *deposition* that defendant had the green light?" The witness answers "Yes." What is this admissible to prove?

2) *Extrinsic evidence of PIS inadmissible to impeach on collateral matter.* Same case. Witness denies giving the inconsistent deposition testimony about the green light. Defendant offers the deposition transcript. Admissible?

3) *Foundation requirement: extrinsic evidence admissible only if witness given opportunity to explain or deny.* Same case. Defendant does not cross witness about his deposition testimony. Witness is then excused. During his case-in-chief, defendant offers the pertinent portion of witness' deposition transcript. Admissible?

c. *Impeachment with Evidence of Bias, Interest, Motive.* Prosecution for drug dealing. On cross-exam of prosecution witness, defense asks, "Isn't it true that you were also arrested for drug dealing but offered a plea bargain if you testified against defendant in this case?" The witness answers "Yes." Admissible?

1) *Foundation requirement: extrinsic evidence admissible if witness given opportunity to explain or deny.* Same case. Witness denies being offered a plea bargain. Defendant offers the plea bargain agreement. Admissible?

d. *Impeachment with Conviction for Crime Involving False Statement.* All convictions (felonies and misdemeanors) for crimes of false statement (e.g. perjury, forgery, fraud) are admissible. No balancing of unfair prejudice against probative value except for convictions more than 10 years old (see bottom p. 25).

1) Prosecution for tax fraud. Defendant testifies and admits his tax return did not report all his income, but claims this was unintentional. Prosecution offers evidence that Defendant previously was convicted of filing a false police report. Admissible to prove Defendant has the character of a liar and, thus, intentionally lied on his tax return?

2) Same case. Is the conviction admissible to impeach Defendant's credibility as a witness? Does it matter if it was a felony or misdemeanor?

3) Same case. Does the court have the discretion to exclude the conviction evidence for all purposes since it would cause unfair prejudice if the jury uses it to infer Defendant lied on his tax return?

e. *Impeachment with Conviction for a Crime Not Involving False Statement.* Felonies that do not involve false statement (e.g., murder, robbery, rape) may be admissible to impeach but court may exclude for unfair prejudice. Misdemeanors that do not involve false statement are inadmissible to impeach.

1) Same case. Prosecution offers evidence that Defendant was previously convicted of rape, a felony. Admissible? Can the court exclude for unfair prejudice?

2) Same case. Prosecution offers evidence that Defendant was previously convicted of disorderly conduct, a misdemeanor. Admissible?

f. *Final points on Conviction Impeachment.* If the conviction is otherwise admissible under the above rules, the conviction may be proved with extrinsic evidence. If the conviction is otherwise admissible under the above rules, but it is more than 10 years since the date of conviction or release from prison (whichever is later), it is inadmissible unless probative value outweighs unfair prejudice

1) Bank robbery prosecution. Defendant testifies, denying involvement. Prosecutor offers a copy of a judgment showing defendant was released from prison in 1988 after serving time for felony perjury. Admissible?

g. *Impeachment with Non-Conviction Misconduct Evidence Bearing on Truthfulness.* Acts of misconduct that did not result in a conviction are admissible to impeach in both civil and criminal cases *if the acts involved lying.* Extrinsic evidence to prove the acts is inadmissible. Impeacher only may cross-examine witness about her misconduct.

1) Action for breach of contract. On cross of plaintiff, defense asks "Isn't it true that you lied on your driver's license application?" Plaintiff answers, "Yes." Admissible?

2) Prosecution for bank robbery. Defendant testifies and denies involvement. Prosecutor asks defendant about lying on his driver's license application but defendant denies it. Prosecutor offers the application. Admissible?

3) Same case. Prosecutor asks defendant if he stole office supplies at work. Defendant admits to the theft. Admissible?

h. *Impeachment with Reputation and Opinion Regarding Truthfulness. Extrinsic evidence admissible.* Personal injury action. Plaintiff testifies he suffers back pain because of the accident. Defense witness testifies he lives in plaintiff's community and has known plaintiff for years. Witness testifies that he believes plaintiff is a liar and is known in the neighborhood as "Shifty." Admissible?

IV. Hearsay.

Hearsay is usually inadmissible. You will be tested on when evidence is hearsay. You can tell if evidence is hearsay if you keep in mind why hearsay is inadmissible. It is inadmissible because the speaker ("declarant") cannot be cross-examined when she speaks out of court. Without cross-examination we cannot tell if declarant is lying or mistaken about the facts in her statement. *But this is a problem only if the evidence is used to prove those facts.* That's when it is hearsay. If it is used to prove anything else, we do not need to cross-examine declarant, because it does not matter if declarant is lying or mistaken about facts we are *not trying to prove.* This is when it is *not hearsay.*

A. Definition of Hearsay. Out of court statement offered to prove the truth of the matter asserted in that statement. Statement = verbal or written expression of a person or conduct by a person intended to communicate (called "assertive conduct").

  1. *Is there a statement?* Prosecution for bank robbery. To prove defendant committed the crime, a police officer testifies that, at a line-up of suspects, he asked the victim if the perpetrator was present and the victim pointed at the defendant. Statement?

  2. Same case. To prove defendant committed the robbery, a police officer testifies that a bloodhound trained to track a scent followed a trail from the crime scene and "pointed" at defendant. Statement?

  3. Same case. To prove defendant committed the robbery, a traffic officer testifies that he arrested the defendant for speeding just after the bank robbery because, when he pointed his radar gun at the defendant's car, the indicator on the gun said, "vehicle is going 100 mph". Statement?

  4. Same case. To prove defendant committed the robbery, a police officer testifies that a computer printout of police files stated, "defendant has three prior robbery convictions". Statement?

5. *Is the statement out of court?* Same case. Defendant had previously been convicted of the bank robbery but the conviction was overturned on appeal and he is now being retried. During retrial the prosecution offers a transcript of the testimony of a witness given in the first trial. Is this an out of court statement?

B. *The tough part of the definition: Assuming an out of court statement, is it offered to prove the truth of the matter asserted?* Three step approach: (i). Find the statement, (ii). Ask what is it offered to prove, (Does the question tell you? If not, consider who offered the evidence and what it would relevant to prove in that party's case. *That* is what it the statement is offered to prove.) (iii). Given what it's offered to prove, will jury be misled if the out of court speaker was lying or mistaken? If the answer is yes, it is hearsay. If the answer is no, it is not hearsay.

1. Action for breach of contract. Defendant denies entering into the contract. Plaintiff offers the out-of-court statement of defendant's secretary, who said "I saw the defendant sign the contract." Hearsay? (Notice that, if the secretary was lying or mistaken, the jury would be misled.)

2. *Not hearsay because statement has independent legal significance.* Same case. Witness testifies she heard defendant say to plaintiff "I accept your offer." Hearsay? (Notice that Contract law does not care if defendant was lying or mistaken. It only cares that he said, "I accept".)

3. Defamation action. Plaintiff offers the testimony of witness who states he heard defendant say "Plaintiff cheats on his wife!" Hearsay?

Other examples of words with *independent legal significance*: "That is my land" in an adverse possession case. "I am giving you this car as a gift" in a dispute over ownership of the car.

4. *Not hearsay because statement offered to show effect on listener.* Action for infliction of emotional distress. Plaintiff, a 78 year-old lady, testifies that when she was in the doctor's office he picked up a file and said "I have wonderful news, you are pregnant!" Other evidence will show doctor read the wrong file. Hearsay?

5. Personal injury action. Plaintiff's car plunged off defendant's bridge. Defense is contributory negligence. Defendant testifies that on road leading to bridge a sign reads "Bridge Out." Hearsay if offered to prove contributory negligence? Hearsay if offered to prove the bridge was out?

6. *Not hearsay because statement offered to show speaker's (or writer's) knowledge of facts stated.* Prosecution for bank robbery. To prove defendant was a member of the gang that robbed the bank, prosecutor offers evidence that the gang leader when arrested had in his pocket a piece of paper on which is written what defendant admits is his correct address and phone number. Hearsay?

7. *Not hearsay because statement is circumstantial evidence of state of mind.* Murder prosecution. Defense is insanity. Defense witness testifies that, on the night victim was found with wounds on his neck, Defendant said "I am Dracula." Hearsay? Compare: "I feel like killing someone."

8. *Hearsay even if out-of-court declarant is now in court witness.* Same case. To prove who committed the homicide, prosecutor asks a witness "what did you tell the police?" Witness says "I told them I saw the defendant bite the victim in the neck." Hearsay? On MBE, watch for "not hearsay because it is the witness' own statement". *Wrong answer!*

C. Exceptions & Exemptions to the hearsay rule. Even if the evidence is hearsay under the basic definition, it might still be admissible. The FRE create *exemptions* to the usual definition of hearsay. Evidence falling within an exemption is admissible because it is not hearsay. Even where the evidence is hearsay, the FRE also provide exceptions that make the hearsay admissible. Here is what this all means: On the MBE you need to distinguish between these two alternative answers: "hearsay but admissible" and "admissible because not hearsay". The former is correct answer for *exceptions*. The latter is correct answer for *exemptions*. Multiple hearsay or hearsay within hearsay = each level must be within exception or exemption.

1. *Admission of Party Opponent.* This is an *exemption* and, thus, *not hearsay*. Party Admission = statement by party, or by someone whose statement is attributable to a party, offered by a party opponent.

   a. *Distinguish party admission from statements against interest exception.* Prosecution for tax evasion. Prosecution offers into evidence a financial statement defendant submitted to bank to get a loan. Statement indicates annual income over $1,000,000. Hearsay?

   b. *Party admissions not subject to personal knowledge requirement or opinion rule.* Wrongful death suit based on airplane crash. Plaintiff calls secretary of defendant, owner of the airline. Secretary testifies that, when he informed defendant of crash, defendant shouted, "Damn, we were negligent again!" Hearsay? Admissible?

   c. *Vicarious party admissions. Statement by (i) authorized spokesperson of party or (ii) employee of party concerning matter within scope of employment and made during employment relationship.*

      1) *Authorization can be expressed or implied.* Toy Co. is sued for selling dangerous products. Plaintiff offers (i) press release issued by defendant's marketing department stating that new toy gun fires real bullets, and (ii) statement of defendant's Vice President that defendant was saving 5¢ on each baby teething toy by using lead paint. Hearsay?

2) Negligence action against UPS. Plaintiff testifies UPS truck crashed through her bedroom window and driver said, "I fell asleep while driving." Hearsay?

3) Other vicarious party admissions: Adoptive admission (nonparty makes statement and party indicates belief in its truth) and Co-conspirator statement (made during course and in furtherance of conspiracy). All are *not hearsay.*

2. *In addition to party admissions, there are the following three exemptions from the usual hearsay definition. These exemptions apply to an out of court statement from a declarant who now testifies at trial*: (i) prior inconsistent statement given under oath at trial or deposion (p. 23), (ii) prior consistent statement offered to rebut charge of recent fabrication or improper influence or motive (p. 21), (iii) statement of identification of a person made after perceiving the person (e.g., "That's the guy who robbed me."). *All are not hearsay under FRE.*

3. *Former testimony exception.* Testimony given by a person in earlier proceeding or deposition is admissible if (i) the party *against* whom the testimony is now offered had, during the earlier proceeding, an *opportunity* to examine that person and the *motive* to conduct that exam was similar to the motive the party has now, **or** (ii) in a *civil* case, the party against whom the testimony is now offered was not present in the earlier proceeding but has a close privity-type relationship with someone who was a party to that earlier proceeding (a "predecessor in interest") and who had an opportunity and a similar motive to examine the witness in that earlier proceeding. Declarant must be unavailable.

Declarant is unavailable if (i) court exempts declarant from testifying due to privilege, (ii) declarant is dead or sick, (iii) proponent of statement cannot procure declarant's attendance by process or other reasonable means, (iv) declarant refuses to testify despite court order, or (v) declarant's memory fails.

a. *Opportunity to examine.* An airplane crashes, killing all passengers. Estate of passenger "X" sued Airline for wrongful death and an expert testified at that trial against Airline concerning defects in the airplane design. The expert is now dead. Estate of passenger "Y", who died in the same crash, subsequently sues Airline for wrongful death and offers against Airline the former testimony of the expert witness given in *X v. Airline*. Admissible in *Y. v. Airline*?

b. *Similar motive to examine.* Same case. *X v. Airline* (the first proceeding) was a civil nuisance suit against Airline for noise pollution. Is expert's testimony offered against Airline in that case now admissible against the Airline in the wrongful death case, *Y v. Airline*?

c. *Deposition testimony.* Same case except the former testimony was given in a deposition in the same wrongful death case (*Y v. Airline*) in which it is now offered into evidence at trial. Admissible?

d. *Predecessor in interest.* Expert witness testified for Airline in first wrongful death case, X v. Airline. That witness then died. Airline now offers transcript of that testimony in the second wrongful death case, Y v. Airline. Admissible?

4. *Declaration against interest exception.* Hearsay statement is admissible if, at time it was made, it was against the financial interest of declarant or would have subjected declarant to criminal liability. If the statement is offered to exculpate accused (i.e., by showing someone else confessed to the crime), there must be corroborating evidence to admit the statement. Declarant must be unavailable.

Distinguish party admissions. Party admission is statement of party (or statement of another person attributed to a party) while a declaration against interest can be made by anyone. Declaration against interest must be against interest when made. No such requirement for party admission.

a. Prosecution for tax evasion. Defendant filed tax return stating he had no income. The prosecution offers into evidence a loan application defendant submitted to a bank. Defendant stated on the application, "I earn $1,000,000 per year." Was this a declaration against interest? Is it admissible under any other theory?

b. Prosecution for murder. Defendant offers into evidence a letter he received from a friend living in Argentina. The letter states, "I committed the murder." There is no other evidence connecting the friend to the crime. Admissible?

5. *Dying declaration exception.* Hearsay statement by one believing he is about to die & describing cause or circumstances leading to impending death is admissible in civil action and in homicide prosecution. Declarant need not die but must be unavailable.

    a. Civil suit contesting validity of will. Plaintiff offers testimony of witness who says he came upon accident scene and found decedent hanging out the windshield of his car. Witness testifies decedent said, "I'm a goner. My will was the product of undue influence...," whereupon he expired. Admissible?

    b. Prosecution for attempted murder. Prosecutor offers evidence that, an hour after Victim was shot, he said, "I'm not going to make it. Defendant did this to me." Victim then lapsed into a coma and has not regained consciousness. Admissible?

    c. Prosecution for murder in which defendant allegedly also shot but did not kill a second victim. Prosecutor offers evidence that the surviving victim, who is now in a coma, said at the scene, "Im not going to make it. Defendant killed my buddy and me." Admissible?

6. *Excited utterance exception.* Hearsay statement relating to startling event or condition is admissible when made while declarant was still under stress of excitement caused by event or condition. No need to show declarant unavailable.

    a. Personal injury action arising out of auto-truck collision. A passenger in car, the only surviving witness, lapsed into a coma upon impact. Two years later passenger suddenly emerged from the coma, sat upright in bed, and screamed, "Watch out for that truck, it's driving the wrong way!" Excited utterance?

7. *Present sense impression exception.* Hearsay statement is admissible if describing or explaining an event or condition made while declarant was perceiving the event or condition or immediately thereafter. No need to show declarant unavailable.

    a. Murder prosecution. Defendant claims self-defense because Victim acted in a threatening manner. Witness testifies she made phone call to Victim on night of the murder and Victim said, "Joe [the defendant] just walked in the room and it looks like he wants to show me his survival knife. I'll call you back." Is the statement admissible to show defendant was in the room with a knife?

8. *Exception for declaration of then existing physical or mental condition.* Hearsay statement of declarant's then existing physical or mental condition or state of mind is *admissible to show the condition or state of mind.* But a statement describing a memory or belief is *not admissible to prove the fact remembered or believed.* Thus, "I remember/believe that the defendant shot the victim" is not admissible to prove defendant shot the victim. No need to show declarant unavailable.

   a. Prosecution for theft of car. Defendant claims owner gave car to defendant as a gift. Defense offers statement of owner made the day before defendant drove off with the car, "I intend to give the car to Joe [the defendant] for his birthday tomorrow." Admissible to show owner's state of mind?

   b. Same case. If the statement is admissible to prove the speaker's intention, can the jury also infer the speaker acted in accordance with his intention and gave defendant the car as a gift?

   c. Same case. The day after defendant took the car, owner said, "I remember that yesterday I gave Joe the car for his birthday." Admissible to prove the owner gave defendant the car as a gift?

9. *Exception for statement of past or present mental or physical condition made for medical diagnosis or treatment.* Hearsay statement by one person concerning the past or present mental or physical condition, or its cause, of that person or any other person, is admissible if made for and pertinent to medical diagnosis or treatment. No need to show declarant unavailable.

   a. Personal injury action. Plaintiff testifies that he told doctor, "My back is killing me. I was hit by a car driven by someone with a suspended license." Admissible?

b. Same case. Plaintiff told another patient in the emergency room, "I was feeling fine before this happened." Can the other patient testify as to what plaintiff said?

c. Action for medical malpractice. Mother asks child to describe his symptoms so she can call the doctor. Child says to his mom, "My head hurts." Mom then calls the doctor and says, "My son has a temperature of 103 and he says his head hurts."

10. *Business records exception.* Hearsay is admissible if it is (i) a record of events, conditions, opinions or diagnoses (ii) kept in course of regularly conducted business activity (iii) made at or near time of matters described (iv) by person with knowledge of the facts in that record, (v) it was regular practice of business to make such record. Court may exclude if untrustworthy.   No need to show declarant unavailable.

a. *Business records exception can cover multiple levels of hearsay.* Personal injury action. Plaintiff offers hospital records, which include statement of surgeon, "Surgery to repair broken keester partly successful. Neurologist reports surgery could not repair severed nerve." Admissible?

b. Same case. Plaintiff offers another part of hospital records, which state "Patient admitted with broken keester. Patient reports he was hit by car driven by someone with a suspended license." Admissible?

c. *Records created in anticipation of litigation are not business records.* Same case. Fearing he and the hospital will be sued, Surgeon writes a memo to his files stating, "Surgery went as well as could be expected and nobody committed malpractice." Admissible?

11. *Public records exception.* Hearsay record of a public office is admissible if within *one* of the following categories: (i) record describes activities and policies of the office; (ii) record describes matters observed pursuant to duty imposed by law (but not police reports in criminal cases); or (iii) record contains factual findings resulting from investigation made pursuant to authority granted by law, unless untrustworthy. In criminal case, prosecution cannot use (iii). No need to show declarant unavailable.

   a. Civil action against the police department for wrongful termination. Plaintiff, a former police officer, offers the police department manual to show that the department did not follow its own policies when he was fired. Admissible?

   b. Criminal prosecution for vehicular homicide. Prosecution offers into evidence police report stating that police officer investigating the accident saw an empty vodka bottle in the cup-holder next to driver's seat in defendant's car. Admissible? What if this same report was offered by plaintiff in the civil tort case brought against defendant?

   c. Civil wrongful death action against airline arising out of airplane crash. Plaintiff offers into evidence report of National Transportation Safety Board in which it concluded, "Cause of crash was pilot error." Admissible? What if report contained statement of witness, "I saw an empty vodka bottle in the cockpit."

12. *Judgment of previous conviction.* Hearsay statement describing felony conviction (eg, copy of the judgment of conviction) is admissible in both civil and criminal cases to prove any fact essential to the judgment, but when offered by prosecution for purposes other than impeachment, judgments against persons other than the accused are inadmissible. No need to show declarant unavailable.

a. Prosecution for being a felon in possession of a firearm. Defendant denies he is a felon. The prosecutor offers into evidence a certified copy of the judgment of conviction of defendant for robbery, a felony. Admissible?

b. Prosecution for murder. Defendant denies the victim is dead. Prosecutor offers into evidence a certified copy of the judgment of conviction of defendant's accomplice who was previously tried and found guilty of the same murder. Admissible to prove the victim died?

D. Confrontation Clause. Even if hearsay law does not make the evidence inadmissible, the Confrontation Clause (CC) of the US Constitution might make inadmissible an out of court statement offered by the prosecution against defendant in a criminal case. Under *Crawford v. Washington,* the CC excludes an out-of-court statement if declarant does not testify at the trial, is now unavailable, the statement is "*testimonial*", and defendant had no chance to cross-examine declarant about the statement when it was made. The full meaning of "testimonial" is unclear, but it at least applies to statements made in court and statements made to further a police investigation aimed at producing evidence for a *prosecution*. Statements to police to deal with an *ongoing emergency* are non-testimonial and their admission does not violate the CC.

1. Prosecution for murder. The perpetrator shot victim in a large shopping mall the day before Christmas. When the police arrived the shooter was still at large in the mall and posed a danger to others. Victim told the police, "I going fast. The guy who shot me was dressed as Santa." Admissible"?

2. Same case. When the police arrived they arrested Defendant, who was working as a department store Santa, because a co-worker saw a gun hidden in his beard. The police then interviewed Victim, who said, "I going fast. The guy who shot me was dressed as Santa." Admissible"?

V. Writings and other Physical Evidence.

   A. Authentication. Every item of non-testimonial evidence (e.g., writings, photos, guns) must be *authenticated*. This means proving it is what the proponent of that evidence claims it to be. Burden of proof is low—"sufficient to sustain finding."

     1. *Signatures.* Breach of contract action. Defendant denies entering into the contract. Plaintiff offers a letter of acceptance that he claims is signed by defendant. What does plaintiff have to prove to authenticate the letter? How does plaintiff prove this?

       a. *Admission.* Plaintiff asks defendant, "This is your signature on the letter, isn't it?"

       b. *Eyewitness testimony.* Witness says, "I saw defendant sign the letter."

       c. *Expert opinion.* Handwriting expert compares disputed signature with a genuine example and declares the signatures were made by the same person.

       d. *Lay opinion.* Lay witness has seen defendant sign his name elsewhere and says the disputed signature is defendant's.

       e. *Circumstantial evidence.* Plaintiff testifies he mailed offer to defendant and four days later this letter (Exhibit A) arrived, postmarked defendant's home town, made specific reference to details in the offer letter, and purported to accept it.

         1) Ancient documents rule. Authenticity is established if (i) document is 20 years old or more, (ii) does not on its face present any irregularities (e.g., erasures), and (iii) was found in a place of natural custody (i.e., where you would expect such documents to be found).

       f. *A genuine exemplar.*

       g. Plaintiff authenticates the letter in one of the ways described above. Defense experts and lay witnesses dispute signature is defendant's. Is letter admissible?

2. *Self-authenticating writings.* For certain writings, authentication is unnecessary. These include certified copies of public documents (deeds), acknowledged documents (i.e., documents where the original signature is attested before a notary to be valid), official publications (government pamphlets), newspapers, periodicals, business records, and trade inscriptions.

   a. *Trade inscription = tag or label that purports to have been attached in course of business and indicates ownership, control or origin.* Plaintiff claims he drank a bottle of Whoopsi Cola with an eyeball in it. Defendant denies it was a bottle of their soda. Plaintiff offers the bottle, imprinted with the words "Whoopsi Cola." Self-authenticating?

3. Photos. *Watch for personal knowledge problem. Does fact testified to = fact perceived?*

   a. Suit for injuries suffered in auto accident. Plaintiff shows eyewitness photo of the intersection taken by newspaper reporter one year before accident. Plaintiff offers photo so jury can see the street layout. Plaintiff asks witness, "Does this photo *fairly & accurately depict* what the intersection looked like at the time of the accident?" Witness says "Yes." Defendant objects, claiming only photographer can authenticate. How should the court rule?

   b. *Compare:* Plaintiff asks the witness "Is this a photo of the intersection taken at the time of the accident?"

4. *Authentication of non-unique items.* How do you authenticate items that are facially indistinguishable from other like items (e.g., bag of white powder, generic handgun). To authenticate, proponent must lay *chain of custody* demonstrating that this is *the specific item* proponent claims it to be.

    a. Prosecution for cocaine possession. Prosecutor offers Exhibit A, bag of white powder, claiming it is same bag found on defendant. Cop testifies he found a bag of white powder on defendant and gave it to police evidence custodian. Custodian then testifies he put bag in a safe until he gave it to police chemist. Chemist testifies he determined powder was cocaine and then returned bag to the evidence custodian. Custodian testifies he kept the bag in a safe until today, when he brought it to trial. He then identifies Exhibit A as that bag. Are the bag and the test results admissible?

B. **Best Evidence Rule.** Applies only where evidence offered to prove the *contents of a writing*. Writings = not only documents but also videos, photos, x-rays, audio recordings, computer disks, or *any tangible collection of data*. The rule requires original, but with many exceptions.

    1. When is evidence being offered to prove contents of a writing?

        a. *Case turns on contents of legal instrument.* Action for breach of written contract. Defendant admits making contract but denies breach. Plaintiff testifies that defendant delivered goods on the tenth while *written contract calls for delivery on the first.* Does the best evidence rule apply?

        b. *Knowledge obtained from writing.* Defendant charged with murdering his wife. Officer testifies that, when defendant was arrested, he had a letter which read "Your wife is having an affair with the 82nd Airborne Division." Does the best evidence rule apply?

c. Same case. Witness to the murder testifies as to the date of death. Defense makes best evidence rule objection on grounds the date of death is contained on a written death certificate. Does best evidence rule apply?

d. Same case. Coroner testifies that x-ray of victim's body showed her neck was broken. Does the best evidence rule apply?

e. *Voluminous documents exception. Can be summarized if originals available for inspection.* Antitrust suit. Accountant testifies that he examined thousands of invoices in defendants' files and only once did the sales price exceed the price fixed by defendants. Admissible over a best evidence objection?

2. Assuming the best evidence rule applies, what type of evidence is admissible to prove the contents of a "writing"?

a. Originals. *Computer printouts and, in the case of public documents, certified copies are considered originals.*

b. *Duplicates usually also admissible. "Duplicate" = a copy of original produced by same impression that produced the original (eg, a carbon copy) or by a machine (e.g., photocopier or camera).* Malpractice suit. Defendant doctor offers a carbon copy of his post surgery notes to show how he performed the surgery. Admissible? How about a photocopy? A handwritten copy?

    c. *Exception to admissibility of duplicates or other written evidence that is not the original: this evidence is not admissible where there is genuine question as to authenticity of original.* Same case. Plaintiff claims that original of the post surgery notes was altered to omit reference to the fact the doctor closed the incision with library paste. Is a photocopy of the notes admissible?

    d. *Testimony regarding contents of writing may be admissible where original lost or destroyed, unless bad faith by proponent of testimony.* Prosecution for treason. Prosecution witness testifies to contents of a note in which defendant outlined details of his plan to sell stealth bomber secrets to the Swiss, who are developing a chocolate bar that produces invisible acne. Defendant ate the note when FBI kicked in his door. Is the testimony admissible over a best evidence objection? What if defendant offered the testimony?

VI. Privileges. The FRE give the courts power to establish privileges. The federal courts recognize attorney-client, spousal, psychotherapist-patient, and social worker-client privileges. In civil actions under diversity jurisdiction, *state* privileges apply in federal court.

    A. *Attorney-Client Privilege.* A communication between attorney and client or their representatives intended by client to be confidential and made to facilitate legal services is privileged in all civil and criminal proceedings unless waived by the client.

    1. When is a communication from a corporation employee to the corporation's attorney privileged? The privilege applies to communications from employees/agents if the corporation *authorized the employee/agent to communicate to the lawyer.*

2. *Communications by and between what people are privileged?* Personal injury action.
    Plaintiff's attorney sends plaintiff to a doctor retained by the attorney to report to the
    attorney about plaintiff's injuries. Are statements made by client to doctor protected
    by the attorney client privilege? Is doctor's report to the attorney privileged?

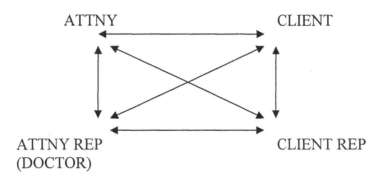

ATTNY CLIENT

ATTNY REP CLIENT REP
(DOCTOR)

3. *Communication must be intended by client to be confidential. Objective standard of
    intent.* Same case. Defendant testifies that, at a new year's eve party, plaintiff
    shouted to his lawyer across a crowded room, "Can't I lose this phony neck brace just
    for one night?" Privileged?

4. Same case. Defendant was speaking to his attorney on the phone and did not know
    the phone was wiretapped. Privileged?

5. Same case. Defendant was speaking to his attorney in the presence of the attorney's
    paralegal and an employee of the client assigned to work on this case. Privileged?

6. *Purpose of communication must be professional legal services.* Same case. Lawyer testifies he met plaintiff at a party and, when plaintiff discovered he was speaking to an attorney, plaintiff tried to get some free legal advice and asked, "Are phony medical expenses tax deductible?" Privileged?

7. Same case. Plaintiff interviews Lawyer and discusses the case but decides not to hire Lawyer. Is the discussion privileged?

8. *The privilege survives.* Same case. Plaintiff hired Lawyer and then discussed case. Is the discussion privileged if the Plaintiff later fires Lawyer? What if Plaintiff dies?

9. Exceptions. Privilege does not apply where (i) professional services sought to further what client knew or should have known to be a *crime or fraud,* or (ii) communication relates to alleged *breach of duty between lawyer and client,* or (iii) two or more parties consult an attorney on a *matter of common interest* and the communication is offered by one of these parties against another.

   a. *Crime or fraud exception.* Prosecution for murder. Prosecution calls defendant's attorney who offers to testify that defendant said to him, "I just shot my parents. Should I claim insanity or self-defense?" Privileged? What if the defendant said to his attorney, "I plan to shoot my parents tomorrow. Get me a visa to South America." Privileged?

b. *Breach of duty between lawyer and client.* Action for malpractice by Client against Lawyer. Client claims Lawyer committed malpractice by failing to file complaint before statute of limitations expired. Lawyer offers to testify that, as she was about to file the complaint the day before the statute of limitations expired, Client said, "I changed my mind. I don't want to sue." Privileged?

B. *Psychotherapist-Patient & Social Worker-Client Privileges.* A communication between psychotherapist and patient, or licensed social worker and client, intended by patient/client to be confidential and made to facilitate rendition of professional psychological services is privileged in all civil and criminal proceedings unless waived by the patient/client. Same basic rules as for Attorney-Client privilege, i.e., patient/client must have intended that communication be confidential and purpose of communication must have been to facilitate professional services.

C. Doctor-patient privilege. There is no doctor-patient privilege under the FRE but most states, including California, have adopted the privilege. Remember that, in a federal court action arising under diversity jurisdiction, you will apply state privilege law on the MBE. Also, sometimes an MBE question will simply assume the existence of the doctor-patient privilege. Where the privilege applies, here is the law:

A patient has a privilege to prevent disclosure of information *confidentially* conveyed to a physician where the patient conveyed the information for the *purpose of obtaining diagnosis or treatment* and the information was *pertinent to diagnosis or treatment*.

1. *Information must be intended by patient to be confidential.* Personal injury action. Joe testifies defendant ran the red light. Defendant wishes to show that Joe has bad eyesight. In a prior unrelated case, Joe's attorney sent him to be examined by an eye doctor so the doctor could testify as an expert in that case. Is the information conveyed by Joe to the doctor during the eye examination privileged in the current personal injury action?

2. *Information conveyed to doctor must be pertinent to diagnosis or treatment.* Same case. Joe went to an eye doctor for medical treatment, not to get expert witness testimony. During the eye examination, Joe told doctor "I started having eye trouble when I was sent to prison for perjury." Are the results of the eye examination privileged? Is Joe's statement privileged?

3. Exceptions. Privilege does not apply (i) where the patient puts his physical condition in issue, as in a personal injury suit, (ii) where physician's services sought to aid in crime or fraud or to escape capture after a crime or tort, (iii) in case alleging breach of duty arising out of physician-patient relationship, as in a malpractice acton. Some states (including California) do not recognize the privilege in criminal cases.

D. Spousal Privileges. (i) Spousal testimonial privilege permits witness to refuse to testify against his/her spouse as to anything. Applies only in criminal cases. (ii) Spousal confidential communication privilege protects confidential spousal communications during marriage. Applies in both criminal and civil cases.

For both privileges, there must be a legally valid marriage. Neither privilege applies in civil action between spouses or in criminal prosecution where one spouse is charged with a crime against the other spouse or one of their kids.

1. Murder prosecution. Defendant's girlfriend saw defendant stab victim. While on bail, defendant and girlfriend marry. Can wife refuse to testify against defendant at trial?

2. Same case. Wife *wants* to testify against husband. Can he stop her?

3. Same case. Defendant was married to a different woman at time of stabbing. They are divorced at time of trial. At trial, defendant's former wife wants to testify that, when he came home the night in question, defendant said "I stabbed a guy tonight." Privileged?

VII. Judicial Notice. Process of establishing facts without presenting evidence. Two issues: (i) Facts appropriate for Judicial Notice, (ii) Procedure for taking Judicial Notice.

A. *Facts appropriate for Judicial Notice*: Courts can take judicial notice of facts not subject to reasonable dispute because they are either (i) generally known within the jurisdiction, or (ii) capable of accurate and ready determination by resort to sources whose accuracy cannot reasonably be questioned.

1. *Generally known facts.* Action for personal injuries. Plaintiff alleges that, at a Fourth of July party, defendant handed plaintiff a firecracker and ignited it, causing burns to plaintiff's hand. After conclusion of plaintiff's case, defendant moves to dismiss on the ground plaintiff offered no evidence to prove that an exploding firecracker can cause a burn. Can the court take judicial notice?

2. Same case. Plaintiff also alleges that the trauma of the exploding firecracker caused his hair to fall out. Assuming the judge was a barber before going to law school and knows that such a trauma can cause hair loss, may he take judicial notice of that fact?

3. *Facts established by sources of unquestionable accuracy.* Same case. Defendant alleges he was attending Sunday church services that day and was not at the party. May the judge consult a calendar and take judicial notice of the fact that the Fourth of July was not a Sunday?

B. *Procedure for taking Judicial Notice.* Party must request judicial notice to compel judicial notice and, if not requested, court has discretion to take judicial notice. If requested in civil case, court instructs jury it must accept noticed fact as conclusive. In criminal case, court instructs jury it may, but is not required to accept judicially noticed fact. Judicial notice may occur at any time, even on appeal.

CALIFORNIA DISTINCTIONS

I. Introduction.

    A. *When Do You Apply California Law?* Do not apply California evidence law on the MBE, where FRE applies. Apply California law *only* on an essay and *only* if the essay question directs you to do so. Otherwise, *apply the FRE on the essay.*

    B. *How different is California and federal evidence Law?* Most of the California Evidence Code (CEC) is similar, if not identical, to the FRE. The differences are described below. If there is no difference described below, *assume the law is the same.* An important difference in criminal cases is created by the California Constitution.

    C. *In a criminal case, mention the "Truth in Evidence" amendment to California Constitution (Proposition 8).* This makes all relevant evidence admissible in a criminal case, even if it is objectionable under the CEC. The constitution overrules the CEC.

    Important Exceptions to Prop. 8 (i.e., these objections are not overruled by Prop. 8): (i) exclusionary rules under US Constitution such as the Confrontation Clause, (ii) hearsay law, (iii) privilege law, (iv) limits on character evidence to prove the defendant's conduct, (v) limits on character evidence to prove the victim's conduct, (vi) the secondary evidence rule (California's version of the Best Evidence Rule), and (vii) CEC 352 (court's power to exclude if unfair prejudice substantially outweighs probative value).

        1. *Three step approach to applying California law on essay:* (i) raise all objections under CEC, (ii) for each objection, mention if Prop. 8 overrules the objection (Is the evidence relevant? Do one of the exceptions to Prop. 8 apply?), (iii) if evidence seems admissible under Prop. 8, balance under CEC 352.

II. Relevance.

    A. Relevance defined. *Federal and California:* Evidence is relevant if it has any tendency to make the existence of any fact that is of consequence to the determination of the action more or less probable than it would be without the evidence. *California only:* the fact of consequence also must be in dispute.

        1. Murder prosecution. Defendant admits to shooting the victim but pleads insanity. Prosecution witness testifies he saw defendant shoot victim. Relevant?

B. Exclusion of relevant evidence for policy reasons.

1. *Subsequent remedial measures or repairs. Federal and California:* Evidence of safety measures or repairs after an accident is inadmissible to prove negligence. *Federal only:* such evidence is also inadmissible to prove defective design in a products liability action based on theory of strict liability.

   a. Products liability action against toy manufacturer. Plaintiff alleges toy's sharp corners caused injury. To prove defective design, plaintiff offers evidence that defendant redesigned toy to remove sharp corners. Admissible?

2. *Settlements, offers to settle and related statements. Federal and California:* Evidence of settlements, offers to settle, and related statements are inadmissible to prove liability or fault. *California only:* discussions during mediation proceedings also inadmissible.

3. *Payment or offers to pay medical expenses. Federal and California:* Evidence of payments or offers to pay medical expenses is inadmissible when offered to prove liability for the injuries in question. *California* also makes inadmissible admissions of fact made in the course making such payments or offers. *Federal law* only excludes such statements if part of a settlement offer.

   a. Plaintiff falls down stairs in defendant's building. Defendant visits plaintiff in the hospital and says "I'll pay your hospital bill. I shouldn't have dropped that banana peel on the stairs." Admissible?

   b. Same case. Defendant says "If you will sign a release, I will pay your hospital bill. I shouldn't have dropped that banana peel on the stairs." Admissible?

4. *Expressions of sympathy. California* makes inadmissible in civil actions expressions of sympathy relating to suffering or death of an accident victim. But statements of fault made in connection with such an expression are not excluded. No comparable *Federal* rule.

   a. Personal injury action arising out of automobile collision. Defendant claims he was not at fault and that plaintiff was not hurt. Plaintiff offers evidence that at the scene of the accident defendant said to plaintiff, "I am so sorry you are badly hurt. I should not have run the red light." Admissible?

5. *Pleas later withdrawn, offers to plea, and related statements.* Inadmissible under both Federal Rules and CEC. *But does Prop. 8 make this admissible in California?* The law is unclear. On an essay, raise the issue and mention that, even if Prop. 8 applies to such evidence, the court still may exclude for unfair prejudice.

III. Character Evidence

  A. Character evidence in *civil* cases. Inadmissible to prove conduct. No *California exceptions. One exception under Federal Rules only:* where claim is based on sexual assault or child molestation. In such a case, defendant's prior acts of sexual assault or child molestation *are* admissible to prove defendant's conduct in this case.

    1. Civil tort action for assault arising out of rape. To prove defendant committed the tort, plaintiff offers evidence defendant committed other acts of sexual assault in the past. Admissible under Federal law? Under California law?

  B. Character evidence in *criminal* cases. Two major issues: Is character evidence admissible to prove conduct of defendant? Of the victim? Remember, there are separate doors to the admissibility of such evidence. Both are closed when the prosecution begins its case. Usually only the defendant can open these doors. Usually they are opened separately.

1. Admissibility of evidence of *defendant's* character to prove his conduct. *Federal and California:* Prosecution cannot be first to offer such evidence. Usually, prosecution may only rebut after defendant opens door by offering character evidence. *Prop. 8 does not change this rule in California.*

   Exceptions where prosecution may be first to offer evidence of defendant's character to prove defendant's conduct: (1) Federal and California—in cases of sexual assault or child molestation, prosecution may offer evidence that defendant committed other acts of sexual assault or child molestation, (2) Federal only—where court has admitted evidence of victim's character offered by accused, prosecution may offer evidence that accused has same character trait, (3) California only—in prosecution for crime of domestic violence, prosecution may offer evidence that defendant committed other acts of domestic violence, and (4) California only—where court has admitted evidence of victim's character for violence offered by accused, prosecution may offer evidence that accused has violent character (a narrower version of #2).

   a. *Trial begins with the door closed.* Defendant is charged with *non-sexual* assault of an elderly woman. He claims self-defense because she attacked him first. Defendant has a long criminal record of violent assaults. During its case in chief, the state offers evidence of this criminal record. Admissible in federal or state court?

   b. *Federal and California exception for sexual assault cases.* Defendant is charged with *sexual* assault of an elderly woman. He denies committing the assault. During its case in chief, the state offers evidence that defendant has committed other sexual assaults. Admissible in federal or state court?

   c. *California exception for domestic violence.* Defendant is charged with assaulting his wife, an act of domestic violence. He denies committing the assault. During its case in chief, the prosecution offers evidence defendant previously assaulted his wife. Admissible in federal or state court?

d. *When does evidence of victim's character open door to evidence of defendant's character? Broad Federal and narrow California exceptions.*

    1). Prosecution for assault. Victim claims that Defendant hit her. Defendant claims Victim hit Defendant first and that Defendant acted in self-defense. Defendant offers evidence that Victim has violent character. May prosecution now offer evidence that Defendant also has violent character?

    2). Prosecution for theft of diamond ring. Victim claims defendant stole her ring. Defendant claims ownership of the ring and claims it was Victim who stole it and that defendant just took it back. Defendant offers evidence that Victim has character for dishonesty. May prosecution now offer evidence that Defendant has character for dishonesty?

e. *On direct examination, reputation and opinion are OK, but not specific instances. On cross examination, all are admissible under FRE. CEC admits only reputation and opinion to prove defendant's character, whether on direct or cross.*

    1). Prosecution for assault. Defendant calls witness who testifies that, in his opinion, the defendant is gentle. On cross-exam, prosecutor asks "Did you know that the defendant kicked his evidence professor?" Admissible under FRE? The CEC? Prop. 8?

2. Admissibility of evidence of *victim's* character to prove his conduct. *Federal and California:* Most of the same rules apply. Prosecution cannot be first to offer character to prove conduct (the trial begins with the door closed). *Prop. 8 does not change this rule in California. Federal exception:*, in a homicide case the prosecution can be first to offer evidence that victim had peaceful character if defendant offers evidence victim attacked first. *Federal and California:* Defendant can be the first to

offer character of victim to prove conduct, then prosecution may rebut (the door is open). Under *FRE* reputation and opinion evidence admissible; no specific instances on direct, but OK on cross. In *California,* reputation, opinion, and specific instances permitted on both direct and cross.

a. *Trial begins with the door closed to victim's character.* Defendant is charged with *non-sexual* assault of an elderly woman. He alleges self-defense, claiming she attacked him first. During its case in chief, prosecution offers evidence that the little old lady who is alleged victim has a reputation for being peaceful and gentle. Admissible under California law? Under federal law? What if this was a homicide prosecution and defendant testified the elderly woman attacked first?

b. *Defendant can open the door.* Same case. Defense calls witness to testify that the little old lady is called "Psycho" back at the rest home because she has a reputation for being violent. Admissible under federal law? California?

c. *On direct, no specific instances under Federal Rules but OK under CEC.* Same case. On direct examination defense witness testifies that the victim once attacked her roommate. Admissible under federal law? California?

3. *Rape shield statute.* Limits defense evidence of alleged victim's character when offered to support defense of consent. *California rule is similar to Federal.* Prop.8 does not apply to evidence barred by this rule.

IV. Testimonial Evidence.

    A. Competency. Both Federal and California law require witnesses testify based on personal knowledge, have the ability to communicate, take an oath or make an affirmation to tell the truth, and claim to recall what they perceived. *California*: witness also must understand legal duty to tell the truth.

        1. *Grounds for disqualifying witnesses. Federal and California:* All witnesses are competent except for judge and jurors. *California* also disqualifies witnesses who were hypnotized before trial to help refresh recollection except, in a criminal case, witness hypnotized by police using procedures that protect against suggestion.

    B. Expert opinion. *Federal and California:* 5 requirements for admissibility. Opinion must be (i) helpful to jury, (ii) witness must be qualified, (iii) witness must believe in opinion to reasonable degree of certainty, (iv) opinion must be supported by a proper factual basis, and (v) opinion must be based on reliable principles reliably applied to the facts.

    Federal and California law differs on application of the last requirement to scientific opinions.

    Federal Daubert/Kumho Standard—Reliability of scientific opinions determined by *four factors*: publication/peer review, error rate, results are tested and there is ability to retest, and reasonable level of acceptance. As to non-scientific opinions, reliability determined ad hoc looking at facts and circumstances of the case.

    California Kelley/Frye General Acceptance Standard—Reliability of scientific opinions determined by *one factor*: the opinion must be based on principles generally accepted by experts in the field. This standard is not altered by Propostion 8 because it is a standard of *relevance*. (Remember, Proposition 8 only makes evidence admissible if it is relevant.) Kelley/Frye inapplicable to non-scientific opinions and medical opinions, reliability of which is based on facts and circumstances of the case.

        1. Murder prosecution. Defendant is Professor Gold. Prosecution expert offers to testify that a new DNA testing technique reveals perpetrator must be a bald law professor. While the validity of the technique is not generally accepted among scientists in the field of genetics, it has been *peer reviewed and published* in scientific journals, has been *tested and is subject to retesting,* has a *low error rate,* and has *a reasonable level of acceptance.* Admissible?

2. *Learned treatise hearsay exception. Federal:* Admissible to prove anything if treatise is accepted authority in field. *California:* Only admissible to show matters of general notoriety or interest, meaning this exception is very narrow and almost never applicable.

D. Evidence of Witness Credibility: Impeachment

1. *Impeachment by Prior Inconsistent Statement of witness now testifying at trial. Federal and California:* Not hearsay if offered only to impeach. *Federal:* If given under oath at trial or deposition, also not hearsay to prove truth of facts asserted, otherwise hearsay and inadmissible to prove those facts. *California:* Hearsay if offered to prove truth of facts asserted but admissible under exception, which extends to *all inconsistent statements of witness, whether or not under oath.*

   a. Action for personal injuries in auto accident. Plaintiff's witness testifies defendant ran the red light. On cross, defendant asks "Didn't you tell the police that defendant had the green light?" The witness answers "Yes." What is this relevant to prove? What is it admissible to prove?

   b. Same case. On cross, defendant asks "Didn't you testify at your deposition that defendant had the green light?" The witness answers "Yes." What is this admissible to prove?

2. *Impeachment with Prior Felony Conviction. Federal:* All felonies involving false statement (e.g. perjury, forgery, fraud) are admissible...no balancing of unfair prejudice against probative value except for old convictions (see p. 58). Convictions for felonies not involving false statement may be admissible but court must balance. *California:* All felonies involving "moral turpitude" are admissible but court must balance; felonies not involving moral turpitude are *inadmissible in California.* Prop. 8 does not make such felonies admissible because *convictions must involve a crime of moral turpitude to be relevant for impeachment.*

   Moral turpitude = crimes of lying, violence, theft, extreme recklessness, and sexual misconduct, but not crimes for merely negligent or unintentional acts.

a. Prosecution for tax fraud. Defendant testifies and admits his tax return did not report all his income, but claims this was unintentional. Prosecution offers evidence Defendant previously was convicted of felony perjury in an unrelated case. Admissible in federal and state court to impeach Defendant as a witness? Does court have discretion to balance probative value against unfair prejudice?

b. Same case. Prosecution offers evidence that Defendant was previously convicted of felony child molestation in an unrelated case. Admissible in federal and state court to impeach Defendant as a witness? Does court have discretion to balance probative value against unfair prejudice?

c. Same case. Prosecution offers evidence Defendant was previously convicted of felony involuntary manslaughter in an unrelated case. Admissible in federal and state court to impeach Defendant as a witness? What is the effect of Prop. 8 in California?

3. *Impeachment with Prior Misdemeanor Convictions. Federal:* All misdemeanors involving false statement are admissible…again there is no balancing of unfair prejudice against probative value except for old convictions (see p. 58). All other misdemeanor convictions are inadmissible to impeach. *California:* The CEC makes misdemeanor convictions inadmissible to impeach. But because of Prop. 8, misdemeanors can be admitted in a criminal case if involving a crime of moral turpitude (lying, violence, theft, extreme recklessness, and sexual misconduct), subject to balancing probative value v. unfair prejudice. This means misdemeanors are inadmissible in California to impeach in a *civil* case.

a. Action for breach of contract. Defendant testifies he never entered into a contract with plaintiff. On cross-examination, plaintiff asks "Isn't it true that you were convicted last year of a misdemeanor for lying on your application for a driver's license?" Defendant answers "Yes." Admissible in federal and state court?

b. Prosecution for bank robbery. Defendant testifies he was in another city when the robbery happened. On cross-examination, prosecutor asks, "Isn't it true that you were convicted last year of misdemeanor theft of a church poor box?" Defendant answers, "Yes." Admissible in federal and state court?

4. *Final points on conviction evidence (felony and misdemeanor).* If the conviction is otherwise admissible under the above rules, extrinsic evidence can be used under Federal and California law to prove the conviction. If the conviction is otherwise admissible under the above rules, but it is more than 10 years since the conviction or release from prison (whichever is later), it is inadmissible under Federal law unless probative value outweighs prejudice. No such specific rule in California. But under above rules California courts may balance, which permits consideration of any factor bearing on probative value, including age of conviction.

a. Prosecution for bank robbery. Defendant testifies and denies involvement. Prosecutor offers a certified copy of a judgment showing defendant was released from prison in 1988 after serving time for felony perjury. Admissible?

4. *Non-Conviction Misconduct Bearing on Truthfulness.* *Federal:* Admissible in civil and criminal cases, subject to balancing; must be act of lying; extrinsic evidence inadmissible but may ask witness about her misconduct on cross. *California:* Inadmissible under CEC but Prop 8 makes it admissible in criminal cases if relevant; to be relevant the misconduct must be act of moral turpitude (lying, violence, theft, extreme recklessness, or sexual misconduct); both cross-examination and extrinsic evidence permitted, subject to balancing.

   a. Action for breach of contract. On cross of plaintiff, defense asks "Isn't it true you lied on your driver's license application?" Plaintiff answers, "Yes." Admissible?

   b. Prosecution for bank robbery. Defendant testifies and denies involvement. Prosecutor asks defendant about lying on his driver's license application but defendant denies it. Prosecutor offers the application into evidence. Admissible?

   c. Same case. Prosecutor asks defendant if he stole office supplies at work. Defendant admits to the theft. Admissible?

V. Hearsay. *California:* Hearsay law is exempt from coverage of Truth in Evidence Amendment to California Constitution (Prop. 8). This means that, even in a criminal case, the usual rules of evidence apply.

A. Exceptions/Exemptions to the Hearsay Rule. While federal law has both exemptions to the hearsay definition and exceptions to the rule making hearsay inadmissible, California law has only exceptions.

1. *Admission of party opponent. Federal and California:* Admission = statement by party, or someone whose statement is attributable to a party, offered by a party opponent. *Federal: exemption* to usual hearsay definition and, thus, not hearsay under Federal Rules. *California:* hearsay but admissible under *exception* in California.

59

a. *Vicarious party admissions. Federal and California:* Statement of authorized spokesperson for party is treated as admission of that party. *Federal:* Statement by employee of party is party admission of employer if statement concerned matter within scope of employment and made during employment relationship. *California:* Statement by employee of party is party admission of employer only where negligent conduct of that employee is basis for employer's liability in the case under *respondeat superior.* In other words, *employer is responsible for employee's words only if also responsible because of that employee's conduct.*

1). Negligence action against UPS. Plaintiff testifies UPS truck crashed through her kitchen window and driver said, "I fell asleep while driving." Admissible?

2) Same case except driver acted properly and accident was caused by faulty brakes. Driver said, "The company mechanic sometimes forgets to check the brakes." Admissible?

2. *Prior inconsistent statement of witness. Federal and California:* PIS not hearsay if offered just to impeach. *Federal:* If given under oath, exemption to usual hearsay definition and not hearsay even if offered to prove truth of facts asserted, otherwise hearsay and inadmissible to prove those facts. *California:* Hearsay if offered to prove truth of facts asserted but admissible under exception, which extends to *all inconsistent statements of witness, whether or not under oath.* (See p. 56 for hypos).

3. *Prior consistent statement of witness now testifying at trial.* Admissible under both Federal and California law if made before bribe or inconsistent statement. Not hearsay under FRE *exemption* to hearsay definition; hearsay but within *exception* under CEC.

4. *Declaration against interest exception. Federal and California:* A statement by unavailable declarant is admissible if, at time it was made, it was against financial interest of declarant or would have subjected declarant to criminal liability. *Federal only:* In a criminal case, evidence offered to exculpate defendant (e.g., a confession of an unavailable declarant) defendant must offer "corroborating circumstances" showing that the declarant's statement is trustworthy. *California only:* Also within the exception is a statement against social interest because it risks making declarant an object of "hatred, ridicule, or social disgrace in the community."

a. Action for divorce. To prove adultery by husband, Donald Trump, Wife offers statement of Paris Hilton, a permanent resident of a psychiatric hospital in Europe, made during an interview for America's Most Disgusting Celebrities: "I got drunk and had an affair with Trump." Admissible?

Federal and California: Declarant is unavailable if court exempts declarant from testifying due to privilege, declarant is dead or sick, or proponent of statement cannot procure declarant's attendance by process or other reasonable means. Following are two additional bases for unavailability applicable only under *Federal* law only: declarant refuses to testify despite court order, declarant's memory fails on the subject of her statement. If declarant suffers total memory loss or refuses to testify out of fear, *California* regards declarant as unavailable.

5. *Former testimony exception.* Testimony given in earlier proceeding or deposition by a witness now unavailable is admissible in current proceeding if:

Federal and California: party against whom testimony is now offered was a party in the earlier proceeding, had *opportunity* to examine the witness, and its *motive* to conduct that exam was similar to motive it has now, or

Federal only: in a *civil* case, party against whom testimony is now offered was not a party in the earlier proceeding but is in a privity-type relationship with someone who was a party to that earlier proceeding (a "*predecessor in interest*") and who had an opportunity and an interest to conduct that exam similar to the interests of the party against whom testimony is now offered, or

California only: in a *civil* case, party against whom testimony is now offered was not a party in the earlier proceeding but a party in that earlier proceeding had an opportunity to examine the witness and an interest to conduct that exam similar to the interests of the party against whom the testimony is now offered, or

California only: the former testimony is offered *against* the person who offered it in evidence in her own behalf in the earlier proceeding, or against a successor in interest of such person.

Related California law: deposition testimony given in the same civil action in which the hearsay is offered at trial is admissible for all purposes if the deponent is unavailable at trial or lives more than 150 miles from the courthouse. *Otherwise, the former testimony exception does not apply to deposition testimony given in the same case in which the hearsay is offered at trial.*

a. *Federal predecessor in interest v. California similar interest standards.* An airplane crashes, killing passengers X and Y. Estate of X sues for wrongful death and Expert testified for Airline in that case. Expert then died. Estate of Y now sues Airline and Airline offers transcript of Expert's testimony. Admissible?

b. *FT offered against party who offered it in previous proceeding.* First proceeding was civil nuisance suit brought in small claims court against Airline for noise pollution. Airline offered Expert's testimony in that case. Expert is now dead. Estate of Y now offers that testimony in wrongful death case against Airline. Admissible, even though issues in this case are different?

6. *Dying declaration exception. Federal:* Declaration by person who believes he is about to die and describes cause/circumstances leading to his death is admissible in a civil action and in a homicide prosecution if declarant unavailable. Declarant need not die. *California:* Exception applies in all civil and criminal cases and *declarant must be dead.*

7. *Present sense impression exception.* No need to show declarant unavailable. *Federal:* A statement describing or explaining an event or condition made while declarant was perceiving the event or condition or immediately thereafter. *California exception is narrower:* A statement explaining conduct of the declarant made while the declarant was engaged in that conduct.

a. Murder prosecution. Defendant claims self-defense because, he claims, Victim acted in a threatening manner. Witness testifies she called Victim on night of the murder. Victim and witness were talking on the phone when Victim said "Joe [the defendant] just walked in the room and it looks like he wants to show me his survival knife. I am smiling and waving at him. I'll call you right back." Is the statement admissible to show defendant was in the room with a knife? Admissible to show Victim was acting in a friendly way?

1) *Related California Exception: Statement describing infliction or threat of physical abuse (the "OJ Exception"). Watch out for Confrontation issue!* Statement made at or near time of injury or threat, by unavailable declarant, describing or explaining infliction or threat, in writing or recorded or made to *police* or medical professional, under trustworthy circumstances.

2) Murder prosecution. The government offers the sound recording of a telephone call Victim made to 911 in which she calmly stated, "My former husband [Defendant] kicked me in the head 20 minutes ago." When the police arrived Victim was unconscious. She later died of a brain injury. Admissible under Federal or California hearsay law to show the Defendant kicked Victim? If admissible under hearsay law, is there a Confrontation Clause objection?

8. *Excited utterance exception. Federal and California:* Statements relating to startling event or condition are admissible when made while declarant was still under stress of excitement caused by event or condition. No need to show declarant unavailable.

9. *Exception for declaration of then existing physical or mental condition. Federal and California:* A statement of declarant's then existing physical or mental condition or state of mind is *admissible to show the condition or state of mind.* But astatement describing a memory or belief is *not admissible to prove the fact remembered or believed.*

10. *Exception for statement of past or present mental or physical condition made for diagnosis or treatment.* No need to show declarant unavailable. *Federal:* A statement describing past or present mental or physical condition of the declarant or of another person is admissible if made for and pertinent to medical diagnosis or treatment. *California exception is narrower:* A statement of past *or* present mental or physical condition is admissible if made for medical diagnosis or treatment, *but only if the declarant is a minor describing an act of child abuse or neglect.*

a.   Personal injury action. Plaintiff, an adult, offers to testify that when he was taken to emergency room he told the doctor, "My back is killing me." Admissible?

b.   *Related California exception:* A statement of declarant's past physical or mental condition, including a statement of intention, is admissible to prove that condition if it is an issue in the case—no requirement that statement be made for medical purposes. Declarant must be unavailable.

   1). Same case. Plaintiff told a second patient in the emergency room, "I was feeling fine before the accident." If plaintiff is now in a coma, can the other patient testify as to what plaintiff said?

11. *Business records exception.* No need to show declarant unavailable. *Federal:* Record of events, conditions, opinions or diagnoses kept in course of regularly conducted business activity is admissible if made at or near time of matters described, by person with knowledge of the facts, and it was regular practice of business to make such record. Court may exclude if untrustworthy. *California exception does not refer to opinions or diagnoses, but courts still will admit simple opinions and diagnoses:* A record of events or conditions kept in course of regularly conducted business activity is admissible if made at or near time of matters described, by a person with knowledge of the facts in that record, and record is trustworthy.

a.   Action for physical & psychological injuries arising out of auto accident. Plaintiff offers hospital record in which orthopedic surgeon stated "Plaintiff has broken leg" and in which psychiatrist stated "Plaintiff is suffering from post traumatic stress syndrome, which is likely to be permanent." Admissible?

12. *Public records exception.* No need to show declarant unavailable. *Federal:* The record of a public office is admissible if it within *one* of the following categories: (i) the record describes the activities or policies of the office; (ii) the record describes matters observed pursuant to duty imposed by law (but not police reports in criminal cases); or (iii) the record contains factual findings resulting from an investigation made pursuant to authority granted by law, unless untrustworthy. In a criminal case, prosecution cannot use (iii). *California does not place same restrictions on prosecution:* Record made by a public employee is admissible if making record was within scope of her duties, record was made at or near the time of the matters described, and circumstances indicate trustworthiness.

    a. Criminal prosecution for vehicular homicide. Prosecution offers into evidence police report stating that police officer investigating the accident saw an empty vodka bottle in the cup-holder next to driver's seat in defendant's car. The bottle, with defendant's fingerprints on it, has already been admitted. Admissible?

13. *Exception for judgment of conviction.* No need to show declarant unavailable. *Federal:* A felony conviction is admissible in both civil and criminal cases to prove any fact essential to the judgment, but when offered by prosecution for purposes other than impeachment, judgments against persons other than the accused are inadmissible. *California:* The specific exception for convictions applies only in civil cases. Prop 8 does not change this hearsay law. But Prop. 8 permits the prosecutor or defendant in a criminal case to impeach a witness using a *criminal conviction (felony or misdemeanor) if it involves moral turpitude.* Further, a certified copy of a judgment of conviction is admissible under the California public records exception in both civil and criminal cases.

    a. Prosecution for being a felon in possession of a firearm. Defendant denies he is a felon. The prosecutor offers into evidence a certified copy of the judgment of conviction of defendant for robbery, a felony. Admissible?

VI. Writings and other Physical Evidence.

   A. Authentication.

      1. Ancient documents. If document is (*Federal* 20, *California* 30) years old or more, does not on its face present irregularities (e.g., erasures), and was found in a place of natural custody (i.e., where you would expect such documents to be found), authenticity is established.

      2. Self-authenticating writings. For certain writings, authentication is unnecessary. These include certified copies of public documents (deeds), acknowledged documents (i.e., documents where the original signature is attested before a notary to be valid), official publications (government pamphlets), newspapers, periodicals, business records (*Federal only*), and trade inscriptions (*Federal only*).

   B. Best Evidence Rule (*Called "Secondary Evidence Rule" in California*). Exempt from Prop. 8 in *California*. This means that, even in a criminal case, the Secondary Evidence Rule applies. This rule applies only where evidence is offered to prove the *contents of a writing* (defined to include any tangible collection of data). The rule requires proof of contents with original, but with many exceptions.

      1. Other than the original, what tangible evidence is admissible to prove contents of a writing? *Federal:* Duplicates usually also admissible. "Duplicate" = a copy of original produced by same impression that produced the original (e.g., a carbon copy) or by a machine (e.g., photocopier, camera). Handwritten copy is not a duplicate. *California:* Admits duplicates and other written evidence of contents of original, such as handwritten notes.

      2. When is testimony admissible to prove contents of a writing? *Federal and California:* Testimony regarding contents of writing may be admissible where original lost or destroyed, unless bad faith by proponent of testimony.

VII. Privileges. *California:* Most privilege law is exempt from coverage of Truth in Evidence Amendment to California Constitution. This means that, even in a criminal case, the usual rules of privilege apply. *Federal:* In a civil suit brought in federal court under diversity jurisdiction, *state* privilege law applies.

A. *Attorney-Client Privilege. Federal and California:* A communication between attorney and client or their representatives intended by client to be confidential and made to facilitate rendition of professional legal services is privileged unless waived by the client.

When is a communication from a corporation employee to the corporation's attorney privileged? *Federal:* privilege applies to communications from employees/agents if they were authorized by the corporation to make the communication to the lawyer on behalf of the corporation. *California:* privilege applies to communications from employee/agent if she is the natural person to speak to the lawyer on behalf of the corporation in the matter (*e.g.*, the corporation's in-house counsel or CEO), or employee/agent did something for which the corporation may be held liable, and the corporation instructed her to tell its lawyer what happened. As applied, there is no significant difference in the scope of these standards.

1. *No privilege for mere witness who happens to be an employee.* Action for personal injuries arising out of collision between Corporation's delivery truck and another vehicle in Corporation's parking lot. Employee of Corporation happened to be parking his car at the time and witnessed the accident. His supervisor orders him to write a statement for the Corporation's lawyers describing what he saw. Privileged?

2. Exceptions. *Federal and California:* Privilege does not apply where (i) professional services were sought to further *crime or fraud,* or (ii) two or more parties consult an attorney on a *matter of common interest* and the communication is offered by one of these parties against another, or (iii) communication relates to alleged *breach of duty between lawyer and client. Additional exception in California only:* privilege does not apply where lawyer reasonably believes disclosure of communication is necessary to prevent crime that is likely to result in death or substantial bodily harm.

   a. Client meets with his attorney and states, "I want you to look for some tax shelters for me because my rich parents are about to have a fatal accident." The attorney called the police, who arrived at defendant's home too late to prevent the "accident." Is the client's statement admissible?

B. *Doctor-Patient and Psychotherapist-Patient Privileges.* *Federal:* There is a psychotherapist-patient privilege but no doctor-patient privilege. (But remember, sometimes MBE questions assumes existence of Doctor-Patient Privilege.) *California:* Both privileges exist.

1. Exceptions. *Federal and California exceptions for both privileges:* (i) where the patient puts his physical or mental condition in issue, as in a personal injury suit, (ii) where professional services were sought to aid in crime or fraud or to escape capture after a crime or tort, (iii) in case alleging breach of duty between patient and doctor or psychotherapist, as in a malpractice action. *California only:* (i) psychotherapist privilege does not apply if the psychotherapist has reasonable cause to believe that the patient is a danger to himself or others, and that disclosure is necessary to end the danger, (ii) doctor-patient privilege does not apply in criminal cases or to information that doctor is required to report to a public office (*e.g.*, gun-shot wounds and some communicable diseases).

C. *Spousal Privileges.* (i) Spousal testimonial privilege permits witness to refuse to testify against his/her spouse as to anything. *Federal:* applies only in criminal cases. *California:* applies in civil and criminal cases and spouse of party is privileged not even to be called to witness stand. (ii) *Federal and California:* Spousal confidential communication privilege may apply in any case and protects confidential spousal communications during marriage.

D. *Other California Privileges.* California also recognizes (i) privilege for confidential communications between a counselor and a victim of sexual assault or domestic violence, (ii) privilege for penitential communications between penitent and clergy, and (iii) immunity from contempt of court for news reporter who refuses to disclose sources.

VIII. Judicial Notice

A. *Procedure for taking Judicial Notice.*

1. Party must request judicial notice to compel judicial notice and, if not requested, court has discretion to take judicial notice. *California exception: whether requested or not, court must take judicial notice of matters generally known within jurisdiction.*

2. *Federal:* In civil case, court instructs jury that it must accept judicially noticed fact. In criminal case, court instructs jury it may accept judicially noticed fact, but is not required to do so. *California:* Court instructs jury that it must accept judicially noticed fact in both civil and criminal cases.

Performance Test Workshops

Professor Peter Jan Honigsberg

barbri®

Performance Test Workshops

By

Professor Peter Jan Honigsberg

PERFORMANCE TEST WORKSHOP 1

BAR EXAM SCHEDULE

	TUES.	WED.	THURS.
AM	3 ESSAYS	100 MBE	3 ESSAYS
PM	PERFORMANCE TEST	100 MBE	PERFORMANCE TEST

<u>GRADING</u>

Grades range from 40% to 100%

---

6 Essays @ 100 points   =   600

2 Performance Tests @ 200 points   =   <u>400</u>

1000
total points
on written portion

PARTS OF PERFORMANCE EXAM

Library

Client's File

Task Memo

SKILLS TESTED ON PERFORMANCE EXAM

Legal Analysis

Fact Gathering

Fact Analysis

Tactics/Problem Solving

Ethical Considerations

- - - - - - - - - - - - - - - -

Communication

<u>**SAMPLE TASK MEMO**</u>

Popper & Sayles, LLP

245 Vaughn Drive
Rosslyn, Columbia 22222

MEMORANDUM

TO: Applicant

FROM: Robert Popper

DATE: July 26, 2007

RE: Tanya and Mark Gross v. Baker

Our clients are Tanya and Mark Gross, children of Claude Gross, a prominent local businessman who recently died. Shortly before his death, while hospitalized and mentally deteriorated, he married his companion, Maxine Baker, and amended his will to leave her most of his property. Tanya and Mark believe that both actions are invalid and do not want Ms. Baker to benefit from taking advantage of Claude's debilitated condition.

Maxine Baker was represented by Rudolph Philmore in an action that Tanya and Mark brought to enjoin their father's marriage to Ms. Baker. I will contact him shortly to see if we can settle these matters prior to filing a lawsuit. Please prepare a letter to Mr. Philmore that persuasively explains that our clients should get their father's entire estate because:

    A. The bequest to Claude's first wife Irene is no longer effective; and

    B. The bequest to Maxine is invalid; and

    C. The marriage to Maxine should be annulled because of Claude's incapacity.

Do not discuss fraud or undue influence. Also, in connection with your discussion of the validity of the bequest to Maxine (Part B above) do not discuss Claude's mental capacity to execute the codicil. Another associate is looking into those issues.

This case will be won or lost on our ability to marshal facts to support our legal position. The ability to weave the facts of our clients' case into our argument and to anticipate the factual arguments that will be raised against our position, therefore, are critical.

SAMPLE TASK MEMO

Jackson County
Office of the General Counsel
1293 Jonesboro Road
Ana, Columbia

July 24, 2001

TO: Applicant

FROM: Ann Ruger, General Counsel

RE: Jerome Sloane

We have been asked by Dr. Sylvia Garwin, Director, Jackson County Department of Health & Human Services, whether we can involuntarily commit a patient, Jerome Sloane, to the Jackson County Hospital. We have considerable experience with involuntary commitment of patients for psychiatric reasons. The problem here, however, is that the patient is refusing treatment for tuberculosis (TB). I've included the relevant Columbia statue dealing with contagious diseases. Keep in mind that it was passed in 1912 and I'm not sure of its continuing vitality.

I will be meeting with Dr. Garwin tomorrow to advise her what options are available for dealing with Mr. Sloane. Please draft a memorandum addressing the following:

Task A: Under the given factual circumstances, what persuasive arguments Dr. Garwin's department can make to lawfully commit Mr. Sloane to the County Hospital for treatment (1) until he completes his treatment program entirely or (2) at least until he is no longer contagious.

Task B: In connection with each of those options, what statutory and constitutional authority there is that would allow such a commitment and what standards and procedures Dr. Garwin's department would need to follow.

Task C: In the event the court does not commit Mr. Sloane for the period of time necessary to complete his treatment program entirely or even until he is no longer contagious, what other creative solutions the County might consider to protect the public and ensure that Mr. Sloane completes his treatment program entirely.

Remember, Dr. Garwin is an experienced public health official familiar with legal matters. She will want as much detail in your legal analysis as I would.

COLUMBIA STATE UNIVERSITY

College Park, Columbia 55512

Office of University Counsel

MEMORANDUM   February 25, 1992

To: APPLICANT, ASSISTANT UNIVERSITY COUNSEL

From: Gary Leedes, University Counsel

Re: Legislation Creating a Civil Action for Offensive Speech

President Gibbs has directed our office to try to convince State Representative Patrick Beaty, Chairman of the House Judiciary Committee, to introduce legislation creating a civil action in Columbia for damages for speech attacking another's race, religion or national origin. The President believes such legislation will help curb the rise of harassment of foreign students we have experienced on our campus.

As you know, the United States District Court in Doe v. Columbia State University enjoined enforcement of the University's anti-discrimination policy drafted by our staff. As a result of this court action, the University is without any effective means of dealing with the increasing incidents of intimidating, hostile or demeaning behavior directed at our foreign students.

President Gibbs has spoken with Representative Beaty about this matter. While Beaty is concerned about the increasing incidence of harassment, he appears reluctant to use the legislative process to stem this conduct. Our task is to convince him that from legal and policy perspectives a tort making persons liable for offensive words and conduct is appropriate legislation.

I have arranged with Beaty to send him a draft of a proposed statute and a letter setting forth our reasons for seeking this legislation. I prepared a rough draft of the legislation. Please do the following:

1.   Prepare a memorandum for me analyzing my draft. Please explain whether the suggested language meets the University's goals and is consistent with constitutional requirements. Redraft the proposed statute if you believe changes are required to meet the University's goals. Be sure to explain how those changes improve the legislation and are consistent with constitutional requirements.

2.   Prepare a letter from me to Representative Beaty that addresses his concerns and will persuade him of the need for legislation creating a civil action for racist speech. It is important at this stage that we convince Beaty that the problems we are facing are serious and that the tort approach is necessary and will be effective.

OUTLINE OF "COLUMBIA STATE UNIVERSITY" TASK MEMO

1. Memo analyzing draft of legislation

    Does language meet university's goals?

    Is it consistent with constitutional requirements?

    Redraft statute if changes required to meet university's goals

        Explain how changes:

            Improve legislation

            Are consistent with constitutional requirements

2. Letter to Rep. Beaty

        Address his concerns

        Persuade him of need for civil action for racist speech

        Convince him:

            Problems are serious

            Tort approach is necessary

            Tort approach will be effective

SAMPLE GENERAL DIRECTIONS

OCHOA v. CMH

INSTRUCTIONS

1. You will have three hours to complete this session of the examination. This performance test is designed to evaluate your ability to handle a select number of legal authorities in the context of a factual problem involving a client.

2. The problem is set in the fictional State of Columbia, one of the United States.

3. You will have two sets of materials with which to work: a File and a Library.

4. The File contains factual materials about your case. The first document is a memorandum containing the instructions for the tasks you are to complete.

5. The Library contains the legal authorities needed to complete the tasks. The case reports may be real, modified, or written solely for the purpose of this performance test. If the cases appear familiar to you, do not assume that they are precisely the same as you have read before. Read each thoroughly, as if it were new to you. You should assume that cases were decided in the jurisdictions and on the dates shown. In citing cases from the Library, you may use abbreviations and omit page citations.

6. You should concentrate on the materials provided, but you should also bring to bear on the problem your general knowledge of the law. What you have learned in law school and elsewhere provides the general background for analyzing the problem; the File and Library provide the specific materials with which you must work.

7. Although there are no restrictions on how you apportion your time, you should probably allocate at least 90 minutes to reading and organizing before you begin preparing your response.

8. Your response will be graded on its compliance with instructions and on its content, thoroughness, and organization.

APPROACH

1.   Read the General Directions

2.   Read the Task Memo

3.   Outline the Task Memo

4.   Tear Out the Task Memo

5.   Tear Out and Read Instruction Sheet (if one is provided)

6.   Read and Outline the Library and File

7.   Complete All of the Above in 85 Minutes

8.   Take 5-10 Minute Break / Review Task Memo / Think Organization

9.   Write Answer in 85-90 Minutes

Westside Community Corporation

LIBRARY

SAMPLE HONIGSBERG GRID:

FACTS & ISSUES

AUTHORITIES	Facts (of each case)	*Issue #1 (e.g. defamation)	*Issue #2 (e.g. right of privacy)	*Issue #3 (if necessary)	*Issue #4 (if necessary)
Name of First Case					
Name of Second Case					
Name of Third Case (if necessary)					
Name of Fourth Case (if necessary)					
Name of Fifth Case (if necessary)					

*Identify **by name** at the top of your grid each issue you intend to include. The legal issues usually come from the cases.

<u>Westside Community Corporation</u>

THE FOUR OR FIVE SHEETS OF PAPER YOU SHOULD HAVE BEFORE YOU WHEN YOU WRITE YOUR ANSWER

Task Memo (torn out)	Document Instruction sheet (torn out - if one is included in the file)	Outline of Task Memo	Outline of Library (Using torn out table of contents for organization) *or* Honigsberg Grid	Outline of File (Using torn out table of contents for organization)

Reminder: Take 5-10 Minute Break

Then: Write Answer in 85-90 Minutes

EXAMPLES OF LEGAL ANALYSIS DOCUMENTS
THE BAR EXAMINERS HAVE USED ON PREVIOUS PERFORMANCE EXAMS

Memo of Law

Memo of Points & Authorities

(Brief in Support of Motion)

(Persuasive Memo)

Trial Brief

Appellate Brief

Memo to Judge

Client Letter

Letter to Opposing Attorney

Position Paper

(e.g., Persuasive Letter to Agency)

Theory of the Case Memorandum

Case Plan

Early Neutral Evaluation Proceedings

<u>DOCUMENT INSTRUCTION SHEET</u>

COLUMBIA PRISON ASSISTANCE PROGRAM
An Equal Justice Project of the Columbia Bar Association

MEMORANDUM   August 1, 1992

To: To All Lawyers
From: Director of Litigation
Re: <u>Persuasive Briefs</u>

To clarify the expectations of the program and to provide guidance to lawyers, all persuasive briefs, including Briefs in Support of Motions (also called Memoranda of Points and Authorities), whether directed to an appellate court, trial court, or administrative officer, shall conform to the following guidelines.

All briefs shall include a concise statement of the jurisdictional (i.e., statutory or other) basis for the case and a Statement of Facts. Select carefully the facts that are pertinent to the legal arguments. The facts must be stated accurately, although emphasis is not improper. The aim of the Statement of Facts is to persuade the tribunal that the facts support our client's position.

The program follows the practice of writing crafted subject headings which will illustrate the arguments they cover. The argument heading should succinctly summarize the reasons the tribunal should take the position you are advocating. A heading should be a specific application of a rule of law to the facts of the case and not a bare legal or factual conclusion or a statement of an abstract principle. For example, <u>Improper</u>: THE PRISONER'S RIGHTS WERE VIOLATED. <u>Proper</u>: REQUIRING THE PETITIONER TO TAKE PSYCHOTROPIC MEDICATION IN THE ABSENCE OF A HEARING ESTABLISHING VIOLENT BEHAVIOR CONSTITUTES CRUEL AND UNUSUAL PUNISHMENT UNDER THE EIGHTH AMENDMENT.

The body of each argument should analyze applicable legal authority and persuasively argue how the facts and law support our client's position. Authority supportive of our client's position should be emphasized, but contrary authority also should generally be cited, addressed in the argument, and explained or distinguished. Do not reserve arguments for reply or supplemental briefs.

The lawyer should not prepare a table of contents, a table of cases, a summary of argument, or the index. These will be prepared, where required, after the draft is approved.

ALTERNATIVE DOCUMENT INSTRUCTION SHEET – JULY 2009

Sundquist & Davis
Attorneys at Law
12 Manning Blvd.
Columbia City, Columbia

MEMORANDUM

To: Attorneys

From: Executive Committee

Re: **Persuasive Briefs in Support of Motions for Summary Judgment**

To clarify the expectations of the firm and to provide guidance to attorneys, all persuasive briefs in support of motions for summary judgment to be filed in state court shall conform to the following guidelines.

All of these documents shall start with a Statement of Uncontested Facts that itemizes the facts that are material to support our motion and explains why each of the material facts is undisputed. The attorney must sift through the facts in the file and draft a statement that persuasively shows that there is indeed no genuine issue of material fact. This requires a careful comparison of the opposing side's characterization of the facts in the file. The format and style shall be as follows:

> Fact #1:   The May 1, 2005 memorandum was signed by the President of the company. Undisputed Because: The President of the company admitted this fact in paragraph 2 of her affidavit.
>
> Fact #2:   The meeting between James and Spellman occurred on March 1, 2006. Undisputed Because: This fact is alleged in paragraph 10 of the plaintiff's complaint and is admitted in paragraph 14 of the defendant's answer.

Following the Statement of Uncontested Facts, the attorney must then argue, applying the law to the facts, and move on to show that, in light of the uncontested facts, our client is entitled to judgment as

26

a matter of law.

This office follows the practice of writing carefully crafted subject headings that illustrate the arguments they cover. The argument heading should succinctly summarize the reasons the tribunal should take the position the attorney is advocating. A heading should be a specific application of a rule of law to the facts of the case and not a bare legal or factual conclusion or statement of an abstract principle. For example, **IMPROPER:** DEFENDANT HAD SUFFICIENT MINIMUM CONTACTS TO ESTABLISH PERSONAL JURISDICTION. **PROPER:** A RADIO STATION LOCATED IN THE STATE OF FRANKLIN THAT BROADCASTS INTO THE STATE OF COLUMBIA, RECEIVES REVENUE FROM ADVERTISERS LOCATED IN THE STATE OF COLUMBIA, AND HOLDS ITS ANNUAL MEETING IN THE STATE OF COLUMBIA HAS SUFFICIENT MINIMUM CONTACTS TO ALLOW COLUMBIA COURTS TO ASSERT PERSONAL JURISDICTION.

The body of each argument should analyze applicable legal authority and persuasively argue how the facts and law support our position. Authority supportive of our position should be emphasized, but contrary authority should generally be cited, addressed in the argument, and explained or distinguished. Do not reserve arguments for reply or supplemental briefs. Attorneys should not prepare a table of contents, a table of cases, or the index. These will be prepared after the draft is approved.

<u>ALTERNATIVE DOCUMENT INSTRUCTION SHEET</u>

CHILTON COUNTY DISTRICT ATTORNEY
PRE-TRAIL UNIT
Chilton County Courthouse
Chilton, Columbia 01010

FROM: Marie Padilla, Unit Chief

RE: <u>Persuasive Briefs and Memoranda</u>

<u>Office Memorandum 121</u>

TO: All Members of the Unit

     All persuasive briefs or memoranda such as memoranda of points and authorities to be filed in support or opposition of pre-trial motions shall conform to the following guidelines.

     1.   <u>Statement of Facts.</u> All of these documents shall contain a Statement of Facts. Select carefully the facts that are pertinent to the legal arguments. The facts must be stated accurately, although emphasis is not improper. The aim of the Statement of Facts is to persuade the tribunal that the facts supports our position.

     2.   <u>Questions Presented.</u> Following the Statement of Facts, the document shall include a section entitled Question(s) Presented. Your objective in this section is to state the precise question or questions presented in the case. Simply to present the question "was there probable cause?" or "was the confession voluntary?" is insufficient. We want to present the questions as a combination of the legally relevant facts combined with the precise point of law. For example, <u>Improper:</u> DID THE ARRESTING OFFICER HAVE PROBABLE CAUSE TO DETAIN THE DEFENDANT? <u>Proper:</u> WAS THE ARRESTING OFFICER , WITH A DETAILED DESCRIPTION OF THE ASSAILANT AND A GENERAL DESCRIPTION OF THE VEHICLE IN WHICH THE ASSAILANT LEFT THE SCENE OF THE CRIME, JUSTIFIED IN STOPPING A VEHICLE WHICH FIT THE DESCRIPTION AND WAS COMING FROM THE AREA IN WHICH THE CRIME TOOK PLACE? As with the Statement of Facts, the issues must be stated accurately, although emphasis is not improper.

     3.   <u>Summary of Argument.</u> After the Question(s) Presented, there must be a brief Summary of Argument. In not more than one brief paragraph per issue, the Summary must succinctly and persuasively encapsulate the argument in the State's favor.

4.   <u>Argument.</u> Following the Summary of Argument, the Argument should begin. The Unit follows the practice of writing carefully crafted subject headings that illustrate the arguments they cover. The argument heading should succinctly summarize the reasons the tribunal should take the position you are advocating. A heading should be a specific application of a rule of law to the facts of the case and not a bare legal or factual conclusion or statement of an abstract principle. For example, <u>Improper:</u> THE EVIDENCE IS SUFFICIENT TO CONVICT THE DEFENDANT. <u>Proper:</u> EVIDENCE OF ENTRY THROUGH AN OPEN WINDOW IS SUFFICIENT TO SATISFY THE "BREAKING" ELEMENT OF BURGLARY.

The body of each argument should analyze applicable legal authority and persuasively argue how the facts and law support our position. Authority supportive of our position should be emphasized, but contrary authority should generally be cited, addressed in the argument, and explained or distinguished. Do not reserve arguments for reply or supplemental briefs.

You need not prepare a table of contents, a table of cases, or the index. These will be prepared by the support staff.

PERFORMANCE TEST WORKSHOP 2

NOTE: This is the task memo of Snyder v. Regents of the University of Columbia. The full exam is in your California Performance Test Book.

POLACEK & SCHEIER
5700 North Prospect, Suite 2600
Springville, Columbia

MEMORANDUM

To: Applicant
From: R. J. Morrison
Re: Snyder v. Regents of the University of Columbia
Date: February 28, 2008

We have been retained by Dr. Norm Snyder to represent him in claims arising from his removal as Chairperson of the Department of Medicine at the University of Columbia. The Regents of the University terminated him as head of the Department following his very vocal and public opposition to the relocation of the Medical School from its current location here in Springville to Palatine, some 20 miles away. The termination is to become effective almost a month from today. He will retain his professorship after his termination as Chair.

Dr. Snyder wishes to pursue injunctive relief to stop his termination, if possible. Please write me an objective memorandum in which you analyze the likelihood of obtaining a preliminary injunction based on retaliatory employer action in violation of Dr. Snyder□s First Amendment right to free speech under the State of Columbia Constitution. For tactical reasons, we are going to rely on the Columbia State Constitution rather than the United States Constitution. We will do so because the Columbia State Constitution is more protective of public employee First Amendment rights. Since the facts will be woven throughout your memorandum, limit your statement of facts to a brief one- paragraph summary.

SNYDER V. REGENTS – ANSWER

To: R.J. Morrison

From: Applicant

Re: Snyder v. Regents of University of Columbia Retaliatory Employer Action

Date: February 28, 2008

Statement of Facts

Dr. Norm Snyder is a tenured Professor and Chair of the Department of Medicine at the University of Columbia located in Springville, Columbia. The Department of Medicine is one of eight Basic Science departments and sixteen clinical departments that make up the School of Medicine at the University. In 2004, the University began consideration of a plan to move the School of Medicine to Palatine, Columbia, 20 miles from its current location. Dr. Snyder was opposed to this plan because it would unnecessarily isolate the Med School from its Basic Science colleagues, be fiscally irresponsible, and detrimental to the lower income members of the community. After using the appropriate channels at the University to voice his dissent, Dr. Snyder wrote a "Letter to the Editor" in the Springville Star Bulletin on December 28, 2007, urging members of the public to attend a public hearing regarding the proposed move. In response to Dr. Snyder's dissent and letter, the Regents of the University of Columbia voted unanimously to terminate his position as Chair of the Department of Medicine. As a tenured professor, Dr. Snyder retains his position at the University within the Department, but stands to incur substantial damage to his reputation and professional interests. The decision to terminate his position will become effective on March 27, 2008. Dr. Snyder has retained our firm to determine whether he has a cause of action for a preliminary injunction against the University for its retaliatory actions taken after he voiced his dissent to the plan to move the School of Medicine.

Likelihood of Obtaining a Preliminary Injunction

In order to succeed in obtaining a preliminary injunction, Dr. Snyder will have to demonstrate that this case meets the standard for obtaining a preliminary injunction. Dr. Snyder must demonstrate: 1) he has a substantial likelihood of prevailing on the merits; 2) he will suffer an irreparable harm in the absence of the injunction; 3) the threatened harm to him outweighs any damage the injunction may cause to the University; and 4) if the court issues the injunction, it will not be adverse to the public interest. Elkins v. Hamel (2007)

1. Substantial Likelihood of Prevailing on the Merits

Dr. Snyder must be able to demonstrate that his claim has a substantial likelihood of prevailing on the merits. To prove this, we must establish that Dr. Snyder has a proper claim for infringement of his First Amendment rights under the Columbia State Constitution. In the public employment context, courts in Columbia have adopted the four-part Boyer test to evaluate a constitutional claim for First Amendment retaliation by a public employer in the State of Columbia. See Elkins v. Hamel (2007); Harlan v. Yarnell (2002). Columbia courts recognize that public employees retain their First Amendment rights under the Columbia Constitution, subject to the employer's right to maintain a safe and orderly workplace. This allows a public employer to impose restraints on job-related speech in a way that would be unconstitutional if applied to a member of the general public. Elkins.

Under the Boyer 4 part test, the court must determine 1) whether the speech involves a matter of public concern; if so; 2) the court must weigh the employee's interest in the expression against the government employer's interest in regulating the speech of its employees to maintain an efficient and effective workplace. If the employee prevails on both of these questions, the court will proceed to the remaining two steps: 3) the employee must show the speech was a substantial factor driving the challenged governmental action. If the employee succeeds; 4) the employer must show that it would have taken the same action against the employee even in the absence of the protected speech. See Elkins; Harlan.

Matter of Public Concern

The court will look at the whole record and review the content, form, and context of the speech to determine if it was a matter of public concern. Elkins. In doing so, the court will consider the motive of the speaker: was Dr. Snyder speaking with the intent to redress a personal grievance that he had or was he commenting for a broader public purpose? Harlan. If Dr. Snyder was speaking merely on matter of personal interest, the speech is not protected. The speech must be something that not only relates to a matter of public interest, but informs the issue in a way that is helpful to the public in evaluating the government conduct.

Dr. Snyder may assert that his letter was a matter of public concern because he was commenting on an issue that has an impact on the entire community of Springville. First, separating the Med School from the rest of the Basic Science departments would isolate members of the faculty. A university is founded on collaboration and the exchange of ideas. Interdepartmental cooperation is often necessary to advance the field of study, especially in the sciences, where members of the faculty can collaborate together to discover new treatment methods. This would be a matter of public concern because separating the medical school may inhibit the University's ability to promote medicine and the development of new treatments beneficial to the community.

We can also argue that his speech is a matter of public concern because there are negative financial consequences to the community. The bonds that were passed to support the construction of the new School will take 40 years to pay off and the current community will not receive a benefit anytime soon. The community has an interest in how public funds are being appropriated, especially if that appropriation will not benefit the community. The community has a fiscal interest in how the move is being paid for. The Harlan court noted that speech regarding the misuse of state funds by a professor at a public university constituted a matter within the public concern.

Most importantly, however, the new school would be located 20 miles from the urban center of Springville. Currently, the school of medicine treats many of the town's indigent citizens. Moving the school would have a detrimental impact on low income members of the community because there is not adequate public transportation between Springville and Palatine, the proposed site. This would prevent low income citizens from receiving necessary medical treatment that they can afford. As a public institution, the medical school likely offers low cost treatment, especially to those who cannot afford to pay. Without the medical school in town, these citizens may be forced to go without health care. We can argue that this situation is similar to Harlan, where a professor filed a grievance against another professor for various charges, including misappropriation of funds and abuse of students. The court found that because the professor was addressing subjects that had a broader public purpose, it was a matter of public concern.

The University will assert that Dr. Snyder's concern is personal, not public, and that he wants to redress a personal grievance. The Regents will argue that Dr. Snyder is angry that the University rejected his proposal to split the medical school in two, leaving some faculty in Springville and some in Palatine. They will also argue that he is angry because his position was not adopted by the University and he sent a letter to the editor with a personal grudge against the administrators. It is true that Dr. Snyder was not satisfied with the Regents' rejection of his proposal. He admits that he is stubborn and feels very strongly that the relocation plan was misguided. But we can overcome this argument by citing previous decisions by the Regents that Dr. Snyder has disagreed with, yet implemented without further objections. Several years ago, the Regents made a decision to reorganize the Health Sciences Center. Dr. Snyder was adamantly opposed to this reorganization and went through a similar campaign to try and prevent that decision from taking place. But after he was outvoted and the Regents proceeded with their plan, Dr. Snyder, as Head of the Department of Medicine, implemented their decision wholeheartedly. Dr. Snyder agrees that the administration should implement policy whether they agree with it or not. The important fact in this situation is that the plan has not yet been decided because the debate within the community continues.

The University may also argue that Dr. Snyder received a personal benefit, was personally motivated, if the school did not relocate. This argument is similar to the one that was made in Harlan. But this case is distinguishable from Harlan, because it involves a matter that affects the entire community. In Harlan, the University alleged that it was merely a matter relating to an internal department dispute because Harlan wanted to achieve a benefit of establishing the "internal order" of the department. But the court rejected this argument because the fact that the plaintiff might receive an incidental benefit from his speech does not transform it into a purely personal grievance. Dr. Snyder was already head of the Department, and by keeping the School of Medicine in Springville, he would not receive a promotion or a better position within the school. The University cannot allege that he is working for a personal benefit.

Due to the harsh impact that this proposal will have on the indigent members of the community and their ability to obtain medical care, the court would likely find that this was a matter of public concern. The fact that Dr. Snyder previously implemented policy decisions that he disagreed with shows that he is capable of working within the system and that he had no personal bias or motive when sending the letter.

Weighing Dr. Snyder's Interest in Commenting -- Against the University's Interest in Promoting an Efficient and Effective Workplace

Under the second prong of the Boyer test, the court will look at several factors to weigh each side's interest, including: 1) whether the speech would or did create problems in maintaining discipline or harmony among coworkers; 2) whether the employment relationship is one in which personal loyalty and confidence are necessary; 3) whether the speech impeded Dr. Snyder's ability to perform his responsibilities; 4) the time, place, and manner of his speech; and 5) whether the matter was one on which debate was vital to informed decision-making.

1. Discipline and Harmony in Workplace

The University will contend that Dr. Snyder's position has created tension among members of the faculty and has created disharmony in the University. Several faculty members have expressed to the Chancellor and Dean that they are intimidated by Dr. Snyder because of his insistence that the relocation decision should not happen. They will argue that this creates discipline problems because his ability to perform as a department chair has been impaired. The University will cite Elkins in support of their position, where the court found that the discipline and harmony within the police station was vital to community interests and outweighed the officers' right to speech.

But Dr. Snyder can rely on Harlan, where the court found that "healthy levels of dissent and debate are essential to the vitality of institutions." The court noted that academic institutions in particular are meant to "foster critical thinking skills in its students," and one way to accomplish this is for members of the university to engage in healthy debate within the institution itself. The court must consider whether the speech of the employees would cause undue disruption of the ability of the university to function. The University contends that Dr. Snyder's authority has been undermined by his vocal dissent. This argument is weakened by the fact that Dr. Snyder has previously opposed plans submitted by the Regents yet has been able to effectively lead the department for over 20 years. The letter from the Regents terminating Dr. Snyder notes his years of service, which proves that his speech would not undermine the discipline and harmony because it has not done so in the past. Dr. Snyder's argument is further bolstered by the fact that 45 of 50 members of the Med School faculty signed a petition in support of Dr. Snyder's position. This severely undercuts the University's argument that there is disharmony in the University.

2. Necessity of Personal Loyalty and Confidence

The necessity of having personal loyalty from an employee to his superiors depends on the nature of the employee-employer relationship in question, Harlan. The Harlan court found that in an academic institution, the relationship between a professor and his superiors did not require loyalty and confidence.

We can argue that this situation is akin to Harlan because the eight departments in the School of Medicine act autonomously. Dr. Snyder is the chair of one department, the Department of Medicine. Although there are bimonthly meetings with Mr. Simmons and the department chairs, the departments basically run themselves. And there is even less contact between the chairs and Chancellor Blake. Dr. Snyder indicated that he sees Chancellor Blake very infrequently. The need for there to be personal loyalty and confidence between Dr. Snyder and his superiors is not as necessary as in the police department. In Elkins, the court emphasized that it was necessary for the officers to follow the command of the captain and ranking officers because the public safety was at stake. But in an academic institution, the need for loyalty and confidence is lessened.

The University will counter that the medical school is distinguishable from a regular university because public health is at stake. The University will contend that the situation does resemble Elkins because, as doctors, it is necessary for them to follow their superiors in order to protect patients and members of the community. This argument is weakened by the fact that the doctors do not rely on the University administration for orders on how to perform their job. The situation is distinguishable from Elkins, where the police captain gives orders to an officer, who must then follow those orders to protect public safety. At the University, even though public safety and health are at stake, the administration does not give orders to the doctors on how to treat patients. The fact that health is involved does not take it out of the holding of Harlan. This situation is distinguishable from Elkins, where it was necessary for there to be loyalty and confidence among members of the police force, because they were charged with protecting the public, and having a clear chain of authority was important, because a fellow officer or a member of the public could be injured or killed if the rank and file was not properly followed. There is not a similar need within the Department because they work autonomously.

3. Whether the Speech Impeded Dr. Snyder's Ability to Perform

The University has indicated that Dr. Snyder's speech did impair his ability to perform as a department chair. It asserted that his ability to lead the department has been undermined and affected by his speech because certain faculty members are intimidated by him and do not feel comfortable going to him directly to express their concerns. This is an important argument, because if Dr. Snyder cannot effectively manage the department, the University will be able to show that his speech impeded his ability to perform his job. Dr. Snyder can rebut the University's allegations by showing the petition signed by the 45 out of 50 faculty members, i.e., approximately 90% of the current faculty. If some are intimidated by him, it is a small minority within the department. Additionally, Dr. Snyder may have enemies who are disagreeing with him just to disagree. They are people who said they feel intimidated because they want to be on the opposite side of the issue and may be acting for personal reasons and not out of true feelings of intimidation by Dr. Snyder. Calling members of the faculty to testify on his behalf would show that he is widely respected among colleagues and staff.

Furthermore, the Harlan court found that speech of a professor does not affect his ability to perform if he can carry on office hours, teaching classes, serving on committees and participating in outside activities related to his profession. Dr. Snyder's ability to perform as chair of the department has not been impeded by his speech. He has been able to attend faculty and university-wide forums and speak to members in the community. But, at the same time, he has headed a huge project within the Department aimed at developing a new method of dialysis that is faster and can be performed at home. This project involves coordinating graduate assistants and lab space. He has been in negotiations with several major pharmaceutical companies in order to secure funding for this research. We can argue that his ability to act as chair has not been disturbed by his speech regarding the proposal.

Dr. Snyder has also asserted that, in the past, he has fully implemented decisions with which he did not agree, and which he had protested before the decision was made. It seems that Dr. Snyder has a fairly good argument that his ability to perform will not be substantially impaired, especially based on his previous actions in supporting University decisions once they had been made. However, it can't be denied that vigorous opposition of a plan definitely can result in an adverse impact on the opponent's ability to perform, once the plan is adopted. Everyone will remember his vigorous opposition, and there is necessarily a serious question of trust, especially when the opposition has been as broad and vigorous as Dr. Snyder's is in this case.

In evaluating both sides of the issue, Dr. Snyder's speech probably did adversely affect his ability to perform to some degree. However, the exact extent to which his ability to perform appears to be at most minimal, since as discussed above, he was able to operate as an effective department chair, continue with his duties and responsibilities and be at the helm of an important research project.

4. Time, Place, and Manner

Public forums are an appropriate place for expression of opinions, but if the speech occurs through proper channels, the court is more likely to uphold the speech as being the proper time, place, and manner for the expression. For a considerable period of time, Dr. Snyder confined his speech to the proper channels for objection within the University system. Dr. Snyder first began his opposition to the proposed project by submitting a comprehensive report that he widely circulated among the medical school faculty in 2004. He also attended and presented his position at faculty and university-wide forums held in 2004 and 2005. In addition to these actions, Dr. Snyder also met with Jack Blake, Chancellor of the Health Sciences Center, and Paul Simmons, Dean of the School of Medicine. After his meeting, he also circulated a petition among the faculty, which 45 out of 50 signed in support of his position. Dr. Snyder did not send the letter to the editor until all of these actions had been taken and he had been unable to persuade the "powers that be" that the proposed relocation was "ill conceived, financially reckless, and detrimental to the needs of our indigent citizens." Dr. Snyder urged the public to look further into the matter at his website, and then attend the public hearing which the Board of Regents would be having regarding this issue.

Although, Dr. Snyder's letter to the editor may be construed as having gone outside the proper channels within the University system, and that he resorted to very strong language to convey his feelings about the relocation, the letter was regarding a public hearing that was critical to the community. Thus, Dr. Snyder was just reinforcing the University's attempt to gauge public opinion by calling their attention to the hearing.

This situation is similar to Harlan, where Professor Harlan followed proper university protocols for voicing his opinion, including attending faculty meetings and airing concerns to the Dean of the College. The Harlan court found that the fact that Professor Harlan followed the authorized procedures and appealed to appropriate authorities. This prong of the balancing of interest weighs in Dr. Snyder's favor because he did not go to the public and air his complaint without first addressing it through proper channels at the University. He had raised his position for years before submitting his letter to the editor for the Star Bulletin on December 8, 2007.

5. Vital to Decision-Making

Under this factor, the court must decide whether the matter is essential to the decision-making process. Here we can argue it is vital to the process because members of the community were unaware of the proposal. The Regents were holding a public hearing on the proposal but it is not clear if they invited members of the public or advertised the meeting. The Springville Star Bulletin article notes that the Regents are expected to make a decision at the close of public testimony. But how can the Regents make an informed decision if there are no members of the public there to support or argue against the proposal? Dr. Snyder's letter merely informed the public about an issue that affected them and invited them to come and speak out in favor or against the proposal.

Weighing these factors, the court will likely find that Dr. Snyder's interest in the speech outweighs the University's interest in an efficient workplace because it does not have a substantial impact on his ability to perform and the workplace is not disrupted.

Dr. Snyder Must Show the Speech Was a Substantial Factor Driving the University's Action

Since Dr. Snyder prevailed on the first two steps of the Boyer test, the court will proceed to the remaining two steps: Under the third Boyer factor, the court will look at whether the speech was a motivating factor for the adverse or retaliatory employment action taken by the employer. The Regents in their letter contend that the decision was not based on his speech, but on disharmony in the faculty. But the alleged disharmony was created by the speech. There appears to be no other reason to remove Dr. Snyder as chair of the department. The fact that he was negotiating a multi-million dollar deal with pharmaceutical companies indicates that he was performing his job adequately and bringing in revenue and new research opportunities to the University. Like Harlan, there is no question that the decision to remove Dr. Snyder from his position was motivated by his speech against the proposal.

The Regents Must Show it Would Have Taken Same Action Against Dr. Snyder Even in the Absence of Protected Speech

If the employee satisfies the other elements of the Boyer test, the burden shifts to the employer to show that the employment action would have been taken regardless of whether the employee was engaged in the protected speech. There must be some other reason that the

44

employer had for taking the action. The University cannot show that the action would have been taken despite the speech.

2. Irreparable Harm in the Absence of Injunction

Elkins opined that the loss of any First Amendment freedoms, even for a minimal period, was an irreparable harm. But in the context of a preliminary injunction, Dr. Snyder must show that there is a danger of recurrent violation of his legal rights. The court, in dicta, suggested that in the employment context, courts are loathe to grant preliminary injunctions because injuries often associated with employment discharge or discipline such as such as damage to reputation, financial distress and difficulty finding other employment, do not constitute irreparable harm. A court will hesitate to grant a preliminary injunction where the employee can be made whole by monetary damages after a full trial.

However, here, Dr. Snyder stands to lose his contacts for his research, which would cause the loss of millions of dollars. His research on a new method of dialysis goes beyond his personal interest. Not only will the local community benefit from Dr. Snyder's research, but also the public at large. His research will directly affect those who rely on dialysis on a daily basis. The local community will especially benefit as they will have direct access to Dr. Snyder and his breakthrough research. Dr. Snyder's professional standing and his ability to get research grants, publication opportunities, and future royalties from licenses will be affected. Unlike lost wages, or harm to reputation, the ability to get a research grant or opportunity for research cannot be quantified in a dollar amount. Although the University may contend that Dr. Snyder's alleged injuries are not definite and certain, Dr. Snyder has progressed far enough in his negotiations with the pharmaceutical companies to be able to reasonably quantify the consequences of the University's actions on his ability to keep progressing forward with all of his research and projects.

Dr. Snyder, the community and the public at large will suffer irreparable harm that cannot be addressed just by monetary damages. First Amendment freedoms combined with a loss of invaluable medical research and millions of dollars should compel the court to grant a preliminary injunction.

3. Threatened Harm Outweighs Any Damage the Injunction May Cause to Party Opposing It – Balancing of Harms

A preliminary injunction necessarily involves an analysis of probabilities and an evaluation of potential injuries. Because a preliminary injunction is issued before there has been a trial on the merits, Dr. Snyder will have the burden of showing that his irreparable injury outweighs any injury the University might suffer if the court grants the injunction. The court will look at the course of action that will minimize the loss to each side and the risk of error.

The University may contend that it will suffer irreparable harm if it is required to keep Dr. Snyder in a position to which he is no longer entitled. The University may further argue that it will not have Dr. Snyder's cooperation in the move, thus having him continue in his role as department chair will continue the disharmonious climate that has been created by his opposition to the relocation plan. However, it seems clear that the University will not suffer much harm, if any at all. Under the balancing of harms, if the University is forced to take Dr. Snyder back, it seems unlikely that they will suffer injury because Dr. Snyder has previously accepted and implemented decisions with which he disagreed. He agrees that it is important for the faculty to put up a united front when it comes to policymaking. Any dissension in the faculty may be based on personal bias and not true intimidation and furthermore, as discussed above, Dr. Snyder has the support of the majority of the faculty.

Dr. Snyder stands to lose a great deal because he will lose licenses from pharmaceutical companies to do his research. These are opportunities that he may never be able to regain. The Elkins court said to look at the risk of making a wrong decision. If it makes a wrong decision in favor of the University, Dr. Snyder will be irreparably harmed. But if the court rules in favor of Dr. Snyder and is incorrect, the University's harm at most will be minimal, because once again, Dr. Snyder has agreed that he will implement the policy regardless of his personal opinions and concerns.

Overall, it seems that the threatened irreparable injury to Dr. Snyder substantially outweighs any injury to the University.

4. The Injunction Will Not be Adverse to the Public Interest

A court will not issue a preliminary injunction if the injunction is adverse to the public interest. This again involves somewhat of a balancing test – is the public interest stronger in favor of the injunction or in opposition to it? The Supreme Court in Elkins stated that the public "has a strong interest in the vindication of an individual's constitutional rights, particularly in encouraging the free flow of information and ideas under the First Amendment."

The Elkins court suggested that an injunction granted against the police department would have been against the public interest because there is a strong interest in having an efficient and dependable law enforcement system. Although the public has an interest in the efficient operation of the University, it does not seem like granting the injunction will interfere with University operations and it seems likely that the public has a strong interest in the continuation of Dr. Synder's research.

Here, the injunction will not be adverse to the public, but quite the contrary, because it will allow a prominent member of the faculty to continue research on dialysis, improving the lives of current and future dialysis patients. This would be a significant benefit to the community. If Dr. Snyder is terminated, his research will cease and may not be able to continue, causing the public to lose out on a possible medical breakthrough.

Therefore, a court should conclude that Dr. Synder's request for an injunction will not be adverse to the public interest and should be granted.

FACT GATHERING

Theory or Ultimate Fact

Elements or Factors

Facts

(D P T -- Documentary, Physical, Testimonial)

Sources

(Tools / Means -- if Required)

Organization   =   **Element – by – Element, or**
                                      Factor – by - Factor

SAMPLE TASK MEMO

MEMORANDUM

To: Applicant

From: Annabelle Lee

Date: July 27, 2004

RE: **Jake Donovan and Bargain Mart, Inc.**

As you know, I participate on a monthly basis at the River City Bar Association Ask-A Lawyer night. At the last session two weeks ago, I met with Jake Donovan. He feels that he has been a victim of a scam involving a "check deferment" service provided by Bargain Mart, Inc., a local appliance store.

I need you to do some preliminary work on any potential statutory claims Mr. Donovan may have against Bargain Mart, Inc. Please prepare a memorandum that identifies the potential claims Mr. Donovan might bring against Bargain Mart, Inc.

Separately for each potential claim:

1. Set forth the statutory requirements to establish the claim;

2. Analyze whether the facts that we know establish the statutory requirements; and,

3. Identify what additional facts, if any, we must seek through investigation or discovery, and how the additional facts might help establish the particular statutory requirements.

At this point, do not discuss what remedies, such as damages or injunctive relief, might be available. We will figure out the remedies aspect at a later time.

<u>**SAMPLE TASK MEMO FROM FACT GATHERING EXAM**</u>

Britzke, Klare & Pushkin

22 Myron Avenue

Thomsonville Heights, Columbia

MEMORANDUM   **July 27, 1989**

To:	**Applicant**
From:	**Marsha Pushkin**
Re:	<u>**Stolier File**</u>

We represent Celia Stolier and are trying to help her establish the right to regular visitation with her granddaughter, Joanna Wallach. The child's mother, Elizabeth Lawton, died several years after divorcing David Wallach, the father. After the mother's death, the father was awarded custody and his second wife has adopted Joanna. Since then the parents have refused to permit our client to see her granddaughter and her every request to do so has been thwarted. My attempts to get an agreement for visitation through the parents' lawyer have similarly been rejected as the correspondence in the file makes clear.

There is a history of bad feelings between our client and her former son-in-law and it is clear to me that she has done nothing to improve that situation. He is apparently prepared to make ugly allegations about her, but nevertheless, since she is very anxious to reestablish what appears to have been an excellent relationship with the child, she wants us to press forward on her behalf.

I think that we are now at the stage where litigation is the only choice left. We will try to get the Family Division of Superior Court to require monthly weekend visitation for our client. In preparation for that, I have done some legal research and collected cases, statutes and court rules which will help us in figuring out exactly what to do next.

I have met twice with our client, discussed the case with opposing counsel and exchanged letters with him, interviewed Ms. Stolier's brother-in-law, and tried to gather other information. There is no doubt that the facts here are seriously in dispute. It is clear to me that we are going to have to work hard to develop the facts necessary to convince the court to issue the order our client needs.

Before we draft the Petition for Visitation, I need your thoughts on how we should go about gathering the facts. I am assuming that we will have to engage in extensive investigation and discovery.

What I need from you is a well-organized, thorough but not unduly repetitive statement as to how we can obtain the evidence needed to show the court that our client should be granted the right to visit her grandchild. Please do not burden this memorandum with a general discussion of the legal right to visitation, as I am aware of those requirements. Instead, the memorandum should set forth the legal elements which we must establish in order to prevail, the items of evidence we will need to prove or disprove facts related to each of these elements, and the sources of such evidence. The memorandum should also set forth the means, including appropriate discovery procedures, of obtaining and making use of the needed items of evidence.

You should discuss facts of which we are already aware and items of evidence we may now have as well as those that might be discovered and/or obtained upon further investigation. For example, one of the elements to be established is that the grandchild Joanna has a desire to visit her grandmother. A fact of which we are aware and that needs to be proved in relation to that element is that Joanna has written a letter expressing that desire. An item of evidence to prove that fact is the letter written by Joanna that is in the File and which was given to us by our client. Discovery procedures that might be used in connection with this item of evidence would be to have it authenticated by asking our client Celia Stolier if she can identify Joanna's handwriting or requesting an admission of authenticity from our adversary, David Wallach. A fact which might be discovered upon further investigation is that Joanna may have told one of her teachers that she wished she could see her grandmother. A means of obtaining evidence to support that fact would be interviewing and, if appropriate, taking depositions from one or more of Joanna's teachers. These examples should give you an idea of what your memorandum should contain.

**FIRST PAGE OF SAMPLE INVESTIGATION PLAN ANSWER
(BASED ON SAMPLE PERFORMANCE TEST <u>STATE V. REED</u>)**

MEMORANDUM #1:

1.   Statutory Rape Charge

Section 18-76 of the Criminal Code defines statutory rape to include these elements:
- (I)   Engaging in sexual conduct
- (ii)   With someone between the ages of 15 and 18, and
- (iii)   The actor is more than 48 months older or in a position of authority.

Engaging in sexual conduct: Although Tom says that he had been intimate with Bonnie, we still need to know whether the state has any evidence to support its case (since the state has the burden of proof). Thus, we need to see whether Bonnie ever mentioned to anyone that she did indeed sleep with Tom. Perhaps she told a friend at the lodge, or perhaps she wrote a letter to a friend in her hometown. We should examine her diary and see whether she really does make damaging statements in it about her relationship with Tom.

Also, were there any medical examinations or are there any other medical records that might have some information on whether they had slept together?

It is possible that even when she spent the night in the motor home, she spent it in a different bed? We need to check the motor home and see whether there are any other beds, and we should ask Tom whether Bonnie ever brought a sleeping bag and slept on the floor. Also, did she really "move in."? Please check on how many of her things were still at her room in the lodge.

Between 15 and 18: Is Bonnie really under 18? See if you can get a copy a of her birth certificate. Did she tell anyone that she was 18 or over? If there is a state law on the minimum age to serve drinks (see research memo below), and if the minimum age is 18, how did she get the job serving drinks? Perhaps she lied about her age or used some phony I.D. Also, if she did go to college, find out whether they have records showing her age.

Tom more than 48 months older or in position of authority: Let's get Tom's birth certificate too to check his age. Also, is there any way that the state could argue that Tom was in a position of authority over Bonnie? Check to see whether she ever did any work for him. Look at the payroll books and perhaps even talk to the lodge owner.

Mens rea: Although the statutory rape statute speaks in terms of strict liability and an appellate court has interpreted the statute as one of strict liability, it is possible that another appellate court would fashion a more reasonable mens rea construction, as has been done in several jurisdictions. Thus, we should check whether Bonnie indicated in any manner to Tom that she was at least 18 years old. Perhaps she hinted at it when she said that she had been in college for a year. If she made such misrepresentations and if it was

TASK MEMO FROM A MULTISTATE PERFORMANCE TEST

Law Office of Andrew J. Reed
509 Dawkins Avenue
Marina, Franklin 33405
(555)581-7108

MEMORANDUM

To: Applicant

From: Andrew Reed

Date: July 25, 2000

Subject: Letitia Pauling v. Del-Rey Wood Products Co.

Our client Letitia Pauling worked for a small, local company called Del-Rey Wood Products for three years. She was recently fired. She came to see me complaining that she and her co-workers had regularly worked between 50 and 60 hours per week and that the company had never paid any of the workers time and a half for overtime.

I filed suit against Del-Rey alleging that Del-Rey violated the Fair Labor Standard Act (the "Act") by failing to pay time and a half after 40 hours a week. In its answer to the complaint, Del-Rey denies that it or its employees are covered by the Act. If there is no coverage, Del-Rey has no obligation to pay overtime, and Ms. Pauling has no claim.

Some of Ms. Pauling's co-workers who are still employed by Del-Rey have expressed interest in joining the lawsuit. There is certainly a basis in what Ms. Pauling told me to assume that the Act applies to Del-Rey's employees, but, since Del-Rey has denied it, we need to pin it down. Before I take this matter any further and possibly jeopardize the co-worker's relationships with Del-Rey, I want to send a set of interrogatories to find out whether the act applies. There are two bases for establishing the application of the Act to employees: "enterprise coverage" and "Individual coverage."

Here's what I'd like you to do:

1.   Please draft for my review a set of six clear and sharply focused interrogatories designed to obtain information on whether there is any basis for asserting "individual coverage" of the Del-Rey employees under the Fair Labor Standards Act. I'm working on the interrogatories for "enterprise coverage," and I've attached three I've finished as examples. Your task is to focus on "individual coverage" and nothing else.

2.   To help me understand why you are proposing each interrogatory, follow each one with a short statement of why you are proposing it and how, based on the law and the facts, it will help us determine whether "individual coverage" exist under the Act. I've included such statements with the three interrogatories I drafted to give you an idea of what I'm looking for.

Our word processing program will supply the correct format, introductory remarks, definitions and the like, so you need not concern yourself with such matters.

CONTINUED FROM MULTISTATE PERFORMANCE TEST

MEMORANDUM

To: Applicant

From: Andrew Reed

Date: July 25, 2000

Subject: Enterprise Coverage Interrogatories

Here are the first three interrogatories I've drafted regarding "enterprise coverage." I'll write other ones later, but this ought to give you an idea of how I want you to go about drafting the interrogatories for the "individual coverage" issue.

INTERROGATORY NO. 1: State in dollars the gross annual volume of sales or business done by Del-Rey Wood Products Co. for each of the past three years.

Reason for proposing: One of the components of enterprise coverage is showing annual dollar volume of $500,000. If that dollar volume can be established vis-à-vis Del-Rey alone, we will have established the threshold statutory requirement under § 203 (s) (1) (A) (ii).

INTERROGATORY NO. 2: State the names of all persons, corporations, partnerships, or other entities having an ownership interest in, or who is an officer, director, or shareholder of, Del-Rey Wood Products Co., D & R Furniture Manufacturing Co., and D & R Enterprises.

Reason for proposing: We need to know the relationships among the three companies to establish that the three entities are related through unified operations or common control, as suggested by the facts and required by § 203(r)(1).

INTERROGATORY NO. 3: In each of the past three years, what has been the combined gross annual dollar volume of sales or business done by Del-Rey Wood Products Co., D & R Furniture Manufacturing Co., and D & R Enterprises?

Reason for proposing: If these companies together do in fact constitute an "enterprise," their combined dollar volume is relevant to the $500,000 threshold.

SAMPLE TREATISE FROM A MULTISTATE PERFORMANCE TEST
WALKER ON DISCOVERY
A Primer On Discovery Techniques

In civil litigation, depositions, interrogatories, request for production of documents, and request for admissions are primary discovery tools used by parties to lawsuits. The purpose of this text is to inform attorneys whose experience is limited or those who need a refresher on discovery techniques. Careful attention to the techniques will facilitate the process of gathering information at a relatively low cost.

*****

Written Interrogatories: Written interrogatories are, plainly and simply a series of written requests for information submitted by one party to another. The recipient is required to respond in writing and under oath and to disclose all pertinent information known to it, reasonable available to it, and within its possession and control. Interrogatories may not be sent to nonparties, although they may request information known to the recipient about nonparties.

An interrogatory may be phrased as a question (e.g., "What goods does ABC, Inc. manufacture?") or as a declarative statement (e.g., "Describe the goods that ABC, Inc. manufactures."). In order to be effective and to avoid objections that they are vague or overbroad, interrogatories must be sharply focused and unambiguously worded.

For example, in an employment discrimination case, the plaintiff might want to obtain information on other employees who have charged the employer with discrimination and what documentary evidence there is of the charges. The following interrogatory would probably be subject to an objection for vagueness and overbreadth:

INTERROGATORY NO. 1: Please describe each document that contains information regarding the names and addresses of the employees of ABC, Inc. who have filed charges of employment discrimination with the EEOC.

Performance Test Workshops

A more focused inquiry will avoid the objection and be more likely to produce the information sought. For example:

> INTERROGATORY NO. 2: What is the name and address of each employee who, within the past two years, has filed with the EEOC a charge of employment discrimination against ABC, Inc.?

Interrogatories may be sequential and may have subparts that seek information related to the main thrust of the interrogatory. For example:

> INTERROGATORY NO. 3: Within the past two years, have any employees of ABC, Inc. filed against ABC, Inc. charges of employment discrimination with EEOC?

> INTERROGATORY NO. 4: If the answer to the preceding interrogatory is in the affirmative, please state the following with regard to each such employee of ABC, Inc.:
> a.   The name, address, and telephone number of the employee;
> b.   The name of the custodian of ABC, Inc.'s records regarding ABC, Inc.'s investigation of and response to each of such charge filed with the EEOC.

Care must be taken, however, in using interrogatories with subparts. Because there is the potential that counsel might abuse the process by serving burdensome interrogatories, many courts, by local rule, limit the number of interrogatories a party may serve. Typically, the local rules treat each subpart of an interrogatory as a separate interrogatory for purposes of measuring the number of interrogatories served; e.g., Interrogatory No. 4, above, would be counted as two interrogatories.

Although interrogatories cannot be used to require the recipient to *produce* documents (i.e., make documents available), they can be used effectively to seek *identification* of relevant documents. For example:

> INTERROGATORY NO. 5: Describe the computerized and/or manually prepared records that are used in your company to keep track of racial, ethnic, and gender make-up

of your work force.

Such interrogatories can be followed up later with written request for production of documents.

The key to the productive use of interrogatories is for the proponent to think carefully about the specific underlying facts he or she wishes to elicit in order to support the legal elements of the claim and to draft straightforward, plainly worded inquiries. It is best to request the information in small doses. One can always send follow-up interrogatories if further explication is necessary. Convoluted or complex inquiries that encompass too many topics or too much subject matter are ordinarily a waste of time and will not draw useful answers. *See, e.g.,* Interrogatory NO. 1, above.

***

FACT ANALYSIS

- **The law is given or agreed upon and is used to help focus and organize the document**

- **The facts are analyzed or argued within the structure of the law**

<u>**SAMPLE INSTRUCTION SHEET**</u>

COLUMBIA PRISON ASSISTANCE PROGRAM
An Equal Justice Project of the Columbia Bar Association

MEMORANDUM   April 10, 1991

To: All Lawyers

From: Director of Litigation

Re: <u>Closing Arguments/Jury Trials</u>

You should begin with an understanding of the legal principles that will applied to the facts in the case. In some cases, you will be provided with jury instructions. In other cases, the instructions will not yet be drafted and you will have to rely upon an analysis of legal authority. The instructions or legal authority will give you the framework for your closing argument. However, the closing argument should not discuss or make reference to these authorities; a closing argument is not a legal brief or an essay. The argument must show how the evidence presented meets the legal standards which are or will be set forth in the jury instructions. The argument is based on the evidence presented, not histrionics or personal opinion. Write out your argument exactly as you plan to give it.

It's important that the argument be in your own words, but remember that you're communicating with a group of lay people. Your job is to help them understand how the law relates to the facts presented, and to persuade them that they have no choice but to find for your client. In doing that, you should consider the following:

- State explicitly the ultimate facts that the jurors must find in order for your client to prevail.

- Organize the evidence in support of the ultimate facts.

- Incorporate relevant legal principles or jury instructions into your argument.

- Discuss the sufficiency of the evidence and the credibility of witnesses.

- Draw reasonable inferences from the evidence to support positions you have taken.

- Anticipate opposing counsel's arguments and point out weaknesses in his case.

- Refer to equities or policy considerations that merit a finding for our client.

The most important factors are organization and persuasiveness; if you immerse the jury in a sea of unconnected details, they won't have a coherent point of view to discuss in the jury room. Never hold back any argument assuming that you will have a second opportunity to make it on rebuttal.

SAMPLE INSTRUCTION SHEET

MEMORANDUM   July 30, 1994

TO: To All Lawyers
FROM: Executive Committee
SUBJECT: Opening Statements

The purpose of an opening statement is to explain to the fact finder, in plain language, the evidence that you have a good faith basis to believe will be introduced and how that evidence fits into the theory of your case.

All opening statements, whether to be given in a jury trial, bench trial or administrative hearing, shall conform to the following organizational structure:

· Introduce the participants.

· State the theory of your case in a way that will command the fact finder's attention

· Develop a logical organization of the substantive part of the statement. The substantive portion of the statement should be organized by presenting a narrative statement in the nature of a story, with reference to specific witnesses and documents within the narrative. This type of narrative is often chronological (e.g., a chronology of a car accident) or a series of related topics (e.g. in a custody case: mother, father, home, school, etc.).

· Anticipate defenses and reveal and appropriately deal with weaknesses in our case. Personalize institutions and unsavory clients and witnesses.

· Do not argue the law, but limited references may be helpful (e.g., plaintiff will not be able to meet its burden of . . .)

· Tell the fact finder what you want it to do (e.g., return a specific verdict).

Remember this is an opening statement, not a closing argument. Arguments are inferences you ask the fact finder to draw and are improper in opening statements. On the other hand, do not be timid about emphasizing the evidence that is important to our case, e.g.,

Improper: It isn't sex discrimination just because a less experienced male employee got the promotion instead of the plaintiff.

Proper: A better qualified male employee was promoted. He was less experienced, but had a higher performance rating.

SAMPLE INSTRUCTION SHEET

Finley, Frost and Van Cleave
Attorneys at Law
7814 Harrowgate
Clinton, Columbia

MEMORANDUM   January 22, 1994

TO: Attorneys

FROM: Lynda Frost

RE: Jury Instructions

This firm follows the policy of insuring that jury instructions are viewed as an integral part of our persuasive presentation. As such, the instructions must be carefully crafted to present the law to the jury in a clear and understandable manner consistent with the theory of our case. To accomplish this, jury instructions must conform to the following standards:

The instructions must be understandable by the average layperson. Remember the instructions will be read by the judge to the jury. You, for example, may have had months to learn torts; the jury may have minutes.

The instructions must be clear.

The instructions must be particularized to the specific case being litigated. The jury will have sat through the entire trial having heard about specific people, corporations, transactions and occurrences. The instructions, therefore, will be more easily understood and will provide much more guidance if they refer to the specific people, corporations, transactions, or occurrences involved in the law suit.

Since the instructions must be adopted and delivered by the judge as a neutral third party, they cannot be argumentative, or misstate or distort the controlling legal authority. The objective is to fairly state the law while emphasizing factors that support a favorable result for our client.

The jury instructions must fairly state the law, yet be consistent with the legal and factual theory of your case. For example, the fact that we may represent a defendant in a personal injury action does not mean that we do not submit a jury instruction that addresses the plaintiff's obligation to establish a prima facie case. We will draft our version and then argue to the court why it is more appropriate than plaintiff's version.

While form instructions are often helpful, they can do no more than provide a general guide. Form instructions, given their generality, will never have sufficient particularity to the facts of our specific case.

The following instructions are examples that meet the above standards. They are taken from several of our cases involving negligent infliction of emotional distress.

• The plaintiff, Nancy Crater, is entitled to recover damages for serious emotional distress if a cause of such serious emotional distress was the negligent conduct of the defendant, Stanley Manufacturing, Inc. Serious emotional distress is an emotional reaction which is not an abnormal response to the circumstances. It is found where a reasonable person would be unable to cope with the mental distress caused by the circumstances. The elements of a cause of action for negligent infliction of serious emotional distress are:

1.   The defendant engaged in negligent conduct;
2.   The plaintiff suffered serious emotional distress;
3.   Such negligent conduct of the defendant was a cause of the serious emotional distress.

• If you find that Harry Jones, as an adjacent landowner to the Chesterfield airport, suffered emotional distress as a result of the noise from aircraft landing, taking off and in-flight, you may award damages to the plaintiff.

• If you find that the employee of the defendant, Speedy Process Service, made an invalid service of the writ on Mary Williams and thereafter knowingly filed a false affidavit of valid service, you may award damages to the plaintiff for negligent infliction of emotional distress.

SAMPLE JURY INSTRUCTIONS

Introductory instructions will be given on the duty of the jury, including its duty to follow the judge's instructions on the law, drawing inferences from circumstantial evidence, weighing conflicting testimony, and judging the credibility of witnesses. Other approved instructions follow:

(1)   The contestants (Mrs. Crenshaw's children) have the burden of establishing a preponderance of the evidence all of the facts necessary to prove the grounds of contest.

By a preponderance of the evidence is meant such evidence as, when weighed with that opposed to it, has more convincing force and the greater possibility of truth. In the event that the evidence from each side is equally balanced so that you are unable to say that the evidence on either side of a ground of contest preponderates, then your finding upon that ground of contest must be against the contestant.

(2)   Every person of sound mind, over the age of 18 years, and not acting undue influence, has the right to make a will directing the disposition of her property upon her death in any way she sees fit. Mrs. Crenshaw, the decedent, was under no obligation to make such disposition as will meet with the approval of a judge or jury.

The right to dispose of property by will is a fundamental right assured by law and does not depend upon a wise use of the right.

A will cannot be set aside simply because dispositions in the will may appear to you to be unreasonable or unjust.

(3)   A will that is made by a person who is not of sound mind is not valid. However, in this case the court has decided Mrs. Crenshaw was of sound mind and therefore had the capacity to dispose of her property by will. That matter has been decided for you by the court and is no longer in issue.

(4)   A will that is obtained by undue influence is not valid and may not be admitted to probate. Your sole responsibility in this case is to determine whether Mrs. Crenshaw's will was obtained by undue influence.

Undue influence consists of acts or conduct by which the mind of the decedent is overcome by the will of another person.

Mere general influence is not undue influence. In order to constitute undue influence, it must be used directly to obtain the will. It must amount to coercion destroying Mrs. Crenshaw's free will, substituting for her own another person's will and compelling Mrs. Crenshaw to make a disposition she would not otherwise have made.

(5)   In determining the issue of undue influence, you may consider, among other things, these questions:

1. Do the provisions of the will prefer strangers in blood to the persons who would naturally be considered by Mrs. Crenshaw, the decedent?

2. Does the will unduly benefit Richard and Alice Waterman, the chief beneficiaries thereof?

3. Is there a variance between the terms of the will and Mrs. Crenshaw's expressed intentions?

4. Was there an opportunity afforded by the Watermans' relationship to Mrs. Crenshaw to influence Mrs. Crenshaw?

5. Was Mrs. Crenshaw's mental and physical condition such as to permit her free will to be overcome?

6. Were the Watermans active in procuring execution of the will?

(6) If you find that a confidential relationship existed between Mrs. Crenshaw and Richard or Alice Waterman, that the Watermans or either of then were acting in obtaining the will and that either of them unduly profited from it, you shall presume that the will was obtained by undue influence of either or both of the Watermans. That presumption may be overcome by the Watermans if they establish by a preponderance of the evidence that the will was not the result of undue influence.

A confidential relationship exists whenever trust and confidence is reposed by one person in the integrity and fidelity of another.

VARIATION ON TESTING FACT ANALYSIS

Task Memo U.S. v. Ramirez

Please do the following:

(1) Write a memorandum to persuade Judge Kelly to exercise his discretion to issue a Judicial Recommendation Against Deportation. Be certain that your memorandum suggests factors the judge should consider in exercising his discretion, and organizes and states the facts relevant to these factors persuasively. Any factual arguments must, of course, be based on evidence we will present to Judge Kelly. At the hearing, we will rely solely on the testimony or use of affidavits from Scooter, Veronica, Dennis Cooper, Milt Mankewitz, and Armando Cruz. We will also be able to rely on the Pre-Sentence Investigation Report with attached Wyoming documents.

(2) Write a brief memorandum on whether there are legal arguments available to us should the request for a JRAD be denied and deportation proceedings instituted. Restrict yourself to the pending court proceeding or possible deportation proceedings.

SAMPLE DECLARATION

DECLARATION OF GLORIA GREEN

Gloria Green, under penalty, declares that the following is true and correct:

1. I am an aunt of plaintiff's Elizabeth and Debbie Powell; I am the sister of their late mother, Martha; and I am the guardian of plaintiff Elizabeth Powell.

2. Although I did not live with Martha and Ronald Powell, I visited them frequently during their marriage and had many opportunities to observe their family.

3. From the time of Ronald Powell's marriage to Martha, he held out Elizabeth as his daughter. Until his death, she lived in his home.

4. From the time of marriage, Elizabeth began to use the name of Elizabeth Powell. I heard Ronald introduce her many times as "my daughter, Elizabeth."

5. Ronald treated Elizabeth as though she was his child, even though, as far as I know, he never formally adopted her. He took her to school and shopping; taught her to ride a bike and swim; and helped her with her homework. For all the world, he was her father. Elizabeth believed Ronald was her father; he was the only father she ever knew.

6. After Debbie was born, Ronald treated Elizabeth in the same manner as Debbie. It was impossible for anyone to know that only Debbie was his natural daughter, and only a few close friends and members of the family, like myself, knew that Elizabeth was not Ronald's natural daughter.

7. Ronald always provided for both Debbie and Elizabeth, and continued to take care of and support Elizabeth, without any support from her natural father, even after Martha's death. He paid to have both girls attend a private school. A small insurance policy he had from work (for $500) listed both Debbie and Elizabeth as co-equal beneficiaries.

8. As far as I know, neither Ronald nor Martha ever requested that Elizabeth's natural father provide for her financial support. Elizabeth's natural father's whereabouts are unknown to me.

9. I know that Ronald would have wanted to see that both Debbie and Elizabeth were treated alike. As much as I love Debbie, it would not be Ronald's wish that only Debbie be included among his heirs.

10. Ronald had a preoccupation with fires. The Powell house had fire extinguishers and smoke detectors in every bedroom and the kitchen. He insisted that *all* of Elizabeth's and Debbie's clothing be fireproof. Ronald told me many times that he would never stay in "cheap" motels because they were "fire traps."

_____

Gloria Green

INSTRUCTION SHEET

CENTRAL COLUMBIA
LEGAL SERVICES

MEMORANDUM

TO: All attorneys & paralegals

FROM: Executive Committee

RE: Affidavits in Support of Motions or Other Requests for Judicial or Administrative Action

Affidavits should meet the following requirements:

1. Affidavits are to be limited to statements of fact. Those facts should be those necessary to support the legal position asserted in the motion or other request.

2. The facts should be presented in numbered paragraphs and each numbered paragraph, to the extent possible, should contain only one factual statement.

3. Only those facts which are personally known to the affiant and which are truthful, logically relevant and material shall be included.

Assume that the person signing the affidavit will be subject to cross-examination concerning the contents of the affidavit. Particular care must be taken to insure that person's credibility will not be impeached.

The materials you rely upon may not always contain precisely the facts you need. There often are, however, other facts that can be inferred from existing statements of the person who will sign the affidavit. If you have a good faith basis to believe that he or she has personal knowledge of those inferred facts, include them. We will then check with the person to confirm he or she actually does have personal knowledge of the inferred fact.

Captions, signature lines, and sworn acknowledgment will be added by support staff.

DRAFTING CAUSES OF ACTION

INSTRUCTION SHEET FROM MULTISTATE PERFORMANCE TEST

MILLER & KILLEBREW LLP

OFFICE MEMORANDUM

To: Attorneys
From: Tania Miller
Re: Drafting Causes of Action
Date: September 5, 2004

In pleading a cause of action, firm practice requires attorneys to draft the minimum allegations necessary to plead the required legal elements of the claim, presented in separately numbered paragraphs. The practice of pleading the required legal elements minimizes the risk of the court dismissing an action for failure to state a claim.

For example, a complaint for negligence must usually allege four elements: that the defendant had a duty, that the defendant breached that duty, that the defendant's breach was the proximate cause of injury to the plaintiff, and that this injury caused the plaintiff to suffer compensable damages. The following complaint for negligence provides an example of a negligence pleading consistent with the firm's pleadings practice:

1. When driving his car on the streets of Franklin City, Joe McMann owed other persons using the streets the duty to drive his car as a reasonable and prudent person would.
2. On December 5, 2002, Joe McMann breached his duty by driving his car at a speed in excess of the posted speed limit and through a red light at the corner of First Avenue and K Street in Franklin City.
3. When Joe McMann breached his duty his car struck Sally Young, who was a pedestrian lawfully walking in a crosswalk at the intersection of First Avenue and K Street.
4. As a result of Joe McMannn's breaching his duty, Sally Young suffered serious bodily injury and other damages.

DRAFTING TRANSACTIONAL DOCUMENTS

TASK MEMO FROM MULTISTATE PERFORMANCE TEST

Reilly, Ingersol & Powell, PC

Attorney's – at –Law   (555) 999-4567
300 Willis Road   (555) 999-4555 (Fax)
Jackson City, Franklin 33399   e-mail: **rip@aol.com**

MEMORANDUM   July 29, 1999

To: Applicant
From: Robert Reilly
Re: Emily Dunn

Yesterday I net with Emily Dunn, who was recently widowed. She has asked me to prepare a
new will for her. The transcript of the interview should give you a good overall sense of what
Mrs. Dunn is trying to accomplish. Looking back over it, however, I see some potential holes on
my understanding of her precise intentions. In particular, I'm concerned about how she wants to
deal with the disposition of potential insurance proceeds, her gifts of stock, the equalization of
gifts to her grandchildren, and the distribution of the residuary estate. The ambiguities are not
surprising. There are always some unresolved details that we must review with a client at a
subsequent meeting. At such meeting, however, I find it useful to have a draft of the will to help
clients refine their choices. I'd like you to do the following:

1. Draft the introductory and all disopositive clauses for Mrs. Dunn's proposed new will. Please
set them forth on separately numbered paragraphs and in order consistent with our firm's Will
Drafting Guidelines. Don't concern yourself with the definitional and boilerplate clauses.

2. In drafting the dispositive clauses regarding the four areas I've said I'm concerned about, you
will have to fill in the gaps left in the interview by making some assumptions about exactly what
Mrs. Dunn wants. Therefore, in drafting a dispositive clause that requires an assumption about
the insurance, the stock, the grandchildren, or the residuary estate, following that clause write a
short explanatory paragraph that does two things:

    A.   Tells me what assumptions you've made about the facts and Mrs. Dunn's intentions;

    B.   Tells me why, based on those assumptions, you drafted the particular clause the way
        that you did.

INSTRUCTION SHEET TAKEN FROM MULTISTATE PERFORMANCE TEST

Locher, Lawson & Klein, P.A.

MEMORANDUM   September 8, 1995

To: All Attorneys
From: Robert Lawson
Re: **Will Drafting Guidelines**

Over the years, this firm has used a variety of formats in drafting wills. Effective immediately. All wills drafted by this firm should follow this format:

PART ONE: Introduction

1. Set forth the first of the introductory clauses with a statement declaring it to be the testator's will and the name and domicile of the testator.
2. Include an appropriate clause regarding the revocation of prior testamentary instruments.
3. Include a clause naming the testator's immediate family members and identifying their relationship to the testators (parent, siblings, spouse, children, grandchildren, nephews, and nieces).

PART TWO: Dispositive Clauses (to be set forth in separate subdivisions or subparagraphs by class of bequest.) See the attached excerpt fro *Walker's Treatise on Wills* for the definitions of the different classes of bequest. Bequest should be set forth in the following order, using the appropriate heading:

1. Specific Bequest
    a. Real Property
    b. Tangible personal property
    c. Other specific bequests
    d. Any other clauses stating conditions that might affect the disposition of specific bequests
2. General bequest
3. Demonstrative bequest
4. Residuary bequest

PART THREE: Definitional Clauses. Clauses relating to how words and phrases used on the will should be interpreted.

PART FOUR: Boilerplate Clauses. Clauses relating to the naming of fiduciaries and their administrative and management authority, payment of debts and expenses, tax clauses, attestation clauses, and self-proving will affidavits.

FROM MULTISTATE PERFORMANCE TEST

Attachment A
Will Drafting Guidelines

Walker's Treatise on Wills

CLASSIFICATION OF BEQUEST:

Section 500.   All bequest under wills are classified as either (1) specific, (2) general, (3) demonstrative, or (4) residuary.

Section 501.   A *specific* bequest is a bequest of a specific asset

Section 502.   A *general* bequest (typically a gift of money) is a bequest payable out of general estate assets or to be acquired for a beneficiary out of general estate assets.

Section 503.   A *demonstrative* bequest is a bequest of a specific sum of money payable from a designated account. To the extent that the designated account is insufficient to satisfy the bequest, the balance is paid from the general funds of the estate.

Section 504.   A residuary bequest is a bequest that is neither general, specific, nor demonstrative and includes bequests that purport to dispose of the whole of the remaining estates.

LAST WILL AND TESTAMENT

I am Emily Dunn, a resident of Jackson City, Franklin. This is my Last Will, and I revoke all pervious wills and codicils.

ONE: A. I give all of my tangible personal property to my husband, Charles Dunn, if we are married to each other at the time of my death.

B. I give my family home located at 23 Ipswich Lane, Jackson City, Franklin to my husband Charles Dunn, if we are married to each other at the time of my death.

C. At the present time my husband is Charles Dunn, and we have two children, Andrea and Jonathan

D. I give 500 shares of Wilson Corporation stock to my cousin, Alice Dunn.

E. If Alice Dunn does not survive me. I give those 500 shares to her son, Drew Dunn.

F. I give the Claude Monet painting I inherited from my grandfather to the Franklin Museum of Art.

TWO   The remainder of my estate shall be disposed of in the following manner:

A. I give the sum of $25,000 to Bea Willis who for many years was my governess and who now lives in Sarasota, Florida.

B. I give the sum of $50,000 to Thomas Hardman who for 25 years served my parents faithfully as a gardener, provided he is married at the time of my death.

C. The balance of my residuary estate I give to my husband, Charles Dunn, or if he does not survive me or if we are not married at the time of my death, I give the balance of my residuary estate equally to our two children if they survive me, or all thereof to the survivor, or if none of my children survives me, I give the balance of my residuary estate to the Franklin Museum of Art.

THREE: A. I nominate First Federal Bank as Executor of my estate. I empower my Executor to exercise all administrative and management powers conferred on it as Executor by the laws of the State of Franklin. I direct that my Executor not be requires to post a bond.

IN WITNESS WHEREOF, I, Emily Dunn, have signed this, my Last Will, in the 18th day of January, 1965.

Witnesses   *Margaret Carnegie*   *Emily Dunn*

Judy Carter

PREMARITAL PROPERTY AGREEMENT

This agreement is entered into this 25th day of September, 1979, in Golden City, Columbia, between ROGER WINTHROP STERN and ANNETTE ELY LOCKWOOD. The parties contemplate marriage on or about October 5, 1979, and by this agreement seek to define their marriage. In furtherance of this purpose, the parties mutually agree as follows:

I. At the present time each of the parties has separate property consisting of real property, investments in stocks and bonds, bank accounts, and a lifetime's accumulation of personal items. Roger's holdings are substantial and include a controlling interest in a busies now managed by others; Annette's are less substantial, but have provided a comfortable income during her widowhood. Each wishes to retain the power to managed and control this separate property and to dispose of the same by will, while at the same time recognizing the rights and obligations that flow from marriage.

II. It is the intent of the parties that Annette's rights under the community property laws of this state be fully protected, and that in the event Roger predeceases her, she will have sufficient property as the result of their marriage to enable her to maintain the lifestyle to which she has become accustomed. To this end Roger specifically agrees that, within 30 days of the parties' marriage, he will do the following:

A.   Transfer to Annette an undivided interest in his home at 77 Firwood Drive, Golden City, valued at approximately $400,000, so that he and Annette hold this residence as joint tenants with right of survivorship. He will also pay off the balance of the mortgage on this property.

B.   Procure and thereafter pay all premiums on a life insurance policy in the amount of $200,000, which policy will name Annette as sole beneficiary.

C.   Open a joint savings account between himself and Annette and thereafter maintain a balance of at least $30,000, that being the amount agreed on by the parties as necessary to provide a smooth transition in the event of Roger's death.

D.   Open a joint checking account between himself and Annette and thereafter deposit all sums necessary to enable the parties to meet monthly expenses and enjoy a comfortable and gracious lifestyle during their marriage.

III. It is agreed by the parties that the value of the property transferred to Annette under Paragraph II, if she should survive Roger, equals or exceeds the value of any community property that might be acquired after marriage, and Annette specifically accepts these transfers, once they become final, as full satisfaction of her community property rights.

IV. It is also agreed by the parties that during the marriage Annette's separate property shall remain her separate property, and that she alone will be entitled to all rents and profits therefrom, whether or not some part of this income might be characterized as community property.

V.   Finally, it is further agreed by the parties that beyond the specific transfers above mentioned, neither shall have any interest in the separate property of the other, and in particular, each party specifically waives the right to inherit from the estate of the other.   Each of the parties has a child or children from a previous marriage, and it is understood that each has willed or intends to will most if not all of his or her separate estate to these children.

In witness whereof, the parties have signed this agreement this 25th day of September, 1979.

_____   _____
ROGER WINTHROP STERN   ANNETTE ELY LOCKWOOD

(The agreement was properly executed under Columbia law.)

TRUST

Andrew Cook of DeVane, Columbia, as Trustor, and Jean Hemphill of DeVane, Columbia, as Trustee, agree as follows:

1. The Trustor hereby transfers and delivers to the Trustee the property listed in Schedule "A", which is attached to this document [not included in this example], together with all his interest in the property described in Schedule "A". The Trustee shall hold the property, together with any additions to the property as provided in this trust agreement as a Trust Estate. The Trustee shall invest and reinvest the property and shall distribute the net income {hereinafter called "income"} and principal for the benefit of the Trustor's children, Michael and Elizabeth.

2. Until Michael and Elizabeth both reach their thirtieth birthdays, the Trustee shall expend both income and principal to such extent and in such manner as she in her sole discretion deems advisable for the beneficiaries' welfare, comfortable support, maintenance, and education. The Trustee shall also add any excess income to principal and invest it as such.

3. When both beneficiaries have reached their thirtieth birthdays, the Trustee shall terminate and the principal and any accrued or undistributed income shall be transferred and delivered to the beneficiaries, in equal amounts, free of trust.

4. If a beneficiary should die prior to the time he or she is entitled to receive distribution of the Trust Estate, one-half of the principal and one-half of any accrued or undistributed income shall be distributed to the beneficiary's then living children, in equal shares. If there is no living child of the beneficiary, then the beneficiary's share shall be distributed to the Homeless Foundation in Columbia.

5. Neither the principal nor income of the Trust Estate held by the Trustee shall be subject to assignment or other anticipation by any beneficiary of this trust. Nor shall any beneficiary's interest be subject to any attachment by garnishment or by any other legal proceeding or action for any debt or other obligation of a beneficiary to this Trust.

6. This Trust shall not be revoked or terminated by Trustor or any other person, nor shall it be amended or altered by Trustor or any other person.

PROBLEM SOLVING

1.   **Identify problem in terms of the client's goals.**

2.   **Identify options (alternatives, courses of action)**

3.   **Identify and analyze consequences for each option (legal and non-legal consequences).**

4.   **If requested – select and implement best option**

Performance Test Workshops

SAMPLE INSTRUCTION SHEET

Rubineau and Boyle
Attorneys at Law
1200 Second Street
Fort Gaines, Columbia 89334

MEMORANDUM   February 24, 1994

To: All Lawyers
From: Executive Committee
Re: <u>Pre-Counseling Letter Guidelines</u>

Often members of the firm will be required to conduct a counseling session with a client who is confronted with several significant and difficult choices. In such a situation, the lawyer is advised to prepare and deliver to the client a Pre-Counseling Letter. In addition to helping prepare the client for the counseling session, the letter will serve as an organizing aid for the lawyer conducting the session.

All pre-counseling letters will use the following format:

- State your understanding of the client's goals.

- Identify all courses of action the client can take or that may be taken against the client.

- For each course of action, identify the possible consequences or results, whether legal, economic, or personal.

- Be sure to explain the possible consequences or results, why they are possible, and how likely they are to occur. This will require a discussion of the interrelationship of the law and facts. Remember that most pre-counseling letters are written to lay clients. Although discussion of underlying law is necessary, you must structure this discussion having in mind the client's level of sophistication.

- Where a possible course of action, consequence, or result is unclear, identify what additional information we need, why we need it, and how it can be obtained.

SAMPLE INSTRUCTION SHEET

LAW OFFICES OF LYNN R. DAWSON

5922 Jeanette Drive
Cordesville, Columbia

MEMORANDUM

To: All Attorneys

From: Executive Committee

Re: **Opinion Letter Guidelines**

Often the firm's attorneys must prepare an opinion letter to communicate its views to a client. An opinion letter should follow this format:

• State the facts that led to the client's need for advice.

• State your understanding of the client's goal or goals.

• Identify options the client has or the actions the client could take to achieve those goals.

• Objectively analyze each of the client's options or possible actions in light of the applicable law and the relevant facts. Be sure to identify the likely success in achieving the client's goals of pursuing each option or action.

• Although you must discuss the law, you should do so as clearly and straightforwardly as possible, in language that allows the client to follow your reasoning and the logic of your conclusions.

ETHICAL CONSIDERATIONS

TWO POSSIBILITIES

1. **Law is in the library.**

2. **No law in the library, but attorney's behavior in the file is questionable.**

    Identify Problem

    Suggest Options

    Recommend one option

BETWEEN TODAY AND OUR NEXT MEETING

Write Out:

1. *In re Sunrise Galleria Mall* -- **in the CGAB and to be graded by Barbri.**

2. *Zwier v. Sea Quest* -- **appears next in this In-Class Workbook.**

3. Simulated Bar Performance Exam – to be assigned later in your Paced Program, and appears near the end of this In-Class Workbook.

On Day 3, we will review the *Zwier v. Sea Quest* exam along with the Simulated Bar Performance Exam. Be sure to bring your answers to *Zwier* and the Simulated Bar Performance Exam along with this In-Class Workbook to our next meeting.

PERFORMANCE TEST WORKSHOP SIMULATED EXAM

Zwier v. Sea Quest

Zwier v. Sea Quest (Cayman) Limited, et al.

INSTRUCTIONS

FILE

Zwier v. Sea Quest (Cayman) Limited, et al.

INSTRUCTIONS

1. You will have three hours to complete this session of the examination. This performance test is designed to evaluate your ability to handle a select number of legal authorities in the context of a factual problem involving a client.

2. The problem is set in the fictional state of Columbia, one of the United States. You are an associate in a law firm representing Sea Quest (Cayman) Ltd.

3. You will have two sets of materials with which to work: A File and a Library. You will be called upon to distinguish relevant from irrelevant facts, analyze the legal authorities provided, and prepare outlines identifying the relevant legal elements and the information to be sought during witness interviews.

4. The File contains a copy of the complaint as well as factual information about your case in the form of six documents. The first document is a memorandum to you from Michael Allen Wolf containing the instructions for the documents you are to prepare.

5. The Library contains a Columbia statute and two cases. They may be real, modified, or written solely for the purpose of this examination. Although the materials may appear familiar to you, do not assume that they are precisely the same as you have read before. Read them thoroughly, as if all were new to you. You should assume that the cases were decided in the jurisdictions and on the dates shown.

6. Your responses must be written in the answer book provided. In answering this performance test, you should concentrate on the materials provided, but you should bring to bear on the problem your general knowledge of the law. What you have learned in law school and elsewhere provides the general background for analyzing the problem; the File and Library provide the specific materials with which you must work.

7. In citing cases from the Library, you may use abbreviations and omit citations.

8. Although there are no restrictions on how you apportion your time, you should probably allocate at least 90 minutes to organizing and writing your documents.

9. This performance test will be graded on your responsiveness to instructions and on the content, thoroughness, and organization of the memorandum and analysis you are asked to prepare. In grading the answers to this question, we anticipate that the following approximate weights will be assigned to each part.

A: 50%
B: 50%

Herbert, Wolf & Stubbs
Attorneys at Law
700 Columbia Center
Richland, Columbia

MEMORANDUM   February 21, 1995

To: Applicant
From: Michael Allen Wolf
Re: Zwier v. Sea Quest (Cayman) Limited, et al.

We have been requested to handle part of a law suit filed against Sea Quest (Cayman) Ltd. As you will see from the attached complaint, suit has been brought here in the United State District Court for the Northern District of Columbia. Sea Quest is incorporated in the Cayman Islands, located just south of Cuba. A second defendant, Scuba Tours International, is located in Indianapolis, Indiana and has separate counsel. We were contacted by Sea Quest's Cayman Islands attorney to see if we can get the suit dismissed

What I would like you to do is focus on two parts of our plan to seek dismissal. I want to be able to argue that the federal district court here in Columbia does not have personal jurisdiction over Sea Quest and in the alternative, that the suit should be dismissed on the basis of forum non conveniens. Specifically, please do the following:

1.   Draft a memorandum to me in which you

   a)   identify the factors the court will consider in deciding our motion to dismiss based upon lack of personal jurisdiction over Sea Quest.

   b)   for each factor, identify the facts in the file that support our position.

   c)   for each factor, identify what additional facts we need and where we might find them. Please be specific about the facts we need and the likely sources. For example, don't just say we need more facts about Sea Quest's purposeful interjection; instead, go through each issue, fact and source, as in the following example:

   1. Did Defendant Sea Quest act or complete a transaction in Columbia by which it invoked the benefits and protection of Columbia law?

      a)   Did Sea Quest advertise its services in Columbia?

97

        (1)   Via newspapers or TV. Ask Reginald Jones and depose appropriate STI employee.

        (2)   Via . . .

   b)   . . . .

2.   Based on the information presently available, draft affidavits to be signed by Reginald Jones and Francis Swift to support our motion that the suit be dismissed on the basis of forum non conveniens. I expect that Jones and Swift will give us information to support our position that trial of the case in Columbia will be inconvenient to our client. Having identified the facts known to us, identify what additional information we should seek to include in the affidavits to support a finding of forum non conveniens. In this latter task, please identify, in the form of a statement which could be included in an affidavit, the information the existence of which we need to determine. Place the information that needs to be determined in a bracket within the statement. Then, once we learn the missing fact, we can decide whether actually to include the statement in the affidavit.

For example, even though we don't know that the Cayman Islands allows an action for negligently causing injury, your draft of the Jones' affidavit would include, "The justice system in the Cayman Islands [recognizes or does not recognize] a cause of action for recovery of damages for negligently causing injury to the person of plaintiff in negligently inflicting emotional distress." I have included a couple of cases that should guide you in these tasks. In addition, I spoke with Reginald Jones, Sea Quest's Cayman lawyer and Nancy O'Brien, STI's lawyer. A partial transcript of each phone conversation is attached as well as a couple of documents Jones faxed along with the complaint.

Herbert, Wolf & Stubbs
Attorneys at Law
700 Columbia Center
Richland, Columbia

MEMORANDUM

To: All Attorneys and Paralegals

From: Executive Committee

Re: <u>Affidavits in Support of Motions or Other Requests for Judicial or Administrative Action</u>

Affidavits should meet the following requirements:

> 1. Affidavits are to be limited to statements of fact. Those facts should be those necessary to support the legal position asserted in the motion or other requested.
>
> 2. The facts should be presented in numbered paragraphs and each numbered paragraph, to the extent possible, should contain only one factual statement.
>
> 3. Only those facts which are personally known to the affiant and which are truthful, logically relevant and material shall be included.

Assume that the person signing the affidavit will be subject to cross-examination concerning the contents of the affidavit. Particular care must be taken to insure that person's credibility will not be impeached.

The materials you rely upon may not always contain precisely the facts you need. There often are, however, other facts can be inferred from existing statements of the person who will sign the affidavit. If you have a good faith basis to believe that he or she has personal knowledge of those inferred facts, include them. We will then check with the person to confirm he or she actually does have personal knowledge of the inferred fact.

Captions, signature lines, and sworn acknowledgment will be added by support staff.

1

UNITED STATES DISTRICT COURT

NORTHERN DISTRICT OF COLUMBIA

2

3

4   Paul Zwier,   )
              Plaintiff,   )

5   )
    v.   )

6   )   COMPLAINT
    Sea Quest (Cayman) Ltd., and   )   C.A. No. 1945N

7   Scuba Tours International,   )
              Defendants.   )

8   _____)

9   1. Plaintiff, Paul Zwier, is a citizen of the State of Columbia.

10   2. Defendant, Sea Quest (Cayman) Limited, is incorporated under the laws of

11   the Cayman Islands with its principal place of business in the Cayman Islands

12   3. Defendant, Scuba Tours International, is incorporated under the laws of the

13   State of Indiana, with its principal place of business in the State of Indiana.

14   4. The matter in controversy exceeds, exclusive of interest and costs, the sum

15   of fifty thousand dollars.

16   5. Sea Quest operates a boat and dive operation in the Cayman Islands.

17   6. Sea Quest maintains a corporate office on Cayman Brac, one of three main

18   islands forming the Cayman Islands

19   7. Scuba Tours International is a travel agency located in Indianapolis, Indiana.

20   specializing in travel arrangements for scuba diving trips.

21   8. Sea Quest participates in a continuing commercial relationship with Scuba

22   Tours International to provide accommodations and scuba diving services on the
    Cayman Islands.

23   9. On August 14, 1993, Plaintiff's mother, as a birthday present, made

24   arrangements for a scuba diving trip through Scuba Tours International.

25   10. Plaintiff left Columbia International Airport on November 21, 1993, and

26   flew to the Cayman Islands.

27

100

1   11. Plaintiff stayed and went diving with Sea Quest.

2   12. On November 27, 1993, Plaintiff went scuba diving off the coast of Little

3   Cayman Island. After surfacing from his first dive, Plaintiff felt a swelling in his head

4   and became dizzy and began to vomit.

5   13. The nearest hospital to Little Cayman is on Cayman Brac, a one-hour boat

6   ride away.

7   14. The nearest pressure chamber to treat dive-related accidents is on Grand

8   Cayman and is a 30-minute flight from Cayman Brac.

9   15. Sea Quest employees refused to return the boat to Cayman Brac to seek

10   medical help for the plaintiff.

11   16. Two hours after the first symptoms Sea Quest crew members transferred

12   Plaintiff to another boat operated by a different company that was going back to

13   Cayman Brac.

14   17. Plaintiff spent one week in the hospital on Cayman Brac.

15   18. As a result of Sea Quest's failure to return immediately to Cayman Brac,

16   Plaintiff suffered permanent nerve damage to his inner ear, resulting in significant and

17   permanent injury.

18   Defendants' negligence and negligent infliction of emotional distress have

19   caused permanent injury to plaintiff.

20   Wherefore plaintiff demands judgment against defendants for the sum of

21   $1,250,000, interest, and costs.

22

23   Signed: *Samuel Lew*
                                     Samuel Levin
24   Attorney for Plaintiff
                                     207 Williams Drive
25   Richland, Columbia

26

27

28

1

PARTIAL TRANSCRIPT OF TELEPHONE INTERVIEW
WITH REGINALD JONES, ESQ.

2

3 . . . .

4   BY REGINALD JONES (RJ): Unfortunately, Michael, I don't have much information

5 other than that contained in the complaint. Sea Quest's owner, Francis Swift, was served

6 last week and I just got a copy today.

7   BY MICHAEL ALLEN WOLF (MAW): I got the FAX of the complaint, and it does not

8 say much. By the way, how was he served?

9   RJ: Swift made a trip to Miami during the holidays and was served at the airport.

10 Flights to Miami are frequent and lots of people here make the trip regularly. It's convenient

11 for shopping and the like. Is service something we can get this dismissed on?

12   MAW: Possibly, but unlikely. If there is personal jurisdiction, then service within the

13 States is probably going to be okay under Columbia law. What was the point of Swift's trip?

14 Medical, shopping, what?

15   RJ: I don't really know. The trip was most likely for shopping or business. He may

16 have relatives there. He was born and raised here but some of his family may have moved

17 to the States. I doubt it was medical. We have a first-rate medical system here. Fact is,

18 we're having a problem with people from the States. A fair number of retirees have bought

19 condominiums down here, say they take up residency, and then come down for the

20 medical treatment and medication purchases. Socialized medicine and all. Fact is, I'll bet

21 Zwier's week in the hospital on Cayman Brac cost him all of $25 U.S.

22   MAW: No kidding. What is it exactly you want us to do, handle the litigation?

23   RJ: At this point, I'm only authorized to retain you to see if we can't get the suit

24 dismissed outright or at least transferred to some place more convenient.

25   MAW: Well, I'll look into that immediately. We'll need someone to do an affidavit on

26 the availability and other aspects of the Cayman Islands' system.

27

28

1   RJ: That's no problem. I can do that. I've been a lawyer in Britain for ten years and

2   then another 15 years here in the Cayman Islands. If the case is ever tried here, we'll use

3   a local trial lawyer. Assuming the suit goes forward, we obviously would prefer to try the

4   case here in the Cayman Islands. There are fewer cases, so the docket moves quickly, and

5   the judgments are for much less money. Besides which, this is a small operation. If Francis

6   has to spend lots of time in the States, it's going to ruin the business.

7   MAW: Tell me about the company.

8   RJ: It's really pretty small. It has two boats that each hold 16 divers and two crew

9   members. These boats make day trips out of Cayman Brac. They typically leave in the

10   early morning and stay out long enough for two dives. The divers then come back and stay

11   on the island.

12   MAW: Was one of these where Zwier was injured?

13   RJ: Apparently not. They have a third boat that is what's known in the industry as

14   a live-aboard. It's 110 feet long and has cabin space for 16 divers and four crew: captain,

15   cook, engineer, and expert dive master. It goes out for five or six days at a time. That's

16   what Zwier was on.

17   MAW: What's something like that cost?

18   RJ: Maybe two or three million. It's converted from being used to serve oil rigs. In

19   fact, the Captain used to run it for the oil company and went with it when Smith bought it.

20   MAW: What does a week on the boat run?

21   RJ: Average probably $1,300 U.S.

22   MAW: Tell me something about the Cayman Islands.

23   RJ: The Cayman Islands is a dependency of Great Britain. Actually, it's officially

24   referred to as a British Dependent Territory. A citizen of a British Dependent Territory is a

25   citizen of the United Kingdom and Colonies. The Cayman Islands is administered by a

26   governor who is appointed by the British monarch. The United Kingdom represents

27   Caymanian diplomatic interests and is responsible for its military defense.

28

1   MAW: How big?

2   RJ: Three islands. In decreasing size, Grand Cayman, Cayman Brac, and Little

3   Cayman. Total population is around 25,000, most of these here on Grand Cayman. About

4   1200 live on Cayman Brac. Maybe 20 permanent residences on Little Cayman.

5   MAW: What's the court system like? British common law?

6   RJ: Yes, it is patterned after that of Great Britain. In addition, the Common Law of

7   England is recognized and applied by the courts in all cases where there has not been a

8   specific local enactment.

9   MAW: What's the relationship with Scuba Tours?

10   RJ: In the summer of 1990, Sea Quest and I negotiated a long-term contract with

11   STI by which STI would be the exclusive booking agent for the Sea Quest live-aboard. STI

12   frequently lists trips to the Cayman Islands in its advertising brochures and has included

13   specific references to Sea Quest.

14   MAW: How about the Zwier trip? Was it definitely booked through STI?

15   RJ: Yes. The only customers he takes out on the live-aboard are through STI. STI

16   puts together each group that goes out on the Sea Quest; they're responsible for getting

17   at least 75% occupancy. STI does all the work. For example, Francis says that the only

18   paperwork on the Zwier trip was a copy of the voucher Zwier brought with him. I'll FAX that

19   to you. Honestly, I haven't pushed too hard to get the basic facts yet. I figured I needed to

20   contact someone like you first thing. After you take a look at this, I can relay questions to

21   Francis or better yet, you can call him direct.

22   MAW: Is there any question whether Zwier was on the boat?

23   RJ: No. Francis said he remembers the incident quite well. You don't have major

24   dive accidents every day. The poor guy had to get a boat back to the States because the

25   doctors didn't want to risk additional ear damage if an airplane became depressurized.

26   Zwier was also apparently traveling with a companion who negotiated a reduced rate on

27

28

1   a return trip because the one with Zwier was cut short. He remembers talking to the

2   companion maybe six months later and hearing about what happened all over again.

3   MAW: What happened anyway?

4   RJ: We're still not sure. Of course, they checked all of the equipment after the

5   accident and couldn't find anything wrong. They don't know whether Zwier was sick

6   before he went diving or whether it was just one of those things. Francis and the dive

7   master are convinced that it's just one of the inherent risks of scuba diving. Sometimes

8   you and the diver do everything right, and the results still turn out bad.

9   MAW: Who is representing STI?

10   RJ: I'm not sure, but it is probably Smith and O'Brien in Indianapolis. I worked with

11   them on the contract with STI, but like I said, that was in 1990.

12   MAW: Do you have a copy of that agreement?

13   RJ: I'll see if I can find it. I'm not sure I have it.

14   MAW: Thanks.

15

16

17

18

19

20

21

22

23

24

25

26

27

28

1

PARTIAL TRANSCRIPT OF INTERVIEW WITH NANCY O'BRIEN

2

3   BY NANCY O'BRIEN (NO): As I said, I am not prepared to discuss this matter in any

4   I depth. I just received the complaint myself and I have serious questions about whether

5   there is a possibility of a cross claim against Sea Quest.

6   BY MICHAEL ALLEN WOLF (MAW): I hear you. I would just like to know something

7   about STI.

8   NO: Let me be straight with you, Mr. Wolf. Our position is that STI is little more than

9   a telephone service for Sea Quest. It is a travel agency that does business under several

10   names. STI specializes in scuba trips, but the overall operation covers general travel

11   services. When you speak of STI, you refer only to a name we use for advertising

12   purposes. You know, in those listings that target scuba divers.

13   MAW: But what do you mean by telephone service?

14   NO: The company has 25 telephones. Eight to ten different hotels, scuba operations

15   and the like are listed under the same number. When anyone calls the number, they simply

16   answer, "Hello, Travel." If, for example, the person calling inquires, "Is this STI?" the clerk

17   answers, "Yes."

18   MAW: You advertise for Sea Quest?

19   NO: STI sends out literature supplied by its clients to people who ask for it on the

20   telephone.

21   MAW: Ads in magazines, newspapers?

22   NO: I'm not sure what you are driving at, Mr. Wolf. As I said, STI doesn't exercise

23   all that much control. When a customer calls STI, it is willing to answer any question that

24   the party at the other end of the line may want to know. Generally speaking, they want to

25   know the prices, and they want literature sent. STI will then send out the literature to the

26   prospective guest. If they're interested in making a reservation, STI will talk to them about

27

28

1   the reservation, and STI will accept the same, provided they send a deposit. No

2   reservation will be taken simply on a mere telephone call.

3   MAW: But STI does more than that.

4   NO: STI takes down the name and the address, telephone number, date when

5   they plan to go, and how long they plan to stay. The clerk will discuss with them the

6   type of accommodation they want. And, at the end, well, STI tells them, "Well, you send

7   us a deposit and you will receive a receipt and a confirmation of the reservation."

8   MAW: Who sends the receipt and confirmation?

9   NO: STI

10   MAW: STI has an exclusive contract with Sea Quest, don't they?

11   NO: There is a written agreement between STI and Sea Quest. Now, I am sorry,

12   but I have a court appearance. We'll have to finish this later, after I have had more time

13   to look into it and talk to my client.

14   MAW: Thank you for your time.

15

16

17

18

19

20

21

22

23

24

25

26

27

28

SCUBA TOURS INTERNATIONAL

Indiana's Largest

Fax (317) 555-1234

1 (800) 555-CUBA

To:_____

This travel voucher will act as confirmation of receipt of $1,250, full purchase price for full accommodations and diving aboard **Sea Quest (Cayman) Ltd.**, November 21, 1993 through November 30, 1993. Services to include:

· Accommodations aboard **Sea Quest**

· All meals (excluding alcoholic beverages)

· Weights, tanks and unlimited diving

· Transfers from Cayman Brac Airport to boat

_____

Scuba Tours International

Travelers are reminded that airfare is **not** included in this voucher. Our travel agents remain ready to make your airline arrangements. Please call.

Limitation of Liability: Divers agree to assume the risk for any injuries resulting from the inherently risky activity of scuba diving and agree to hold both Sea Quest and STI harmless for the consequences of any such injury

Travel Agents of America

SCUBA TOURS INTERNATIONAL
Indiana's Largest
FAX (317) 555-1234
1(800) 555-CUBA

January 21, 1995 Newsletter

Okay, happy campers, two great deals this month:

<u>CORAL SEA NOMAD</u>
One hundred and fifty feet of diving luxury in one of the most exotic locations in the world. Spaces are limited. Call now. $2200 - $2500 for 10 day trips.

<u>SEA QUEST</u>

<u>The New Standard in Live-Aboard Diving</u>

Come join us diving the pristine waters of Little Cayman Island. View the spectacular Bloody Bay Wall. Swim with the Mantas and enjoy the companionship of experienced divers. All for less per dive than you would pay at the best shore-based operations. $1,3000 - $1,500 for 7-day trip.

CALL AND WE'LL MAKE YOUR TRIP ONE TO REMEMBER

Travel Agents of America

Mr. Wolf, I also found this recent newsletter from **STI.**
                                    R.J.

Zwier v. Sea Quest (Cayman) Limited, et al

Library

STATUTE OF COLUMBIA

Title 12, §2004

A court of this state may exercise jurisdiction on any basis consistent with the constitution of this state and the Constitution of the United States.

<u>Mercier v. Sheraton International, Inc.</u>
United States Court of Appeals, 1st Cir. (1991)

Susan and George Mercier appeal the district court's dismissal of their diversity breach of contract suit against Sheraton International, Inc. ("Sheraton International"). The district court dismissed the diversity action on grounds of forum non convenient concluding that the Republic of Turkey was a more suitable alternative jurisdiction in which to pursue this suit.

I.   Facts and Procedural History

At all times relevant to this suit, Susan and George Mercier--daughter and father--were United States citizens. At the time the suit was brought, Susan Mercier was a New York citizen; her father was a Florida citizen. Sheraton International is a Delaware corporation with its principal place of business in Massachusetts.

Sometime in 1983, the Merciers and Hamilton Bauer (on behalf of Sheraton International) signed a Memorandum of Understanding that provided the basic terms for the establishment and operation of a casino in the Istanbul Sheraton. The Memorandum essentially provided that in return for an annual fee paid to Sheraton International, the Merciers would be permitted to operate a casino in the hotel. There is disagreement about whether all terms of the Memorandum were satisfied.

Susan Mercier settled in Turkey and began to prepare for the casino's opening. In January 1986, however, she was involved in a violent altercation with a Turkish national who had served as her translator. Susan Mercier claims that the Turkish national attacked her when she rejected his marriage proposal; however, it appears that her alleged attacker filed charges with the Turkish authorities. As a result, Susan Mercier fled Turkey. An October 1986 State Department telex reported that Susan Mercier had been charged with assault, a felony, and would probably be arrested if she reentered Turkey.

It appears that, in the fall of 1987, Sheraton International entered into an agreement with Leisure Investments P.L.C. (Leisure), a British company. The agreement provided for Leisure to be the sole operator of a casino. Casino operations commenced, without the Merciers, sometime in 1988.

The Merciers first filed suit in the United States District Court for the District of Massachusetts against Sheraton International. Sheraton International moved for dismissal on grounds of forum non conveniens. The district court granted Sheraton International's motion to dismiss.

II. Discussion

A. Standard of Review and Governing Principles

The Supreme Court has set out the appropriate analysis for a district court to undertake when presented with a motion to dismiss on grounds of forum non conveniens. A district court may dismiss a case when an alternative forum has jurisdiction to hear the case, and when trial in the chosen forum would establish oppressiveness and vexation to a defendant out of all proportion to plaintiff's convenience, or when the chosen forum is inappropriate because of considerations affecting the court's own administrative and legal problems.

A finding that there is a suitable alternative forum is usually justified as long as the defendant is amenable to process in the other forum. In rare circumstances--such as when the alternative forum does not permit litigation of the subject matter of the dispute--an alternative forum may be inadequate, even if service can be accomplished.

Once having concluded that an adequate alternative forum exists, a district court is then to consider whether the balance of convenience and judicial efficiency favors litigating the claim in the alternative forum. The district court should undertake this inquiry mindful that the forum non conveniens doctrine's principal purpose is to ensure that trials are convenient, both for the parties and for the court.

The Supreme Court has identified a number of private and public interest factors that are to guide this aspect of the district court's inquiry. The private interest factors include relative ease of access to sources of proof; availability of compulsory process for attendance of unwilling, and the cost of obtaining attendance of willing witnesses; possibility of view of premises, if view would be appropriate to the action; all other practical problems that make trial of a case easy, expeditious and inexpensive; and questions as to the enforceability of a judgment if one is obtained. The public interest factors include the administrative difficulties flowing from court congestion; the local interest in having localized controversies decided at home; the interest in having the trial of a diversity case in a forum that is at home with the law that must govern the action; the avoidance of unnecessary problems in conflict of laws, or in application of foreign laws; and the unfairness of burdening citizens in an unrelated forum with jury duty. The plaintiff's forum choice should rarely be disturbed, thus, the moving defendant must establish that the private and public interests weigh heavily on the side of trial in foreign forum.

With these principles in mind, we now turn to the merits of the appeal.

B.   Adequate Alternative Forum

The district court concluded that the Republic of Turkey was an adequate alternative forum. In doing so, it relied principally on an affidavit submitted by Sheraton International. The affidavit was taken by Yucel Sayman, a professor of law and practicing attorney in Istanbul. After summarizing his professional qualifications, and explaining his (correct) understanding that the Merciers were making claims for breach of contract and tortious interference with contract, Sayman states:

> The courts of Istanbul are competent to hear the claims stated in the Complaint filed by the Merciers in the above-captioned proceeding. In such a civil proceeding before our courts the litigants are guaranteed the same sort of procedural safeguards I understand they enjoy in the United States. They are entitled to be heard, to present evidence, and to cross-examine their opponent's witnesses. The judgment of the trial court is subject to review by an appellate tribunal called, "Yargitay"--Court of Appeals. Our constitution grants standing to foreign nationals, such as the Merciers, to prosecute such commercial claims in our courts.

Before the district court, the Merciers objected that this affidavit was insufficient to establish that Turkey is an adequate alternative forum. In particular, they argued that the Sayman affidavit was deficient because it did not discuss (1) Turkey's substantive law of contract, (2) statute of limitations and fee arrangements, and (3) whether Turkey would take jurisdiction of a dispute in which neither party is a Turkish national. The Merciers renew these objections on appeal. Moreover, even should these issues be resolved in Sheraton International's favor, the Merciers contend that Susan Mercier's difficulties with the Turkish unavailable for all practical purposes.

Finally, the Merciers direct our attention to authority apparently not provided to the district court suggesting that Turkey has a one-year statute of limitations that would bar the claims sought to be pursued in the present action.

We believe the district court erred. We are mindful of the Merciers' failure to provide competing evidence that an adequate alternative forum does not exist; nevertheless, it remains the moving defendant's burden to establish that an adequate alternative forum does exist. As we conclude that the affidavit through which Sheraton International attempted to meet its burden contains substantial gaps, we believe the district court acted prematurely in finding that Turkey is an adequate alternative forum.

While cognizant of the district court's discretion in such issues, we believe that the affidavit failed to satisfy fully the initial burden which must be shouldered by a defendant seeking a forum non conveniens dismissal. Among the affidavit's most notable defects is its failure to state expressly that Turkish law recognizes claims for breach of contract and tortious interference with contract--or some analogous action.[1] A general recitation such as Sayman's that the alternative forum can adjudicate "commercial claims," simply fails to provide a sufficient basis upon which confidently to conclude that Turkey will take cognizance of this dispute.

The affidavit is even more defective with respect to statute of limitations issues: it wholly fails to address this question. We note that, at the oral argument of this appeal, Sheraton

International's counsel expressed a willingness to waive Sheraton International's right to raise in Turkish courts any statute of limitations claim that would not be available should the action go forward in Massachusetts. That concession is insufficient. Even given a willingness on Sheraton International's part to abandon such defenses, the Merciers must be given an opportunity to address the question whether Turkish courts would accept such a waiver[2] and, if they would not, to argue the effect of such a refusal to the Court deciding the forum non conveniens motion.

Our conviction that the district court erred in finding that Turkey is an adequate alternative is bolstered by the district court's own findings. The district court stated that its decision was partially premised on the conclusion that, Susan Mercier's difficulties notwithstanding, George Mercier remained free to bring their case in Turkey. The district court noted, however, that "Susan must be afforded an opportunity to present her evidence through affidavits and depositions, etc. Assuming that she is able to do so, I believe a Turkish court will be able to competently and fairly judge the Merciers' complaint." Having stated its belief that Susan Mercier's testimony was essential to the prosecution of this case, the district court failed to attach any conditions to its dismissal that would ensure that such testimony would be considered. By "assuming" that Susan Mercier would be

---

1 We recognize that the Supreme Court has cautioned against refusing to dismiss on forum non conveniens grounds simply because a foreign forum does not recognize an identical cause of action. However, the Court also stated that dismissal would not be appropriate where the alternative forum does not permit litigation of the subject matter of the dispute. Thus, it is in incumbent upon the defendant moving for dismissal on forum non conveniens grounds to establish that there is a meaningful cause of action available in the proposed alternative forum.

2 The notion that the Turkish courts might refuse to recognize Sheraton International's voluntary abandonment of statute of limitations defenses might seem off to those familiar with American practice, where such waivers are regularly recognized. However, we find the possibility of such a refusal no more implausible than the well-accepted American rule barring a federal court from accepting a defendant's waiver of jurisdictional defects.

allowed to present testimony, rather than requiring an affirmative demonstration to that effect, the district court mistakenly relieved the moving defendant of its burden of assuming the district court that all conditions essential to establishing an adequate alternative forum exist.

Finally, the rather summary fashion in which the affidavit announces its conclusions inspires little confidence. This fact standing alone--or any of the other defects of the Sayman affidavit standing in isolation--might not warrant reversal. Cumulatively, however, they suggest sufficient uncertainty about Turkey's capacity and readiness to entertain this suit that defendant should have been required to provide further evidence and assurances to the district court before dismissal was granted. At a minimum, the district court should have granted a dismissal conditioned on the Turkish courts' actually taking cognizance of a substitute action.

The Merciers urge us to decide that Turkey is incapable of ever serving as an adequate alternative forum. The Merciers advance two grounds for such a conclusion. First, they highlight Susan Mercier's personal difficulties and argue that her flight from, and refusal to return to, Turkey will preclude meaningful prosecution of the Mercier claims. However, we share the district court's doubts that Susan Mercier's personal difficulties with the Turkish system--as opposed to a showing of Turkish justice's systematic inadequacy--can provide an appropriate basis for a finding that Turkey is an inadequate forum.

We leave this issue open for exploration on remand, however, in light of the district court's previously expressed view that Susan Mercier's testimony is essential to the case. Should it be the case that Turkish courts will refuse to admit the affidavit or deposition testimony of Susan Mercier due to her fugitive status, the district court on remand may be justified in concluding that Turkey is an inadequate alternative forum. However, absent an absolute, or near-absolute, prohibition on the admission of such testimony that would gut the core of the Merciers' action--thus rending Turkey inadequate--we believe restrictions on Susan Mercier that flow from her flight from Turkey do not make Turkey inadequate. In particular, if the district court reasonably determines that (1) Susan Mercier's testimony would be admitted by a Turkish court, or, (2) her testimony is not essential to the presentation of the Merciers' claim, we would then find merit in the district court's conclusion that George Mercier's ability to serve as surrogate by bringing an action in Turkey adequately addresses Susan Mercier's difficulties.

The Merciers also urge that we find Turkey inadequate based on considerations of Middle East upheaval and via judicial notice of the "injustice prevalent in the Turkish legal system when a

118

foreigner (especially a woman) opposes a Turkish man." The record provides no basis for us to suspect, much less take judicial notice of, an American woman's patent inability to secure basic justice in the Turkish courts. We cannot say, therefore, that the district court erred in refusing to find Turkey inadequate on this basis.

We therefore conclude that, while Sheraton International did not carry its affirmative burden of showing that Turkey is an adequate alternative forum, the Merciers have failed to demonstrate that under no circumstances could Turkey be an adequate forum. At a minimum, therefore, remand is warranted so that the district court may conduct additional factual inquiry, and perhaps--should the district court conclude it is appropriate--fashion a conditional dismissal that will ensure the Merciers' ability to prosecute their claim. However, before announcing such a disposition we must consider the Merciers' additional contention that, even should Turkey be an adequate alternative forum, a proper balancing of the private and public interests at stake compels retention of the case in Massachusetts. Should this be the case, dismissal would be improper, even if Turkey should prove to be an adequate alternative. We turn now to this issue.

C. The Private and Public Interest Factors Balancing

1. Private Interest Factors

Sheraton International argued before the district court that an analysis of the relevant private interest factors reveals that Turkey is a more convenient forum for litigating this action. Sheraton International relied principally on the fact that the principals of Sheraton International's "owning company" are in Turkey, and not amenable to compulsory process that would ensure that their testimony is available. The district court disagreed. It found that Sheraton had failed to establish that these witnesses would be unwilling to come to the United States or to provide depositions on a voluntary basis. It also found that the translation and travel expenses Sheraton International faces if the case goes forward in Massachusetts are roughly equal to those that the Merciers face if the case proceeds in Turkey. The district court then concluded that this general equipoise, combined with the presumption favoring a plaintiff's choice of forum, dictated that the private interest factors weighed in favor of retaining jurisdiction.

We think it within the district court's discretion to have concluded that the burdens of arranging for witness attendance are likely to be about equal. We therefore accept that finding. In turn, we accept the district court's conclusion that the private interest factors weigh in favor of retaining jurisdiction, primarily on the strength of the substantial deference due a domestic plaintiff's choice of forum.

2. Public Interest Factors

The district court concluded that the public interest factors weighed heavily in favor of dismissing the Massachusetts action with a view to having it litigated in Turkey. In reaching this conclusion the district court relied on (1) the crowded state of its own docket compared to that in Turkey, (2) the minimal importance of the action to Massachusetts, and (3) the difficulties that the district court would face in mastering and applying Turkish law. The Merciers challenge each element of the district court's analysis.

On the present record, we do not disagree with the district court's conclusion that several of these facts point toward dismissal. We believe, however, the district court erred in weighing the relevance of the parties' citizenship and residence to the public interest factor analysis.

The Merciers' United States citizenship and residence--plus Sheraton International's similar citizenship and residence--are factors that make this a controversy local to the United States, if not necessarily to Massachusetts. In turn, conducting the case in the United States would serve the substantial public interest of providing a convenient United States forum for an action in which all parties are United States citizens and residents.

III. Conclusion

For the foregoing reasons, the judgment of the district court is vacated and the case is remanded to the district court for further consideration consistent with this opinion.

Sinatra v. National Enquirer, Inc. and Clinic La Prairie
United States Court of Appeals, 9th Cir. (1988)

Appellee Frank Sinatra brought suit against Clinic La Prairie, S.A. ("Clinic") over statements made by the Clinic's employees that were published in a national tabloid. Clinic employees, when interviewed in Switzerland by reporters for the magazine, the National Enquirer, falsely stated that Sinatra visited and was given youth regeneration treatments at the Clinic. The Clinic unsuccessfully entered a special appearance to challenge the district court's assertion of in personam jurisdiction over it. The Clinic renews its jurisdictional challenge on appeal from a judgment for Sinatra.

The question on appeal involves whether statements made by employees of a Swiss clinic to a Florida corporation's reporter about a California resident, which are the foundation for an article published in a nationally circulated magazine, are sufficient minimum contacts to establish personal jurisdiction in California.

BACKGROUND

Frank Sinatra is a well-known entertainer in the recording, television, and motion picture industries, who resides in California. The Clinic is a Swiss corporation, operating a medical clinic in Montreux, Switzerland. The Clinic has operated an information and reservation center in Kansas City, Missouri since 1976. Richard Van Vrooman set up the information center, represented the Clinic in the United States, and handled all reservations in the United States. Van Vrooman also coordinated the Clinic's extensive North American advertising efforts in which advertising was placed in various periodicals of national circulation. Van Vrooman was the Clinic's sole representative in North America. The Clinic contests these facts and contends that it merely entered into a contract with New Life, a Missouri corporation, located solely in Missouri corporation, located solely in Missouri, to provide information to persons in the United States through a national toll-free or "800" telephone number. According to the Clinic, Van Vrooman is the owner of New Life; the Clinic does not own or control any part of New Life; and no owner, employee, or officer of New Life is an owner, employee or officer of the Clinic.

On September 27, 1984, representatives of the Enquirer contacted the Clinic inquiring about an alleged visited by Sinatra, The Clinic referred the representatives to Van Vrooman. After speaking to an Enquirer editor, Van Vrooman informed the Clinic that the Enquirer would send an editor to Switzerland to do a full feature on the Clinic if the Clinic would allow the Enquirer to print a statement that when the Clinic was asked if Sinatra had been a patient, the Clinic refused to confirm or deny the statement. Van Vrooman also informed the Clinic of the Enquirer's circulation, its general readership, and of the fact that the Clinic could successfully solicit clients through an article published in the magazine. At the request of the Clinic's director, Van Vrooman attempted to contact Sinatra in California in order to solicit him to come to the Clinic.

In early October of 1984, an Enquirer reporter traveled to Switzerland. The president, chief of medicine, director, and other members of the Clinic met with the reporter and made several false statements concerning Sinatra's alleged stay at the Clinic, including details of their personal contact with him. Sinatra never visited the Clinic, nor did he receive any treatment from the Clinic.

The National Enquirer, on the cover of its October 23, 1984 issue, published a photograph of Sinatra with the headline, "Sinatra Injected with Youth Serum--He's Secretly Treated with Sheep Cells at Swiss Clinic" on the front page. The article falsely stated that Sinatra had been admitted to the Clinic where he had received a youth regeneration treatment that included an injection with "live cells from black sheep fetuses."

At the conclusion of Sinatra's case and argument, the district court entered judgment in Sinatra's favor, awarding $350,000 in compensatory damages and $100,000 in punitive damages.

DISCUSSION

The due process clause of the Fourteenth Amendment requires that the defendant must have minimum contacts with the forum state "such that the maintenance of the suit does not offend traditional notions of fair play and substantial justice. "International Shoe Co. V. Washington (U.S. 1945).

This circuit applies a three-part test to evaluate whether a court may exercise specific jurisdiction:

    1.   The non-resident defendant must do some act or consummate some transaction with the forum or perform some act by which he purposefully avails himself of the privilege of conducting activities in the forum, thereby invoking the benefits and protections of its laws.

    2.   The claim must be one which arises out of or results from the defendant's forum-related activities.

    3.   The exercise of jurisdiction must be reasonable.

I.   Purposeful Availment through Forum-Related Activities.

Purposeful availment analysis examines whether the defendant's contacts with the forum are attributable to his own actions or are solely the actions of the plaintiff. In order to have purposefully availed oneself of conducting activities in the forum, the defendant must have performed some type of affirmative conduct which allows or promotes the transaction of business within the forum state. For example, the solicitation of business in the forum state that results in business being transacted or contract negotiations will probably be considered purposeful availment. Moreover, the decisions of this court have interpreted the Supreme Court holdings as modifying the purposeful availment rubric to allow the exercise of jurisdiction over a defendant whose only "contact" with the forum is the "purposeful direction" of a foreign act having effect in the forum state.

In this case, the Clinic has directed its activities at California by using Sinatra's name in an effort to promote its business. The Swiss acts or directions that had a California effect consist of: (1) the misappropriation of the value of Sinatra's name through interviews conducted in Switzerland between Clinic employees and Enquirer reporters, in which the Clinic supplied false information about Sinatra's treatment at the Clinic; (2) the Clinic's California advertising efforts to attract patients; and (3) the Clinic's knowledge of Sinatra's residence in California. In addition, California is the situs of Sinatra's injury.

We must consider the economic reality of the defendant's activities that form the basis for the assertion of jurisdiction. The Clinic participates in conduct which allows or promotes the transaction of business within the forum state. The Clinic mounted significant advertising efforts in California by placing ads in San Diego Magazine, Town & Country, the Wall Street Journal, and elsewhere. The Supreme Court, in defining the nature of the "substantial connection," which must exist "between the defendant, the forum, and the litigation," listed several factors which indicate purposeful direction. Additional conduct of the defendant may indicate an intent or purpose to serve the market in the forum state: advertising in the forum state, establishing channels of communication for providing regular advise to customers in the forum state, or marketing the product through a distributor who has agreed to act as the sales agent in the forum state. Asahi Metal Industry Co., Ltd. v. Superior Court of California (1985) (O'Connor, J. Plurality opinion).

Here, the misappropriation is properly viewed as an event within a sequence of activities designed to use California markets for the defendant's benefit. The Clinic instructed Van Vrooman to advertise and approved the ads placed. By use of toll-free telephone number, California customers were given access to information, advice, and reservations concerning the Swiss Clinic. Clearly, the Clinic was

123

more that merely aware that its services were known to or used by California clients. In effect, the Clinic created controlled, and actively used the reservation and advertising system that brought customers from the United States to Switzerland. The Clinic treated many California residents and Van Vrooman's deposition establishes that a significant percentage of the Clinic's United States clientele are California residents.

Given the Clinic's commercial activity in the forum state, it should have reasonably anticipated being brought into court in California. In addition, the Clinic's acts in Switzerland clearly had a tortious effect in California. Therefore, we conclude that the Clinic, through its pursuit of California clients by advertising, part of which involved the misappropriation of Sinatra's name in order to benefit the Clinic through the implied endorsement, possessed sufficient minimum contacts with California to justify the district court's exercise of jurisdiction over it.

II.   Reasonableness

Reasonableness is considered as a separate factor in determining the existence of limited personal jurisdiction. The court examines seven factors to determine reasonableness: the extent of purposeful interjection; the burden on the defendant; the extent of conflict with sovereignty of the defendant's state; the forum state's interest in adjudicating the suit; the most efficient judicial resolution of the dispute; the convenience and effectiveness of relief for the plaintiff; and the existence of an alternative forum. The application of these factors is not mechanical. In determining whether the exercise of personal jurisdiction reasonable, the court must balance the seven factors.

Extent of Purposeful Interjection

The factor of purposeful interjection is analogous to the purposeful direction analysis discussed above. Because we have determined that the Clinic purposefully directed its activities toward

California residents, we cannot conclude that it did not deliberately avail itself of the benefits of California laws or markets for its services.

Burden on the Defendant

The unique burdens placed upon one who must defend oneself in a foreign legal system should have significant weight in assessing the reasonableness of stretching the long arm of personal jurisdiction over national borders. However, modern advances in communications and transportation have significantly reduced the burden of litigating in another country. The continuing contacts between

124

the Clinic's United States-based agent and California translate into less of a litigation burden than if the Clinic maintained no physical presence or agent within the United States. The burden on Sinatra to litigate in Switzerland is as great as that on the Clinic to litigate in California.

Conflict with Sovereignty of the Defendant's State

The factor of conflict with the sovereignty of the defendant's state is not dispositive because, if given controlling weight, it would always prevent suit against a foreign national in a United States court. The Supreme Court, though, has cautioned against extending state long arm statutes in an international context. This circuit has also stated that litigation against an alien defendant creates a higher jurisdictional barrier than litigation against a citizen from a sister state because important sovereignty concerns exist. In Asahi, the Court found the exercise of jurisdiction unreasonable in part because Asahi exercised little control over the marketing decisions or day-to-day activities of the manufacturer doing business in California. By contrast, Van Vrooman operated as the Clinic's agent in the United States. Van Vrooman actively solicited business in California and considered California one of the Clinic's best sources of American clients.

Therefore, the possibility of an interruption of or interference with international commerce does not exist in this action because the Clinic maintains a continuing business relationship with its United States agent. By the Clinic's extensive advertising efforts and the maintenance of the toll-free information number, the Clinic has manifested an intent to serve and to benefit from the United States market.

Forum State's Interest in Adjudicating the Suit

California maintains a strong interest in providing an effective means of redress for its residents tortiously injured by commercial misappropriation. California possesses a clear interest in protecting Sinatra as a California resident; thus, this case is different from the weak state interests present when nonresidents sue in California courts. California's interest in providing effective redress for its residents supports the reasonableness of an exercise of jurisdiction in this case.

Efficient Judicial Resolution

California is the most efficient forum to hear this case. The employees of the Clinic who supplied the information to the Enquirer are located in Switzerland, but they are the only foreign witnesses or parties involved in this suit. Van Vrooman, the agent of the Clinic, resides in Missouri. The National Enquirer is a Florida corporation whose reporters are located across the nation.

Additionally, establishing that the statements were made is only one aspect of the evidence required to resolve the claims. Expert testimony as to the value of the Enquirer's article to the Clinic and as to the value of Sinatra's name in general is also required. Sinatra's career is centered in California and industry valuation experts are most likely located in the United States. Because the witnesses and evidence are primarily located in the United States, the United States is the most efficient forum for resolution of this dispute. Thus, efficiency concerns weigh in favor of the exercise of jurisdiction in the United States.

Convenience and Effectiveness of Relief for Plaintiff

The maintenance of a suit outside of California would be inconvenient and costly for Sinatra. Sinatra has not shown that the misappropriation cannot be effectively remedied in Missouri or Switzerland. Although location of the evidence and witnesses argues for the maintenance of this suit in the United States, this factor does not necessarily weigh in favor of California as a forum without further proof by Sinatra.

Existence of an Alternative Forum

No regulatory or policy interests are served by the exercise of jurisdiction in Missouri, making it unlikely that Missouri possesses a strong interest in providing a forum to resolve this suit. Moreover, whether another reasonable forum exists becomes an issue only when the forum state is shown to be unreasonable, which it has not been shown to be.

After balancing the relative significance of each factor, we have determined that the district court's exercise of jurisdiction over the Clinic was reasonable.

CONCLUSION

On these facts we hold that the exercise of jurisdiction over the Clinic was reasonable. The decision of the district court is therefore AFFIRMED.

END OF EXAM

Zwier v. Sea Quest (Cayman) Limited, et al. - Sample Answer 1

MEMORANDUM

To:	Michael Allen Wolf
From:	Applicant
Re:	Columbia's Courts' Personal Jurisdiction over Sea Quest

INTRODUCTION

Title 12, § 2004 of the Columbia statutes, provides that a Columbia court may exercise jurisdiction on any basis that is consistent with the Columbia Constitution and the Constitution of the United States.

The due process clause of the Fourteenth Amendment of the United States Constitution requires a defendant to have minimum contacts with the forum state "such that the maintenance of the suit does not offend traditional notions of fair play and substantial justice." International Shoe Co. V. Washington (U.S. 1945). In Sinatra v. National Enquirer, Inc. and Clinic La Prairie (1988), the ninth circuit uses a three-part test to determine whether a court may exercise specific jurisdiction. First, the non-resident defendant must do some act or consummate some transaction with the forum or perform some act by which he purposefully avails himself of the privilege of conducting activities in the forum, thereby invoking the benefits and protection of its laws. Second, the claim must arise out of or results from the defendant's forum-related activities. Finally, the exercise of jurisdiction must be reasonable.

1.   Does the Columbia court have jurisdiction based on service of process?

Sea Quest was served in Miami. Although Sea Quest has actual notice, service of process within Columbia does not make this issue moot.

2.   Did Sea Quest do some act or complete a transaction in Columbia by which it invoked the benefits and protections of Columbia law?

a.   Did Sea Quest advertise its services in Columbia?

Via newspapers and TV? Ask Reginald Jones. Ask Swift. Do computer search. Ask Columbia travel agents if they received any advertisements.

b.   Did Sea Quest utilize STI to solicit business in Columbia?

Research relationship between STI and Sea Quest. Did long-term contract between STI and the exclusive booking agency include advertisements? STI lists Sea Quest in its advertising brochures. Did Sea Quest pay STI for this?

Via getting copy of the contract from Reginald. Interview STI agents responsible for printing materials.

4. Does STI's supplying of information in the United States constitute purposeful availment by Sea Quest?

O'Brien stated that STI supplies information only when requested. Check if this is true, or if STI solicits business. It appears that STI only answers questions and accepts names for bookings. Check if STI agents aggressively push Sea Quest or if they only book Sea Quest if the customer requests it.

a.   Via talking to STI sales representatives.

b.   Via calling STI to see how they handle incoming calls. Ask about scuba tours in general. See if they mention Sea Quest. Then ask about Sea Quest in particular. Use neutral party, who can write an affidavit, to make telephone call.

4.   Did Sea Quest purposefully avail itself of Columbia laws by accepting bookings from Columbia residents?

Did Sea Quest even know the plaintiff was a Columbia resident? Via Sea Quest and STI. Did Sea Quest or STI know whether plaintiff's mother, who made the reservation, was a Columbia resident?

What percentage of STI's bookings for Sea Quest are Columbia residents?

a. Via booking addresses from STI's files and from Sea Quest's files. Via return addresses.

b. Via whether STI has an 800 number. If it does, check the phone bills to see which calls are from Columbia.

Does Sea Quest do business in Columbia that does not involve STI?

Via interviews with Sea Quest's officers and crew members who may know where Sea Quest's customers come from. Check Sea Quest files.

Check percentage of STI's business is with Sea Quest. Check STI records and Sea Quest records. Interview agents. Did Sea Quest have the intent to serve the market in Columbia? Does Sea Quest provide "regular" advice to customers or does it merely caters to their demands?

By promoting Sea Quest and soliciting business for Sea Quest, is STI truly a sales agent for Sea Quest?

Has a Columbian resident ever sued Sea Quest before? If so, Sea Quest may have notice that it could be sued again.

Via Columbia court records; ask Swift.

How close is the claim related to Sea Quest's forum-related activities?

a. Were representations made to the plaintiff in the United States that influenced his decision to make the trip? Did plaintiff's mother see any U.S. advertising?

Depose plaintiff's mother. Locate the STI agent that talked to plaintiff's mother and booked the trip.

b. Check how companion received a discount return trip. Did Sea Quest follow up after plaintiff returned to the U.S.?

5. Would the exercise of jurisdiction be reasonable?

a. Was Sea Quest's purposeful interjection extensive?

Find out if Sea Quest's advertisements were placed in Columbia or targeted Columbia residents.

b. Burden on Sea Quest?

Sea Quest is a small company. Find out if Sea Quest has any physical presence in the U.S. How often does Swift come to the U.S.? Why? Ask Swift. How much are transportation costs? Check Sea Quest records.

Would the plaintiff be burdened by traveling to Cayman? Is he restricted from flying due to any medical reason?

c. Sovereignty concerns?

Since tourism is one of the largest industries in Cayman, jurisdiction to decide matters that affect Cayman companies towards American tourists would significantly impact Cayman. We should emphasize the sovereignty concerns of Cayman. Sea Quest did not anticipate conforming to American laws. Check whether the laws in Cayman regarding negligence are different from Columbia law. If it is different, it may be unfair to impose a different standard on Sea Quest, after the fact.

If Columbia law is similar, it will help our forum non conveniens argument; if Columbia law is different, it helps our personal jurisdiction argument.

d.   Does Columbia have an interest in providing a forum for its citizens?

Although Columbia has an interest in providing a forum for redress for its citizens, it may not have a strong interest in adjudicating a scuba diving suit. If such a case does not add to the body of Columbian law the interest of Columbia is much less.

Check how often these issues arise. Does Columbia have a significant tourist industry? Does it include scuba diving. Check Chamber of Commerce publications to find out more information regarding tourism in Columbia.

e.   Is Columbia an efficient forum for this case?

The employees of STI involved in this case are in Indiana. Find out where the plaintiff is. Find out where plaintiff's mother is. It would be more efficient for judicial resolution to hear the case where all of the witnesses to the actual "negligence" are: Cayman. The boat, the equipment, and experts on the standard of care for scuba divers and providers are in Cayman. Check to see if there are scuba clubs in Cayman where we could find these experts.

f.   Can convenience and effectiveness of relief be obtained in Columbia?

Compare the cause of actions available in Cayman and in Columbia; check the sizes of the damage awards and speed of trials. Jones indicated that the size of damages are smaller in Cayman and that trials are quicker. The research we do on the Swift and Jones affidavits will help.

      g.   Alternative forum?

Use the information in Jones' affidavit to show that Cayman is ready and able to hear plaintiff's suit.

STI appears to just supply information to seemingly educated customers that already know what they want. If this is the case, then Sea Quest is less likely to have purposefully availed itself of Columbia. Since STI is located in Indiana, its advertising is probably not targeted in Columbia. Further, if advertising is not provided for in the contract between STI and Sea Quest, then perhaps Sea Quest did not solicit business in Columbia, instead STI did.

Lastly, if STI and Sea Quest do little business with Columbia residents, then a lawsuit in Columbia was not foreseeable. In addition, STI only makes reservations. According to their voucher, it does not provide either package deals or airfare. Finally, the voucher states that customers assume the risk of the inherently dangerous activity of scuba diving. Thus, the suit is even less foreseeable.

Personal jurisdiction against Sea Quest is unreasonable for all of the reasons mentioned in the affidavits. The suit would be more convenient in Cayman and the courts in Cayman are ready and able to hear the suit. Therefore, we have a strong argument against personal jurisdiction.

AFFIDAVIT OF REGINALD JONES

1.   I, Reginald Jones, Esq., am counsel for Sea Quest, Ltd. in the Cayman Islands.

2.   I am a member of the bar in Cayman and have practiced in Cayman for (years). I am familiar with the justice system and the laws in Cayman.

3.   The Cayman Islands is a British Dependent Territory. A citizen of the Cayman Islands is a citizen of the United Kingdom and Colonies. The governor of the Cayman Islands is appointed by the British monarch.

4.   Similar to the United States, the law of Cayman is patterned after the Common Law of England. The Common Law of England is applied by the Cayman courts in all cases where there is no specific local enactment.

5.   The Cayman courts are familiar with American law. Due to the geographic location and strong commercial ties, a number of disputes involving American law have been litigated in Cayman (check this).

5.1   The Cayman courts are friendly to American plaintiffs.

6.   Due to the small size of the Cayman Islands, the site of the accident is not far from the courthouse located (on Grand Cayman?).

7.   Defendant Sea Quest would accept service of process in Cayman because it is a Cayman Corporation.

8.   Defendant STI (would, would not) accept service of process in Cayman. If STI stipulates to personal jurisdiction, the Cayman courts (would, would not) accept it.

9.   The subject matter of the dispute would be litigable in Cayman. Cayman (does, does not) recognize a cause of action for negligence and negligent infliction of emotional distress.

10.   Cayman (does, does not) recognize a cause of action breach of warranty in service contracts.

11.   Cayman (does, does not) provide compulsory process in civil cases to enable litigants enabling parties to obtain witnesses. Witnesses (do, do not) have to be paid to testify.

12.   The following elements make up actions for negligence, intentional and negligent infliction of emotional distress, breach of contract, battery, and false imprisonment under Cayman law: (list elements).

13.   Cayman law (does, does not) recognize vicarious liability of an employer for an employee. Cayman law (does, does not) bind a principal to statements made by an agent.

14.   Cayman law provides for the following damages: (List types of damages available)

15.   The statute of limitations under Cayman law is (list number of years for each cause of action). Therefore, the statute of limitations (has, has not) run for each type of action.

16.   For those types of actions in which the statute of limitations has run, Cayman law (does, does not) recognize a waiver of the statute of limitations by defendant.

17.   Jury trial (is, is not) available for this type of action.

18.   Cayman law (does, does not) allow a defendant to be indemnified by another. It (does, does not) provide for joint and several liability. It (does, does not) permit the corporate veil to be pierced for (tort, contract) plaintiffs.

19.   Judgments obtained in Cayman courts (are, are not) enforceable in the United States.

20.   Cayman courts use rules of procedure that (are, are not) similar to the Federal Rules of Civil Procedure as follows: the use of affidavits to present testimony when witnesses are unavailable; the right of plaintiffs and defendants to be heard, to present evidence, to cross-examine their opponent's

witnesses; discovery access.

21.   Litigants in Cayman civil actions (are, are not) permitted to appeal.

22.   A Cayman court (would, would not) accept jurisdiction of a dispute in which one of the parties is a foreign national.

23.   Cayman courts are less congested than United States courts. In Cayman, the average length of time between filing of a suit and judgment is (___) months.

24.   Cayman courts handle far fewer cases than United States courts. They average (___) cases per year. Each case is given an average of (___) days of trial time.

25.   The qualifications of judges in Cayman (are, are not) similar to those of American (state, federal) judges.

26.   The Cayman Islands has a significant tourist industry and (does, does not) have a strong interest in determining cases involving its tourist industry. There is a significant body of law that has developed around safety in scuba activities (check to see if true). (___) scuba accidents, on the average, are litigated in Cayman courts every year. In addition, there is a complex regulatory scheme involving tourist charter companies and the Cayman courts are familiar with this scheme.

27.   Cayman law (does, does not) recognize the assumption of risk defense. It (does, does not) recognize the following defenses: (once someone gets aboard a charter boat, is there a duty of care owed? Is a charter company liable if it provides defective scuba equipment? Are the duties of common carriers similar to the duties of such entities in the United States? Are jury verdicts as high? Do any special defenses limit the liability of a charter company? Would Sea Quest's liability for bad medical care at the hospital differ significantly)?

28.   If a litigant is unable to come to Cayman in person to the trial, Cayman courts (do, do not) allow that person to present declarations and affidavits as evidence instead.

AFFIDAVIT OF FRANCIS SWIFT

1.   I, Francis Swift, am the owner of Sea Quest, (Cayman) Ltd. ("Sea Quest").

2.   Sea Quest is incorporated under the laws of Cayman Islands with its principal place of business in Cayman Brac, Cayman.

3.   Sea Quest's designated agent for service of process is agent _____, (who is, is not) a citizen of Cayman and subject to service of process in Cayman.

4.   Sea Quest's total assets are valued at (under $_____) (omit this line if the total sounds too high).

5.   Sea Quest is a small business. It operates an (exclusive, non exclusive) boat and dive operation in the Cayman Islands. Sea Quest has no corporate offices in the United States. (Sea Quest has only one corporate office, in Cayman Brac).

6.   Sea Quest's assets consist of three boats. Sea Quest employs only (total number of employees, and occupations) and are (citizens or residents) of the Cayman Islands.

7.   On the day of the alleged incident, the occupants of the boat chartered by plaintiff were (list crew members, plaintiff, his). With the exception of plaintiff and his companion, all are residents of the Cayman Islands (check).

8.   All diving equipment was used the day of the alleged incident is located in the Cayman Islands (check).

9.   The hospital plaintiff was taken to is located in the Cayman Islands, on Grand Cayman.

10.   The boat chartered by plaintiff is located in the Cayman Islands. The expense of transporting the boat to the United States would be $_____ (total sum, including lost revenue).

11.   The boat that transported plaintiff to the hospital is located in the Cayman Islands.

12.   Airfare from Cayman to Columbia averages $_____ per person. The total cost of transporting all witnesses in my employ would be $_____. It is a (____) hour flight from Cayman to Columbia.

13.   I was born and raised in Cayman. I travel to the United States (rarely, and usually only to Miami for purposes of _____ - check this).

14.   My employees do not travel to the United States for business (check this).

15.   Litigating this matter in the United States would involve considerable expense and hardship to me and my employees. It would involve considerable expense, time off from work, loss of revenue since my boats would be idle, and my office would be unattended while my staff traveled back and forth to Columbia.

Zwier v. Sea Quest (Cayman) Limited, et al. - Sample Answer 2

MEMORANDUM

To: Michael Allen Wolf

From: Applicant

Re: <u>Zwier v. Sea Quest (Cayman) Ltd., et al.</u>

        Lack of Personal Jurisdiction

I.   Personal Jurisdiction

Title 12, § 2004, Columbia's personal jurisdiction statute, permits an exercise of personal jurisdiction on any constitutional basis. A defendant must have sufficient minimum contacts with the forum state "such that the maintenance of the suit does not offend traditional notions of fair play and substantial justice." <u>International Shoe</u>.

Under <u>Sinatra</u>, the court will apply a three part test:

a.   Purposeful availment

The defendant must act in a way which purposefully avails himself of the privilege of conducting activities in the forum and thereby involving the benefits and protections of its laws.

b.   Arising out of the act

The claim must be one which arises out of or results from the defendant's act within or connected to the forum.

c.   Reasonableness

In determining the reasonableness of an exercise of jurisdiction, the court examines the following seven factors:

        1.   extent of purposeful interjection;

        2.   burden on the defendant;

139

3.   conflict with the sovereignty of defendant's state;

4.   forum state's interest;

5.   most efficient judicial resolution;

6.   convenience/effectiveness of relief for plaintiff; and

7   existence of an alternative forum.

II.   Facts in our favor

A.   Purposeful Availment

The claim filed by Mr. Zwier is based on an alleged injury suffered in Cayman, not Columbia. Sea Quest used STI, a "telephone service" type of travel agency. The facts have not been verified yet, however, this may tie Sea Quest to some purposeful availment.

B.   Arising Out of the Act

While there may be an arguable case for purposeful availment, the "arising out of prong" of the test does not seem to be met.

Mr. Zwier vacationed in Cayman for almost a week before his injury. He felt ill in Cayman on Nov. 27, off the coast of Little Cayman and his medical treatment began and continued for a week in Cayman Brac. Unlike the effect in the <u>Sinatra</u> case, Mr. Zwier is making a tort claim based on actions which took place in Cayman, not in Columbia.

C.   Reasonableness

1.   Extent of interjection - only one of Sea Quest's three boats is involved in this claim.

2.   Burden on defendant - STI is not necessarily an agent of Sea Quest. Francis Swift owns a small operation of diving boats. If he has to come to Columbia, he will suffer significant losses to his business.

3. Sovereignty conflict - English common law v. Columbia law.

4. Forum state's interest -

5. Efficient resolution - Since the Cayman courts are less congested than Columbia courts, cases move more quickly. In addition, all witnesses to the "accident" are, or were, in Cayman, not Columbia. Medical personnel and the first treating doctors are in Cayman. Finally, even STI is in Indiana, not Columbia.

6. Convenience for plaintiff/effectiveness of relief -

7. Alternative forum -

The most important factors in our favor are "arising out of the act" and, under the "reasonableness" prong, the burden on the defendant and an efficient resolution in Cayman.

III.   Facts needed

A.   Purposeful Availment

1.   Did Sea Quest act or complete a transaction in Columbia by which it invoked benefits and protections of Columbia law?

a.   Solicitation of business
    1.   Did STI send its flyers to Columbia?
    2.   Did Sea Quest request STI to solicit business in Columbia?

        Via Reginald Jones, Nancy O'Brien, or an STI employee about agreements between STI and Sea Quest and whether STI was Sea Quest's authorized agent.

Via documentary evidence (i.e., written agreement between STI and Sea Quest) from Jones, O'Brien or other STI personnel.

    b.   Percentage of business from Columbia

Via records from Sea Quest and STI. Ask Swift and O'Brien.

B.   Arising out of the Act

    1.   Did Zwier come to Cayman from STI/Sea Quest package?
Depose Zwier. Send interrogatories to Zwier. Get voucher from Swift (mentioned in file).

    2.   Did Zwier ever injure himself diving before?
Depose/send interrogatories to Zwier. Check Zwier's medical records. Request medical information from Zwier's Cayman treaters. Get statements from Cayman treaters regarding Zwier's contemporaneous statements to them about previous injuries, etc.

C.   Reasonableness

    1.   Extent of purposeful interjection (see purposeful availment, above).
How much of Sea Quest's business comes from STI? Ask Jones or Swift. Get Sea Quest records of customers. Get STI records.

    2.   Burden on defendant
        a.   Find out extent of Sea Quest's business from STI, (see above).

        b.   Injury to Sea Quest if the trial is in Columbia. Ask Swift for statement of business impact based on his unavailability. Request business records from Sea Quest. Ask Swift and Jones.

142

3. Conflict with sovereign

   Find out STI's relationship with Sea Quest to determine applicability of <u>Asaki</u>. Request business records from Sea Quest. Ask Swift and Jones.

4. Forum state interest

   Verify Columbia's interest. Make sure Zwier is a Columbia resident. Via public records.

5. Efficient Judicial Resolution

   a. Clogged courts in Columbia.

      Check Columbia court records for back log.

   b. Presence of witnesses/parties

      Verify STI's citizenship. Ask O'Brien or check Indiana records. Ascertain residency of witnesses by checking Sea Quest's records for Sea Quest personnel who were present with Zwier and other customers at the time of the alleged injury (hopefully, some divers live in Cayman and no others live in Columbia!). Ask treating doctors in Cayman about their residency and their availability to travel to Columbia.

   c. Experts.

      Locate diving experts in Cayman.

6. Convenience/Effectiveness for Plaintiff

   a. Find out if plaintiff may now travel more comfortably. Depose and send interrogatories to Zwier. Ask experts or doctors in Cayman about plaintiff's ability to travel.

   b. Check law for this type of claim in Cayman.

      Research law to make sure this claim may be maintained in Cayman by a non-resident/non-citizen who allegedly suffered injury here.

7. Alternative Forum

Show that Cayman is an appropriate forum. Witnesses, experts and defendant Sea Quest's are all present in Cayman. Make sure there is an adequate remedy under Cayman law.

AFFIDAVITS (DRAFT)

I, Francis Swift, hereby attest to the following facts:

1.   I am the owner of Sea Quest (Cayman) Limited.

2.   I was born, raised, and am a current resident of the Cayman Islands.

3.   I have personal knowledge of the following facts:

4.   The Cayman Islands is a dependency of Great Britain. As a citizen of the Cayman Islands, I am a citizen of the United Kingdom and Colonies.

5.   I own and operate Sea Quest (Cayman) Limited ("Sea Quest") and have done so for (number of) years.

6.   (I have never been to the state of Columbia.)

7.   Because the pressures of my business require my constant and personal attention, I (rarely) travel to the United States.

8.   Since I started Sea Quest, I have only left the Cayman Islands (number of) times in the past (number of) years.

9.   Sea Quest (lost a quantifiable amount of business) the last time I left the Cayman Islands for more than (three) days.

10.   (All of) Sea Quest's equipment is located in the Cayman Islands.

11.   (All inspections and certifications of Sea Quest's equipment) are performed in the Cayman Islands.

12.   (All) business records of Sea Quest are located in the Cayman Islands.

13.   It would be difficult, costly, and potentially dangerous to move Sea Quest's diving equipment, (especially the air tanks.)

14.   I do not have any (assets, property, and bank accounts) in the United States.

15.   Sea Quest does not have any (assets. property, or accounts) in the United States.

16.   My employees (names) were on the Sea Quest live-aboard ship on the day of plaintiff Zwier's alleged injury.

17.   (Names) are residents of the Cayman Islands and, therefore, citizens of Great Britain.

18.   (Names) have been my employees for (number of) years. They are the main crew of Sea Quest live-aboard.

19.   On my income from Sea Quest, I support (my family) and I have (a side relative or other personal factor) which makes it especially difficult for me to leave the Cayman Islands for any length of time.

I, Reginald Jones, hereby attest to the following facts:

1.   I am an attorney for Sea Quest (Cayman) Limited ("Sea Quest").

2.   I have a total of twenty-five years of experience practicing British law, including ten years in Britain and fifteen in the Cayman islands.

3.   I have personal knowledge of the following facts:

4.   The Cayman Islands is a British Dependent Territory. It is administered by a governor appointed by the British monarch.

5.   The court system in the Cayman Islands is patterned after Great Britain's.

6.   The Common Law of England is recognized and applied by the Cayman courts in all cases where there has not been a specific local enactment.

7.   The Cayman courts (recognize or do not recognize) a cause of action for recovery of damages for negligently causing injury to the person of plaintiff in negligently inflicting emotional distress.

8.   The Cayman courts (recognize or do not recognize) a cause of action for recovery of damages for negligently causing injury to the person of the plaintiff.

9.   The Cayman courts (recognize or do not recognize) the application of "respondent superior" based on imposing vicarious liability on an employer or business for the negligence of its employees during the course of their employment.

10.   The doctrine of "respondent superior" liability (is or is not) recognized in the Cayman Islands to the same extent as the doctrine is recognized in the United States.

11.   The Cayman courts (allows or does not allow) non-citizens to pursue tort claims against

Cayman citizens.

12.   The Cayman courts (allows or does not allow) the same or substantially similar discovery procedures as those permitted in the United States.

13.   The authorities in the Cayman Islands (impose strict requirements for the transportation of dangerous materials, including oxygen tanks, across its borders.)

14.   The justice system in the Cayman Islands is fast-moving. The average civil case takes only (number of months) from filing to resolution.

15.   The average docket load for each judge is (number of cases).

16.   The Cayman courts (provide for or do not provide for) compulsory process to the same extent as the United States.

17.   The statute of limitations for tort claims like plaintiff's (is or is not) the same or longer than the comparable statute in the United States. Filing a claim in any other jurisdiction (tolls or does not toll) the statute of limitations on such claims.

18.   The Cayman courts (permit or do not permit) testimonial evidence, to the same extent as the United States.

19.   The Cayman courts (do or do not) limit a plaintiff's recovery in a tort action by any regulation or law except in similar ways to the United States.

PERFORMANCE TEST WORKSHOP 3

TASK MEMO

BURRIS, CHASE, KALEVITCH & ROHR

Attorneys and Counselors
Sunrise Professsional Centre – Suite 500
Sunrise, Columbia 55551

TO: Applicant

FROM: Tony Chase

SUBJECT: Sunrise Galleria Mall Curfew

DATE: February 24, 2000

As you may know, the management of the Sunrise Galleria Mall recently announced that it will impose a 6:00 p.m. curfew on minors under the age of seventeen who are not accompanied by apparent or guardian. We represent a group of teenagers and parents who object to the proposed curfew because it will interfere with variety of activities in which the young people are engaged with the knowledge and permission of their parents.

After the Mall's intentions were made public, I telephoned Leslie Kelleher, counsel for Sunrise Galleria, to express the concerns of our clients and to ask for a copy of the text of the curfew. Ina letter that accompanied the copy of the rule she forwarded to us, Leslie explained that the Galleria's exclusionary policy is similar to curfews adopted by several other mega-malls. She pointedly noted that those shopping centers have successfully resisted challenges to nighttime bans on unaccompanied teenagers.

Our Supreme Court has held that the Columbia Constitution provides access to private shopping centers to persons exercising free speech rights. Nonetheless, I'm not confident we would ultimately prevail in an action that seeks to completely eliminate all elements of a curfew. Moreover, the high cost of litigating the matter is a factor we must consider in counseling our clients, none of whom has significant resources.

I want to present Leslie Kelleher with an alternative to the Mall's absolute ban on unaccompanied teens while permitting our clients to pursue their legitimate objectives.

Here's what I'd like you to do:

1. Draft an alternative to the complete curfew contained in the Mall's Parent Escort Policy that allows our clients to continue their present evening activities and engage in other appropriate endeavors, and meets the Mall's needs as we understand them. Write only the actual language you propose for the alternative Parent Escort Policy; don't write how you would do it or why.

2. Prepare a letter to Leslie Kelleher for my signature designed to persuade her:

    a)   that the Mall's proposed absolute ban on unaccompanied teenagers is unconstitutional,

    b)   that our proposed curfew alternative will pass constitutional scrutiny, and

    c)   that our alternative formulation meets the Mall's needs as we understand them.

We will, of course, enclose in the letter to Leslie Kelleher our draft of the Parent Escort Policy.

Thanks for your help.

TASK MEMO TO ZWIER V. SEA QUEST: FROM PERFORMANCE TEST SIMULATED EXAM

Herbert, Wolf & Stubbs
Attorneys at Law
700 Columbia Center
Richland, Columbia

MEMORANDUM   February 21, 1995

To: Applicant
From: Michael Allen Wolf
Re: Zwier v. Sea Quest (Cayman) Limited, et al.

We have been requested to handle part of a law suit filed against Sea Quest (Cayman) Ltd. As you will see from the attached complaint, suit has been brought here in the United State District Court for the Northern District of Columbia. Sea Quest is incorporated in the Cayman Islands, located just south of Cuba. A second defendant, Scuba Tours International, is located in Indianapolis, Indiana and has separate counsel. We were contacted by Sea Quest's Cayman Islands attorney to see if we can get the suit dismissed

What I would like you to do is focus on two parts of our plan to seek dismissal. I want to be able to argue that the federal district court here in Columbia does not have personal jurisdiction over Sea Quest and in the alternative, that the suit should be dismissed on the basis of forum non conveniens. Specifically, please do the following:

1.   Draft a memorandum to me in which you

   a)   identify the factors the court will consider in deciding our motion to dismiss based upon lack of personal jurisdiction over Sea Quest.

   b)   for each factor, identify the facts in the file that support our position.

   d)   for each factor, identify what additional facts we need and where we might find them. Please be specific about the facts we need and the likely sources. For example, don't just say we need more facts about Sea Quest's purposeful interjection; instead, go through each issue, fact and source, as in the following example:

      1. Did Defendant Sea Quest act or complete a transaction in Columbia by which it invoked the benefits and protection of Columbia law?

153

a)	Did Sea Quest advertise its services in Columbia?

    (1)	Via newspapers or TV. Ask Reginald Jones and depose appropriate STI employee.

    (2)	Via . . .

b)	. . . .

2.	Based on the information presently available, draft affidavits to be signed by Reginald Jones and Francis Swift to support our motion that the suit be dismissed on the basis of forum non conveniens. I expect that Jones and Swift will give us information to support our position that trial of the case in Columbia will be inconvenient to our client. Having identified the facts known to us, identify what additional information we should seek to include in the affidavits to support a finding of forum non conveniens. In this latter task, please identify, in the form of a statement which could be included in an affidavit, the information the existence of which we need to determine. Place the information that needs to be determined in a bracket within the statement. Then, once we learn the missing fact, we can decide whether actually to include the statement in the affidavit.

For example, even though we don't know that the Cayman Islands allows an action for negligently causing injury, your draft of the Jones' affidavit would include, "The justice system in the Cayman Islands [recognizes or does not recognize] a cause of action for recovery of damages for negligently causing injury to the person of plaintiff in negligently inflicting emotional distress." I have included a couple of cases that should guide you in these tasks. In addition, I spoke with Reginald Jones, Sea Quest's Cayman lawyer and Nancy O'Brien, STI's lawyer. A partial transcript of each phone conversation is attached as well as a couple of documents Jones faxed along with the complaint.

Zwier v. Sea Quest (Cayman) Limited, et al. - Sample Answer 1

MEMORANDUM

> To: Michael Allen Wolf
>
> From: Applicant
>
> Re: Columbia's Courts' Personal Jurisdiction over Sea Quest

INTRODUCTION

Title 12, § 2004 of the Columbia statutes, provides that a Columbia court may exercise jurisdiction on any basis that is consistent with the Columbia Constitution and the Constitution of the United States.

The due process clause of the Fourteenth Amendment of the United States Constitution requires a defendant to have minimum contacts with the forum state "such that the maintenance of the suit does not offend traditional notions of fair play and substantial justice." International Shoe Co. V. Washington (U.S. 1945). In Sinatra v. National Enquirer, Inc. and Clinic La Prairie (1988), the ninth circuit uses a three-part test to determine whether a court may exercise specific jurisdiction. First, the non-resident defendant must do some act or consummate some transaction with the forum or perform some act by which he purposefully avails himself of the privilege of conducting activities in the forum, thereby invoking the benefits and protection of its laws. Second, the claim must arise out of or results from the defendant's forum-related activities. Finally, the exercise of jurisdiction must be reasonable.

1.   Does the Columbia court have jurisdiction based on service of process?

Sea Quest was served in Miami. Although Sea Quest has actual notice, service of process within Columbia does not make this issue moot.

2.   Did Sea Quest do some act or complete a transaction in Columbia by which it invoked the benefits and protections of Columbia law?

155

a.   Did Sea Quest advertise its services in Columbia?

Via newspapers and TV? Ask Reginald Jones. Ask Swift. Do computer search. Ask Columbia travel agents if they received any advertisements.

b.   Did Sea Quest utilize STI to solicit business in Columbia?

Research relationship between STI and Sea Quest. Did long-term contract between STI and the exclusive booking agency include advertisements? STI lists Sea Quest in its advertising brochures. Did Sea Quest pay STI for this?

Via getting copy of the contract from Reginald. Interview STI agents responsible for printing materials.

5. Does STI's supplying of information in the United States constitute purposeful availment by Sea Quest?

O'Brien stated that STI supplies information only when requested. Check if this is true, or if STI solicits business. It appears that STI only answers questions and accepts names for bookings. Check if STI agents aggressively push Sea Quest or if they only book Sea Quest if the customer requests it.

a.   Via talking to STI sales representatives.

b.   Via calling STI to see how they handle incoming calls. Ask about scuba tours in general. See if they mention Sea Quest. Then ask about Sea Quest in particular. Use neutral party, who can write an affidavit, to make telephone call.

4.   Did Sea Quest purposefully avail itself of Columbia laws by accepting bookings from Columbia residents?

Did Sea Quest even know the plaintiff was a Columbia resident? Via Sea Quest and STI. Did Sea Quest or STI know whether plaintiff's mother, who made the reservation, was a Columbia resident?

What percentage of STI's bookings for Sea Quest are Columbia residents?

a.   Via booking addresses from STI's files and from Sea Quest's files. Via return addresses.

b.   Via whether STI has an 800 number. If it does, check the phone bills to see which calls are from Columbia.

Does Sea Quest do business in Columbia that does not involve STI?

Via interviews with Sea Quest's officers and crew members who may know where Sea Quest's customers come from. Check Sea Quest files.

Check percentage of STI's business is with Sea Quest. Check STI records and Sea Quest records. Interview agents. Did Sea Quest have the intent to serve the market in Columbia? Does Sea Quest provide "regular" advice to customers or does it merely caters to their demands?

By promoting Sea Quest and soliciting business for Sea Quest, is STI truly a sales agent for Sea Quest?

Has a Columbian resident ever sued Sea Quest before? If so, Sea Quest may have notice that it could be sued again.

Via Columbia court records; ask Swift.

How close is the claim related to Sea Quest's forum-related activities?

a.   Were representations made to the plaintiff in the United States that influenced his decision to make the trip? Did plaintiff's mother see any U.S. advertising?

Depose plaintiff's mother. Locate the STI agent that talked to plaintiff's mother and booked the trip.

b.   Check how companion received a discount return trip. Did Sea Quest follow up after plaintiff returned to the U.S.?

5.   Would the exercise of jurisdiction be reasonable?

a.   Was Sea Quest's purposeful interjection extensive?

Find out if Sea Quest's advertisements were placed in Columbia or targeted Columbia residents.

b.   Burden on Sea Quest?

Sea Quest is a small company. Find out if Sea Quest has any physical presence in the U.S. How often does Swift come to the U.S.? Why? Ask Swift. How much are transportation costs? Check Sea Quest records.

Would the plaintiff be burdened by traveling to Cayman? Is he restricted from flying due to any medical reason?

c.   Sovereignty concerns?

Since tourism is one of the largest industries in Cayman, jurisdiction to decide matters that affect Cayman companies towards American tourists would significantly impact Cayman. We should emphasize the sovereignty concerns of Cayman. Sea Quest did not anticipate conforming to American

158

laws. Check whether the laws in Cayman regarding negligence are different from Columbia law. If it is different, it may be unfair to impose a different standard on Sea Quest, after the fact.

If Columbia law is similar, it will help our forum non conveniens argument; if Columbia law is different, it helps our personal jurisdiction argument.

d.   Does Columbia have an interest in providing a forum for its citizens?

Although Columbia has an interest in providing a forum for redress for its citizens, it may not have a strong interest in adjudicating a scuba diving suit. If such a case does not add to the body of Columbian law the interest of Columbia is much less.

Check how often these issues arise. Does Columbia have a significant tourist industry? Does it include scuba diving. Check Chamber of Commerce publications to find out more information regarding tourism in Columbia.

e.   Is Columbia an efficient forum for this case?

The employees of STI involved in this case are in Indiana. Find out where the plaintiff is. Find out where plaintiff's mother is. It would be more efficient for judicial resolution to hear the case where all of the witnesses to the actual "negligence" are: Cayman. The boat, the equipment, and experts on the standard of care for scuba divers and providers are in Cayman. Check to see if there are scuba clubs in Cayman where we could find these experts.

f.   Can convenience and effectiveness of relief be obtained in Columbia?

Compare the cause of actions available in Cayman and in Columbia; check the sizes of the damage awards and speed of trials. Jones indicated that the size of damages are smaller in Cayman and that trials are quicker. The research we do on the Swift and Jones affidavits will help.

       g.   Alternative forum?

Use the information in Jones' affidavit to show that Cayman is ready and able to hear plaintiff's suit.

STI appears to just supply information to seemingly educated customers that already know what they want. If this is the case, then Sea Quest is less likely to have purposefully availed itself of Columbia. Since STI is located in Indiana, its advertising is probably not targeted in Columbia. Further, if advertising is not provided for in the contract between STI and Sea Quest, then perhaps Sea Quest did not solicit business in Columbia, instead STI did.

Lastly, if STI and Sea Quest do little business with Columbia residents, then a lawsuit in Columbia was not foreseeable. In addition, STI only makes reservations. According to their voucher, it does not provide either package deals or airfare. Finally, the voucher states that customers assume the risk of the inherently dangerous activity of scuba diving. Thus, the suit is even less foreseeable.

Personal jurisdiction against Sea Quest is unreasonable for all of the reasons mentioned in the affidavits. The suit would be more convenient in Cayman and the courts in Cayman are ready and able to hear the suit. Therefore, we have a strong argument against personal jurisdiction.

AFFIDAVIT OF REGINALD JONES

1.   I, Reginald Jones, Esq., am counsel for Sea Quest, Ltd. in the Cayman Islands.

2.   I am a member of the bar in Cayman and have practiced in Cayman for (years). I am familiar with the justice system and the laws in Cayman.

3.   The Cayman Islands is a British Dependent Territory. A citizen of the Cayman Islands is a citizen of the United Kingdom and Colonies. The governor of the Cayman Islands is appointed by the British monarch.

4.   Similar to the United States, the law of Cayman is patterned after the Common Law of England. The Common Law of England is applied by the Cayman courts in all cases where there is no specific local enactment.

5.   The Cayman courts are familiar with American law. Due to the geographic location and strong commercial ties, a number of disputes involving American law have been litigated in Cayman (check this).

5.1   The Cayman courts are friendly to American plaintiffs.

6.   Due to the small size of the Cayman Islands, the site of the accident is not far from the courthouse located (on Grand Cayman?).

7.   Defendant Sea Quest would accept service of process in Cayman because it is a Cayman Corporation.

8.   Defendant STI (would, would not) accept service of process in Cayman. If STI stipulates to personal jurisdiction, the Cayman courts (would, would not) accept it.

9.   The subject matter of the dispute would be litigable in Cayman. Cayman (does, does not)

recognize a cause of action for negligence and negligent infliction of emotional distress.

10.   Cayman (does, does not) recognize a cause of action breach of warranty in service contracts.

11.   Cayman (does, does not) provide compulsory process in civil cases to enable litigants enabling parties to obtain witnesses. Witnesses (do, do not) have to be paid to testify.

12.   The following elements make up actions for negligence, intentional and negligent infliction of emotional distress, breach of contract, battery, and false imprisonment under Cayman law: (list elements).

13.   Cayman law (does, does not) recognize vicarious liability of an employer for an employee. Cayman law (does, does not) bind a principal to statements made by an agent.

14.   Cayman law provides for the following damages: (List types of damages available)

15.   The statute of limitations under Cayman law is (list number of years for each cause of action). Therefore, the statute of limitations (has, has not) run for each type of action.

16.   For those types of actions in which the statute of limitations has run, Cayman law (does, does not) recognize a waiver of the statute of limitations by defendant.

17.   Jury trial (is, is not) available for this type of action.

18.   Cayman law (does, does not) allow a defendant to be indemnified by another. It (does, does not) provide for joint and several liability. It (does, does not) permit the corporate veil to be pierced for (tort, contract) plaintiffs.

19.   Judgments obtained in Cayman courts (are, are not) enforceable in the United States.

20.   Cayman courts use rules of procedure that (are, are not) similar to the Federal Rules of Civil Procedure as follows: the use of affidavits to present testimony when witnesses are unavailable; the

right of plaintiffs and defendants to be heard, to present evidence, to cross-examine their opponent's witnesses; discovery access.

21.   Litigants in Cayman civil actions (are, are not) permitted to appeal.

22.   A Cayman court (would, would not) accept jurisdiction of a dispute in which one of the parties is a foreign national.

23.   Cayman courts are less congested than United States courts. In Cayman, the average length of time between filing of a suit and judgment is (__) months.

24.   Cayman courts handle far fewer cases than United States courts. They average (__) cases per year. Each case is given an average of (__) days of trial time.

25.   The qualifications of judges in Cayman (are, are not) similar to those of American (state, federal) judges.

26.   The Cayman Islands has a significant tourist industry and (does, does not) have a strong interest in determining cases involving its tourist industry. There is a significant body of law that has developed around safety in scuba activities (check to see if true). (__) scuba accidents, on the average, are litigated in Cayman courts every year. In addition, there is a complex regulatory scheme involving tourist charter companies and the Cayman courts are familiar with this scheme.

27.   Cayman law (does, does not) recognize the assumption of risk defense. It (does, does not) recognize the following defenses: (once someone gets aboard a charter boat, is there a duty of care owed? Is a charter company liable if it provides defective scuba equipment? Are the duties of common carriers similar to the duties of such entities in the United States? Are jury verdicts as high? Do any special defenses limit the liability of a charter company? Would Sea Quest's liability for bad medical care at the hospital differ significantly)?

28.   If a litigant is unable to come to Cayman in person to the trial, Cayman courts (do, do not) allow that person to present declarations and affidavits as evidence instead.

AFFIDAVIT OF FRANCIS SWIFT

1.   I, Francis Swift, am the owner of Sea Quest, (Cayman) Ltd. ("Sea Quest").

2.   Sea Quest is incorporated under the laws of Cayman Islands with its principal place of business in Cayman Brac, Cayman.

3.   Sea Quest's designated agent for service of process is agent _____, (who is, is not) a citizen of Cayman and subject to service of process in Cayman.

4.   Sea Quest's total assets are valued at (under $_____) (omit this line if the total sounds too high).

5.   Sea Quest is a small business. It operates an (exclusive, non exclusive) boat and dive operation in the Cayman Islands. Sea Quest has no corporate offices in the United States. (Sea Quest has only one corporate office, in Cayman Brac).

6.   Sea Quest's assets consist of three boats. Sea Quest employs only (total number of employees, and occupations) and are (citizens or residents) of the Cayman Islands.

7.   On the day of the alleged incident, the occupants of the boat chartered by plaintiff were (list crew members, plaintiff, his). With the exception of plaintiff and his companion, all are residents of the Cayman Islands (check).

8.   All diving equipment was used the day of the alleged incident is located in the Cayman Islands (check).

9.   The hospital plaintiff was taken to is located in the Cayman Islands, on Grand Cayman.

10.   The boat chartered by plaintiff is located in the Cayman Islands. The expense of transporting the boat to the United States would be $_____ (total sum, including lost revenue).

11.   The boat that transported plaintiff to the hospital is located in the Cayman Islands.

12.   Airfare from Cayman to Columbia averages $_____ per person. The total cost of transporting all witnesses in my employ would be $_____. It is a (____) hour flight from Cayman to Columbia.

13.   I was born and raised in Cayman. I travel to the United States (rarely, and usually only to Miami for purposes of _____ - check this).

14.   My employees do not travel to the United States for business (check this).

15.   Litigating this matter in the United States would involve considerable expense and hardship to me and my employees. It would involve considerable expense, time off from work, loss of revenue since my boats would be idle, and my office would be unattended while my staff traveled back and forth to Columbia.

Zwier v. Sea Quest (Cayman) Limited, et al. - Sample Answer 2

MEMORANDUM

To: Michael Allen Wolf

From: Applicant

Re: <u>Zwier v. Sea Quest (Cayman) Ltd., et al.</u>

Lack of Personal Jurisdiction

I. Personal Jurisdiction

Title 12, § 2004, Columbia's personal jurisdiction statute, permits an exercise of personal jurisdiction on any constitutional basis. A defendant must have sufficient minimum contacts with the forum state "such that the maintenance of the suit does not offend traditional notions of fair play and substantial justice." <u>International Shoe</u>.

Under <u>Sinatra</u>, the court will apply a three part test:

a. Purposeful availment

The defendant must act in a way which purposefully avails himself of the privilege of conducting activities in the forum and thereby involving the benefits and protections of its laws.

b. Arising out of the act

The claim must be one which arises out of or results from the defendant's act within or connected to the forum.

c. Reasonableness

In determining the reasonableness of an exercise of jurisdiction, the court examines the following seven factors:

1. extent of purposeful interjection;

2.   burden on the defendant;

3.   conflict with the sovereignty of defendant's state;

4.   forum state's interest;

5.   most efficient judicial resolution;

6.   convenience/effectiveness of relief for plaintiff; and

7   existence of an alternative forum.

II.   Facts in our favor

A.   Purposeful Availment

The claim filed by Mr. Zwier is based on an alleged injury suffered in Cayman, not Columbia. Sea Quest used STI, a "telephone service" type of travel agency. The facts have not been verified yet, however, this may tie Sea Quest to some purposeful availment.

B.   Arising Out of the Act

While there may be an arguable case for purposeful availment, the "arising out of prong" of the test does not seem to be met.

Mr. Zwier vacationed in Cayman for almost a week before his injury. He felt ill in Cayman on Nov. 27, off the coast of Little Cayman and his medical treatment began and continued for a week in Cayman Brac. Unlike the effect in the <u>Sinatra</u> case, Mr. Zwier is making a tort claim based on actions which took place in Cayman, not in Columbia.

C.   Reasonableness

1.   Extent of interjection - only one of Sea Quest's three boats is involved in this claim.

2.   Burden on defendant - STI is not necessarily an agent of Sea Quest. Francis Swift owns a small operation of diving boats. If he has to come to Columbia,

he will suffer significant losses to his business.

3.   Sovereignty conflict - English common law v. Columbia law.

4.   Forum state's interest -

5.   Efficient resolution - Since the Cayman courts are less congested than Columbia courts, cases move more quickly. In addition, all witnesses to the "accident" are, or were, in Cayman, not Columbia. Medical personnel and the first treating doctors are in Cayman. Finally, even STI is in Indiana, not Columbia.

6.   Convenience for plaintiff/effectiveness of relief -

7.   Alternative forum -

The most important factors in our favor are "arising out of the act" and, under the "reasonableness" prong, the burden on the defendant and an efficient resolution in Cayman.

III.   Facts needed

A.   Purposeful Availment

1.   Did Sea Quest act or complete a transaction in Columbia by which it invoked benefits and protections of Columbia law?

a.   Solicitation of business
   1.   Did STI send its flyers to Columbia?
   2.   Did Sea Quest request STI to solicit business in Columbia?

      Via Reginald Jones, Nancy O'Brien, or an STI employee about agreements between STI and Sea Quest and whether STI was Sea

Quest's authorized agent.

Via documentary evidence (i.e., written agreement between STI and Sea Quest) from Jones, O'Brien or other STI personnel.

b.   Percentage of business from Columbia

Via records from Sea Quest and STI. Ask Swift and O'Brien.

B.   Arising out of the Act

1.   Did Zwier come to Cayman from STI/Sea Quest package?
       Depose Zwier. Send interrogatories to Zwier. Get voucher from Swift (mentioned in file).

2.   Did Zwier ever injure himself diving before?
       Depose/send interrogatories to Zwier. Check Zwier's medical records. Request medical information from Zwier's Cayman treaters. Get statements from Cayman treaters regarding Zwier's contemporaneous statements to them about previous injuries, etc.

C.   Reasonableness

1.   Extent of purposeful interjection (see purposeful availment, above).
       How much of Sea Quest's business comes from STI? Ask Jones or Swift. Get Sea Quest records of customers. Get STI records.

2.   Burden on defendant
       a.   Find out extent of Sea Quest's business from STI, (see above).

       b.   Injury to Sea Quest if the trial is in Columbia. Ask Swift for statement of business impact based on his unavailability. Request

169

business records from Sea Quest. Ask Swift and Jones.

3. Conflict with sovereign

Find out STI's relationship with Sea Quest to determine applicability of Asaki. Request business records from Sea Quest. Ask Swift and Jones.

4. Forum state interest

Verify Columbia's interest. Make sure Zwier is a Columbia resident. Via public records.

5. Efficient Judicial Resolution

a. Clogged courts in Columbia.

Check Columbia court records for back log.

b. Presence of witnesses/parties

Verify STI's citizenship. Ask O'Brien or check Indiana records. Ascertain residency of witnesses by checking Sea Quest's records for Sea Quest personnel who were present with Zwier and other customers at the time of the alleged injury (hopefully, some divers live in Cayman and no others live in Columbia!). Ask treating doctors in Cayman about their residency and their availability to travel to Columbia.

c. Experts.

Locate diving experts in Cayman.

6. Convenience/Effectiveness for Plaintiff

a. Find out if plaintiff may now travel more comfortably. Depose and send interrogatories to Zwier. Ask experts or doctors in Cayman about plaintiff's ability to travel.

b. Check law for this type of claim in Cayman.

Research law to make sure this claim may be maintained in Cayman by a non-resident/non-citizen who allegedly suffered injury here.

7.   Alternative Forum

Show that Cayman is an appropriate forum. Witnesses, experts and defendant Sea Quest's are all present in Cayman. Make sure there is an adequate remedy under Cayman law.

AFFIDAVITS (DRAFT)

I, Francis Swift, hereby attest to the following facts:

1.   I am the owner of Sea Quest (Cayman) Limited.

2.   I was born, raised, and am a current resident of the Cayman Islands.

3.   I have personal knowledge of the following facts:

4.   The Cayman Islands is a dependency of Great Britain. As a citizen of the Cayman Islands, I am a citizen of the United Kingdom and Colonies.

5.   I own and operate Sea Quest (Cayman) Limited ("Sea Quest") and have done so for (number of) years.

6.   (I have never been to the state of Columbia.)

7.   Because the pressures of my business require my constant and personal attention, I (rarely) travel to the United States.

8.   Since I started Sea Quest, I have only left the Cayman Islands (number of) times in the past (number of) years.

9.   Sea Quest (lost a quantifiable amount of business) the last time I left the Cayman Islands for more than (three) days.

10.   (All of) Sea Quest's equipment is located in the Cayman Islands.

11.   (All inspections and certifications of Sea Quest's equipment) are performed in the Cayman Islands.

12.   (All) business records of Sea Quest are located in the Cayman Islands.

13.   It would be difficult, costly, and potentially dangerous to move Sea Quest's diving equipment, (especially the air tanks.)

14.   I do not have any (assets, property, and bank accounts) in the United States.

15.   Sea Quest does not have any (assets. property, or accounts) in the United States.

16.   My employees (names) were on the Sea Quest live-aboard ship on the day of plaintiff Zwier's alleged injury.

17.   (Names) are residents of the Cayman Islands and, therefore, citizens of Great Britain.

18.   (Namcs) have been my employees for (number of) years. They are the main crew of Sea Quest live-aboard.

19.   On my income from Sea Quest, I support (my family) and I have (a side relative or other personal factor) which makes it especially difficult for me to leave the Cayman Islands for any length of time.

I, Reginald Jones, hereby attest to the following facts:

1. I am an attorney for Sea Quest (Cayman) Limited ("Sea Quest").

2. I have a total of twenty-five years of experience practicing British law, including ten years in Britain and fifteen in the Cayman islands.

3. I have personal knowledge of the following facts:

4. The Cayman Islands is a British Dependent Territory. It is administered by a governor appointed by the British monarch.

5. The court system in the Cayman Islands is patterned after Great Britain's.

6. The Common Law of England is recognized and applied by the Cayman courts in all cases where there has not been a specific local enactment.

7. The Cayman courts (recognize or do not recognize) a cause of action for recovery of damages for negligently causing injury to the person of plaintiff in negligently inflicting emotional distress.

8. The Cayman courts (recognize or do not recognize) a cause of action for recovery of damages for negligently causing injury to the person of the plaintiff.

9. The Cayman courts (recognize or do not recognize) the application of "respondent superior" based on imposing vicarious liability on an employer or business for the negligence of its employees during the course of their employment.

10. The doctrine of "respondent superior" liability (is or is not) recognized in the Cayman Islands to the same extent as the doctrine is recognized in the United States.

11. The Cayman courts (allows or does not allow) non-citizens to pursue tort claims against

Cayman citizens.

12.   The Cayman courts (allows or does not allow) the same or substantially similar discovery procedures as those permitted in the United States.

13.   The authorities in the Cayman Islands (impose strict requirements for the transportation of dangerous materials, including oxygen tanks, across its borders.)

14.   The justice system in the Cayman Islands is fast-moving. The average civil case takes only (number of months) from filing to resolution.

15.   The average docket load for each judge is (number of cases).

16.   The Cayman courts (provide for or do not provide for) compulsory process to the same extent as the United States.

17.   The statute of limitations for tort claims like plaintiff's (is or is not) the same or longer than the comparable statute in the United States. Filing a claim in any other jurisdiction (tolls or does not toll) the statute of limitations on such claims.

18.   The Cayman courts (permit or do not permit) testimonial evidence, to the same extent as the United States.

19.   The Cayman courts (do or do not) limit a plaintiff's recovery in a tort action by any regulation or law except in similar ways to the United States.

Pages 177-186 are intentionally left blank.

Pages 177-186 are intentionally left blank.

Pages 177-186 are intentionally left blank.

Pages 177-186 are intentionally left blank.

Pages 177-186 are intentionally left blank.

Pages 177-186 are intentionally left blank.

Pages 177-186 are intentionally left blank.

Pages 177-186 are intentionally left blank.

Pages 177-186 are intentionally left blank.

Pages 177-186 are intentionally left blank.

LAW OFFICES OF LYNN R. DAWSON

5922 Jeanette Drive
Cordesville, Columbia

MEMORANDUM

To: Applicant

From: Lynn Dawson

Date: July 27, 2006

Re: **Breene and Frost**

Our client, Jim Breene, is a patent lawyer who works principally as a consultant to other lawyers in patent litigation. He was retained by the firm of Willing, Mayer & Frost to assist Julia Frost in presenting a patent infringement case on behalf of one of Frost's clients.

Breene and Frost entered into a fee-splitting arrangement pursuant to which, according to Breene, Breene would get 50% of whatever fee Willing, Mayer and Frost received from the litigation. The agreement is enforceable, raising no formation, Statute of Frauds, or subject matter issues.

Recently, Breene received and cashed a check for $128,000 purportedly tendered in "full satisfaction" of Breene's share of the fees. Breene claims this is far short of the full amount to which he is entitled and seeks our advice concerning what he should do.

Please draft for my signature an opinion letter, following the format and guidelines described in the firm's memorandum on opinion letters, explaining to Breene what options are available to him and which one we recommend to him.

LAW OFFICES OF LYNN R. DAWSON

5922 Jeanette Drive
Cordesville, Columbia

MEMORANDUM

To: All Attorneys

From: Executive Committee

Re: **Opinion Letter Guidelines**

Often the firm's attorneys must prepare an opinion letter to communicate its views to a client. An opinion letter should follow this format:

• State the facts that led to the client's need for advice.

• State your understanding of the client's goal or goals.

• Identify options the client has or the actions the client could take to achieve those goals.

• Objectively analyze each of the client's options or possible actions in light of the applicable law and the relevant facts. Be sure to identify the likely success in achieving the client's goals of pursuing each option or action.

• Although you must discuss the law, you should do so as clearly and straightforwardly as possible, in language that allows the client to follow your reasoning and the logic of your conclusions.

"Client Interview Plan" Task Memo

1.   Please review my interview plan and draft a memo commenting on my interviewing decisions. My interview goals are to understand the client's desires, to gather the facts necessary to accomplish them, and to establish the type of relationship that will best facilitate both the interview and the long-term relationship I optimistically anticipate with this client. Please be specific. Indicate which approaches you agree with and, where appropriate, suggest specific alternatives, additions, deletions or modifications and state the reasons for your suggestions. Please be sure to give me your thoughts on each of my proposed interviewing tactics, the specific language I plan to use, as well as follow-up topics I intend to pursue. I've had the interview plan typed on line-numbered paper for ease of reference.

2.   In a second memo, please critique the key dispositive provisions of the various trust instruments I have drafted. Please suggest specific additions, deletions, and modifications and briefly explain the reasons for your suggestions. I want to insure these documents conform to Columbia law and will accomplish Cook's goals as I understand them. The relevant administrative provisions will be added later; don't concern yourself with them. You can also ignore the tax consequences when reviewing these documents. Again, I've had the documents typed on line-numbered paper for ease of reference.

I have scheduled a meeting with Mr. Cook early next week, so I would appreciate receiving your memos as quickly as possible. Please be completely candid when analyzing my plans. I'm eager to do a good job and welcome criticism.

First Page of Interview Plan

Note: Indented materials in brackets are my decisions concerning interviewing tactics. I intend to follow the quoted language as closely as possible. The indented items after quoted language are follow-up topics I plan to pursue. Please give me your advice on all three categories of material; be sure to comment on both those which you do agree and those with which you don't agree.

> [Have receptionist escort Cook to my office after buzzing me. Greet him at door and seat him at small conference table so we may more easily review the drafts of the various trust documents. Begin interview in very professional manner to impress Cook I have prepared for the interview and know what I am doing. Attempt to do so by omitting any small talk and by presenting draft of documents.]

"I've studied the material provided by your niece and developed a strategy for implementing your decisions. I think we should proceed by reviewing the goals you hope to achieve for your children, the special problems posed by Denise's condition, the gift to Dr. Finkle's hospital and the matter of the youngster in Baltimore. Let's begin with the two younger children. I've made a copy of the key provisions the trust instrument we should use to set up the program for Michael and Elizabeth. Why don't you look this over [Hand copy to Cook] while I explain what it's designed to do."

> - Explain that first paragraph of trust would include the $20,000 gifts for Michael and Elizabeth from Mr. and Mrs. Cook (a total of $40,000 in the first year) which qualify for federal gift tax exception.
> - Second and third paragraphs retain funds within control of Trustee until children reach 30 years. Trustee given discretion of how much money to give children each year, but education is one of discretionary standards.

INSTRUCTION SHEET

McIntyre, Yost and Amrein, LLP
INTERNAL MEMORANDUM

TO: Associates

FROM: Myron Taylor

RE: Oppositions to Motions for Summary Judgment

DECLARATIONS

All facts asserted in opposition to motions for summary judgment must be supported by admissible evidence established in declarations or by judicial notice.

Declarations must:

- Be limited to facts relevant to the motion for summary judgment.
- Include only admissible evidence that the declarant could testify to if called as a witness.
- Be concise and direct statements of facts; a declaration should not be a summary of everything the declarant knows.
- Be drafted before the memorandum of points and authorities; then, the statements of undisputed and disputed facts and argument can cite to the declarations by paragraph number, and need not repeat all of the facts.

MEMORANDUM OF POINTS AND AUTHORITIES

The Memorandum of Points and Authorities in Opposition to Motion for Summary Judgment consists of five different sections, as follows:

Section I. Introduction: This consists of a concise one-paragraph summary of the nature of the underlying case, the basis for the summary judgment motion, and the basis for the opposition.

Section II. Response to Moving Party's Statement of Undisputed Facts: This is in two column format. In the first column we restate the alleged Undisputed Facts. In the second column, we respond with "Agree" or "Disagree," indicating whether we agree or disagree that the fact alleged to be undisputed is in fact undisputed.

Section III. Responsive Party's Statement of Disputed Facts: This is a two-column section identical in format to the Moving Party's Statement of Undisputed Facts (Section II of their Memorandum). In the first column, we state those facts we believe are disputed. The second column lists citations to evidence that establish these facts.

Section IV. Response to Moving Party's Arguments: In this section, we draft arguments that respond point by point to the arguments made in the moving party's Memorandum of Points and Authorities in Support of Motion for Summary Judgment. In support of our arguments, we cite to our Disputed Facts by the number assigned in Section III, and to relevant cases to support our legal assertions. We also make any additional arguments that support the position that there are triable issues of fact or that there are legal issues precluding entry of judgment as a matter of law.

Section V. Conclusion: This is a brief statement asking the court to find in our favor.

EXAMPLE OF DEFENDANT'S STATEMENT OF UNDISPUTED FACTS

II. DEFENDANT'S STATEMENT OF UNDISPUTED FACTS

Statement	Citation of Evidence
1. Defendant is the administrator of decedent's estate.	Declaration of Grant Keefe, ¶ 1
2. Defendant is decedent's nephew	Declaration of Grant Keefe, ¶ 2
3.Defendant reviewed decedent's papers and documents, and personal effects, and found no writing signed by decedent promising interests in her estate to plaintiff.	Declaration of Grant Keefe, ¶ 3
4.Defendant spent significant time with decedent in the months before she died.	Declaration of Grant Keefe, ¶4
5.Defendant had many conversations with decedent in which she discussed defendant and plaintiff and Megan Finch.	Declaration of Grant Keefe, ¶5
6.Decedent indicated that she felt she had more than provided compensation to plaintiff for the services he provided.	Declaration of Grant Keefe, ¶6
7.Decedent indicated that she would not leave a will as she knew and desired that defendant would inherit everything if she died intestate.	Declaration of Grant Keefe, ¶7
8. Decedent died on August 26, 1999.	Declaration of Grant Keefe, ¶8
9. his action was filed on January 11, 2002	Request for Judicial Notice of Complaint

<u>SAMPLE INSTRUCTION SHEET</u>

MEMORANDUM   July 29, 1995

To: Applicant
From: Leslie Kelleher
Re: Case Plan

This memo provides guidance to all associates in developing uniform Case Plans. When I request a case Plan, what I want is a memorandum explaining clearly and concisely the steps that I should take in order to handle the case from beginning to end, including researching the law, investigating and developing the facts, and taking any other necessary actions.

The case plan must cover the following:

· What is the overall goal to be achieved?

· What legal issues need to be researched? As to each legal issue, what legal research needs to be done?

· For each legal issue, what factual issues, if any, need to be resolved?

· For each factual issue, 1) what additional facts do we need and 2) how and from what source do we obtain these facts?

Where formal discovery devices are available, state what specific devices should be employed. Do not ignore informal discovery devices such as interviews of potential witnesses or asking for copies of documents.

Be sure to indicate the order in which the steps should be taken. For example, in a product liability action you might suggest that we should take a party's deposition before serving interrogatories. State why this is so. For example, there are a limited number of interrogatories available and follow-up questions are not allowed.

Therefore, the deposition which is more open ended and allows follow-up questions should be done first. Then based on this information, the interrogatories can be used to clarify more specific and possibly narrower details.

In writing the Case Plan for investigating, researching and preparing a case for resolution, be as specific as possible. In a custody case, for example, do not just tell me I need to do informal and formal discovery to establish that placement with our clients is in the best interests of child. Tell me what statutory or case law is relevant, what factual considerations should be brought to bear to establish those interests, and specifically how (e.g., deposition, affidavit, interrogatories, requests for admission, etc.) and from whom we should obtain and present the facts.

<u>**SAMPLE INSTRUCTION SHEET**</u>

GALENA COUNTY RULES OF COURT

5. EARLY NEUTRAL EVALUATION RULES

5-1. Description.

In Early Neutral Evaluation (ENE) the parties and their counsel make compact presentations of their claims and defenses, including key evidence, and receive a nonbinding evaluation by an experienced neutral lawyer with subject matter expertise.

5-2. The ENE Session.

(a) At least ten days before the ENE session, each party shall file an ENE Statement that describes briefly the substance of the suit, addressing the party's views of the key liability issues and damages and discussing the key evidence.

(b) At the ENE session, the evaluator shall:

> (1) permit each party, orally and through documents or other media, to present its claims or defenses and to describe the principal evidence on which they are based;

> (2) help the parties identify areas of agreement and, where feasible, enter stipulations;

> (3) assess the relative strengths and weaknesses of the parties' contentions and evidence, and explain carefully the reasoning that supports these assessments.

(c) If requested by one or more of the parties, within 10 days after the session, the evaluator shall provide a written opinion that:

> (1) includes a statement of facts that carefully selects only the facts pertinent to the legal and factual issues evaluated in the opinion;

> (2) states the legal and factual issues presented to the evaluator;

(3) assesses the relative strengths and weaknesses of the parties' contentions and evidence, and explains carefully the reasoning that supports the evaluator's assessments; and

(4) draws a conclusion as to the likely outcome in the pending litigation on each legal and factual issue presented to the evaluator and requested to be addressed in the opinion.

(d) The ENE session shall be informal. Rules of evidence shall not apply. There shall be no formal examination or cross-examination of witnesses.

5-3. Confidentiality. The court, the evaluator, all counsel and parties, and any other persons attending the ENE session shall treat as "confidential information" the contents of the written ENE Statements, anything that happened or was said, any position taken, any view of the merits of the case formed by any participant in connection with any ENE session, and any opinion or assessment of the evaluator.

<u>**SAMPLE INSTRUCTION SHEET**</u>

**CENTRAL COLUMBIA
LEGAL SERVICES**

TO: All Staff Attorneys

RE: Theory of the Casc Memorandum

A theory of the case is a working hypothesis of how the law and facts will fit together to support the result sought by our client. The statement of facts should include, in addition to a statement of those facts presently known, a statement of those facts that need to be developed. The statement of law is a summary explanation of why specific legal authorities compel a decision in our client's favor on the basis of those facts. Although it is to be stated in detailed and definite terms, the theory of the case is necessarily provisional, and may be revised and refined as fact development proceeds.

In writing the theory of the case memo, the staff attorney must begin with one or more overarching statements of what we will ask the court to hold. For example, in an age discrimination in employment case, an overarching statement of the plaintiff's case theory might be:

> The defendant employcr is liable under the Federal Age Discrimination in Employment Act for damages, injunctive relief, and attorney's fees for having terminated our client because of his age. Our client will make out a <u>prima facie</u> case based on the facts that he was in a protected age category at the time of his termination, was qualified to perform the job, was replaced by a younger person, and was terminated in a work force reduction which disproportionally impacted persons over 40 years old. Defendant's effort to establish that our client was unqualified to perform the assigned work will fail to rebut the <u>prima facie</u> case.

Next, each element of the case theory must be identified. Any legal principles that affect an element of the case theory must be briefly analyzed. Known facts that support an element of the case theory must be stated and facts that need to be developed must be identified.

In the preceding age discrimination example, this analysis would be as follows:

- <u>Element:</u> A showing of disparate impact alone establishes a <u>prima facie</u> case of age discrimination.

- <u>Analysis:</u> In <u>Greggs v. Maryland Power</u>, the United States Supreme Court held that disparate impact alone establishes a <u>prima facie</u> case of race discrimination, because it raises a permissive inference with regard to a protected class. The same analysis should apply in age discrimination cases, because of congressional intent to create a protected class.

- <u>Known facts:</u> 12 of 20 persons terminated in plaintiff's department were over 40 years old.

- <u>Facts to be developed:</u> age distribution of defendant's overall work force reduction and remaining work force.

TRIAL PREPARATION WORKSHEET

OFFICE OF THE PUBLIC DEFENDER
County of Alpamayo
State of Columbia

To: Applicant

From: Hubie Brown, Misdemeanor Supervisor

Date: February 25, 1999

Subject: People v. Mata

Now that you have completed our training program, you are ready for your first trial. I will be your trial supervisor for the trial of our client, Teddy Mata, who is charged with misdemeanor battery. The trial is set for next week.

The file is fairly complete: complaint, police report, student-intern interview of Mata and declaration from a witness, Pat Powers. As usual, the police officers have refused to speak with our interns or investigators, and therefore we can't get anything more from them until the trial. At the trial setting conference, the People said that they would call only Officer Mendoza and the victim, Kenneth Jones.

I met Teddy Mata briefly when he came to the office to meet with the student-intern for his interview. Teddy is an articulate retired taxi driver, with, as you'll see from his interview, strong views on the atmosphere of fear and violence that, he says, too many older citizens live with every day. In our short meeting, we had a lively discussion of Teddy's objection to the defense by this office of those accused of mugging the old or infirm. Teddy is insistent that he was just defending himself when he struck the 17 year old victim, and that we "owe" him the same defense we give "muggers". This background explains in part the necessity of a trial for a relatively minor offense.

The next step is for you to study the file and work that's been done and complete the Trial Preparation Worksheet, which is attached. Do not fill out the attached sample worksheet, but provide the information in a separate document precisely following the sample worksheet format.

OFFICE OF THE PUBLIC DEFENDER

TRIAL PREPARATION WORKSHEET- MISDEMEANOR

NAME OF DEFENDANT:_____

I. CHARGES: PENAL CODE SECTIONS:

A._____

B._____

C._____

II. ELEMENTS OF EACH CHARGE TO BE PROVED BY THE PEOPLE:

Charge A	Charge B	Charge C
1.	1.	1.
2.	2.	2.
3.	3.	3.
4.	4.	4.
5.	5.	5.
6.	6.	6.

III. OUTLINE OF THE PEOPLE'S CASE

List subpoenaed and likely witnesses and anticipated testimony.

Witness	Summary of Expected Testimony	Element Proved

IV. ELEMENTS OF EACH AFFIRMATIVE DEFENSE TO BE PROVED BY THE DEFENDANT:

Defense 1	Defense 2	Defense 3
1.	1.	1.
2.	2.	2.
3.	3.	3.
4.	4.	4.
5.	5.	5.
6.	6.	6.

V. DEFENSE CASE:

List witnesses and summarize testimony of defense witnesses.

Witness	Summary of Expected Testimony	Element negated or satisfied

II   CROSS EXAMINATION:

List People's witnesses and identify evidence to be elicited to support defense theory (e.g., witness at crime scene failed to identify defendant) or harmful evidence that must be challenged (e.g., witness is biased, had no opportunity to observe, cannot recall, can be otherwise impeached).

Witness	Testimony to be elicited or challenged	Element negated or satisfied

VII.   THEORY OF THE CASE

The theory of the case is a working hypothesis of how the law and facts will fit together to support the results sought by the client. The theory is used for preparation and is integrated into all aspects of the trial, since it provides the basic outline of how the law and facts (both pro and con) weave together to lead to a result favorable to the client. For example, it defines the jury instructions to be requested and the content of witness examination. An effective statement of the theory of the case would combine the factual analysis of a closing argument with the legal analysis that supports the client's position. Write a summary of the theory of the case using the following organization:

- Start with one or more decisive statements of what we will ask the court or jury to decide.

- Identify each element of the case theory

- Briefly analyze legal principles that affect each element.

- State known facts that support an element and identify facts that need to be developed.

Remember the rule that all factual assertions must be supported by evidence admitted at trial.

PRACTICE PERFORMANCE TESTS IN CALIFORNIA PERFORMANCE TEST BOOK:

Professional Responsibility

Professor Marina Hsieh

PROFESSIONAL RESPONSIBILITY

By

Professor Marina Hsieh

I. COVERAGE ON THE CALIFORNIA BAR

A. What body of law to apply.

1. The State Bar "Instructions Regarding Professional Responsibility" state:

"Applicants should be prepared to answer questions that test knowledge of the California Rules of Professional Conduct [_____], relevant sections of the California Business and Professions Code, and leading federal and state case law on the subject in addition to the ABA Model Rules of Professional Conduct [_____] and ABA Model Code of Professional Responsibility [_____]. Professional responsibility issues may be included in conjunction with any subject tested on the examination."

2. Unless the question directs you to use California law, you should answer according to legal theories and principles of general application, i.e., the ABA Model Rules. Most recent calls have directed you to "answer according to both California and ABA authorities," so you must study both.

3. The CA Bar does not cover the Code of Judicial Conduct.

B. Essay Tip: Don't chase phantom PR questions.

II. ORGANIZING YOUR ESSAY

A. The building block:

"The lawyer has a duty of ____(fill in a duty)____ to ____(fill in a person or thing)____.

1. The bulk of duties are those owed to your client(s). These are:

Confidentiality	
Loyalty	
Financial Responsibility	—> Client(s). Do each separately!
Competence	
…& other reasonable things	

2. Duties to entities other than your client(s). Mix and match:

Candor/Truthfulness	Court
Fairness	Adversaries (parties & their counsel)
Dignity/Decorum	—> Legal profession
…& other reasonable things	Third parties
	Public

Mnemonic: _____

B. Building an essay. Within the call of the question, outline by identifying every major duty that you have to _____. Then, for each of these, look for conflicting duties to other clients or entities. Organize your answer by discussing these conflicting duties in a cluster, then move to the next major duty to your client and its related cluster of duties. Finally, resurvey the problem for any miscellaneous duties, *e.g.,* to the public or profession, that you haven't discussed yet.

—Use headings and skip lines!

III. THE DUTY OF CONFIDENTIALITY (TO YOUR CLIENT)

A. General rule: You can't reveal anything "_____ _____" of a client without her consent. The rationale is to maximize candor and trust, allowing the adversarial system to work.

1. Scope. The duty of confidentiality applies _____ whether the client requested it be kept "confidential" or whether its revelation might harm or embarrass the client.

2. Timing and Disclaimers.

Shania liked DivorceLaw Firm's website so she filled out an online form with her background facts. Above the "SUBMIT" button a list of "Terms" stated: "I agree I am not forming an attorney-client relationship or a confidential relationship by submitting this question." LawFirm discovered they already represented Shania's husband in the divorce. Now what? The duty of confidentiality can attach

_____

_____, or even if none is formed. If no employment results, the party seeking to disqualify a lawyer bears the _____ of proving confidences were actually imparted.

Here, the duty attached because this website disclaimer was *not* in sufficiently plain terms. Result: LawFirm must _____ from all representations! Compare: "I understand and agree that LawFirm will have no duty to keep confidential the information I am now transmitting to LawFirm."

Once attached, your duty of confidentiality _____ _____, even after formal representation ends, and even after death!

B. Distinguish Attorney-client privilege, the overlapping, but _____ evidentiary rule that allows you to refuse to produce or testify about confidential communications related to the representation from your client or her agents to you. Confidentiality applies _____ of the information, and prohibits disclosures that could reasonably lead to discovery of information related to the representation.

C. Exceptions. There are major exceptions to the ethical duty of confidentiality.

1. Consent. If the client _____, a lawyer may reveal otherwise confidential information.

Your client Jason has synthesized a new steroid, and hires you to get a patent on the drug. May you reveal his invention to the Patent Office? _____. You have "_____" to reveal what's necessary to render your legal services.

2. Defending yourself.

Jason (i) sues you for malpractice, (ii) brings disciplinary actions against you, and (iii) refuses to pay you, forcing you to sue him for your fees. May you reveal confidential information in any of these proceedings? _____; all of these circumstances, as well as seeking an ethics opinion, fall into the exception for revealing information necessary _____

_____

3. If compelled by final court order, law, or other ethical duties. E.g., your duty to uphold the law permits an exception to prevent certain some crimes:

a. Death or substantial bodily harm.

What if Jason told you his adulterated drugs have caused the death of a ball player and pose a mortal danger to others still taking it? May you reveal his ongoing distribution to anyone? _____

_____, if you reasonably believe disclosure is necessary to prevent a crime likely to result in reasonably certain

_____.

—*In CA you must first, if reasonable in the circumstances, (i) make a
_____ to persuade the client not to commit the
act, and (ii) inform the client of your decision to reveal his confidences.

b. Fraud or financial crimes.

Jason tells you that he has stopped distributing roids because he's found that
bribing ball players makes for even more lucrative betting on the games. May
you reveal his intentions to prevent his future crime? ABA: Yes, if he used or is
using _____ to commit the crime, *and*
the disclosure would prevent or mitigate substantial financial loss.

*CA: _____

IV. THE DUTY OF LOYALTY TO YOUR CLIENT: CONFLICTS OF INTEREST

A. The black letter law

1. You have a duty of loyalty to your client. If an interest of you, another client, or
a third party _____
to loyal representation, you have a conflict of interest. Flag and discuss
_____ and _____ conflicts.

—If conflicts emerge only after representation begins, disclose them and get
further consent.

2. Rule: You must not take on the representation unless:

a. _____
_____ despite a potential or actual conflict; *and*

b. You _____ each affected client. If your duty of _____
prevents you from fully disclosing information the client needs to understand
the conflict, then consent may not be possible; *and*

c. The client _____.

—Specific conflicts rules fall into various types: Some categories of conflicts are
objectively never reasonable, others may be reasonable with client consent. CA
liberally allows case-by-case screening and client consent to overcome many
conflicts. Some fact patterns fall outside the ethical rules don't trigger any conflict.

3. "_____" means that you and all the members
of your firm share conflicts. This includes any group of lawyers that work together
closely or share responsibilities, *e.g.,* private firms or corporate law departments.
*CA follows these rules for *disqualification*, but does not subject a lawyer to
discipline for imputed conflicts.

— Exceptions: When one lawyer's conflicts arise from previous government
service, work for adverse parties at a previous firm, or a purely personal
relationship, the conflict need not disqualify colleagues. In these cases, an
"_____" may make representation reasonable by blocking

off any contact on the matter between the lawyer with the conflict and other lawyers of his firm.

—Issue spotter tip: Look for your colleagues' conflicts as well as your own.

4. You are ordinarily responsible even for conflicts about which you are ignorant. The exception is for _____ under a court, agency, or non-profit program, where you are responsible only if you know the representation involves a conflict.

5. Remedies: (depends on the posture of the case, but consider): _____
_____
_____

Now, consider major fact patterns where rules address what's "reasonable":

B. Conflicts between lawyer and client.

1. Business transactions or adverse interests: "_____
_____." You may enter into business with a client or obtain an interest adverse to hers only if: (a) the terms are **F**air to the client, (b) fully **D**isclosed in understandable writing, (c) the client has an **O**pportunity to consult an outside lawyer, and (d) your client provides written **C**onsent.

a. Transactions

In representing a start-up company, its law firm agreed to accept "payment" in the form of shares of stock equal to the value of the services provided. Assuming that the services have been valued reasonably, and the transaction is documented, may it do so? _____
_____
_____

—Be particularly cautious if the investment is by individual firm members, or if the acquisition represents a major asset that might distort the firm's advice to the company, *e.g.,* regarding disclosure of adverse information.

b. Board service

There is no automatic bar to serving on a Board of Directors of a corporate client, although it is now strongly discouraged, as it is likely to compromise duties of _____
Service to a non-profit legal services organization is allowed.

Attorney Shaha is a member of the Board of Directors of World Bucks, Inc. Paul, World's CEO, asks Shaha to defend him in an investigation of his alleged embezzlement of company money. May Shaha represent him? _____.
Shaha has a _____ to the corporation in her personal capacity as a member of the Board. _____
_____

2. Limiting liability. You cannot limit your client's right to report you for ethical or other professional violations. Similarly, you cannot limit your _____ liability when you enter into a relationship with your client relationship with your client, unless the client is independently represented in making the agreement.

—If a client later does make a malpractice claim against you, you can only settle after _____
_____

3. Publication rights contracts.

Halfway through his trial, Scott offers to sell his lawyer rights to his story to raise some needed cash. Can the lawyer accept? ABA: _____
_____

—*CA: _____. CA case law discourages contracts before the end of proceedings, but tolerates them if the judge is satisfied that the client clearly understands and consents.

4. Loans and advances to your client. ABA: No financial assistance, except for: costs and litigation expenses when representing an indigent, and the _____
_____ in contingent fee cases.

—*CA prohibits the promise of paying a *prospective* client's debts, but allows loans in all matters (including non-litigation matters) for any purpose after the lawyer is hired if there is _____

5. Use of information. Use or communication of information relating to the representation of a client to her disadvantage and without consent violates the duties of both _____

6. Gifts to the lawyer or lawyer's family. You must not solicit a substantial gift from a client, or draft a legal instrument for a client who is not your close relative if it _____
_____.

7. Close relationships with the lawyer for the other side. You can't oppose a party represented by your relative without informed client consent. "Close relations" include: _____, i.e., your parent, child, sibling, and spouse. *CA explicitly recognizes other "intimates," *e.g.*, shackmates.

—This conflict is not imputed to other firm members, nor is:

8. Trial counsel as a necessary witness. The ABA is more restrictive: you cannot serve as counsel and witness in the same trial unless your appearance as a witness won't _____ the client and (i) your testimony is uncontested or regarding the nature and value of services rendered; or (ii) if your _____
_____ to the case means withdrawal would impose substantial hardship on the client.

—*CA prohibits attorneys from testifying only in _____ if the client refuses written consent.

C. Conflicts between Clients. Generally, you may represent clients with potential conflicts with proper consent, but it rarely proper if their interests are in actual conflict.

1. Issue spotter tip: Always check for breaches of _____ in multiple client representation.

2. Opposite sides of the same matter / imputed DQ.

Your law firm represents Texaco in labor matters, although you have done no work for it. Lundwall, a former Texaco employee, asks you to help him sue Texaco for cutting off his benefits. Can you do so? _____
_____
_____

3. Opposing present client's interests.

Assume your firm's only contact with Texaco is representing it in a securities action. May you now take the labor claim of Lundwall v. Texaco? * _____
_____.

— Statutory exception: CA does not extend this prohibition to representing a policyholder and his _____ as joint clients, where the insurer's interest in each matter is only as an indemnity provider:

Your law firm has been retained by NorCal InsCo to represent Daniel Driver in tort action. May you now represent *Patty Plaintiff* in an unrelated case against Dave Daredevil and NorCal InsCo, his insurer? _____
_____
_____

4. Two clients with inconsistent positions.

You find yourself arguing both for and against the constitutionality of mandatory sentencing laws in two different appeals. Is that OK? _____
_____, but if either would be disadvantaged you must _____.

5. Multiple clients in the same matter.

Examples of representing multiple clients or matters in which you might _____
_____ are representing:

—A corporation and any of its directors, officers, employees, or shareholders;

—Both spouses in a divorce or will.

Kevorkian's insurance company has hired you to defend him and it in a malpractice action. Note this presents a _____,
but is acceptable with reasonable consent.

Now, however, Kevorkian tells you that he was indeed using medically "unorthodox practices" on the plaintiff that are not covered by his malpractice insurance policy. Is there now an actual conflict between Kevorkian and his insurance company? _____

Best remedy? _____

You must at least withdraw from representing InsCo because you have relevant, _____ information from Kevorkian that you cannot use in pursuing undivided loyal representation of InsCo.

—In criminal matters, dual representation may also impede the Sixth Amendment's guarantee of "effective assistance of counsel."

6. New clients in matters related to former clients'.

If confidential information from a former client might be relevant to work on a new client's matter, you may be violating your continuing duty of _____ as well as your duty of _____ to your former client. You cannot take on a new client with interests materially adverse to a former client without the _____
_____.

Kevin asks you to represent him in his divorce from Britney, but your senior partner once represented Britney in business dealings. OK? _____
_____
_____

What if your partner had only represented a real estate venture in which Britney was a limited partner? _____
_____
_____

—Ask: do the representations overlap in function, scope or information?

In defending Britney in the past against copyright infringement charges, you were privy to all of her private recording notes. Can you use that knowledge today to represent Christina in a similar action *against* Britney? _____
_____
_____

—Imputed disqualification: If you left your firm, can it now represent Christina in her action against Britney? Not if: (i) the matters are substantially related or the same, and (ii) _____
_____

At your new firm, your conflicts will not extend to your colleagues if you: (1) are timely and effectively _____, (2) receive no direct part of the fee, and your former client receives (3) notice and (4) _____
_____ of compliance with these conditions.

7. Former government lawyer now in private practice.

a. *CA _____ from later working for the defendants of those cases. Case law allows screening of other government colleagues.

b. The ABA bars a government lawyer who worked "_____
_____ " on a "_____", i.e., a specific dispute between specific people over specific issues, from working on the same

8

"matter" later in private practice. This conflict may be allowed with informed consent by the government agency.

You've left the federal Equal Employment Opportunity Commission where you worked on regulations prohibiting religious discrimination. At your new firm, can you litigate the meaning of those regulations? _____

_____

What if your work at the EEOC was bringing an anti-discrimination suit against Halliburton? You've now joined the private firm defending Halliburton in that case. May you represent Halliburton? _____, not without _____ of your Government employer.

c. Imputed disqualification.

May other members of your firm? _____ , _____ the three ABA conditions for an exception to imputed disqualification of colleagues of former government lawyers are met:

1) _____; and

2) You do not share any part of the fee in the matter (pre-arranged salaries or partnership shares are OK); and

3) _____.

d. Judicial officers besides attorneys.

What if you were a judicial clerk on the Ninth Circuit and worked on the *EEOC v. Halliburton* case? The same rules apply to _____

_____

D. Conflicts due to Third Party interference.

1. General rule: _____

_____

2. Compensation for your services from a third party is permitted only with informed client consent.

3. Organizational clients. A lawyer must act in the best interest of the _____, even if an officer, employee, or other associated person acts to the contrary.

a. Recent Federal laws increased obligations of securities lawyers:

You are in-house counsel at Reron. You discover that the Chief Operating Officer materially violated securities laws. You _____ the matter to the CEO or Chief Legal Counsel of the company. If they do not respond, you must go to the Board or the _____ in the company.

—Finally, if you reasonably believe it necessary to _____ fraud, perjury or substantial injury to the organization or investors, or to _____ financial injury from a violation that involved your services, you _____ disclose confidential information to the Securities Exchange Commission without client consent.

b. New ABA Rules similarly mandate "reporting up," and permit limited "reporting out." *Although CA still prohibits outside reporting, federal preemption means a CA lawyer may comply with federal law.

V. YOUR FINANCIAL DUTIES TO YOUR CLIENT

A. Attorney fees.

1. In non-contingent fee cases, agreements must include: how the fee is calculated; what services are covered, and the lawyer and client's duties.

—*CA requires more than the ABA: agreements _____
_____, unless (i) the fee is under $1000, (ii) with a corporate client, (iii) for routine services for a regular client, or (iv) it's an emergency or impractical.

2. In contingent fee cases:

a. Written fee agreements must be signed by the client and contain:

1) _____; and

2) _____; and

3) _____
_____

—*CA also requires that agreements state:

4) How work not covered by the contingency fee will be paid, and

5) That lawyers' fees are _____.

b. Types of actions allowing contingent fees:

Under ABA Rules, contingent fees may not be used in: _____
_____ or _____ cases. *CA is silent on criminal cases, and OKs contingent fee divorces "provided the fee arrangement won't encourage the breakup of an otherwise savable marriage."

c. Termination before contingency / judgment.

Bud fires Vinny from his personal injury case after he decides he's not nearly as good as the guys in the movies. Vinny's put in a good year of work, although the case has not gone to trial or settled. If Vinny had a contingent fee agreement with Bud, can he recover any fees? _____
_____
_____

3. When are fees too high? ABA Rule: Fees must be _____, taking into account the labor, novelty, difficulty, skill and timing required, result obtained, the experience of and other demands on the attorney, fee arrangement, etc.

*CA Rule: _____

Bud hires Vinny to represent him in a subsequent malpractice action against his doctors. Vinny drafts a new contract that providing that Vinny will receive 1/3 of the recovery as a contingent fee, and that if Bud fires Vinny or refuses a settlement offer that Vinny believes is "fair and reasonable," then Bud will immediately pay Vinny $600 per hour for all work done to date. OK?

—Contingent fee: _____.

—Refusal of settlement offer as grounds to W/D? _____.

—$600/hr. payment? _____

If it's functionally a penalty or forfeiture, then it is not enforceable.

—* CA requires a lawyer to participate in _____
if the client requests it. The ABA encourages arbitration.

4. Fee splitting. Focus on the party/entity with whom you are sharing fees:

   a. It is generally OK to split fees with other _____
   _____

   b. You may split fees with _____
   only if the total fee is ethical and there is written disclosure and client consent.
   The ABA further requires the division be _____ to the
   work done by each attorney, unless each is jointly responsible for the action.

   Jacob gets a great personal injury case, but is annoyed that the case is based in LA, which he regards as a grid locked armpit. He refers the case to Meyer, who does all the work and wins a million bucks. Can Meyer send Jacob a Hummer as thanks for the referral? ABA: No, Jacob did no work, so it's _____
   _____. *CA: _____
   _____

   c. Fee splitting with _____ is generally not allowed
   (protects your judgment and prevents the unauthorized practice of law.)

   —Exceptions to fee splitting with non-lawyers are for (1) _____
   _____ paid to a deceased lawyer's firm or heirs for his work, (2)
   fees passed on salaries and pensions to non-lawyer employees, and (3) sharing
   of court-awarded legal fees with a _____
   that employed or recommended the lawyer.

   —A lawyer may pay the usual charges of a qualified lawyer _____
   _____.

5. Partnership with non-lawyers in providing legal services is prohibited for any
practicing lawyer. _____ cannot be partners, shareholders,
officers, or control or direct a lawyer's professional judgment.

—You can arrange reciprocal referrals with other professionals if they are _____ _____, and you explain the arrangement to the client.

—If "_____"are provided by a separate entity controlled by you, you must tell the client that lawyer-client protections do not apply. If you *personally* provide those related services, you are subject to the ethical rules.

"Foreclosure Solutions" employs non-lawyers to consult with homeowner clients about loan renegotiations. Its ads promise legal services, but clients cannot choose their lawyer and are not told what legal fees are generated. Andy Attorney partners with Foreclosure for $150 a case to file boilerplate pleadings to delay foreclosure and if foreclosure begins, to send a boilerplate letter suggesting bankruptcy. Ethical violations? _____. Attorney solicited via an agent, provided incompetent legal services, formed a _____, aided them in the unauthorized practice of law, and _____ with them.

—To avoid these dangers, Attorney needs to generate the business himself, review each case for appropriate legal action, and control and supervise the consultants' work.

B. Disclosure of Professional Liability Insurance

Although not a disciplinary offense, the ABA allows administrative suspensions for failure to report whether you _____ on your annual registration statement. *CA requires, at the time of engagement, written disclosure of the absence of insurance directly to any client foreseen to need more than four hours of work.

—Exceptions are for government and in-house lawyers.

C. Client trust accounts.

1. You have a duty to safeguard your _____ by labeling and storing it in a safe place such as an office safe or bank safe deposit box.

2. Money held for the client must be placed in a _____ _____. These include moneys received on his behalf, advances for costs, expenses and fees. No borrowing or commingling of funds with your personal money allowed!

   a. Normally, use an individual, interest bearing trust account to hold client funds; the interest belongs to the client.

   b. Smaller funds held for a short period of time for several clients at once can be deposited into a "_____ client trust account." The interest (IOLTA) on this checking account will first pay the bank's service charges, and the remainder goes to _____ to fund legal services for the poor.

   c. If you have a fee dispute or if a third party has a lawful claim over your client's funds or property in your custody, you _____ the disputed portion in the client trust account until resolution of the claim.

3. You have a duty to keep good records for your client, to render accountings, notify him of moneys received on his behalf, and pay promptly money due to him. *CA requires you to keep records of client property for _____ after final distribution and to make records available to the State Bar for audits.

VI. COMPETENCE & OTHER COMMON SENSE DUTIES TO YOUR CLIENT

A. Duty of competence.

1. You have a duty to render competent service to your client. If you don't, you are subject to: (i) discipline by the Bar, (ii) disqualification as counsel in a litigated matter, and (iii) civil malpractice liability.

Competence means: _____
_____
_____

—If you don't know the relevant law, you can't take on a matter unless: you can put in the time to learn it without undue expense or delay to your client, or you associate with a lawyer competent in the area.

2. Distinguish malpractice: A malpractice action is a civil case brought by a plaintiff for money damages; a disciplinary action is administrative and brought by State Bar to discipline you and protect the public.

a. A malpractice plaintiff must prove a legal claim. In simple negligence cases, the malpractice plaintiff must show a breach of a _____, which for the general practitioner is the skill, care and judgment that a reasonably prudent general practitioner in the region would have used in the circumstances.

b. While an ethical violation may be relevant evidence of malpractice, it does not create a presumption of it.

B. Duty of diligence. You have a duty to diligently, promptly and _____ pursue your case to completion.

C. Duty to communicate. You have a duty to keep your client informed about the case, including _____

—If a settlement offer is made to joint clients, you must convey the offer to all and make sure they agree on the division of the settlement before accepting.

D. Accepting representation. The general rule is that you are free to accept or to reject any case. "A lawyer is not a bus."

1. You _____, as part of your duty to the public and profession: (a) the case of the defenseless or oppressed "if your only reason to refuse is selfish," and (b) a fair share of work without charge. ABA rules urge 50 hours of *pro bono* work a year for truly indigent clients.

2. Conversely, you _____if you would
_____.

Typical problems are if you are not in the physical or mental shape to take the case (violating the duty of _____ to the client).

E. Scope of representation. The client makes decisions about her _____ _____ (*e.g.*, whether to testify in a criminal case, accepting a settlement). The lawyer makes decisions on _____ _____ (*e.g.*, choice of motions, what discovery to seek). If you disagree, you can limit the scope of representation, with client consent.

—The scope of representation does not include assisting a client in conduct you know is criminal or advising the client how to act illegally and get away with it!

F. Duties on withdrawal from representation.

1. Mandatory withdrawal. You must withdraw from a pending case if: _____ _____ _____, e.g., if continuing would require assisting in a crime.

Attorney Vinny tells Bud that his research shows that there's no viable malpractice claim against Bud's doctors. Bud insists that Vinny continue, saying, "I don't care if I don't win, I just wanna make dose scum pay their lawyers as much as I paid dem." Must Vinny withdraw? _____ _____ _____

2. Permissive withdrawal. You may withdraw from a case if you convince the court there is _____, and your withdrawal will not cause undue delay or disruption. Recognized causes include a client's _____ _____, or his insistence on actions you find "repugnant" or imprudent. The ABA also recognizes when the representation will result in an unreasonable financial burden or when, after warning, the client fails substantially to fulfill an obligation to you. *CA more liberally allows withdrawal if your client simply breaches an agreement as to fees or expenses.

3. Procedures for withdrawal. In order to quit, you must:

   a. Provide _____, and

   b. You also must promptly return:

      1) Any unspent fee and expense advances, and

      2) _____.
      Include everything needed to pursue the case, even work product, and even if the client has not paid! *CA forbids withholding your client's materials for your money!

G. Other Duties. Be reasonable and sensible.

—In 2002, the ABA added a Rule prohibiting _____ _____ unless you had a preexisting sexual relationship. *CA Rule 3-120 also excuses preexisting relationships, and allows spouses and even new relations, with cautions.

VII. DUTIES OF CANDOR TO THE PUBLIC & DIGNITY OF THE PROFESSION: ADVERTISING & SOLICITATION

A. General Essay writing tip. Separately identify duties that can run to multiple entities. *E.g.,* advertising may breach your duty of candor to the public, but also your duty to preserve the dignity of the profession. Give each a separate heading!

B. The basic idea. A state can regulate attorney advertising and solicitation subject to the lawyer's Constitutional right to free speech. This is protected under the limited _____ doctrine of the First Amendment.

A state bar rule prohibits lawyers from using direct mail to solicit personal injury or wrongful death clients within 30 days of an accident. Stewart, the sole owner of "Went For It" lawyer referral service, sued the Bar for the alleged right to go for it early and often. Is the restriction Constitutional? _____ , _____ :

1. _____
(*e.g.,* preserving the dignity of the legal profession, or citizen privacy); and

2. _____ ; and

3. _____ .

C. Advertising. This refers to a lawyer's communication with the public at large.

  1. Advertising must not be false or misleading.

    a. Don't mislead or omit material information.

      Ally advertises that she prepares "simple wills" for $300. However, 95% of the wills she writes involve "complications" that require additional fees. Is her ad misleading? _____ .

    b. Don't raise unjustified expectations or make unverifiable comparisons. *CA presumes improper any ad that contains _____ _____

    No testimonials or endorsements may be used unless there is an express disclaimer that they are not a GWP.

  2. Claims of legal specialties. You can explain your fields of practice, such as "practice limited to federal courts." But you may not advertise claims of specialization unless you are a "_____." The CA Board of Legal Specialization requires the "4 E's": Experience, an Examination, Education, and Evaluations. ABA rules allow certification by approved organizations, which must be identified in communications.

  3. Advertising must not _____ or solicit someone who has indicated that she wants to be left alone. Targeted direct mail is OK, but must meet exact guidelines for labeling as "Advertising Material."

  4. Every ad must be _____ as advertising and, if applicable, "a dramatization" or "impersonation." It must _____ at least one lawyer responsible for its contents. You must _____ of the content and placement of any ad for 2 years.

5. *CA presumptions. CA Rule 1-400 lists additional specific actions presumed to be advertising violations, *i.e.*, they shift the burden to the lawyer to disprove a violation.

D. Solicitation refers to individualized contact with a layperson.

1. The rule, with built-in exceptions:

Do not seek professional employment for _____
_____
_____
with whom you have no prior professional, personal or family relationship.

Attorney Ann lurks in a chat room designed "to offer emotional support for victims of Hurricane Katrina." She then introduces herself as a lawyer and offers to answer legal questions. Prohibited solicitation? *CA: _____. CA reads "live or telephone" narrowly. ABA: _____, because solicitation extends to "_____
_____."

*CA does presume that communications made at the scene of an accident or en route to a medical facility are improper, as are communications to potential clients that you should know are not in the physical or mental state to exercise reasonable judgment.

Is Attorney Ann's chat room overture unethical under this standard? _____

2. "Runners and cappers" (agents) can't do anything that a lawyer can't do.

A lawyer sent a non-lawyer friend into a hospital, dressed as a member of the clergy, to provide injured patients with comfort—and the lawyer's business cards in case they needed assistance in suing a wrongdoer. OK? _____
_____
_____

VIII. DUTY OF CANDOR TO THE COURT & FAIRNESS TO YOUR ADVERSARY

A. Basic idea. A lawyer is prohibited from engaging in conduct involving
_____.
Even within our adversarial system these duties generally create an ethical obligation that can override conflicting duties of _____ and _____ to your client.

B. Duty to present facts and evidence truthfully. You must refuse to make a false statement of material fact, or offer evidence you know is false to a tribunal, or _____ a false statement of material fact or law that you previously made or presented to the tribunal.

1. Client perjury. You must not knowingly facilitate client perjury.

—If the matter is a _____ case, you must refuse to call the client as a witness if you know he intends to perjure himself.

—However, _____ have a ____ Amendment right to testify on their own behalf and a _____ Amendment right to the effective assistance of counsel. Counsel also has an ethical obligation to protect her client's confidences. How do you balance these rights?

Ted tells you that he intends to testify falsely that he has never owned a typewriter to type manifestos against technology. What should you do? _____ _____:

    a. Counsel Ted to testify truthfully or not to take the stand, then if that fails,

    b. You may _____,
then if that fails,

    c. *CA view (case law): _____
_____
(*E.g.*, don't facilitate with questions, argue points later to the jury)

    ABA: _____. The Constitutional right to counsel and the duty of confidentiality do not protect perjury.

—What if, only after the proceeding ends, Ted tells you that he lied? Take reasonable remedial measures, *e.g.*, counsel him to recant, but your duties _____ _____ (after the time for appeal has run.)

2. You must not counsel or assist a witness to testify falsely or to become "unavailable." Unless local law prohibits it, you may pay basic expenses of a witness and reasonable fees for expert witnesses, so long as payment is not contingent on the content of the testimony.

The morning that Ted's brother is to testify, you discover that he intends to lie and state that Ted was with him across the country that day. If he refuses your advice to testify truthfully, what do you do? _____ _____

3. If you do not know, but only have a reasonable belief, that testimony is false, these rules are _____.

C. Duty to produce evidence.

1. Basic idea. You must not suppress any evidence that you or your client has a legal obligation to reveal or produce, regardless of your duty of loyalty. You must not _____ _____

Neo comes to Attorney Morphius' office with a kilo of cocaine and $100,000 cash as a retainer. He tells Morphius, "I'm rich, but it's all blood money. I want out." What must Morphius do with the drugs? _____ _____ (police or DA) because it is contraband. The money? _____. If he's reasonably certain it's the instrumentality of a crime he should turn it over.

May Morphius disclose what Neo told him about selling the cocaine? _____
_____

Erik brings you a shotgun saying he used it to kill his father. He is charged with murder, and you are served a subpoena for the production of physical evidence received from your client. Must you turn over the gun? _____

_____

May you disclose what Erik told you about the gun? _____!

—Draw a line between physical evidence and confidential information!

2. Interference with evidence.

What if Erik told you that he threw the emptied gun into the bushes behind his house? Your investigator finds it but leaves it untouched. Must you tell the authorities about it? _____

If your investigator retrieves the gun and examines it, may she then be compelled to produce it for the authorities? _____. May she also be compelled to testify where she found it? _____, because an attorney or his agent may be compelled to testify as to the original location or condition of evidence that he _____

_____

May you reveal the source of the information about the gun's location? _____

_____

—A lawyer may retain evidence for a reasonable time to prepare his client's case, *e.g.,* to conduct tests so long as they will not alter or destroy the evidence.

3. Prosecutors have a special duty to _____
_____. Your ethical duty
_____ the Constitutional *Brady* obligation, requiring disclosure without regard to impact on outcome or admissibility of information.

4. Volunteering information: "_____" proceedings are unusual communications with the judge without your adversary present. Your ethical duties of candor to the court and fairness to your (absent) adversary require you to reveal relevant information, overriding the normal presumption that you not reveal facts harmful to your client's case.

D. Duty to state the law truthfully. Knowingly making a false statement of law to the court is subject to discipline. You have an obligation to be candid about the law and to cite to _____, if it's from a controlling jurisdiction and directly on point. Presenting frivolous claims or defenses is subject to discipline.

E. Duty to uphold the law.

1. Assisting in a crime. If continued representation would require *you* to commit or assist in committing a crime, you _____ withdraw! (If your client persists in actions that you reasonably believe are criminal or fraudulent, but *you* are not assisting, you _____ withdraw.)

2. Preventing your client from committing a crime.

— If your client is going to commit a crime reasonably likely to result in reasonably certain _____, your disclosure of confidences is _____.*In CA, be sure to follow safeguards in III.C.3.a. before disclosure.

— If your client's crime would only cause _____ _____, and *if* your services were employed in the crime, the ABA permits disclosure. *CA forbids any disclosure for these crimes.

IX. ADDITIONAL DUTIES OF FAIRNESS

A. The general rule. The lawyer has a duty to behave _____ in all dealings, whether or not engaged in the practice of law. When there are no explicit rules, you must act to promote _____ in the integrity and efficiency of the legal system and profession.

B. Dealing fairly with others.

1. Documents sent inadvertently.

During litigation, you open an E-mail from opposing counsel and find not the expected discovery schedule attached, but an outline of your opponent's strategy for deposing a key witness. May you forward it to your client? _____ _____ _____.You must not copy, disseminate the document; or use it to your advantage; you will be disqualified!

— Counsels' obligation to safeguard client's confidences includes reasonable electronic security and steps to prevent disclosure and to rectify errors.

2. Communication with adversaries and third parties. You must not _____ to people or mislead them as to your interests. You must not violate the legal rights of a person in order to obtain evidence, or use means with no purpose but to delay, burden or embarrass them.

3. Communication with represented people. Unless authorized by law, you must not communicate with a person you know is represented by counsel on the subject of your inquiry _____. (This rule does not apply if the party is seeking a second legal opinion.) *CA limits this to "parties" represented by counsel.

Your client claims that Beatrice Corp. negligently disposed of industrial byproducts, giving her child a deadly leukemia. Must you have Beatrice's corporation counsel's consent before you interview its site manager? _____. In CA consent is required for interviews of an officer, director or managing agent. The prohibition extends to any current employee whose communication might _____ _____ the organization or constitute _____ on its part.

Must you have consent before interviewing a former employee? _____, although care should be taken to respect your opponent's attorney-client privileges.

An unrepresented, non-employee who will testify for Beatrice? _____.

C. Dealing with the press.

You have a duty not to interfere with a defendant's right to a fair trial. You may respond to the press and public's right to know, but you and your agents must avoid out of court statements that you reasonably should know _____

_____

—Exceptions are for: matters in the public record or routine booking information, warning the public, informing them of an ongoing investigation or asking for help, and statements required to protect your client from substantial undue prejudice from

_____

—In addition, prosecutors and their associates must not make comments that have a substantial likelihood of heightening public condemnation of the accused.

D. Special duties of prosecutors.

The basic duty of a prosecutor is to seek justice, not just to win cases. Prosecutors have higher ethical obligations than criminal defense or civil attorneys. Among other duties, such as providing exculpatory evidence, they must _____

_____

X. PRESERVING THE DIGNITY OF THE COURT AND ADDITIONAL DUTIES

A. Duty to preserve the impartiality and decorum of the tribunal.

1. Don't try to influence anybody improperly. Before and during trial you must not talk to any prospective or empanelled _____. After trial is over, if local law permits, you may _____ any consenting juror at a reasonable time and place. In CA you must tell them they have a right to refuse an interview and to have a copy of any resulting court declaration.

2. No "chicanery": _____

_____! *E.g.*, referring to inadmissible material or matters unsupported by evidence, asserting personal knowledge of facts at issue.

3. Duty to preserve the decorum of the tribunal. Refrain from abusive or obstreperous conduct, belligerence, or theatrics. The rules state: "A lawyer may stand firm against abuse by a judge but should avoid reciprocation...."

B. Duty to expedite cases.

1. Under ABA Rules, you have an affirmative duty to expedite cases. In *CA you _____ to harass an adversary, or for your own personal gain or convenience.

2. You have a duty to follow valid procedural rules or court orders, unless you are making a _____ to their validity. You must not abuse or obstruct discovery.

C. Additional duties to the profession and public.

1. A "lawyer" must not engage in the unauthorized – or unlicensed – practice of law to safeguard the public from incompetence. Practice in a state while suspended

or in which you are not admitted is a violation unless allowed by law, a "_____" order by the local court, or under limited exceptions.

A Texas firm wrote and marketed in CA E-Broke software, which asks users to input answers and then determines what bankruptcy schedules and exemptions to file, and prepares petitions. Is this unauthorized practice of law in California? ____. The program activities were "_____ _____."

a. ABA rules on _____ allow temporary practice by an out-of-state lawyer in good standing if (i) the lawyer _____ who actively participates in the matter, or (ii) the services relate to _____ _____, or (iii) the matter arises out of matters reasonably related to the lawyer's practice in a state where she is admitted and are not services where the forum requires a *pro hac vice* appearance.

b. *CA structures its more restrictive rules governing out-of-state lawyers by practice area. They generally require the lawyer to _____ with the CA Bar, pay dues, get continuing legal education, and be subject to CA ethics rules.

2. Policing misconduct. ABA rules _____ _____ to "the appropriate professional authority" any other lawyer's or judge's violation of the Rules in any legal or non-legal context if it raises a substantial question as to that person's honesty, trustworthiness, or fitness.

*CA does not require external reporting, but can discipline you for knowing about a fellow firm member's disciplinary violation and _____ _____. (*E.g.,* counseling the lawyer, or telling a supervisor.) CA also requires _____ of the lawyer's being charged with a felony or certain crimes, found civilly liable for fraud or breach of fiduciary duty, disciplined in another jurisdiction, or under certain conditions, sued for malpractice or sanctioned.

XI. DUTIES OF SUBORDINATE LAWYERS

A. Subordinates. If you are under the control or supervision of another attorney, *e.g.,* a senior partner, who ratifies or orders you to take an action violating the ethical rules, is that OK? _____!

1. Your ethical responsibility if it is a clear violation: _____ _____

2. Your ethical responsibility if it is a debatable problem: _____ _____

3. Your supervising partner's ethical responsibility: If he ratified the action or knew of the conduct and failed to take action, _____

B. **Managing partners** must also make reasonable efforts to ensure that everyone's conduct in a firm comports with the professional obligations of a lawyer, including

---

/////

Real Property

Professor Paula Franzese

PROPERTY
By Paula Franzese
Professor of Law

I. Summary of Freehold Estates

Estate	Language to Create	Duration	Tranaferability	Future Interest
1. Fee Simple absolute	"To A and his heirs." "To A."	Absolute ownership, of potentially infinite duration.	Devisable, descendible, alienable	None
2. Fee Tail	"To A and the heirs of his body"	Lasts only as long as there are lineal blood descendants of grantee	Passes automatically to grantee's lineal descendants	Reversion (if held by grantor); Remainder (if held by third party).
3. Defeasible Fees: A. Fee simple determinable	"To A so long as …" "To A until …." "To A while …." (Language providing that upon the happening of a stated event, the land is to revert to the grantor)	Potentially infinite, so long as event does not occur.	Alienable, devisable, descendible, subject to condition.	Possibility of Reverter (held by grantor).
B. Fee Simple subject to condition subsequent	"To A. but if X event happens, grantor reserves the right to reenter and retake." Grantor must carve out right of reentry.	Potentially infinite, so long as the condition is not breached and, thereafter, until the holder of the right of entry timely exercises the power of termination.	Same	Right of Entry/Power of Termination (held by grantor)
C. Fee simple subject to an executor limitation	"To A, but if X event occurs, then to B."	Potentially infinite, so long as stated contingency does not occur.	Same	Executory Interest (held by third party).
4. Life Estate	"To A for life." "To A for the life of B."	Measured by life of transferee or by some other life (*pur autre vie*).	Alienable, devisable and descendible if *pur autre vie* and measuring life is still alive.	Reversion (if held by grantor); Remainder (if held by third party).

THE PRESENT ESTATES

We are concerned here with four categories of freehold estates, so named because they grew out of the English system of feudalism:

    I.   The Fee Simple Absolute;

    II.   The Fee Tail;

    III. The Defeasible Fees (of which there are three species); and

    IV. The Life Estate.

The bar examiners will expect you to know three things with respect to each of these estates:

    1.   What language will create the estate?

    2.   Once identified, what are the estate's distinguishing characteristics? In other words, is the estate *devisable*, meaning, can it pass by will? Is the estate *descendible*, meaning, will it pass by the statutes of intestacy if its holder dies intestate (without a will)? Is the estate *alienable*, meaning, is it transferable inter vivos, or during the holder's lifetime?

    3.   Which future interests, if any, is the estate capable of?

I.   The Fee Simple Absolute

    1) How to create: "To A" or "To A and his heirs."

           Today, those common law words "and his heirs" _____ _____.

           Thus, "to A" suffices to create the fee simple absolute.

    2) Distinguishing characteristics:

           This is _____ of potentially infinite duration. It is freely, _____, _____ and _____.

3)   Accompanying future interest?

Example 1:   O conveys "to A" or "to A and his heirs." A is alive and well. What do A's heirs have?

_____. Only _____ has absolute ownership. This leads us to the Bruce Willis rule of property: _____.

Thus, while A is alive, he has only _____ _____. They are powerless.

II.   The Fee Tail

1)   How to create: "To A and the heirs of his body."

2)   Distinguishing characteristics:

Virtually abolished in the U.S. today. Virtually never tested. Historically, the fee tail would pass directly to:

_____

_____.

Today, the attempted creation of a fee tail creates instead: _____.

3)   Accompanying future interest?

_____. In O, the grantor, it was called _____.

In a third party (someone other than O), it was called _____.

III.   The Defeasible Fees:

1)   The Fee Simple Determinable:

i)   How to create: "To A for so long as . . ." "To A during . . ." "To A until . . ."

Grantor must use _____.

If the stated condition is violated, _____ _____.

ii)   Distinguishing characteristics:

This estate, like all of the defeasible fees, is _____,
_____ and _____, but always
subject to the condition.

Example 2:   Paul conveys Blackacre "to Ringo so long as the
               premises are used as a recording studio." Ringo has:
               _____.

               Suppose that Ringo in turn conveys to Mick, who seeks
               to convert the recording studio into a bowl-a-rama. May
               Mick do so?

               Hence, the Mick Jagger rule of property:

               *You may convey less than what you started with,
               but you can't convey more. In other words,*
               _____
               _____.

iii) Accompanying future interest?

It is _____ in the
grantor.

Example 3:   Frank Sinatra conveys Sinatra Palace "to Orville
               Redenbacher, so long as popcorn is never made on the
               premises." Classify the interests.

               Orville has: _____.

               Frank has: _____.

F S D P O R

4

2) The Fee Simple Subject to Condition Subsequent:

    i) How to create: "To A, but if X event occurs, grantor reserves the right to re-enter and retake."

       Here, grantor must use clear durational language ***and*** _____
_____.

       Example 4:   Ross conveys "To Rachel, but if coffee is ever consumed on the premises, grantor reserves the right to re-enter and retake."

          Rachel has: _____.

          Ross has: _____.

    ii) Distinguishing characteristics:

       This estate is NOT _____, but it can be cut short at the grantor's option, if _____
_____.

    iii) Accompanying future interest?

       _____, synonymous with
_____.

3) The Fee Simple Subject to Executory Limitation:

    i) How to create: "To A, but if X event occurs, then to B."

       Example 5:   "To Barry Manilow, but if Manilow ever performs music on the premises, then to Mandy."

          Barry has: _____.

          Mandy has: _____.

ii) Distinguishing characteristics:

This estate is just like the fee simple determinable only now, if the condition is broken, the estate is _____ in favor of _____.

iii) Accompanying future interest?

_____.

AS CONCERN THE DEFEASIBLE FEES, NOTE TWO IMPORTANT RULES OF CONSTRUCTION:

1) **Words of mere desire, hope, or intention are insufficient to create a defeasible fee.**

Courts disfavor restrictions on _____.

Thus, courts will not find a defeasible fee unless _____
_____.

Example 6: In each of these instances, A is vested with a fee simple absolute, and <u>NOT</u> a defeasible fee: "To A for the purpose of constructing a day care center"; "To A with the hope that he becomes a lawyer"; "To A with the expectation that the premises will be used as a Blockbuster video store."

2) **Absolute restraints on alienation are void.**

An absolute restraint on alienation is an absolute ban on the power to _____, that is not linked to _____
_____.

Example 7:   O conveys: "To A so long as she never attempts to sell."

A has: _____.

O has: _____.

Example 8:   O conveys: "To A so long as she does not attempt to sell until the year 2012, when clouds on the title will be resolved."

(Note: Here the restraint is linked to a reasonable, time-limited purpose. Thus, it is _____.)

A has: _____.

O has: _____.

IV. The Life Estate

1) How to create:

This is an estate that must be measured in _____ _____, and NEVER _____.

i) O conveys: "To A for life."

A has: _____.

A is known as: _____.

O has: _____, meaning that at the end of A's lifetime, the estate reverts back to O or O's heirs.

Contrast with: "To A for 50 years, if she lives that long," or "To A for life, but in no event more than 10 years," both of which create the term of years (a leasehold interest), and NOT the life estate.

ii) The life estate *pur autre vie*:

A life estate measured by a life _____

_____.

"To A for the life of B."

Example 9: O conveys: "To Madonna, for the life of David Letterman."

Madonna has: _____.

O has: _____. At the end of _____ _____life, the estate reverts back to O or O's heirs.

Example 10: O conveys "to Madonna for life." Madonna then sells her entire interest to David Letterman. (Note that it is permissible for a life tenant to sell her interest. But remember the Mick Jagger rule: You can't convey more than you've got. The holder of a mere life estate cannot presume to sell more than that.)

Thus, David Letterman has: _____

_____.

O has:_____. At the end of _____ life, the estate reverts back to O or O's heirs.

2) Distinguishing characteristics of the life estate:

The life tenant's entitlements are rooted in the important doctrine of **waste**.

Note two general rules:

a. The life tenant is entitled to: _____

_____.

b.   The life tenant must not _____

_____.

There are three species of waste:

i)   **Voluntary or affirmative waste. This is:** _____

_____.

a)   Voluntary waste and natural resources:

The general rule: The life tenant must not consume or exploit natural resources on the property (such as timber, oil, or minerals), unless one of four exceptions applies, remembered by **PURGE**.

1.   **PU:** _____, meaning that prior to the grant,

_____.

Here, the life tenant may continue to exploit, unless otherwise agreed.

Note: Prior Use and the Open Mines Doctrine: If mining was done on the land before the life estate began: _____
_____, but is limited to _____. Thus, the life tenant must not open any new mines.

2.   **R:** _____. The life tenant may consume natural resources for _____ and _____.

3.   **G:** _____. The life tenant may exploit if _____.

4.   **E:** _____, meaning _____
_____.

ii) Permissive waste, or neglect. This occurs when: _____

_____

_____.

    a)   Permissive waste and the obligation to repair:

       The life tenant must simply _____ the premises in reasonably good repair.

    b)   Permissive waste and the obligation to pay all ordinary taxes: The life tenant is obligated to pay all ordinary taxes on the land, to the extent of income or profits from the land. If there is no income or profit, the life tenant is required to pay all ordinary taxes to the extent of

       _____.

iii) Ameliorative waste:

The life tenant must not engage in acts that will enhance the property's value, unless: _____.

3)   The life estate's accompanying future interest?

If held by O, the grantor, it is called a _____. If held by a third party, it is a _____.

FUTURE INTERESTS

There are six categories of future interests, and we classify them based on whether they are retained by the grantor or instead, by a transferee.

Future Interests Capable of Creation in the Grantor

There are only three future interests capable of creation in the grantor.

1) **The Possibility of Reverter:** It accompanies only the _____

_____.

2) **The Right of Entry, also known as the Power of Termination:** It accompanies only the _____.

3) **The Reversion:**

A reversion is the future interest that arises in a grantor who transfers an estate of lesser quantum than she started with, other than a fee simple determinable or a fee simple subject to condition subsequent.

Example 11:   O, the holder of a fee simple absolute, conveys:

"To A for life." O has conveyed less than what she started with. She has a reversion.

"To A for 99 years." O has conveyed less than what she started with. She has a reversion.

"To A for life, then to B for 99 years." O has still conveyed less than that with which she started. (Remember that the fee simple absolute can endure forever.) O has a reversion.

Future Interests in Transferees

If our future interest is held by someone other than the grantor, it has to be either:

11

I. A **vested remainder** (of which there are three species: (i) the indefeasibly vested remainder, (ii) the vested remainder subject to complete defeasance (also known as the vested remainder subject to total divestment), and (iii) the vested remainder subject to open).

II. A **contingent remainder**; OR

III. An **executory interest** (of which there are two species: (i) the shifting executory interest, and (ii) the springing executory interest).

OUR THREE TASKS IN ASSESSING FUTURE INTERESTS IN TRANSFEREES:

I. We must distinguish vested remainders (of which there are three kinds), from contingent remainders;

II. We must distinguish the three kinds of vested remainders from each other; and

III. We must distinguish all remainders from executory interests.

I. The difference between vested remainders and contingent remainders:

First, what is a remainder?

A remainder is a future interest created in a grantee that is capable of becoming possessory upon the expiration of a prior possessory estate created in the same conveyance in which the remainder is created.

Remember that remainderman is sociable, patient and polite:

1. Remainderman is sociable. He never travels alone.

   In other words, remainderman always accompanies a preceding estate of _____. That preceding estate is usually a _____ or a _____.

   For example, "To A for life, then to B," or "To A for ten years, then to B."

2. Remainderman is patient and polite, meaning: Remainderman never follows a defeasible fee.

Remainderman cannot cut short or divest a prior transferee. In other words, if your present estate is a defeasible fee, your future interest is NOT a remainder. Instead, it will be _____.

REMAINDERS ARE EITHER VESTED OR CONTINGENT.

A remainder is *vested* if it is *both* created in an ascertained person and is not subject to any condition precedent.

A remainder is *contingent* if it is created in an unascertained person *or* is subject to a condition precedent, or both.

1. The remainder that is contingent because it is created in as yet unborn or unascertained persons.

    Example 12:   "To A for life, then to B's first child." A is alive. B, as yet, has no children.

    Example 13:   "To A for life, then to B's heirs." A is alive. B is alive. Because a living person has no heirs, while B is alive his heirs are unknown.

    Example 14:   "To A for life, then to those children of B who survive A." A is alive. We don't yet know which, if any, of B's children will survive A.

2. The remainder that is contingent because it is subject to a condition precedent.

    A condition is a condition precedent when it appears _____ the language creating the remainder or is woven into the grant to remainderman.

Example 15:   "To A for life, then, if B graduates from college, to B." A is alive. B is now in high school. Before B can take, he must graduate from college. He has not yet satisfied this condition precedent.

B therefore has: _____.

O has: _____. (If B never graduates, O or O's heirs take.)

If B graduates from college during A's lifetime: B's contingent remainder is transformed automatically into an

_____.

Example 16:   "To A for life, and, if B has reached the age of 21, to B." A is alive. B is 19 years old. Again, B must satisfy a condition precedent before B can take. B therefore has:

_____.

O has: _____. (If B never reaches 21, the estate reverts back to O or O's heirs.)

If B attains the age of 21 during A's lifetime: B's contingent remainder is transformed automatically into an

_____.

3. Contingent remainders and:

    i. The Rule of Destructibility of Contingent Remainders:

        At common law, a contingent remainder was destroyed if it _____

        _____ at the time _____

        _____.

    Example 17:   "To A for life, and if B has reached the age of 21, to B."
                    Now, A has died, leaving behind B, who is still only 19 years old. Assess the state of the title.

    Historically, at common law:

            B's contingent remainder _____. Thus,
            _____ would take in fee simple absolute.

14

Today: The Destructibility Rule has been _____. Thus, if B is still under 21 when A dies, _____ hold the estate subject to B's springing executory interest. Once B reaches 21, B takes.

ii.   The Rule in Shelley's Case: At common law, the rule would apply in one setting only:

Example 18:   O conveys "To A for life, then, on A's death, to A's heirs." A is alive.

Historically: The present and future interests _____, giving A _____.

Note: The Rule in Shelley's Case is a rule of law, and not a rule of construction.

It would apply even in the face of _____.

Today: The Rule in Shelley's Case has been virtually abolished. Thus, today, when O conveys "To A for life, then to A's heirs:"

A has _____.

A's as yet unknown heirs have _____.

O has _____, since A could die without heirs.

iii.   The Doctrine of Worthier Title (also known as the rule against a remainder in grantor's heirs):

This doctrine is still viable in most states today. It applies when O, who is alive, tries to create a future interest in his heirs.

Example 19: -   O, who is alive, conveys "To A for life, then to O's heirs."

If the Doctrine of Worthier Title did <u>not</u> apply, A has _____ and O's heirs have _____, because O is still alive and a living person has no heirs.

Instead, because of the Doctrine of Worthier Title, the contingent remainder in O's heirs is _____. Thus, A has _____ and O has _____.

The doctrine endeavors to promote _____

_____.

Note: The Doctrine of Worthier Title is a rule of construction, and not a rule of law.

Grantor's intent _____. If grantor clearly intends to create a contingent remainder in his heirs, _____

_____.

II. Distinguish the three kinds of vested remainders:

Note: Only remainders can be vested.

1. The indefeasibly vested remainder: The holder of this remainder is certain to acquire an estate in the future, with _____.

    Example 20:   "To A for life, remainder to B." A is alive. B is alive.

    A has: _____.

    B has: _____.

    What if B predeceases A?

    At common law, B's future interest _____

    _____.

2. The vested remainder subject to complete defeasance (also known as the vested remainder subject to total divestment).

Here, remainderman exists. His taking is NOT subject to any _____ _____. However, his right to possession could be cut short because of _____.

Here, note the difference between a condition precedent, which creates a contingent remainder, and a condition subsequent, which creates a vested remainder subject to complete defeasance. To tell the difference, apply the "Comma Rule": When conditional language in a transfer follows language that, taken alone and set off by commas, would create a vested remainder, the condition is a condition subsequent, and you have a vested remainder subject to complete defeasance.

Example 21:   O conveys: "To A for life, remainder to B, provided, however, that if B dies under the age of 25, to C." A is alive. B is 20 years old.

A has: _____.

B has: _____.

C has: _____.

If B is under 25 at the time of A's death: _____.

However, B must live to 25 for his estate to retain his interest. Otherwise, B's heirs lose it all, and C or C's heirs take.

O has: _____, because it is possible that neither C nor C's heirs will exist if and when the condition is breached.

By contrast, if the conditional language appears before the language creating the remainder, the condition is a condition precedent, and you have a contingent remainder.

Example 22:   O conveys "To A for life, and if B has reached the age of 25, to B."

A is alive. B is 20 years old.

A has: _____.

B has: _____, because his taking is subject to _____. B must be _____ before he can take possession.

O has: _____. (If B dies under 25, the estate reverts back to O or O's heirs.)

If B is still alive but under 25 at the time of A's death, _____. Instead, the estate reverts back to _____, who holds it subject to _____. (If and when B reaches 25, B divests O.)

3.   The vested remainder subject to open:

Here, a remainder is vested in a group of takers, at least one of whom is:

_____.

But each class member's share is subject to partial diminution because:

_____

_____.

Example 23:   "To A for life, then to B's children." A is alive. B has two children, C and D.

What do C and D have?

A CLASS IS EITHER OPEN OR CLOSED

A class is open if: _____.

A class is closed when: _____

_____.

How will you know when the given class has closed?

Apply the common law rule of convenience:

    The class closes whenever any member _____.

In the preceding example ("To A for life, then to B's children." A is alive. B has two children, C and D), when does the class close?

    At _____ death, and also, according to the rule of convenience, at _____ death, no matter that _____ is still alive. Why? That's when C and D can demand possession. It's called a rule of convenience because _____

    _____.

    Once A dies, a child of B born or conceived thereafter will not share in the gift.

        The exception: The womb rule: _____

        _____.

What if C or D predeceases A?

III. Distinguish remainders from executory interests:

What is an executory interest?

It is a future interest created in a transferee (a third party), which is not a remainder and which takes effect by either cutting short some interest in another person ("shifting") or in the grantor or his heirs ("springing").

    1.   Shifting executory interest:

        It always follows _____ and cuts short someone other than _____.

Example 24:   "To A and her heirs, but if B returns from Canada sometime next year, to B and his heirs."

B has: _____.

Why doesn't B have a remainder? _____.
_____.

A has: _____.

Does the conveyance violate the rule against perpetuities? _____

_____

_____.

Example 25:   "To A, but if A uses the land for nonresidential purposes at any time during the next 20 years, then to B."

B has: _____.

A has: _____.

Does the conveyance violate the rule against perpetuities?

_____.

2.   Springing executory interest:

Example 26:   O conveys: "To A, if and when he marries." A is unmarried.

A has: _____.

O has: _____.

Does the conveyance violate the rule against perpetuities? _____

_____.

Example 27:   O conveys: "To A, if and when he becomes a lawyer." A is in high school.

A has: _____.

O has: _____.

Does the conveyance violate the rule against perpetuities? _____

_____.

THE RULE AGAINST PERPETUITIES ("RAP")

I.   The Rule:

Certain kinds of future interests are void if there is any possibility, however remote, that the given interest may vest more than 21 years after the death of a measuring life.

II. Four-Step Technique for Assessing Potential RAP Problems:

1.   Determine which future interests have been created by the conveyance. The RAP potentially applies **only** to contingent remainders, executory interests, and certain vested remainders subject to open. The RAP does <u>NOT</u> apply to:

_____

_____

_____

_____

Example 28:   "To A for life, then to A's children." A is alive. She has no children.

The as yet unborn children have: _____.

2. Identify the conditions precedent to the vesting of the suspect future interest.

   In the preceding example, what has to happen before a future interest holder can take?

   _____.

3. Find a measuring life. Look for a person alive at the date of the conveyance and ask whether that person's life or death is relevant to the condition's occurrence.

   In the preceding example, who qualifies as a measuring life?

4. Ask: Will we know, with certainty, within 21 years of the death of our measuring life, if our future interest holder(s) can or cannot take? If so, the conveyance is good. If not (if there is any possibility, however remote, that the condition precedent could or could not occur more than 21 years after the death of a measuring life), the future interest is void.

   The preceding conveyance, therefore: _____. We will know, at the instant of A's death, if A has left behind a child or not.

   Example 29:   "To A for life, then to the first of her children to reach the age of 30." A is 70. Her only child, B, is 29 years old.

   Apply the four steps:

   1. Classify the future interest.

   2. What are the conditions precedent to the vesting of the future interest?

   3. Find a measuring life.

4. Will we know, with certainty, within 21 years of the death of our measuring life, if a future interest holder can take? In other words, is there any possibility, however remote, that A would not have a child to reach 30 until more than 21 years after A's death? _____. The common law RAP is miserable. It presumes that anything is possible. What parade of horribles could invalidate this future interest? _____, who is 29, could die tomorrow. Thereafter, A could have another child, no matter that A is 70. (This is called the Fertile Octogenarian Rule. It presumes that a person _____ _____.) A could die in labor, or, A could live. We just don't know for sure, today, whether the condition precedent to any potential newborn's taking—the child's turning 30—will be satisfied within 21 years of A's death. Thus, we are left with:

A has _____.

O has _____.

III. Two Bright Line Rules of Common Law RAP:

1. **A gift to an open class that is conditioned on the members surviving to an age beyond 21 violates the common law RAP.**

    "Bad as to one, bad as to all." To be valid, it must be shown that the condition precedent to every class member's taking will occur within the perpetuities period. If it is possible that a disposition might vest too remotely with respect to any member of the class,

    _____.

    Example 30:   "To A for life, then to such of A's children as live to attain the age of 30." A has two children, B and C. B is 35 and C is 40. A is alive.

    B and C's_____
    are voided by _____

    _____

    _____.

    Thus, under the common law RAP, we are left with:

    _____.

2. Many shifting executory interests violate the RAP. An executory interest with no limit on the time within which it must vest violates the RAP.

Example 31: "To A and his heirs so long as the land is used for farm purposes, and if the land ceases to be so used, to B and his heirs."

1. Classify the future interest.

2. What are the conditions that will trigger B's entitlement?

3. Find a measuring life.

4. Will we know with certainty, within 21 years of the death of our measuring life, if a future interest holder can take?

No. A might abide by the condition during her lifetime. The condition may not be breached, if ever, until hundreds of years have passed.

Once the offensive future interest is stricken, we are left with: "To A and his heirs so long as the land is used for farm purposes."

Thus, A now has: _____.

O now has: _____.

Is there a RAP problem? _____

_____

_____.

Compare the preceding example to: "To A and his heirs, but if the land ceases to be used for farm purposes, to B and his heirs."

Same result as in the preceding example, except that now, once the offensive future interest ("to B and his heirs") is stricken:

_____

_____.

Thus, the entire conditional clause _____.

Therefore, A now has: _____.

O has: _____.

The charity-to-charity exception:

A gift from one charity to another: _____

_____.

Example 32:   "To the American Red Cross, so long as the premises are used for Red Cross purposes, and if they cease to be so used, then to the YMCA."

Ordinarily, the YMCA would have an invalid _____

_____.

However, because of the charity-to-charity exception to the RAP:

_____.

Thus, the American Red Cross has _____
subject to the YMCA's valid _____.

IV. Reform of the RAP:

1. The "wait and see" or "second look" doctrine:

Under this majority reform effort, the validity of any suspect future interest is determined on the basis of the facts as they now exist, _____

_____.

This eliminates the "_____" or "_____
_____" line of inquiry.

2. The Uniform Statutory Rule Against Perpetuities (USRAP):

Codifies the common law RAP and, in addition, provides for: _____

_____.

3. Both the "wait and see" and USRAP reforms embrace:

A. The cy pres doctrine: "_____."

If a given disposition violates the rule, a court may reform it in a way _____

_____.

B. The reduction of any offensive age contingency to 21 years.

CONCURRENT ESTATES

There are three forms of concurrent ownership:

I. The joint tenancy:
                        Defined:

II. The tenancy by the entirety:
    Defined:

III. The tenancy in common:
    Defined:

I. The Joint Tenancy

A. Distinguishing Characteristics:

1.

2.

B. Creation of a Joint Tenancy:

1) The four unities:

Remember this **"T-TIP"**

Joint tenants must take their interests:

T: _____

T: _____

I: _____ and

P: _____.

2) Grantor must clearly express the right of survivorship.

Joint tenancies are _____. Thus, in addition to the _____, grantor must clearly state _____ _____.

3) Use of a straw.

   Example 33:   Dave holds Blackacre in fee simple absolute. He wishes to hold it as a joint tenant with his best friend Paul. How must Dave proceed?

   To satisfy the four unities, Dave must _____ _____.

   Step One: _____.

   Step Two:_____ _____ _____.

   (Now, all four unities are present, including the unities of _____ and _____.)

C. Severance of a Joint Tenancy:

   Remember **"SPAM"**: **S**ale, **P**artition **A**nd **M**ortgage

   1) Severance and Sale:

      i. **A joint tenant can sell or transfer her interest during her lifetime.**

          May she do so secretly? _____ _____.

          One joint tenant's sale severs the joint tenancy as to the seller's interest because it: _____.

          Thus, buyer is: _____.

          To the extent that we started with more than two joint tenants in the first place: _____, as between the other, non-transferring joint tenants.

Example 34:   O conveys Blackacre "To Phoebe, Ross, and Monica as joint tenants with the right of survivorship."

Each owns:

Phoebe then sells her interest to Chandler. What is the state of the title?

Phoebe's act severs the joint tenancy as to _____ interest. Ross and Monica still hold _____, and Chandler holds _____ as their _____.

Later, Ross dies, leaving behind his heir, Rachel. What is the state of the title?

Monica takes _____.

Thus, Monica now holds 2/3s with Chandler, who holds 1/3. Monica and Chandler are _____ _____.

Rachel takes _____.

ii. In equity, a joint tenant's mere act of entering into a contract for the sale of her share will:

_____

_____

This is because of the doctrine of: _____, which provides that **"equity regards as done that which ought to be done."**

Example 35:   O conveys Blackacre to "Ringo, Paul, and John as joint tenants with the right of survivorship." This form of concurrent estate is: _____ _____.

29

On January 1, Ringo enters into a contract for sale of his interest in the joint tenancy to George, with the closing to take place on April 1. When does the severance as to Ringo's interest occur, and why?

2) Severance and Partition:

Remember three variations:

i) By voluntary agreement:

ii) Partition in kind:

iii) Forced sale:

3) Severance and Mortgage:

The rule: One joint tenant's execution of a mortgage or a lien on his or her share will sever the joint tenancy as to that now encumbered share only in: _____

_____.

By contrast, the majority of states follow _____

_____, whereby a joint tenant's execution of

a mortgage on his or her interest _____

_____.

Example 36: Paul, John, and George are joint tenants. Suppose now that Paul mortgages his interest in the joint tenancy. Will this sever the joint tenancy as to Paul's interest?

In a minority jurisdiction to follow the title theory of mortgages:

In a majority jurisdiction to follow the lien theory of mortgages:

II.   The Tenancy by the Entirety

i)   How to create:

In those states to recognize the tenancy by the entirety, it arises presumptively:

_____

_____.

ii)   This is a very protected form of co-ownership:

Remember "CAN'T TOUCH THIS."

a)   Creditors:

b)   Unilateral conveyance:

Neither tenant, acting alone, can defeat the right of survivorship by:

_____.

Example 37:   Tony and Carmella, married to each other, own Blackacre as tenants by the entirety. Tony then secretly transfers his interest to Uncle Junior. What does Uncle Junior have?

III. The Tenancy in Common

Remember three features:

i)   Each co-tenant owns: _____, and each has a right: _____.

ii)   Each interest is _____, _____ and _____. There are no _____ _____ between tenants in common.

iii) The presumption favors: _____.

Rights and Duties of Co-Tenants

Greg and Marcia own Blackacre as tenants in common. Greg contributed 90% of the purchase price and Marcia 10%.

1)   **Possession:** Greg takes a can of white paint and divides up the premises. "Marcia," he says, "you can use and enjoy that 10% on that side of the line, and only that." Are Greg's actions permissible?

Each co-tenant is entitled to _____.

If one co-tenant wrongfully excludes another co-tenant from possession of the whole or any part, he has committed _____

_____.

2) **Rent from co-tenant in exclusive possession:** Marcia leaves Blackacre voluntarily, for a three-month tour of Europe with her cheerleading squad. On her return, she demands rent from Greg for the three months in which he enjoyed exclusive possession. Will she prevail?

Absent ouster, a co-tenant in exclusive possession: _____

_____.

3) **Rent from third parties:** Greg leases Blackacre's basement to Alice, a tenant. Is Marcia entitled to a portion of the rental income?

A co-tenant who leases all or part of the premises to a third party:

_____

_____.

4) **Adverse possession:** Marcia, so enthralled by a family trip to the Grand Canyon, decides to stay there for the next 20 years. In her absence, can Greg acquire title to the whole through adverse possession?

Unless he has ousted the other co-tenants, one co-tenant in exclusive possession for the statutory adverse possession period: _____

_____.

Why not? The _____ element of adverse possession is absent. There is no hostility because there was _____.

5) **Carrying costs:** What are Marcia and Greg's respective responsibilities with respect to Blackacre's carrying costs?

Each co-tenant is responsible for his or her fair share of _____ (such as _____ and _____), based upon: _____.

6) **Repairs:** A football, thrown in Marcia's direction, goes through Blackacre's front window. Marcia, who has repaired the window, now seeks contribution from Greg. Will she prevail?

The repairing co-tenant enjoys: _____

_____

_____,

provided that she has: _____

_____.

Greg must contribute: _____.

7) **Improvements:** Marcia has wallpapered Blackacre's den with life-size posters of her idol, Davy Jones. She now seeks contribution from Greg, for his fair share of the costs of her "improvements." Will she succeed?

During the life of the co-tenancy, there is: _____

_____.

However, at partition, the improving co-tenant is entitled to a _____, equal to: _____

_____.

Attendantly, at partition, the so-called "improver" bears full liability for:

_____

_____.

8) **Waste:** A co-tenant must not commit waste. (Recall the three species of waste: voluntary, permissive and ameliorative.)

9) **Partition:** A joint tenant or tenant in common has a right to bring an action for partition.

LANDLORD/TENANT LAW

I. The Four Leasehold or Nonfreehold Estates

1) The Tenancy for Years (also known as the Estate for Years or the Term of Years):

i) This is a lease for: _____

_____.

When you know the termination date from the start, you have

_____.

ii) Because a term of years states from the outset when it will terminate:

_____.

Example 38: L leases Blackacre to T "from January 1, 2007 to July 1, 2007." Which form of tenancy exists here?

Why?

How much notice is needed to terminate the tenancy?

iii) A term of years greater than one year: _____,

_____because of the Statute of Frauds.

2) The Periodic Tenancy:

i) This is a lease which continues for: _____

_____.

ii) The periodic tenancy can be created expressly. For example, L conveys:

_____

_____.

35

iii) The periodic tenancy can also arise **by implication,** in any one of three ways:

    a. **Land is leased with no mention of duration, but provision is made for** _____.

        Example 39:   T rents an apartment from L, beginning June 1. Nothing is said about duration. T pays rent each month. What tenancy exists here?

    b. **An oral term of years in violation of the Statute of Frauds creates:** _____, measured by the way _____.

        Example 40:   L and T negotiate on the telephone for a commercial lease. They orally agree on a five-year lease with rent at $1,000 a month.

        Is this a tenancy for years?

        What if T sends L a check for $1,000 and L accepts it?

        T's first rental payment renders his interest: _____ _____, with the intervals based on: _____ _____.

    c. **The holdover: In a residential lease, if L elects to hold over a T who has wrongfully stayed on past the conclusion of the original lease:**

        _____

        _____.

        Example 41:   T holds over after the expiration of her one-year lease, but sends another month's rent check to L, who cashes it. What tenancy now exists? _____

        _____.

iv) How to terminate a periodic tenancy: _____

_____.

How much notice? At common law, _____

_____.

Thus, in a month-to-month periodic tenancy: _____.

In a week-to-week periodic tenancy: _____.

The one exception: If the tenancy is from year-to-year or greater:

_____.

Note: By private agreement, the parties may lengthen or shorten these common-law prescribed notice provisions.

Note: The periodic tenancy must end at the conclusion of a natural lease period.

Example 42: L leased Blackacre to T on January 1, 2003, for a periodic tenancy of month-to-month. On May 15, 2003, T sends written notice of termination. T is bound until:

_____.

3) The Tenancy at Will:

i) This is a tenancy for: _____.

For example, "To T for as long as L or T desires."

ii) Unless the parties expressly agree to a tenancy at will, the payment of regular rent will cause a court: _____

_____.

iii) The tenancy at will may be terminated: _____

_____

_____.

4) The Tenancy at Sufferance:

It is created when T has _____,
past the expiration of the lease. We give this wrongdoer a leasehold estate
(the tenancy at sufferance), to permit L to _____.

The tenancy at sufferance lasts only until L either _____ or
_____.

II. Tenant's Duties: 1) T's liability to third parties;
2) T's duty to repair;
3) T's duty to pay rent.

1) T's liability to third parties:

T is responsible for keeping the premises: _____
_____.

T is liable for injuries sustained by _____, even
where _____
_____.

Example 43:   L leases a building to T, expressly promising to maintain the
premises in a state of good repair. T's invitee trips over a
loose floorboard and sues T. If invitee sues T, what result?
_____.

(It does not matter that T may seek indemnification from L.
Vis-à-vis the plaintiff, who is a guest, _____.)

2) T's duty to repair:

a) T's duty to repair when the lease is silent:

i)   The standard:

ii) T must not commit waste:

Remember the three species of waste:

1) Voluntary waste:

2) Permissive waste:

3) Ameliorative waste:

iii) The law of fixtures:

When a tenant removes a fixture: _____.

A fixture is a once movable chattel that, by virtue of its annexation to realty:

_____

_____.

Common examples:

T MUST NOT _____, NO MATTER
THAT _____.

FIXTURES PASS WITH OWNERSHIP OF THE LAND.

Example 44:   Janet Jackson, a tenant, installs a beautiful heirloom chandelier in the dining room. At the conclusion of the leasehold, as she is about to remove it, Landlord demands that the chandelier stay put. If the chandelier qualifies as a fixture,

_____.

How to tell when a tenant installation qualifies as a fixture:

a. Express agreement controls:

b. In the absence of agreement, T may remove a chattel that she has installed so long as: _____

_____.

If removal will cause substantial damage, then **in objective judgment** T has shown:

_____

_____.

b) **T's duty to repair when T has expressly covenanted in the lease to maintain the property in good condition for the duration of the lease:**

At common law, historically: _____

_____

_____.

Today, the majority view: _____

_____.

3) **T's duty to pay rent:**

a) **T breaches this duty and is in possession of the premises:**

The landlord's only options are to _____ or _____. If the landlord moves to evict, she is nonetheless entitled _____ from the tenant until the tenant, who is now _____ _____, vacates.

LANDLORD MUST NOT: _____, such as

_____

_____.

Self-help is flatly outlawed, and is punishable _____ and

_____.

b) T breaches this duty but is out of possession:

For example, T wrongfully vacates with time left on a term of years lease.

Remember S I R:

i) **S**urrender:

L could choose to treat T's abandonment as _____

_____.

What is surrender?

If the unexpired term is greater than one year: _____

_____.

ii) **I**gnore the abandonment and hold T responsible for _____
_____, just as if T _____.
This option is available only in a _____ of states.

iii) **R**e-let the premises on the wrongdoer tenant's behalf, and hold him or
her _____.

Majority rule:

L must at least _____.

This is a _____.

III. Landlord's Duties

1) Duty to deliver possession:

The majority rule requires that L put T _____ of the premises. Thus, if at the start of T's lease a prior holdover T is still in possession, L _____ and the new T

_____ .

2) The implied covenant of quiet enjoyment:

Applies to <u>both</u> _____ and _____ leases.

T has a right to _____ , without interference from L.

a) Breach by actual wrongful eviction:

This occurs when _____

_____ .

b) Breach by **constructive eviction:**

For example, every time it rains, Dido's apartment floods. She has a claim for constructive eviction if three elements are met.

To recall the elements of constructive eviction, remember **S I N G:**

i) **S**ubstantial Interference:

ii) **N**otice:

iii) **G**oodbye:

Is landlord liable for acts of other tenants?
General rule:

Two exceptions: 1)

2)

3) The implied warranty of habitability:

Applies <u>only</u> to _____ leases.

The implied warranty of habitability is non-waivable.

i) The standard:

The appropriate standard may be supplied by _____ or
_____.

The sorts of problems to trigger breach of the implied warranty of
habitability include: _____

_____

_____.

ii) T's entitlements when the implied warranty of habitability is breached:

Remember **M R** ^{3}: **Move, Repair, Reduce, Remain.**

M: _____.

R: _____, allowable by statute in a
growing number of jurisdictions. T may make the reasonable repairs
and deduct their cost from future rent.

R: _____ or withhold all rent until the
court determines fair rental value. Typically, T must place withheld
rent _____ to show her good faith.

R: _____, pay rent and affirmatively
seek money damages.

4) **Retaliatory eviction: If T lawfully reports L for housing code violations, L**
is barred from penalizing T, by, for example,

_____

_____.

IV. The Assignment versus the Sublease

1) In the absence of some prohibition in the lease, a T may freely transfer his or
her interest in whole (thereby accomplishing an _____) or in
part (thereby accomplishing a _____).

In the lease, L can prohibit T from assigning or subletting without L's:
_____.

However, once L consents to one transfer by T, L waives the right to object to
future transfers by that T, _____
_____.

2) The assignment:

Example 45:   T1 has 10 months remaining on a two-year term of years. T1 transfers all 10 months to T2. This is:

_____.

As a result, L and T2 are: _____.

This means that L and T2 are liable to each other for all of the covenants in the original lease that "_____

_____."

Common examples: _____

_____

_____

L and T2 are **not** in _____,

unless: _____

_____

_____.

L and T1 are no longer in _____.

However, they remain in_____.

Thus, L and T1 are _____ liable to each other.

Example 46: L leases Blackacre to T1. T1 assigns to T2. T2 assigns to T3. T3 then engages in flagrant abuse to the premises.

Can L proceed against T3, the direct wrongdoer?

Can L proceed against T1, the original tenant?

Can L proceed against T2?

3) The sublease:

L and sublessee are in neither privity of estate nor privity of contract.

V. Landlord's Tort Liability

1) The common law of caveat lessee:

The norm:

2)   The five most important exceptions to the common law:

Remember: When tenant learns of these exceptions to the harsh common law, he or she **CLAPS.**

a)   **C**ommon areas:

b)   **L**atent defects rule:

c)   **A**ssumption of repairs:

d)   **P**ublic use rule:

L who leases public space (such as:_____),
and who should know, because of _____ and
_____ that T will
not repair, is liable for any defects on the premises.

e)   **S**hort term lease of furnished dwelling:

SERVITUDES

A SUMMARY OF SERVITUDES

Forms of Servitude	Method of Creation	Parties Bound	Remedy
Affirmative Easements	P-I-N-G P- Prescription (use that is continuous, open and notorious, actual under a claim of right that is hostile for request statutory period). I- Implication (implied from prior use; at time land is severed, a use of one part existed from which it can be inferred that an easement permitting its continuation was intended N- Necessity (division of a tract deprives one lot of means of access out). G – Grant (writing signed by grantor).	Easement appurtenant is transferred automatically with dominant tenement. Easement in gross for commercial purposes is assignable.	Injunction or Damages
Negative Easements (L-A-S-S: Light, Air Support and Streamwater).	Can be created only by writing signed by grantor.		Injunction or Damages

Form of Servitude	Method of Creation	Parties Bound	Remedy
Real Covenants	Writing signed by grantor.	Burden of promise will run to successor of burdened lot if WITHN requirements are satisfied: Writing, Intent, Touch & concern, Horizontal and vertical privity and Notice. Benefit of promise will run to successor of benefited lot is WITV: Writing, Intent, Touch and concern and Vertical privity.	Damages
Equitable Servitudes	Writing signed by grantor (unless implied by General Scheme Doctrine).	Successors bound if WITNes: Writing, Intent, Touch and concern, Notice (privity not required).	Injunction.
Reciprocal Negative Servitudes (General Scheme Doctrine).	According to majority, in a subdivision, residential restriction contained in prior deeds conveyed by common grantor will bind subsequent grantees whose deeds contain no such restriction if: At start of subdividing, grantor had (i) common scheme and (ii) unrestricted lot holders had notice. (Note: Minority rule will not bind subsequent grantees unless their lots are expressly restricted in writing.)	Where common scheme exists, subsequent purchasers with notice are bound.	Injunction.

I. Easements

1) Defined: the _____ of a nonpossessory property interest that entitles its holder to some form of use or enjoyment of another's land, called_____.

   Common examples: the privilege to lay utility lines on another's land; the easement giving its holder the right of access across a tract of land.

2) Easements can be affirmative or negative.

   a) Most easements are affirmative:

   b) Negative easements: The negative easement entitles its holder to prevent the servient landowner from doing something that would otherwise be permissible. Negative easements are generally recognized in only four categories:

   Remember **L A S S :**

   L:

   A:

   S:

   S:

   NEGATIVE EASEMENTS CAN ONLY BE CREATED EXPRESSLY, BY WRITING SIGNED BY THE GRANTOR. THERE IS NO NATURAL OR AUTOMATIC RIGHT TO A NEGATIVE EASEMENT.

3) An easement is either appurtenant to land or it is held in gross.

 a) The easement is appurtenant when it benefits its holder in his physical use or enjoyment of his property. How will you know when you've got an easement appurtenant?

 Example 47: A grants B a right of way across A's land, so that B can more easily reach his land. B's land is benefited by the easement. In easement parlance, it is the dominant tenement. A's land is serving B's easement. It is the servient tenement. Notice that two parcels are involved.

 B has:_____.

 b) The easement is in gross if it confers upon its holder only some personal or pecuniary advantage that is not related to his use or enjoyment of his land. Here, servient land is burdened. However, there is no benefited or dominant tenement.

 Common examples:

4) The easement and transferability:

 a) The appurtenant easement passes automatically with the dominant tenement, regardless of whether it is even mentioned in the conveyance.

51

Example 48:   A has an easement entitling her to cut across B's lawn to get more easily to her land.

This is: _____.

A's land is: _____.

B's land is: _____.

Now A sells her parcel to Mr. X, with no mention of the easement. Does Mr. X enjoy the easement?

_____

_____.

Note that the burden of the easement appurtenant also passes automatically with the servient estate, unless the new owner is: _____

_____.

b)   An easement in gross is not transferable unless it is for commercial purposes.

Example 49:   A has an easement entitling her to swim in B's lake.

This is: _____.

Is it transferable? _____.

Example 50:   Starkist has an easement to use B's lake to fish for bait for Starkist's tuna company.

This is:

_____.

Is it transferable? _____.

5)   Creation of an affirmative easement:

Remember **P I N G:**

P:

I:

N:

G:

a)   By grant:

An easement to endure for more than one year _____
_____ that complies with the formal elements of a
deed.

This is because of _____. The writing to
evidence the easement is called _____.

b)   By implication (also known as the easement implied from existing use):

Example 51:   A owns two lots. Lot 1 is hooked up to a sewer drain
located on lot 2. A sells lot 1 to B, with no mention of B's
right to continue to use the drain on A's remaining lot 2.
The court may nonetheless imply an easement on B's
behalf if:

1) the previous use _____
_____ and

2) the parties expected _____
_____ because it is
reasonably necessary to _____
_____.

c)   By necessity: The landlocked setting. An easement of right of way will be
implied by necessity if grantor conveys a portion of his land

_____

_____.

d) By prescription: An easement may be acquired by satisfying the elements of _____.

Remember **C O A H:**

C:

O:

A:

H:

Note: Permission defeats the acquisition of an easement by prescription. An easement by prescription requires that the use be hostile.

6) The scope of an easement is determined by:

Example 52: A grants B an easement to use A's private road to get to and from B's parcel, Blackacre.

B has: _____.

A's parcel is: _____.

Subsequently, B purchases the adjacent Greenacre, with its small marina. May B unilaterally expand the use of the easement to benefit Greenacre?

_____

_____.

7) Termination of an easement:

Remember **END CRAMP:**

a) **E**stoppel: Here, the servient owner materially changes his or her position in reasonable reliance on the easement holder's assurances that the easement _____.

       Example 53:   A tells B that A will no longer be using her right of way across B's parcel. In reasonable reliance, B builds a swimming pool on B's parcel, thereby depriving A of the easement. In equity:

b) **N**ecessity: Easements created by necessity expire as soon as: _____ _____. However, if the easement, at-tributable to necessity, was nonetheless created by express grant:

_____.

       Example 54:   O conveys a portion of his ten-acre tract to A, with no means of access out except over a portion of O's remaining land. The parties reduce their understanding to express writing. Thereafter, the city builds a public roadway affording A access out. The easement:_____.

c) **D**estruction of the servient land, other than through the willful conduct of the servient owner:

d) **C**ondemnation of the servient estate:

55

e) **R**elease: A written release, given by _____ to the _____.

f) **A**bandonment: The easement holder must demonstrate by <u>physical action</u>:

_____.

Note: Abandonment requires physical action by the easement holder.

Example 55: A has a right of way across B's parcel. A erects a structure on A's parcel that precludes her from ever again reaching B's parcel. That is the sort of action to signify abandonment. By contrast, mere nonuse, or mere words, are insufficient to terminate by abandonment.

g) **M**erger doctrine (also known as unity of ownership):

The easement is extinguished when title to _____ and title to_____ become vested in the same person.

Example 56: A has a right of way across B's parcel, to enable A to better reach her parcel. A's land is: _____
_____. A is: _____
_____.

B's land is: . _____

Later, A buys B's parcel. The result:

Note: If complete unity of title is achieved, the easement is extinguished. Even though there may be later separation of title:

_____

_____

_____.

For example, assume now that A later sells the parcel over which she once enjoyed the right of way. The easement:_____

_____

_____.

h) **P**rescription: The servient owner may extinguish the easement by interfering with it in accordance with the elements of _____

_____.

Remember COAH:

C:

O:

A:

H:

Example 57:　A has an easement of right of way across B's parcel. B erects a chain link fence on B's parcel, thereby precluding A from reaching it. Over time, B may succeed in extinguishing the easement through:

_____.

II.　The License

1)　Defined:

2) Licenses are not subject to: _____. Thus, you do not
    need a _____ to create a license.

3) Licenses are _____, at the will of the licensor,
    unless _____ to bar revocation.

4) The classic license cases:

    i)   The ticket cases:

             Tickets create _____.

    ii) Neighbors talking by the fence:

             Example 58:   Neighbor A, talking by the fence with neighbor B, says,
                              "B, you can have that right of way across my land." This
                              oral easement:

                              _____
                              _____.

                              An oral easement creates instead _____

                              _____.

    iii) Estoppel will apply to bar revocation only when the licensee has
         invested _____ in
         reasonable reliance on the license's continuation.

III. The Profit

1. The profit entitles its holder to enter the servient land and take from it:

_____

_____.

2. The profit shares: _____.

IV. The Covenant

1) Defined: The covenant is a promise to do or not do something related to land. It is UNLIKE the easement because it is not the grant of a property interest, but rather _____ or promise regarding land.

2) Covenants can be negative (known as restrictive covenants): The restrictive covenant is a promise to refrain from doing something related to land. For example:

Covenants can be affirmative: The affirmative covenant is a promise to do something related to land. For example:

3) How to know whether to construe the given promise as a covenant or as an equitable servitude: _____

_____

_____.

4) In covenant parlance, one tract is burdened by the promise and another is benefited.

When will the covenant run with the land? In other words, when is it capable of binding successors?

Example 59:   Neighbor A promises neighbor B that A will not build for commercial purposes on A's property. A's parcel is burdened by the promise. B's parcel is benefited. Later, A sells her burdened parcel to A-1. B sells his benefited parcel to B-1. Now, A-1 has commenced manufacture of a steak sauce plant on the premises. B-1 wishes to proceed against A-1 for money damages. Will B-1 succeed? *It depends on whether the facts support the conclusion that the burden and benefit run.*

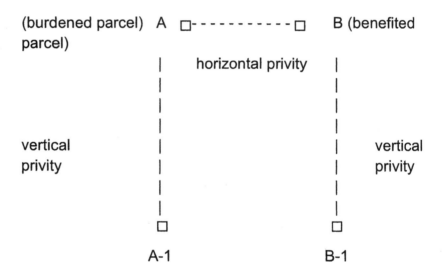

In answering, two separate contests must be resolved:

First, does the burden of A's promise to B run from A to A-1?

Remember W I T H N:

The elements necessary for the burden to run:

i)   **W**riting:

ii)   **I**ntent:

Note: Courts are generous in finding the requisite intent.

iii)   **T**ouch and concern the land:

The promise must affect the parties' legal relations as _____, and not simply as members of _____.

Note: Covenants to pay money to be used in connection with the land (such as homeowners' association fees) and covenants not to compete do touch and concern the land.

iv)   **H**orizontal and vertical privity:

Horizontal privity refers to the nexus between: _____ _____.

It requires that they be in _____, meaning that they were in a _____ or _____or _____ relationship.

Vertical privity refers to the nexus between _____. It simply requires some _____, such as: _____.

The only time that vertical privity will be absent is if A-1 acquired her interest through: _____.

v) **Notice:**

Second, does the benefit of A's promise to B run from B to B-1?

Remember W I T V:

i) **W**riting

ii) **I**ntent

iii) **T**ouch and Concern

iv) **V**ertical Privity

Note: Horizontal privity is not required for the benefit to run.

V. Equitable Servitudes

1) Defined: The equitable servitude is a promise that equity will enforce against successors. It is accompanied by _____.

2) To create an equitable servitude that will bind successors:

Remember W I T N E S:

i) **W**riting

ii) **I**ntent

iii) **T**ouch and Concern

iv) **N**otice

NOTE: PRIVITY IS NOT REQUIRED TO BIND SUCCESSORS.

3) The implied equitable servitude—the general or common scheme doctrine:

Example 60: A subdivides her land into 50 lots. She sells lots 1 through 45 through deeds that contain covenants restricting use to residential purposes. A then sells one of the remaining lots to a commercial entity, B, by deed containing no such covenant. B now seeks to build a convenience store on his lot. Can he be enjoined from doing so?

Yes, if the two elements of the general or common scheme doctrine apply. Under the common scheme doctrine, the court will imply a reciprocal negative servitude to hold the unrestricted lot holder to the restrictive covenant.

The two elements of the general or common scheme doctrine:

i) When the sales began, the subdivider (A): _____

_____

_____.

ii) The defendant lotholder (B) _____

_____.

There are three forms of notice potentially imputed to defendant:

Remember A I R:

A: Actual notice, meaning: _____

_____.

I: Inquiry notice, meaning: _____

_____.

R: Record notice, meaning the form of notice sometimes imputed to buyers on the basis of: _____.

Note: With respect to record notice, the courts are split. Some take the view that a subsequent buyer is on record notice of the contents of prior deeds transferred to others by a common grantor. The better view, taken by other courts, is that the subsequent buyer does NOT have record notice of the contents of those prior deeds transferred to others by the common grantor.

4) Equitable defenses to enforcement of an equitable servitude:

a) Changed conditions:

The changed circumstances alleged by the party seeking release from the terms of an equitable servitude must be: _____

_____.

What is never good enough? _____

ADVERSE POSSESSION

1) The basic concept: Possession for a statutorily prescribed period of time can, if certain elements are met: _____.

2) The elements of adverse possession:

Remember C O A H:

For possession to ripen into title it must be:

i) **C**ontinuous:

ii) **O**pen and Notorious:

iii) **A**ctual:

iv) **H**ostile:

NOTE: POSSESSOR'S SUBJECTIVE STATE OF MIND IS IRRELEVANT.

3) Tacking:

One adverse possessor may tack on to his time with the land his predecessor's time, so long as _____, which is satisfied by _____, such as _____.

Tacking is NOT allowed when: _____.

Example 61:   O owned Blackacre in 1980 when A entered adversely. A was on her way to satisfying the elements of adverse possession when, in 1986, Mr. X ousted her. Mr. X stays on the land through 2000. Our jurisdiction has a 20-year statute of limitations. In 2000, who owns Blackacre?

4) Disabilities:

The statute of limitations will not run against a true owner who is afflicted by a disability at: _____.

Common disabilities include: _____ _____.

Example 62:   O owned Blackacre in 1980 when A entered adversely. In 1990, O went insane. In 2000, O recovered. Our jurisdiction has a 20-year statute of limitations. In 2000, who owns Blackacre? _____, assuming that she has met the COAH elements. O cannot claim the benefit of the disability because: _____ _____.

LAND CONVEYANCING: THE PURCHASE
AND SALE OF REAL ESTATE:

Every conveyance of real estate consists of a two-step process.

Step I: The land contract, which endures until step II.

Step II: The closing, where the deed becomes our operative document.

I.   The land contract

1)   The land contract and the Statute of Frauds:
     i)   The standard:

     ii)   When the amount of land recited in the land contract is more than the actual size of the parcel:

           Example 63:   B enters into a contract to purchase a farm. The contract recites that the farm is 100 acres. When B has a survey done, B learns that the farm is actually 98 acres. What is B's remedy?

     iii) The one exception to the Statute of Frauds: THE DOCTRINE OF PART PERFORMANCE. If, on your facts, you have two of the following three, the doctrine is satisfied and equity will decree specific performance of an oral contract for the sale of land:

           a)

           b)

                 and/or

           c)

2) The problem of risk of loss:

Apply the doctrine of equitable conversion: _____
_____.

Thus, in equity, once the contract is signed: _____,
subject of course to the condition that he pay the purchase price at closing.

One important result flows from this: **Destruction.** If, in the interim between contract and closing, Blackacre is destroyed through no fault of either party:

_____

_____.

3) Two implied promises in every land contract:

a) Seller promises to provide marketable title:

i) The standard:

ii) Three circumstances will render title unmarketable:

1. Adverse possession: If even _____ of the title rests on adverse possession, it is _____. Seller must be able to provide _____.

2. Encumbrances:

Marketable title means _____.
Thus, _____
render title unmarketable, unless _____
_____.

Note: Seller has the right to satisfy an outstanding mortgage or lien at the closing, with the proceeds of the sale. Thus, buyer cannot claim title is unmarketable because it is subject to a mortgage prior to closing, so long as the parties understand that the closing will result in the mortgage being satisfied or discharged.

3. Zoning violations:

b) Seller promises not to make any false statements of material fact:

The majority of states now also hold seller liable for:

_____
_____.

If the contract contains a general disclaimer of liability (for example, "property sold as is" or "with all faults"):_____
_____.

4) The land contract contains no implied warranties of fitness or habitability.

The common law norm is: _____.

One important exception: The implied warranty of fitness and workmanlike construction applies to the sale of a new home by a builder-vendor.

II. The Closing

Our controlling document is now: _____.

How does the deed pass legal title from seller to buyer? It must be "LEAD": Lawfully Executed And Delivered.

1) Lawful execution of a deed:

i) The standard:

Note: The deed need not recite _____, nor must _____ pass to make a deed valid.

ii) The description of the land:

Example 64:   The deed recites that O conveys "all of O's land," or "all of O's land in Essex County." Would such descriptions suffice?

Example 65:   O conveys "some of my land in Sussex County." Does such a description satisfy the standard?

2)   The delivery requirement:

   i)   The delivery requirement could be satisfied when: _____ _____.

   It is permissible here to use _____, _____or _____.

   ii)   However, delivery does not necessarily require: _____ _____.

   The standard for delivery is a legal standard, and is a test solely of ____ _____. Ask: Did grantor have _____ _____, irrespective of whether or not _____ _____.

   iii)   Recipient's express rejection of the deed: _____.

   Example 66:   As a surprise graduation gift, A's Aunt Gertrude executes a deed conveying Blackacre to A. A responds, "I can't accept such a lavish gift." Blackacre belongs to: _____.

iv) If a deed, absolute on its face, is transferred to grantee with an oral condition: _____.

      Example 67:   O conveys a deed to Blackacre that is absolute on its face, but says to grantee, "Blackacre is yours only if you survive me." This oral condition is:

v) Delivery by escrow: _____.

      Grantor may deliver an executed deed to a third party, known as an
_____, with instructions that the deed be delivered to grantee once _____
_____. Once the conditions are met:
_____.

      The advantage of escrow: If grantor dies or becomes incompetent or is otherwise unavailable before the express conditions are met: _____
_____.

3) Covenants for title and the three types of deed:

a) **The quitclaim:** It contains _____.
Grantor isn't even promising _____
_____. This is the worst deed buyer could hope for.

b) **The general warranty deed:** The best deed a buyer could hope for.

The general warranty deed typically contains all six of the following covenants. The first three are present covenants, meaning: a present covenant is breached, if ever, _____.

Thus, the statute of limitations for breach of a present covenant begins to run _____.

i) **The covenant of seisin:**

ii) **The covenant of right to convey:**

iii) **The covenant against encumbrances:**

The next three covenants are future covenants, meaning: a future covenant is not breached, if ever, until _____ _____. Thus, the statute of limitations for breach of a future covenant will not begin to run _____.

iv) **The covenant for quiet enjoyment:**

v) **The covenant of warranty:**

vi) **The covenant for further assurances:**

c) **The statutory special warranty deed:**

Provided for by statute in many states, this deed contains two promises that grantor makes only on behalf of himself. (Note: Grantor makes no representations on behalf of his predecessors in interest.)

1) _____

_____

and

2) _____

_____

THE RECORDING SYSTEM

Our model: The case of the double dealer.

O conveys Blackacre to A. Later, O conveys Blackacre, the same parcel, to B. O, our double dealer, has skipped town. In the battle of A vs. B, who wins?

Remember two brightline rules:

1) **If B is a BONA FIDE PURCHASER, and we are in a NOTICE jurisdiction, B wins, regardless of whether or not she records before A does.**

2) **If B is a BONA FIDE PURCHASER and we are in a race-notice jurisdiction, B wins if she records properly before A does.**

First, recording acts exist to protect only _____ and _____.

A bona fide purchaser is one who:

    i)

    and

    ii)

Two routine value questions:

1)   The bargain basement sale:

    Example 68:   B paid $50,000 cash for Blackacre, when its fair market value is estimated at $100,000. Is B a purchaser for value?

2) The case of the doomed donee:

Example 69: B is O's heir, or devisee, or donee. In a recording statute question, B:

The three forms of notice that a buyer may potentially be charged with are:

A I R:

A:

I:

R:

i) Actual notice:

ii) Inquiry notice:

a. Whether he looks or not, B is on inquiry notice of:

_____ .

The buyer of real estate has a duty to _____
before transfer of title, to see, for example, whether anyone else is in
possession. If another is in possession, _____
_____, regardless of whether buyer actually
bothered to inspect or not.

Thus, in our model, _____, B
would be on inquiry notice of that fact, thereby defeating B's status as

_____.

b. If a recorded instrument makes reference to an unrecorded transaction,
grantee is on inquiry notice of: _____

_____.

iii)   Record notice:

B is on record notice of A's deed if at the time B takes,

_____.

In our model, what if A has not recorded, or has not recorded properly at the time B takes? Assume that B is a bona fide purchaser. Does B win?

It depends on_____ the jurisdiction has enacted. In a notice state, _____. In a race-notice state, to win B must be a BFP and B must also _____.

The Recording Statutes:

1)   The Notice Statute: "A conveyance of an interest in land shall not be valid against any subsequent purchaser for value, without notice thereof, unless the conveyance is recorded."

    If, at the time B takes, he is a _____, he wins. It won't matter that A may ultimately record first, before B does. It won't matter, in the A vs. B contest, that B never records.

2)   The Race Notice Statute: "Any conveyance of an interest in land shall not be valid against any subsequent purchaser for value, without notice thereof, whose conveyance is first recorded."

    To prevail, B must 1) _____ and B must 2) _____.

Example 70:   On March 1, O conveys to A, a bona fide purchaser who does not record. On April 1, O conveys the same parcel to B, a bona fide purchaser, who does not record. On May 1, A records.

Who takes Blackacre in a notice jurisdiction?

Who takes in a race-notice jurisdiction?

Back to our original model, note that in either a notice or race-notice jurisdiction, B's status as a subsequent bona fide purchaser will be defeated if A had promptly and properly recorded before B takes. In other words, A's proper recordation: _____, thereby defeating their status as _____.

To give record notice to subsequent takers, the deed must be recorded properly, within: _____, which refers to that sequence of recorded documents:_____. In most states, the chain of title is established through a title search of _____.

Note three discrete chain of title problems:

I.   The Shelter Rule:

One who takes from a BFP will prevail against any entity that the transferor-BFP would have prevailed against. In other words, the transferee "takes shelter" in the status of her transferor, and thereby "steps into the shoes" of the BFP even though she otherwise fails to meet the requirements of BFP status.

Example 71:   O conveys to A, who does not record. Later, O conveys to B, a BFP, who records. B then conveys to C, who is a mere donee or who has actual knowledge of the O to A transfer. In the contest of A vs. C, who prevails?

_____ wins, in both a notice and race-notice state, because of _____. C steps into the shoes of _____, who was a BFP who recorded first.

II. The Problem of the Wild Deed:

Example 72:   **O sells Blackacre to A, who does not record. Then, A sells to B. B records the A-to-B deed.**

Note: The A to B deed, although recorded, is NOT connected to the chain of title, because _____

_____.

The A to B deed, therefore, is a _____.

The rule of the wild deed: *If a deed, entered on the records (A to B), has a grantor unconnected to the chain of title (O to A), the deed is a wild deed. It is incapable of giving record notice of its existence.*

O, our initial grantor and dirty double dealer, then sells Blackacre to C. Assume that C has no actual or inquiry knowledge of the O-to-A or A-to-B conveyance. C records.

O has skipped town. In the contest of B vs. C, who prevails?

_____ wins, in both a notice and race-notice state. C wins in a notice state because at the time C takes she is a _____.

C wins in a race-notice state because she is _____ who _____.

III. Estoppel By Deed:

Example 73:   In 1950, O owns Blackacre. He is thinking about selling it to X, but for now decides against it. In 1950, X, who does not own Blackacre, sells it anyway, to A. A records.

In 1960, O finally sells Blackacre to X. X records.

In 1970, X, a double dealer, sells Blackacre to B. B records.

i)   As between X and A, who owned Blackacre from 1960-1969?

_____ did, because of the rule of **estoppel by deed:** One who conveys realty in which he has no interest (here, X), is estopped from denying the validity of that conveyance if: _____

_____.

ii)   Who owns Blackacre in 1970?

_____, as long as he is _____.

B wins in a notice system because he is a _____. B wins in a race-notice system because he is a _____ who _____.
How so? A's 1950 recording is a nullity. A recorded too early. B's title searcher would not find A's deed. Why not? Because one is entitled to assume that no one sells land until they first own it. Thus, B's title searcher would not discover X's 1950 pre-ownership transfer to A.

MORTGAGES:

Our model: C, a creditor, is thinking of lending O $50,000. O offers Blackacre as collateral.

1)   **How does one create a mortgage?**

A mortgage is the conveyance of a security interest **in land**, intended by the parties to be: _____

_____.

A mortgage is the union of two elements:

i)

ii)

By way of vocabulary, debtor is: _____, and creditor is: _____.

The mortgage typically must be in writing to satisfy the Statute of Frauds. This is the _____.

2) **The equitable mortgage:**

Example 74:   O owns Blackacre. Creditor lends O a sum of money. The parties understand that Blackacre is the collateral for the debt. However, instead of executing a note or mortgage deed, O hands Creditor a deed to Blackacre that is absolute on its face. This is called:

_____.

As between O and Creditor:

What if Creditor proceeds to sell Blackacre to bona fide purchaser X?

_____ owns the land. O's only recourse: _____

_____

_____.

3) **Once a mortgage has been created, what are the parties' rights?**

Unless and until foreclosure, debtor-mortgagor has: _____
_____.

Creditor-mortgagee has: _____.

4) All parties to a mortgage can transfer their interests.

The mortgage automatically follows: _____.

i) The creditor-mortgagee can transfer his interest by:

(1) _____

_____

or

(2) _____

_____.

If the note is endorsed and delivered, the transferee is eligible to become: _____. This means that he takes the note free of any_____

_____.

"Personal defenses" include:

_____

_____

_____.

Thus, the holder in due course may foreclose the mortgage despite:

_____.

By contrast, the holder in due course is still subject to "real" defenses that the maker might raise.

MAD FIFI[4], *the Real Defenses:*

M _____

A: _____

D: _____

F
I
F: _____

I: _____

I: _____

I: _____

I: _____

To be a holder in due course of the note, the following criteria must be met:

a) the note must be _____, made payable to the named mortgagee;

b) the _____ must be indorsed, signed by the named mortgagee;

c) the_____ must be _____ to the transferee. A photocopy is unacceptable;

d) the transferee must take the note _____, without notice of any _____;

and

e) the transferee must pay _____ for the note, meaning some amount that is more than nominal.

ii)   **If O, our debtor-mortgagor, sells Blackacre, which is now mortgaged:**

_____

_____

_____.

Example 75:   On January 10, Madge took out a $50,000 mortgage on Blackacre with First Bank. First Bank promptly and properly recorded its interest on January 10. Thereafter, on January 15, Madge sold Blackacre to Buyer. Buyer had no actual knowledge of the lien. Buyer promptly and properly recorded its deed.

Does Buyer hold subject to First Bank's mortgage? _____. **All recording statutes apply to mortgages as well as deeds.** Thus, _____.

Does it matter which recording statute this jurisdiction has enacted? _____. In a notice state, Buyer takes subject to the lien because: _____.

In a race-notice state, Buyer takes subject to the lien because: _____ _____ _____.

Example 76:   Assume now that on January 10, Madge took out a $50,000 mortgage on Blackacre with First Bank. On January 15, Madge sold Blackacre to Buyer. Buyer had no knowledge of the lien. On January 20, First Bank recorded its mortgage in Blackacre. On January 30, Buyer recorded his deed to Blackacre. Does Buyer hold subject to First Bank's mortgage? **This time, it depends on which recording statute has been enacted.**

In a race-notice jurisdiction: _____

_____

_____.

In a notice jurisdiction: _____

_____

_____.

In a notice state, a subsequent BFP prevails over a prior grantee or mortgagee who has not yet recorded properly at the time the BFP takes.

iii) **Who is personally liable on the debt if O, our debtor-mortgagor, sells Blackacre to B?**

If B has "assumed the mortgage":

Both _____ and _____ are personally liable.

_____ is primarily liable.

_____ remains secondarily liable.

If B takes "subject to the mortgage":

_____ assumes no personal liability.

Only _____ is personally liable.

But, if recorded, _____.
Thus, _____

_____.

5) **Foreclosure:**

Assuming that our mortgagee-creditor must look to the land for satisfaction, how must he or she proceed?

The mortgagee must foreclose by: _____
_____. At foreclosure, the land is sold. The sale proceeds go to satisfying the debt.

What if the proceeds from the sale of Blackacre are less than the amount owed?

By contrast, what if there is a surplus?

Example 77:   Assume that Blackacre has a fair market value of $50,000 and is subject to three mortgages executed by its owner, Madge. First Bank, with first priority, is owed $30,000. Second Bank, with second priority, is owed $15,000, and Third Bank, with third priority, is owed $10,000. Assume that First Bank's mortgage is foreclosed, and that Blackacre is sold for $50,000. How will the funds be distributed?

Off the top: _____

_____

_____.

The sale proceeds are then used to pay off the mortgages in the order of their priority. Each claimant is entitled to satisfaction **in full** before a subordinated lienholder may take. Thus, First Bank takes: _____. Then, Second Bank takes: _____. The remaining balance is applied toward:

_____.

Third Bank should be able to proceed for a deficiency judgment.

Now assume the same facts as above, except that Blackacre is sold at First Bank's foreclosure sale for $60,000. What result?

_____

_____.

6) **Effect of foreclosure on various interests:**

i) Foreclosure will terminate interests junior to the mortgage being foreclosed but will not affect senior interests. (This means that junior lienholders will be paid in descending order with the proceeds from the sale, assuming funds are leftover after full satisfaction of superior claims. Junior lienholders should be able to proceed for a deficiency judgment. But once foreclosure of a superior claim has occurred, with the proceeds distributed appropriately, junior lienholders can no longer look to Blackacre for satisfaction.)

Those with interests subordinate to those of the foreclosing party are:

_____.

The debtor-mortgagor is also considered a: _____
_____, particularly if creditor wishes to proceed against debtor for a personal deficiency judgment.

Failure to include a necessary party results in the preservation of that party's claim, despite the foreclosure and sale. Thus, if a necessary party is not joined, _____

_____.

ii) Foreclosure does not affect any interest senior to the mortgage being foreclosed. The buyer at the sale takes subject to such interest. This means that buyer is NOT _____,
but, as a practical matter, if the senior mortgage is not paid, sooner or later, _____

_____.

Example 78: Assume the same set of facts as in the previous hypothetical: Blackacre has a fair market value of $50,000 and is subject to three mortgages executed by its owner, Madge. First Bank, with first priority, is owed $30,000. Second Bank, with second priority, is owed $15,000, and Third Bank, with third priority, is owed $10,000. Now, however, suppose that it is Second Bank's mortgage that is being foreclosed. (First Bank's mortgage exists, but it is either not in default or its holder has not yet taken action to foreclose it.)

Foreclosure does not affect any interest senior to the mortgage being foreclosed. Thus, foreclosure of Second Bank's mortgage:

_____
_____. First Bank's

mortgage will continue: _____

_____.

Is the foreclosure sale buyer personally liable to First Bank?

_____

_____.

The foreclosure sale buyer has a strong incentive to:

_____

How is bidding apt to proceed at the foreclosure sale brought by Second Bank? Buyer should bid up to _____, which represents

_____
_____.

How will the proceeds from the sale be distributed?

_____

_____

_____

_____.

7) **Priorities:**

i) As a creditor, you must _____.

ii) Once recorded, priority is determined by the norm of _____

_____.

iii) The purchase money mortgage: A mortgage given to secure a loan that enables the debtor to acquire the encumbered land.

Example 79:   C lends O $100,000 so that O can purchase Blackacre. C takes as collateral a security interest in Blackacre, the very parcel that C's extension of value enabled O to acquire.

C is: _____.

Assuming that C records properly, he has: _____

_____.

The purchase money mortgagee's "superpriority":

Example 80:   C1 lends $200,000 to O, taking a security interest in all of O's real estate holdings, "whether now owned or hereafter acquired." (This clause is called _____ _____. It is permissible.)

C1 records the mortgage note. Six months later, C2 lends O $50,000 to enable O to acquire a parcel known as Blueacre, taking back a security interest in Blueacre and recording that interest. Subsequently, O defaults on all outstanding obligations. All that he has left is Blueacre. Who has first priority in Blueacre, C1 or C2?

iv) Subordination agreements:_____

_____

_____.

8) Redemption:

i) **Redemption in equity:** Equitable redemption is universally recognized up to the date of sale. At any time prior to the foreclosure sale:

_____

_____.

Once a valid foreclosure has taken place: _____

_____

How is the right of equitable redemption exercised?

_____

_____.

What if the mortgage or note contained an acceleration clause? An acceleration clause permits the mortgagee to declare the full balance due in the event of default. If the mortgage contains an acceleration clause:

_____

_____.

May a debtor/mortgagor waive the right to redeem in the mortgage itself? _____

This is known as: _____

_____.

ii) **Statutory redemption:** Recognized in one-half the states, statutory redemption gives the debtor-mortgagor a statutory right to redeem for some fixed period after the foreclosure sale has occurred (typically six months to one year). Where recognized, statutory redemption applies: _____. The amount to be paid is usually:

_____

_____.

In most states, to recognize statutory redemption, the mortgagor will have the right:

_____.

When a mortgagor redeems, the effect is to:

_____

_____.

LATERAL SUPPORT

If land is improved by buildings and an adjacent landowner's excavation causes that improved land to cave in, the excavator will be liable only if:

_____.

Strict liability does not attach to the excavator's actions unless plaintiff shows that, because of defendant's actions, _____

_____.

(In other words, for strict liability to apply, plaintiff must show that the improvements on his land (for example, the shrubs, the fountain, the structures) did not contribute to his land's collapse.)

WATER RIGHTS

I. **The two major systems for determining the allocation of water in water-courses, such as streams, rivers, and lakes:**

1) **The riparian doctrine:**

The water belongs to those who own the land: _____.

These people are known as: _____, who share the right

_____.

Thus, one riparian will be liable if his or her use: _____

_____.

2) **The prior appropriation doctrine:**

The water belongs initially to the state, but the right to divert it and use it can be acquired by: _____, regardless of whether or not he happens to be: _____.

Rights are determined by: _____. The norm for allocation is: _____. Thus, a person can acquire the right to divert and use water from a watercourse merely by being the first to do so. Any productive or beneficial use of the water, including use for _____, is sufficient to create the appropriation right.

II. **Groundwater, also known as percolating water: Water beneath the surface of the earth that is not confined to a known channel.**

The surface owner is entitled to make _____. However, the use must NOT be _____.

III. **Surface Waters: Those which come from rain, springs or melting snow, and which have not yet reached a natural watercourse or basin.**

The common enemy rule:

A landowner may change drainage or make any other changes/ improvements on his land to combat the flow of _____. Many courts have modified the common enemy rule to prohibit:

_____.

POSSESSOR'S RIGHTS

The possessor of land has the right to be free from trespass and nuisance.

1) Trespass:

2) Private nuisance:

        Note: Unlike trespass, nuisance does NOT require _____
_____. Thus, _____ and
_____ could give rise to a _____, but
not a _____.

        Nuisance and the hypersensitive plaintiff:

        Example 81:   A operates a dog kennel located near a power plant. A
notices that her dogs are chronically agitated, causing her to
lose business. She learns that the power plant emits a high
frequency sound heard by animals but not humans. A sues
the plant for nuisance. What result?

EMINENT DOMAIN

1) Defined: Government's _____ to take
private property for _____ in exchange for
_____.

2) Explicit takings: acts of governmental condemnation.

For example, the government condemns your land to make way for a
public highway.

3) Implicit or regulatory takings: a governmental regulation that, although not intended to be a taking, has the same effect.

> Example 82: You buy land in North Carolina for development. Three months later, the government imposes a ban on all development. Note that you have not been the target of an overt condemnation. Still, you argue that the regulation is an implicit taking. It has worked an _____ _____.

4) The remedy for a regulatory taking: government must either:

i)

or

ii)

ZONING

1) Defined: Pursuant to its police powers, government may _____ _____.

2) The variance: The principal means to achieve flexibility in zoning.

The variance is granted or denied by _____.

3) The nonconforming use: A once lawful, existing use now deemed nonconforming by a new zoning ordinance. It cannot be _____ _____ unless _____. Otherwise, it could be deemed _____.

4) Unconstitutional exactions:

   i) Defined: Exactions are _____ _____ in exchange for granting permission to build.

       Example 83:   You are a developer seeking permission to build a 200-unit residential development in the town of Utopia. The town tells you that it will grant you the requisite permit if you agree to provide several new streetlights, a small park and wider roads. To pass constitutional scrutiny, these exactions must: _____ _____ _____.

                  If they are not, the exactions are unconstitutional.

Remedies

Professor Steve Calandrillo
Professor Richard Conviser

REMEDIES

Professor Steve Calandrillo
Professor Richard Conviser

HOW TO SPOT A REMEDIES QUESTION

The "call-of-the-question" line will do one of three things:

One: Use the word " <u>Remedy/Remedies</u> "

Two: Use the word " <u>Relief.</u> "

Three: State a <u>an Injunction, specific performance.</u>
e.g., specific performance.

◆

Bar Exam Tip: The remedies issues will be incorporated into a substantive law fact pattern. The most relevant areas for bar exam purposes are torts and contracts (and the related property areas).

The question may be a pure remedies question or a crossover. The "tip-off" will be found in how the call-of-the-question lines are worded.

◆

The remedies issues are also a lock to be tested on the Multistate Bar Exam.

---

3 STEPS TO APPROACH A REMEDIES QUESTION

STEP 1

Determine what _substantive area_ of law is involved

torts, contracts

and

What _specific type problem_ problem is at issue within that substantive area, *i.e.,* what tort or what type contract.

Bar Exam Tip: The fact pattern may be susceptible to more than one substantive law interpretation, *e.g.*, torts <u>and</u> contracts.

STEP 2

Make sure that _P will win the case. Why? Bc no remedies if no case._
e.g., a tort committed, a contract breached.

Bar Exam Tip: On crossover questions P will **<u>always</u>** have a good case.

STEP 3

Determine what _remedies_ require discussion.
This **<u>must</u>** be done in the right chronological order as follows:

◆

at law **FIRST:** _Legal_ Remedies *(# Damages, compens, nominal, punitive)*

      SECOND: _Restitutionary_ Remedies (2 categories)

      THIRD: _Pure equitable_ Remedies *injunction, recission, reformation, specific performance*

◆

Bar Exam Tip: There are **two** types of restitutionary remedies, **legal** and **equitable**. The legal remedies **<u>must</u>** be considered **<u>first</u>**.

THE TORT REMEDIES

1. LEGAL REMEDIES

   DAMAGES

2. RESTITUTIONARY REMEDIES

   A. LEGAL RESTITUTIONARY REMEDIES

   RESTITUTIONARY DAMAGES
   REPLEVIN
   EJECTMENT

   B. EQUITABLE RESTITUTIONARY REMEDIES

   CONSTRUCTIVE TRUSTS/
   EQUITABLE LIENS

3. EQUTIABLE REMEDIES

   INJUNCTIVE RELIEF

1. LEGAL REMEDIES (TORTS)

DAMAGES

Definition: *Defendant is ordered to pay money to plaintiff.*
[(i) compensatory (ii) nominal (iii) punitive]

FIRST TYPE OF DAMAGES: COMPENSATORY

BASIC CONCEPT

These are based on the _____ to the **plaintiff**. (They put the injured party in the position he/she would have been in had the injury not occurred.)

4 REQUIREMENTS CHECKLIST

1st) CAUSATION

This refers to _____ causation. (The **"but for"** test)

2nd) FORESEEABILITY

This refers to _____ causation. (The injury must have been **foreseeable at the time of the tortious act**.)

3rd) CERTAINTY

Damages can**not** be too _____.

BAR EXAM TIPS

Tip 1: _____ losses have to be established with <u>more</u> certainty than _____ losses.

Tip 2: If there is a "_____" record that helps to provide certainty.

X: old vs. new business.

Hypo: Defendant causes plaintiff's restaurant to burn to the ground. Restaurant has been in business for three years. Vs. three days.

_____

Tip 3: For **future** damages, plaintiff must show that they are <u>more likely to happen than not</u>. This is the "_____" rule.

Hypo: Injured plaintiff is an outstanding undergraduate student who has been accepted to law school. Basis of future lost income calculation?

_____

4th) <u>UNAVOIDABILITY</u>

Plaintiff must take _____ steps to **mitigate** the damages.

<u>Hypo:</u> Plaintiff injured in car accident. What should plaintiff do?

_____

♦ ♦ ♦ ♦ ♦

COMPENSATORY DAMAGES – PARTICULAR PROBLEM AREA:

<u>PERSONAL INJURY TORTS</u>

I. <u>THE *"CERTAINTY"* RULES:</u>

<u>ECONOMIC LOSSES (SPECIAL DAMAGES)</u>
    X: Medical Expenses/Lost Earnings

Basic certainty rules _____ here, *i.e.,* calculation must be with **sufficient** certainty.

<u>Vs. NON-ECONOMIC LOSSES (GENERAL DAMAGES)</u>
    X: Pain and Suffering, Permanent Disfigurement

Basic certainty rules do _____ apply here. The jury may award **any amount it wishes**
    subject to proper instructions.

II. <u>FORM OF JUDGMENT PAYMENT</u>

The award **<u>must</u>** be a _____ payment.
Installment payments are **<u>not</u>** allowed.

<u>2 "CALCULATION" ITEMS":</u>

<u>Calculation Item 1</u>: The award **<u>must</u>** be _____ to **present value**.

<u>Calculation Item 2</u>: _____ is **<u>not</u>** taken into account. Under the <u>modern view</u> it is.

Write: "The judgment must be a single lump sum payment that will be discounted to present
    value without taking inflation into account (except under the modern rule)."

5

SECOND TYPE OF DAMAGES: NOMINAL

BASIC CONCEPT

These are awarded where **plaintiff** has _____.
They serve to establish or to vindicate the plaintiff's rights.

Hypo: Defendant regularly walks across dirt road on plaintiff's land to get to a bus.

THIRD TYPE OF DAMAGES: PUNITIVE

BASIC CONCEPT

These are awarded to _____ the **defendant**.

THE *THREE* RULES

1st **RULE:** In order to get punitive damages, plaintiff must have **first** been awarded
_____ or _____ damages.

Note: Punitive damages can also be attached to **restitutionary** damages.

2nd **RULE:** In order to get punitive damages, defendant's type **fault** must be greater than
_____.

3rd **RULE:** Generally, punitive damages are awarded in an amount **relatively**
_____ to actual damages. (As actual damages go up, punitive damages
go up.) U.S. Supreme Court would limit punitive damages to a **single digit** multiple of
actual damages unless conduct facts are extreme.

THE RESTITUTIONARY REMEDIES

BASIC CONCEPT

These remedies are based on the theory that the **defendant**

should not be _____.

RESTITUTIONARY DAMAGES
"LEGAL" RESTITUTIONARY REMEDY

BASIC CONCEPT

These are based on the _____ to the **defendant**.
And the amount is calculated based on the **value of the benefit**.

Contrast this with *compensatory* damages which focus on the **injury to the plaintiff**.

"COMPENSATORY" vs. "RESTITUTIONARY" DAMAGES

THREE BAR EXAM FACT PATTERN POSSIBILITIES

1) Only *compensatory* damages are available.

Hypo: Defendant destroys plaintiff's car. Remedy?

_____

2) Only *restitutionary* damages are available.

Hypo: P buys land with private dirt road through middle. Defendant manufacturing company drives trucks across road on plaintiff's vacant property to get to railroad reducing trip from ten miles to one-half mile. Remedy?

_____

Note: Nominal damages might technically be available on these facts.

3) Both *compensatory* and *restitutionary* damages are available.

Hypo: Defendant steals your machine to use in its business. Remedy?

_____

_____

Can you be awarded **both**? _____

Bar Exam Tip: How to Write Your Answer:

Write about _____ . Give plaintiff the _____ .

Bar Exam Tip: **Punitive** damages **can** be attached to **restitutionary damages** as long as the underlying cause of action is in tort.

REPLEVIN
"LEGAL" RESTITUTIONARY REMEDY

Definition: *Plaintiff recovers possession of specific personal property.*

Replevin requires a 2 part test.

Establish that: (1) The plaintiff has a right to _____ .

(2) There is a _____ by defendant.

MOST LIKELY BAR EXAM ISSUE:

"Timing" of Recovery
Plaintiff can recover the chattel _____ the trial.

Bar Exam Tip: If this is in issue, **mention in your answer** that:

(i) Plaintiff will have to **post** a _____ .

(ii) Defendant can defeat an **immediate** recovery by posting a _____ _____ . (The defendant can then keep the chattel until after the trial.)

Note: The **sheriff** repossesses the property for plaintiff.

Bar Exam Tip: Replevin is **almost always** coupled with _____ (compensatory or restitutionary) for lost use or benefit to the defendant during the time of detention.

EJECTMENT
"*LEGAL*" RESTITUTIONARY REMEDY

Definition: *Plaintiff recovers possession of specific real property.*

> **Ejectment requires a 2 part test.**

Establish that: (1) The plaintiff has a right to _____.

(2) There is a _____ by defendant.

MOST LIKELY BAR EXAM ISSUE:

Status of Defendant
Ejectment is available **only** against defendant who has _____ of property.

Hypo: Defendant crosses plaintiff's lawn on way to bus every day.

_____

Hypo: (i) Defendant is adverse possessor. (ii) Holdover tenant at expiration of lease term.

_____

Note: The **sheriff** ejects defendant from property.

Bar Exam Tip: Ejectment is **almost always** coupled with _____ (compensatory or restitutionary) for lost use or benefit to defendant during time of wrongful withholding.

CONSTRUCTIVE TRUSTS AND EQUITABLE LIENS
"*EQUITABLE*" RESTITUTIONARY REMEDIES

Definitions:

Constructive Trust: *Imposed on improperly acquired property to which defendant has **title**. Defendant serves as "trustee" and must return the property to the plaintiff.*

Equitable Lien: *Imposed on improperly acquired property to which defendant has **title**. Property will be subject to an immediate court-directed sale. The monies received go to the plaintiff. If the proceeds of the sale are less than the fair market value of the property when it was taken, a **deficiency judgment** will issue for the difference and can be used against defendant's other assets.*

9

Bar Exam Tip: Please note that constructive trusts and equitable liens can be used only when the fact pattern indicates that the defendant has **title** to the property.

Hypo: Doofus improperly acquired **title** to Bowater's property. Doofus is now **insolvent**.

THE RULES

RULE 1: Inadequate _____ alternative.

Basic Alternative: _____

The 2 Reasons:

(i) Defendant is _____; or

(ii) For **constructive trusts:** The property is *unique*.

RULE 2: _____ is allowed.

Hypo: Doofus sold the property for $50,000, which he put in a bank. What can Bowater do?

_____

_____

RULE 3: _____ prevail over plaintiff.

Hypo: Doofus sold the property to Lulu, a BFP. Bowater wants to have a constructive trust imposed on the property. Can he?

_____

_____

RULE 4: Plaintiff will prevail over _____ creditors.

Note: To the extent you have a deficiency judgment in connection with an equitable lien, you stand on equal footing with other unsecured creditors.

CHOICE OF REMEDY:
CONSTRUCTIVE TRUST OR EQUITABLE LIEN?

(i) If the property value subsequent to taking goes _____, **go with a constructive trust.**

(ii) If the property value subsequent to taking goes _____, **go with an equitable lien.**

(iii) When defendant's property can**not** be traced _____ to plaintiff's property, **only an equitable lien is available**.

> Hypo: Doofus misappropriates money and uses it to remodel his house. Since title to the home was not obtained by use of the money, the proper remedy is an equitable lien on it.

_____

_____

THE EQUITABLE REMEDY

INJUNCTIVE RELIEF
"EQUITABLE" REMEDY

Definition: *Defendant is ordered (enjoined) to do or refrain from doing something.*

THRESHOLD INQUIRY

Determine if you're required to discuss *"permanent"* or *"temporary/preliminary"* injunctive relief.

Permanent Injunction: Issued **after** full trial on merits.

Temporary (Preliminary, Interlocutory) Injunction: Issued **pending** trial on merits.

Bar Exam Tip: **If in doubt:** Go with a _____ injunction.

TEMPORARY INJUNCTIVE RELIEF

Temporary/preliminary injunctive relief requires a 2 part test.

PART 1

Establish that there is _____ injury.

Exam Fact Discussion: Facts must be discussed in a _____ context. In short, one must show that he or she will incur irreparable injury while waiting for a full trial on the merits – and that's why he or she needs relief **now**.

Note: Balancing of Hardships: Irreparable injury is weighed against any hardship defendant will suffer if a temporary injunction is granted.

> ## PART 2

Establish plaintiff's _____ of success.
(Plaintiff must establish this "probability.")

Bar Exam Tip: **Bond Requirement:** If a preliminary injunction is sought on the exam: Mention that the court should impose a bond requirement on plaintiff to reimburse defendant if the injunction injures him/her and the plaintiff does not succeed.

> ### _TEMPORARY/PRELIMINARY INJUNCTION_
> ### _MODEL BAR EXAM ANSWER_
>
> **Temporary Injunction: In issue is whether plaintiff can obtain temporary/preliminary injunctive relief. To do so, plaintiff must meet a 2-part test:**
> **(i) Irreparable Injury: (Discuss facts in time-frame context.)**
> **(ii) Likelihood of Success: (Discuss the "probability." Impose bond requirement.)**

Bar Exam Writing Tip: Same structure for **Replevin** and **Ejectment.**

> ## CONTRAST – TEMPORARY RESTRAINING ORDER
> ## WITH TYPICAL TEMPORARY INJUNCTION

Temporary Restraining Order (TRO): Issued **pending** a hearing to determine whether preliminary injunction should issue.

The Test for Obtaining a TRO: _____ to that for preliminary injunction.

TRO proceeding can be *ex parte*. Thus

    (i)   **Notice:** _____ required.

    (ii)   **Adversarial Proceeding:** _____ required.

Note: Please note that even though a TRO can be issued *ex parte*, if there's an opportunity to give the defendant notice and a chance to appear and contest the injunction, a good faith effort must be made to do so.

Note: TROs are limited to *10 days* (14 in federal court). Must have regular tempoary injunction hearing by then.

```
┌─────────────────────────────────────────┐
│      PERMANENT INJUNCTIVE RELIEF         │
└─────────────────────────────────────────┘
```

```
┌─────────────────────────────────────────┐
│        THE PERMANENT INJUNCTION         │
│           5-PART CHECKLIST              │
└─────────────────────────────────────────┘
```

```
┌─────────────────────────────────────────┐
│                 FIRST                   │
│   INADEQUATE LEGAL REMEDY ALTERNATIVE   │
└─────────────────────────────────────────┘
```

THE 3 LEGAL REMEDY ALTERNATIVES
      (1) **REPLEVIN**

      (2) **EJECTMENT**

      (3) **MONEY DAMAGES**

1st ALTERNATIVE: REPLEVIN

Q: Why Would It Be Inadequate? *[2 Reasons]*

    (i)   The _____ may not be able to recover it, *e.g.,* find or identify the chattel.

    (ii)   Defendant can file a _____ (and then, *e.g.,* run off with or destroy chattel in the interim.)

2nd ALTERNATIVE: EJECTMENT

Q: Why Would It Be Inadequate?

    The _____ may refuse to act.

    <u>Hypo:</u> Defendant builds structure which slightly encroaches on plaintiff's property. Will sheriff rip it down? _____

3rd ALTERNATIVE: MONEY DAMAGES

Q: Why Would They Be Inadequate? *[4 Reasons]*

    (i)   They're too _____.

    (ii)   Defendant is _____.

    (iii) _____ injury.

Hypo: Factory emits clouds of smoke containing metallic particles harmful to the lungs. Are money damages adequate?

_____

_____

(iv) Avoiding a _____ of actions.

Bar Exam Tip: How to Spot the Fact Pattern: They will tell you there has been:

_____

_____

Bar Exam Tip: It is much **easier** to show money damages are inadequate if plaintiff is protecting an interest in **land**, *e.g.,* injunctive relief against nuisance, trespass to land.

> ## SECOND
> ### *PROPERTY RIGHT/PROTECTABLE INTEREST REQUIEMENT*

Traditional Rule: Equity will grant relief only where a protectable _____ right is involved.

Modern View: You don't even need a property right – any _____ interest will suffice.

How to Write Bar Exam Answer

If applicable on the facts you should write about _____ the _____ and the _____. If conflicting results go with the latter.

THIRD
FEASIBILITY OF ENFORCEMENT

Characterization Note: 2 Types of Injunctions

(1) *Negative Injunction:* _____.

(2) *Mandatory Injunction:* _____

_____.

Rules:

(1) *Negative Injunction:* There is **no** enforcement problem.

(2) *Mandatory Injunction:* There **may be** an enforcement problem based on **(i)** the difficulty of supervision, or **(ii)** concern with effectively ensuring compliance.

THE 3 EXAM FAVORITE "MANDATORY" INJUNCTION FACT PATTERNS

1) Act involves the application of **great taste, skill, or judgment**.

Bar Exam Answer: Injunction _____.

2) A **series** of acts **over a period of time**.

Bar Exam Answer: Injunction _____ unless plaintiff's case is otherwise _____.

3) An **out-of-state** act is required.

Bar Exam Answer:

(i) **Resident** Defendant: Injunction _____.

(ii) **Non-Resident** Defendant: Injunction _____.

```
┌─────────────────────────────────┐
│ ┌─────────────────────────────┐ │
│ │          FOURTH             │ │
│ │   BALANCING OF HARDSHIPS    │ │
│ └─────────────────────────────┘ │
└─────────────────────────────────┘
```

Plaintiff's *benefit* vs. Defendant's *hardship* if relief granted.

THE 4 BALANCING OF HARDSHIPS RULES

1)   **There must be _____ between defendant's detriment and plaintiff's benefit.**

2)   **Even then, there will be <u>no</u> balancing if defendant's conduct was _____.**

   <u>Hypo:</u> Doofus informs Bowater that he's going to build a building going up to their joint boundary line. Bowater returns from vacation to discover that, due to Doofus' willful conduct, the now completed building encroaches slightly onto his property. What result?

   _____

   _____

   _____

3)   **If you decide to balance hardships, in whole or in part, consider awarding plaintiff**

   _____.

4)   **Hardship to the _____ is also taken into account.**

   <u>Hypo:</u> A factory spews out clouds of smoke and fumes. There is no cost effective way to sufficiently abate this nuisance. An injunction would force the factory to close down. It is located several miles from a small town and employs 500 persons. The only nearby structure is Plaintiff's small home. Result?

   First: Discuss the _____ hardship.

   Second: Discuss the _____ hardship.

   Third: _____ the injunction.

   Fourth: Award the plaintiff _____.

Bar Exam Tip: Balancing of hardships defense is **almost always** a primary discussion item when the tort is **<u>nuisance</u>** or **<u>trespass to land</u>**.

```
┌─────────────────────┐
│ ┌─────────────────┐ │
│ │     FIFTH       │ │
│ │    DEFENSES     │ │
│ └─────────────────┘ │
└─────────────────────┘
```

A. UNCLEAN HANDS

The Bar Exam Trick Fact Pattern: _____ .

The Rule: The "unclean hands" defense is available **only** if plaintiff's alleged improper conduct is _____ to the lawsuit.

B. LACHES

Preliminary Note: Laches/Statute of Limitations

(a)   Laches is a "running of a period of time" defense. Unlike the statute of limitations, however, which involves the mere passage of time, laches is concerned with the *effect* of the passage of time.

(b)   The laches time period will **never** be greater than the statute of limitations time period. (No need for laches – the statute will bar the claim.)

THE 3 LACHES ISSUES

1)   **When does the "clock start to run"?**

When plaintiff _____ of the injury

2)   **When does the delay cut off the right to relief?**

When it has been **both** _____ **and** _____ to the defendant.

> Hypo: Same as balancing of hardships hypo above, where structure encroaches plaintiff's land. Plaintiff is home the entire time and watches construction proceed.
>
> _____
>
> _____

3)   If laches applies, consider:

_____.

C.   IMPOSSIBILITY

Impossible for defendant to carry out terms of injunction.

D.   FREE SPEECH

If the tort is **defamation** or a **privacy publication branch** tort (false lights, private facts), your best exam answer is:

Injunction _____ based on free speech grounds.

◆ ◆ ◆

PERMANENT INJUNCTION "MEMORIZER"

1.   ____I____   **I**nadequate Legal Remedy

2.   ____P____   **P**roperty Right/Protectible Interest

3.   ____F____   **F**easibility of Enforcement

4.   ____B____   **B**alancing of Hardships

5.   ____D____   **D**efenses

MISCELLANEOUS INJUNCTIVE RELIEF PROBLEMS

A. CRIMES:

_____.

(Check to see if the conduct could be characterized as a tort.)

B. WHO WILL BE BOUND BY AN INJUNCTION?

(1) _____

(2) _____ and _____ acting with notice

(3) Others acting "_____" with notice

> Hypo: Manufacturer makes Michael Jordan t-shirts without Jordan's permission and is enjoined from doing so. Vendor at stadium buys t-shirts for resale and continues selling them even though he knows of the injunction. Result?

_____

C. "ERRONEOUS" INJUNCTION
If there is an erroneous injunction, does one have to obey it? _____.

Therefore, what one must do is have it _____ or _____.

D. CONTEMPT   [This issues for *disobeyance of a court order.*]

Civil Contempt (*to coerce*)

Money (Fine)

Imprisonment: Defendant "_____" to the jailhouse, *i.e.*, can get out by agreeing to comply.

Criminal Contempt (*to punish*)

Money (Fine)

Imprisonment: Can_____ get out of prison. Remain for set amount of time.

♦♦♦

Bar Exam Tip: Injunctive relief is **almost always** coupled with _____ for injuries incurred in the **time period prior** to obtaining the injunction.

```
┌─────────────────────────────────────────────────────┐
│ ┌───────────────────────────────────────────────┐   │
│ │   SPECIFIC TORT FACT PATTERN POSSIBILITIES      │   │
│ │    EXAMSMANSHIP:  GENERAL THOUGHTS              │   │
│ └───────────────────────────────────────────────┘   │
└─────────────────────────────────────────────────────┘
```

2 SETS OF BASIC BAR EXAM QUESTIONS

1ˢᵗ SET:

    1) Has/is **plaintiff** been/being _____?

    2) Has **defendant** derived a _____?

    3) Does **plaintiff** want the property _____?

    4) Does **plaintiff** need an _____?

    Bar Exam Note: Remember, these questions are **not** mutually exclusive.

2ⁿᵈ SET:

    1) Do the wrongs relate to the _____ only?

    2) Do the wrongs relate to the _____ only?

    3) Do the wrongs relate to **both** the _____ and the _____?

HOW TO HANDLE COMPENSATORY DAMAGES MEASURES

BAR EXAM COMPENSATORY DAMAGES LANGUAGE

"Plaintiff is entitled to compensatory damages to put her in the position she would have been in had this wrong and resulting injury not occurred. On these facts . . . [include common sense fact application here] . . . ."

SPECIFIC TORTS: POTENTIALLY AVAILABLE REMEDIES
THE "CHEAT SHEET"

PROPERTY TORTS
PERSONAL/REAL

PERSONAL PROPERTY TORTS

THE 3 BASIC BAR EXAM FACT PATTERNS

1)   **DESTROYED PROPERTY**

AVAILABLE REMEDIES

   (i)   **Compensatory Damages**

2)   **DAMAGED PROPERTY**

AVAILABLE REMEDIES

   (i)   **Compensatory Damages**

*3)   **DISPOSSESSION**

AVAILABLE REMEDIES

   (i)   **Compensatory Damages**

   (ii)   **Restitutionary Damages**
            If defendant benefits

   (iii)   **Replevin**

   (iv)   **Mandatory Injunction**
            If chattel *unique* and damages and replevin won't work

   (v)   **Constructive Trusts/Equitable Liens**
            Particularly if defendant is *insolvent* and/or *"tracing"* facts are involved

   (vi)   **Self-Help**
            Reasonable force to recapture

REAL PROPERTY TORTS

THE 5 BASIC BAR EXAM FACT PATTERNS: (Encroachment & Nuisance most common)

1) **SIMPLE TRESPASS**
AVAILABLE REMEDIES
- **(i)** **Nominal Damages**
- **(ii)** **Restitutionary Damages**
- **(iii)** **Injunction:** Avoiding multiplicity of actions

2) **DESTRUCTION/DAMAGE OF REALTY**
AVAILABLE REMEDIES
- **(i)** **Compensatory Damages**
- **(ii)** **Injunction**

3) **DISPOSSESSION**
AVAILABLE REMEDIES
- **(i)** **Compensatory Damages**
- **(ii)** **Restitutionary Damages**
- **(iii)** **Ejectment:** Since it's available, no injunction
- **(iv)** **Constructive Trusts/Equitable Liens**

*4) **ENCROACHMENT**
AVAILABLE REMEDIES
- **(i)** **Compensatory Damages**
- **(ii)** **Injunction:** Probably emphasize balancing of hardships

Bar Exam Note: **No** Restitution

*5) **NUISANCE**
AVAILABLE REMEDIES
- **(i)** **Compensatory Damages**
- **(ii)** **Injunction:** Probably emphasize balancing of hardships

Bar Exam Note: **No** Restitution

PERSONAL INJURY TORTS

AVAILABLE REMEDIES

(1) Compensatory Damages

Economic Losses/Special Damages (*e.g.,* lost wages): Certainty rules apply.

Non-Economic Losses/General Damages (*e.g.,* pain & suffering): Certainty rules do not apply.

Lump Sum Payment: Discounted to present value. *Inflation* not taken into account.

(2) Injunction

Only against prospective intentional tortious conduct.

FRAUD

AVAILABLE REMEDIES

(1) Damages

(2) Constructive Trusts/Equitable Liens

Important Bar Exam Tip: Always consider **(i)** whether punitive damages should be awarded **and** **(ii)** if it also could be analyzed as contracts case.

THE CONTRACT REMEDIES

1. THE LEGAL REMEDIES

DAMAGES

2. THE RESTITUTIONARY REMEDIES

A. LEGAL RESTITUTIONARY REMEDIES

RESTITUTIONARY DAMAGES
REPLEVIN
EJECTMENT

B. EQUITABLE RESTITUTIONARY REMEDIES

CONSTRUCTIVE TRUSTS/
EQUITABLE LIENS

3. THE EQUITABLE REMEDIES

SPECIFIC PERFORMANCE
RESCISSION
REFORMATION

THE LEGAL REMEDIES

DAMAGES
"LEGAL" **REMEDY**

FIRST TYPE OF DAMAGES: COMPENSATORY

Once again, these are based on the **injury to the plaintiff**.

The 4 requirements [**(i)** *causation* **(ii)** *forseeability (tested at time of formation)* **(iii)** *certainty* **(iv)** *mitigation*] are also basically the same analytically as for torts.

DIRECT DAMAGES

Those damages that flow **inherently** from the wrong.

Bar Exam Tip: The most common measure of damages is the **expectation** measure.

CONSEQUENTIAL DAMAGES

Available for *related* damages **foreseeable** at the time of **formation**.

Bar Exam Favorite Fact Pattern: The _____ fact pattern.

SECOND TYPE OF DAMAGES: NOMINAL

_____.

THIRD TYPE OF DAMAGES: PUNITIVE

_____.

Bar Exam Tip: If defendant's conduct is **willful**, you should always try to see if you can characterize it as a _____ case.

THE LIQUIDATED DAMAGES CLAUSE FACT PATTERN:

2 PART TEST FOR VALIDITY:

Part 1: Damages are _____ at time of contract formation.

Part 2: This was a _____ of what they would be. If amount is excessive this would be a *"penalty."*

RESULTS:

(i) **If Valid:** Only liquidated amount available
(ii) **If Invalid:** Only actual damages available

Bar Exam Trick Fact Pattern:

Clause provides that one can get *either* actual damages *or* liquidated damages.

THE RESTITUTIONARY REMEDIES
TO PREVENT UNJUST ENRICHMENT

LEGAL RESTITUTIONARY REMEDIES
    RESTITUTIONARY DAMAGES
    REPLEVIN
    EJECTMENT

EQUITABLE RESTITUTIONARY REMEDIES
    CONSTRUCTIVE TRUSTS/
    EQUITABLE LIENS

THE BASIC BAR EXAM RESTITUTIONARY "CONTRACT" FACT PATTERN

Contract "fails" _after_ plaintiff has rendered *performance* (partial or complete).

2 WAYS THIS OCCURS ON THE BAR EXAM:

    1) **The contract is** _____.

    2) **The contract is** _____.

1) UNENFORCEABLE CONTRACTS

The contract is unenforceable due to, *e.g.,* mistake, lack of capacity, statute of frauds, illegality.

The 2 Questions:

1) **Can plaintiff get restitutionary damages for property/money given to, or services rendered for, defendant?**

_____

> Hypo 1: Plaintiff sells store fixtures to Defendant for new store, pursuant to an unenforceable contract. Defendant decides not to open store and repudiates contract.

_____

> Hypo 2: Plaintiff renders services pursuant to an unenforceable contract. Their value is greater than the contract rate. Can Plaintiff recover it? _____

2) **Can plaintiff get the property back?**

_____

2) BREACHED CONTRACTS

Bar Exam Threshold Inquiry: **Who** is the _____? Is she the **non-breaching** or **breaching** party?

Plaintiff As *"NON-BREACHING"* Party:

The 2 Questions:

1) **Can plaintiff get restitutionary damages for property/money given to, or services rendered for, defendant?**

    _____, for the **value** of the benefit

    Note: Again, the value of the recovery may be **greater** than the contract rate.

2) **Can plaintiff get the property back?**

    _____, if it is **unique** or defendant is **insolvent**.

Vs. Plaintiff As *"BREACHING"* Party:

Hypo: Contract for land, price = $100,000. Plaintiff, after paying 30% of the purchase price, defaults.

Can plaintiff get any restitutionary damages?

Traditional View: _____

Modern View: _____

But: (a) **Cannot** be greater than contract rate and (b) is **reduced** by any damages suffered by defendant as a result of the breach.

SPECIFIC PERFORMANCE
"EQUITABLE" REMEDY

Definition: *Defendant is required to perform the contract.*

> **THE SPECIFIC PERFORMANCE
> 6-PART CHECKLIST**

> **FIRST
> *CONTRACT IS VALID/
> CERTAIN & DEFINITE***

Plaintiff must be able to show the contract is valid.

Bar Exam Note: In order to obtain specific performance plaintiff must be able to show the contract terms with more **certainty and definiteness** than would be the case in an action for money damages at law.

> **SECOND
> *CONTRACT CONDITIONS OF PLAINTIFF
> MUST BE SATISFIED***

Plaintiff must be able to show her contract conditions have been fulfilled (already performed, ready and able to perform, or excused from performing).

THE 2 FAVORITE BAR EXAM "CONDITIONS" FACT PATTERNS

Bar Exam Tip: **Both** fact patterns typically involve **land sale contracts.**

1. DEFICIENCIES FACT PATTERN
Seller can<u>not</u> deliver the agreed upon consideration.
(Usually involves the <u>quantity</u> of land.)

<u>Threshold Inquiry:</u> **Who is the plaintiff? Is it the _____ or _____?**

    a. ***SELLER* as Plaintiff**

        (i)   <u>**Can**</u> enforce the contract if the defect is _____.

        (ii)   Can<u>**not**</u>, however, enforce the contract if the defect is _____.

            <u>unless:</u> The seller can _____.

    b.   ***BUYER* as Plaintiff**

        (i)   <u>**Can**</u> enforce the contract even if the defect is _____.

        (ii)   Can<u>**not**</u>, however, enforce the contract if the defect is _____.

Bar Exam "Imperative": If you decide that specific performance should be granted under the rules above even though a defect still remains, you **must** include a sentence noting that the court will _____ the purchase price to take into account this defect in consideration.

Bar Exam Buzzword: _____ in the purchase price.

2. TIME OF THE ESSENCE CLAUSE FACT PATTERN
Buyer does <u>not</u> meet contract condition of timely performance.

THE "FACT LINE-UP"

    (i)   There **<u>will</u>** be a _____.

    (ii) The contract **<u>will</u>** contain an _____
          _____. (If this is not contained in fact pattern, this problem is <u>not</u> at issue.)

    (iii) This clause **<u>will</u>** contain a _____.
          (In short, it will provide for the forfeiture of all performance rendered
          to date if performance is not timely.)

    (iv) There **<u>will</u>** have been _____ which is now
          potentially subject to forfeiture.

> **Note:** Who partially performs land sale contracts? It's the buyer who has made payments towards the purchase price.

(v) Buyer **will** have made a _____.

> ***This triggers the time of the essence clause and its forfeiture provision. Seller wants to keep both the land and any performance rendered to date.***

(vi) Buyer **will** bring a lawsuit for specific performance.

WHAT RESULT?

Note: Equitable Maxim: "Equity _____ Forfeitures."

What Factors Court Can Look at to Avoid the Harsh Result of a Forfeiture?
    (1)   **Loss** to seller is **small**.
    (2)   **Tardiness** is *de minimis*.
    (3)   **Waiver** (seller has accepted late payments in past).
    (4)   Buyer would suffer **undue hardship**.

Bar Exam Tip 1:
    On the bar exam you should _____ award specific performance.

Bar Exam Tip 2:
    In your answer, you should note that under the **modern trend** courts would give plaintiff **restitutionary relief *if*** specific performance were ***not*** granted.

> ### *THIRD*
> ### *INADEQUATE LEGAL REMEDY ALTERNATIVE*

What Is The Basic Alternative? _____

Why Would They Be Inadequate? *[The Four Reasons]*
    (1)   Damages are **speculative**.
    (2)   Defendant is **insolvent**.
    (3)   **Multiple suits** are necessary.
    (4)   The thing bargained for is **<u>unique</u>**.

THE FAVORITE BAR EXAM ISSUE: THE "UNIQUENESS" PROBLEM

The Concept: If the property is "unique," then even if plaintiff received money damages, he could not simply go out and buy it. It would not be available.

Threshold Inquiry: Determine whether contract was for the sale of *real* or *personal* property.

a. REAL PROPERTY

The Rule: Land is _____!!

The Bar Exam Trick Fact Pattern: Every parcel of land will be made to look _____.

The Special "Seller's" Rule: Sellers of land **can** get specific performance even though all they have coming is money (*i.e.,* the purchase price).

b. PERSONAL PROPERTY

General Rule: Personal property is _____ (and damages are adequate).

Exceptions:

(1) **One of a Kind or Very Rare**

Hypo: Doofus contracts to buy a Rembrandt painting from Bowater, who now refuses to transfer it. Specific performance?

_____

(2) **Personal Significance to Buyer**

Hypo: I contract to buy from you my old purple felt-tip pen which I used to write my bar exam. Can I get it if you refuse to convey?

_____

Bar Exam Tip: _____.

(3) **Circumstances Make Chattel Unique**

Hypo: (i) OPEC decides to dramatically cut down oil production, causing severe gas shortages. Can buyer get specific performance of contract to purchase gasoline?

_____

(ii) Seller, however, contends that there was nothing unique about gasoline when the contract was entered into.

_____

_____

BAR EXAM FAVORITE ISSUE
LIQUIDATED DAMAGES CLAUSES

General Rule: A liquidated damages clause does _____ make money damages adequate. Specific performance is still available.

Exception: Where the clause provides that this is to be the "_____."

FOURTH
MUTUALITY OF REMEDY

Hypo: Bowater, 17 years of age, enters into a contract to buy land from Doofus, an adult. Doofus refuses to convey, and Bowater brings an action for specific performance. Result?

FIRST

Determine and discuss that you have a mutuality fact pattern. This is one where defendant argues: _"Plaintiff should not be able to enforce this contract against me because I could not enforce it against him."_

SECOND

Set out the rule. "Court will **reject** the mutuality argument if it feels **secure** that the plaintiff _____ and _____ perform."

THIRD

Grant specific performance. In your answer, have the decree provide for _____ performance.

FIFTH
FEASIBILITY OF ENFORCEMENT

PERSONAL SERVICES CONTRACT ENFORCEABILITY

RULE: They are _____ **specifically enforceable**.

Reasons: (1) **Enforcement** Problem
(2) **Involuntary Servitude**

VS. COVENANTS NOT TO COMPETE

RULE: These _____ enforceable if a **2-part test** is met:

(1) The services are _____, and
(2) The _____ (**geographic** & **duration**) is reasonable

SIXTH
DEFENSES

EQUITABLE DEFENSES

1) **UNCLEAN HANDS**

2) **LACHES**

3) **UNCONSCIONABILITY**

(i) **More** than simply a *"bad deal."* There must also be some *"smell factor"* facts that brought it about.

(ii) Tested at the **time of contract formation**.

CONTRACT DEFENSES

1) **MISTAKE**

2) **MISREPRESENTATION**

3) **STATUTE OF FRAUDS** ↓

BAR EXAM FAVORITE:
STATUTE OF FRAUDS/PART PERFORMANCE DOCTRINE PROBLEM

How Do You Spot The Problem?

(i)   The contract **must** involve _____. It could be either a land sale contract or one to make a testamentary disposition of land.

(ii)   This contract **will** have been an _____ contract.

Defendant now raises the **Statute of Frauds** as a **defense** to specific performance.

Once you have spotted and set out the problem, discuss the Rule.

The Rule: If one has rendered **(i)** *valuable part performance*, **(ii)** *in reliance on the contract*, this will take the case out of the Statute of Frauds and specific performance will be granted.

What is Valuable Part Performance?

(i) Payment (in whole or part)   *Any _____ of the top*

(ii) Possession   *three taken together.*

(iii) Valuable Improvements

(iv) Valuable Services

♦ ♦ ♦ ♦ ♦

SPECIFIC PERFORMANCE "MEMORIZER"

1. _____C_____ Contract is Valid

2. _____C_____ Conditions of Plaintiff Satisfied

3. _____I_____ Inadequate Legal Remedy

4. _____M_____ Mutuality of Remedy

5. _____F_____ Feasibility of Enforcement

6. _____D_____ Defenses

RESCISSION
"EQUITABLE" REMEDY

Definition: *The original contract is considered voidable and rescinded.*

Rescission requires a 2-step analysis.

STEP 1
DETERMINE IF THERE ARE GROUNDS FOR RESCISSION

1.   **GROUNDS: GENERAL:** **(i)** Mistake **(ii)** Misrepresentation **(iii)** Coercion **(iv)** Undue influence **(v)** Lack of capacity **(vi)** Failure of consideration **(vii)** Illegality.

    What do these grounds have in common?

    They all relate to contract _____.

2.   **MISTAKE**

    MUTUAL MISTAKE:

    (i)   **Material Fact:** *Rescission* _____.

    (ii)   **Collateral Fact** (going to quality, desirability, or fitness of property for a particular purpose): *Rescission* _____.

    Hypo: Bowater and Doofus enter into a contract for the sale of a warehouse building which they both mistakenly believe is in good condition. In fact, it has major structural problems. Rescission?

    _____

    Hypo: Bowater enters into a sale contract with Doofus for a warehouse. Both believe its <u>only</u> use is as a warehouse. One week later, developer offers Doofus three times the sale price because he intends to convert it into expensive loft apartments. Rescission?

    _____

UNILATERAL MISTAKE:

Rescission _____.

Exception: General:

The **non-mistaken** party _____ of the mistake.

> Hypo: Contractor submits a bid for a construction project, negligently leaving out a major cost item. The bid is far, far less than competing bids and is accepted. Rescission?
>
> _____

Modern Trend Exception

The **mistaken** party would suffer **undue hardship** if there is no rescission.

3.   MISREPRESENTATION

Recission: _____

In order to get rescission based on misrepresentation grounds, the plaintiff must show that they have **actually relied** upon the misrepresentation.

STEP 2
DETERMINE IF THERE ARE VALID DEFENSES
---

1.   UNCLEAN HANDS

2.   LACHES

NON-DEFENSE (Will Not Work)

Negligence of plaintiff is **not** a good defense.

2 SPECIFIC ITEMS:

1)   ELECTION OF REMEDIES

Plaintiff Sues For Damages "First": Rescission is _____ allowed.
This is regarded as an **affirmance** of the contract.

Plaintiff Sues For Rescission "First": Damages _____ allowed.

Note: Plaintiff can even sue for **both at the same time**, but must **elect** the preferred remedy <u>before</u> judgment.

2) **AVAILABILITY OF RESTITUTION**

If a plaintiff who is entitled to rescission has **previously** rendered performance on the contract (*e.g.*, performance of services, advance on purchase price), **she can get compensated for it or get the property back via <u>restitution</u>.**

REFORMATION
"EQUITABLE" REMEDY

Definition: *Changes written agreement to conform with the parties' original understanding.*

Reformation requires a 3-step analysis.

STEP 1 ***DETERMINE IF THERE IS A VALID CONTRACT***

STEP 2 ***DETERMINE IF THERE ARE GROUNDS FOR REFORMATION***

1. **MISTAKE**

MUTUAL MISTAKE:

Reformation _____

UNILATERAL MISTAKE:

Reformation _____

Exception: Where the **non-mistaken** party _____ of the mistake.
    (This is regarded as fraud or inequitable conduct.)

Please Note: Unlike the rescission exception, this does not encompass the situation where the non-mistaken party <u>should</u> have known of the mistake.

2.   **MISREPRESENTATION**

Reformation _____.   Rewriting reflects **expressed intent** of the parties.

STEP 3
DETERMINE IF THERE ARE VALID DEFENSES

---

1.   **UNCLEAN HANDS**

2.   **LACHES**

NON-DEFENSES (Will Not Work)

(i)   Negligence of Plaintiff
(ii)   Statute of Frauds
(iii)   Parol Evidence Rule

RESCISSION "MEMORIZER"

[ ]

1.   __G__   Grounds for Rescission

2.   __D__   Defenses

REFORMATION "MEMORIZER"

[ ]

1.   __V__   Valid Contract

2.   __G__   Grounds for Reformation

3.   __D__   Defenses

```
┌─────────────────────────────────────────────────┐
│  SPECIFIC CONTRACT FACT PATTERN POSSIBILITIES     │
│     EXAMSMANSHIP: GENERAL THOUGHTS                │
└─────────────────────────────────────────────────┘
```

1) Has **plaintiff** been _____?

2) Has **defendant** derived a _____?

3) Does **plaintiff** want the property _____?

4) Does **plaintiff** want the contract _____?

5) Does **plaintiff** want the contract _____?

6) Does **plaintiff** want the contract _____?

HOW TO HANDLE COMPENSATORY DAMAGES MEASURES:

BAR EXAM COMPENSATORY DAMAGES LANGUAGE

"Plaintiff is entitled to compensatory damages to put her in the position she would have been in had this wrong not occurred. On these facts ... [include common sense fact application here] ...."   [don't forget Consequential damages]

& THRESHOLD INQUIRY FACT ANALYSIS FOR COMPENSATORY DAMAGES

**Ask****:** Which _____ to the contract committed the breach and _____ did they do it?

SPECIFIC CONTRACTS: POTENTIALLY AVAILABLE REMEDIES
THE "CHEAT SHEET"

PERSONAL PROPERTY SALE CONTRACTS

AVAILABLE REMEDIES

(1)   Compensatory Damages

> *Seller's* Breach (Does not convey, delivers damaged goods)
>
> *Buyer's* Breach (Does not pay)

(2)   Restitution

> Favorites: <u>Unenforceable</u>/<u>Breached</u> Contracts

(3)   Specific Performance

> Property <u>not unique</u>, subject to exceptions

(4)   Rescission

(5)   Reformation

REAL PROPERTY SALE CONTRACTS

AVAILABLE REMEDIES

(1)   Compensatory Damages

> *Seller's* Breach (Does not convey)
>
> *Buyer's* Breach (Does not pay)

(2)   Restitution

> Favorites: <u>Unenforceable</u>/<u>Breached</u> Contracts)

(3)   Specific Performance

> Remember:
>
> **1.** Land is <u>unique</u>.
>
> **2.** <u>Both</u> Buyer <u>and</u> Seller can get specific performance.
>
> **3.** Favorites:
>
> > **(a)** <u>Deficiencies</u>/<u>Time of Essence Clause</u> "Conditions" Fact Patterns

(4)   Rescission

(5)   Reformation

CONSTRUCTION CONTRACTS

AVAILABLE REMEDIES

(1) **Compensatory Damages**

> *Owner's* Breach (Does not pay)

> *Builder's* Breach (Non-completion, Defective completion)

(2) **Restitution**

> Only <u>Builder</u> for work done – unless Owner pre-paid

(3) **Specific Performance**

> Only <u>Owner</u> – but very difficult because of enforcement problems

PERSONAL SERVICES CONTRACTS

AVAILABLE REMEDIES

(1) **Compensatory Damages**

> *Employer's* Breach (Wrongfully terminates)

> *Employee's* Breach (Wrongfully quits)

(2) **Restitution**

> Only <u>employee</u> for services rendered – unless employer pre-paid

(3) **Specific Performance**

> "<u>No</u>": Employment contract

> "<u>Yes</u>": Valid covenant not to compete

Wills and Trusts

Professor Ira Shafiroff

**California Wills
Professor Ira Shafiroff
Southwestern Law School**

Introduction

There are a total of 17 concepts in the law of wills:

1. Intent
2. Mistake
3. Components of the will
4. Formalities of execution for attested wills
5. Formalities of execution for holographs
6. Choice of law
7. Codicils
8. Revocation by physical act
9. Revocation by instrument
10. Revocation by operation of law
11. Revocation by change in property holdings
12. Contracts to not revoke or make a will
13. Restrictions on testamentary dispositions
14. Intestate succession
15. Distribution of the estate: who takes?
16. Distribution of the estate: what does the beneficiary take?
17. Will substitutes

Thus, we approach wills conceptually from:
INTENT to FORMATION to REVOCATION to DISTRIBUTION

FIRST CONCEPT: INTENT

4 Issues: Capacity
                Insane delusion
                Fraud
                Undue influence

[I]   Capacity
      [A]   The capacity to make a will is the lowest capacity recognized in law.
      [B]   At the *time of execution*, testator must satisfy four elements:
           [1]   Testator must be at least 18 years of age.
           [2]   Testator must be able to understand the extent of her property.
           [3]   Testator must know the natural objects of her bounty:
                [a]

                [b]

                [c]

                [d]   And those whose interests are affected by the will.
           [4]   Testator must know the nature of her act:
                [a]   Testator must know that she is executing is a will.
                [b]   However, testator does not have to know all of the legal technicalities of the will.
                [c]   Example:

      [C]   Consequences of no capacity:
           [1]

           [2]   Property, therefore, will pass by intestate succession.
           [3]   Exception: If testator had a valid prior will that was purportedly revoked by a second will, (the one for which testator did not have capacity), then the first instrument will be probated because if testator did not have capacity, the second will could in no way have revoked the first.
      [D]   Bar exam tip:

[1]

[2]

[3] Note that the mere appointment of a conservator or diagnosis of mental disorder is not alone sufficient to show incapacity; go through the 4-prong test.

[4] Example: "Because testator was diagnosed with a mental disorder, this is relevant to establish that at the time of execution, testator did not know the natural objects of her bounty because . . . [now apply the facts]."

[II] The Insane Delusion

[A] A will can also be attacked if *at the time of execution* the testator was suffering from an insane delusion.

[B] Four elements needed to establish testator was suffering from an insane delusion:

[1]

[2]

[3] There is no evidence to support the belief, not even a scintilla of evidence.

[4] Delusion must have affected testator's will.

[C] Consequences of finding an insane delusion:

[1]

[2] As to that part, it will go to the residuary devisee, or if none, or if the residue itself was infected by the delusion, by intestate succession.

[3] What is the residuary gift?

[a] The residuary gift is that part of the will not otherwise expressly disposed of.

[b] For example, the will reads, "Blackacre to A, Whiteacre to B, and the residue to C." C is the residuary devisee. C gets the balance of testator's estate. C's gift may be worth $1 or $1 billion.

[D] Distinguish lack of capacity from a delusion:

[1]   No capacity is a very severe problem because it goes to testator's entire essence (not knowing one's spouse).

[2]   With a delusion, however, while testator has a problem, it is a narrow one and testator is otherwise perfectly normal (believing one's spouse is unfaithful).

[III]   Fraud

[A]   Elements: 5 elements to fraud:

[1]   There must be a representation;

[2]   Of material fact;

[3]   Known to be false by the wrongdoer;

[4]   For the purpose of inducing action or inaction; and

[5]   In fact induces the action or inaction desired.

[B]   Three types of fraud on the bar exam:

[1]   Fraud in the execution

[2]   Fraud in the inducement

[3]   Fraud in preventing testator from revoking the will

[C]   Fraud in the execution

[1]   Defined

[a]

[b]   Testator is given a document to sign that purportedly is non-testamentary in nature, but in fact it is, and testator signs it.

[1)]   Example: Testator is given a document to sign, purportedly a power of attorney, but in fact it is a will, and testator signs it.

[2]   Consequence of finding fraud in the execution:

[a]

[b]   Thus, the property passes by intestate succession, unless there is prior will that was validly executed.

[c]   If there was a prior will that was validly executed, the instant will, as a consequence of the fraud, could in no way have revoked the prior valid will.

[D]   Fraud in the inducement

[1]   Defined:

[2]   Example: Son learns that testator is going to soon execute a will leaving all of her property to a charity. The son approaches testator and states, "Did you hear that the FBI is investigating that charity for cheating elderly citizens out of their savings?" The son knows that this is a lie, and is doing so because the son wants testator to leave nothing to charity and everything to the son, and this is exactly what happens: Son gets everything and the charity gets nothing.

[3]   Consequence of finding fraud in the inducement:
[a]

    [b]   As to that part, the court has three options:
        [1)]   Give the property to the residuary devisees, if any; or
        [2)]   If there is no residue, to the heirs at law by intestate succession; or
        [3)]   Constructive trust remedy (see trusts lecture for a fuller discussion of constructive trusts). A constructive trust is a remedy to prevent fraud or unjust enrichment. In the scenario of fraud in the inducement, the court will deny probate to the portion of the will induced by fraud and allow the property to go either to the residuary devisees or the heirs at law (see above) *and then* make those devisees or heirs a constructive trustee. The constructive trustee has one duty: to transfer the property to the intended beneficiary, as determined by the court. Here, in the "FBI" hypothetical, the son, as the heir, will be a constructive trustee who will have only one duty—to transfer the property to the charity. Note that the constructive trust remedy is the only remedy that works here: not probating the will without more gives the son (the wrongdoer) the property by intestate succession. Hence, the constructive trust.

[4]   Distinguish fraud in the execution from fraud in the inducement:

           [a]   In fraud in the execution:

           [b]   In fraud in the inducement: Testator intends the document to be his will, however, the contents are affected by misrepresentation.

[E]   Fraud in preventing testator from revoking

    [1]   This is a variation of fraud in the inducement.

    [2]   Example: Testator's will leaves everything to son, but testator later changes her mind and wants to leave everything to charity. Due to son's fraud (the lie that the charity is being investigated by the FBI) testator does not revoke the will. Because of the fraud, there is no revocation.

    [3]   Consequence of fraud in preventing testator from revoking:

           [a]

           [b]   Simultaneously, the court also will decree that the heir is a constructive trustee who has one duty: to transfer the property to the intended beneficiary as determined by the court. Here, in the hypo above, son is a constructive trustee and charity gets the property via the constructive trust remedy.

[IV]   Undue Influence

    [A]   Defined:

    [B]   Established in three ways: On the bar exam, you always will be able to discuss the first two, and almost certainly be able to discuss all three:

        [1]   Prima Facie Case

        [2]   Presumption

        [3]   Statutory

    [C]   Prima Facie Case: 4 elements:

        [1]   Susceptibility: Testator has a weakness such that he is able to have his free will subjugated. The weakness can be anything:

           [a]

[b]

[c]

[d]   Any weakness of the testator.

[2]   Opportunity: the wrongdoer had access to the testator. If the wrongdoer is testator's friend, business associate, etc. there is always access. On the bar exam, opportunity just needs to be stated as part of the rule, but it is never an element in dispute.

[3]   Active participation (sometimes referred to as the wrongdoer having a "disposition" to exert influence): it is the wrongful act that gets the gift. Active participation can be the wrongdoer's use of force, or threat of force, or blackmail, or dragging the 90-year old testator to the wrongdoer's attorney.

[4]   An unnatural result: the wrongdoer is taking a devise, and this person ordinarily would not be expected to take a devise. Typically, it is one who has no relationship to the testator.

    [a]   Example:

[D]   Presumption: 3 elements

    [1]   A confidential relationship exists between testator and the wrongdoer.

        [a]   California recognizes all of the common law confidential relationships:

            [1)]

            [2)]

            [3)]

            [4)]

            [5)]

[b] In addition, in California, a confidential relationship arises whenever one person reposes trust in another. Thus, a confidential relationship can exist between two close friends.

[2] Active participation. See above.

[3] An unnatural result. See above.

[E] Consequences of finding undue influence (by prima facie case or by presumption):

[1]

[2] The part affected goes to:

[a] The residuary devisees if any, or, if none;

[b] To the heirs at law by intestate succession; or

[c] Via constructive trust remedy: The tainted part of the will goes to the residuary devisees, if any, or if none to the heirs at law. Simultaneously, the residuary devisees or heirs are made constructive trustees (on the ground of preventing unjust enrichment) who have only one duty: to transfer the property to the intended beneficiary.

[d] Which remedy will the court use? The one which gets the best result.

[F] Distinguish undue influence from fraud in the inducement:

[1] Fraud:

[2] Undue influence: the wrongdoer is being perfectly honest: "Leave me all your property or I will kill your family." There is honesty here, albeit a wrong.

[G] Statutory Presumption of Undue Influence

[1] California law statutorily presumes that a provision of an instrument (will, trust, or deed) making a donative transfer to the following persons is the product of undue influence:

[a] The person who drafted the instrument; or

[b] A person in a fiduciary relationship with the transferor (e.g. a trustee or lawyer) who transcribed the instrument or caused it to be transcribed; or

[c] A "care custodian" of a "dependant adult," but only if the instrument was executed during the

period in which the care custodian provided services to the transferor, or within 90 days before or after that period; or

[d]   A person who is a spouse, domestic partner, or blood relative related within the "third degree" of any person described in [a] through [c], above; or

[e]   A person who is a cohabitant or employee of any person described in [a] through [c], above;

[f]   A partner, shareholder, or employer of a law firm in which the drafter has an ownership interest.

[2]   The statutory presumption is *conclusive* with respect to a donative transfer to the person who drafted the instrument, or if the gift is to someone who is related to or associated with the drafter, as described in sections [d], [e], or [f], above. However, the statutory presumption is *rebuttable* by clear and convincing evidence with respect to a donative transfer to a fiduciary or care custodian, as described in [b] or [c].

[3]   The statutory presumption does not apply to:

[a]   A donative transfer to a person who is the spouse, domestic partner, or a cohabitant of the transferor, or to a person related by blood, within the "fourth degree," to the transferor (e.g. caregiver is transferor's spouse); or

[b]   An instrument that is drafted or transcribed by a person who is the spouse, domestic partner, or cohabitant of the transferor, or by a person related by blood, within the "fourth degree," to the transferor (e.g. drafter is transferor's adult child); or

[c]   An instrument reviewed by an independent attorney, who counsels the transferor about the nature and consequences of the intended disposition and executes a certificate stating that the attorney concludes that the disposition is not the product of undue influence; or

[d]   A transfer that does not exceed $5,000, if the estate is over $100,000 (i.e., a "small" gift when there is a "big" estate).

[4]   Consequences of finding undue influence under the statutory presumption:

[a]   The transferee is deemed to have predeceased the transferor without spouse, domestic partner, or issue. Thus, the gift "lapses" or fails, meaning that the transferee does not take.

[b]   As to that lapsed gift, it passes to the residuary devisee if any, or, if no residue, or if the lapsed gift is itself the residue, to the heirs at law by intestate succession. [See below, Fifteenth Concept in the Law of Wills, for discussion of lapse.]

[5]   Definitions

[a]   "Care custodian" is a person who provides health or social services (e.g., administration of medicine, wound care, cooking, assistance with hygiene, shopping, or companionship) to a dependent adult. The term does *not* include a person who provided services without compensation if the person had a personal relationship with the dependent adult at least 90 days before providing those services.

[b]   "Dependent adult" is a person who at the time of executing the instrument was 18 years or older and [i] was unable to provide for his or her personal needs, or [ii] due to a deficit in mental function, had difficulty managing his or her own a financial affairs or resisting undue influence.

[b]   "Degrees of relationship" from a transferor are as follows: [i] first degree: children, parents; [ii] second degree: grandparents, grandchildren, siblings; [iii] third degree: great-grandparents, great-grandchildren, aunts and uncles, nephews and nieces; [iv] fourth degree: grand nephews and nieces, first cousins, great aunts and uncles.

[H]   Bar Exam Hypo:

[1]   Invalidate the gift on three theories of undue influence:

      [a]   Prima facie case undue influence
      [b]   Presumption of undue influence
      [c]   Statutory presumption of undue influence
     [2]   Discuss all three on the bar exam

SECOND CONCEPT: MISTAKE

6 issues: Mistake in content
Mistake in execution
Mistake in inducement
Mistake in description (ambiguity)
Mistake in the validity of a subsequent testamentary instrument
(Dependent Relative Revocation)
Mistake involving living children (pretermission)

[I]   Mistake in Content
    [A]   Defined:

    [B]   Whether relief is given depends on the type of mistake: omission or addition.
        [1]   Mistake in omission: words are accidentally left out.
            [a]   Example: Testator's will states, "Blackacre to John." But testator actually wanted Blackacre to go to "John and Mary."
            [b]   No remedy is given: Mary's name is not added.
            [c]   Reason:

        [2]   Mistake in addition: words are accidentally added.
            [a]   Example: Testator wants to execute a will that says, "Blackacre to John," but the will actually reads, "Blackacre to John and Mary." This is an accidental addition.
            [b]   Remedy may be given.
            [c]   The court may strike out Mary's name.
            [d]   Reason:

[II]   Mistake in Execution
     [A]   The testator signs the wrong document.
     [B]   This occurs in one of two situations.
         [1]   First situation: Testator mistakenly signs his will believing it is a non-testamentary instrument.
             [a]   Example:

             [b]   Consequence: the will is not probated because testator did not intend the document to be a will.
         [2]   Second situation: Reciprocal wills or mutual wills: a reciprocal will or mutual will is when you have 2 testators, each with his or her own will and each leaves everything to the other.
             [a]   Example: Husband's will leaves everything to wife, and vice versa. Husband mistakenly signs Wife's will and Wife mistakenly signs Husband's will. Husband dies.
             [b]   Consequence: the court may reform the will in this unique situation of reciprocal wills, especially if the testators are Husband and Wife or domestic partners. Thus, for example, where Husband's name appears, the court will substitute the Wife's name, and vice-versa. Reasoning: it is equitable.

[III]   Mistake in Inducement
     [A]   A particular gift is made or not made on the basis of testator's erroneous beliefs.
         [1]   Example: Testator would like to leave John $1000, but does not do so because testator erroneously thinks John is dead. In fact, John is alive.
         [2]   Rule:

         [3]   Reasoning is based on maintaining the integrity of the Statute of Wills (i.e. the California Probate Code).
         [4]   Exception: Relief will be given in one narrow exception:

[5]   Example: Testator's will reads: "I leave John nothing because John is dead. But were John not dead, I would leave John $1,000." Here, both the mistake (John is dead) and what testator would have done but for the mistake (leave John $1,000) appear on the face of the will. Thus, John will take $1,000.

[IV]   Mistake in Description (Ambiguity)
[A]   Mistake in description defined:
[1]

[2]   Examples:
[a]   Two persons fit the description: "I leave my property to my cousin John." Testator has 2 cousins named John, a first cousin and a second cousin.
[b]   Two things fit the description: "I leave my beach-house to X." Testator has 2 beach houses, one on the east coast and one on the west coast.
[c]   Nothing fits the description:

[B]   Consequences of a mistake in description
[1]   Distinguish between latent and patent ambiguities.
[a]   Latent ambiguity: on the face of the will there is no problem. Everything seems fine on the face of the will. You introduce parol evidence to establish the ambiguity, then you introduce the evidence a second time to determine testator's intent (which cousin John testator meant).
[b]   Patent ambiguity: the ambiguity is apparent on the face of the will: For example, testator's will reads: "I have two cousins by the name of John; I leave $1,000 to my cousin John." Some older cases

stated that no remedy is given in the case of a patent ambiguity.

[2] Modernly, in California, by statute:

    [a] We introduce parol evidence for *any type* of ambiguity—latent or patent—to determine what testator's intent was.

    [b] So now, we would introduce parol evidence to ascertain which cousin John testator meant in the last hypothetical dealing with a patent ambiguity.

[V] Mistake in the Validity of a Subsequent Testamentary Instrument (Dependent Relative Revocation)

    [A] This is Dependent Relative Revocation (DRR)

    [B] The basis of DRR:

        [1]

    [C] A preliminary foundation to understanding DRR requires that you understand two fundamental principles:

        [1] A will can be revoked by physical act. A physical act includes burning, tearing, destroying or canceling (crossing out or lining out with a pen or pencil). Example: Testator executes a will and subsequently, with the intent to revoke it, rips it up. Testator has revoked his will by physical act.

        [2] A will also can be revoked by a subsequently executed will. Example: Testator executes Will #1. Thereafter, testator executes Will #2, which expressly revokes Will #1. Will #2 has revoked Will #1.

    [D] The heart of DRR is that [i] testator executes Will #1, [ii] then executes Will #2 and [iii] subsequently revokes Will #1, thinking that Will #2 effectuates his intent. But testator is *mistaken*. Will #2 either is invalid as a will, or, if it is valid as a will, fails to effectuate testator's intent. DRR allows the court to ignore the revocation of Will #1 on the grounds that testator revoked Will #1 because testator *mistakenly* believed Will #2 effectuated his intent.

    [E] Example:

        [1] Testator executes Will #1, a valid will. Thereafter, testator executes Will #2, which is *virtually identical* to

#1 (changes executor or makes small change in a large estate). But #2 is invalid as a will (because, for example, there is only 1 witness instead of 2). Testator mistakenly believing #2 is valid revokes #1 by physical act (e.g. by destroying it). Testator thereafter dies.

[2]   Consequences:

[a]

[b]

[c]   Consequently, in our initial analysis, testator dies intestate.

[d]   But Will #1, in fact, can be probated under DRR.

[e]   Rationale for DRR is that [i] testator simply made a mistake in the revocation of Will #1 and [ii] notwithstanding the mistake, we know what testator's intent is because testator stated his testamentary plan, not once, *but twice* (the two wills are very similar, if not identical). As between intestacy or Will #1, testator would want Will #1 probated (remember it is virtually identical to Will #2).

[F]   Rule for Dependent Relative Revocation:

[1]   If testator revokes her will, or a portion thereof,

[2]   in the *mistaken* belief that a substantially identical will or codicil effectuates her intent,

[3]   then, by operation of law,

[4]   the revocation of the first will be deemed conditional, dependent, and relative to the second effectuating testator's intent.

[5]   If the second does not effectuate testator's intent, the first (by pure legal fiction) was never revoked.

[G]   Two situations of DRR for the bar:

[1]   First situation:

        [a]   Two substantially identical wills, #1 and #2, #2 is invalid as a will, and #1 is revoked by physical act.

        [b]   Look to DRR to probate Will #1.

    [2]   Second situation:

        [a]   Testator executes Will #1 and subsequently executes Will #2 (or a codicil), which is *valid* and substantially the same as #1 and revokes #1, but #2 (or the codicil), although valid, cannot effectuate testator's intent (because, for example, of the interested witness rule, *or because there was a mistake in omission in Will #2*).

        [b]   Look to DRR to probate Will #1.

[H]   Miscellaneous matters

    [1]   Remember that Will #1 and Will #2 must be *substantially the same*. (In the case of a mistake in omission in Will #2, but for the mistake in omission, the two wills are substantially the same.)

    [2]   If Will #1 is revoked by physical act by being destroyed (thus, Will #1 no longer exists), Will #1 can still be probated under California's lost will provisions:

        [a]   These provisions state that a lost will or accidentally destroyed will can be probated if at least one witness testifies as to the terms of the will.

        [b]   The witness does not necessarily have to be one of the attesting witnesses.

        [c]   For example:

[VI]   Mistake Regarding Living Children (Pretermission)

    [A]   This is a type of pretermission problem regarding children.

    [B]   Pretermission defined:

        [1]

[2]   Rule: A child is pretermitted if born or adopted after all testamentary instruments are executed and not provided for in any testamentary instrument.

    [a]   Testamentary instrument means will, codicil, and a revocable inter-vivos trust established by testator during testator's lifetime.

    [b]   A pretermitted child takes an intestate share of the estate (which includes the assets in testator's inter-vivos trust).

[3]   Corollary: A child born or adopted before all testamentary instruments are executed and not provided for in any instrument is not pretermitted. Of course, such a child takes nothing.

[4]   Exception to corollary: A child born or adopted before all testamentary instruments are executed and not provided for in any of the instruments is treated as if pretermitted if *the only reason* the child was not provided for in the testamentary instrument is because testator erroneously thought the child to be dead or not existent—i.e. testator made a *mistake*.

[6]   On bar exam:

THIRD CONCEPT: THE COMPONENTS OF THE WILL
(WHAT MAKES UP THE WILL?)

5 issues: Integration
                Incorporation by reference
                Facts of independent significance
                Writing disposing of limited tangible personal property
                Pour-over wills

[I]   Integration
    [A]   Defined
        [1]

        [2]   If you have a will written on only one piece of paper, there is no issue of integration.
        [3]   But if testator executes a 10-page will, the question arises: what papers make up the will?
    [B]   Two elements required for papers to be integrated:
        [1]   Intent: Testator must have intended for the papers in question to be part of the will; and
        [2]   Presence: The paper must have been actually or physically present at the time of execution.
        [3]   Example: Testator goes to lawyer's office to execute his typed 10-page will. Upon reading it testator states to lawyer that page five does not manifest his intent. Lawyer tells testator to execute the will as it is, and promises tomorrow to have the secretary type a new page five which will be inserted and which will manifest testator's intent. This happens. The next day the secretary types new page five and inserts it in the will. Testator dies. What result? Answer: Only pages 1-4 and 6-10 are probated.
            [a]   Old page 5: is not probated, because it was not integrated:

        [b]   New page 5: is not probated because it was not integrated:

        [c]   What will be probated are pages 1-4 and 6-10.

   [4]   Proving integration: 2 different ways:

        [a]   Establish a physical connection among all the pages: If the papers are stapled together, it is inferred that testator intended the papers to be part of the will and were physically present at the time of execution.

        [b]   Establish a logical connection: Does the last word on page 1 make sense in relation to the first word on page 2? If so, integration is inferred.

[II]   Incorporation by Reference

   [A]   The theory of incorporation by reference is that a non-integrated writing is given testamentary effect and becomes part of the will. As such, it is now admitted into probate.

        [1]   Example: Testator's will states, "I leave my property to the grantee named on the ABC deed."

        [2]   Problem: From the 4 corners of the will, we do not know who the grantee of the deed is. Can't we always admit in parol evidence to ascertain his or her identity? No, because the integrity of the Statute of Wills (California Probate Code) would be undermined. But in this hypo, we actually can admit the deed into probate and, thus, determine who the beneficiary is. How can we do so? We can do so under the doctrine of incorporation by reference.

   [B]   Elements to incorporation by reference: Four Elements:

        [1]   A document or a writing;

        [2]   The document or writing must have been in existence when the will was executed;

        [3]   The document must be clearly identified in the will; and

        [4]   Testator must have intended to incorporate the document into the will.

        [5]

[C]   In the hypo, the deed is a writing, in existence when the will was executed, clearly identified in the will, etc. Thus, the deed will become part of the will and admitted into probate. Consequently, the grantee named in the deed can now be identified and take the devise provided for in the will.

[D]   Problem: What if in the hypo above (devising property to the grantee named on the ABC deed) the deed to be incorporated is an invalid deed?

        [1]   This is irrelevant.

        [2]   Reason:

                [a]   Thus, you can incorporate by reference an invalid deed, an invalid contract, or even an invalid will of the testator or of a third person.

[III]   Facts of Independent Significance

    [A]   Theory and definition of doctrine:

        [1]   Who a beneficiary is, or what gift is given, may be given meaning by facts of significance independent from testator's will.

        [2]   Example:

        [3]   The problem: from the 4 corners of the will we cannot determine the identity of the church. Can we admit parol evidence? Remember that we can't admit parol evidence whenever we want to because we are concerned about maintaining the integrity of the Statute of Wills (the California Probate Code).

        [4]   However, here we *will* be able to admit into evidence the identity of this church? Why?

        [5]   Because the church that testator was a member of at the time of his death is a fact of significance independent of testator's will.

        [6]   People join churches for religious reasons, social reasons, psychological reasons, etc.

[7]   But people do *not* join a church just to validate a devise in a will; they join a church for reasons *independent* of the will.

[8]   Because of these independent reasons for joining a church, there is truthfulness to such fact or act. Therefore, this fact or act is susceptible of independent verification. As such, there is no concern for fraud.

[9]   Thus, this fact of significance, the church that testator was a member of at the time of his death, will be ascertained (from records or testimony) and will be admitted into evidence in the probate of testator's will.

[10]   Summary:

[B]   When to use this doctrine:

[1]   Ask yourself this question:

[2]   In the above hypo, the answer is yes.

[3]   Example: Testator's will states, "I leave all my property to the people who are in my employ at the time of my death." Is it a fact of independent significance? Yes.

   [a]   Reason: From the 4 corners of the will we do not know who these people are. Yet, it is a fact of independent significance. Why?

   [b]   Because even without the will, these people would exist: they would be in testator's employ because people have employees for a variety of reasons: to make money, to make their job easier, etc. But people do not hire workers just to validate a devise.

   [c]   As such, we can admit this parol evidence (the people in testator's employ at the time of his death) and use these facts to fill in the blanks to testator's will.

[4]   Example: Testator's will states, "I leave my car to John." The car is fact of independent significance. At testator's death, John will take whatever car testator owned

because people own cars for many reasons, none of which have anything to do with the law of wills.

[5] The fact or act can be a future fact or act or a past fact or act.

    [a] Example: Testator's will states, "I leave all my property to people I had Thanksgiving dinner with in 1999."

    [b] This is a past fact, independent of testator's will.

[6] But consider this hypo, where neither incorporation nor independent significance will work:

    [a] Example:

    [b] Incorporation by reference will not work because the note was not in existence at the time the will was executed.

    [c] Independent significance will not work because without the will, this note would not exist. The note is not a fact of *independent* significance.

[IV] Writing Disposing of Limited Tangible Personal Property

    [A] Effective for decedents dying on or after January 1, 2007, under new California Probate Code section 6132, a writing, whether or not it can be incorporated by reference or is a fact of independent significance, may be admitted into probate and, thus, given testamentary effect.

    [B] 4 elements needed under section 6132:

        [1] First Element: The writing must be (i) referred to in the will, (ii) dated, and (iii) either signed or handwritten by the testator (but even if the writing is not dated or neither handwritten nor signed by the testator, the writing can still be admitted into probate and given testamentary effect if extrinsic evidence establishes the testator's intent regarding disposition of the items described in the referenced writing);

        [2] Second Element: The writing must describe the items and recipients (beneficiaries) with reasonable certainty;

        [3] Third Element: The writing may be executed *before or after* the will;

[4]   Fourth Element: The writing directs the disposition of tangible personal property (*excluding* cash and property used primarily in a trade or business) valued, at the time of testator's death, at not more than $5,000 per item and not more than $25,000 *in the aggregate*.

[5]   Example: Testator's will states: "I give my car to the person who is identified on a note I executed yesterday." The writing (i.e. the note), signed and dated by testator, states: "2003 Honda CR-V: Mary Jones." At the time of testator's death, the car is not business property and is worth not more than $5,000. On the bar exam, discuss whether the writing can be admitted into probate, thus allowing Mary to take the gift, on three theories (discuss all three):

[a]   Incorporation by reference: We have a writing, in existence when the will was executed, clearly identified in the will, and intended by testator to be incorporated. Thus, incorporation works.

[b]   Facts of independent significance: Apart from the will, the note has no significance. While the car can be a fact of independent significance, the name of the beneficiary clearly is not. Thus, this is just a variation of, "I leave all my property to the people I will name on a note tomorrow" (see handout, above, discussing facts of independent significance). In short, but for the will, this note would not exist. Thus facts of independent significance will not work.

[c]   Section 6132: Irrespective of incorporation and independent significance, the writing is referred to in the will; dated, and signed by the testator; describes the property and the recipient with reasonable certainty; and is personal tangible property not used in testator's business worth not more than $5,000. Thus, section 6132 works.

[C]   If the value of an item of tangible personal property described in the writing exceeds $5,000, that item is not subject to section 6132 and that item passes to the residuary clause of the will (and if none, by intestate succession). Such an item is not counted towards the $25,000 limit.

[D]   If any person designated to receive property in the writing dies before the testator, the property passes as directed in the writing and, in the absence of directions, the disposition lapses. See below for lapsed gifts.

[E]   Note: The testator may make subsequent handwritten or signed changes to any writing (no witnesses are required for this). If there is an inconsistent disposition of tangible personal property as between writings, the last writing controls.

[V]   Pour-Over Wills
  [A]   The problem:
    [1]   Example: On January 1, testator executes a document creating the ABC Trust, an inter-vivos trust (an inter-vivos trust in this context is a trust created by testator during testator's lifetime). On January 2, testator executes his will. In the will, testator devises part or all of his estate, "To the trustee of the ABC Trust, to be administered pursuant to the terms of that trust." Testator dies. What we have here is a "pour-over will." That means that part or all of testator's estate is devised to the trustee of the inter-vivos trust, to be administered pursuant to the terms of that trust.
    [2]   But appreciate the problem that we have in the above hypo:
      [a]   Who is the trustee of this trust?
      [b]   Who are the beneficiaries?
      [c]   What are the terms of the trust?
      [d]   From the four corners of the will, we do not know. And remember, generally speaking, we cannot just admit parol evidence whenever we want to because we are concerned with maintaining the integrity of the Statute of Wills, that is, the California Probate Code.
  [B]   How, then, do we validate the pour-over provision? (That is, how do we get the trust instrument admitted into probate?) There are three ways.
    [1]   Incorporation by reference:
      [a]

      [b]

[c]

[d]

[e]   Thus, the trust instrument will be admitted into probate and the pour-over provision will be validated.

[2]   Independent Significance:

[a]   Even without the will, we would still have this inter-vivos trust.

[b]   The trust instrument, therefore, is a fact of significance *independent* from the will.

[c]   Thus, the pour-over provision can be validated on this theory, too.

[3]   Uniform Testamentary Additions To Trusts Act (UTATA):

[a]   So long as you have a valid trust, which was in existence before the will was executed, or at the time of execution, the pour-over provision is valid by statute.

[b]   The pour-over provision is valid simply because the statute says it is valid.

[C]   Example: On January 1 testator creates the inter-vivos trust. On January 2 testator executes the will, devising part or all of her estate to "the trustee of the ABC Trust, to be administered pursuant to the terms of the trust." On January 3, testator modifies the trust. Thereafter, testator dies.

[1]   How do we validate the pour-over provision?

[a]   Incorporation will *not* work:

[b]   Facts of independent significance works: The trust as modified is still a fact of significance independent from the will. Even without the will, there would be this trust.

[c]   UTATA works: Under the act, a pour-over provision is valid even if the trust is subsequently modified. Why? Because the statute says so.

[2]   On the bar exam, discuss *all three theories* for a pour-over situation.

[3]   Note: It is *highly unlikely* that California Probate Code section 6132 (dealing with a writing that disposes of limited amounts of personal property; see above) would ever apply to validate a pour-over situation on the bar exam. The reason is that for section 6132 to apply, we would need the *highly unusual* fact pattern of a trust instrument which has a corpus of not more than $25,000 of non-business, non-cash personal property with individual items not exceeding $5,000. In the highly unlikely event that you get a pour-over situation with such facts, then you also would validate the pour-over provision by discussing section 6132 (in addition to incorporation by reference, independent significance and UTATTA). But, again, this is an unlikely factual scenario on the bar exam.

FOURTH CONCEPT: FORMALITIES OF EXECUTION FOR ATTESTED OR FORMAL WILLS (WITNESSED WILLS)

3 Issues: Elements for an attested will
              Interested witness problem
              Conditional wills

[I]   Elements for an Attested Will (5 elements, the "traditional formalities"):
    [A]   The first element:

    [B]   The second element: The will must be signed by one of the following three people:
        [1]   Testator
            [a]   Nicknames ("Dad") are okay.
            [b]   "X" is okay if testator is illiterate.
        [2]   A third person, in testator's presence and at testator's direction. This arises if testator is incapacitated.
        [3]   By a conservator pursuant to a court order
    [C]   The third element: The signing by testator, the third person, or the conservator must be done in the presence of two witnesses, both present at the same time.
        [1]   What if testator had previously signed alone or in the presence of just one of the witnesses? Does testator have to sign again in the presence of the two witnesses? The answer is no.
        [2]   In such case, testator simply *acknowledges* his signature ("This is my signature") or *acknowledges* the will ("This is my will"), in the presence of the two witnesses, both present at the same time.
    [D]   The fourth element: The witnesses must sign the will during the testator's lifetime.
    [E]   The fifth element:

[F]   NOTE: For testators dying *on or after* January 1, 2009
        (irrespective of when the will was executed), California's "clear
        and convincing" standard applies if the will does not satisfy
        elements 3, 4, or 5, of the "traditional formalities" approach,
        above. In such case, the will can still be admitted into probate if
        the proponent of the will establishes by "clear and convincing
        evidence" that at the time the testator signed the will, he or she
        intended the will to constitute his or her will. [Note that this
        clear and convincing standard is *not* the same as the Uniform
        Probate Code's "harmless error" rule.]

        [1]   Example 1: re element 3 (T must sign or acknowledge in
                the presence of 2 witnesses, both witnesses present at the
                same time): T signs his will in the presence of Witness #1
                only. The next day, T acknowledges his will or signature
                in the presence of Witness #2 only. Thereafter, T dies.
                On these facts, T did not execute his will in compliance
                with the "traditional formalities," discussed above.
                Nonetheless, if the proponent of the will can establish by
                clear and convincing evidence that T intended the will to
                be his will when T signed it, the will is admitted into
                probate.

        [2]   Example 2: re element 4 (witnesses must sign during T's
                lifetime): T signs his will in the presence of the 2
                witnesses, but the witnesses forget to sign the will. T
                thereafter dies. The witnesses sign *after* T's death. On
                these facts, T did not execute his will in compliance with
                the "traditional formalities" discussed above. But again,
                if the proponent of the will can establish by clear and
                convincing evidence that T intended the will to be his
                will when T signed it, the will is admitted into probate.

        [3]   Example 3: re element 5 (witnesses understand that the
                document they sign is T's will): T, without declaring the
                document to be his will, signs his will in the presence of
                the 2 witnesses, but only Witness #1 understands that the
                document is T's will; Witness #2 signs the document but
                does not know what the document is. T thereafter dies.
                Again, the will was not executed in compliance with the
                "traditional formalities" but if the proponent can establish
                by clear and convincing evidence that that T intended the

29

will to be his will when T signed it, the will is admitted into probate.

[G] Approach for formalities of execution on the California Bar Exam:

[1] First, always analyze the problem under the "traditional formalities" as indicated in [I][A]-[E], above.

[2] Second, if there is a problem with compliance under the "traditional formalities" approach for elements [I][C]-[E] (elements 3, 4, or 5), then use the "clear and convincing" standard for elements, *but only if the testator died on or after January 1, 2009.*

[3] Note that the clear and convincing standard *cannot* be used for [I][A]-[B] (elements 1 or 2).

[4] Note also that it is not fully clear if the "clear and convincing" standard applies to codicils. On the bar exam, if you have a codicil that presents a witness execution problem (*and* the testator died on or after January 1, 2009), handle the problem as you would for a will: [i] first apply the traditional formalities analysis, [ii] and then apply the clear and convincing standard.

[H] Note the following in California (under even the more rigorous traditional formalities standard):

[1] The witnesses do not have to sign in the presence of each other.

[2] The witnesses do not have to sign in the presence of testator.

[3] Testator does not have to declare to the witnesses, "this is my will" because California does not have a so-called "publication" requirement. Nonetheless, something about the execution process must convey to the witnesses the information necessary for them to understand that the document being signed is the testator's will. (But even if the witnesses do not understand that the document is testator's will, for testators dying on or after January 1, 2009, under the new "clear and convincing" standard, this should not be a problem.)

[4] Neither testator nor the witnesses have to sign at the end of the will: Signing *anywhere* on the will is okay in California.

[5]   But must the Testator sign the will before the witnesses sign? Typically, chronologically speaking, the normal course of events is that testator signs the will and *then* the witnesses sign the will. But what if the witnesses sign the will before the testator signs? The California statute is ambiguous as to whether the testator must sign before either or both of the witnesses.

    [a]   Some courts in other jurisdictions have construed similar state statutes as implicitly imposing a requirement that the testator sign first.

    [b]   More recent cases in other jurisdictions, however, have held that even if the witnesses sign first, the will is still valid so long as the testator signs before either witness leaves the room.

    [c]   On the bar exam, for testators dying *before* 2009, if you get a hypo where the witnesses sign before the testator, tell the bar examiners the following: "If there is no issue of fraud or mistake, the will should be deemed valid under California's 'substantial compliance' doctrine (that is, if there is no fraud or mistake, the will is validly executed if there is substantial compliance with the Probate Code, even if not literal compliance)."

    [d]   For testators dying *on or after* January 1, 2009, in addition to the preceding analysis, *also* tell the bar examiners that if the proponent establishes by clear and convincing evidence that T intended the will to be his or her will, the document is admitted into probate.

[I]   Meaning of "presence"

    [1]   Testator must sign or acknowledge in the "presence" of two witnesses. What means presence? It means one of two things:

        [a]   Sight presence: The witnesses see testator sign; or

        [b]   Conscious presence: Testator signs or acknowledges within the witnesses hearing and the witnesses know what is being done.

        [c]   But note, that for testators dying on or after January 1, 2009, the failure of the testator to sign or acknowledge in the presence of two witnesses

31

does not mean that the will cannot be probated; such a will still may be admitted into probate under the "clear and convincing" standard, discussed above.

[II]   Interested Witness
    [A]   Interested witness defined:
        [1]

    [B]   Consequences of finding an interested witness:
        [1]

        [2]   But unless there are two other disinterested witnesses, a presumption arises that the witness-beneficiary secured the gift by wrongdoing.
        [3]   If witness-beneficiary rebuts the presumption of wrongdoing, no problem: witness-beneficiary takes the gift.
        [4]   If witness-beneficiary cannot rebut the presumption of wrongdoing, he or she takes the amount as does not exceed what would be given by intestacy.
        [5]   Example: Gift is $1000 and intestacy would be $600. If the presumption is not rebutted, witness-beneficiary takes $600.
    [C]   The presumption of wrongdoing is inapplicable if witness-beneficiary is taking only in a fiduciary capacity.
        [1]   Example:

[III] Conditional Wills
    [A]   Defined
        [1]   A conditional will is one whose validity is made conditional by its own terms.
        [2]   Example: Testator's will states:

[3]   The will is to be probated only if the condition is
         satisfied: that testator die in Europe on his vacation.

[B]   Conditional wills can be formal (attested) wills or holographic
         wills.

FIFTH CONCEPT: FORMALITIES OF EXECUTION FOR HOLOGRAPHIC (HANDWRITTEN) WILLS

3 Issues: Elements for a valid holograph
             Testamentary intent
             Dates

[I]   Elements for a Valid Holograph (2 elements):
    [A]   First element:

           [1]   The signature can be anywhere in the will.
           [2]   As to what constitutes a signature, see rules regarding attested or formal wills, above.
    [B]   Second element:

           [1]   The "material provisions" are:
               [a]   the gifts made, and
               [b]   the beneficiaries' names.
           [2]   Example of material provisions: Testator's will states, "$1000 to Mary Smith."
               [a]   The gift ("$1,000") and the name of the beneficiary ("Mary Smith") are what must be in testator's handwriting.
               [b]   Introductory clauses: are not material terms.
               [c]   Appointment of an executor: is not material because the court can appoint an administrator.
               [d]   If witnesses sign, their signatures are superfluous and, therefore, irrelevant.

[II]   Testamentary Intent
    [A]   In a holographic will, a statement of testamentary intent ("This is my last will") need not be on the face of the will and in testator's handwriting.

[B]   There are, however, three problems related to a statement of testamentary intent:

    [1]   What if testator signs and executes a writing that lists just the names of people and next to each name, an asset that testator owns?

        [a]   Is this a holographic will, or is it just a list?

        [b]   Extrinsic evidence is admissible to determine testator's testamentary intent.

        [c]   For example:

    [2]   What if testator writes a series of letters?

        [a]   Is this just a series of letters, or is it a holographic will?

        [b]   The series of letters can constitute one will under *integration*.

        [c]

    [3]   What if the testamentary intent ("this is my last will and testament") is part of a commercially printed form will?

        [a]   The California Probate Code expressly states this is not a problem.

        [b]   "Any statement of testamentary intent contained in a holographic will may be set forth either in the testator's own handwriting or as part of a commercially printed form will." [Cal. Prob. Code section 6111(c).]

[III]   Dates

    [A]

    [B]   But lack of a date can create a problem with:

        [1]   Inconsistent wills; and

        [2]   Capacity.

    [C]   Problem of lack of dates and inconsistent wills:

[1] If an undated holograph is inconsistent with the provisions of another will (either a dated holographic will, a dated witnessed will, or an undated witnessed will), the undated holograph is invalid *to the extent of the inconsistency*—unless the undated holograph's time of execution is established to be after the date of execution of the other will.

  [a] What if there are two undated holographs?

  [b] If you can't establish which one came last, neither holograph is probated *to the extent of the inconsistency.*

[D] Problem of lack of dates and capacity

  [1] If a holograph is undated, and if it is established that the testator lacked testamentary capacity at any time during which the will *might have been executed*, the holograph is invalid—unless it is established that it was executed at a time when the testator had testamentary capacity.

SIXTH CONCEPT: CHOICE OF LAW

2 issues: Illustration of the problem.
               Can the will be admitted into probate in California?

[I]   Illustration of the Problem
     [A]   Example:
          [1]   Testator is a domiciliary of New York. Testator goes to North Carolina to have his will executed. Thereafter testator becomes a domiciliary of California and dies here in California.

[II]   Can the Will be Admitted into Probate in California?
     [A]   Is testator's s will deemed valid with respect to the formalities of execution so that it can be admitted into probate in California?
     [B]   The will can be admitted into probate in California if *any one* of the following three rules is satisfied:
          [1]   If the will complies with California's formalities of execution, the will is admitted into probate in California.
          [2]   If the will does not comply with the formalities of execution under California law, but it complies with the formalities of execution of the *place where the will was executed*, the will is admitted into probate in California. Thus, if the will complies with the formalities of execution under North Carolina law, the will is admitted into probate in California.
          [3]   If the will does not comply with any of the above but it complies with formalities of execution of the *place where testator is domiciled at the time of execution*, the will is admitted into probate in California. Thus, if the will complied with the formalities of execution under New York law, the will is admitted into probate in California.
     [D]   Summary: The will is admitted into probate in California if the will complies with the formalities of execution of:
          [1]

[2]

[3]

SEVENTH CONCEPT: CODICILS

3 issues: Defined
Republication
Revocation of codicils

[I]   Defined
    [A]

[II]   Republication
    [A]   Defined:
        [1]   A codicil republishes a will. This means that a codicil causes the will to speak from the date that the codicil is executed on (also called "down-dating").
        [2]   On the bar exam, republication comes into play in two scenarios: [i] pour-over wills and incorporation by reference and [ii] pretermission problems.
    [B]   Pour-over wills and incorporation by reference:
        [1]   Example: On January 1, testator executes an inter-vivos trust. On January 2, testator executes a will with a pour-over provision. On January 3, the trust is amended.
        [2]   On these facts, incorporation by reference will *not* work because the trust as modified was not in existence when the will was executed.
        [3]   New fact added:

        [4]   Because the codicil republishes the will, the codicil causes the will to speak from January 4.
        [5]   Thus, incorporation by reference now works because the trust as modified was in existence on the date that the will is deemed executed, which now is January 4.
    [C]   Pretermission problems:

[1] Example: Year 1 the will is executed (everything to charity). Year 2 child is born or testator marries or enters into a domestic partnership (child, spouse, or domestic partner is pretermitted). Year 3 a codicil is executed which republishes the will.

[2] Because the codicil republishes the will, the will now speaks from Year 3.

[3] As such, there is no pretermission because the birth, marriage, or domestic partnership is deemed to have taken place before the will was executed.

[4] Note that there is an *alternative* theory to prevent pretermission on the facts given in the above example: Because a codicil *is itself* deemed to be a testamentary instrument, the birth of the child or marriage or domestic partnership took place *before* the codicil was executed. This alone (without any discussion of republication) precludes the finding of a pretermission.

[5] On the bar exam, when you have a pretermission problem and a subsequent republication of the will by the codicil, discuss *both* theories to preclude an omitted child, spouse, or domestic partner from taking under our pretermission laws: [a] the codicil republished the will, *and*, in the alternative, [b] the codicil itself is a testamentary instrument, thus the birth, marriage, or domestic partnership took place *before* the codicil (testamentary instrument) was executed, consequently precluding any pretermission attack by the child, spouse, or domestic partner.

[III] Revocation of Codicils
 [A] Rules regarding revocation of codicils:
  [1] If testator executes a will, then executes a codicil, and subsequently revokes his codicil, there is a rebuttable presumption that testator intended to revoke only his codicil.
  [2] On the other hand, if testator executes a will, then executes a codicil, and testator subsequently revokes the will, there is a rebutable presumption that testator intended to revoke the will *and* codicil.

EIGHTH CONCEPT: REVOCATION BY PHYSICAL ACT

4 issues: Elements
              Cancellations & Interlineations
              Duplicate wills
              Mutilated wills

[I]   Elements for Revocation by Physical Act (3 elements):
        [A]   First Element: Will must be burned, torn, cancelled, destroyed
                or obliterated.
                [1]   Cancellation: lining out or crossing out with a pen or
                        pencil.
                [2]   Obliteration:

        [B]   Second Element: Testator must have the simultaneous intent to
                revoke.
                [1]   If testator accidentally destroys his will, thereafter finds
                        out about it and says, "That's okay because I wanted to
                        revoke it anyway," the will is *not* revoked.
                [2]   Reason:

        [C]   Third Element: The act must be done either by testator, or by
                some one in testator's presence and at his direction.
                [1]   For what means "presence," see discussion above in
                        Fourth Concept : Formalities of Execution for a Formal
                        Will.

[II]   Cancellations and Interlineations
        [A]   Definitions
                [1]   Cancellation: crossing out or lining through.
                [2]   Interlineation:

        [B]   Example: Testator executes a typed formal (attested) will that
                states, "I leave $1,000 to Mary." Testator then takes his pen,

41

crosses out the $1,000 and interlineates "$1,500" just above the $1,000. Testator signs his name. Question: Do we have a holographic codicil on top of a formal will? Answer: No.

[1]   The $1,500 gift is invalid as a holograph because the material provisions (gifts and names of the beneficiaries) are not in testator's own handwriting.

    [a]   The gift ($1,500) is in testator's own handwriting.

    [b]   But the name of the beneficiary (Mary) is not in testator's own handwriting: "Mary" is typed.

    [c]   Moreover, the $1,000 gift has been revoked by physical act (cancellation).

    [d]   Mary, therefore, takes nothing.

[2]   But in a little twist to our traditional view of dependent relative revocation (DRR) (we previously stated that the two documents must be very similar), we can save Mary's gift so that Mary takes the original $1,000:

    [a]   The revocation of the $1,000 was conditional, dependent, and relative to the $1,500 being effective.

    [b]   Because the $1,500 was not effective, by operation of law, the $1,000 was never revoked.

    [c]   Put another way, would testator rather Mary take nothing or $1,000? Clearly, testator would rather Mary take $1,000. Why? Because testator has indicated that he would want Mary to take $1,500. If Mary can't take $1,500, let her at least take $1,000.

[3]   But compare: If the original gift to Mary was $1,500 and testator cancelled this out and the interlineation was $1,000, can DRR be used to give Mary the original $1,500?

    [a]   When the interlineation is *less than* the cancelled provision, DRR will not be used.

    [b]   Mary will take nothing.

[C]   Example: Testator executes a *holographic will* that states, "I leave $1,000 to Mary." Testator then takes his pen, crosses out the $1,000 and interlineates just above the $1,000, "$1,500." (Note that for this hypo we can even stipulate that testator does *not* sign his name again.)

[1]   On these facts, we have a revocation of the $1,000 by physical act (crossing out) and a *valid* new disposition: Mary takes the $1,500. Why?

[2]   Because testator's prior signature is deemed *adopted* at the time the interlineation is made and all the material terms are in T's own handwriting.

[D]   Cancellation to increase a gift is prohibited.

[1]   Rule:

[2]   Example: "I leave my farm to X and Y." Testator subsequently cancels out Y's name. What does X take?

[a]   X takes ½ of the farm.

[b]   The other ½ goes to the residuary devisees or, if none, by intestacy.

[E]   An interlineation or other handwritten addition to a typed (attested) will that does not qualify as a holographic codicil may nonetheless be a valid cancellation.

[1]   Example: Testator executes a valid typed formal will. Subsequently testator writes "Null and Void" across the face of the will.

[a]   Without a signature accompanying this "Null and Void" addition, the addition cannot be deemed a holographic codicil to the typed formal will.

[b]   Nonetheless, writing "Null and Void," even without a signature, is a valid cancellation of the typed formal will.

[III] Duplicate Wills

[A]   Understanding the problem:

[1]   What we are talking about here is duplicate originals, *not* a photocopy of the signatures.

[2]   Illustration: Testator and witnesses sign the will, then they do it again on a duplicate original. Thus, testator signs and witnesses sign on duplicate #1; then they sign again on duplicate #2. Consequently, there are 2 sets of original signatures.

[B]   Rule

[1]   If testator, or someone in testator's presence and at his direction, revokes by physical act one of the duplicate originals, then the other duplicate original also is revoked, as a mater of law.

[2]   The term "presence" here is defined in the same manner as in the Fourth Concept: Formalities of Execution.

[IV]   Mutilated Wills

[A]   Problem: What is the consequence of finding a will in a mutilated condition?

[1]   If a will is found in a mutilated condition at testator's death, and when last seen it was in testator's possession, there is a rebutable presumption:

[2]   Example: Testator has a safety box in a bank, and is the only one with access. At testator's death the will is found to be in a mutilated condition. It is presumed that testator mutilated the will with the intent of revoking the will.

NINTH CONCEPT: REVOCATION BY SUBSEQUENT WRITTEN INSTRUMENT

2 Issues: Manner of revoking
              Revival

[I]   Manner of Revoking
      [A]   Question: How many ways can Will #1 be revoked by Will #2?
            Answer: Two ways: Express and Implied.
            [1]   Express revocation:
                  [a]   Will #1 can be revoked by Will #2 if Will #2
                        expressly revokes Will #1.
                  [b]   Example: If Will #2 states, "I hereby revoke all
                        previously executed wills," then Will #1 is
                        revoked.
            [2]   Implied revocation:
                  [a]

                  [b]   If Will #2 totally disposes of all of testator's estate,
                        there is nothing for Will #1 to act upon.
                  [c]   Thus, by implication, Will #2 has revoked Will #1.

[II] Revival
      [A]   Revival can be best understood by examining the concept
            within the two situations in which revival can arise.
            [1]   Situation #1: Revocation by physical act.
                  [a]   Example: Testator executes Will #1. Testator
                        thereafter executes Will #2, which revokes #1
                        (expressly or impliedly). Testator thereafter
                        revokes #2 by physical act (example, by
                        cancellation or tearing).
                  [b]   Issue: In Situation #1, is Will #1 automatically
                        revived—restored or back in operation?
                  [c]   In California, Will #1 is *not* automatically revived;
                        rather, Will #1 is revived only if testator manifests
                        an intent to revive Will #1. Oral statements by

testator at the time Will #2 was revoked are admissible. Thus, when testator revokes Will #2 and states, "Now Will #1 is back in operation," then Will #1 is revived. But if testator states, "Now everything is back the way I want it," this is not clear: Is Will #1 is back in operation, *or* does testator mean that now he dies with no will?

[2]   Situation #2: Revocation by subsequent instrument.

    [a]   Example: Testator executes Will #1.Testator subsequently executes Will #2, which revokes Will #1 (expressly or impliedly). Testator subsequently revokes Will #2 by codicil.

    [b]   Issue: Is Will #1 automatically revived, that is, restored or back in operation?

    [c]   In California:

TENTH CONCEPT: REVOCATION BY OPERATION OF LAW

4 issues: Omitted child
Omitted spouse
Omitted domestic partner
Final dissolution of marriage or domestic partnership

[I]   Omitted or Pretermitted Child
    [A]   Definition, Consequence, and Exceptions
        [1]   Defined:

                [a]   Testamentary instrument includes [i] a will, [ii] a codicil, or [iii] a revocable intervivos trust created by the decedent during decedent's lifetime.
        [2]   Consequence of finding an omitted child: Child receives a share of the decedent's estate equal in value to that which the child would have received if the decedent had died without ever having executed any testamentary instrument (will, codicil, or intervivos trust). Thus, to put it more plainly, the child receives an intestate share of assets decedent owned at death *plus* the assets held in any intervivos trust.
                [a]   For the child to take this statutory share, other gifts will have to be abated or reduced.
                [b]   Hence, revocation by operation of law.
        [3]   3 Exceptions: if any of the following exceptions exist, the child will not take this statutory share:
                [a]   First exception:

[1)] Example: Testator's will states, "I presently have no children, but if I ever do, they are to take nothing." The intent to disinherit appears from the will itself. Thus, any after-born child takes nothing.

[b] Second exception: At the time of execution of the testamentary instrument, the decedent had one or more children and transferred by will or revocable inter vivos trust substantially all of his estate to the parent of the omitted child.

[1)] Example: Testator and X have a child, C1. Testator executes a will and leaves substantially all of his estate to X. Testator and X now have C2. Testator dies. Analysis: C1 is not pretermitted because C1 was born before the will was executed. Moreover, C2 will take nothing: When the will was executed, Testator already had one child, C1, and gave substantially all of his estate to the parent of the omitted child, X. The plan is clear: X will take financial care of all children that Testator and X have together.

[c] Third exception: The decedent provided for the child by transfer outside the testamentary instrument with the intention that the transfer is to be in lieu of any testamentary provision.

[1)] Example:

[II] Omitted Spouse
  [A] Definition, Consequences, and Exceptions
    [1] Defined:

[a] Testamentary instrument includes [i] a will, [ii] a codicil, or [iii] a revocable intervivos trust created by the decedent during the decedent's lifetime.

[2] Consequence of finding an omitted spouse: spouse receives a statutory share of the decedent's estate equal in value to that which the spouse would have received if the decedent had died without ever having executed any testamentary instrument (will, codicil, or intervivos trust). Thus, to put it more plainly, the omitted spouse receives a statutory share of assets decedent owned at death *plus* the assets held in any revocable inter vivos trust. This statutory share that the omitted spouse receives is as follows:

[a] The one-half of the community property owned by the decedent at death or in any revocable inter vivos trust (thus, because the omitted spouse already owned the other one-half, the omitted spouse now ends up with 100% of the community property).

[b] The one-half of the quasi-community property owned by decedent at death or in any revocable inter vivos trust (thus, because the omitted spouse already owned the other one-half, the omitted spouse now ends up with 100% of the quasi-community property).

[c] A share of the separate property of the decedent equal in value to that which the spouse would have received if the decedent had died without ever having executed any testamentary instrument (will or trust), but in no event is the share to be more than one-half the value of the separate property in the estate.

[3] For the omitted spouse to take this statutory share, other gifts will have to be abated (reduced).

[4] Hence, revocation by operation of law.

[5]   3 Exceptions: If any apply, the omitted spouse will not take the aforementioned statutory share:

      [a]   First exception:

            [1)]   Example: Testator's will states, "I presently am not married, but if I ever do marry, my spouse is to take nothing from my will." The intent to disinherit appears from the will itself. Any person testator subsequently marries takes nothing.

      [b]   Second exception: Decedent provided for the spouse by transfer outside of the testamentary instruments with the intention that the transfer be in lieu of any testamentary provision.

            [1)]   Example: After decedent and spouse marry, decedent purchases an annuity for the spouse. In such case, decedent has provided for the spouse in lieu of any testamentary instrument. The spouse does not take anything else.

      [c]   Third exception: Omitted spouse signed a waiver.

[6]   Waiver

      [a]   Waiver defined:

      [b]   What can be waived?

      [c]   Any and all probate rights can be waived: the right to take a probate homestead, a family allowance, an intestate share, and any other probate transfer rights, *including* the right to take as an omitted spouse.

[7]   3 elements for a waiver:

[a] Waiver must be in writing, signed by the waiving spouse before or during marriage; and

[b] Full disclosure by decedent of decedent's finances; and

[c]

[1)] But even if there is no disclosure by the testator or independent counsel by the waiving spouse, the waiver still is enforceable if [i] the waiving spouse had or should have had knowledge of the testator's finances, or [ii] if the waiver was in fact fair.

[2)] Example of fair waiver: Waiving spouse gave up $100,000 worth of rights at the time waiver was executed and received $100,000.

[3)] But in no event will the waiver be enforced if the waiver is:

[III] Omitted Domestic Partner

 [A] Domestic partners defined:

  [1] Partners must be [i] of the same sex, or [ii] of the opposite sex and at least one person is at least 62 years of age, AND

  [2] Partners must have filed a declaration of domestic partnership with the Secretary of State.

 [B] Recent legislation gives domestic partners the same rights and obligations as married persons.

 [C] Thus, domestic partners may hold property as community property or quasi-community property.

 [D] Consequently, the rules for omitted domestic partners are the same as for omitted spouses.

[IV] Final Dissolution of Marriage or Domestic Partnership:

 [A] Four rules regarding testamentary gifts:

  [1] By operation of law, there is a revocation of the devise to the spouse or domestic partner if there is an annulment or

final dissolution of marriage, or termination of domestic partnership.

[2]

[3] The devise is reinstated if the will is unchanged and the testator remarries the former spouse, or reestablishes another domestic partnership with the former domestic partner.

[4] These rules do not apply if the will expressly states otherwise:

[a] Example:

ELEVENTH CONCEPT: REVOCATION BY CHANGE IN PROPERTY HOLDINGS (ADEMPTION)

4 issues: Classification
Ademption by extinction
Ademption by satisfaction
Advancements

[I]   Classification of 4 types of gifts:

    [A]   Specific devise:

        [1]   A specific devise is a gift of a particular item.

        [2]   There is something unique about it.

        [3]   Testator must have the *intent* the beneficiary take this particular thing, and nothing else. Because testator is dead, we must look to objective manifestations of testator's intent.

        [4]   Examples:

            [a]

            [b]

            [c]   "100 shares of my Xerox to Bob" is specific because of the word, "my," indicating something unique. Although publicly traded stock typically is a general gift (discussed below), by stating "100 shares of *my* Xerox to Bob," testator has attached some uniqueness to it. So, too, if testator listed the serial numbers of the shares.

            [d]   "100 shares of Amalgamated Fuzz to Bob" is a specific gift if Amalgamated Fuzz is a closely held corporation: if not publicly traded, there is a uniqueness to the gift.

    [B]   General devise:

        [1]   A general devise is payable out of the general assets of the estate.

        [2]   There is nothing unique or special about this gift.

[3]   Example:

[4]   This a general gift because there is nothing unique about publicly traded stock.

[5]   In a general devise, the executor can make good the gift to the beneficiary by giving beneficiary either the 100 shares of Microsoft or the fair market value of 100 shares of Microsoft as measured by its value at the time of testator's death.

[C]   Demonstrative devise:
[1]

[2]   It is a gift from a particular fund, but if that is not enough, the executor can resort to general property.

[3]   Example: "To John I leave $1000 from my account at Bank of America." If there is only $900 in the account at the Bank of America, this is how the executor pays John:

[a]   First from the account at the Bank of America ($900)

[b]   Then the balance ($100) comes from general assets if necessary.

[D]   Residuary devise:
[1]   All other property not expressly disposed of in the will. It is easy to recognize.

[2]   Examples:
[a]

[b]

[E]   Why classify gifts? Three reasons:
[1]   For ademption by extinction problems: Only specific gifts adeem by extinction. Thus, if a gift is classified as general, there is no issue of ademption by extinction.

[2]   For ademption by satisfaction problems: Typically, only general gifts adeem by satisfaction: (You can have a specific gift adeem by satisfaction, too, but this is not common. See below).

[3]   For abatement problems: There is a priority whereby gifts to beneficiaries have to be cut back or abated to come up with the statutory share for the omitted child or omitted spouse or omitted domestic partner.

[F]   Note: It is easy to classify a residuary gift or demonstrative gift. Thus, on the bar exam, the fight is always about whether the gift is specific or general.

[II]   Ademption by Extinction

[A]   Common law test: Ademption by extinction is when a specific gift fails because testator did not own the property at testator's death.

[1]   It was a simple mechanical test.

[2]   If the testator did not own the specific property at his death, the gift failed, or adeemed by extinction.

[3]   Thus, intent was important only for determining whether gift was general or specific.

[B]   California: Intent is important not just for determining whether a gift is general or specific, but a *second time* in determining whether testator intended the gift to fail.

[1]   There may be situations where testator does not own the property at death, but testator did not intend the gift to fail.

[2]   Thus, in California, we do not use a simple mechanical test.

[C]   There is no ademption by extinction in California in the following situations. The common thread is that testator did not *intend* the gift to fail:

[1]   Securities changing form: This arises because of mergers, stock splits, stock dividends, or reorganizations of corporations and stock is re-issued.

[a]   Example: Testator devises a specific gift of 100 shares of ABC stock to beneficiary. Thereafter, during testator's lifetime, there is a reorganization or merger so that the 100 shares of ABC stock are exchanged by the corporation for 1000 shares of XYZ stock. When testator dies, testator owns 1000 shares of XYZ stock.

[b] In California, there is no ademption by extinction. Beneficiary takes the 1000 shares of XYZ stock. Why?

[c]

[2] Conservator sells off the assets.
  [a] Example: Testator devises Blackacre (a specific gift) to beneficiary. Thereafter, a conservator is appointed and, with court approval, the conservator sells off Blackacre.
  [b] In California, there is no ademption by extinction. Beneficiary takes the net sales price of Blackacre. Why?
  [c]

[3] Eminent domain award, casualty award, or an installment sale of property in which testator holds the deed of trust as security for the sale.
  [a] In California, there is no ademption by extinction with respect to the eminent domain proceeds, insurance proceeds, or installment payments paid *after* testator's death.
  [b] What about those proceeds paid during testator's lifetime? See if you can trace.
  [c] If you can trace the proceeds into one bank account (especially if there were no other transactions in that bank account outside of that initial deposit from the eminent domain award, casualty award, or installment sale) then the beneficiary may argue that by making the proceeds easily traceable, testator intended no ademption by extinction. Testator intended beneficiary to take all the proceeds, even those payable during testator's lifetime.
  [d] If tracing is not possible, then you probably have an ademption by extinction with respect to those proceeds paid during testator's lifetime.

[4] In all other situations:

[a]

[b]

[III] Ademption by Satisfaction
[A] Definition:

[1] Example: Testator executes his will leaving a $1,000 devise to beneficiary. Testator later goes to beneficiary and says, "I've left you a $1,000 devise in my will. But why should you have to wait for me to die? Here is $100 on account."

[a] If we conclude that the $100 is a satisfaction, then when testator dies, beneficiary will not receive the $1,000 per the will.

[b] Rather, beneficiary will take only $900.

[B] How to establish a satisfaction: 4 alternative ways:
[1]

[2] Testator declares in a contemporaneous writing that the gift is a satisfaction.

[3] Beneficiary acknowledges in a writing (at any time) the satisfaction.

[4] The property given in the satisfaction is the same property that is the subject of a specific gift to the beneficiary. This is an ademption by satisfaction and *also* by extinction, because the property no longer exists in testator's estate.

[C] What if beneficiary receives a satisfaction but predeceases the testator?

[1] Rule: Where the issue of the predeceased beneficiary takes the devise under the anti-lapse statute (see below), the issue of the predeceased beneficiary is treated as if he or she had received the satisfaction, unless testator's will or contemporaneous writing states otherwise.

[2]   Example: Testator devises $1000 to his brother, Abel. Testator subsequently makes a satisfaction of $700 to Abel. Abel predeceases testator. Abel is survived by a son, Baker. Unless testator's will or contemporaneous writing states otherwise, Baker takes only $300 ($1,000-700).

[D]   How to value the satisfaction if not made in cash?

    [1]   If the value of the satisfaction is expressed in the contemporaneous writing of the testator or in a contemporaneous writing of the beneficiary, that value is conclusive.

    [2]   In all other cases, the property is valued at its fair market value, measured at time the transferee came into possession of the property.

[IV]   Advancements

[A]   Definition: Recall that a satisfaction is an inter-vivos down payment on a devise. An advancement is similar:

    [1]   Thus, a satisfaction deals with a testacy situation (decedent dies with a will), whereas an advancement deals with an intestacy situation (decedent dies without a will).

    [2]   The concept is identical and the rules for advancements are nearly the same as for the rules for satisfactions.

    [3]   Example: Intestate goes to the heir-apparent and states, "When I die you will inherit approximately $1,000 from me. But why should you have to wait. Here is $100 on account."

        [a]   Assuming that a $100 advancement has been made, when the intestate dies, the heir will not inherit the full $1,000.

        [b]   Rather, the heir will inherit $900. Why?

        [c]   Because the heir has received this down payment of $100 during the lifetime of the intestate.

[B]   Establishing an advancement: 2 alternative ways:

[1]   Intestate declares in a contemporaneous writing that the gift is an advancement.

[2]   Heir acknowledges in a writing (at any time) that the gift is an advancement.

[C]   What if heir-apparent receives an advancement but predeceases the Intestate?

[1]   The issue of the heir-apparent is *not* treated as having received an advancement, unless the advancement provides otherwise.

[2]   This is the opposite of a satisfaction.

[D]   How to value the advancement if not made in cash?

[1]   If the value of the advancement is expressed in the contemporaneous writing of the intestate or in a contemporaneous writing of the heir-apparent, that value is conclusive.

[2]   In all other cases, the property is valued at the fair market value at time the time the transferee (heir) came into possession of the property.

TWELFTH CONCEPT: CONTRACTS (TO MAKE A WILL OR DEVISE, OR TO NOT MAKE A WILL OR DEVISE)

5 issues: Scenario
Requirements
When the cause of action accrues
Joint and mutual wills
Remedies available to promisee

[I]   Scenario
    [A]   Example: Testator executes a will that states, "I leave Blackacre to Abel." Can testator revoke the gift and execute another will leaving Blackacre to Baker?
        [1]

        [2]   But what if there is a contract between testator and Abel, providing that testator will not revoke his will?
        [3]   In such case, if testator revokes, testator is in breach of contract and, upon testator's death, Abel may sue testator's estate for breach of contract.

[II]   Requirements for a Contract to Not Revoke (or to Make a Will)
    [A]   Five alternative ways in California:
        [1]   The will or other instrument (e.g. a trust) states the material provisions of the contract.
            [a]   Example: Testator's will states: "In consideration of the $5000 Abel has given me, I have promised to devise Blackacre to Abel, and I hereby do devise Blackacre to Abel."
        [2]

            [a]   In such case, the terms of the contract may be established by extrinsic evidence, including oral testimony.

        [b]   Example: Testator's will states, "Pursuant to my contract, this is my will."
- [1)]   What are the terms of the contract?
- [2)]   Who is the promisee?
- [3)]   What consideration was given?
- [4)]   Is the entire will affected by the contract, or only certain provisions?

        [c]   The point is that because there is express reference in the will to a contract ("Pursuant to my contract, this is my will"), the terms of the contract (Blackacre to Abel) can be established by extrinsic evidence, and that evidence is not limited to written evidence. It can include oral testimony. Thus, in this regard, the statute of frauds is *not* a problem, and this is so even if the subject matter of the contract is real property.

    [3]   There is a writing signed by the decedent evidencing a contract.

    [4]   There is clear and convincing evidence of an agreement between decedent and promisee that is enforceable in equity. (This is estoppel.)

    [5]   There is clear and convincing evidence of an agreement between decedent and a third person for the benefit of the claimant that is enforceable in equity. (This is estoppel, too.)

[III]   When the Cause of Action Accrues
    [A]   General Rule
        [1]

        [2]   Rationale: No cause of action arises at the time of breach because a moment before decedent dies, decedent can execute a new will which would be in compliance with the contract. In such case, the promisee has no damages.

    [B]   Exception to the general rule:
        [1]   The cause of action accrues during decedent's lifetime if the decedent is engaging in conduct which would be a fraud on the promisee.

        [2]   Example: Testator enters into a contract with Abel to devise Blackacre to Abel. Thereafter, testator prepares to sell Blackacre with the intent to dissipate the funds.

              [a]   On these facts, Abel may be irreparably harmed if the sale goes through.

              [b]   Consequently, Abel may be able to secure an injunction to either prevent the sale of the property or, failing that, to enjoin testator from dissipating the funds from the sale.

[IV]   Joint and Mutual Wills

    [A]   Definitions

        [1]   Joint Will:

              [a]   The provisions do not have to be reciprocal.

              [b]   When the first person dies, the will is probated. When the second person dies, the will is probated again.

        [2]   Mutual Wills (also known as Reciprocal Wills):

              [a]   Example: Husband and Wife execute their own separate wills. Husband leaves everything to Wife. Wife leaves everything to Husband.

        [3]   Joint and Mutual Wills: Reciprocal provisions on one instrument.

    [B]   Rules

        [1]   The execution of a joint will, or mutual will, or a joint and mutual will does *not* create a presumption of a contract to not revoke or make a will.

        [2]   But it may be evidence of a contract, in conjunction with other factors.

[V]   Remedies Available to Promisee

    [A]

[B] Specific performance: plaintiff can seek to force the executor to comply with the terms of the contract.

[C] Constructive trust remedy: the court can probate the will as it is, giving the property to the devisee, and make the devisee a constructive trustee, who will have only one obligation: to transfer the property to the promisee of the contract.

THIRTEENTH CONCEPT: RESTRICTIONS ON TESTAMENTARY DISPOSITIONS

3 Issues: Definitions
Spousal/domestic partner protection
Unworthy heirs or beneficiaries

[I]   Definitions
    [A]   Community Property
        [1]   Defined by way of exclusion:
        [2]   All property acquired during marriage or domestic partnership while domiciled in California that is not separate property.
    [B]   Separate property
        [1]   Property that is acquired before marriage or domestic partnership, and during marriage or domestic partnership by gift, bequest, devise, and descent, together with the rents, issues, and profits thereof.
    [C]   Quasi-Community Property
        [1]   All personal property wherever situated, and all real property situated in California, acquired by a decedent while domiciled elsewhere that would have been community property if the decedent had been domiciled in this state at the time of its acquisition.
        [2]   In the absence of death or divorce or termination of domestic partnership, it is treated as separate property of the acquiring spouse or the acquiring domestic partner. [Note that the probate definition for quasi-community property is different from the definition for divorce. For divorce purposes, quasi-community property is all real property, wherever located. For decedents' estates purposes, quasi-community property is limited to real property located in California.]

[II]   Spousal/Domestic Partner Protection
    [A]   Protection is given to the surviving spouse or domestic partner based upon our community property system.
    [B]   Four rules to protect the surviving spouse or domestic partner.

[1] Protection regarding community property:

[a] Testator can dispose of only ½ of the community property (surviving spouse or surviving domestic partner owns the other half).

[2] Protection regarding quasi-community property:

[a] Testator, assuming testator is the spouse or domestic partner who acquired the quasi-community property, can dispose of only ½ of the quasi-community property (surviving spouse or surviving domestic partner owns the other half at death of testator).

[b] Note that the non-acquiring spouse or domestic partner has no testamentary power to dispose of the acquiring spouse's or domestic partner's quasi-community property during the lifetime of the acquiring spouse or domestic partner.

[3] Widow's election (which includes a widower and a surviving domestic partner):

[a] Arises when testator attempts to dispose of more than ½ the community property or ½ the quasi-community property.

[b] In such case, the widow (or widower or surviving domestic partner) may invoke the widow's election. This means that:

[c] The survivor may accept the gift given in testator's will in lieu of his or her statutory right (½ community property and ½ quasi-community property); this is called taking "under the will."

[d] Or, the survivor can renounce all benefits given in the will and confirm his or her rights to ½ the community property and ½ quasi-community property; this is called taking "against the will."

[e] Example: Husband's will states:

[f] In the above example, Wife can take under the will and accept the will's provisions (give up her ½ of the community property and take all of Husband's

separate property), or take against the will (renounce the separate property gift and retain her ½ interest in community and quasi-community property).

[4] Protection regarding illusory transfers of quasi-community property and the widow's (or surviving domestic partner's) election:

[a] General rule: An inter-vivos transfer by the decedent (the acquiring spouse or the acquiring domestic partner) of the quasi-community property to a third person without consideration *is* allowed.

[b] Reason:

[c] Exception to rule: The transfer will *not* be allowed, however, when the transfer of the quasi-community property is deemed illusory and the surviving spouse or domestic partner invokes the widow's election.

[d] The transfer is deemed illusory when the decedent (the acquiring spouse or acquiring domestic partner) retained some interest or control over the property. The interest can be an ownership interest, a use, or a co-tenancy.

[e] In such case, upon the death of the decedent (the acquiring spouse or domestic partner), the surviving spouse or domestic partner may require the transferee to restore ½ of the quasi-community property to the decedent's estate.

[III] Unworthy Heirs or Beneficiaries: Killers

[A] Certain killers cannot take any benefits under the will or by intestacy. Which killers?

[B] Those who feloniously and intentionally kill the decedent.

[C] Proof needed:

[1] A conviction (which includes a plea of guilty) is conclusive.

[2] In all other cases, the probate court determines guilt by a preponderance of the evidence.

[D] Consequence of finding that the killing was felonious and intentional:

[1] Killer is deemed to have predeceased the decedent, and the anti-lapse statute does not apply.

[2] See below for the anti-lapse statute.

[3]

[E] Problem of one joint tenant feloniously and intentionally killing the other joint tenant:

[1] There is a severance of the joint tenancy so that the killer does not have a right of survivorship.

[2] But note, the killer does not lose his or her ½ interest in the property.

[F] Problem of a beneficiary feloniously and intentionally killing the insured:

[1]

FOURTEENTH CONCEPT: INTESTATE SUCCESSION

6 issues: Surviving spouse/domestic partner
                All others
                Per capita/representation
                Adopted children
                Non-marital children
                Half-bloods

[I]   Surviving Spouse/Domestic Partner
     [A]   Community Property: Surviving spouse or domestic partner inherits decedent's ½ of the community property.
          [1]   Note surviving spouse or domestic partner already owned ½ of the community property.
          [2]   Thus, the surviving spouse or domestic partner ends up with 100% community property.
     [B]   Quasi-Community Property: Surviving spouse or domestic partner inherits decedent's ½ of the quasi-community property.
          [1]   Note the surviving spouse or domestic partner owned ½ quasi-community property at decedent's death.
          [2]   Thus, the surviving spouse or domestic partner ends up with 100% of the quasi-community property.
     [C]   Separate Property: Surviving spouse or domestic partner inherits decedent's separate property as follows:
          [1]   If decedent leaves no issue, parents, brother or sister, or issue of a deceased brother or sister, all to surviving spouse or domestic partner.
          [2]   If decedent is survived by one child, or issue of a predeceased child, ½ to surviving spouse or domestic partner and ½ to child or child's issue.
          [3]   If decedent is survived by 2 or more children, or issue of predeceased children, 1/3 to surviving spouse or domestic partner and 2/3 to the children or their issue.
          [4]   If decedent is survived by no issue, but leaves parent or parents or their issue, then ½ to parent or parents or their issue, ½ to surviving spouse or domestic partner.

[II] All Others (Intestate Leaves No Surviving Spouse or Domestic Partner)
   [A] Intestate scheme
      [1]

      [2]

      [3]

      [4]

      [5]

      [6] Issue of a predeceased spouse or domestic partner:
         [a] Definition of a predeceased spouse or domestic partner: a spouse or domestic partner who died while married to or in partnership with the decedent; it is *that* spouse's or domestic partner's issue, i.e., decedent's former step-children.
      [7] Next of Kin
      [8] Parents of a predeceased spouse or domestic partner: This is the decedent's former in-laws.
      [9] Issue of parents of a predeceased spouse or domestic partner.
      [10] Escheat

[III] Per Capita/Representation Problem
   [A] Whenever issue take by intestacy, or if a will or trust provides for issue to take without specifying the manner, they take in the manner provided in section 240 of the Probate Code. This means:
      [1] Issue of the same degree take "per capita," or equally and in their own right.
         [a] Example: X (Intestate) has children A, B, and C and they are all alive at X's death. Each child takes takes 1/3, per capita, meaning each takes equally and in his or her own right.
      [2] Issue of more remote degree take "per capita with representation."

[a]   Example: X has 2 children: A and B. Both predecease X. A leaves child C, who survives X. B leaves children D and E. D survives X, but E predeceases X. E leaves children F and G, both of whom survive X.

[b]   Under section 240, we make our distribution [i] at the first level someone is living and give shares to all living people at that generation, *and* [ii] to deceased members of that generation who leave issue.

[c]   Thus, in our hypo, because no one is alive at A and B's level, we drop to down to C's level to begin making our distribution. C is alive, as is D. So we allocate a share for C and a share D. We also allocate a share for E because, while E is dead, E has left issue, F and G. Thus, we allocate a total of three shares: to C, D, and E. Thus, we give: 1/3 to C; 1/3 to D; and 1/3 for E, whose share will be split between F and G (1/6 each). C and D each take 1/3 per capita (in their own right), while F and G step into the shoes of E and take E's share by right of representation.

[B]   If a will or trust calls for a distribution "per stirpes" or "by right of representation," or by "representation," we make a different distribution.

[1]   Such terminology requires a "strict per stirpes" distribution , as per section 246 of the Cal. Prob. Code.

[2]   That means you make the distribution at the first generation or first level, even if everyone is dead, so long as they left issue. The issue then step into the shoes of their predeceased ancestor.

[a]   Example: In the above example, we make our distribution at the first level, even if everyone is dead.

[b]   Thus, we allocate a share for A and a share for B: C, therefore takes ½, while D and E split ½ (each take ¼). F and G then split E's ¼ share between them. Thus, at the end, C takes ½, D takes ¼, and F and G split ¼ (⅛ each for F and G), all taking "per stirpes."

[IV] Adopted Children
      [A]

      [B] Regarding the adopted child's natural parents, the adoption
           severs the relationship.
           [1] Exception: The relationship to the natural parent is not
                severed if the adoption is by the spouse or domestic
                partner of the natural parent, or after the death of either
                of the natural parents.
                [a] Example: H1 marries W. They have a child C. H1
                     dies. W marries H2. H2 adopts C. C inherits not
                     just from W and H2, but also from H1's line.
      [C] As to stepchildren or foster children
           [1] The child is treated as having been adopted if 3 elements
                are satisfied:
                [a] The relationship began during the child's minority;
                [b] It continued throughout the parties' lifetimes; and,
                [c] It is established by clear and convincing evidence
                     that the stepparent or foster parent would have
                     adopted but for a legal barrier.
                [d] Example of a legal barrier:

      [D] Equitable adoption
           [1] Also known as adoption by estoppel.
           [2] Arises when the parties hold themselves out as parent and
                child.

[V]   Non-Marital Children
      [A] In California, marital status of the parents is irrelevant.
      [B] The key is whether a parent-child relationship existed,
           irrespective of marital status.
      [C] In a domestic partnership, a parent-child relationship is
           established as to the non-birthing partner by means of one of
           several presumptions:

[1] A child born during the domestic partnership is presumed to be the child of the non-birthing domestic partner.

[2] If the non-birthing domestic partner and the birthing domestic partner formed (or even just attempted to form) a domestic partnership in a lawful manner *after* the child's birth and [i] the non-birthing domestic partner is named on the birth certificate, or [ii] the non-birthing domestic partner makes a voluntary promise to pay child support or is ordered to do so by a court, then a parent-child relationship is presumed to be established between the child and the non-birthing domestic partner.

[VI] Half bloods
[A] Defined: Relatives who have only 1 common parent, and not 2.
[B] Example: Half-siblings
[C] Rule: Relatives of the half blood inherit the same as the whole blood.

FIFTEENTH CONCEPT: DISTRIBUTION OF THE ESTATE: WHO CAN TAKE?

3 Issues: Posthumous Children
Lapse and anti-lapse
Simultaneous death

[I]   Posthumous children
    [A]   A posthumous child is a child conceived during the lifetime of the intestate or testator, but born after the death of the intestate or testator.
    [B]   Posthumous children are deemed heirs of the intestate and beneficiaries of testator's will.

[II]   Lapse and Anti-Lapse
    [A]   For a beneficiary to take a devise, beneficiary must survive the testator; dead people do not take. This is common sense. This brings us to the rule of lapse, and the anti-lapse statute
    [B]   Rule of Lapse:
        [1]   If it is required that the beneficiary survive the testator, what happens if the beneficiary predeceases the testator?
        [2]   Example:

            [a]   What happens to A's gift?
            [b]   It is distributed under the rule of lapse.
        [3]   Rule of lapse: If the beneficiary does not survive the testator, beneficiary's gift lapses, or fails. Thus, if a gift lapses, unless a contrary intent is expressed in the will, the gift falls into the residue, if there is one; if it is already part of the residue, it goes to other co-residuary devisees. Otherwise, the gift goes by intestacy.
    [C]   Anti-Lapse Statute:
        [1]   If the anti-lapse statute applies, the rule of lapse will not apply.
        [2]   California's Anti-Lapse Statute: Applies only if the devisee who predeceased the testator was "kindred" of

the testator, or kindred of a surviving, deceased or former spouse or domestic partner of the testator, and this predeceased devisee leaves issue. In such case, the issue of that predeceased devisee will step into the shoes of that predeceased devisee.

[3]   Example:

[4]   In the absence of a contrary provision of the will, the gift to the brother will not lapse but go to the issue of the brother.

[5]   Note: For the anti-lapse statute to apply, devisee must be "kindred" (blood relative) of the testator or testator's spouse or domestic partner—but the devisee cannot be the spouse or the domestic partner.

[6]   Note also: the issue of the predeceased devisee who take under the anti-lapse statute take in the manner provided in section 240: those of the same degree take "per capita," while those of more remote degree take by "per capita with representation" (see above for discussion).

[7]   In California, both the rule of lapse and the anti-lapse statute applies to wills *and also* to revocable trusts.

[8]   In California, the anti-lapse statute also applies to class gifts. Example: Testator executes a will devising Blackacre "to my children." At the time the will was executed, Testator had three children, A, B, and C. After Testator's will is executed, C predeceases Testator. C leaves children C1 and C2. Thus, at Testator's death, the survivors are: A, B, C1, and C2. Under California's anti-lapse statute, C's gift does not lapse; rather, C1 and C2 take C's devise. Thus, A gets 1/3, B gets 1/3, and C1 and C2 take C's 1/3 (C1 and C2 each taking 1/6).

[III]   Simultaneous Death
    [A]   Recall that under the rule of lapse, dead people cannot take by will or trust or intestacy.
    [B]   Simultaneous death involves the following problem: If the devolution of property is dependent on one person surviving another, and it cannot be determined by clear and convincing

evidence who survived whom, then it is deemed the one person did not survive the other. This is the Uniform Simultaneous Death Act which California has adopted.

[C]   Its application can be best understood in the following 5 situations:

[1]   Testator and devisee die under circumstances of simultaneous death, a plane crash, for example. You cannot tell by clear and convincing evidence that devisee survived the testator—not even for one second. If you can establish by clear and convincing evidence that devisee survived testator for even a second, devisee takes. But if you cannot so establish by clear and convincing evidence that devisee did survive testator, the Uniform Simultaneous Death Act provides that devisee is deemed to have predeceased the testator. Thus, the devisee will not take. What will happen to the gift? The gift will either lapse (see above), or be distributed under California's anti-lapse statute.

[2]   A and B, are joint tenants with right of survivorship, and die under circumstances of simultaneous death: you cannot tell by clear and convincing evidence who survived whom. In such case, you sever the joint tenancy: ½ the joint tenancy property goes to A's estate and ½ the joint tenancy property goes to B's estate.

[3]   Spouses or domestic partners have wills and own community property or quasi community property and die under circumstances of simultaneous death: you cannot tell by clear and convincing evidence who survived whom. In such case the community property and quasi-community property will be severed:

[a]   ½ community property and ½ quasi-community property will be distributed through one spouse's or one domestic partner's estate; and

[b]   ½ the community property and ½ quasi-community property will be distributed through the other spouse's or the other domestic partner's estate.

[4]   A life insurance policy and the insured and beneficiary die under circumstances of simultaneous death: you cannot tell by clear and convincing evidence that the

beneficiary survived the insured. What happens in such case? If it cannot be so established that the beneficiary survived the insured, then the beneficiary is deemed not to have survived the insured. What happens?

[a]   See if there is an alternative beneficiary named.

[b]   If there is no alternative beneficiary, the policy proceeds are paid to the insured's estate: to the residuary devisees in the will if there are any, but if none, the proceeds will go to the insured's heirs.

[c]   But Note: if the policy premiums are paid for with community property or quasi-community property and the insured and beneficiary are spouses or domestic partners, then ½ the proceeds go to the husband's or one domestic partner's estate, and ½ the proceeds go to the wife's or the other domestic partner's estate.

[5]   The intestate and heir die and the 120-hour rule: Here the rule is a little different. For any heir to take, the heir must survive the intestate by 120 hours. If it cannot be determined by clear and convincing evidence that the heir has survived the intestate by 120 hours, it is deemed that the heir did not survive the intestate, and the heirs are determined accordingly. This 120-hour rule does not apply if the property would escheat.

SIXTEENTH CONCEPT: DISTRIBUTION OF THE ESTATE: WHAT DOES A BENEFICIARY TAKE?

5 issues: After-acquired property
              Increase during Testator's lifetime
              Increase after Testator's death and during probate
              Abatement
              Exoneration

[I]   After-Acquired Property
        [A]   A will passes all property the testator owned at death, including after-acquired property.
        [B]   After-acquired property defined:

        [C]   Example: In 1990, testator executes a will leaving, "All of my estate to Mary." At the time the will was executed, testator's net worth is $1,000. When testator dies in 2003, testator has a net worth of $1 million. Because a will can dispose of after-acquired property, Mary will take the full $1 million, not just the $1,000 or the property owned by testator at the time the will was executed.

[II]   Increase During Testator's Lifetime
        [A]   Rule: Stock dividends or splits paid during testator's lifetime go to the beneficiary if the stock is owned by testator at testator's death.
        [B]   Example:

                [1]   Beneficiary gets the 100 shares and the stock dividends.
                [2]   Note that for purposes of this rule, it does not matter whether the shares are general or specific.

[III]   Increase After Testator's Death and During Probate
        [A]   Regarding specific devises, all increase goes to the beneficiary:

[1]

[2]

[3]

[4]   Cash dividends
[5]   Interest on indebtedness

[B]   As a general rule, general devisees do not receive any increase.
   [1]   Exception: General pecuniary gifts (gifts expressed in a dollar amount, such as "$10,000 to Abel,") earn interest on such gifts not distributed one year after testator's death. Thus, for example, if testator died January 1, 2005 and the estate was not distributed until June 30, 2006, general devisees would receive interest for six months (from January 1, 2006 though June 30, 2006). The interest received is a formula based on the legal rate.

[IV]   Abatement
[A]   Defined:

[B]   When abatement arises:
   [1]   When it is necessary to pay for the share of the omitted child or omitted spouse or omitted domestic partner.
   [2]   When there is an omitted child or omitted spouse or omitted domestic partner, the gifts of devisees have to be decreased to come up with the statutory share of the omitted child or omitted spouse or omitted domestic partner.
   [3]   Thus, whenever you have an omitted child or omitted spouse or omitted domestic partner, there will almost certainly be the related issue of abatement.

[C]   Order of abatement for omitted children and omitted spouses and omitted domestic partners:
   [1]   First abate property not passing by the decedent's will *or* revocable inter-vivos trust.

[2] Then abate from all beneficiaries of testator's will *and* revocable inter-vivos trust pro rata, in proportion to the value of the gift received.

    [a] Example: An estate is valued at $90,000. Testator had three children: A, B, and C. A and B were provided for in the will and given $45,000 each. Child C was pretermitted. C's statutory share is $30,000 (1/3 of $90,000). A and B will have their gifts abated by $15,000 each.

[3] No distinction is made between specific, general, and residuary gifts.

[4] Exception for specific gifts: the court can exempt the specific gift if abating the specific gift would defeat the *obvious intention* of the testator. This obvious intention must appear from the language in which the specific devise is created, or from the general terms of the will or trust.

    [a] There are no cases indicating what means "obvious intention."

[5] Note that there is no favoring of relatives over non-relatives.

[6] Note that the order of abatement for omitted children and omitted spouses and omitted domestic partners is *not* the order of abatement to pay off *general debts* of the decedent. The order to pay off *general debts* of the decedent is: [i] intestate property; [ii] residuary gifts; [iii] general gifts to non-relatives; [iv] general gifts to relatives; [v] specific gifts to non-relatives; [vi] specific gifts to relatives. To the extent they can be satisfied from the designated fund, demonstrative gifts are treated as specific gifts.

[V] Exoneration
    [A] Defined:

    [B] Common law view: If testator devised a specific gift subject to an encumbrance (e.g. a mortgage) for which testator was personally liable, the executor was required automatically to pay off the debt before passing the property to the beneficiary.

[C]   California view:

[1]   In California, the devisee takes the specific gift subject to the encumbrance, unless the testator's will states that the specific gift is to be exonerated. Moreover, a general direction "to pay all my just debts" is not sufficient to exonerate. If the gift is exonerated, in the absence of a contrary intention in the will, other specific gifts do not abate.

SEVENTEENTH CONCEPT: WILL SUBSTITUTES

2 issues: Gifts causa mortis
              Totten trusts

[I]   Gifts causa mortis
    [A]   Defined:

    [B]   Property that can be the subject of a gift causa mortis: personal property only; no gifts of real property.
    [C]   Donor must make a delivery of the property to donee.
        [1]   Delivery can be one of three forms: Actual, symbolic, or constructive delivery.
            [a]   Actual delivery or manual delivery: The corpus itself is transferred to donee. Example: $1,000 cash is given to donee.
            [b]   Symbolic delivery: Something representative of the corpus is given to the donee. Typically it is a writing evidencing ownership. Example: Cash is not available for a manual delivery, but giving the donee a bank document evidencing ownership of the account, such as the quarterly statement of interest earned in the account.
            [c]   Constructive delivery:
                [1)]   Common law view: what is given to the donee is a key, that unlocks a box or room, in which is located the corpus, which is too big or bulky for a manual delivery. The key can be literal, or figurative, such as a treasure map that would lead one to the buried treasure. Thus, the heart to a common law constructive delivery is the opening of access to a room wherein is the corpus, that is that is too big, or bulky, or otherwise unavailable.
                [2)]   Modern view: A constructive delivery

will be found whenever the donor has done everything possible to effectuate a delivery, and there is no issue of fraud and mistake.

[D]   If donor survives the peril, the gift is revoked by operation of law.

[II]   Totten Trusts

[A]   Later in Trusts lecture.

Trusts Lecture
Professor Ira Shafiroff
Southwestern Law School

INTRODUCTION

Ten concepts in the law of trusts:

1. Private Express Trust
2. Charitable Trust
3. Pour-over wills
4. Miscellaneous trusts
5. Restraints on Alienation
6. Resulting Trusts
7. Constructive Trusts
8. Trustee Powers and Duties
9. Modification and Termination of Trusts
10. Income v. Principal Problems

FIRST CONCEPT: PRIVATE EXPRESS TRUST

7 issues: Private express trust defined
              Property of the trust, or corpus
              The beneficiary
              The trustee
              Manifestation of intent
              Creation
              Legal purpose

[I]   Private Express Trust Defined
      [A]   A fiduciary relationship with respect to property whereby one person, the trustee, holds legal title for the benefit of another, the beneficiary, and which arises out of a manifestation of intent to create it for a legal purpose.

[II]   Property of the Trust
      [A]   Rule: Any presently existing interest in property that can be transferred can be the corpus of a trust.
      [B]   Examples:
           [1]

           [2]

           [3]

           [4]

           [5]

      [C]   Illusory interests cannot be the subject matter of a trust.
           [1]   Examples:
                [a]   Future profits to a business.
                [b]   A debt that settlor owes beneficiary is not property and cannot be the corpus of a trust; a debt is a liability, not property.

[c]   A mere expectancy: what settlor expects to inherit or receive as a gift because a mere expectancy is not property.

[III] The Beneficiary (i.e. Who Can Be the Beneficiary of a Private Express Trust?)

[A] Rule: Any ascertainable person or group of people can be the beneficiary of a private express trust. Person includes a legal person.

[1] Corporations can be the beneficiary of a private express trust.

[2] Unincorporated associations

[a]   Common law: unincorporated associations could not be the beneficiary of a private express trust.

[b]   Modern law: an unincorporated association can be the beneficiary of a private express trust.

[3] Class gifts are valid, but watch out for a class that is too big. For example, all of the people of the state of California is too big; even if ascertainable it simply cannot be administered. But it might be a charitable trust (see below).

[4] A child conceived when the interest was created and later born is deemed an ascertainable person.

[5] Watch out for a violation of the Rule Against Perpetuities:

[a]   Example:

[b]   B's interest can vest 10,000 years from now, which is certainly more than any life in being plus 21 years. Hence, B's interest is stricken. A is left with a fee simple (and, as you will see later, the trust may be terminated because A is the only beneficiary of the trust).

TRUSTS

[IV] Trustee
  [A] Rule: A trust must have a trustee, but the court will not allow the trust to fail solely because there is no trustee or a trustee refuses to serve.
  [B] The court, in such case, will appoint a trustee.
  [C] Until a trustee is appointed, the settlor or the settlor's estate will hold legal title.

[V] Manifestation of Trust Intent
  [A] There must be *present* manifestation of trust intent made by the settlor. You cannot manifest an intent for a trust to arise in the future.
  [B] No magic words, however, are needed to create a trust. Settlor does not have to use the words "trust," "trustee," or "beneficiary."
  [C] Although no magic words are needed to create a trust, precatory words, by themselves are not sufficient to create a trust.
    [1] Precatory words defined:
      [a]

      [b] Precatory words are not mandatory words, which is required for a trust.
    [2] Example 1: S gives $100,000 to his brother, with "the direction and order that he use it for my sister."
      [a] The words are mandatory, not precatory.
      [b] As such, a trust has clearly been created.
    [3] Example 2: S gives $100,000 to his brother, "with the hope and desire that he will use it for my sister."
      [a]

      [b] The words used are not mandatory; they are precatory.
      [c] Precatory words by themselves are not sufficient to create a trust.
    [4] Example 3: Same facts as in Example 2, but add this fact: S was supporting his sister before transferring the money to the brother, but stopped supporting his sister after the money was transferred to the brother.
      [a]

[b] Here, in Example 3, that S stopped supporting sister after the transfer to the brother would be probative to show that S intended the money to be used in trust for the benefit of the sister, and that S was merely using his words imprecisely and did intend to create a trust.

[5] If you conclude that the words are precatory and the parol evidence is not sufficient to cause a trust to be created, then the transferee owns the property in fee simple.

[D] Trusts of personal property do not have to be in writing. The Statute of Frauds applies only to real property.

[VI] Creation: How to Create a Private Express Trust

[A] Two time frames are important: A trust created to take effect at settlor's death and during settlor's lifetime.

[1] Trust created to take effect at settlor's death:

[a] If settlor wants to create a trust to take effect at settlor's death, the only way settlor can do that is by complying with the Statute of Wills, i.e. the local probate code. Thus, our settlor is really a testator. Thus, a part of testator's will has a provision for a testamentary trust, a trust which will take effect at testator's death.

[b] Example: Testator's will states:

[2] The other time frame settlor can create a trust is during his lifetime: If settlor wants to create a trust to take effect during his lifetime, there are two ways to accomplish this: Transfer in Trust and Declaration in Trust.

[a] Transfer in Trust: In a transfer in trust, a third person is the trustee. [i] For a trust of *real property*, the settlor must execute and deliver a deed transferring title to the trustee. The writing requirement is due to the Statute of Frauds. [ii] For a trust of *personal property*, there must be delivery

5

to the trustee of the trust property at the time settlor manifests the intent to create the trust. The delivery can be actual, symbolic or constructive. (See discussion regarding gift causa mortis in the wills lecture for types of delivery). Note: If there is no delivery to trustee, there is no trust. Moreover, a promise to deliver the corpus in the future is *not* a delivery.

[b]   Declaration in Trust: Settlor herself is the trustee. [i] In a declaration of trust for *real property*, again, there must be some writing satisfying the Statute of Frauds indicating that settlor also is the trustee. [ii] In a declaration in trust of *personal property*, because the settlor is the trustee, there is no issue of delivery: One cannot deliver property to oneself. So if settlor is going to be the trustee in a declaration in trust of personal property, the only thing we have to look to is the present manifestation of trust intent. Example: Settlor executes a trust instrument that states:

[VII] Legal Purpose
   [A]   Rule: A trust may be established for any legal purpose.
   [B]   What if the trust is for an illegal purpose or, if not illegal, violative of public policy? In such case, distinguish between illegality at creation from illegality subsequently after creation.
      [1]   Illegality at creation: try to excise the bad from the good. If you can, the trust will stand.
         [a]   Example:

         [b]   Such a trust is violative of public policy.
         [c]   Result: Court will excise illicit condition. Thus, Abel would take the trust free of the condition.

[2] Illegality at creation: If it is not possible to excise the illicit condition and sever the good from the bad, the court has two options: the court will do whatever achieves the best result:

[a] First option of the court: Simply invalidate the trust at its inception. Thus, the trust is not recognized. Settlor remains the owner of the property.

[1)] Example:

[2)] Analysis: The court will invalidate the trust, so that settlor's creditors can attach the assets.

[b] Second option of the court: Allow the trustee to keep the property for himself or herself.

[1)] Reason:

[3] Illegality after creation: If a trust becomes illegal after creation, a resulting trust is decreed. We discuss resulting trusts in depth later. But for now it is sufficient to state that a resulting trust is an implied in fact trust based on the presumed intent of the parties. Once a court decrees a resulting trust, the resulting trustee has only one obligation: to transfer the property back to the settlor if the settlor is alive, and if not, to the settlor's estate (meaning, the residuary devisees, if any, and if none, to the settlor's heirs at law). Thus, if a trust is created that was perfectly legal at the time of creation but subsequently becomes illegal due to a change in law, we have a resulting trust in favor of the settlor if settlor is alive, and if not, to the settlor's estate.

SECOND CONCEPT: CHARITABLE TRUSTS

5 Issues: Definition
                    Creation
                    Beneficiary
                    Rule Against Perpetuities
                    Cy Pres

[I]   Definition of a Charitable Trust
      [A]   Statute of Elizabeth: Trusts for education, alleviation of poverty, alleviation of sickness, to help orphans.
      [B]   Restatement: Any trust which confers a substantial benefit upon society.
      [C]   Examples of charitable trusts include trusts to:
           [1]

           [2]

           [3]

           [4]

[II]   Creation of a Charitable Trust
      [A]   How to create a charitable trust
           [1]   It is created in the same way that a private express trust is created: you need a [i] manifestation of trust intent, which can be done [ii] at testator's death by will or [iii] during settlor's lifetime by declaration of trust or by transfer in trust [iv] of a presently existing interest in property that can be transferred [v] for a legal chartiable purpose.

[III]   Beneficiary of a Charitable Trust
      [A]   Identification of the beneficiary
           [1]   In a charitable trust, there is no ascertainable person or group of people who are the beneficiaries, as in a private express trust.

[a]   Why is this?

[b]

[2]   Note that while an individual may receive an incidental benefit, the focus is on society.

    [a]   Example: A trust is established to endow a chair at a university.

    [b]   Analysis: While a professor may receive a benefit from a trust to endow a chair at a university, the trust is not a private express trust, but a charitable trust because society benefits when education is advanced.

[B]   Where the beneficiary is of a small group of people, is this a charitable trust, or a private express trust?

    [1]   Example: Settlor creates a trust to alleviate poverty among his poor relatives. Is this a charitable trust or a private express trust? Answer: a split of authority.

        [a]   One view: it is a private express trust because:

        [b]   Other view: it is a charitable trust because:

    [2]   Why care if the trust is a private express trust or a charitable trust? Because of the Rule Against Perpetuities and Cy Pres.

[IV] Rule Against Perpetuities

    [A]   The common law Rule Against Perpetuities still applies in many jurisdictions, but the Rule does not apply to charitable trusts.

        [1]   Thus, a trust to alleviate poverty among settlor's poor relatives, assuming this is a private express trust, will violate the common law Rule Against Perpetuities because it can vest more than 21 years after a life in being; it could vest 1000 years from now.

[2]   A charitable trust, on the other hand, is not affected by the Rule. Thus, a charitable trust, such as a university chair, can endure forever.

[V]   Cy Pres
    [A]   Introduction to the problem:
       [1]   Example:

       [2]   This is a good charitable trust. But let us assume that there is not enough money in the trust to do this.
       [3]   What happens if a charitable trust is impossible to carry out? There are two alternative solutions:
          [a]   A resulting trust: the corpus is returned to settlor if alive, and if not, to settlor's estate (which means, to the residuary devisees if any, and if none, to the intestate takers).
          [b] Cy pres.
    [B]   Cy pres means:

       [1]   In cy pres, if the court finds that settlor had a general charitable intent (to help the poor who are sick) and only the mechanism for effectuating that intent is not possible or practicable (a free hospital), the court can modify the mechanism, cy pres, as nearly as possible, to effectuate settlor's general intent.
       [2]   Here, the court can change the mechanism from a free hospital to a free out-patient clinic, if we stipulate that there is enough money to build and fund a free clinic. This is classical cy pres.
       [3]   In Summary: If settlor manifests a general charitable intent, but the mechanism for effectuating that intent is not possible or practicable, the court can modify the mechanism cy pres, as nearly as possible, to effectuate S's general charitable intent.
       [4]   How do we know if settlor's charitable intent was general (so that cy pres can be used), or specific (so that the trust fails and we have a resulting trust to return the property back to the settlor or settlor's estate)?

[a]

[b] Remember, if settlor has a specific charitable intent, cy pres cannot be used. The following example will illustrate this point.

[5] Example when cy pres cannot be used:

[a] Settlor creates a charitable trust for Syracuse University Medical School.

[b] This is a valid charitable trust.

[c] Years later, after settlor's death, the medical school ceases to exist.

[d] Syracuse University wants to use the trust for their health science school. Can they under cy pres?

[e] Only if settlor had a general charitable intent: to help education, in general, or even Syracuse University in general.

[f] Here is the evidence available: [i] Settlor graduated from Syracuse University Medical School; [ii] taught there; [iii] was a dean there; and [iv] settlor gave much money to Syracuse University Medical School during his lifetime and seldom gave any money to any other charity during his lifetime.

[g] On these facts, the court would not invoke cy pres because settlor has a specific charitable intent.

[h] The consequence is that we have a resulting trust: because settlor was dead, back to the settlor's estate.

[6] Only the court invokes cy pres, not the trustee on his own.

[7] Trustee may petition the court, but only court has the cy pres power.

THIRD CONCEPT: POUR-OVER WILLS

[I] Scenario
   [A] Settlor creates an inter-vivos trust, with a provision in her will devising part or all of the estate to the trustee of the trust.
   [B] The pour-over provisions are validated in three ways:
      [1] Incorporation by reference;
      [2] Facts of independent significance; and
      [3] UTATTA (Uniform Testamentary Additions to Trusts Act).
   [C] See wills lecture.

FOURTH CONCEPT: MISCELLANEOUS TRUSTS

2 issues: Honorary trusts
            Totten trusts

[I]   Honorary Trusts
    [A]   Defined:

        [1]   Because there is no ascertainable beneficiary, it cannot be a private express trust.

        [2]   Because there is no substantial benefit to society, it cannot be a charitable trust.

        [3]   What, then, is an honorary trust?

        [4]   It is simply a goal of the settlor.

        [5]   The trustee is not required to carry out settlor's goal, but has the power to carry it out.

        [6]   Thus, the trustee is on his honor only to carry out settlor's intent.

    [B]   Examples of honorary trusts:

        [1]

        [2]

        [3]   A trust to advance an unusual political ideology.

    [C]   Problems with honorary trusts:

        [1]   Trustee may, in an honorary trust, refuse to carry out settlor's wishes and the trust then fails.

            [a]   Thus, with respect to an honorary trust to further fox hunting, if trustee says, "this is the craziest thing I have ever heard of and I won't be a part of this," the trust fails and we have resulting trust in favor of the settlor, or, if she is dead, to settlor's estate.

[b] This failure of a trust because the trustee refuses to serve *never* happens with a private express trust or a charitable trust: if a trustee in these types of trusts refuses to serve, the court will appoint a new trustee.

[2] Typically there are Rule Against Perpetuities problems with honorary trusts.

[a] Without going into the Rule Against Perpetuities in depth, suffice to say there is no measuring life for these trusts and, consequently, they virtually always violate the Rule Against Perpetuities.

[b] Because these trusts violate the Rule Against Perpetuities some courts strike the trust at its inception, and as a consequence, we have a resulting trust.

[c] In other states, courts allow the honorary trust to endure for 21 years and then a resulting trust follows to end the trust. This is the approach of the Restatement of Trusts and the Uniform Probate Code.

[II] Totten Trust

[A] Defined: A Totten trust is also referred to as tentative bank account trust, whereby the named beneficiary takes whatever is left in the account at death of the owner of the account.

[B] But a Totten trust really is a misnomer because:

[1] The depositor/trustee owns the account during the depositor's lifetime and owes the named beneficiary no fiduciary duties whatsoever.

[2] It really, therefore, is just a will substitute.

[3] It is more accurate to call it a Totten account.

[4] A Totten trust or Totten account is always a type of savings account with a bank or other financial institution.

[C] Example: A Totten account reads:

[1] Mary Smith is the settlor/depositor.

[2] Mary Smith has full control during her lifetime.

[3]   Mary Smith does not owe John Jones any fiduciary duty whatsoever.

[4]   Mary Smith can do with the money anything she wants to during her lifetime.

[5]   John Jones takes whatever is left, if anything, on Mary Smith's death.

[D]   Issue: Does the settlor/trustee in a Totten trust or Totten account do something during her lifetime to elevate this lowly Totten account with no fiduciary duties to a full-blown private express trust with the full range of fiduciary duties?

[1]   Answer: Look to the actions of the depositor/trustee for a manifestation of trust intent.

[a]

[b]   Thus, if Mary Smith tells John Jones, "I have created this trust for you," or words to that effect, Mary has manifested an intent to create a trust and elevated this lowly Totten account to a full-blown private express trust, with the full range of fiduciary duties.

FIFTH CONCEPT: RESTRAINTS ON ALINENATION

4 issues: Introduction to the problem
              Spendthrift trusts
              Support trusts
              Discretionary trusts

[I]   Introduction to the Problem
      [A]   Hypothetical #1: Voluntary alienation.
            [1]   Settlor creates a private express trust for beneficiary
                  ("B"), which provides B is to receive all accrued interest
                  income every December 31. At the end of this year, on
                  December 31, we stipulate that B will receive $10,000.
                  Around November, B needs money and cannot wait until
                  December 31. B, therefore, goes to a money broker or a
                  bank and transfers his interest (the right to receive
                  $10,000 on December 31) to the bank for $5,000. Can B
                  do this? Yes. Property interests can be sold or transferred.
                  This is what is known as voluntary alienation: B can sell
                  his right to future payments. B can sell his right to
                  receive this year's payment, or even his right to receive
                  every interest payment for the rest of B's life. That is the
                  nature of property.
      [B]   Hypothetical #2: Involuntary alienation.
            [1]   Settlor creates a private express trust for beneficiary
                  ("B"), which provides B is to receive all accrued interest
                  income every December 31. B does not pay his bills,
                  however. Creditors in November want to seize all of the
                  accrued interest. They don't want to wait until B gets the
                  money because once B gets the money, B will spend the
                  money, leaving the creditors out of luck. Thus, the
                  creditors want to attach the money owed directly from
                  the trustee. Can they do it? Yes. That is the nature of
                  property, too. Not only can property be voluntarily
                  alienated, but it can be involuntarily alienated: attached
                  by creditors after proper legal proceedings.
      [C]   In summary:

[1]   The beneficiary of a private express trust can voluntarily alienate his interest in property (transfer his right to future payments), and creditors can involuntarily alienate a B's interest in property (attach or seize a beneficiary's right to future payments).

[2]   Now let us see how this can change if the trust has a spendthrift, support, or discretionary provision.

[II]   Spendthrift Trust (Spendthrift Provision of a Private Express Trust)

[A]   Definition of a spendthrift trust:

[B]   How to recognize this on the Bar Exam:

[1]   The terms of the trust must essentially include the definition:

[2]   Example: "No beneficiary of this trust shall be allowed to voluntarily transfer his right to future payments, and no creditor shall be allowed to attach any beneficiary's right to future payments."

[3]   The fact pattern must include the definition.

[C]   Three testable issues on Spendthrift trusts:

[1]   Voluntary alienation: Can the beneficiary ever voluntarily alienate or transfer his right to future payments, notwithstanding the spendthrift provisions?

[a]   Answer: No, as a general rule.

[b]   This would defeat the terms of the trust.

[c]   But sometimes a court will recognize the assignment on the ground that the beneficiary merely has given the trustee a direction or order to pay the beneficiary's agent or representative, i.e. the assignee. In such case, prior to the time of payment, beneficiary would have the right to revoke the order or direction.

[2]   Involuntary Alienation: Can creditors ever attach the beneficiary's right to future payments, notwithstanding the spendthrift provisions?

[a]   Answer: No, as a general rule.

[b] Common law exceptions: Preferred creditors can attach the beneficiary's right to future payments, notwithstanding the spendthrift provisions. The key is that they are not typical creditors.

[c] Examples of common law preferred creditors:

[1)]

[2)]

[3)]

[4)]

[5)]

[6)] A tort judgment creditor. Example: Beneficiary ("B") negligently injures X. X can satisfy his judgment against B by proceeding against the trust and attach B's right to future payments. Reason: When settlor created the spendthrift trust, it was to insulate B from his spendthrift ways, from spending all of his money in one fell swoop. It was not for the purpose of insulating B from his negligent acts.

[d] In addition to these common law exceptions for preferred creditors, there is also the rule in many jurisdictions that *any* creditor (even if not a preferred creditor) has the right to attach "surplus," as measured by the beneficiary's "station in life."

[e] What is "surplus" and what is the "station in life" standard?

[f] Suppose beneficiary ("B") needs $25,000 a year to live, to maintain her station in life, that is, her standard of living. Suppose also that the trust

generates $75,000 of income for the B. The difference, $50,000, is surplus and in many jurisdictions that can be attached by any creditor, not just a common law preferred creditor.

[g] Note that the beneficiary's station in life is *not* based on an objective test. It is subjective, although only reasonable amounts are considered. Thus, gambling expenses would not be considered.

[3] Can the settlor ever create a spendthrift trust for himself or herself (create a self-settled spendthrift trust)?

[a] As to involuntary alienation: [i] In the overwhelming number of jurisdictions, the trust itself is valid, but the spendthrift provisions are not recognized. To recognize a self-settled spendthrift trust for the purpose of insulating oneself from one's own creditors violates public policy. [ii] In a few jurisdictions, however, a settlor is allowed to create a spendthrift trust for himself, thus insulating himself from his own creditors.

[b] As to the voluntary alienation: There is a split of authority: [i] Most jurisdictions will ignore the provision restricting voluntary alienation and allow the settlor to voluntarily alienate her interest. [ii] But some jurisdictions will not allow settlor to transfer her right to future payments; the rationale here is policy driven: that enforcement of the spendthrift provision protects the settlor/beneficiary from himself or herself.

[III] Support Trusts (Support Provisions of a Private Express Trust)
[A] Definition of a support trust:

[B] How to recognize it on the Bar Exam:
[1] The terms of the trust must include the definition.

19

[2] Example: "Trustee is required to use only so much of the income or principal as is necessary for the beneficiary's health, support, maintenance, and education."

[3] The fact pattern must include the definition.

[C] Three testable issues on Support trusts:

[1] Voluntary alienation: Can the beneficiary ever voluntarily alienate or transfer his right to future payments, notwithstanding the support trust provisions?

[a] Answer: No. Why? To allow any type of assignment would defeat the purpose of the trust and violate settlor's intent.

[b] Thus, beneficiary cannot transfer his right to future payments in a support trust.

[2] Involuntary alicnation: Can creditors ever attach the beneficiary's right to future payments, notwithstanding the support trust provisions?

[a] Answer: See rules for spendthrift trusts: rules are the same. (Generally no attachment. But there are preferred creditors, who can attach the beneficiary's right to future payments.)

[3] Can the settlor ever create a support trust for himself or herself (create a self-settled support trust)?

[a] Answer: See rules for spendthrift trusts.

[IV] Discretionary Trusts (Discretionary Provisions of a Private Express Trust)

[A] Definition:

[B] How to recognize this on the Bar Exam:

[1] The terms of the trust must include the definition.

[2] Example: Settlor will create a trust, the terms of which will state, "Trustee shall have full, sole, and absolute discretion in determining when to pay the beneficiary and how much to pay the beneficiary."

[3] The fact pattern must include the definition.

[C] Three testable issues on discretionary trusts:

[1]   Voluntary alienation: Can beneficiary ever transfer his interest, his right to future payments, notwithstanding the discretionary trust provisions? This is what you should tell the bar examiners:

[a]   On the one hand, no: Beneficiary cannot voluntarily transfer his right to future payments because, the question may be asked, what exactly is the beneficiary assigning? The beneficiary may not get anything.

[b]   But, on the other hand, if in fact there was an assignment, then the assignee steps into the shoes of the beneficiary. Because the beneficiary could not force payment by the trustee, neither can the assignee. However, if the trustee has notice of the assignment and does decide to pay, then the trustee must pay the assignee or be held personally liable.

[2]   Involuntary alienation: Can creditors ever attach the beneficiary's right to future payments, notwithstanding the discretionary trust provisions? This is what you should tell the bar examiners:

[a]   On the one hand, creditors cannot attach the beneficiary's right to future payments because there is nothing to attach. The trustee may never allocate anything to the beneficiary. The beneficiary could not force payment, and neither can the creditors. Thus, there is nothing to attach by the creditors.

[b]   On the other hand, if the trustee has notice of the debt and the creditor's judgment against the beneficiary, and the trustee does decide to pay, he must pay the creditors or be held personally liable.

[3]   Can settlor ever create a discretionary trust for herself? Answer: See rules for spendthrift trusts.

[D]   Example: "Trustee in his sole and absolute discretion, shall pay the amount needed for the beneficiary's support and maintenance." How do you handle this for the bar exam?

[1]   Tell the bar examiners:

[2]   Then tell the bar examiners:

SIXTH CONCEPT: RESULTING TRUSTS

2 issues: Definition
                How a Resulting Trust Arises

[I]   Definition of a Resulting Trust
    [A]   A resulting trust is an implied in fact trust and is based upon the presumed intent of the parties. If a resulting trust is decreed by the court, the resulting trustee will transfer the property to the settlor if the settlor is alive, and if not, to the settlor's estate, i.e. to the residuary devisees if any, and if none, to the intestate takers (the heirs).

[II]   How a Resulting Trust Arises: 7 situations:
    [A]   First situation: When a private express trust ends by its own terms, and there is no provision for what happens to the corpus thereafter.
        [1]   Example:

                [a]   This is a perfectly good private express trust.
                [b]   But what happens to the property after the daughter gets her law school education?
                [c]   The trust instrument is silent in this regard.
                [d]   We presume the settlor wants the property back.
                [e]   Thus, once daughter gets her education, the trust ends and we presume that the settlor wants the property back: back to settlor if she is alive, and if not, to her estate.
    [B]   Second situation: When a private express trust fails, because there is no beneficiary.
        [1]   In such case, we presume settlor wants the property back: to settlor if alive, and if not, to settlor's estate.
    [C]   Third situation: When a charitable trust ends because of impossibility or impracticability (see above) and Cy Pres cannot be used.
        [1]   Example:

[D]   Fourth situation: When a private express trust fails because after creation, the trust becomes illegal (see above).

[E]   Fifth situation: When there is excess corpus in a private express trust.

    [1]   Example: Settlor creates a valid private express trust, but due to excellent investing, there is more than enough corpus available to accomplish the trust purpose. With respect to that excess corpus, we have a resulting trust.

[F]   Sixth situation: When we have a "purchase money resulting trust"

    [1]   Example:

        [a]   If A and C are not closely related: there is a rebuttable presumption that C is holding as a purchase money resulting trustee for the benefit of A. But this is only a rebuttable presumption.

        [b]   If A and C are closely related: there is a rebuttable presumption that A simply made a gift to C.

[G]   Seventh situation: Semi-secret trusts: a semi-secret trust arises when the will makes a gift to a person to hold as trustee, but does not name the beneficiary.

    [1]   Example:

        [a]   The will on its face shows a trust intention, but the beneficiary cannot be ascertained.

        [b]   To admit in the evidence to establish the terms of the trust violates the Statute of Wills (the local probate code).

        [c]   Courts typically decree a resulting trust: the property goes back to testator's estate: the

residuary devisees, if any, and if none, the heirs at law.

[d] This outcome is to be distinguished from "secret trusts" where the courts allow in parol evidence to establish the identify of the beneficiary (see material on constructive trusts).

SEVENTH CONCEPT: CONSTRUCTIVE TRUSTS

2 issues: Definition
              How a Constructive Trust Arises

[I]   Defined
    [A]   A constructive trust is really a misnomer because it is not a trust.
    [B]   Rather, a constructive trust is simply:

    [C]   When a court decrees a constructive trust, the wrongdoer will have only one obligation: to transfer the property to the intended beneficiary as determined by the court.
    [D]   A constructive trust, therefore, is a means to disgorge a wrongdoer of his ill-gotten gains.

[II]   How a Constructive Trust Arises: 4 situations:
    [A]   First situation:

              [1]   With respect to those ill-gotten profits, the trustee will be a constructive trustee.
              [2]   As such, the trustee will have to turn those profits over to the intended beneficiaries of the trust, as decreed by the court.
    [B]   Second situation: With respect to the law of wills, when there is fraud in the inducement or undue influence:
              [1]   Refer back to the lecture earlier.
              [2]   Remember that a remedy that the court has for fraud in the inducement or undue influence is that the court can deny the will probate and make the heir a constructive trustee who will have only one obligation: to transfer the property to the intended beneficiary, as determined by the court.
    [C]   Third situation:

[1]   Secret trust defined: The will on its face makes a gift outright to A, but the gift is given on the basis of an oral promise by A to use the property for the benefit of B.

[2]   Example: Testator goes to A and says, "A, I shall devise $100,000 to you, if you promise to use this money for the benefit of B." A states to testator that he (A) will comply. Thereafter testator executes his will that states, "I devise $100,000 to A."

    [a]   When testator dies, from the four corners of the will, it seems that A owns the $100,000 for himself, free of any trust.

    [b]   Parol evidence is admissible to show that the beneficiary was B.

    [c]   Thus, A will not be allowed to keep the property. A will become a constructive trustee who will have only one obligation: to transfer the property to B.

    [e]   But note: For semi-secret trusts (see above), courts will not impose a constructive trust. Rather they impose a resulting trust (back to testator's estate).

    [f]   On the bar exam, whether you have a semi-secret trust ("I devise $100,000 to Abel as trustee" and no beneficiary is named), or secret trust ("I devise $100,000 to Abel"), discuss the rules for *each* (give the rule for semi-secret trusts and then give the rule for secret trusts), then apply the appropriate doctrine to the facts at hand.

[D]   Fourth situation: Oral Real Estate Trusts (also known as Breach of Promise):

[1]   Example: S goes to A and states, "If I transfer Blackacre to you by deed, will you hold Blackacre for the benefit of B?" A agrees. Thereafter S executes a deed in favor of A and delivers it to A.

    [a]   From the four corners of the deed, A seemingly owns the property in fee simple absolute, free of any trust.

    [b]   Further, if B claims the property, A can raise the Statute of Frauds as an affirmative defense to keep the property for himself.

[c] But, there are three situations where the transferee, A, will not be allowed to invoke the Statute of Frauds to keep the property. In such case, A will be decreed a constructive trustee who will have only one obligation: to transfer the property to the intended beneficiary, B.

[1)] A fiduciary relationship between S and A. If there was a fiduciary relationship between S and the oral real estate trustee A, A will not be allowed to invoke the Statute of Frauds. A will be decreed a constructive trustee, who will have only one obligation: turn the property over to the intended beneficiary, as decreed by the court.

[2)] There was fraud in the inducement on A's part. Thus, S went to A and said, "If I transfer Blackacre to you in fee simple, do you promise to hold Blackacre for the benefit of B," and A says yes, while he is thinking to himself: "What a fool. I can't believe this guy is doing this." This is fraud in the inducement. A will not be allowed to invoke the Statute of Frauds to keep the property. A will be decreed a constructive trustee: turn the property over to the intended beneficiary, B.

[3)] There was detrimental reliance by B, the intended beneficiary: If B relied to his detriment on the existence of this oral real estate trust, then B will get the property from A via a constructive trust. What constitutes detrimental reliance? Look for B taking possession and making improvements. Possession alone is not enough.

[E] Note that constructive trusts also appear as cross-overs with Remedies.

EIGHTH CONCEPT: TRUSTEE POWERS AND DUTIES

3 issues: Trustee powers
Trustee duties owed to the beneficiary and remedies
Trustee duties owned to third persons

[I]   Trustee Powers
    [A]   Trustee has all enumerated powers.
    [B]   Trustee has all implied powers, too.
        [1]   Implied powers: helpful and appropriate to carry out the trust purpose.
        [2]   Examples of implied powers:
            [a]

            [b]

            [c]

            [d]

[II]   Trustee Duties Owed to Beneficiaries
    [A]   Duty of Loyalty
        [1]   Definition: Requires that the trustee administer the trust for the benefit of the beneficiaries (implicitly, trustee must be impartial), having no other consideration in mind.
        [2]   Corollary:

        [3]   Examples of self-dealing:
            [a]   Trustee prefers one beneficiary, his child, over the other beneficiaries
            [b]   Trustee sells trust property to trustee's spouse
            [c]   Trustee-lawyer hires himself
        [4]   Consequences of finding breach of the duty of loyalty or self-dealing:

        [a]   If there is a loss, the trustee is "surcharged," meaning that the trustee has to make good the loss.

        [b]   If the trustee makes a personal profit, then with respect to those ill-gotten profits, the trustee is a constructive trustee: must turn over those profits to the intended beneficiary.

[B]   Duty to Invest: Split of authority: There are three alternative rules of the duty to invest. Discuss *all three* on the bar exam.

    [1]   State lists: Some states have lists which trustee must follow in the absence of directions in the trust. Good investments in these jurisdictions are:

        [a]

        [b]

        [c]

        [d]

        [e]   Never invest in a new business.

        [f]   Never invest in second deeds of trust in real estate.

    [2]   Common law prudent person test: The duty to invest requires the trustee to act as reasonably prudent person investing his own property, trying to maximize income while preserving corpus. If the trustee holds himself out as having greater skill, he is held to that higher standard.

        [a]   Key: Each individual investment is scrutinized.

        [b]   Good investments under the common law test:

            [1)]

            [2)]

            [3)]

            [4)]

            [5)]

            [6)]   Never invest in a new business.

[7)]   Never invest in second deeds of trust in real estate.

[3]   Uniform Prudent Investor Act: Adopted by most states: The act simply provides that the trustee must invest as a "prudent investor."

     [a]   Key: Unlike the rules above (the state lists approach and the common law prudent person test), each individual investment is *not* scrutinized, but, rather, performance is measured in the context of the *entire* trust portfolio. Thus, any investment is not per se invalid. Consequently, even derivatives or futures contracts (investments absolutely prohibited under state lists standard or the common law reasonably prudent person standard) may be appropriate in the context of an entire portfolio.

[4]   Miscellaneous rules regarding the duty to invest:

     [a]

     [b]   Under the first two rules (state lists and the common law prudent person test), no speculating allowed.

     [c]   What if trustee breaches the duty to invest? In any jurisdiction, trustee must make good the loss. If there is a profit, the beneficiaries affirm the transaction. If the trustee makes two investments that breach the duty to invest, one makes money and the other loses money, the trustee is surcharged for the loss while the beneficiaries affirm the transaction that made money. No netting allowed by the trustee.

[C]   Duty to Earmark

[1]   Defined:

[a]   Example: If trustee owns share of stock and it is properly earmarked, the stock will be registered to "John Smith, as trustee of the ABC trust."

[2]   Consequences of trustee breaching the duty to earmark:

[a]   Common law approach: If trustee breaches the duty to earmark and there is a loss, the trustee is held personally liable. No causal relationship required between failure to earmark and a loss. Thus, if the stock market crashes and there is a loss, trustee is held personally liable, even though the failure to earmark did not cause the loss (the market would have crashed even if the trustee had earmarked).

[b]   Modern approach: If there is a failure to earmark and there is a loss, the trustee is held personally liable only if the loss was caused by the failure to earmark. Thus, for example: If trustee fails to earmark and she holds the trust property in her own name and her own personal creditors subsequently attach and end up keeping that asset, then the failure to earmark caused the loss and under either the common law or modern approach, the trustee would be held personally liable.

[D]   Duty to Segregate

[1]   Defined:

[2]   Moreover, the duty to segregate also requires that the trustee not co-mingle the funds of Trust A with the funds of Trust B.

[3]   If trustee breaches the duty to segregate, the trustee can be removed and be held liable for any loss.

[E]   Duty Not to Delegate

[1]   Defined: The trustee can rely on professional advisors in reaching a decision, but the trustee cannot delegate decision-making authority to these advisors.

[a]   Example: Trustee can rely on advice of competent counsel in determining whether to prosecute a lawsuit. However, the trustee is not allowed to sign

a blank pleading and tell the lawyer, "You do what you think is best."

       [b] Under the common law, a trustee could not delegate the duty to invest to a professional money manager.

       [c] Modernly, a trustee can delegate this duty (e.g. to a manager of a mutual fund).

   [2] Moreover, while a trustee cannot delegate to a third person, the trustee also cannot delegate to another trustee.

   [3] Under the common law, in the absence of a contrary provision in the trust instrument, trustees must act unanimously.

   [4] Modernly, trustees can act by majority decision.

[F] Duty to Account

   [1] Defined:

       [a] If the trustee fails to render an accounting to the beneficiaries, the beneficiaries would file an action for an accounting.

[G] Duty of Due Care

   [1] Defined:

   [2] You will almost always be able to discuss this duty when the trustee breaches his or her fiduciary duties on the bar exam.

[H] Remedies of beneficiary for breach of duty or duties:

   [1] Damages.

   [2] Constructive trust remedy.

   [3] Tracing and equitable lien on property (see Remedies outline).

   [4] Ratify the transaction if good for beneficiary.

   [5] Remove trustee.

[I] Final Points

[1]   Look for three or four duties breached on bar exam; you never get just one, or even two.

[2]   Again, remember, you will always be able to discuss due care, so don't leave it out.

[III] Liability of Trustee to Third Persons (Liability in Contract and Liability in Tort)

[A]   Liability in Contract

[1]   Common law rule:

[a]   Trustee is sued in his personal capacity. Consequently, the trustee's personal assets are at stake. But the trustee can get indemnification from trust assets if the trustee acted within his or her powers and was not personally at fault.

[b]   The only time the trustee would be sued in his representative capacity (i.e., trustee's personal assets are not at risk) is if the contract itself provided that in the event of a breach by the trustee, the trustee is to be sued in his representative capacity. It was not enough under the common law that the trustee signed the contract, "John Smith, as trustee of the ABC Trust."

[2]   Modern law rule:

[a]   If the other person to the contract, the promisee, knows that the trustee is entering into the contract in his representative capacity, then the trustee must be sued in his representative capacity. Thus, the trustee's personal assets are not at stake.

[b]   Thus, if the trustee signs the contract, "John Smith, as trustee of the ABC Trust," under the modern rule, the trustee must be sued in his representative capacity.

[B]   Liability in Tort

[1]   Common law rule:

[a]   The trustee is sued in his personal capacity.

[b]   If the trustee was without personal fault, however, the trustee can get indemnification from trust assets. Thus, if an agent committed the negligent

act, or if this is a case of strict liability, then the trustee can obtain indemnification.

[2] Modern law rule:

[a] The trustee is sued in his individual capacity and is personally liable for torts *only* if the trustee is personally at fault (i.e. acted negligently or otherwise committed a tort). Thus, if an agent committed the negligent act or if this is a case of strict liability, the trustee is sued in his representative capacity.

NINTH CONCEPT: MODIFICATION AND TERMINATION OF TRUSTS

4 issues: Modification by the settlor
                Modification by the court
                Termination of revocable trusts
                Termination of irrevocable trusts

[I]   Modification by the Settlor
     [A]

     [B]   Settlor also has the power to modify if the settlor has the power to revoke.
         [1]   This is because the power to revoke is the greatest power a settlor can have.
         [2]   It would make no sense to say that settlor has the power to revoke the trust, but not the power to modify the trust. Why? Because if settlor has the power to revoke, settlor can revoke and then set up the trust newly constituted, as settlor wants the trust be—as modified. Thus, whenever settlor has the power to revoke, settlor has, by implication, the power to modify.
         [3]   When does the settlor have the power to revoke? See below.

[II]   Modification by the Court
     [A]   There can be modification by the court regarding charitable trusts and the cy pres power: changing the mechanism to further settlor's general charitable intent.
     [B]   There also can be modification of charitable trusts or private express trusts regarding the court's deviation power.
         [1]   Deviation power (also known as Doctrine of Changed Circumstances):
             [a]   When the court exercises its deviation power, the court changes the administrative or management provisions of the trust.

[b]

[c]   Example: Settlor creates a valid private express trust, providing that the trustee can invest only in bonds and cannot invest in stocks. The trust was created during the Great Depression, when the stock market collapsed. In 1955, after the stock market rebounded and during a time of high inflation, the trustee petitions the court to allow investing in stocks because without such investing, within 20 years inflation will outpace the investments presently authorized to the point where the trust will not be able to pay trust expenses, let alone pay income to the beneficiaries. Will the court under these circumstances allow deviation to allow investment in stocks?

[2]   2 elements must be established for the court to use its deviation power:

[a]   Unforeseen circumstances on the part of the settlor, and

[b]   Necessity (deviation needed to preserve the trust).

[c]   Example: In the above hypo, if we stipulate that settlor [i] could not foresee the rate of inflation and the resurgence of the stock market and [ii] without deviation, the trust will go broke, the court will allow deviation: trustee will be authorized by the court to deviate from the trust instrument and invest in stocks.

[III]   Termination of Revocable Trusts

    [A]   When does settlor have the power to revoke?

        [1]   Majority Rule:

        [2]   Minority Rule: Settlor has the power to revoke, unless the trust is expressly made irrevocable.

[IV]   Termination of Irrevocable Trusts

    [A]   Three ways an irrevocable trust can terminate prematurely, that is, before the time set for termination in the trust instrument:

        [1]   Settlor and all the beneficiaries agree to terminate.

            [a]   "All the beneficiaries" means you must account for contingent remaindermen: guardian *ad litem* (a guardian appointed to represent those parties to a suit who are incapacitated by infancy or otherwise) must be appointed to represent them.

        [2]   All the beneficiaries agree to terminate and all the material purposes have been accomplished.

            [a]   Reason: Equity will not see a trust continue to carry out a minor or insignificant purpose. What about the insignificant purposes that have yet to be accomplished? The court will make certain that sufficient assets are set aside to accomplish these purposes. However, you do not need a $100 million trust kept alive to accomplish a $100 purpose.

            [b]   Remember to account for unborn beneficiaries with a guardian *ad litem*.

        [3]   By operation of law: passive trusts and the Statute of Uses:

            [a]   Statute of Uses comes into play when you have a private express trust with a corpus of real property, and the trust is passive (the trustee has no active duties and is just holding bare legal title).

            [b]   In such case, under the Statute of Uses, the beneficiaries get legal title by operation of law, and thus the trust terminates.

            [c]   Not all jurisdictions recognize the Statute of Uses.

            [d]   What of a passive trust of stock or other personal property? Answer: Statute of Uses does not apply, but, by analogy, the principles of the Statute of Uses should apply because equity should not see a useless act done.

TENTH CONCEPT: INCOME & PRINCIPAL (UNIFORM PRINCIPAL AND INCOME ACT)

3 issues: Income and expenses allocated to the life tenant
Income and expenses allocated to the remainderman
Adjustment power of trustee

[I]   Income and Expenses Allocated to the Life Tenant
   [A]   The life tenant gets the following income:
      [1]

      [2]

      [3]

   [B]   The life tenant's interest pays for the following expenses:
      [1]   Interest on loan indebtedness
      [2]   Taxes
      [3]   Minor repairs (e.g. paint job)

[II]   Income and Expenses Allocated to the Remainderman
   [A]   Remainderman gets the following income:
      [1]

      [2]

      [3]

   [B]   Remainderman's interest pays for the following expenses:
      [1]   Principal part of loan indebtedness
      [2]   Major repairs or improvements (new wing on a building)

[III]   Adjustment Power of Trustee
   [A]   Trustee can disregard the above stated rules regarding allocation of income to life tenant and remainderman if a different allocation is necessary to administer the trust fairly.

[B]   Example: If the only income from the trust is from the sale of trust assets, trustee may allocate some of the income to the life tenant.